THE COMPOSER
AS INTELLECTUAL

THE COMPOSER AS INTELLECTUAL

Music and Ideology in France
1914–1940

JANE F. FULCHER

OXFORD
UNIVERSITY PRESS
2005

OXFORD
UNIVERSITY PRESS

Oxford University Press, Inc., publishes works that further
Oxford University's objective of excellence
in research, scholarship, and education.

Oxford   New York
Auckland   Cape Town   Dar es Salaam   Hong Kong   Karachi
Kuala Lumpur   Madrid   Melbourne   Mexico City   Nairobi
New Delhi   Shanghai   Taipei   Toronto

With offices in
Argentina   Austria   Brazil   Chile   Czech Republic   France   Greece
Guatemala   Hungary   Italy   Japan   Poland   Portugal   Singapore
South Korea   Switzerland   Thailand   Turkey   Ukraine   Vietnam

Copyright © 2005 by Oxford University Press, Inc.

Published by Oxford University Press, Inc.
198 Madison Avenue, New York, New York, 10016

www.oup.com

Oxford is a registered trademark of Oxford University Press

All rights reserved. No part of this publication may be reproduced,
stored in a retrieval system, or transmitted, in any form or by any means,
electronic, mechanical, photocopying, recording, or otherwise,
without prior permission of Oxford University Press.

Library of Congress Cataloging-in-Publication Data
Fulcher, Jane F.
The composer as intellectual: music and ideology in France 1914–1940 / Jane F. Fulcher
p. cm.
Includes bibliographical references and indexes.
ISBN-13 978-0-19-517473-1
ISBN 0-19-517473-9
1. Music—France—20th century—History and criticism. 2. Composers—France.
3. Music—Social aspects—France. 4. Music—Political aspects—France. I. Title.
ML270.5.F83 2005
780'.944'09041—dc22   2004049521

1 3 5 7 9 8 6 4 2

Printed in the United States of America
on acid-free paper

For my mother,
Carol Fulcher

ACKNOWLEDGMENTS

I am extremely grateful to a number of colleagues, in several disciplines, who have been of indispensable help by so generously offering me intellectual exchange, their own materials, bibliographic suggestions, and moral as well as professional support. I am particularly indebted to the historians Carl E. Schorske, Arno J. Mayer, Christophe Charle, Jacques Revel, Roger Chartier, and Michael Steinberg. I also wish to thank Leon Botstein for providing me with the opportunity to present and develop my ideas concerning Claude Debussy by inviting me to advise the Bard Music Festival the year that it was devoted to Debussy. I am grateful to historians Christophe Prochasson, Steve Schloesser, Marie-Claude Genet-Delacroix, Joel Blatt, and Maurice Agulhon for the materials and advice they gave me.

Colleagues in my own field of musicology have been equally generous and supportive, and I especially wish to thank Philip Gossett, Richard Leppert, Pamela Potter, Marian Green, and Brian Hart. I am also grateful for the information, sources and support provided by Leslie Sprout, Nigel Simeone, Bridget Conrad, Joël-Marie Fauquet, Martin Marks, Myriam Chimènes, Glenn Watkins, Barbara Kelly, Andrea Musk, Ronald Wiecki, David Grayson, and the late François Lesure. My students at Indiana University also helped to stimulate my ideas and to provide me with valuable information through their own research projects, and so I wish to thank them, and particularly Gary Laycock and Jennifer Smull.

My friends and colleagues in Paris were a continual source of both inspiration and practical help in all domains of my research; I am thus extremely grateful to Elizabeth Bartlet, Leslie Wright, Annegret Fauser, Sabina Ratner, Marie Rolf, Esteban Buch, and Earl and Donna Evleth. Equally supportive were my colleagues, in several departments, at Indiana University, especially Gilbert Chaitin and Rosemary Lloyd in the Department of French, Thomas Mathiesen and the late A. Peter Brown in Musicology, and Marianne Kielian-Gilbert, Gretchen Horlacher, Robert Hatten, and Mary Wennerstrom in Music Theory.

In addition, I am indebted to those colleagues who provided me with the stimulating opportunity to present and discuss my ideas at Princeton and Yale Universities, the University of North Carolina at Chapel Hill, Trinity College, and the University of Cincinnati, as well as at the Sorbonne, the Ecole des Hautes Etudes en Sciences Sociales, and the Centre National de la Recherche Scientifique in Paris. I thus wish to thank Scott Burnham, Leon Plantinga, Gail Hilson Woldu, Edward Nowacki, and, once again, Roger Chartier, Jacques Revel, and Christophe Charle.

Also of considerable and generous aid in various aspects of my research and the development of my ideas were art historian Mark Antliff, and several sociologists whose planning of and participation in a conference on opera and society was particularly stimulating for me: Victoria Johnson, Thomas Ertman, and Craig Calhoun. I remain extremely grateful to another sociologist, the late Pierre Bourdieu, who never flagged in his support or help, who offered me the opportunity to present my material to his seminar, and who published material relating to this study in his journal.

I also wish to thank those colleagues who were of essential assistance in the development of this manuscript in all its stages, and whose professional advice I have greatly valued. This book would not have been possible without the expert computer assistance of Melissa Beaver, who patiently and enthusiastically helped me through several stages of its growth and revision. Nancy Toff, of Oxford University Press, was always generous with her help and advice, practical and intellectual, in both her fields of expertise, publication and the music history of this period. I am also most grateful to my editor, Kim Robinson, for her valuable assistance in all phases of the preparation and publication of this book, as well as to the three scholars whom she so insightfully selected to read it.

I remain indebted, as well, to my previous editor, Maribeth Payne, for her enthusiasm, advice, and guidance in my previous book and in the transition to the publication of this one.

Several institutions also made this study possible through their financial and practical assistance over the period of its genesis and development, from 1986 to the present.

I am thus grateful to the National Endowment for the Humanities and the Wissenschaftskolleg zu Berlin for their fellowships for individual research, and to the Institute for Advanced Study in Princeton, New Jersey, where I was the Edward T. Cone Member in Music Studies for 2003–4. I also wish to thank the French Centre National de la Recherche Scientifique for its research fellowship, and the Ecole des Hautes Etudes en Sciences Sociales for its support and the opportunity to present my ideas.

I am equally grateful for the assistance I received from the Office of Research and the University Graduate School and the Program in West European Studies at Indiana University.

Finally, I wish to thank my family for their continual belief and generous help in every aspect of my career, particularly my mother, to whom this book is dedicated, my sister, Carol Ann Fulcher, and brother-in-law, Frederick Pepper.

CONTENTS

Introduction
    The Artist as Intellectual?, 3
    The Composer, Public Issues, and Symbols, 4
    The Political and Symbolic Background, 10
    The State, National Symbols, and the Dialogue, 11
    Two Histories and Their Intersection, 17

1: Wartime Nationalism, Classicism, and Their Limits

    Part 1: State Hegemony and Musical Culture: Institutions and Propaganda
    French Identity and the Classic Myth, 19
    The Myth and Music in Wartime, 22
    Imagining the French Community through Opera, 23
    Defining the "Classic Masters" in Concerts, 26
    "Defending" French Music and Its "Purity," 31
    Professional Interests versus Cultural Politics, 33
    The Orthodox Discourse and Its Boundaries, 34
    Wartime Ideology and Musicology, 40
    French Editors, the Canon, and the Classics, 42
    Resistance to the War and Its Culture, 45

Part 2: Intellectual and Creative Responses
How to Defend "la Musique Française," 46
Nationalist Orthodoxy: D'Indy versus Saint-Saëns, 48
Charpentier's Double-Voiced Schemes, 50
Debussy's Dialogue with Orthodoxy, 52
Ravel's Inflections of Tradition: The *Tombeau*, 65
Satie's Subversions: Language and the Dialogic in *Parade*, 70
The Birth of the "Next Generation," 84

2: The National or Universal in the Twenties

Part 1: Conservative Hegemony and Political-Cultural Conflict
Memory and the Nationalists' Agenda, 86
Commemoration, Spiritualism, and the Classic in Music, 86
Political and Symbolic Confrontations, 89
Consecration, Concerts, and the Orientation of Taste, 91
The Opera of Conservative Ideas, 96
Reclassifications in Scholarship and Criticism, 108
New Goals in French Musical Education, 113
The Complex Case of Nadia Boulanger, 116
Forging the French Image Abroad, 117
Cultural Responses of the Far Right and Left, 118
Politics through Culture, 118
The Action Française and "Intelligence," 119
The "Schola d'Action Française," 122
The Left: Universalism and the "Classic," 123
Syndicalism, Music, and the Fêtes du Peuple, 126

Part 2: French Composers as Intellectuals and the Issues
The Older Generation and Its Choices, 133
D'Indy: Innovation versus Dogma, 134
Ravel: Reasserting the Universal and the Modern, 136
Satie and Leftist Individualism: *Socrate*, 146
The Adversative Modernism of Youth, 152
Wiéner's Challenge through Repertoire, 152
The Generation of 1914 in Music, 154
The Counterculture and Its Supporters, 156
Cocteau: Protecting Modernism with Nationalism, 162
Collet and the Myth of Les Six, 167
Legitimizing Modernity through Tradition: Boulanger and Stravinsky, 169
Les Six and Neoclassicism: Reality versus Myth, 172
Auric: The National or the Universal?, 173
Milhaud and the Transcendent Collectivity, 175
Honegger and the Dilemma of the "National," 184
Poulenc: Modernity and Tradition, 188

Durey: Aesthetic and Political Integrity, 191
Tailleferre and Dual Marginality, 193
Nationalism, Xenophobia, and Revenge on "the Modern," 195

3: The "Defense" of French Culture in the Thirties

Part 1: The Popular Front: Culture as Politics
Programs and Ideals of the Government, 199
Antifascism and the Politics of the Spectacle, 199
The Political and Cultural Background, 201
The New Role of French Left Intellectuals, 203
The Ideology of Culture in 1936, 205
Themes, Myths, and Programs of the Popular Front, 207
Redirecting French Musical Culture, 209
French Musicians as Intellectuals of the Left, 211
Roussel and the Fédération Musicale Populaire, 211
Koechlin: Style and Ideological Investment, 215
The "Defense" of Musical Culture, 219
Attacks on Tradition and "la Grande Musique," 221
The Influence of Romain Rolland, 223
Les Six as Cultural Advisors, 223
Aesthetics, Style, and "Engagement," 226
Le 14 juillet: Politics and Representation, 234
Performance and Ideology: The 1937 Exposition, 237

Part 2: Political and Symbolic Challenges to the Government
The Conservative and Profascist "Defense" of Culture, 242
Political Dissension and the Symbolic Battle, 242
Profascist and Romantic Currents, 243
The Oppositional Musical Aesthetic, 245
The Return of "d'Indysme" and "Wagnerisme," 247
Attacks on Government Programs and on Les Six, 249
Ideological Constructions of Ravel, 252
Other Composers Appropriated, 255
Political Tensions with the Government among Composers, 258
Poulenc and Sauguet: Political and Aesthetic Resistance, 258
The Case of Poulenc's *Litanies à la vierge noire,* 261
Honegger's Aesthetic and Political "Nonconformism," 265
From *Jeanne au bûcher* to Frontisme, 270

4: The Return to Spirit

Part 1: Redefinitions of Symbolic Legitimacy
The Decline of a Politics and an Aesthetics, 275
Reconstruction of Ravel and the Context, 275
Delegitimizing Musical Neoclassicism, 277

Revalorizing Tradition and "Spirit," 281
Reclassification of Genres, 283

Part 2: The Search for "Oppositionality"
French Youth and "Revolutionary Spiritualism," 285
The Nonconformist Movement and Its Impact, 285
Leftist Spiritualism and Youth, 287
The Conservative Catholic Avant-Garde, 288
Music in Nonconformist Journals, 289
Nonconformism and Musical Innovation: Recontextualizing Jeune France, 291
The Framing Manifesto and Its Discourse, 293
The Choice of Intellectual Sponsors, 295
Beyond Modernism: Olivier Messiaen, 296
Beyond "Orientalism" to the Cosmic: André Jolivet, 302
Critical Readings on the Right and the Left, 308

Part 3: Seeds of the Vichy and Resistance Aesthetics
Redefining "Frenchness" in Music, 310
Jeanne au bûcher in 1939, 312
Resistance Despite the Odds, 314

Conclusion
The Subtle Symbolic Dialogue and Its Impact, 319
The Convergence of French Music and Politics, 321
From Political Utterance and Discourse Back to "Text," 322

Notes, 325
Bibliography, 427
Index, 463

THE COMPOSER
AS INTELLECTUAL

INTRODUCTION

THE ARTIST AS INTELLECTUAL?

Ever since Julien Benda's impassioned indictment of apostate intellectuals in *La trahison des clercs* (1927), there has largely been consensus on the intellectual's true "charge." Edward Said, for example, concurs with Benda that the intellectual attempts to be "the conscience of mankind," implacably and courageously upholding "eternal standards of truth and justice."[1] Inherent in this conception is the intellectual's oblivion to both professional and material advantage: acting as moral adjudicator, the intellectual speaks out publicly, and regardless of the consequences. Perpetually vigilant, he or she intrepidly exposes half-truths, received ideas, faulty logic, or empty rhetoric—integrally including that dispensed by "power."[2]

These associations, of course, developed originally in the period of the Dreyfus affair, which Benda himself experienced, and which helped to solidify the social rubric "intellectual." For by the later 1890s, amid efforts to establish the innocence of a Jewish army officer accused of treason, the essential characteristics of the then derisively labeled "intellectuals" emerged. They were in search of truth, based upon empirical or verifiable fact, and concomitantly insisted upon justice for all, established by the basic principle of the French Revolution. In doing so they negated "raison d'Etat," or blind credence in the nation and its institutions of "authority," which in the period of the Dreyfus affair still included both the French army and the church.[3]

For Benda, however, intellectuals were betraying their role in the decade that followed World War I—many by continuing slavishly to serve "the national interest," as they had throughout the war. Now engulfed by the political "passions" not only of nation, but of race and class, intellectuals had ignominiously abandoned their sacred duty for the sake of personal and professional interests. In short, instead of boldly contesting dogma, stereotypes, slogans, and "orthodox party lines," many now espoused them, in effect, colluding "to make hegemony work."[4]

Recent intellectual historians, while in principle endorsing Benda's "universalist" definition, have questioned its limits and its uncompromising idealism, which exclude certain types of intellectuals. Gramsci, for example, put forth the classification of the "organic intellectual," or those who are defined by new collective goals, appearing in connection with an emergent social class. Moreover, Erich Auerbach argues that intellectuals rather than categorically rejecting their affiliation with a national culture, can retain a critical "affiliation" with it.[5] And, more recently, Jacques Julliard and Michel Winock, among others, have posited the category of intellectual who promotes national unity, including certain French circles in the mid-1930s.[6]

Far more problematic, however, in both past and present definitions, is the question of which groups may be subsumed by this rubric, or "who" serves an "intellectual function" and how. Benda himself explicitly included artists in his denunciation of intellectual treason, and more recently Said has treated writers of fiction, including Jonathan Swift, as "intellectuals." For the major issues that Swift addressed in his writing, according to Said, are those within the intellectual domain—or "anything connected with human aggression or organized human violence." Swift served an "intellectual function" in describing stereotypes, or by adopting and therefore exposing the discourse that "made it possible for England to mistreat Ireland so cavalierly."[7] In sum, for Said, within whatever genre, through whatever stylistic devices, the intellectual is essentially the author of a language that attempts "to speak the truth to power." For he or she knows both how and when to "intervene" in language in order to expose its misrepresentations, its euphemisms, and its socially baleful obfuscations. But the intellectual is also someone with a developed ability to "represent"—to embody or articulate "a message, a view, an attitude, a philosophy, or opinion."[8]

THE COMPOSER, PUBLIC ISSUES, AND SYMBOLS

The implications of such a broad definition complement the more capacious description of potentially "intellectual" professions posited by Jacques Julliard and Michel Winock. For, as they argue, intellectuals are, first, those who through their specific activity propose a "direction to society"—an analysis or moral standard, which their previous work qualifies them to offer. Second, they practice professions that inherently predispose them to the treatment of general ideas or philosophies concerning both society and its most appropriate means of governance. And, finally, they have "clout" because they bring to their political or ideological involvement a reputation and renown that they have gained elsewhere, in their own fields.[9]

Of particular significance here is that for Julliard and Winock the professions thus subsumed include not only science, philosophy, literature, and art, but also music. Their *Dictionnaire des intellectuels français* makes this clear, if only implicitly, by its notable inclusion of a number of entries on prominent twentieth-century French composers. The implications of this inclusion are substantial, and I was forced to consider them in depth when requested to write articles for the dictionary on several of these composers, all of whom figure centrally here.[10] This endeavor led to the title of my study and to the thesis or the premise which informs it: that we may better understand these composers, their motivations, and all the levels of their work, within their context as "intellectuals." For they were indeed intellectuals, deeply engaged with public issues, symbols, and ideologies, and their evolution in this period cannot be explained by "pure" stylistic development, or sporadic influence from other arts. This is not to say that all composers in this period were highly politicized, nor that their artistic choices were dictated exclusively by ideological considerations; but the contemporary issues were significant factors for the prominent composers I have selected for study, and whose work and choices can be more fully explained in this light.

Composers faced the same questions as French intellectuals in other fields, but the most important issue for them was how to respond to the state's ideological projections through the unique register provided by their art. They also confronted the responses or cultural constructions of the government's opponents, who contested the identity thus being enunciated through culture and addressed the key issues surrounding it. Sought out by political groupings, including those in power, they were frequently importuned to use their capacity for cultural "representation" to legitimize an ideological stance. In a culturally centralized nation like France this had implications for performance or for official "favors," and some put aesthetic integrity first, later realizing the political implications of their refusal. Others stuck firmly to their already established political-aesthetic principals, and thus incurred the same professional risks as committed intellectuals in different fields. Often, their positions were not communicated verbally but expressed through symbolic gestures, as well as by stylistic decisions, that can only be understood completely within such a context.

This hermeneutic premise necessarily counters the still dominant tendency in the historiography of twentieth-century music, which concentrates on internal stylistic evolution, and has consequently dismissed many of these composers. For the standard of evaluation in established historiography remains clearly that of "success" in bequeathing techniques to subsequent major composers throughout the twentieth century. Such an approach therefore emphasizes compositional "method" and how it fits a teleological conception of ineluctable musical "progress" or necessity.[11] It is less concerned with the style, or with the content and meaning of the works themselves, and, by extension, with the cultural context that originally imbued them with resonance. Works that are apparently engaged are frequently dismissed as extraneous to "real" musical development, treated as embarrassing aberrations worthy of only anecdotal treatment.

The exception, of course, is Marxism: within Marxist musical historiography ideology is taken seriously, although most often construed reductively—as a form of "false consciousness," especially when associated with the bourgeoisie. Indeed, several of the existing studies that treat the composers of interwar France at length have been written from Marxist or revised Marxist perspectives, and they have generally been diatribes, dismissive of their work. The most prominent is that of Theodor Adorno, who equates all French neoclassicism with Stravinsky's, reviling it as essentially infantile, socially affirmative, and devoid of content. From Adorno's perspective the neoclassic is monolithic, a crystallized social formation, and, like all tradition, inherently inimical to the critical spirit. Within his essentialist manner of associating ideological orientations with aesthetic values and styles, contestation within neoclassicism is invisible—a theoretical impossibility.

Adorno's discourse does not recognize semiotic strategies within a social field of power; it focuses on the way in which the individual seeks freedom, is able to preserve an "un-fixed" identity. Within his "negative dialectic," repressive classic forms and the rational reconciliation they embody must be "dissolved" through innovations in processes, which oppose authority, totality, or structure. His paradigm, then, is the composer's new organization and working through of the material: this, as in Schoenberg, is what he identifies with the advanced, autonomous artwork. Given Adorno's focus on the dialectic of technique and material, the destruction of fixed meaning, or emancipation from false resolution, cannot occur within a formal tradition.

The fact that these composers did work within tradition has provided the basis for several studies that presume their "bourgeois" identities, and thus similarly attack their work. One recent book, focused on the group Les Six, indicts their purported "quest for pleasure," associating their so-called neoclassicism with frivolity, good humor, and pure egoism. Moreover, it argues that their eclectic intermingling of cultural levels, genres, and styles was an expression of their class—its uncertainty as to social place, and its fear of the future and of change. Attempting to restore or rewrite past chefs-d'oeuvres, they sought to reverse both history and time, and created a reactionary art, devoid of profundity, which "counts for nothing" in twentieth-century music.[12]

Long unexamined and unchallenged in music, the theoretical premises upon which such arguments rest have already come under assault in almost all the other academic fields. As several recent historians have averred, Marxism, as an interpretive paradigm, has unequivocally declined with the collapse of communist systems and the challenge of postmodern theories. Even within Marxism itself, older beliefs in class determination and historical teleology have been shaken in light of Louis Althusser's challenging new reading of Marx. For Althusser argues that Marx perceived not simple economic determinism but rather the close interaction of social processes, or "over determination," a term that Althusser borrowed from Freud. From this perspective we are compelled to examine the imbrication of political, economic, and cultural factors, and to recognize the openness and evolution of identity, as opposed to its roots in class interests. For an individual may inhabit a number of different social identities at once; moreover, the factors in identity-formation, which is fluid, include both race and gender.

In light of these new departures, I shall attempt to shift the questions as well as the theoretical paradigms through which we approach these composers, and reexamine them in terms of the complexity of their identities and their intellectual responses. None were ideological "puppets"; rather, they responded to the symbols and debates around them, which we are obliged to examine from the perspective of recent studies, historical and theoretical, in other fields. My approach, which utilizes postmodern insights into the flexibility of both identity and of meaning, is relational, or contextual, and incorporates Pierre Bourdieu's perceptions of semiotic strategies within a social field of power. For Bourdieu's sociological perspective on power, or hegemony, and its deployment of symbols allows us to comprehend not only the state, but also its cultural dialogue with both groups in opposition and artist-intellectuals. Most pertinent to this study is Bourdieu's seminal concept of "symbolic domination"—the attempt to maintain social hierarchies through the definition of symbolic legitimacy and thus "symbolic capital." Bourdieu's concomitant concept of "symbolic violence" refers to the invisibility of this imposition, which reproduces the existing social order but without physical violence. It occurs not only within a colonial context but in class relations, as well as in relations between the sexes, as Bourdieu demonstrated so vividly in *La domination masculine*.

It also occurs politically, for groups in power impose representations, which provoke a wide range of responses across a broad spectrum, from dominations, or acceptance, to contestation. Given this awareness, we can no longer dismiss the French government's involvement in music as a simple quest for "gloire," or for "return" on its financial investment. For power is a broad and fluid phenomenon and can manifest itself, for example, in the establishment of the criteria for symbolic or cultural legitimacy, and, by extension, for official "consecration." Dissension erupts when there is inescapable misadaptation or disjunction between dominant systems of classification and experience in the social world. While, for the most part, musicology is still locked in either a narrow and literal or a philosophical conception of the political, Bourdieu (like Foucault) identifies it in systems of representation and in challenges to them. For Bourdieu (as opposed to Adorno), our perception of the symbols that "authority" has inculcated for political ends—in many possible styles—is a prerequisite for interpreting culture and deciphering politics. In a country like France, where the state has traditionally made a substantial investment in culture, we must then unlock the language of symbolic domination and the idioms through which social actors respond. From this dialogic perspective, styles or symbols we have previously considered to be apolitical should necessarily be reconsidered, and the structure of symbolic opposition revealed.[13]

This is what I attempt in my study of how specific French composers, as intellectuals, responded in a period of state manipulation of culture, and of political messages enunciated through it. For as the title of each chapter indicates, the major intellectual questions of both decades had direct implications for state policy in the arts, for the responses of political adversaries, and for the stylistic choices of French composers. They lived in an era of mass politics, when political leaders realized that "the political" had to be expressed through symbols, including those of high culture. French composers in this period were aware that ideological visions were being projected onto styles, and some responded symbolically by manipulating the musical meanings established by official culture or by its opponents. Again, actions or gestures, conceived within the framework of ambient symbols or meanings, could be preferable to words in situations of tension, and, in some cases, as Ravel found, more effective. Through culturally meaningful acts as well as through confrontations with the ideological connotations of style, in addition to artistic collaborations with specific intellectual circles, important composers did act as intellectuals.

Ideology, then, as I use the term in this study, is not "false consciousness" in the Marxist sense, but rather, in that of Karl Mannheim, a system of ideas at the basis of a political or social theory. Its impact on French music was multiple—manifest in the cultural initiatives of both power and its opponents, in the choices made by composers, in journalistic interpretations, and in politically partisan constructions. French composers felt all these ideological forces in addition to their own inner tensions, or the pull between conscious ideological intent and aesthetic, artistic demands. I maintain, then, that although its workings were subtle, ideology was no less important an influential factor in musical evolution in France than it was in interwar Germany, Italy, or Soviet Russia. For music became entangled in the sophisticated cultural practices of politics in France in these years, and particularly in attempts to exploit its potential for constituting political representations or images. It was thus an integral part of symbolic modes of ideological communication within the political culture of France in the period from the First to the Second World War.

French intellectuals in all fields were well aware of how ideological orientations were being communicated through the symbolism of style and genres, not only in music but in the other arts as well. Recognizing the stakes, they, together with composers, became deeply engaged in the intellectual, symbolic battle that affected both political perceptions and the evolution of French music. But here we must also be aware of the diverse responses of individual composers and generations, as well as the changing or contradictory impulses that could exist within composers as their social identities evolved.

In addition, we must recognize that composers entered into political or ideological issues using both their prose and their music as a means to address or subtly comment on contemporary ideological-stylistic debates. In some cases their verbal articulations or writings contradicted the symbolic message of their styles, for the creative or "autonomous" personality, which refuses all orthodoxies, could conflict with the rational intellect. Indeed, since the romantic era, artists from Friedrich Schiller to Robert Lewis Stevenson have recognized this bifurcation, seeking ways to explain it metaphorically. Both Schiller and Stevenson emphasized the distinction between an artist's reason and his creative faculties, or, as Schiller described them, his "transient extravagances" or nonreflective aesthetic impulses. Which, we might ask, is more authentic when it comes to responding to ideological issues? Is it Stevenson's "Brownie," his "unseen collaborator" whom "I keep in the back garret, while I get all the praise"?[14] Is intellect in art, then, a "common enterprise," as Stevenson so eloquently put it—a collaboration between the two parts of the self—one rooted in rational reasoning and the other in aesthetic logic? As Mikhail Bakhtin perceived, great art is founded upon the process of dialogue, or the refusal of orthodoxy, of monologic consciousness, in favor of dialogic consideration of possibilities. If artists are true intellectuals, then, is it sometimes that less controlled or self-questioning side that prevails and articulates truth? These are among the questions that I seek to raise in this study.

Further questions concern other aspects of the creative process, or the transformation from intent to realization, a question that is similarly at the center of postmodern explorations into language. Here we must also consider the tensions between intellectual abstraction and art, or between communication with a specific intent and the experiential or "poetic" components of artistic symbols. Ideology may provide an impetus, but its schematizing or simplifying goals inherently thwart the nuanced and personal, the "complicating" or pluralizing character of great art. For art seeks concrete experience, emotions and passions as opposed to abstraction; it strives for immediacy and closeness, whereas ideology is by nature general and inclusive. Ideas, in sum, undergo transformation in the aesthetic process, in the ineluctable movement from theories to experience, or to the emotional coherence of a creative application. This is perhaps one meaning of the now famous phrase of Stephen Spender, "The politics of the artist is the politics of the apolitical, decided on for the sake of life and art and not of politics."[15]

The vision projected by art, then, is inherently inimical to that of "theory," for a transubstantiation accompanies the movement into the symbolic, the aesthetic realm. But other transmutations may occur in the gap between the artist's conscious ideas and the artistic "message," as a result of both collaborations and shifting performative circumstances. For we cannot assume an identity of intent between the composer and the author of a text he sets, or between composer, librettist, and stage designer, as in opera. All these semiotic factors interact to shape the utterance, within the performative context, the political conjuncture, and the current framework of stylistic meaning. As intellectuals, then, composers made artistic decisions within an ideologically charged and volatile context, and their conscious intent was not always that which emerged, for all of the reasons that we have considered.

Our perception of the meaning of their decisions, of course, is dependent upon recognition of those cultural symbols deployed by political power as it evolved and interacted with the symbols of adversaries. These symbols had direct implications for music, most notably in the case of classicism, which became the "national style" during both World War I and the twenties, but whose interpretation was contested by the government's critics. Participating in these contestations were specific French composers who were apprised of the issues and knowingly inflected, manipulated, or "disrupted" dominate chauvinistic meanings, thus serving an "intellectual function." But their tactics were as subtle as those of the state, which often acted in an indirect manner to "orient" French taste in the direction of the state's cultural, symbolic goals.

Significantly, recent studies have argued that starting with World War I the French state systematically expanded its domain, and particularly its techniques of intervention in culture. After the war, it continued to enlarge the realm of political dialogue with its ideological adversaries centrally to include the language of the arts, or high culture. In France, as in Germany, the state continued to occupy the same extended cultural terrain that it had carved out in wartime, and more actively to shape political representation and national cultural identity. The cultural dynamic of the prewar period was therefore reversed, for before the war the nationalist leagues had "invaded" French culture and henceforth set the terms of the dialogue. Since, as we shall see, their cultural arguments and symbols had triumphed by 1914, only to be adapted by the state, it is here essential, briefly, to review this phenomenon. Moreover, this was the period when French composers, as a result of their ideological engagement in the Dreyfus affair, began to be cognizant of their "intellectual" role.

THE POLITICAL AND SYMBOLIC BACKGROUND

Having legally lost their battle in the Dreyfus affair, French nationalists proceeded to target the arts as a realm through which to further their traditionalist interpretations of essential French values. Cultural criticism henceforth became a covert form of political intervention, or a means through which to articulate and diffuse their distinctive conception of "authentic" French identity. Indeed, the Right considered literature and art to be "the principle model and support of politics," expressive of "the ideal form and fundamental nature of the national community and the people."[16] Recent studies have shown that long before the war nationalist critics of art as well as writers applied such politicized conceptions and thus subtly influenced aesthetic directions. In fact, throughout the decade preceding the war, the conceptual and aesthetic terrain was being prepared for a return to tradition and a reassertion of classicism as France's distinct "national style."

Since the French musical world became caught up in this cultural "project," being aggressively invaded and used by French nationalist leagues, the Republic was forced to respond.[17] The state now proceeded to use music as an important venue for political representation, and a means of communicating spiritual authority, thus making it a nexus for ideological debate.

In music the institutional dimension was particularly distinctive, for, to a greater extent than in other fields, a single state institution dominated professional training, and thus "consecration." At the time, the Conservatoire National de Musique, which controlled "legitimate" education in music, found itself confronted by a nationalist challenger, the Schola Cantorum. The latter's eventual director, Vincent d'Indy, was a prominent member of the Ligue de la Patrie Française, and through the school he sought to develop a musical culture to oppose the state's. He marshaled the prestige and resources of the league, and played upon the widespread criticism of the pedagogical limitations of the Conservatoire to legitimize his own school of music. Eventually the institutional opposition that resulted generated a structural opposition, at once professional and ideological, that would pervade much of the French musical world.[18]

Especially significant here is that the Schola Cantorum did not just define musical values that it considered to be "national," it established a "code" that associated them with genres, styles, repertoires, and techniques. Hence, while literature diffused nationalist "ideas" as embodied creatively in fictional form, and the visual arts engaged with politically charged images, music opened up another powerful realm: it "manifested" nationalist values through a potent symbolism that was inherently bivocal—or invoking both politics and art—an insight that the state would deftly appropriate in wartime.[19] Moreover, the Schola developed a resonant new discourse that transcended cold political abstractions by conflating the political, religious, and aesthetic, which the Republic would also eventually borrow. And finally, the Schola created a canon not only for pedagogical purposes, but one which it "staged," framed by a discourse on its political significance, as later would the state.

French nationalist leagues taught the Republic that music could be invaluable as a form of "representation"—that it could help shape perceptions when surrounded by a discourse which imbued it with ideological meaning. For it could engage the realm of what Freud refers to as "primary process thought," or that which is associated with "projection, fantasy, and the incorporation of disparate ideas."[20] And so music was particularly useful for the nationalist Right in the wake of the Dreyfus affair, as again in wartime, for all that it conflated could not be addressed effectively through rational critique in the French republican tradition.

The Third Republic, which before the affair has not systematically imprinted its values through music, henceforth responded in kind, making it an agent in the political-symbolic battle. It thus developed its own historical conceptions based upon French popular, secular, and revolutionary traditions, which it similarly associated with a canon, as well as with specific genres, repertoires, and techniques.[21] But as the republican elite had waxed more conservative by the eve of the war, many nationalist conceptions, including those concerning French art, were subtly appropriated by official discourse. And so with the war and the triumph of traditionalist values, the state employed the nationalist "code," as well as the nationalists' discourse, and their techniques of "framing" the French musical canon. In addition, with the growing prestige of the stalwart Ligue de l'Action Française, the prewar adversarial stance concerning "authentic" French culture entered the official mainstream. The league's rhetoric of French art as classic accordingly became doctrine, as did the nationalist belief that a nation's culture, and above all its art, was the quintessential articulation of the indigenous national "soul."

THE STATE, NATIONAL SYMBOLS, AND THE DIALOGUE

Beginning with the war, state officials concurred that music could serve an invaluable role in uniting the French community and "expressing" the nation's mythic "essence." They were also aware that this integrally involved a control of the mode of presentation in order to ensure the right ideological inscription—again, a lesson learned from the nationalist leagues. My first chapter shows that, as a result of these goals, French composers were enlisted to express "patriotic" orthodoxies, and they were expected to do so within established conceptions of the French classic style. In France, as opposed to Germany, then, we may see that the origins of neoclassicism lay not only in responses to the trauma of war, but also in official propaganda through culture. And here recent studies of other French intellectuals in wartime are particularly relevant, for scholars have underlined the difficult choice they faced between acceding to state hegemony, on the one hand, and propaganda, or "resistance." While the majority participated in cultural mobilization in support of the war effort and propaganda—and most prominently the academic community—a minority experienced an intellectual "prise de conscience."[22]

The first chapter thus examines how musical administrators, scholars, and critics played their "patriotic" role by disseminating conservative conceptions concerning French musical classicism, its myths, and its canon. It also shows how musicians participated in the "staging" of music in order to "construct" a conception of great French composers in accordance with this message (in the manner of nationalist leagues)—to control and "frame" the performative context. These official intentions are important, for they helped to establish dominant meanings and symbols, of which French musicians became increasingly and visibly aware. Indeed, some composers resisted these official symbols and meanings, as the first chapter demonstrates: they chafed at the limits of nationalist orthodoxies concerning style, subversively inflecting or baldly confronting them. Like other "mobilized" intellectuals, they experienced inner conflicts and contradictions, and expressed them in various manners, from symbolic public gestures to stylistic strategies. They, too, were forced to confront larger issues that would preoccupy them long after the war, and in particular the proper function of art in a period of imposed or implicit cultural constraints.

Satie, Ravel, and Debussy, I argue, challenged the "authoritarian discourse of monologic consciousness" (in the words of Bakhtin) by either subverting it or introducing another "voice."[23] Critical of French nationalist myths, and well aware of their cultural symbols, they acted as authentic intellectuals in ignoring the professional consequences of their "disruptive" acts. Claude Debussy reflected profoundly, if more discreetly than the others, on "how" to be patriotic, artistically taking issue with his professed nationalist doctrine and maintaining the contradiction with telling irony and integrity. As I show, this "inner dialogy" results in a semiotic complexity and multivalence of meaning, which could accommodate diverse constructions, even in his own lifetime. Satie was far less subtle: in works like *Parade* he satirized the dominant model, ridiculing the "myth" not only of classical hierarchy, but of proportions and "order."

Nationalist hegemony did not end with the war, and the second chapter traces the manner in which the conservative postwar governments intruded on or "influenced" the same expanded cultural territory. National symbolism through culture was no less important in a shaken postwar nation, confronted with social threats from "below" at home and with weakened influence abroad. Previous studies have slighted the pervasively conservative musical culture of the twenties, which marshaled music to the service of national memory and identity, preferring to concentrate on the small avant-garde. This study rather argues that it is essential to see the "whole" to understand any one part, and the former includes the then hegemonic culture, subtly influenced by the state, with which the avant-garde entered into dialogue. We must recognize the stylistic, here neoclassic, norm in order to perceive the responses, or the critical commentary expressed through the congeries of approaches subsumed under "neoclassic style."

To understand not only Ravel, then, but progressive young composers in their attitude toward the past, classic paradigms, and foreign influence, it is important to analyze the "mainstream," the cultural programs and symbols through which the postwar government consolidated conservative dominance. Moreover, we must recall that in the twenties the political opposition to the government ardently contested its nationalist symbols, in the process of developing its own representations through culture. This chapter thus examines the musical aesthetic and programs of the "internationalist" political Left, and the meanings it established in the context of selected repertoires, musical genres, and styles, including "the classic."

Chapter 2 then turns to the responses of two generations of French composers, some of whom confronted the issues and assumed an intellectual role, each in his or her own manner, employing different approaches and stylistic means. For escape was not possible in this period, when questions that were raised not only during the war, but in the midst of the political conflict that followed, impinged on French cultural life. The older generation, which included not only Ravel and Satie, but Roussel and Koechlin, contested the "exclusive" nationalist conception of the classic, and its political connotations. Their choices of classic values were rife with connotations within this system of political representation, and contemporaries, rightly or wrongly, read meaning into their music within this framework. Although different political constructions of "the classic" included models or aesthetic prescriptions, it was composers who made the creative leap from these conceptions, as articulated discursively, to formal or stylistic interpretations. In doing so they traversed that eloquent gap between the substantially different cultural registers of verbal or discursive articulation and symbolic, artistic "representation." Some attempted to translate particular conceptions or models into stylistic terms, while others inflected or reacted to key concepts within specific constructions of the classic.

From this perspective, we may see how Ravel boldly confronted the conventional classic model, which was balanced in form and devoid of irony and of borrowing from "lower" cultural levels or "dangerous" foreign cultures. These included not only the Germanic (of recent date), but those associated with races or nationalities from which France was to be "protected" culturally, such as black American jazz. Ravel not only ignored these proscriptions, he openly flouted them in several works, including *L'enfant et les sortilèges* (which incorporated references to jazz) and his Sonata for Violin and Piano (1927). The latter work, for example, is not only formally innovative and harmonically dissonant in the first movement, but the second, marked "Blues," again openly manifests the influence of American black culture.

Moreover, as I show, Ravel and Satie even went so far as to challenge the glories of colonialism (Ravel's *Chansons madécasses*) and the priority of the community over individual conscience (Satie's *Socrate*) through stylistic means, within the context, as well as through choice of text. Both composers not only aligned themselves publicly with the Left and its universalist, individualist classic creed, but they resisted the political appropriation of music and musicians, including themselves, as Ravel did in refusing the Légion d'Honneur. Finally, while commenting creatively in their work and manipulating the politically symbolic connotations of style, Ravel and Satie both became part of important intellectual "networks," collaborating with other Left intellectuals.

But this chapter also shows that the younger generation, and specifically Les Six, who are often dismissed a frivolous pranksters, similarly confronted the musical "language or power." Responding to the notable exclusions in the dominant culture, they, too, boldly integrated these elements while demystifying and "reinventing" classic style, or making it "critical" within the cultural context. As chapter 2 demonstrates, to focus on the playful "slumming" or rebellion of this avantgarde is to miss its inherently contestatory element as expressed through style within this framework. For in a period when political meaning was invested in culture, a response to such models inescapably carried political implications—an implicit criticism, if not clear alignment.

Milhaud, for example, as a Jew, faced the intellectual issues that were raised directly: for him the French tradition was unquestionably "universal," one that since the Revolution tolerated different religions and races. The classic, as he interpreted it, meant the ancient Greek and Roman civilizations that he, like Freud before him, perceived as shared by Jews and non-Jews alike. Milhaud would inscribe this classicism—the stylistically synthetic, formally innovative, and intellectually critical classicism of the Left—in work like *Esther de Carpentras*. As chapter 2 shows, not all the ideas of Les Six concerning nationalism were those of their mentor Cocteau; rather, they crossed a wide spectrum and were influenced by specific French intellectual groupings.

In addition, while many studies, treating Igor Stravinsky as the quintessential neoclassic, assimilate their goals to his model, I rather stress the difference, or their own cultural message, as well as their debt to his style. Some readers may miss a substantial treatment of Stravinsky, but I have chosen to discuss him only within the context of his influence and effect in this framework. As a foreigner in France (until naturalized in the mid-thirties), Stravinsky did not face the same pressures or intellectual issues as native French composers, and although he held strong political opinions, they exercised a different kind of effect on his art. While some scholars have pointed out that he reinforced, stylistically, the conservative "constructions" of him by figures like Nadia Boulanger, he did not consistently assume an "intellectual" role, in the critical sense of Benda and Said.

Les Six, on the other hand, questioned both the dominant musical language and the cultural, political, and social structures that sustained it in a manner no less radical than the Dadaists, who helped shape their aesthetic. The group's neoclassicism, as I argue, was deeply informed by the Dadaist paradigm of radical disorientation—of respecting traditional cultural frames so that the internal, logical breaks would become more apparent. In the manner of Satie, they invoked aesthetic norms—here traditional and classic—only to thwart expectations, to "dislocate" conventions with all the more incisive effect. Like the Dadaists in other fields, they explored a language of "revolt," or a transformation of techniques of producing meaning in art, and thus questioned the basis of the musical language itself. No less than Dada, their neoclassicism was fundamentally a negation not only of social and cultural institutions, but of constructed "reality" and convention in the wake of the war.[24] Aware of the rise of mass culture, and particularly of popular music, recordings, and radio, they called traditional hierarchies into question at the very moment that conventional conservatory training reasserted tradition. Manifesting their awareness of "the popular" and its cultural-political significance with irony or appreciation, as well as humor, they eventually defined their own new status, as musician-intellectuals.

The third chapter thus demonstrates how the implicitly political stance of Les Six in the twenties became explicit in the thirties, under the Popular Front, when politics was given more obvious cultural expression, further motivating them to become "engaged" intellectuals. They, like other intellectuals, confronted the phenomena of mass political organizations and parties and, like contemporary writers, realized the role they could play with regard to the ideologies they either supported or opposed. Just like their elders in the twenties, they faced the major issues through stylistic means, most defending French democratic values and a "popular," "modern" aesthetic against a contestatory fascist romanticism. But, in addition, several composers of the older generation (including Koechlin and Roussel) helped the state to redefine its aesthetic values in the direction of an accessible yet "progressive" style and adapted their own styles as well. Such stylistic transformation, which most histories construe as "regression" from the standpoint of evolution, was rather, as this chapter argues, perceived in the period and context as culturally innovative.

To demonstrate this I examine the contemporary cultural discourses—not only that promoted by the Popular Front, but also that of its vociferous opposition, which contested both its politics and its aesthetics. As distinct from previous studies, this one argues that musical journals and political spokesmen reveal the extent to which the government and its opponents had fully developed, coherent aesthetics, which were further clarified in the course of the dialogue. This chapter then demonstrates that only such a background allows us to perceive the structure of stylistic meaning and confrontation in the period, against which we may better understand the responses of specific French composers. Not all members of Les Six and the Ecole d'Arcueil supported the government: some sought out or were recruited by other enclaves, for which they provided valuable "cultural capital," and which provided them with publicity and financial backing. These figures included Poulenc, Sauget, and, to a certain extent, Arthur Honegger, who, although he participated in the government's projects, finally aligned himself with a political group that grew hostile to it. Personal and political factors, of course, cannot be separated, and I accordingly attempt to consider both elements, or their intersection, in each case.

Events such as the Spanish Civil War and Mussolini's invasion of Ethiopia provoked a crisis of conscience in most intellectuals, especially Catholic conservatives, including Poulenc and Sauguet. Both now became even more censorious of the Popular Front government, and here it is significant that Poulenc's turn to surrealist texts and to religious composition, or his spiritual and Catholic "reawakening," accompanied both his rejection of the government and its "culture" and his full acceptance of his own sexuality. The personal and political were united in Poulenc's embrace of those musical styles and symbols that now (and formerly at the Schola) represented ideological opposition to secular republican aesthetic values. For Poulenc, unlike his colleagues in Les Six, this opposition was a means of "defending" French culture—not so much against fascist threats as against the "superficial" and rational cultural values of the Popular Front. Accordingly, as I demonstrate, Poulenc went against his own professional interest and was forced to rely on the patronage of those who similarly distanced themselves from the government and the cultural values it sought to promote.

The final chapter then turns to the shift in aesthetic legitimacy and symbolism that, as I demonstrate, accompanied the fall of the Popular Front in 1938.[25] The failure and delegitimization of the Popular Front and the concomitant consolidation of conservative hegemony helped to usher in a profound transformation in musical taste and aesthetics. This cultural evolution of the Republic and its elites, then, provides a background to a fuller understanding of official policies and changing values in French music in the later 1930s. During this period, in official circles, we find a return not only to Scholiste models, but to the discourse of the former political and cultural critics of the Republic on the right. Accordingly, many works, as well as canonic or prominent composers, assumed new significance or political valence, as aesthetic values began to change.

As the title of this chapter indicates, "spirituality" henceforth became a dominant theme within the new discourse, but it was diversely interpreted, carrying different connotations for specific groups. And so the shift in aesthetic hegemony and the tendency to embrace those values previously associated with the conservative and profascist opposition, should not blind us to the significant nuances. The return to the "spiritual," the "noble," and the "human" was not monolithic in meaning, but rather carried diverse ideological implications of which we must be aware.

Even in the midst of political trauma, fear, and a return to the "transcendent," there were those who defended republican values and maintained idealism and hope.[26] An important spectrum of ideas concerning the spiritual and the "human" was articulated around Jeune France, a group of composers whose most prominent members were Jolivet and Messiaen. Accordingly, this chapter shows that the ideals of the group itself were complex and should be studied within the context of the philosophic-literary "nonconformist" movement of the early 1930s. For intertextual reference to the intellectual ideals of these writers is clear not only in the group's manifesto but in its artistic assertion of universal values, religious feeling, and human dignity. Jeune France's distinctive musical modernity was profoundly influenced by the movement's search for ideological-aesthetic alternatives to positions on both the left and the right, by its quest for a path that placed the "individual" or the "person" in new light. Yet, again, their aesthetic was inherently rather than explicitly engaged with the political-ideological context (with a slight delay in music) and the "nonconformists'" concern with human responsibility, true community, and values. This alternative ideology, for Jeune France, provided a guiding and sustaining vision, and led to an inseparable fusion of aesthetic, religious, and ideological elements in their work.

While Messiaen's motivations have generally been interpreted as narrowly religious, in this context, then, we may see that his specific points of emphasis approached nonconformist philosophy in its more conservative enunciations. Similarly, Jolivet's fascination with non-Western religions and larger cosmic forces transcending the national should be seen within the framework of the movement's more democratic or progressive tendencies. Indeed, their chosen intellectual "sponsors," ranging from François Mauriac to Georges Duhamel, included figures who promoted a similar range of values and interests in the literary realm. Here, then, I stress that we must remain alert to the variety and subtlety of responses expressed both in and around music in the later 1930s, which demonstrates that there was no consensual movement toward the "spirit" of Vichy. The future was not uniformly perceived as inevitable, as recent studies have argued, and in music we find not only French self-recrimination but expressions of hope as well as the invocation of inspirational symbols. By examining French musical culture we may thus see that the nation's self-image was by no means unequivocally that of a "rural, feudalized, feminized, and victimized nation," as a historian of French art has recently charged.[27] Music's specific mode or "register" of artistic representation expressed and helped shape another range of themes, values, and tensions that we cannot ignore in the cultural history of the period. Much musical discourse, as well as the stylistic message of numerous composers, enunciated an aspiration, resistance, and vision, which would endure throughout the dark years of Vichy.

TWO HISTORIES AND THEIR INTERSECTION

This book, in sum, attempts to reintegrate two previously separated histories—that of official politics and culture, and responses to them, with that of musical, stylistic development. Cultural symbols in French politics were mobilizing forces that affected two fields at once, and perceiving this is essential to achieving important new musical and historical insights. French musical culture in these years, its dynamic and logic, its particular concerns, divisions, and tensions remain, in part, inscrutable or opaque without these perceptions. So, too, does the evolution of the French avant-garde, which developed in a constant, subtle dialogue with the dominant ideological-aesthetic positions that I examine in this study. From this perspective, then, we may gain a singular view of not only the tensions within the culture, but also of those within the music, leading us to new layers and depths of hermeneutic interpretation.

Each chapter thus begins with an analysis of the predominant cultural themes, images, and stylistic meanings of the period, as manifest in state-sponsored performances and institutions, to which the political opposition responded. I then turn to this opposition to examine the structure of stylistic confrontation, and I analyze both the musical programs and meanings it developed in dialogic relation with those of the state. Finally, each chapter attempts to illuminate how different generations of those French composers whom we may consider intellectuals reacted to these significations in both their prose and their musical compositions. I examine not only their ideological orientations and how these translated into terms of their style, but the contradictions within some of these figures, which are best understood against the background of these conflicts. I also demonstrate how particular works of these composers were both appropriated and "used" (or misused) by either the government or its opposition in the continuing battle over national identity.

In sum, this book seeks to present a distinct interpretation of how French music articulated with ideology as a result of the political-cultural initiatives of the state, and the response of its opponents. It was in this manner, I contend, that ideological orientations became demonstrably associated with aesthetic values, or with tastes and styles in music, provoking specific composers to respond. To understand their responses we must recreate the dialogue of which they were a part, or the interlocutors who are now absent, but whose voices are essential to a full grasp of the "utterance." These works may then assume new culturally and politically semantic dimensions, or a multivocality we have overlooked, when placed within the discourse, symbols, and ideological meanings of their day. From this perspective I argue that many of the composers studied here were not only artists but also intellectuals who responded to the major ideological-aesthetic questions and polemics of their period. They did so diversely and creatively, yet penetrating their complex responses reveals deeper levels of not only their work, but also of French culture in the two tumultuous decades between the World Wars.

1

Wartime Nationalism, Classicism, and Their Limits

Part 1: State Hegemony and Musical Culture: Institutions and Propaganda

FRENCH IDENTITY AND THE CLASSIC MYTH

On 16 December 1915, the director of the recently reopened Paris Opéra displayed his political acumen to a government still skeptical of opera's relevance in wartime. Drawing on innovations in his own private theater, Jacques Rouché mounted a seemingly anodyne work, resembling classic "Opéra-ballet" and bearing the pallid title of *Mademoiselle de Nantes*.[1] The production, in reality, was ingenious—a brilliant departure in wartime propaganda—not through blatant "brainwashing" but through means far more powerful for being so insidiously indirect.

Central to the work's scenario is a concert with musicians and audience dressed in period costume; the former are presenting a performance of French music before the grandchildren of Madame de Montespan. More specifically, the eighteenth-century progeny of this famous mistress of Louis XIV are listening to selections of Lully and Charpentier which illustrate the birth and growth of opera in France. The "homology" between the performances here was charged: the audience that was present in the opera was being manipulated astutely toward identification with what was being represented on the stage. The concert depicted historically was instilling national memory as well as cultural identity, creating a sense of its unity and continuity as the patrimony of all future generations. So too was the performance at the Opéra: the audience in the theater was witnessing its own past on the stage and, in identifying with the historical audience, imbibing the same lesson of French identity and tradition. Its heritage, it learned, was classic; in addition, since the illustrious days of Louis XIV it has been bound instrumentally to state power, defining the French community and insuring its prestige.

In this and similar productions Rouché inserted the Opéra into a network of wartime propaganda through clever mediation, or the attempted control of the production of meaning. This included popular culture as well, for, as French cultural officials understood, different levels of culture offered different "modes" of understanding and had to be surveilled in distinctive ways. Mass culture was widely spread and well financed, particularly the song culture of *café-concerts* and music halls, which, as censors were well aware, could both sustain morale or give voice to dissent. And so they scrupulously reviewed not only the lyrics but actual performances themselves, fully understanding the volatility of meaning in this repertoire as the situation changed. The Opéra was far easier to monitor and control and to marshal toward the goals of propaganda as an official state theater under the bureaucratic management and vigilant eye of Jacques Roché.

Like other institutions, the Opéra was to serve as a realm of national memory and myth, to instill a unified wartime identity in a politically and culturally fractured France.[2] Here the myth was that of French classicism: France was "Latin" and thus classic in culture, but according to a circumscribed notion of the style that was rooted in the ideology of the monarchist Right. The doctrine of the now triumphant Ligue de l'Action Française placed primary emphasis upon the classic aesthetic as indigenously French, thus necessitating the extirpation of any foreign stylistic "infiltration."[3] Its dogma provided a key to crafting a unified cultural myth, rooted in history and thus imparting a sense of the "tradition" for which the war was being fought. Rouché's production engaged this myth, imposing it through symbols, or "representations," as would most other official cultural institutions in wartime, and prominently including those involving music. For with the war came greater state involvement in music, in its symbolism and social context, hence the development of techniques like Rouché's for subtly "orienting" public taste. In addition, the French state would learn how to apply pressures on nonofficial musical institutions, establishing a hegemony that French composers would have to confront, and to which they reacted diversely. In this chapter we will thus trace not only the refraction of this hegemonic myth in musical institutions, but the way French composers responded, invoking it or cleverly resisting it, within the boundaries of wartime strictures.

Throughout French cultural institutions the goal for wartime propaganda was the same: to effect consensus concerning French identity and thus arrive at a unified core of national beliefs. Being the first "total war," it was imperative both to obtain and to maintain the complete cooperation of French civil society—to win public opinion and to sustain it as the conflict continued.[4] This was particularly crucial in the wake of the cultural "war" that followed the Dreyfus affair, when the defeated French nationalist Right belligerently posed the question of "essential" French values. Leagues like Action Française had challenged the legitimacy of republican institutions as incarnations of endemic French identity, true national values, and "authentic" French culture. Well before the war, Action Française had reasserted French culture as classic, although not without resistance to its definition, particularly by the Left.[5]

Now, given the nationalists' triumph, the task was to enlist the collaboration of leaders not only in education but in religion and the arts in implementing wartime doctrine. For all areas had to be "mobilized," consensus as to French "classic" cultural identity had to be achieved, since it was, according to French wartime propaganda, fundamentally a "war of cultures."[6] The combat was thus to be "referenced" in this myth in order to galvanize energies and create a common emotional bond in a still politically contentious nation. To achieve this, the cultural myth had to have its roots in national history, since in France, as in Great Britain, history became the very core of national identity.[7]

French history and classicism were inherently bound in the ideology of Charles Maurras, the founder and principal thinker of the now prestigious nationalist Ligue de l'Action Française. For Maurras, a return to monarchy would be a return to the basic principles of order, which he believed also inhered in all great art. He concluded that beauty was dependent on order, and order on a hierarchy of values; hierarchy, in turn, depended upon an authority to "define and endorse it." And since, by extension, order and authority in politics ought to arise from tradition, that which followed this tradition in art and literature would be most successful. As a result, Maurras supported "absolutist" judgments in art, with the aesthetic model being, above all, seventeenth-century France. He thus equated classicism and traditionalism with his attempt to restore the French monarchical state that, historically, had produced such great art.[8]

For Maurras, as well as for his fellow nationalist, the writer Maurice Barrès, politics and art should be imbued with the same "national spirit" from which each was born. "French" comprised not only a language, but a mode of thought and feeling, common values and traits that bound the community in a political and aesthetic whole. Hence literature and art, for French nationalists, would be "the principal model and support of politics," expressive of "the ideal form and fundamental nature of the national community and the people." Barrès thus placed consistent emphasis on the tight imbrication of nationalist politics and art, stressing especially the role of art in "the mythologizing of the nation."[9] This concept was particularly resonant in wartime France, when Barrès's conviction would become a cornerstone of propaganda, which centered on culture.

Barrès's prestige, like that of Maurras, thus reached its height during the war, and his ideas concerning the "national genius" were widely accepted and deftly vulgarized. Now it was commonly believed that there was a French "style" not only of thought or philosophy, based on classical lucidity and precision, but of expression, which followed similar principles. As a result of such reasoning, the highest forms of culture were no longer to be considered as "universal" but rather as national: art, like intellect, unequivocally had a "patrie."[10] French values or characteristics were henceforth to be considered as fundamentally "classical," in marked distinction to the romantic, now associated with both irrationalism and the German enemy.[11]

Classicism, however, had specific connotations and meanings within this context: it was not associated with Greek universalism or the fundamental principles of ancient Greek philosophy. Rather, it was tied to "Latinity," in contrast to the "Nordic" romanticism and irrationalism of the "Huns," and stood for the purportedly endemic Latin virtues of purity, proportion, and order. Abjuring the egalitarian universalism of republican classicism for the orderly, hierarchical model of Catholicism, this conservative classicism emphasized "balance."[12] Classicism here connoted "discipline, obedience, and self-abnegation," or "a strictly regulated moral and aesthetic order" now essential to the nation's survival.13 Theorists of Action Française thus stressed that the greatest artists did not reject but harmoniously incorporated the influence of their illustrious national predecessors.

Classicism, then, became a national language of both remembrance and of mourning, one that inherently incarnated and poignantly evoked the collective as well as the spiritual.14 As a result of all these conceptions, classicism was linked to the "defense" of French culture, including protection against contamination from elements outside of the "national organism." "Purity" was considered essential and demanded the immediate extirpation of all foreign traits that could "pollute" any component of the mythic "génie national." For Action Française, the most consistent danger in the past arose from "Jewish art," which, even if the artist was a French citizen, brought in an "éclat oriental."15 From this point on, a principal concern in artistic judgment was thus "purity," or the absence of traits construed as foreign, or not endemic to the national classic style.

THE MYTH AND MUSIC IN WARTIME

In music, the classic dogma was tyrannical: it became the task of all institutions to impose its tenets, if through the prism of their specific professional concerns and means or techniques. Hence musical institutions were charged with both national and historical education—with the construction of national memory via a canon, the meaning of which was to be "fixed." Great French composers of the past had to be constructed or "created" within this context, the production of meaning in their music controlled to harness it to the service of the national myth. The national community, as Jacques Rouché showed, could indeed be "imagined" through music, which was distinctively to enunciate, if here ineffably, the principles that underpinned France's "ethos."16

Again, as Rouché perceived, to assume their new role, musical institutions had to mediate in the construction of meaning and taste, controlling the means of transmitting music to help shape the experience of it. Control of conditions of access to music meant experimenting with forms of performance, and here the now conservative Republic learned valuable lessons from the prewar Left and Right. Both had experimented extensively with forms of control of "performative context," or of that which impinges on the experience of musical works to endow them with a specific "cultural sense." To create a political "utterance," they often had "framed" concerts with appropriate discourses, or "keyed" the experience through various symbols to impart it with a political significance.17 In this manner, political meanings were being inscribed in genres, in works, and in style, a practice that could now be appropriated and implemented extensively by the French state. The Right, through these means, had helped to make music a natural agent for collective myth, or emblematic of national identity and embodying a conception of the national past. Here Action Française had played a key role, articulating a conception of the French musical canon as classic, one that, as we will see, was now widely accepted.18

But in French music the problem of factions remained: not all concurred with the dominant doctrine, for different institutions and performance societies conceived the French tradition in varying manners. The central problem was still precisely how to construe French classicism—an issue inherently tied to former passionate conflicts over the political identity of France. Were its roots in the universalism characteristic of the French Revolution, or in the cultural specificity that the Right had unequivocally identified with the Ancien Régime?[19] The problem of reconciling these disputes would fall on the shoulders of French bureaucrats or cultural officials, who now established a hegemonic network of control that musicians would find hard to escape. Indeed, as this chapter reveals, the distinction between public and private musical realms was effaced: both were here subject to state intervention as well as to incessant, if indirect, pressures. The subtle new modalities of state intrusion into a mobilized institutional network created official hegemony in public education and performance, and would eventually impinge on creativity. With all the techniques of intervention, musicians were thus to face the perplexing dilemma, not confronted so baldly since the French Revolution, of whether to embrace ideological conformity or risk dissent. For the musical culture in which they had to function comprised a maze of ideological controls, applied to lectures, concerts, editions, and, of course, the opera, to which we must here return.

IMAGINING THE FRENCH COMMUNITY THROUGH OPERA

Jacques Rouché was well prepared to navigate through the new labyrinth of official injunctions, balancing ideological orthodoxy with a pragmatic sense of what the French public would accept. Here he was unquestionably abetted by the perspicacious actions of Pierre Gheusi, the director of the Opéra-Comique, who had become the assistant to General Gallieni, the military governor of Paris. Gheusi helped to convince Albert Dalamier, the undersecretary of fine arts, of the importance of reopening the theaters for reasons of both employment and public morale. And so, the theaters, closed by the government in November 1914, reopened in early 1915, and the French classical tradition of Racine and Corneille, previously slighted, came to dominate the Comédie-Française. The themes of heroism, tragic nobility, and sacrifice it embodied now naturally assumed new resonance for the French wartime theatrical public.[20] But strict limitation to the French classic tradition, while easily defensible in principal, would not attract the new audience at the Opéra—the public that remained in the city, and that the institution now needed badly. The long-time "habitués" of the Opéra had either left Paris or terminated their subscriptions, opposing the theater's reopening in wartime, as did the powerful Conseil des Ministres.[21] But Rouché was nevertheless able to win the support of important figures, many of whom he knew through his journal, *La grande revue*, including Paul Painlevé, at the Ministère de l'Instruction Publique. He had undoubtedly succeeded in convincing them of the pedagogical function that the Opéra could serve in providing "national instruction" for the "grand public" as well as for unmobilized French youth.[22]

This was precisely the rationale he employed in a letter to the ministry of 25

August 1915, in which he explained his desire to make the Opéra accessible to this public through a series of "matinées." Such an audience would be attracted not only by the lowered ticket prices and more informal dress code, but by programs on Thursday and Sunday afternoons that would demonstrate the vitality of the French tradition.[23] Each performance, he proposed, would comprise varied selections drawn from operas in the repertoire, including "divertissements de danse," and employing period costumes. As Rouché put it, "le public assistera à l'histoire de la musique de l'Opéra; il pourra se convaincre que la tradition française s'affine aujourd'hui plus forte et plus riche que jamais." (The audience will witness the history of music at the Opéra; it will be convinced that the French tradition is refined today, stronger and richer than ever.)[24]

Rouché thus envisaged the music of the past (as presented in these matinées) placed side by side with that of the present, to be performed on other programs. This plan was clearly dictated not only by his desire to display "the French tradition" and its continuing vitality, but by the necessity of adhering to his *cahier des charges* (or contract). The *cahier* of 1915 represented the culmination of official demands that contemporary French music be performed at the Opéra as well as at concert societies. This emphasis had been steadily imposed in directors' contracts since the turn of the century, but now the number of new works demanded was seventeen, as opposed to six in 1901.[25] Rouché's new proposal was thus a means not only to meet the demands of the state for French music of the past and the present, but to imbue this injunction with a timely logic, a historical rationale. And based on his past experience in his own private Théâtre des Arts, Rouché well knew that if presented correctly the historical works could draw the public he sought. Hence, even if the modern works he staged did not meet with public success, the institution would still be publicly justified and remain financially solvent through his proposed "matinées."

Each of these performances was, according to Rouché, to teach the public through representing what he construed as "un moment significatif de l'évolution artistique" (a significant moment of artistic evolution).[26] Already, he had won both approbation and success with this method in his Théâtre des Arts, which had utilized a similar technique in appealing to a middle- and working-class public. On 16 January 1913, *L'humanité* (today the Communist daily but a Socialist organ until 1920, when the Section Française de l'Internationale Ouvrière split into the Communist and Socialist Parties) praised Rouché's "concerts illustrés," featuring musicians in period costumes acting out concerts from the historical past. These concerts, too, specifically sought links between the French past and present by juxtaposing examples of music by, for example, Lully and Fauré.[27] Rouché was already aware that for this new audience the French music of the historical past had to be "transmitted" or mediated through staging that would inscribe it with both historical and political "sense."

Now, in wartime, Rouché had other special criteria in selecting the works: they had to be already in the repertoire, and they had to be works for which performing forces were still available (i.e., not serving in the armed forces).[28] But they also had to mediate between the propagandistic demands of the government and the actual taste of the public, which still largely preferred nineteenth-century works. Rouché's programs thus traced the evolution of the repertoire across the centuries, stressing collective effort, "official" classic values, and the historical emergence of the French canon. *Mademoiselle de Nantes* had illustrated the birth and rapid flowering of opera in France in the age of absolutism, and thus according (aptly) to a classic aesthetic. The *Roman d'Estelle*, on the other hand, represented the revolutionary "moment," depicting a fête at the home of Cherubini, in which selections of his own music were being performed. The technique employed here for fusing the real and depicted audience across the centuries was to end the performance with the collective singing (as during the Revolution) of "Amour sacré de la patrie."[29] Although the Revolution had long been anathema to the Far Right, throughout wartime all rallied to the Republic, and identified its defense in the past with that of the present.

Les virtuoses de Mazarin, on the other hand, returned faithfully to the years of the Ancien Régime, but cleverly called for the performance of works by a wartime ally, in this case Italy. It represented a concert before the young Louis XIV and his mother by a group of Italian artists performing excerpts from Luigi Rossi's *Orfeo* and Monteverdi's *Coronation of Poppea*.[30] The implication here was not only the affinity of the two "Latin" cultures, but the French recognition and patronage of Italian opera, and further development of the Italian operatic "seed."

In the Opéra's regular repertoire Rouché also recognized the need to balance the performance of the modern French works required with those of France's wartime allies. Moreover, he astutely revived excerpts of several great French classic works of the past, which, juxtaposed with works of the present, imparted the same lesson of "the French tradition."[31] The modern works performed, moreover, represented an attempted musical *union sacrée*, for they comprised selections by composers belonging to hostile factions in the prewar period. These included those with nationalist sympathies, such as d'Indy, and those who were linked with the Republic and with the Dreyfusard position, such as Bruneau.[32]

But, once more, these modern French works, drawn from prewar hostile factions or "schools," were balanced by a selection of French "classic" works, in keeping with the new aesthetic dogma. Hence the production of Gossec's revolutionary *L'offrande à la liberté* (1915); *Oedipe à Colonne* by Sacchini (aptly, the work of an Italian composer who made his reputation in France); Gluck's *Iphigénie en Tauride* (act 3, 1916); Le Sueur's *Le sommeil d'Ossian* (1916); *Une fête chez la Pouplinière*, to the music of Rameau and Gluck (1916); and the "historically accurate" production of Rameau's *Castor et Pollux*, all performed defiantly in the midst of the final German bombardment in 1918.[33] These, in turn, were rounded out by popular works of France's allies, and most notably those of Italian and Russian composers of the present and past. They included Tchaikovsky's *Eugene Onegin* (tableaux 2 and 3, 1915), Donizetti's *Don Pasquale* (act 1, 1916), scenes from Mussorgsky and Borodin (1916), Puccini's *Manon Lescaut* (act 4, 1916), and Stravinsky's ballet, *Les abeilles* (1917), based on *Scherzo fantastique*.

Insinuating the "patriotic spirit," however, called not only for a careful selection of works that presented the French musical past, or that of France's allies, in an appropriate light; it also called for more overt displays of wartime propaganda and spirit in the form of now topical operas or *pièces de circonstances*, as in previous periods of crisis. The former included such operas as Paladilhe's *Patrie*, about the martyrdom of Flanders under the Spanish domination, now making implicit reference to the situation in Belgium. Among the *pièces de circonstances* were ephemeral works such as *La victoire en chantant*, Saint-Saëns's patriotic chorus, *La gloire*, and Florent Schmitt's *Chant de guerre*. The real home for such topical works, however, was traditionally the Opéra-Comique, which had originally featured them (along with other repertoire) during the revolutionary period. Now run by a former soldier, Gheusi, together with the Isola brothers, the Opéra-Comique undertook a vigorous program of four to five performances a week, even during the summer.[34]

The directors of the Opéra-Comique, like Rouché at the Opéra, now recognized the potential of the theater to impart propaganda, or to instill wartime values, in addition to providing employment for those not conscripted. Hence they presented many patriotic works that recalled the revolutionary period with which the theater was closely identified, such as the *Chant du départ* and *La marseillaise*. But they also presented old French favorites, now synonymous with the "national spirit," such as Bizet's beloved *Carmen* and Gustave Charpentier's *Louise*.[35] The latter work, significantly, was selected for a special performance in 1917—which took place in honor of General Pershing, the commander-in-chief of the American forces in France. Undoubtedly this performance was meant to help insure American support in terms not only of its armed forces, but of badly needed war loans. *Louise*, once highly controversial because of its association with the "Dreyfusard Republic," now, as presented in this patriotic context, assumed a far different range of political connotations.[36] Here associated with a "picturesque" view of the French and a nostalgic portrait of Paris, it was undoubtedly thought to be both appealing and comprehensible for an American dignitary.

The Opéra-Comique, however, unlike the Opéra under Jacques Rouché, did make one unfortunate choice in its repertoire, and thus found itself subject to wartime censorship. One of the tenets of the latter was that, in the interests of preserving *union sacrée*, anything that might incite either dangerous controversy or civil dissension must be prohibited. Hence Zola and Bruneau's *L'attaque du moulin*, which depicted a violent uprising, was thought to be too dangerous to stage at a time of worker unrest and strikes in Paris. Clearly, the political events of the day became a part of the performative context of such works by "keying" them, or situating them socially within a distinctive interpretive frame. This was not only true at the opera house: works presented in concerts were similarly "reinscribed," not only by the wartime context, but also by conscious techniques of mediation and "framing." For concert societies similarly experienced new modalities of ideological pressure, as well as the dilemma of how to respond, without ignoring the reality of French public taste.

DEFINING THE "CLASSIC MASTERS" IN CONCERTS

French concert societies, like the Opéra, were expected to propagate the dominant myth of a pure, collective, and unified tradition that had its basis in a hierarchical, orderly classicism. For they too were charged with the task of education, or of "fixing" the meanings of French musical works so that the canon, now reconstructed, would resonate with the national myth of the "French cultural community."[37] This similarly implied the necessity of creatively mediating musical experience through various techniques in order to inscribe both works and styles with a "national" significance. Such modalities of "producing" meaning required the mobilization of a network of often subtle controls, the influence of which was felt not only in state institutions but also in the private sector.

As with the Opéra, there was initial hesitation about resuming any public performances, and hence a period when concerts were prohibited by the government. But this view quickly changed. By the end of 1914 concert activities in Paris had already resumed, undoubtedly due to reassurance as to their utility and to the establishment of mechanisms of ideological surveillance. The pianist and teacher, Alfred Cortot, was here to play a central and visible role as the *chef du Service officiel de la propagande musicale* in the Ministère des Beaux-Arts.[38] The ideological usefulness of concerts becomes clear if we examine one of the first concert series to appear, and the way in which it constructed a performative context intended to inscribe national values in chosen works.

On 29 November 1914, the Oeuvre Fraternelle des Artistes presented the first of their Sunday "matinées nationales" in the large amphitheater of the Sorbonne. Organized by Henri Rabaud (who would become the Conservatoire's director upon the death of Fauré), the concerts utilized the "légionnaires" of the Société des Concerts du Conservatoire, and were conducted by Messager and Rabaud, dressed in patriotic blue.[39] The first of the concerts set the tone and established the pattern for the rest of the series: after a performance of national hymns, there was a speech by the dean of the Faculty of Letters, followed by a series of patriotic readings from such nationalist figures as Deroulède and Péguy (as well as by the more moderate Alphonse Daudet, Victor Hugo, and Théodore de Banville). These literary readings were then followed by the performance of works by French composers, including the so-called "modern classics" (or those using classic forms), particularly Franck, Magnard, and Saint-Saëns. Despite the caustic aesthetic disagreements between the followers of Franck (such as d'Indy) and those of Saint-Saëns. both composers were here framed and consecrated as part of France's "Latin" and collective culture.[40] The experience of these musical works was thus "keyed" by the events and readings that preceded it, and by the performance of allied national anthems at the beginning and end, imbuing it, as the organizer of the series sought, with a "national sense." Subsequent concerts followed a similar pattern of tellingly juxtaposing a series of great French literary or propagandistic readings with older or more recent French works.

Again, such a technique was not new: it had been instigated by French nationalist leagues (such as Action Française) in the interest of nationalist propaganda before the war.[41] Characteristically, they had "framed" performances of French works in the nationalist canon by either carefully selected readings (with political implications) or by lectures explaining the music's cultural and thus national significance. Now such constructions of "performative context" were being appropriated by French officials in order to explain the significance of the newly reconstructed and unified "French musical canon." The "matinées nationales" were aimed at a broad or "popular" public, and thus sought to make their "national" significance unmistakable by also ending with collective singing of the "Marseillaise."[42]

Concert life in Paris flourished, in part because of the intersecting functions being served—such concerts provided inspiration, instruction, entertainment, and employment for those musicians not drafted.[43] With many museums closed for safety, concerts offered a unique collective access to the nation's artistic past and thus to a sense of its distinct cultural identity. The musical press, nourishing such endeavors, continued to be active throughout the war, and significantly, most papers, while centered on war news, retained their musical columns. Discussing French music was clearly a way of engaging with the nation's aesthetic values, employing a vocabulary that addressed the emotions, and inspiring pride in the nation's artistic past.

The proliferation of concerts now was astounding: they appeared throughout Paris and were often sponsored by particular interest groups, all of which attempted to ally themselves both with patriotism and with the nation's great musical patrimony. These included the "Concerts Classiques Rouges," held in the Rue de Tournon; the "Matinées Français," at the Palais de Glace; Wurmser's "Concerts Populaires," in the Salle des Agriculteurs; Mme Yvette Guilbert's "Matinées rétrospectives" in the Salle Gaveau; the traditional "Concerts spirituels" in the Eglise de la Sorbonne; and Victor Charpentier's "Association des Grands Concerts" at the Trocadéro.[44]

In addition, the traditional large concert societies in Paris were also active; significantly, the Pasdeloup Concerts, which had ceased in 1884, began again in 1916. At the Odéon, Pierre Monteux directed a series of "festivals" of French music, designed to showcase contemporary French composers such as d'Indy, Debussy, Saint-Saëns, and Ravel.[45] Hence, again, composers previously associated with conflicting prewar schools or "camps," were grouped together as "the French school," and thus assimilated to the same nationalist discourse. This was also true of the traditional large concert societies, which were forced temporarily to fuse because of shortage of facilities, funds, and personnel. Previously, the Concerts Colonne had favored the more "classical" or traditional, Conservatoire-trained composers, while the Concerts Lamoureux concentrated on those who had been influenced by Wagner, as well as on Wagner himself. Now, the Concerts Colonne-Lamoureux gave concerts devoted to Berlioz and Franck (the latter highly influenced by Wagner), as well as to French composers bearing arms, or "morts pour la patrie."[46]

Despite forced cooperation, however, dissension remained deeply embedded in French musical culture, manifest in disputes over the sensitive problem of what to exclude from the repertoire during the war. Principally, this concerned German music, which in the past had been central to French concert life, particularly with the vast popularity of Wagner in France since the 1890s. Now the central questions were "Should all German music be peremptorily banned?" and "Were all German composers now 'the enemy,' even those from the nation's distant cultural past?" This similarly entailed the question of whether any art could be considered "universal," or as transcending the boundaries of a national culture, which was now widely considered as all-determining. Once again, a major issue was "purity," or whether French music should be "protected" from exposure to any "contamination" by foreign music, which had so threatened its unique identity in the past.[47]

Despite attempts to avoid all things German in public, German music did indeed reappear as early as the fall of 1915, in the Salle Gaveau and in the Concerts Colonne-Lamoureux. Indeed, the Concerts Classiques Rogues performed not only Beethoven, Haydn, and Mozart, but also the hotly disputed Wagner as early as 1915. It did not take long to perceive that despite the exigencies of ideological orthodoxy, the French repertoire alone was not sufficient, and the public indeed wanted to hear German music. But the concept of "musique défaitiste," or music that compromised French patriotism, remained, inciting censors to examine programs for the menacing presence of composers considered to be "*boches*" (or Germanic and sometimes modernist). At first this included not only Wagner, still remembered as hostile to France as a result of his satire of the French following the Franco-Prussian War, but also Mozart, Schubert, Handel, Mendelssohn, Bach, Haydn, and Weber. Beethoven was conveniently exempted as "Belgian" because of his supposed Flemish ancestry, which allowed the performance of his now widely loved symphonies in French wartime concert programs.[48]

Also present to balance French music, as in the Opéra, was that of the allied nations, principally Italy, Russia, and, to a lesser extent (because of scanter repertoire), England. Hence the presence on programs of the music of Monteverdi, whom d'Indy had helped to make known in France, as well as Purcell and Handel, the latter justified as essentially "English." Also particularly prominent now was the still popular music of such Russian composers as Borodin, Tchaikovsky, Balakirev, Rimsky-Korsakov, and early Stravinsky. However, as we noted, some concert societies, particularly those politically oriented to the left, such as the Concerts Rouges, had the temerity to perform (initially) "enemy" musicians, including Mozart and Haydn early on.[49]

Hence dissent, in effect, remained in practice, if now within clearly circumscribed limits, and it similarly perdured in theory, as musicians fought out the question of "exclusion" in the press. Most prominent in this debate were longtime professional antagonists Saint-Saëns and d'Indy, who, although both patriotic, disagreed as to the implications this held for the repertoire. Vincent d'Indy continued to defend the performance of the music of those composers whom he considered unequivocally to be the indispensable "German masters." For despite his ardent nationalism, he believed in a "universal" tradition that was based upon the "logical chain of the past," which composers could realize in varying ways in different national contexts. He argued, moreover, that this great tradition, founded in religious music, had passed into German hands in the eighteenth and nineteenth centuries, but had been betrayed by the contemporary Germans, or "Prussians." Wagner, however, he firmly maintained, had helped to "cleanse" French music of more insidious foreign traits, and particularly those that came from the popular, meretricious French-Jewish composers. Unlike Action Française, with which he most emphatically disagreed, d'Indy did not consider Wagner to be of Jewish blood, and thus tainted in his art by "oriental" influence. Hence he defended the performance of Wagner, as against his antagonist Camille Saint-Saëns who, after a passing Wagnerian influence, and thus the accusation of "Wagnerism," had turned against the composer. This helped to inflame the violent polemics concerning Wagner in concert series, including those at the Salle Gaveau, the Concerts Colonne-Lamoureux, and the Matinées Nationales.[50]

During the war Saint-Saëns wrote a series of prominent articles denouncing German and Austrian influence, as well as those French composers, like d'Indy, who still defended it. As early as December 1914, in the widely read L'écho de Paris, Saint-Saëns went so far as to suggest that no German music be played during the war. His articles were subsequently collected and published in 1916 as a virulently anti-German pamphlet, entitled aggressively Germanophilie, and soon incited polemics among composers. For Saint-Saëns here denounces all German artists, even those "universalists" such as Goethe, holding steadfastly that art is by no means universal in nature but rather has a "patrie." As he put it: "Rien des Barbares, rien de leur musique, de leur art, de leur science, rien de leur 'culture' ne doit désormais souiller notre intelligence et notre coeur." (Nothing of the barbarians, nothing of their music, of their art, of their science, nothing of their "culture" should henceforth defile our intelligence and our heart.)[51] Saint-Saëns thus accepted what was now the orthodox position with regard to French culture, and the immediate necessity of defending it from German "contamination" in all areas.

D'Indy stolidly restated his belief in Wagner's indispensable role in a lecture that was subsequently published in La renaissance in June 1915. Again, he asserted his conviction that Wagner had rendered an invaluable service to the French by helping to rid the Opéra of those who were defiling it—"musiciens de mauvais goût, de mauvais style, et de mauvaise musique, dont les auteurs se nomment Auber, Hérold, Halévy et Adam" (musicians of bad taste, of bad style, and of bad music, of which the authors are named Auber, Hérold, Halévy, and Adam).[52] For d'Indy, again, Wagner had helped to rid the Opéra of those composers who wrote in the meretricious style inspired by the Italians, and in particular the seminal figure of Rossini.

Wagner thus helped to restore "dignity" to the Opéra and elevated the mentality of the French, thereby hastening the return of taste for such peerless classical "French" masters as Gluck. The latter, claimed by both the French and Germans, having worked in Paris and Vienna, in addition to Italy, was, in fact, born in central Europe, then "Bohemia." Saint-Saëns, of course, was quick to riposte to d'Indy in an article titled "L'avenir de la musique en France," published in La grande revue in March 1916. Here he confrontationally and ironically proposes that what is really required for the fullest development of "the French school" in music is the restoration of the Théâtre Italien. It could perform the old and newer Italian repertoire, including the works of Mozart—conceived here as "Italian" stylistically—and thus as implicitly opposed to the aesthetic of Wagner. This would lead the French away from the Wagnerian excessive growth of the orchestra, and back toward "song" and endemic French qualities, including gaiety, clarity, and measure. The French themselves, he then proposes, could return to the model of the repertoire of the Opéra-Comique, or to works interlaced with dialogue, although in a more modern style. "Purification" of French music would thus rather come from Italy, considered a "sister" nation, one that had similarly Latin roots, as opposed to the modern, or Prussian "Huns."

"DEFENDING" FRENCH MUSIC AND ITS "PURITY"

Despite Saint-Saëns's and d'Indy's confrontation over the "perniciousness" of Wagner's music, and over how French music should be "regenerated" for the future, they did concur on one key point: the importance of prohibiting the performance, during wartime, of any contemporary German or Austrian musical work, or one that was not yet legally within the public domain. Hence both of them joined and supported a new musical "league" that was formed, with the support of Albert Dalimier, of the Sous-secretariat des Beaux-Arts, in 1916, and which aptly illustrates how wartime pressures to arrive at a classic orthodoxy were implemented within the musical world. This was the Ligue Nationale pour la Défense de la Musique Française, the formation and subsequent activities of which were reported in the propagandistic journal, *La musique pendant la guerre*, founded the previous year. In January 1916 the principal instigator of the league, the jingoistic and opportunistic music critic Charles Tenroc, published the plans and statutes of the league in this journal.

Here, the league's stated goal was primarily to safeguard the (implicitly classic) "patrimoine artistique national," and to foster its development and diffusion, without respect to any particular "school." Its central purpose, nevertheless, was to develop all the possible and necessary means to oust the enemy culturally, and prevent the return of any "infiltrations funestes."[53] In addition, it presumed to pronounce on all questions concerning the still central issue of the future of French music, not only inside, but also outside France. The league would therefore help to determine what would and would not be encouraged at home, and also how French music—and thus France herself—would be represented abroad. Its xenophobic intentions were boldly emblazoned on its brochure, intentions that would continue to resonate throughout the twenties: "La musique de France aux Français."

The president of the league was Charles Tenroc himself, who here was clearly positioning himself for power in the postwar French musical world, and who would succeed, as the influential editor of the *Courrier musical*.[54] However, there were several other "présidents d'honneur," among whom were most of the leading figures within the French musical world, drawn from both the prewar warring factions. These included Camille Saint-Saëns, Théodore Dubois, Gustave Charpentier, Vincent d'Indy, Xavier Leroux, and Charles Lecoq. In addition, they included two politicians, both deputies and copresidents of the Groupe Parlementaire de l'Art, Paul Meunier and Lucien Millerenge. Besides a president, the league had an official secretary as well, another critic of music, Jean Poueigh (who would become Satie's nemesis). This group, according to the statement of the league, intended to act simultaneously in both the musical and political worlds through the following practices and means of action: propaganda, intervention with those in power, demands for reform in specific *cahiers des charges* (official contracts) and rules of the schools, as well as by imposing interdictions on and influencing French editors. Although not presenting itself as political, its very language recalls that of Action Française, for it advocates a battle against "les trusts suspects," which, since the Dreyfus affair, generally implied the non-French, and particularly the Jews.

The league's list of adherents, probably actively recruited, relates closely to the tactics it proposed, for it includes the directors of the Opéra-Comique, the director of the Odéon and of the Trianon-Lyrique, and the director of the Maison Pleyel, among others. The members also included the musicians Francis Casadesus, Gustave Samazeuilh, Raoul Bardac (Debussy's pupil and stepson who did nothing without Debussy's advice), and Victor Charpentier (the brother of Gustave and conductor of the Association des Grands Concerts). Notably absent was Maurice Ravel, for reasons that we will examine, as well as three members of the Institut de France—Widor, Paladilhe, and Fauré. Fauré, while unquestionably patriotic, loyal to the state, the political traditions of France and its culture, rejected the narrow, ethnically defined, exclusive nationalism invoked by the league. But the league still established a tight network of control, one through which French officials and their allies could act upon or influence all French musical life, even that outside the official domain. It created professional pressures that would not disappear with the end of the war, but would continue to act as a subtle curb on musicians in the postwar period. This hegemonic network attempted to "supervise" not only concert programs but musical education, as well as publications, and thus exert direct or indirect influence on creativity.

Several members of the league were associated with a series of "Festivals de Musique Française," begun in 1916, with the support of the Sous-secrétariat des Beaux-Arts. Significantly, Alfred Cortot, the pianist, and now *chef du Service officiel de la propagande musicale* in the Ministère des Beaux-Arts, was a prominent member of the program committee. This is indeed somewhat ironic, given Cortot's earlier ardent Wagnerism, manifest when he was an assistant to Mottl and Richter at Bayreuth and conducted *Tristan* as well as the first Parisian performance of *Götterdämmerung*. But the festivals were less bellicose and exclusive than the league, and so Fauré did agree to join in their organization, together with the more orthodox Saint-Saëns, Charpentier, and Tenroc. Their purpose was not to exclude foreign music, but rather to perform those works by French composers in military service who were lost, wounded, or killed in battle.[55] Although music of the members of both the leading performance societies for new music—the Société Nationale de Musique Française (SNMF) and the Société Musicale Indépendante (SMI)—was presented in the "festivals," certain composers who refused to join the league were excluded, as we will see in the case of Ravel. Yet the attempt to join the formerly antagonistic performance societies in the interest of common national effort and consolidation of resources was destined to fail. For significant disagreement remained over the question of "true" French patriotism and tradition, as well as over the specific interpretation of the "classic" —dissensions that would explode in controversy after the war.

PROFESSIONAL INTERESTS VERSUS CULTURAL POLITICS

Alfred Cortot, as head of "musical propaganda" for the Ministère des Beaux-Arts, sagaciously recruited from within the French musical world, initiated a "consolidation" of musical societies. He sought specifically to fuse the antagonistic Société Nationale de Musique Française and the Société Musicale Indépendante under the umbrella, or leadership, of the former. The Société Nationale, after all, was more venerable and more closely represented the policy of "exclusion" of specific non-French elements, which had now become the official musical goal. The new, or amalgamated, society would thus receive "l'investiture de l'Etat," or effectively, official patronage, bringing a substantial subvention and a formal national "mission." Indeed, it was at the annual distribution of prizes at the Paris Conservatoire that the Sous-secrétaire des Beaux-Arts announced the fusion, to be sponsored by Cortot himself.[56]

Immediately, members of the more liberal Société Musicale Indépendante perceived the menace of the plan: to expunge their freedom to perform contemporary foreign as well as more audacious French works. Such a fusion, they perceived, was intended to consolidate power in the hands of the "conservatives," whose traditionalist aesthetic and doctrine now accorded completely with that of the state. Before the war the SMI had not only presented "progressive" French works that employed bi- and polytonality, but foreign works by composers such as Kodaly, Bartok, Stravinsky, and Schoenberg. Hence, prominent members of the SMI, such as Maurice Ravel, Charles Koechlin, and Emile Vuillermoz, quickly protested the fusion and warned their fellow members that their aesthetic freedom was in danger.[57]

Members of the Société Nationale were equally skeptical about the fusion; d'Indy, in particular, foresaw dissension, and inevitable bitterness within the group. He knew he would no doubt contribute to the dissension, having openly mocked not only bitonality but specific innovations in phrasing and form as representing the Germanic, or the modern "style *boche*." For d'Indy the SMI remained socialist and Dreyfusard in its orientation, an argument he had developed in both political and aesthetic terms in numerous publications before the war. The stakes were thus far more than aesthetic: such a nationalist position was not simply a means to further his artistic beliefs, for these had already become thoroughly politicized. Since the Dreyfus affair, when d'Indy was both a founding and ardent member of the Ligue de la Patrie Française, he perceived, like Barrès and Maurras, his political and aesthetic goals as united.[58]

This, however, was not true of all the members of the Société Nationale, nor of the SMI; some did make the separation both now and again after the war. Albert Roussel, for example, although a member of the Société Nationale, and long associated with the Schola, was increasingly espousing a progressive political and aesthetic stance.[59] And although some members of the SMI, such as Ravel, Roussel, and Koechlin, would soon adopt an aesthetically "advanced" and politically leftist position, the same was not true of others. Emile Vuillermoz, Louis Vuillemin, and Florent Schmitt, loyal members of the SMI, and wary of the Société Nationale during the war, would assume an implicitly nationalist or aesthetically "exclusive" position. Their concern being more musical than political, they would defend their professional positions in the postwar musical world by attacking certain French youth as well as the malignant "foreign infiltrations" they perceived in French music. Hence the dominance now being exercised by the state was powerful precisely because, in the interests of ideological hegemony, it played upon deeply rooted professional concerns.[60] After the war, some would still place their ideological allegiances first, while others would adopt the political position that best appeared to further their professional interests.

Despite the election of Fauré (admired by, and a member of, both societies) as president of the "coalition," the fusion, as many predicted, failed, and each society went its own way. However, the Société Nationale, now led by Fauré, was reorganized under *l'union sacrée* with a more diverse board of directors that included those associated with both prewar republican culture and its nationalist opposition. As René Baton remarked, however, this group (comprising Debussy, Dukas, Duparc, d'Indy, Messager, and Bruneau) was an "assemblée de momies, sans idées, sans but et sans cohésion" (an assembly of mummies, without ideas, without an end, and without cohesion).[61]

With the exception of one concert by the SMI in 1915, neither society actually resumed regular performances during the war until 1917. The Société Nationale, predictably, decided to perform only French works, and, although the SMI did not, it faced the considerable difficulty of obtaining new works from abroad for performance during the war. And while the SMI did present some more "progressive" works, such as Koechlin's Sonata for Violin and Piano in 1917, most younger composers had been drafted, and hence the programs of both societies were, in effect, similar.[62] They featured composers of the older generation, prominent in both societies, such as Debussy, Fauré, Ravel, and d'Indy, now the "pillars" of "modern French music."

Several of these composers, however, masked resistance by superficial conformity, for, although they did espouse classicism, they interpreted it in significantly different ways. Not all adhered to classic orthodoxies, strictures that we will examine further when turning to criticism and scholarship, for disagreement remained over appropriate techniques and treatment of form in a neoclassic style.[63] At issue here, again, was the question of permissible influences from outside France, as well as what true French classicism comprised—whether it embodied "indigenous" Latin traits or Greek universalism.

THE ORTHODOX DISCOURSE AND ITS BOUNDARIES

It was not only through wartime concerts that music was to participate in the propagandistic endeavor of "national" education, or in "imagining" a community—in fixing or redefining its basic values. For evoking the "right" values and meanings in performance presupposed the existence of a shared ideological frame created not only through the performative contexts but through associations ensconced in accompanying lectures. Public lectures played a central role, particularly the new series that were now devoted to French music, some of which were subsequently published, becoming a part of the burgeoning literature on French music. Publications on music were proliferating to reassure the French of their distinguished musical past—one that had been called into question by the Wagnerian mania in France preceding the war. Now both lectures and books were disseminating propaganda concerning the "âme nationale" as expressed in music, and mediating the concert experience by inscribing national meanings in genres, forms, and styles.

They were similarly constructing or reconstructing great composers of the French national past in terms of what were now defined as distinctive French national cultural values and traits. But here too dissension surfaced, and although public pressures clearly circumscribed its limits, music history provided an indirect means through which to criticize dominant conceptions of "the French." Disagreement concerning what "defines" French music, over "true" classical traits, and thus the canon, soon appeared and became part of the battle over musical taste and desired stylistic directions.

One of many series of lectures, typical of the concerns and debates of the period (and fortunately published, so that we may examine it) was delivered in Lyon, in 1916. The lectures were sponsored by one of the numerous groups that now developed to encourage French music, in this case the Lyonnais Amis de la Musique Française, under the leadership of a member of the University of Lyon's Faculty of Law. They were subsequently published in a book edited by the "femme de lettres" Mme J. Bach-Sisley, appearing in 1917 under the title *Pour la musique française: Douze causeries*.[64] As was typical in such a series, the contributors came from several different professional fields, all of which were similarly concerned with instilling ideological orthodoxies with regard to French culture. Especially intriguing about this collection, however, is its preface—by Claude Debussy, who was deeply engaged in preserving French "purity," although he was suffering with terminal cancer.

His text is, in part, ironic, revealing Debussy's tensions with certain key elements of wartime dogma concerning French classicism—tensions that would permeate his compositions of the period. While agreeing wholeheartedly with the necessity of "protecting" French culture and of returning French music to a "purified" state, his interpretation of how to do this was decidedly unorthodox. Debussy, who was long critical of the classical doctrine as taught at the Schola (one he decried as Germanic), perceived the contradiction in enshrining this as the "authentic" French style.[65] Doctrinaire in his belief in the uniqueness of French culture and the necessity of returning to purity, Debussy was stubbornly independent in his construal of "the French" and thus in his view of what French classicism comprised.

Debussy begins compliantly, remarking that for some time now it has been all too clear that French music has suffered from what he refers to as "importations singulières." He then acutely observes that while France was in the process of sacrificing its very best youth, regardless of social class, one heard strange things about Beethoven and Wagner. Here he undoubtedly is referring to the argument that Beethoven was of Flemish ancestry, and hence acceptable, as well as to d'Indy's rhetoric concerning the valuable service that Wagner rendered by "ennobling" French music. Rejecting such reasoning, he proceeds with arresting violence of imagery to observe: "Il s'agit de mauvaises herbes qu'il faut arracher sans pitié, comme un chirurgien coupe une jambe où monte la gangrène." (It is a matter of pulling out the weeds without pity, just as a surgeon cuts off a gangrened leg.)[66]

He then addresses the complex and delicate question as to how to do this, and, again with the Schola Cantorum undoubtedly in mind, he turns to the key issue of form: "Retrouvons notre liberté, nos formes: les ayant inventées pour la plupart, il est juste que nous les conservions; il n'est pas de plus belle. Ne nous essoufflons plus à écrire des symphonies, pour lesquelles nous tendons nos muscles sans résultat bien appréciable. . . . préférons-leur l'opérette." (Let us recover our liberty, our forms: having invented them for the most part, it is right that we conserve them; there are none more beautiful. Let us no longer exert ourselves in writing symphonies, for which we stretch our muscles without an appreciable result. . . . let us prefer the operetta.)[67]

Long a critic of the symphony as a genre that was not endemically French, Debussy is once again positioning himself against d'Indy, who still taught the Beethoven model (as he construed it) at the Schola. While d'Indy continued to promote and to write symphonies himself, Debussy was rather turning to the sonata, in its earliest, or still amorphous state. As opposed to Germanic conceptions, he would here reappropriate the genre as "French" by attempting to utilize French thematic material and to define an appropriate form for it. Debussy, like Maurice Barrès, believed that all constraints—including those of form—should arise from the national past: true liberty lies in recognizing history's necessities.

But Debussy was heterodox in other key points: as opposed to the dominant view of the French as "serious," as well as "master craftsmen" (to rival the Germans), he still argues, as before the war, that they are rather distinguished by "fantasy."[68] As a model of his vision of the French, Debussy turns again to his beloved Chabrier, praising his "fantaisie" in works like the "Marche joyeuse," as well as in his unpretentious songs. And despite the fact that he had previously praised the music of the German, naturalized French, Jacques Offenbach, Debussy here treats him harshly—as a "foreigner" who deformed the text. Although Offenbach had arrived as a teenager, and subsequently made his career in France, Debussy implicitly treats him here as a German Jew, in the manner of Action Française. However, again against the orthodox view, Debussy concludes by asserting the senselessness of the French still striving to write "la grande musique," associated with Germanic conceptions and forms. Here he tartly observes that this has led not only to imbecilic journalistic opinions, but to the construction of "faux grands maîtres," supposedly embodying these traits: ironically, Debussy was among them.[69]

Writers in the newspaper L'action française were currently "constructing" Claude Debussy according to their conception of French music, one heavily influenced by the Schola Cantorum. Critics associated with the league had long supported d'Indy's "traditionalist" teaching, especially his stress on past French masters, although flatly rejecting his argument concerning Wagner. Now, by assimilating Debussy to the Schola's conception of traditional French form and style, they were attempting to ensure his consecration in the canon, which was by no means sure to this point. In 1915, *L'action française* thus ran a series of articles on his music, the content of which is revealed by the title, "La musique française: Claude Debussy."[70]

In these articles Jean Darnaudet attempts to accentuate Debussy's later style, thus dissociating the composer from the pernicious "impressionist" influence, which he condemns as follows: "C'est le système d'art qui sacrifie l'ensemble au détail, qui vient suppléer à l'idée absente ou défaillante par la multiplication et les raffinements de la sensation, qui se rattrape de la faiblesse ou de l'indécision des lignes et des formes générales sur la prodigalité des menues touches et nuances."[71] (It is the system of art that sacrifices the ensemble to the detail, that makes up for the absent or weak idea by the multiplication and refinement of sensations, that makes up for the weakness and indecision of the lines and of the larger form with a prodigality of small touches and nuances.) This was similarly d'Indy's view, as manifest perhaps most provocatively in his allegorical depiction of the impressionists as the "armée de l'erreur" in his opera, *La légende de Saint Christophe*.[72] The "true" French, or authentic, classic style, for Darnaudet, rather emphasizes the "collective"—the formal element or the "whole"—as well as a firm and precise guiding idea throughout. For him, as well as for d'Indy and the Schola, the form and the unity of the whole work directly depend on a clearly defined melody and rhythm, which facilitates the development of themes and the "economy" of tonalities.

Darnaudet, of course, is quick to assert that Debussy's greatest works—those of his recent, or more traditionalist style—are no longer lacking in the spheres of line or rhythm. Hence he concludes that the values of line, rhythm, simplicity, and amplitude of form were reclaiming their place in French music, which was returning to its true classic heritage.[73]

Further revealing of Darnaudet's Germanic conception of classicism is another, related article in which he recognizes (unlike Debussy) the greatness of non-French classical masters, above all Beethoven. For Darnaudet, as well as for d'Indy, this composer was a "good German"—an important distinction—belonging to the classical (eighteenth-century) past that Germany and France shared.[74] As Debussy had astutely perceived, the Schola's conception of the classic was by no means French, but was rooted in the high classical style of later eighteenth-century Germany and Austria. Again, this was also true of the xenophobic critics and writers associated with Action Française, such as Jean Darnaudet, Léon Daudet, and Camille Bellaigue.

Debussy's beliefs and his style indeed differed substantially from the orthodox position, which had nevertheless constructed his image to make him "classic" in this mold. However, in two significant points Debussy did accord with the dominant position: not only should French culture be defended, or kept "pure," but the enemy could be combated most effectively through culture. For, as he concludes his preface, "there are many ways that one can vanquish the enemy, and it is important, above all, to remember that music is both an admirable and fecund means to do so."[75]

The published lectures that follow are equally heterodox in the viewpoints they present; while all incorporate some aspects of the orthodox dogma, some diplomatically take issue with others. All are overtly anti-German, and attempt to illuminate France's "génie national," while offering various opinions concerning what this may be considered to comprise. Prominent here is the lecture by the famed historian of art, and specifically of romanticism, Henri Focillon, who now faced the delicate question of whether romanticism could be considered as "French."[76] This, of course, was related to the already hotly debated issue of whether Berlioz, as a French romantic composer, should occupy a place in the national canon.

Despite the wartime emphasis on the supposedly "Latin" virtues, Focillon argues that while art is sometimes principally balance and clarity, at other times it is rather energy and disorder. And, as he points out, not only is the latter an immortal aspect of the human soul, it indeed is equally a part of the "génie de l'Occident." That France was part of the "Occident," and thus devoid of any "oriental" traits—including the Jewish and Arab—had long been a key element of nationalist dogma. But here Focillon bravely contends, against the now dominant or official position, that the Occident (in which France was central) and the Latin are not necessarily synonymous.[77]

The Action Française, of course, disagreed strenuously, as we may glean in Jean Darnaudet's emphatic excommunication of Berlioz from the French canon, and indeed from the "French school." Like d'Indy, he accused Berlioz of being fundamentally more "poet" than musician, or far too reliant on literature, although his "ideas" in themselves are often superb. The problem lies in the musical form as well as in the insufficiency of its development, in addition to, in general, an "écriture" that is often simply "incorrect." Darnaudet similarly disqualifies Wagner as a model through which to "purge" French music, arguing, as opposed to d'Indy, that his music, like Berlioz's, is superficial and empty. Pierre Lasserre, as we will shortly see, even perceived an "oriental," feminine influence inherent in Wagner's music, thus equating the German, the Jewish, the "effete," and the romantic.[78]

Other essays in the collection, however, like Focillon's, implacably confront such dogma, arguing that the "French manner of expression" is not necessarily classic. Significantly, we find this position articulated in "L'ecole de César Franck" by Maurice Boucher, identified as a professor at the Lycée Ampère. In his presentation Boucher stresses César Franck's emphasis on the importance of sincerity of expression, thus defending the now unpopular view that music is "le récit de notre vie intérieure." But he concludes with a bow to the more orthodox position by attempting to assimilate Franck's music to what were now generally considered the dominant traits in French art—"temperance, modération," and "harmonie." Debussy, in other writings, had firmly disagreed with this interpretation of Franck, arguing that he was indeed a great composer—but that he was fundamentally a "compositeur belge."[79]

Disagreement over who was a "French" composer, and what authentic French traits in music comprised, appear in other books of the period as well as in articles by well-known composers. A case in point is Jean-Aubry's *La musique française aujourd'hui*, which appeared in 1916, with a preface by Gabriel Fauré, who here was compelled to take issue with the author. Georges Jean-Aubry was a noted French music critic and musicologist, and a strong supporter and personal friend of Claude Debussy. Fauré immediately observes that the fundamental idea underlying the book is that to qualify as "truly French," a work must issue from the tradition of Rameau and the *clavecinistes*.[80] This, indeed, had been the position of Debussy and his followers before the war, and one to which many admirers of the composer continued implacably to adhere. But Fauré here firmly favors freedom, while as the Conservatoire's director he defends academic training, pointedly asking, "Isn't everyone free to translate his thought and sensibility through the means that please him?"

Confronting not only wartime dogma, but also attacks on the symphony by Debussy and his followers, he then asks rhetorically, "are not the symphonic works of Saint-Saëns [Fauré's teacher], of Franck, of d'Indy, or Dukas, although conceived in a form of German origin, manifestations of French taste?" For they all exhibit those traits that Fauré, here echoing the orthodox view, believes essential to defining "the French" aesthetically—clarity and a feeling for proportion.[81] Indeed, in maintaining this view, Fauré was defending the original doctrine of the Société Nationale de Musique (of which he was now president)—that the Germans could be beaten on their own grounds, or in their own musical forms. But as we will see, in the twenties, soon after his death, Fauré's firm support for certain French classical traits would lead to a misappropriation or "construction" of him as an orthodox "classicist."

This he most certainly was not, which becomes clear when Fauré again disagrees with the author over the question of utilitarian art, which Jean-Aubry opposes to classical disinterest. To this claim Fauré incisively replies: "Que Wagner ait apporté dans la conception de ses oeuvres des préoccupations philosophiques—et dans leurs oeuvres Franck ou d'Indy des préoccupations morales ou religieuses, Bruneau ou Charpentier des préoccupations sociales, que ces préoccupations aient dépendu d'une volonté réfléchie ou d'une impulsion inconsciente peu importe, s'il en résulte pour nous de grandes, de fortes et de belles émotions."[82] (That Wagner brought philosophical preoccupations to the conception of his works—and Franck and d'Indy moral preoccupations in theirs, Bruneau and Charpentier social preoccupations, that these preoccupations resulted from a considered desire or an unconscious impulse, what does it matter if for us they result in great, strong, and beautiful emotions?)

Fauré, in conclusion, then addresses the question that was increasingly becoming a preoccupation in wartime—the direction that French music would or should take when the conflict was finally over. Here he prognosticates that the war will undoubtedly bring a new aesthetic direction in its wake, and as horrible as it is, it will help return the French to their most basic cultural values. He thus ends with an encomium of French classical traits, which in its rhetoric sounds sagaciously orthodox, although, as we have seen, he construes French classic values with considerable latitude: "l'effroyable tempête que nous traversons nous rendra notre sens commun, c'est-à-dire le goût de la claire pensée, de la forme sobre et pure, la sincérité, le dédain du gros effets, en un mot, toutes les vertus qui peuvent contribuer à ce que notre art tout entier retrouve son admirable caractère."⁸³ (The terrible storm that we are experiencing will return us to ourselves and give us back our common sense, that is, the taste for clear thought, sober and pure form, sincerity, the disdain of big effects, in a word, all the virtues that can contribute to allowing our art to find again, completely, its admirable character.)

Fauré's interpretation of classicism was by no means identical to that of the supporters of the Schola and of Action Française, which concurred in many points, as we have seen. While Fauré did stress clarity of expression and sobriety and purity of form, unlike the Schola he emphasized French understatement and did not advocate stylistic or formal "molds." Always judicious, Fauré well knew the precise extent to which he could and could not inflect the dominant paradigm, while adhering, in principle, to official expectations in wartime. The book that follows is similarly deft in its amalgamation of patriotic rhetoric and its subtle departures from, or reinterpretation of, the now orthodox position.

For Jean-Aubry, Satie is a "classic," embodying the true French tradition—its preference for "line," and particularly its "unpretentiousness," as seen in his small-scale, unassuming works. Here the author resembles Debussy and his followers (the "Debussystes"), and to some extent Fauré, in his stress on the French tendency toward understatement and lack of pretension. But in tune with wartime dogma, Jean-Aubry compensates for his bold departures by his strongly anti-German stance and his attack on those sympathetic to German music—those violating *union sacrée* through aesthetic partisanship.⁸⁴ There were thus many shades of "orthodoxy," and dissent could be couched in technical discussions or balanced by a final affirmation of the basic values of French wartime propaganda. This dissension, again, would emerge more patently and publicly in the realm of composition, and would assume a new life in the postwar period, when official nationalism remained firmly in place.

WARTIME IDEOLOGY AND MUSICOLOGY

The climate, themes, controls, and tensions we have noted were not only to permeate lectures and books on French music during the war, they inevitably penetrated musical scholarship as well. Here too both national and historical education became primary concerns, and indeed attended the very birth, in wartime, of the Société Française de Musicologie. Scholarship in music, just as in other fields, was to be harnessed to the service of the national myth, or to the "projection" of the French community as a cultural entity throughout the ages. French intellectual leaders, including academics and scholars, were expected to contribute to the war effort by helping to mold a resilient "mentalité," thus bolstering morale.⁸⁵

As a discipline now taught in the university, musicology was subject to the same expectations and constraints as the other academic fields, which were deprived of their intellectual autonomy in wartime.⁸⁶ Before the war, the discipline of music history had been rapidly developing in France, spurred by the increasing absorption in "tradition" and in the issue of the French cultural "essence." As a result, many of the presuppositions and goals that were closely associated with the discipline in France had originated in French nationalist thought, which had been refracted musically at the Schola Cantorum. From this nexus the basic assumptions, interests, and questions of the field arose, for here, even before the war, ideology and music history had become inseparable.[87] However, it was not until shortly before World War I that the label of "musicologie" was commonly applied to the scholarly study of the history of music in France. More frequently employed was "musicographe," a designation for those who attempted, as scholars, to situate musical works in their original historical epoch and cultural milieu. But in 1913 an article on the discipline of "musicologie" appeared in Paul-Marie Masson's *Rapport sur la musique française contemporaine*. Significantly, it is by Michel Brênet (the pseudonymn for Marie Bobilier), closely associated with the Schola Cantorum, and identified here as the "doyen" (dean) of musicology in France.[88]

As someone close to the Schola, it is hardly surprising that Brênet's own research had been closely focused on the Ancien Régime, and was informed by basic Scholiste aesthetic conceptions. Nor is it surprising that in the article on musicology Brênet emphasizes the role of the Schola as a fundamental impetus for the original growth of musicology in France.[89] Significantly, the author also here observes the rivalry to which this soon led in France, as official institutions felt obliged to respond to the Schola's scholarly challenge. As an example, she cites their willingness, finally, to admit musicology as one of the subjects worthy of a thesis for the prestigious Sorbonne *doctorat ès lettres*. Yet the Schola remained a dominant force in the discipline as it developed and flowered in France, and indeed the first president of the Société Française de Musicologie would be a figure who was close to the Schola.

Until the First World War the official organization of musicologists in France had not been autonomous, but rather part of a larger, collective international group. In 1904 Lionel Dauriac, J.-G. Prod'homme, and Jules Combarieu, all associated with state institutions, founded the Paris section of the Société Internationale de Musique.[90] This had undoubtedly been stimulated by the Congrès International d'Histoire de la Musique, which Jules Combarieu had helped to organize in conjunction with the 1900 Universal Exposition. But the First World War ineluctably led to a rupture in the international organization, leading the French to create their own independent musicological society. The Société Française de Musicologie was officially founded on 17 March 1917, with the goal—typical of the period—to uncover the musical past of France. Although the primary officers were associated with the Schola, the leadership did include figures in official institutions, thus representing, as propaganda demanded, a kind of scholarly *union sacrée*. Lionel de La Laurencie (close to d'Indy and the Schola) was president, but other members included J.-G. Prod'homme (librarian of the Opéra and secretary of the society), Brênet, de Curzon, Dauriac, Boschot, and Quittard.[91]

The society's goals were ambitious: not only did it wish to reexamine the history of French music, but, in so doing, it sought to contribute to the historical knowledge of France in general. In wartime, this implied studying the evolution of the "âme nationale" as it developed and manifested itself ineluctably in the different French cultural areas. As the society's organizers asserted, music history in France revealed that "le développement des organismes musicaux se rattache de façon étroite a l'évolution politique, sociale et littéraire" (the development of musical organizations in France are closely attached to political, social, and literary evolution).⁹² Again, this was wartime ideology, based on the premise that the "national genius" manifests itself not only in the political and social realms but, concomitantly, in that of culture. Scholarship here too was suitably "mobilized" so that a sense of French music history, as well as of a more comprehensive national canon, could, with the collaboration of intellectuals, now fully emerge. But the collaboration of others, particularly those within the commercial musical world, was essential, and here the officials directing propaganda in the Ministère des Beaux-Arts would lead the way.

FRENCH EDITORS, THE CANON, AND THE CLASSICS

Officials were well aware that a French classic canon that conciliated factions could not be defined without the collaboration of other sectors of the profession, particularly editors of music. Again, the decision was not left to musicians; it was rather the Ministère des Beaux-Arts that would play the central role in ensuring that musical production followed political exigencies. But it was to do so indirectly and gradually, first by attempting to reorient their attention toward the musical past by pragmatically pointing out the financial advantages. In July 1918 the director of the Beaux-Arts, d'Estournelle de Constant, approached the Société des Auteurs, Compositeurs et Editeurs de Musique (SACEM) with a specific request: he asked the society to found an annual prize of one hundred francs, which it would award at the end of the academic year to the outstanding student in music history at the Conservatoire.

This was a savvy means of furthering an interest in music history and past musical styles in an institution in which both had long been notoriously weak.⁹³ The message to be communicated to students by this central professional and commercial organization (upon the urging of officials) was the importance of music history, and of knowledge of past styles. Indirectly, this would assure that not only musical taste but style would develop in the desired direction in the future, and indeed the plan would bear fruit: one of the students who would win the new prize in the postwar period and go on, creatively, to fuse past and present stylistically was the young Olivier Messiaen.

This successful effort on the part of the administration of the Beaux-Arts, however, followed another, unsuccessful attempt at a similar "collective" endeavor, the effort to "popularize" the musical classics in France by making them more widely available, or affordable, through French editions, to a mass public. In keeping with official "taste," which, again, was close to the Schola's, the new "French edition" was to distribute widely not only the French but also the consecrated German classics. For as we have seen, "French classicism," ironically, was generally understood by officials in terms of the high classic German-Austrian style, but with the substitution of certain French traits. Once more, it was this position that Debussy and Fauré, as well as others, continued, subtly, to protest in prose, as well as in their art, as we will see. But it suited the dominant rhetoric since it stressed the "orderly" qualities now being sought throughout French society, as opposed to anarchic or individualistic romanticism. Moreover, it accorded with the rhetoric being so widely diffused in France that the French were traditionally the "protectors" of the classic, particularly after nineteenth-century Germany had betrayed it.

To this point, the French had been dependent on Germany for editions of the German classics, and particularly on the venerable publishing houses of Peters as well as Breitkopf. Before the war, individual editors already proposed the launching of a "popular," accessible edition of the "classics," to be financially competitive with the German editions.[94] Here nationalist chauvinism was already evident, for Durand, and others, held that pedantic German "professors," courted by the editors for their many students, had "deformed" the works with their numerous markings. The French would restore them to their original classical "purity," and in so doing finally respect the authentic "pensée des maîtres."

Despite these reservations about German editions, however, Durand remained the official representative of the Peters edition in France until the war made this impossible. Now, economic interests would work together with professional and ideological needs to foster a French edition of the canonic French and German "classical" works. Durand, of course, was delighted, for the war at last allowed him to realize a long held ambition of producing a true "édition classique populaire française."[95]

As Durand observed, the moment was right to solicit the collaboration of French composers in his "patriotic" project, for few were presently in the frame of mind to compose. Hence he was able to enlist the aid of prestigious composers in his "house" for the project, including, notably, Debussy, Saint-Saëns, Fauré, and Dukas.[96] Debussy, ravaged by cancer, found this a convenient way to compensate Durand for the rapidly mounting monetary advances that he was now being forced to request. Hence Debussy agreed to edit Chopin, having been a pupil of one of Chopin's purported students, and, with somewhat less enthusiasm, to undertake Bach's Sonata for Violin and Keyboard.[97]

The first volume of Durand's edition appeared in October 1914, but soon other editors and composers decided to launch similar profitable "patriotic" projects. D'Indy, once close to Durand, was no longer in his "house," since the editor, after seeing the virulently anti-Semitic pamphlet and libretto to d'Indy's *La légende de Saint-Christophe*, had precipitously dropped the composer. D'Indy thus cooperated with Sénart and, as we might expect, held his own distinctive conceptions of the editorial principles that should apply in arriving at a "pure" edition of the classics.[98]

Yet despite professional hostility, d'Indy did share an "imaginaire national" with Durand, or a sense of French as opposed to German culture, as propaganda had fostered. In a letter of 28 December 1914 to another collaborator on Sénart's competitive edition of the classics, d'Indy articulated his own ideas about editorial principles:

Pour les nuances, supprimer celles trop nombreuses et trop fantaisistes, les "Bearbeitungen"; se rapprocher de celles des manuscrits; écrire des préfaces non pas esthétiques, mais pratiques pour l'exécutant ou élève; établir une édition non de musicographe mais de musicien, conservant le texte du manuscrit original toutes les fois qu'il indique son interprétation, mais se substituant à lui, dans le but pratique de l'exécution digne de l'oeuvre toutes les fois que ces indications manquent.

[For the nuances, suppress those too numerous and fanciful, the "Bearbeitungen"; get closer to those of the manuscript; write prefaces that are not aesthetic but practical for the performer or the student; establish an edition that is not that of a "musicographe" but of a musician, conserving the text of the original manuscript every time it indicates its interpretation, but substituting for it, with the practical end of a performance worthy of the work, whenever the indications lack.][99]

In keeping with the dominant "collective representations" of the Germans, d'Indy here depicted them as pedantic and abstract, as opposed to truly musical, as were the French. It was thus now up to the French to restore the manuscripts to their pristine state, applying not only their indigenous "bon goût" but their honest "bonne foi."[100] D'Indy went on publicly to develop his principles of editorial practice at length in an article of 1 April 1917 in the *Courrier musical*. This was only to further fuel the controversy among competing editors, much to the alarm of the Sous-secrétariat des Beaux-Arts, which perceived a violation of *union sacrée*. Durand thus proposed a collective endeavor, as not only patriotic but a financial necessity, having seen a survey which attested that only collaboration would make the project financially feasible. Hence employing patriotic terms, he now enjoined the other French editors who were engaged in classic editions to "venir sacrifier à l'autel de la collectivité au nom de l'Union sacrée" (come to sacrifice at the alter of the collectivity in the name of the "sacred union").[101] As president of the Chambre Syndicale, Durand was felicitously in the position to solicit the assistance of the Administration of the Beaux-Arts in his new collective venture. Alfred Cortot was thus again to play a key role in an attempt to affect reconciliation within the contentious and implacably competitive French musical world. Aware of Cortot's support for Durand, the latter's enemies now launched a press campaign intended to undermine his credibility through the claim that Durand himself was not "French."[102] Casting doubt on one's patriotism by questioning national and racial "roots" was an insidious practice employed by adversaries both during and after the war.

Despite these slurs, the Sous-secrétaire d'Etat did come to Durand's aid, addressing the project at the annual distribution of prizes at the Conservatoire. He even raised the possibility of "compelling" all those editors who continued to cling to "individualism" to participate in this collective, national endeavor. And just as significantly, he urged French editors to publish vocal and orchestral "classics" as well as works little heard in France, such as Bach's B Minor Mass and his Passions.[103] Now the great Bach was no longer "boche" but rather rechristened as a good "classical" German—one of the pre-Prussian past, whom the French were now destined historically to "save." But Bach "the classic" would be interpreted diversely in the 1920s, and used to justify stylistic practices and departures of markedly different kinds.

The project of a collective edition failed, as had similar endeavors in the French musical world, still rent by competition and hostilities, despite lip service to *l'union sacrée*.[104] Interpretations of the "classic" would continue to differ, beneath the carapace of ideological orthodoxy, which all factions quickly learned to manipulate, as the Ministère des Beaux-Arts soon perceived. Despite the failures, however, French officials had succeeded, at least, in imposing a set of "national" standards and expectations for music in France that would outlast the war. They had made French music synonymous not only with classicism, but with the national community, both of which were to be "protected" from the baleful influence of foreign cultures. Throughout French culture the choices now were thus adherence to orthodoxy, subtly masked dissent, or a dangerous "open" confrontation, which carried the peril of accusations of treason.

RESISTANCE TO THE WAR AND ITS CULTURE

Political agitation continued, within circumscribed parameters during the war, and political life grew more animated as the government gradually gained control of the army.[105] Although patriotism was at its summit, conflict with a more ethnically exclusive nationalism was inevitable and would be accompanied by continuing battles over the interpretation of the French Republic itself. For the Left, as opposed to the Right, French patriotism consisted primarily in the recognition of the grandeur of France's "mission" as protector of universal values. But at first, despite continuing conflicts and distrust between Left and Right, most Frenchmen resigned themselves to the necessity of *l'union sacrée* to assure the national defense.[106] Yet dissent would gradually emerge in civil society as well as at the front, leading to the devastating combination of workers' strikes and military mutinies. For some time already soldiers had begun to loose sight of the war's rationale and to perceive the diminishing possibilities of employment upon their return home from military service.[107]

It was at this point that songs of revolt began to circulate secretly in Paris, and Socialist opposition to the war, which had been quelled at its start, began to resurge. Even within popular culture, a marked tone of resistance became gradually evident, with the more polyvalent song texts and performances assuming a new meaning that was implicitly seditious. *L'union sacrée* was definitively shattered by November 1917, and the prime minister, Georges Clemenceau, positioned himself squarely against the "defeatists."[108]

Disillusionment and disenchantment had already begun to express themselves in the arts, and most radically in the Dada movement, born in Zurich during the war. It confronted the loss of meaning of traditional forms of representation by peremptorily and aggressively denying not only tradition, but indeed meaning itself. "Dadaists" rejected the conception of art as a means of reassurance, transcendence, or evocation of a mythical national past: it was rather purely and simply "provocation."[109]

In France the movement would have special resonance in certain intellectual circles in which there was a growing suspicion of language, or an acute awareness of what it obscured. Lofty phrases, vague generalities, and euphemisms became increasingly suspect as the war continued, and propaganda appeared to drain language of any authentic meaning.[110] Romain Rolland, who, as a pacifist (although not a Dadaist), resided in Switzerland during the war, expressed exactly this in his satirical play, *Liluli*. A farcical critique of the dominant wartime myths, it exposed the concomitant distortions of reality on every level of culture throughout the war.[111]

Pacifism was indeed present from the start, but it only gradually grew overt; at first it was expressed principally through small journals that deftly eluded the harsh censorship code. It was in these journals that not only French youth, but a political and aesthetic avant-garde began to express itself and its vision of both French society and art. Implacably antiofficial, they (like their pacifist counterparts in Germany and Russia) perceived the possibility of artistic renewal in the wake of the upheaval caused by the war.[112]

Gradually two cultures—those of conformity and dissent—confronted intellectuals, including artists, and demanded difficult choices, often between professional interests and ideological beliefs. Although those in both literature and the visual arts faced harsh and specific censorship codes, those in other abstract "symbolic" areas, such as music, would have far more latitude. Again, ever since the Dreyfus affair, French composers considered themselves to be intellectuals, obliged to respond to the issues of their period, in music, prose, or both.[113] Wartime was no exception: more than ever they realized the necessity of choosing between espousing the dominant myth (and the bellicosity behind it) or challenging it in their actions and art. The question of the positions that composers assumed, and what they expressed both in the framework of classicism and current codes of stylistic meaning, is one to which we must now turn.

Part 2: Intellectual and Creative Responses

HOW TO DEFEND "LA MUSIQUE FRANÇAISE"

As we have seen, the network of propaganda and control that French composers confronted had no recent precedent: foreign to their personal experience, it would have been so equally to several previous generations. It impinged directly on them, just as it did on intellectuals and artists, all of whom were faced with specific interdictions on "representations" of the national culture. In searching for ideological hegemony, official culture now functioned through a tightly imbricated system of institutional controls monitoring both intellectual and artistic life. Of cardinal importance within this system was that all representations, either intellectual or cultural, be subordinated to national, as opposed to universal, values, the latter now considered suspect. The arts, approached as an integral part of French national symbolism in wartime, were henceforth subject to both official injunctions and new political "inscriptions," or interpretations.[114]

The belief that art and *patrie* were inseparable now carried important implications for music, which was equally absorbed by the political culture and expected to further national values and interests. Specifically, music, as we have seen, was to serve the national myth of "true" French identity and tradition: it was, as Rouché perceived, to "imagine" the French community and its "classical" culture. But if specific meanings were to be produced or inscribed and thus a political "utterance" created, music had to be mediated, performative context and means of access to it carefully monitored.[115] Here, again, the principal goal was to define French tradition in music as "classic," but construed according to a narrow conception of it already articulated by Action Française.

As we have also noted, there were modes of cultural resistance within French society, which would mount in force in the course of the war and explode in contestation upon its conclusion. French intellectuals, as Martha Hanna has shown, disagreed vigorously on several key points, including the value of the German cultural tradition and the nature of the French classical inheritance.[116] Not surprisingly, then, composers, as intellectuals, responded diversely, some accepting the propaganda concerning classic style, having previously espoused the political perspective to which it was tied. Others, as we will now see, embraced it, but with caveats, realizing that nationalist dogma, while a necessity in wartime, masked both the reality of war and of the French musical past.[117]

A handful were to rebel against it, but the older generation characteristically did so within the framework of the "orthodox" position, contesting dogma by confronting current stylistic codes. They were clearly conscious of the ideological meanings being ascribed to the doctrinaire classic style, and they hence faced the challenge of maintaining both personal and creative integrity while this style was imposed. Whether or not they submitted, all became aware of the choices, being necessarily cognizant of the political pressures now placed on musicians through the myriad modalities of state control.[118]

High culture, including music, then, by no means became "sterile" during the war, or stagnated in official conventionality, as some historians continue to claim.[119] For many composers the imposition of classicism presented a stylistic and technical challenge—that of finding compositional interest within the injunctions of French wartime propaganda. For others the challenge lay in discovering how to manipulate stylistic meanings, with a growing awareness of the perceptions they could awaken in doing so, or of the statements they could articulate through style. If an ideology was inscribed in "orthodox" classicism, another could be communicated in its variants, or through inflections of stylistic orthodoxies, making style a locus of ideological confrontation.

The choice for musicians, unlike artists and writers, therefore, was not that of clear conformity or dissent through words or images; rather, through style they could equivocate more subtly. Words were subject to censorship, but symbols and style could be manipulated with latitude, providing a mode of criticism or of indirect resistance to complete absorption by the nationalist myth. Moreover, since this myth was projected onto the canon and thus onto great French composers of the past, the question of "influence" was particularly sensitive, now carrying ideological implications. For to manifest or avow the influence of one of the canonized French composers meant, in the context of the discourse surrounding them, or modes of presenting them, to ascribe to the "myth."

Here, much could be said through the use of "outside" cultural influences, which, within the discursive context, could make an equally resonant statement. In such a manner French composers could subtly transmit their tensions with the orthodox stylistic expectations and concomitantly communicate their conceptions of true French music, of French culture, and of patriotism. In some cases, as we will see, the results would be complex and semiotically multivalent works which critics during wartime, and in the postwar period, would decipher or "appropriate" in conflicting ways. The most innovative composers would cleverly blur the boundaries between the dominant traditionalist ideals of order and morality, as expressed in conventional artistic tropes, and "cultural modernism."[120] They were thus in tense dialogue with the press, for most critics compliantly buttressed public pressures to conform to baroque or (ironically) Viennese classic models, which d'Indy's Schola Cantorum had long propagated as paradigms.

NATIONALIST ORTHODOXY: D'INDY VERSUS SAINT-SAËNS

As we have seen, musical orthodoxy in wartime was equivocal: even those who espoused the "patriotic" tenets of official institutions could not agree on what they specifically implied for the repertoire. Such was to be the case within the most doctrinaire organization of musicians assembled during the war in Paris, the chauvinist Ligue pour la Défense de la Musique Française. Not only did d'Indy and Saint-Saëns continue their vitriolic exchanges in print, but other members were soon to find that there was little agreement over how to be "French."[121] Two cases here are of particular note, for not only do they concern prominent French composers, but they reveal the variety of ways in which the league's ideals could be interpreted artistically.

Unlike Debussy, Fauré, Ravel, and Satie, who declined to join the league, both Vincent d'Indy and Gustave Charpentier adhered to it publicly and prominently.[122] But they did so for substantially different reasons, and interpreted the ideals of the league in opposite ways, revealing the tensions within *l'union sacrée*, which would explode soon after the war. For d'Indy and the Schola, true classicism had passed from France to Austria and Germany at the time of the French Revolution but had subsequently been betrayed by the Prussians and was now to be reclaimed by the French. Largely due to the influence of d'Indy, Viennese classicism, but filled with French material, now best embodied the classic ideal of a "regulated moral and aesthetic order."[123]

D'Indy's classicism was, unequivocally, that of the traditional, nationalist French Right, associated not with egalitarian universalism but with the "orderly and hierarchical values of Catholicism." Hence their credo was not the "Liberty, Equality, Fraternity" of the French Revolution, but rather "clarity, reason, and moderation," associated with the Ancien Régime.[124] As we have seen, d'Indy's interpretation of French classicism was now widely shared, although, paradoxically, it conflated elements of both French and German classic style. Again, for d'Indy, there were "good" and "bad" Germans, the former being those of the baroque and classical past (extending, for him, through Wagner), and the latter (the "Boches") being more recent German composers, or "Prussians." His national loyalty remained without question; d'Indy stayed in Paris, even through the most difficult days of the war, and resolutely forbid the Schola's nonmobilized faculty and students to flee the city.[125] In an attempt to endorse *l'union sacrée*, he also agreed to teach courses at the Conservatoire, which he had previously attacked, and which was now depleted of students and faculty. Although openly hostile to the aesthetic avant-garde, which he maintained was "unpatriotic," or inspired by the "Boches," he nevertheless impressed even his innovative students with his sincerity and generosity of spirit.

Saint-Saëns rather expressed his loyalty to the nation in other ways, including his official sponsorship of the Conservatoire's Comité Franco-Américain. Founded with the participation of both Lili and Nadia Boulanger, the organization sent packages, letters, musical works, and even corrections of harmony exercises to some three hundred Conservatoire students mobilized at the front. He also gave concerts for the benefit of soldiers, and composed numerous *pièces de circonstances*, consciously making them easy so that they could be transcribed for local bands and other ensembles. These included such works as *L'honneur à l'Amérique* and *Victoire*, the latter a song written at the end of the war, dedicated to the king of Belgium, with words by Paul Fournier.[126]

D'Indy both taught and edited, and, like Saint-Saëns, continued to compose, although in more "classic" genres, now more than ever confirmed in his conviction that French culture must be protected from its "enemies." He finally completed his anti-German and anti-Semitic opera, *La légende de Saint-Christophe*, which he had begun just after the Dreyfus affair. At the same time, he began his Third Symphony; like his second, it was a "symphony of ideas," intended to communicate concepts, or a "message." Here again he followed the symphonic model that he perceived in Beethoven.[127] And, as with his purportedly anti-Dreyfusard Symphony no. 2, although a "program" inspired the work, d'Indy maintained that it was not essential for all to know the "code," or the meanings behind it. As before, it would be his intimates, or his circle of staunch supporters, who would grasp, and thus be responsible for diffusing, the commentary that "explained" the work's ideas.

While the "message" of d'Indy's Second Symphony was avowedly "anti-Dreyfusard," or about the ultimate victory of "tradition," that of the Third Symphony was anti-German. More specifically, it was a work ostensibly inspired by the myth of a classical and "Latin" French culture, as pointedly opposed to that of modern Germany, generally referred to as "boche." In a letter written from Florence to Guy Ropartz, d'Indy pointed out that the work would be short—only thirty-nine to forty minutes, which, he claimed, was to make a point: he wanted clearly to define himself, and indeed the French in general, against "les boches modernes avec leur 'Kolossale-Synfonie' durant trois heures et demie" (the modern "boches" with their "collosal" symphony lasting three and a half hours).[128]

Moreover, in a later letter to Ropartz, d'Indy explains that the "program" or idea inspired the work, although it was not to be circulated or published with the score. According to d'Indy, the symphony, composed between 1916 and 1918, was about his impressions of the war, which he describes as follows, making frequent use of dominant wartime myths: "Ier Move.—La mobilisation de la Marne (the mobilization on the Marne); Scherzo—La gaieté du Front (the gaiety at the front); Andante—L'art latin et l'art boche (Latin art and "boche" art); Finale—La victoire, avec hymne" (the victory, with an anthem).[129]

As historians of the war have observed, the idea of insouciant "gaiety" at the front was a myth, as much as was the idea of France as a "Latin" culture, as opposed to that of the "Huns."[130] But for d'Indy it was a motivating myth to which he wholeheartedly adhered, unlike other composers we will examine, whose relation to it, creatively, was tense. Although dogmatic and doctrinaire in both its conception and composition, d'Indy's Third Symphony was published with only the traditional indications, "Introduction," "Divertissement," "Lent," and "Finale." D'Indy also made a particular point of noting to Ropartz that nothing recalling the music of Stravinsky—too modernistic or "boche"—was to appear in the score. Instead, as he went on to explain, it was intended to resemble a symphony of Haydn, one of the eminently acceptable "good" German composers from the classical past.[131]

But ironically, again, although d'Indy verbally espoused the aesthetic of "purity," the symphony was conceived under strong German influence—from both the distant and the more recent past. Not only is it cast in traditionally German forms, as Debussy dyspeptically emphasized, the treatment of these forms is not that of the "good Germans," but of later nineteenth-century German composers, well after Beethoven. As Glenn Watkins has noted, a German military march evokes the enemy in the first movement, the sound of bugles appear in the Scherzo, and there is a "crude allusion to contemporary German music in the Adagio." The strongly programmatic underpinning bears the imprint of the Lisztian school, and the placing of the Scherzo second, as well as making it and the slow third movement the "centers of gravity," is characteristically German romantic. Indeed, as d'Indy's critics had been quick to note, and continued to stress, his conceptions, as articulated in his treatise, were Germanic, and based fundamentally upon the theorist Hugo Riemann.[132] But d'Indy found creative inspiration in the discursive dogma of "the classic," as well as in the statutes of the Ligue pour la Défense de la Musique Française, while Gustave Charpentier found in both these same sources justification for very different endeavors.

CHARPENTIER'S DOUBLE-VOICED SCHEMES

From the very beginning, Charpentier knew how to manipulate the "official mentality," having been dependent on both academic and official culture as a composer from a humble social background. He had already learned adeptly how to serve his own compositional and social interests while in rhetoric appearing to endorse the official goals of the state. Not only could his successful opera, *Louise*, be "read" or interpreted from both points of view: so too could his popular fêtes, in particular his widely performed *Couronnement de la muse*.[133] This was equally true of his combined "school of music" and "social project" for young working women in Paris, his still thriving Conservatoire Populaire de Mimi Pinson.[134]

It is thus not surprising that Charpentier's response to wartime propaganda would be to create a patriotic project, or an "oeuvre de guerre," which would simultaneously serve his other goals. In 1914, in addition to the social programs that he had initiated with his school, he introduced Les Infirmières de Mimi Pinson, La Cocarde de Mimi Pinson," and L'Ouvroir [Ladies Work Party] de Mimi Pinson. Here he had found another avenue through which to make poor Parisian working girls—badly needed performers in his fêtes—part of the social "mainstream," or (as his critics put it) more "bourgeoise."[135] Now they too could serve the Republic, thus strengthening their social identity as well as their ties of loyalty and their place within the republican political system. The plan was highly effective: La Cocarde de Mimi Pinson (in which young women made patriotic "rosettes" for charity) lasted from 1917 to 1920, receiving subventions from the Conseil Municipal, the Conseil Général, and the Ministère de l'Instruction Publique et des Beaux-Arts.[136]

Much more controversial, however, were Charpentier's creative projects which distinctly projected his leftist—specifically Socialist—conception of the future Republic.[137] Now he publicly proposed the institution of a series of "fêtes laïques," to take place on the anniversary of decisive events, or in celebration of organizations, ideas, or principles. Recalling the fêtes of the French Revolution (and equally revealing of his social vision), he proposed a "fête des corporations, célébrant la force active de la ville" (a festival of corporations, celebrating the active forces of the city). Even more specifically recalling the fêtes of the French Revolution, another series of fêtes he proposed was designed to celebrate seasons and the work with which they were associated: "Les fêtes de la moisson, des vendanges, sont tout indiquées pour la campagne, dans notre Midi notamment. Pour ces fêtes serviraient les divertissements traditionnels, facile à élargir." (The festivals of the harvest, of the grape harvest, are all indicated for the countryside, especially in our "Midi." For these festivals the traditional entertainments would serve, easy to enlarge.)[138]

He also proposed another *fête* that immediately recalls a scene in his opera, *Louise* (which, as we have seen, was popular during the First World War), a "fête de la poésie, du rêve, de l'amour." Charpentier's perceptive idea was thus to replace what he disdainfully termed "froides conférences" and "défilés" which he considered too austere, glorifying only abstractions. Hence he now advocated a celebration of "life," stressing the psychological importance (particularly in a time of war) of embellishing it with the "féerique," or magical element. He imagined "heures d'exaltation embaumées de musique et de poésie, où les arts plastiques, par le décor, par ses groupements, seraient appelés à réjouir des regards." (Hours of exaltation fragrant with music and poetry, where the plastic arts, through the decor and its groupings, would be called on to delight the eyes.)[139]

Although such a conception would indeed be realized later, under the Popular Front, Charpentier's plan was badly timed; it came to public notice at a moment of workers unrest in Paris, followed by strikes, as well as the mutinies on the front. Interpreted as politically and socially partisan, glorifying French workers and the revolutionary heritage, critics perceived it as a violation of *l'union sacrée* (now dissolving) and thus attacked it in the press. Specifically, Action Française bitterly denounced Charpentier, as it long had, because of his "naturalist" aesthetic (associated with Emile Zola) since the time of the Dreyfus affair.[140] Charpentier's outward adherence to wartime propaganda through such gestures as joining the Ligue pour la Défense de la Musique Française, as well as his purportedly patriotic projects, did not fool Action Française. They also perceived that *l'union sacrée*, both politically and aesthetically, was a thin veneer that would soon wear off, revealing the old polarities that preceded the war.

DEBUSSY'S DIALOGUE WITH ORTHODOXY

Although Claude Debussy was far closer to the principles of the Ligue pour la Défense de la Musique Française than Charpentier, since he was now seriously ill with cancer, there was no possibility of his becoming a member. But even if his health had permitted, it is doubtful that Debussy would have adhered, having long made clear his distaste for factions and schools of any kind.[141] Debussy could not abide orthodoxies: he had always to consider and define a position for himself, in keeping with his distinctive interpretation of both the French canon and of wartime cultural exigencies. Like d'Indy, he needed a "myth" of the French in music to spur creativity, but he insisted on defining his own, which only in certain respects resembled that of propaganda. But unlike d'Indy, Debussy would discover his own private tensions with his personal myth while composing, which resulted in a series of complex, contradictory works.

Throughout his career, in both his prose and his music, Debussy unremittingly questioned all "doctrine," particularly that concerning French "traits" in music and the meanings assigned composers and styles. Although someone who believed that "the collective" could ultimately produce individual freedom, he staunchly resisted the crass attempts of officials to "direct" style or to tell the public what to think. Ironically, just as Action Française was "constructing" him as classic, Debussy was continuing to repudiate the Germanic French classicism that they, in essence, espoused. As we have noted, Jean Darnaudet's perception of simplicity, unity, and clear form in his work undoubtedly perturbed the composer, who believed that all form should be both individual and concealed.[142] And Darnaudet's description of "the French" as consisting of clarity, sobriety, sincerity, and purity, Debussy rejected, with the exception of the first and last components. The Schola's conception of the canon and of "la grande musique," endorsed by Darnaudet, had long been targets for Debussy's barbs, which by no means now ceased. A committed and self-avowed "nationalist," Debussy nevertheless maintained his own personal terms and beliefs, which helped to guide his creativity now, as before the war.

In his published prose of the period, Debussy reiterated many of his earlier themes concerning the unquestionable necessity of rediscovering the "authentic" French tradition. And yet his concepts of race, blood, and "purity" recalled the rhetoric of Action Française, with which he continued to have a complex intellectual relation. As we saw in his preface to the collection, *Pour la musique française*, his primary concern was with the immediate extirpation of anything he considered to be "un-French." Debussy's solution here was to return to "authentic" French forms, thus abjuring any that were not endemically French, which included his target of many years, the symphony.

In an article of 11 March 1915, in the ardently nationalist *L'intransigeant*, he states his position on these issues in equally emphatic and bellicose terms: "For many years now I have been saying the same thing: that we have been unfaithful to the musical traditions of our race for more than a century and a half. . . . since Rameau, we have had no purely French tradition. . . . Today, when the virtues of our race are being exalted, the victory should give our artists a sense of purity and remind them of the nobility of the French blood. We have a whole intellectual province to recapture."[143]

Here Debussy's argument closely resembles that of the now prominent Action Française, which similarly stressed intellectual purity, or the importance of preserving the purported "French style of thought." This indeed had been a central issue in the vociferous controversy that preceded the war concerning the "Germanic" influence on the reformed, or "nouvelle Sorbonne."[144]

Debussy's letters in this period continue to reiterate the same set of themes, but with even less circumspection or circumlocution than his statements in print. In a letter to Igor Stravinsky of 24 October 1915, he speaks far less cautiously of the issues of race and of preserving the "purity" of French culture:

> Il faudra nettoyer le monde de cette mauvaise semence. Il faudra tuer ce microbe de la fausse grandeur, de la laideur organisée, dont nous ne nous sommes pas aperçus qu'elle était simplement de la faiblesse. . . . Vous êtes assurément un de ceux qui pourront combattre victorieusement ces autres "gaz" aussi mortels que les autres, contre lesquelles nous n'avions pas de "masques."
>
> [It will be necessary to cleanse the world of this bad seed. It will be necessary to kill this microbe of false grandeur, or organized ugliness, which we have not perceived as simply being a weakness. . . . You are assuredly one of those who will victoriously combat the other gasses that are just as lethal as the other [kind], and against which we had no "masks."][145]

Here Debussy treats Stravinsky as an ally, a Russian artist equally hostile to German postromanticism and to its noxious legacy of "false grandeur" at the Schola. Debussy proceeds earnestly to assure Stravinsky that he is a "great" artist, but then he urges him to be, with all his force, a great "Russian" artist, for "C'est si beau d'être de son pays, d'être attaché à sa terre comme le plus humble des paysans." (It is so beautiful to be of one's country, to be attached to the earth like the humblest peasant.)[146] In thus urging Stravinsky to remain "rooted" in his own soil, Debussy once again sounds (as he had before the war) like the novelist and nationalist Maurice Barrès.[147] His real concern here, however, was that Stravinsky was not only a threat to his preeminence, but that he was becoming far too "boche," an opinion he had expressed ten days earlier in a letter to Robert Godet.

In the course of this letter Debussy complains about the problem of German "infiltration" in France, and particularly the baleful influence of Wagner, which unfortunately continued to loom. Again, he speaks of "cette lourde mainmise sur nos pensées, nos formes" (this heavy hold on our thought, our forms), and then goes on to remark, "Voilà la faute grave, impardonable, difficile à réparer car elle est en nous comme un sang vicié." (Here is the grave fault, unforgivable, difficult to repair because it is in us like vitiated blood.)[148] Debussy's real worry was apparently that Stravinsky would help to further, and perhaps to bring, the insidious German influence directly into France. As we will see in chapter 2, Schoenberg himself would be attacked on such grounds in the 1920s, and within a racial discourse that had been legitimized during the war.

In the rest of his letter to Godet, Debussy reiterates his obsessive concern with the nature of true French music and its implications for both the nation's present and its future. Here, as before the war, he returns to the theme of the old French "*clavecinistes*," a group excluded from the national canons of both republican institutions and the Schola.[149] Omitted because they were not "virile" or "serious," and thus rejected as "enfants ingrats" (unattractive children), Debussy pointedly includes them on the basis of their "grâce profonde," and their "émotions sans épilepsie." Here, in emphasizing their unpretentious, pleasing manner, Debussy recalls Jean-Aubry, although the latter perceived these qualities in Debussy's rival, Satie. Debussy's canon was thus singular, although, like others, he included Rameau; however, he interpreted this illustrious predecessor, and his implications, in a personal manner.[150] Earlier in the letter to Godet, he speaks of the current shared obsession with Rameau, whom no one will admit that they do not know how to perform authentically—which they certainly would not learn from d'Indy.[151]

Debussy's continuing dispute with d'Indy and with wartime propaganda over the "true" French tradition, or what constitutes authentic French classicism, is evident in other correspondence as well. In a letter to Stravinsky of 24 October 1915, he mentions that at the moment he his writing only "musique pure," a term that d'Indy associated with traditional abstract forms. Here he was specifically referring to both his *Douze études pour piano* and to "deux sonates pour divers instruments dans nos véritables formes" (two sonatas for diverse instruments in our true forms).[152] But Debussy's abstract forms, as we will see, bore little resemblance to the "molds" of d'Indy, particularly his sonatas, in which Debussy interpreted the genre in the original free sense of "sounding piece."

Only the day before, he had written to Francis Poulenc about recapturing the old forms: Poulenc was posing as a Belgian music critic in order to obtain Debussy's autograph. In response to Poulenc's provocative question concerning his opinion of the music of Franck, Debussy addresses the subject of form in the following unequivocal terms: "Cher Monsieur, en ce moment nous devons tâcher à ressaisir nos vieilles traditions: celles-là dont nous avons délaissé la beauté qu'elles n'ont cessé de contenir." (Dear Monsieur, at this moment we should try to recapture our old traditions: those whose beauty we have abandoned and which they haven't ceased to contain.)[153] Debussy does, in the end, respond specifically to the question concerning Franck by succinctly retorting that Franck was indeed the greatest of the recent "musiciens flamands."

Despite the certitude of his rhetoric, Debussy's music reveals a continual search for a personal conception of "purity," of French roots, and his place in or relation to this past. Here he equivocated with wartime dogma far more so than in his prose, confronting current significations, questioning his own beliefs and past works, and facing the inconsistencies with irony. But it was the macabre, honest irony of someone confronting imminent death in a traumatic time of war, and hence preoccupied not only with the nation's future, but with his own past and reputation. Debussy's compositions of the war years attempt to define "French tradition," to explore those aspects of France's musical past that he interpreted as "pure," and to unmask both false conceptions and myths.

One series of compositions in this period confronts contemporary propaganda and myth through his musical language, and thus with an impunity not possible in other arts. Here Debussy is intractably locating his roots in the work of French Renaissance composers such as Janequin, whose "realism" previous republican spokesmen like Bruneau had identified as the "true" French tradition.[154] Yet in all of Debussy's wartime works, the emphasis, as propaganda demanded, is no longer on asserting his individuality or indulging in the sensual; it is on "ideas" and his links to the past.

The first of these boldly realistic compositions, at a time when "heroism" and myth were promoted, was his *Berceuse héroïque* (which belies its title), composed for *King Albert's Book*, in 1914. The latter comprised a series of works of art assembled by Hall Caine, an English novelist, as a tribute to the king of Belgium (a favorite ally of the French) and his heroic soldiers in the face of German attack. Caine solicited works from prominent artists and intellectuals from the allied countries, including Elgar, Messager, and Monet, and published them in the *London Daily Telegraph*. Debussy's contribution was later published by Durand (the following year), with the inscription, "Pour rendre hommage à S.M. le Roi Albert de Belgique et à ses soldats." (To pay homage to his Majesty, King Albert of Belgium and his soldiers.)[155]

Here Debussy, like contemporary intellectuals, confronts the problem of honestly "representing" the war, well aware of the limitations of language in capturing the horrific reality of combat. He was also inescapably aware of the standard images that were being disseminated, which often employed the Christian reference of sacrifice and resurrection, or banalized and commercialized the war in antiseptic icons.[156] These he clearly could not accept, and in the piece he rather expresses his personal anguish, in a manner far less subtle, more direct and linear, than in all his previous compositions.

Opening in a stately manner, invoking the rhythms of a slow march and not a *berçeuse*, Debussy then introduces harsh dissonances, including, at one point, simultaneous reference to three different tonalities. But Debussy is even more explicit in meaning through the inclusion of an identifiable quotation—in this case several bars that, poignantly in the context, are drawn from the Belgian national anthem and arrestingly juxtaposed within an almost opposite stylistic context. As

Debussy avowed in a letter to Emile Vuillermoz, in June 1916, it was extremely difficult for him to incorporate the quotation (commonly expected in such works) especially since it did not arouse the same heroic feelings in him as in those who were raised with this anthem. Perhaps because of this he "demartializes" the rhythms, transforming and prolonging them so that, as he put it "il n'y hurle pas" (it doesn't yell), and thus making the quotation all the more poignant. But Debussy also evokes the war vividly in his explicit imitation of distant bugle calls; moreover, although the work is obligingly in traditional ternary structure, Debussy, in honest commentary, suggests a funeral procession.[157]

Although the composition was originally for piano, the now associated Concerts Colonne-Lamoureux performed the *Berçeuse héroïque* in a version that Debussy himself orchestrated for the occasion. But the composer's substitution of the lugubrious style of a funeral march for the "heroic" (despite its title) was apparently too honest for the French public in 1914. What it desired, toward the start of the war, was neither reality nor a statement of anguish, but rather a simple triumphal idiom that Debussy, unlike Saint-Saëns, could not produce. As Marc Ferro has incisively observed, "the cameras that recorded the war never show men in the process of dying. . . . they only show the image of the dead— a much calmed, if also more tragic, image."[158]

But this was only the first of a series of straightforward, if not popular compositions, in which Debussy would find himself unable to adhere to the myth in the face of harsh realities. Despite cool public response, the following year (1915) Debussy composed another somber and realistic work, his *En blanc et noir* for two pianos. Again, he would depict the bald reality of combat, here employing almost expressionistic techniques in an even more dissonant composition that in another composer he would have decried as "boche." And, in an attempt to make his commentary or intended meaning explicit, Debussy employs literary inscriptions, thus creating a kind of "hermeneutic window" onto the work.[159]

The first of the three pieces is prefaced with four lines that are drawn from the libretto of Gounod's *Roméo et Juliette*; hence, although the movement is abstract, the quotation invests it with specific meaning. The lines chosen indicate, if obliquely, Debussy's still ardent sense of personal patriotism: "Qui reste à sa place—Et ne danse pas—de quelque disgrâce—Fait l'aveu tout bas." (He who remains in his place and does not dance, of some disgrace whispers a confession.) The reference here, although veiled today, was widely understood in the period as being to those who attempted to avoid military service on the false pretext of a physical disability.[160] It is also significant that Debussy rebelliously invokes Gounod, who had long been a part of "his" canon, representing the "grace" and the "charm" of the French. Yet this movement, ironically, is more orthodox than before, both in form and in certain stylistic aspects: it is generally tonal (in C major) and contains a sonata-like thematic recapitulation and coda.[161]

Each of the work's movements creates a mood, or an emotional response to the war: the first, marked simply "avec emportement" (with anger), suggests the bold ardour of a wartime patriot. The second, "Lent et sombre," evokes the emotions felt preceding and during battle, and is similarly prefaced by an epigraph, here drawn from a French poet of the past whose work Debussy had set. He had long admired, and in fact identified personally, with François Villon, a French fifteenth-century poet who, like he, made often candid observations from a position of social marginality. Here the lines selected address not the national problems within but the threat from outside, chosen aptly from Villon's "Ballade contre les ennemis de la France." But poignantly and personally, it is dedicated to one of Debussy's deceased associates and friends, Lieutenant Jacques Charlot, who was killed in battle on 3 March 1915.[162]

Thus, stylistically, this piece includes subtle reference to a traditional genre, the *tombeau*, a memory or mourning piece for the dead, particularly characteristic of the French Renaissance. Debussy invokes the genre by employing the effect of a funereal drone, although the harmonies are nonfunctional, and in some cases highly dissonant. Death is indeed represented, but the unspeakably horrific reality of the war is couched in terms of French tradition, although not the one being promoted by propaganda.

Other Renaissance idioms then follow, for, in recalling the "battle pieces" of composers like Janequin (whose works he knew), Debussy evokes the war realistically through suggestions of bugle calls and the rumbling of guns.[163] He even resorts to non-Western pentatonicism, together with clashing seconds, to achieve an almost visceral effect, and to imply that the Germans are not Occidental, but "Oriental," as propaganda demanded. Further buttressing these martial references are the descriptive and simultaneously emotionally explicit markings in the score, such as "alerte," "joyeux," and "sourdement tumultueux" (dully tumultuous). Thus in a manner still characteristic of the symbolists, the composer is describing not external events or images in themselves, but rather the emotional effect they elicit, as filtered through consciousness. Such a description, less of the war than of its emotional realities, including joy, was indirect enough not to be labeled "defeatist," unlike Henri Barbusse's realistic novel, *Le feu* (1916). But it nevertheless differs substantially from the more normative evocations of the period, such as Matthÿs Vermealon's "Poème de la tranchée," to a text of François Porché. Here the emotions aroused by war are approached dramatically and pathetically: after the description of a quiet evening, and a call to prayer, the men prepare for combat against a regular, slow, binary rhythm that becomes more agitated with the "recitation passionée."[164]

Also counter to the norm, Debussy is explicit, yet circumspect, in his employment of musical quotations, a practice he had explored before the war but here carries to a new degree of almost collage-like, cubistic abstraction, as opposed to his earlier seamless interpolations or interweavings. He cites Luther's chorale, "A Mighty Fortress Is Our God" recognizably, to evoke the "Germanic," but here, as propaganda obliged, transmogrified into ponderous, jarring discords. And in order, thereafter, to "cleanse" the atmosphere of these "poisonous fumes," as Debussy put it (recalling his letter to Stravinsky about noxious cultural gasses), he then claims to make a passing reference to the "Marseillaise." As Glenn Watkins has pointed out, however, the anthem is so deftly interwoven into the musical fabric, and without its recognizable rhythmic profile, that it is, in essence, inaudible. Despite the symbolic significance of this poignant quotation, then, Debussy clearly sought to avoid the all too common heroic and blatant reference to the French national anthem. Citations from the "Marseillaise" were indeed the norm throughout the war, and may be seen in more typical works such as Francis Casedesus's *France lève-toi*. [165]

Debussy's piece, however, is not without other conciliatory gestures toward wartime propaganda, for Debussy (as d'Indy) attempts to evoke the mythic brave "gaiety" of the French, as opposed to the humorless Germans, in battle. Yet here he does so not only through reference to the traditionally lighter genre of the scherzo, but through an almost cubistic juxtaposition of French folk songs (introduced earlier) with military bugle calls. The overall atmosphere nevertheless emerges as grim, as Debussy was well aware, for although he attempted to tone it down, his authentic, creative response would not permit this. As he had already learned with his *Berçeuse héroïque*, he had to walk a fine line between the depiction of harsh reality and what was considered "defeatism."[166]

The third piece, marked "Scherzando," ironically, is dedicated to "mon ami, Igor Stravinsky," and modernistically suggests both the physical atmosphere and emotional mood of the war. This results not only from the unmistakably Stravinskian motor rhythms and ostinati that immediately evoke wartime mechanization, but from the epigraph drawn from Charles d'Orléans, "Yvers, vous n'êtes qu'un vilain" (Winter, you are just ugly). While critical of Stravinsky in his letters for his "boche-like" modernism, Debussy could not prevent himself creatively from employing these same techniques when they served his artistic, expressive goal. Debussy, characteristically, explores the future of French music without giving up the past, seeking his "French identity" by looking forward and backward simultaneously. Indeed, there were never any simple dichotomies of traditionalism or modernism in Debussy's work; posed precariously between the past and the future, he sought the "spirit," not the "letter" of tradition.

Clearly, Debussy could not remain conciliatory for long, and he once more confronts wartime myth in his terrifying last song, the "Noël des enfants qui n'ont plus de maison," which he performed at the Société Musicale Indépendante in what would be his last public appearance.[167] Having recently learned of a war atrocity impacting children, he immediately penned his own text, a strikingly unorthodox confrontation with the unmitigated horrors of war. In perhaps his strongest emotional statement of the period, Debussy alternates (paradoxically recalling Schubert's "Erlkönig") between the innocent, the menacing, and the ironic.

Probably originally intended to resemble a popular chanson (*noëls*' having a popular and collective character), and possibly inspired by a poem of Victor Hugo ("L'enfant," in his *Orientales*), the text is cast as a childlike imploration to Santa Claus from traumatized children who had lost their homes in the war.[168] Here Debussy attempted, in part, to explode the still current myth of "heroic, storybook children" (extending back to the Napoleonic wars), and rather confronts the sordid reality. To do so, ironically, he uses the German lied as a model (perhaps unconsciously), for it is evoked through the vivid piano accompaniment (again recalling "Erlkönig") and emotionally charged imagery, so rare in his work. Here anti-German content is perversely expressed within a German stylistic frame, the effect being not one of parody, but rather of inversion, or subversion, of a national genre.

Debussy thus again dialogically undermines his own myth of French cultural purity, and, ironically, in other aspects he manifests obeisance to the dogma of French classicism he had attacked. For striking here is the clarity and balance of the form—ternary with refrain—as well as in the rhythmic and metric clarity and frequently defined tonality (despite the unconventional modulations), suggesting the naive certainties of childhood. These qualities, which Debussy had previously abhorred, are indeed those that the critic for *L'action française* perceived in Debussy's late style, although removed from its textual context. Debussy was ardently patriotic, as we have noted, but it was consistently on his own terms, for he continued critically, or intellectually, to accept or reject specific elements of wartime myth. Hence his work in this period was both contradictory and highly complex, and could be interpreted in myriad ways, during and after the First World War.

This is especially true of Debussy's last work, left unfinished upon his death, the "Ode à la France," which had apparently undergone substantial evolution in the course of the war. Referred to as both oratorio and cantata, it was planned in 1916 for the combined performing forces of soprano, chorus, and orchestra. It falls into the larger genre of hymn, which was popular throughout the war, with prominent examples being those of Lili Boulanger and Camille Saint-Saëns. Boulanger's *Dans l'immense tristesse*, to a text of Geleron de Calonas, calls for national reconstruction and hope, incorporating an old popular song as well as a pathetic *berçeuse*. Debussy's text, by his friend Louis Laloy, was on the subject of Jeanne d'Arc, who was to personify a suffering France, "sacrificed to appease an unjust fate and save future generations."[169] Here she was to stand for current French youth, similarly being sacrificed in the war, although the tone of the work was to change as time progressed and victory seemed imminent. Debussy received the poem for the beginning of the work in January 1917, and planned at that point to title his oratorio "La ballade de pitié du royaume de France"—again evoking the distant French past. However, when Debussy's editor, Jacques Durand, saw what was still a sketch of the work shortly before the composer's death, in 1918, he noted its optimistic, even triumphant tone.[170]

The style envisaged for the work in the sketch recalls that of Debussy's *Le martyre de Saint-Sébastien*, or one close to the Renaissance polyphonic style that he admired since his Prix de Rome days in Italy. Indeed, according to another of Debussy's friends, the conductor D.-E. Inghelbrecht, one of the composer's last desires was to "read" the a cappella works that he (Inghelbrecht) was planning to perform.[171] But further indications as to Debussy's stylistic intentions still remained vague, and it was not until ten years after his death that Laloy attempted to reconstruct the work from Debussy's notes. This he did with the help of a young musician, Marius-François Gaillard, who not only filled in the sketch, but then orchestrated the work, which was performed at the Salle Pleyel on 21 April 1928. What was originally an expression of anxiety was gradually modified by Debussy and then by his mediators into an optimistic, "patriotic" statement.

Although Debussy critiqued the dominant wartime myth in a relatively overt manner, through the manipulation of wartime symbols, in the compositions we have examined, he did so more subtly in another "abstract" series of works. In these he independently examines the orthodox wartime classic myth and defines his own "French classicism," but at times, in the interests of honesty, he betrays even his own doctrine.

Undoubtedly motivated in his choice of genre by his collaboration in Durand's "classic edition," and specifically by his editing of Chopin, Debussy composed his piano *Etudes* in 1915.[172] Just as Chopin, and as he himself did in his own other "classicizing" compositions, he here sought "freedom," or the illusion of it, within large formal symmetries. The first study, for example, is firmly bound tonally, at the beginning and end, by the key of C major, and the fifth and twelfth etudes, formally, are cast in an identifiable ternary structure. But, as in his earlier work, Debussy does not here simply "return" to the past, he rather "translates" it creatively into the terms of his own sensibility and technique. This is evident not only in form, but in the subtle and imaginative way he invokes the eighteenth-century *clavecinistes* who, as we have seen, were a central part of "his" canon. In "Pour les notes repétées," he refers to one of the *clavecinistes'* favored techniques, having already emulated their careful use of ornament and skillfully spaced textures in his previous compositions. Here he creates a traditional "toccata-like" effect, but one that is nevertheless boldly original, with a virtually atonal opening.[173]

In "Pour les sonorités opposées," he experiments with contrasts in harmony, color, dynamics, register, and texture, although in the latter case he stresses treble and bass lines, as in Couperin. The last etude, "Pour les accords," is similarly traditional and daring at once: in a clear ABA structure, it employs polytonal effects and asymmetrical rhythms, here recalling his rival, Stravinsky.[174] At a time when Debussy was worried about Stravinsky's "modernism," which he perceived as dangerously "boche," and despite his best efforts to evoke the "classic," he could not avoid rising to Stravinsky's challenge when it served his purpose.

But Debussy was to be just as unorthodox in his other contemporary "classicizing" compositions, in which he continued to define himself against his contemporaries, and particularly d'Indy and Saint-Saëns. This is especially true in his wartime treatment of sonata form—a genre of which he had once made fun, considering it as synonymous with d'Indy's orthodox "mold."[175] But now, as we have noted, Debussy audaciously reclaims the genre as "French," referring back to its origins (which, in fact, were in Italy) as simply an instrumental piece. It is also significant that Jean Huré, a staunch Debussyste, had defined the sonata, before the war, as any work of "musique pure" larger than a "feuille d'album" or a prelude.[176] In adopting this definition, Debussy was again defining his own approach in opposition to the norm, or demonstrating what a sonata does not necessarily "have" to be. Ironically embracing "la grande musique," he, like his predecessors in the Société Nationale de Musique Française, was convinced that this form, which carried Germanic connotations, could be filled with authentic French content.[177]

According to Jacques Durand, it was after hearing Saint-Saëns's Septet (1881) at the Concerts Durand that Debussy conceived his idea of writing a set of sonatas for different combinations of instruments. As a composer who was always responding to his contemporaries, Debussy was probably aware that Saint-

Saëns (who was also published by Durand) was now writing a series of instrumental sonatas. Hence he projected six sonatas; however, increasingly weakened by cancer, he would succeed in producing only three before his death in 1918. And in writing them he was certainly also aware of the many French "classicizing" sonatas now being composed and performed at the Société Nationale as well as at the Société Musicale Indépendante.[178]

Such a rivalry provided Debussy with yet another occasion to accept or reject specific elements of the dominant conception of classicism, along with the ideological connotations it carried. Here it is important to remember as well that a particularly negative model for Debussy was the "Beethoven sonata," especially the dogmatic conception of it taught at the Schola.[179] Debussy audaciously attempted to reclaim the genre as endemically French, referring back to its origins, as we noted in his prose, as simply an instrumental piece; but, in fact, like his predecessors in the Société Nationale de Musique Française, he adapts the Germanic model to a supposedly French content. Ironically here embracing "la grande musique," he, like his elders at the Société, and as he himself had done earlier in his String Quartet, was meeting the Germans, and attempting to better them, on their own formal grounds.

The first of the set, the Sonata for Cello and Piano, is a highly personal statement, a work that Debussy originally considered titling "Pierrot fâché avec la lune." This was meant to refer not only to the theater of eighteenth-century France, but to Debussy himself, who now personally identified with the sad figure of the traditional clown, Pierrot. Significantly, for eighteenth-century artists, including Watteau and Couperin, Pierrot had become a symbolic embodiment of man's dissatisfaction with his own desire.[180] In addition, Pierrot was traditionally an incarnation of paradox, as well as of the ineffability of expression in a realm beyond rationality, or the multiplicitous and illusory nature of all appearance.

Debussy, in fact, had referred to the figure of Pierrot several times already, in works like his *Fêtes galantes* (to poems of Verlaine) of 1882. But now the trope was particularly meaningful, for Debussy was poignantly aware of the paradox of his own recent stylistic evolution, and of the transience of his personal identity. For Debussy, someone who had come from the social margins, had arrived in "society," yet here was ill at ease, and who had rejected his academic training, but now found himself embracing it, the irony was acrid.[181]

However, there was yet another paradox that Debussy himself did not clearly perceive: in certain aspects his approach approximates the description of a sonata by the Scholiste pianist, Blanche Selva. In her book, *Quelques mots sur la sonate*, she describes the genre as follows:

> Dans la sonate, où la tonalité peut se comparer au lieu de l'action, les thèmes sont des personnages possédant la parole et le geste et se mouvant dans ce lieu. Le rythme est le "geste" et la "mélodie" la "parole." Les personnages ou thèmes concourent tous, par leurs gestes et leurs paroles, à l'action générale qui est l'oeuvre. Par interprétation, le personnage-thème doit être présenté, dès l'abord, avec la rapidité habituelle des gestes, le timbre de sa voix, l'accent de sa parole.[182]

[In the sonata, where the tonality can be compared with the place of action, the themes are the characters possessing word, gesture, and movement within it. The rhythm is the gesture and the melody the word. The characters or themes all converge, by their gestures or words, in the general action, which is the work. Through interpretation the character-theme should be presented from the start with all the characteristics defined, that is to say with the habitual rapidity of gestures, the timbre of the voice, the accent of the speech.]

This is precisely what Debussy does in a startlingly literal sense, for his "character" appears immediately, with his own distinctive traits, and thereafter remains omnipresent. But the character here seems anachronistic—out of place— for the opening melodic material is far different from what one would expect in a sonata, and was even described by contemporaries as evocative of French trouvère melodies. In fact, its opening rhythmic gesture has since been identified as deriving from he "prologue-ouverture" to Rameau's *Les fêtes de Polymnie*, which Debussy himself had edited. Also, as opposed to the conventional sonata, the concentration throughout the movement is not on a harmonic goal, but rather on presenting the "protagonist" in all his facets. (Significantly, the markings in the score include the "vocal" instructions to the "character": "largement déclamé.")

And in place of either traditional lyric continuity or conventional contrasting themes, the various ideas are rather juxtaposed—a practice frequently denounced in the period as "boche." Hence, while the development section does impart tension, the techniques are decidedly not those of the Schola, nor is Debussy's treatment of the recapitulation, which is thematic but not tonal. In short, Debussy has perversely written a sonata-form first movement that dialogically both invokes and violates the standard Viennese classic model. For in keeping with the now dominant aesthetic (as articulated most clearly by Action Française), the proportions, if not the contents, are classic, as Debussy himself was proud to point out. As he put it, attempting judiciously to distinguish his classicism from that of "the mold," "I like its proportions and its form that is almost classical in the good sense of the word."[183]

Classicism had its distinctions, and there were models of the style that he clearly refuted—none more so, perhaps, than that associated with the rigid Germanic model as taught at the Schola. But Debussy's work is classical, according to "his" conception, not only in its economy, but also in its general lightness of texture. In making this choice he invokes the contemporary dogma of the classical as synonymous with the "Latin," but then does so in an unorthodox manner in the sarcastic second movement, with its habanera rhythm and guitar-like pizzicato.

Just as ironic and original melodically is the Sonata for Violin and Piano, which Debussy composed and premiered himself in his last public appearance before his death. Here, perversely, given the dogma concerning the "purity" of French culture, to which he ascribed in his prose, Debussy employs melodies that suggest not only folk song but the "Oriental," or the non-Western. But this was not the first time that Debussy, having denounced foreign influences on the French in print, then paradoxically turned to the non-Western for melodic, harmonic, and formal inspiration. Yet here, even more paradoxical is the fact that, again contradicting his own statements in print, he subjects his material to academic procedures he had once satirized, such as augmentation and diminution.[184] Moreover, the first movement, in ternary form, ends in G minor, having employed conventional contrasts and logical development, and the last movement of the work cyclically recalls the first, in the Franckian, Scholiste manner, as in his early String Quartet (1893).

However, the sarcasm here is directed not at the Schola, but rather, honestly and dialogically, at himself, at his own inner battle with the Conservatoire training he had once naïvely rejected. Increasingly, Debussy was creatively rediscovering certain components of his academic training, a phenomenon that would similarly characterize his wartime Sonata for Flute, Viola, and Harp. Here he employs themes that, for his contemporaries, resembled not only Gregorian chant in their length and rhythmically amorphous quality, but, for some, once again, French troubadour and trouvère melodies.[185] He is, then, in a highly unorthodox sense, again invoking the theme of "Latin" culture, but from a historical perspective, free of the eighteenth-century model. Yet at the same time the sonorities and nondirectional effect created by the texture, harmonic language, and rhythm distinctly suggest the non-Western element.

Equally heterodox is the thematic structure: not only does he employ no fewer than six different thematic ideas in the course of the movement, juxtaposed and treated sectionally: they return in the end, but again without significant variation and in a substantially different order, or simply "rearranged," in a non-Western manner. And in spite of the incorporation of minuet and rondo elements in the following movements, he again mixes these predominantly later-eighteenth-century German features with those that clearly recall the French baroque. Not only does he employ baroque dance styles, and emphasize the period's stylistic traits, but again, in the manner of Couperin, he gives the movements theatrical titles, "Pastorale," "Interlude," and "Finale."

Debussy recognized his inconsistencies, and as he said of his Sonata for Violin and Piano, "You can read between the lines; you will see the traces of that image of the perverse which drives us to choose the very idea we should have rejected." But as Rollo Myers points out, Debussy also observed that the mood which emerges in this sonata was strikingly different from his own mood at the time he composed it, being rather "full of life, almost joyous." He then went on to muse that this may be proof of "how little a man's own feelings are concerned with what is occupying his brain." Here the creative and the conscious were clearly at odds, as in all his sonatas.[186]

Debussy was indeed promoting French tradition, but not in the conventional manner, and with an irony that he himself appreciated, as he openly played with his academic past. His acceptance of this, and his public acknowledgement that he indeed wished to enter "the canon," in spite of his disdain for "models" and schools, would become patent in his last public gesture. As early as 1914 Debussy's candidacy for the prestigious Institut de France had been proposed, and received strong support from members in several different cultural fields. For this was the year that the chair of the organist and composer Charles-Marie Widor became available, since Widor had been named the permanent secretary of the Académie des Beaux-Arts.

However, during most of the war there were no elections at the Institut, and when all believed that the war would soon end, Debussy's wife contacted Widor on his behalf. She indicated her husband's willingness, now, to submit his candidacy, and asked Widor about the specific procedures that would have to be followed.[187] But Saint-Saëns was strenuously opposed, and hence the proposal was further delayed, although most French contemporaries generally assumed that Debussy would, in fact, be elected. However, when he finally sent his official letter of candidacy to the Institut de France, on 17 March 1918, hopeful of becoming an academic authority, he was already on the verge of death. Yet even in these final days, Saint-Saëns continued to do all he could to prevent Debussy's elevation to the rank of "immortal," and thus his entry into the canon.[188]

The fact that both composers firmly believed they embodied the "French classical tradition" is indeed an indication of how contestatory conceptions of it remained in wartime France. And while Debussy sketched only one blatantly "patriotic" work, his cantata "Ode à la France," and Saint-Saëns produced many propagandistic compositions, Debussy was by no means less "engaged." However, he insisted on expressing his beliefs and nationalism in his own terms, through a rigorous and "intellectual" evaluation of French wartime myths, including "the French classic tradition." If this required him to ignore the centripetal cultural forces of wartime, or even to contradict himself, self-contradiction was less important than personal authenticity. The result was a series of compositions that are semiotically complex and thus multivalent in meaning, accommodating diverse constructions, even in his lifetime.

For Debussy's political investment did not destroy his aesthetic integrity, and like all great art, it could be both political and apolitical.[189] Discourse and dialogy were unequivocally present at the moment when Debussy conceived these works—there was a situation of interlocution, a context, which made them specific "utterances" in their period. But the discourse has since become abstract text and entered other "environments"; the works are now autonomous, removed from their original communicative context and "speaking subject." This, as we have seen, was Debussy, the intellectual, not only exposing stereotypes, but "intervening in language," or "speaking truth to power," and at the same time, unflinchingly, to himself.[190]

Because Debussy's death coincided with the last major German offensive, the press, preoccupied with the news of the war, gave the event little coverage. A notice by Adolphe Julien did appear in the learned *Journal des débats*, as did one by the critic Paul Landormy in the more popular *La victoire*. Even at this point, however, not all French critics construed Debussy as either "classic" or unequivocally "French," thus prolonging prewar battles, and violating *l'union sacrée*. One skeptic was another critic, who was close to Action Française, but who, as opposed to Darnaudet, did not perceive the "classicism" of Debussy's late style. Camille Bellaigue, in the *Revue des deux mondes*, continued to condemn the composer, perceiving his music as too individual and thus "unsubstantial," just as he had at the turn of the century. But the process of "consecrating" Debussy as one of the great

French composers, who embodied quintessential French values, was nevertheless now beginning to occur symbolically, even at his funeral, which took place on 29 March 1918. Despite the events of the war, there was some, albeit meager, official representation; as Jacques Durand ruefully observed, a minister (the minister of public instruction) put in a brief appearance.[191] But Debussy's definitive entry into the canon would have to await the early 1920s, when the factions within the older generation lost relevance in the face of the threat of youth, the "foreign," and the "modern."

RAVEL'S INFLECTIONS OF TRADITION: THE *TOMBEAU*

Maurice Ravel, like Claude Debussy, accepted certain elements of the dominant myth, but only on his own terms—as filtered through his highly critical intelligence and creativity. There was no question of Ravel's patriotism: despite his age, he sought to enlist and defend la *patrie*, yet his interpretation of the "patriotic" stemmed not from the conservative, nationalist tradition but from the republican, revolutionary one.[192] For Ravel, then, the mark of patriotism was the willingness to defend the French nation as the protector of universal values, as opposed to its own national interests, or its "particular," historically determined culture. It was such a conception of patriotism that would lead to Ravel's refusal to join the Ligue pour la Défense de la Musique Française, and to the retaliation of the Ligue's tightly bound network.

Ravel was part of a republican tradition that emphasized both reason and individual responsibility, or individual autonomy and the revolutionary conception of human liberty and progress.[193] The war thus marked the beginning of Ravel's intellectual "prise de position," or the growing recognition of the deep political implications of the cultural stance he now assumed. Like Debussy, however, if his intellectual position was unequivocal, his creative response was more subtle, especially the way in which he engaged with and commented on the dominant classic myth.

Maurice Ravel had never been reticent to defy authority openly, a fact that was already clear in his student days, when his independence cost him official consecration. Not only had Ravel (as opposed to the more pragmatic Debussy) failed a record five times to win the Prix de Rome on the basis of his harmonic audacities, he was part of a renegade coterie known as "les Apaches," which maintained "advanced" artistic tastes.[194] Such confrontation with those in power in the hierarchical French musical world continued to manifest itself during the prewar battle of factions, or the "Guerre des chapelles." Despite the increasing dominance of d'Indy and the Schola before the war, Ravel, perhaps more than any other composer, confronted both of them boldly. On numerous occasions, not only in private letters but also in print, he made it clear how insidious he believed their reactionary aesthetic and political doctrine to be.[195]

Although he considered writing a symphony, Ravel, like Debussy, could not bring himself to do so because of its Scholiste connotations, and this remained true during the war. And, again like Debussy, one of Ravel's beloved counter-models to both the Scholistes and to the Conservatoire academics was the music of Emmanuel Chabrier.[196] Ravel's other idol was Debussy himself, whose music he defended despite the fact that Debussy did not reciprocate when Ravel's *Histoires naturelles* was attacked by the Scholistes in 1907. Yet when Debussy's *Images* for orchestra was attacked by the supporters of the Schola, Pierre Lalo and Gaston Carraud, Ravel leapt to his defense in the *Cahiers d'aujoud'hui*. Here he intrepidly challenged their claim that Debussy's work was an "exception," or far too individualistic, and would thus lead to an artistic "impass."[197]

A staunch supporter of innovation, Ravel was present at the tumultuous premiere of *Le sacre du printemps*, and is reported to have defiantly cried "Génie! Génie!" amid the brouhaha. Also reported is the fact that when he attempted to quiet a neighbor so that he could hear the music, the latter angrily retorted that he was a "sale Juif." Perhaps because of certain physical traits, this was an accusation that Ravel would repeatedly confront in the following decades, and to which his response would be uncompromising. While vigorously denying that he was Jewish, Ravel would, in turn, consistently defend and come to the aid of persecuted Jewish composers and performers, having no tolerance for any racial prejudice.[198] But it was in the course of the war and in its polarized aftermath that Ravel gradually drew ideological conclusions from his instinctual or impulsive response to such issues.

The war was a turning point for Ravel. He discovered that his patriotism was based upon principles associated with the Left and the universalism that it had defended since the French Revolution. When the war broke out, Ravel immediately sought to enlist in the army, but was rejected for military service because he was too small. Hoping that his size and weight would not matter, or indeed would be an asset in aviation, Ravel then tried, without success, to become a pilot (despite his turning forty in 1915). He finally had to content himself with driving a truck and helping to care for the wounded, an experience that, given his sheltered life, would be transformative.[199]

Ravel recorded this experience in letters: on 8 October 1916, he wrote to Mme Casella of his "camaraderie" with and admiration for the trench soldiers, drawn predominantly from the lower classes: "De vrais poilus, pas de M. Bourget, de M. Barrès. . . . Révoltés, pessimistes, aveugles, d'un égoïsme bas . . . et qui deviendront des héros dans quelques semaines." (True soldiers, no Misters Bourget or Barrès. . . . Rebellious, pessimistic, blind, of a lowly egoism . . . and who will be heroes in a few weeks.)[200] The reference to Bourget and Barrès is telling, for both were associated with the nationalistic Far Right, and both defended the slaughter chauvinistically from comfortable positions within "the establishment."[201]

Ravel was by no means the only musician to perceive and ridicule their hypocrisy: the same was true of his good friend Albert Roussel, as well as of Jean Marnold (the critic). Roussel, like Ravel, was undergoing a political awakening; associated with the Schola, he now examined, and rejected, his colleagues' predominant political and aesthetic beliefs. In a letter to his wife of 4 January 1916, Roussel makes disdainful reference to a recent article by Barrès (politically close to d'Indy) in *L'écho de Paris*: "C'est un chef-d'oeuvre d'hypocrisie et il porte bien sa signature. Rien de plus méprisable que ce faux monsieur, malgré son talent. Il ne se trouvera donc jamais personne pour le démarquer!"[202] (It is a masterpiece of hypocrisy and it truly bears his signature. Nothing is more contemptible than this false "monsieur," despite his talent. There will never be anyone to bring him down!)

While finding himself growing away from d'Indy, Roussel was still hurt by the latter's indifference, especially d'Indy's lack of response to his letters, after so many years of working together. Like Ravel, Roussel would not only undergo stylistic transformation, he would evolve politically in the same direction after the war—toward the left, and particularly toward French socialism. Already, in a letter to Cipa Godebski of 20 August 1914, Ravel proclaims his support for France, as opposed to Austria and Germany, but wishes "longue vie à l'Internationale et la Paix" (long life to the International and to peace).[203] The tendency toward both pacifism and socialist universality would indeed characterize postwar French socialism politically and culturally, thus attracting both Roussel and Ravel. Despite their shared antipathy for "extremist," or xenophobic, uncritical nationalism, Ravel and Roussel consented to participate in the attempted union of the Société Nationale and the Société Musicale Indépendante. In fact, it was the *chef de la propagande musicale* himself, Alfred Cortot, who sagaciously sought out Ravel to solicit his participation in the project. However, when asked to be a member of the directive committee of the united societies, Ravel hesitated to accept, fearing, as he stated baldly in a letter to Marnold, that this combined society (under the leadership of the Société Nationale) would be "trop nationale."[204] This was undoubtedly a double reference both to the dominance of Scholistes in the Société Nationale and to their exclusive, extreme nationalism.

Although Ravel, in the end, consented, if provisionally, to participate in the ultimately unsuccessful fusion of the two performance societies, he firmly drew the line when it came to joining the Ligue pour la Défense de la Musique Française. Ravel received the league's declaration and invitation while at the front, and, enraged at its principles, responded in the following adamant terms:

> Il serait même dangereux pour les compositeurs d'ignorer systématiquement les productions de leurs confrères étrangers et de former ainsi une sorte de coterie nationale: notre art musical, si riche a l'époque actuelle, ne tarderait pas à dégénérer et s'enfermer en des formules poncifs. . . . J'espère néanmoins "faire acte de Français" et me compter parmi ceux qui voudront y servir.[205]

> [It would even be dangerous for composers systematically to ignore the productions of their foreign colleagues and thus to form a sort of national coterie: our musical art, so rich in the present epoch, would quickly degrade and enclose itself in clichés. . . . I hope, nevertheless, to act as a Frenchman and count myself among those who want to serve.]

Neither during nor after the war would Ravel accept the league's attempt to ban the performance of German or Austrian works not yet in the public domain. He would heartily defend the work of Schoenberg and other foreign modern composers, whatever their nationality or ethnic origins. Unlike Debussy, whose aesthetic inclinations and political beliefs were frequently at odds, Ravel, both in principle and in creative practice, would defend the "universal." The wartime dogma that art did have a *patrie* was for him unacceptable, as was the concomitant doctrine that French classicism had to remain narrowly and exclusively "French." Ravel, like Debussy, would highlight the irony that the dominant model was, in fact, German, and would do so both through ridicule of the Schola and in his commentary through musical style. And again like Debussy, Ravel would gradually define his own authentic position through opposition to other current conceptions of what the French musical tradition comprised.

Ravel began by exploring those epochs of the French musical past that, for him, could serve as a model, and, like Debussy, he did not hesitate to mix the traits of different stylistic periods. For both composers, this was an implicit rejection of the Schola's dogmatism, or its rigid adherence to "molds" that d'Indy derived, essentially, from the Viennese high classic style. This mélange appears already in Ravel's Trio (1914), dedicated to one of his teachers, André Gédalge, and premiered at a concert of the Société Musicale Indépendante on 28 January 1915. Here Ravel (like Debussy) enters into a dialogue with the classicism of Camille Saint-Saëns, the teacher of his own teacher, Fauré, and whom he admired, although by no means uncritically. The first movement, which employs Basque rhythms, is based loosely on sonata form (as opposed to the "mold" of the Schola), while the final movement rather suggests a grandiose baroque passacaglia. Ironically, the work, unusually emotional or personal for Ravel, won the praise of both Scholistes, such as Gaston Carraud, who noted its elegance of form, and opponents of the Schola, such as Jean Marnold.[206]

While composing this piece, Ravel was at work on two other compositions which he described as follows: "1) Une suite française—non ce n'est pas ce que vous croyez: "la Marseillaise" n'y figure point et il y aura une forlane, un gigue, pas de tango cependant 2) Une "Nuit Romantique," avec spleen." [(1) A French suite—no it isn't what you think: the "Marseillaise" doesn't figure into it and there will be a *forlane*, a gigue, no tango, however (2) a "Romantic Night," with spleen.)][207] Ravel's description of the first composition indicates that its "patriotic" components, as well as the nature of its style, would definitely be unorthodox, which was indeed the case. The second work mentioned was inherently "deviant" in its spiteful reference to the "romantic" at a time when this style was generally associated with both individualism and the Germanic.

The first work Ravel described would become the *Tombeau de Couperin*, a composition that belies its title, being avowedly not written in commemoration of Couperin, although Ravel, like Debussy, proudly admired this ancestor not yet in the canon. For Ravel, the piece was rather composed in memory of his friends who had been killed in the war, and as an homage to all French music of the eighteenth century, as provocatively opposed to the official "exclusions." In thus declaring his intent, Ravel was also, like Debussy, subversively invoking the ritualistic genre of the Renaissance-baroque *tombeau*, as opposed to a later classic genre. Moreover, it has been postulated that the inclusion of the *forlane* and the reference to Couperin had been inspired by an article on Couperin by Jules Ecorcheville, who had been killed in the war; this article had appeared in an issue of the *Revue musicale S.I.M.* in 1914, and included an example of a *forlane*.[208]

As a *tombeau*, however, the piece is unorthodox, for traditional *tombeaux* (which were transferred from literature to music by the mid-seventeenth century in France) were generally in a single movement. Most often written for lute, harpsichord, or viol, they honored or enshrined a dead master, in what Carolyn Abbate has aptly referred to as an act of "commemorative mimesis." Ravel's work consists of six pieces, inspired by both baroque and classic forms (as in his Trio)—a Prelude, Fugue, Forlane, Rigaudon, Minuet, and Toccata. Unlike Debussy in his wartime works, Ravel does not seek a personal, emotional involvement with the eighteenth-century French style, but typically remains formal and detached, here in keeping with the genre. And instead of emphasizing classical "forms" and simplicity in the dominant manner, Ravel rather stresses the rhythmic gestures, ornamental practices, and accompaniment figures of Couperin and the eighteenth-century baroque, employing strange, uncharacteristic harmonies, and a strong linear drive. He aptly captures both the acuity of articulation and the transparent, if complex textures of the *clavecinistes*, thus preserving an eighteenth-century sense of syntax, but with his own distinctive harmonic idiom.

Moreover, while some have perceived a rhythmic reference to Rameau in the "Rigaudon," others have noted, ironically, another to the Italo-Spaniard Scarlatti, in the "Forlane," which is based upon a *forlane* by Couperin. Ravel indeed employs dissonance in a manner that resembles Scarlatti, or as a pungent color added to a tonal or modal harmony. Significantly, Ravel well knew the artificiality of borders when it came to culture: of both Swiss and Basque descent, he intrepidly remained proud of his heritage.[209] And in addition to this unorthodox reference to a non-French composer in the work—ostensibly a statement concerning the fluidity of cultural borders—references to the present, not just to the past, appear. Roland-Manuel perceived a specific invocation of Saint-Saëns, and even of Ravel's own "Menuet antique" and "Sonatine" in the "Rigaudon" and "Menuet."

But other cultural challenges punctuate the work, and especially the "Forlane": not only are the harmonies "distorted," but, as Carolyn Abbate has noted, Ravel suggests a *musette*, with its characteristic drone, in several of the contrasting episodes. The effect, she advances, is one of a "mechanism gone awry," or that of a "broken machine," both ironic and terrifying, especially given the specified lack of rubato. But the conceit may also suggest further meanings within the context of wartime culture in France, for "mechanism" has other layers of resonance, as indeed did the *tombeau*. Here the suggestion of mechanism or "automata," as we will also see in Satie's *Parade*, had a chilling reality, given the new mechanisms of killing, now including aviation, of which all, including Ravel, were aware. And so did the invocation of "dead objects," which Abbate perceptively relates to modern anxieties over the reproduction of sound—to sounds that are dead, and yet audible through a personal sound, as they are in the *tombeau*. Given the historicism of French wartime culture, all composers faced the anxiety of reproducing or emulating that which was "dead" creatively, of finding an authentic voice within it. Ravel here provocatively mixes deep irony with the objectivity that defines the genre as a way of maintaining his creative integrity, while expressing his homage in recognized musical forms.[210]

Ravel refused to remain mired in the past, ignoring music of the present day, just as he refused to consider French modern or historical classicism as mutually exclusive. His classicism was that of the French republican tradition, one that associated "the classic" not only with sacrifice but with the still vibrant moral or political principles of ancient Athens.[211] Yet, cleverly, Ravel again produced a work that could please those conservatives who expected obeisance to certain dominant conceptions of French music and of classicism, while managing, like Debussy, to do so on his own terms. Both composers thus commented not only on their affective and stylistic relations to prominent French composers and forms of the past, but also to the current nationalist myths about them. And like Debussy, Ravel similarly combined his own personal style with the French Renaissance past, and with particular reference to Janequin in the first of this *Three Songs for Unaccompanied Mixed Chorus*, "Nicolette." However, it would be in the 1920s that Ravel would make his strongest artistic statement about exclusive nationalist myths, and buttress them with a clear, if implicit, ideological commitment.

SATIE'S SUBVERSIONS: LANGUAGE AND THE DIALOGIC IN *PARADE*

No one was more distrustful of the dominant wartime discourse than Erik Satie, and no one managed to undermine it more completely, and with such consummate skill. If Jacques Rouché had demonstrated how theater could brilliantly serve wartime propaganda, Satie thus demonstrated with equal brilliance how it could serve subversion. Satie's wartime project, like Rouché's, involved representing a performance within a performance in order to awaken perceptions in the audience, although with opposite ideological intent.[212] And while Rouché's project resembled ritual, or the genre of "cultural performance"—a society displaying its own culture to itself—Satie's, on the opposite end of the spectrum, rather resembled far more a "ludic celebration." The latter, associated with the "liminal," or the socially uncategorized and transformative, is characterized by a "surplus of signifiers, a kind of sensory overload created by a Rabelaisian profusion of images and the intermingling of categories."[213] The semantics of such "ludic" spectacles are thus "open, unorthodox, fragmented, and often highly individualized, enabling them to elude control and to transcend or subvert ideology."[214]

This was precisely Satie's goal, one perfectly suited to a collective theatrical work in which there was no real "author," although, historically, Cocteau has most often been "assigned" this function.[215] The central question with regard to the work, then, is what caused this ambiguity of authorship, and hence such "fluidity" of signification, which left the work's message dependent on its performative context. During and after the war *Parade* would be construed in ideologically opposite ways—first as attacking nationalist orthodoxies, and then as embodying or epitomizing its values.

The starting point to understanding this phenomenon must be the nature of the collaboration itself, which brought together those with similar "progressive" aesthetic stances, but different ideological orientations. Cocteau and Apollinaire (who wrote the program notes) both believed that "modern art" could be justified through appeals to nationalist rhetoric, and thus shown to be "patriotic," as opposed to "boche." Satie and Picasso had a different intent: to subvert nationalist and official classic rhetoric, or to extract illicit meanings from the "classic," and thus open up new perspectives on wartime culture. *Parade* provided a means of response to the control of the production of meaning that had characterized French wartime culture, including the theater, as we saw with Rouché and the Opéra. The "utterance" of this semiotically unstable work, seemingly devoid of a "moral center," and combining elements of elite and popular culture, would be largely dependent on both the production and context. Both "factions" among the collaborators were combating the hegemony of conservative, official culture, but for different reasons, and each, in turn, would succeed in its goal. As we will see, Satie's and Picasso's subversive message emerged in wartime, while in the twenties, the work communicated the more acceptable "modernist nationalism" of Apollinaire and Cocteau through its production and "framing."

Cocteau, in a sense, was attempting to do the impossible in his conception of *Parade*: to create a place for the "modern" in French wartime culture, and specifically in theater and music. He realized that justification of the modern had to depend on its being perceived as both patriotic and "French," a rhetorical ploy already attempted in both poetry and the visual arts. In the latter case, certain modernist journals had argued that cubism was indeed the "language of the war," for not only was it suitable for camouflage, it best represented the character of the battlefield and its tragedies.[216] Numerous avant-garde journals were thus claiming that modern art was "patriotic," even in a culture that was, as we have seen, rooted firmly in a specific conception of the French past. These included Ozenfant's *L'élan* (on which Apollinaire collaborated), *Son, idées, couleurs* (also associated with Apollinaire), and *Nord-Sud*, which promoted the modern as "l'art vivant."[217]

All these journals attempted to claim a place for artistic innovation, or for an art that was "of its day," although its "roots" lay in the national past. Hence the modernist argument was that cubism, far from being "boche," now embodied the simple and "rigorous" French style, as opposed to the "decorative mannerism" of German art.[218] Cocteau not only sought to apply these arguments to theater in *Parade*, but to implement a professional and social strategy that would place him in an advantageous position. For he was scheming to become a leader in the French wartime artistic avant-garde by making "cubism acceptable to a wider, more influential 'haute bourgeois' and aristocratic audience."[219] In other words, he hoped to convert the influential French social elite that, before the war, supported Diaghilev's Ballets Russes to support for the new cubist artists. As Cocteau himself explained it:

I understood that there existed in Paris an aristocratic Right and an artistic Left, which were ignorant of and distrustful of each other for no valid reasons, and which it was perfectly possible to bring together. It was a question of converting Diaghilev to modern painting and converting the modern painters, especially Picasso, to the sumptuous decorative aesthetic of the ballet; of coaxing the cubists out of their isolation, persuading them to abandon their hermetics. Montmartre folklore. . . . the discovery of the middle-of-the-road solution attuned to the taste for luxury and pleasure, of the revived cult of French "clarity" . . . such was the history of *Parade*.[220]

But this project of a cultural *union sacrée*, conceived to provide a cultural place, and thus "distinction," to an aristocracy increasingly without function, would be undermined in wartime by the "artistic Left." For here Satie, politically to the Left—a Socialist and soon to become Communist in the twenties—would subvert this intent, and bring both blind nationalism and wartime culture into question.[221]

Cocteau, as opposed to Satie, was close to the wealthy social circles he was courting, hence the perfect person to bring "the monied stylishness of the aristocratic Right together with the radical audacity of the artistic Left."[222] A well-connected member of the *haute bourgeoisie*, Cocteau was already in contact with noted nationalists, who were now very much in fashion, in particular Maurice Barrès and Léon Daudet.[223] Moreover, Cocteau was already an intimate member of the exclusive French social circle that had gathered around the impressario Diaghilev and his Ballets Russes before the war. But Cocteau had also recently entered the "circle of Montparnasse," a group which, as he himself put it, "had given proof of their Leftism, and I had to do the same. I was suspect on the Right, which I was leaving, and suspect on the Left, where I was arriving."[224] Hence Cocteau now attempted to find a political "middle road" for French classicism, and thus to lead the effort to define a model that would conciliate wartime nationalism with the artistic avant-garde.

This concialiation Cocteau, among others, began to attempt rhetorically in his journal, *Le mot*, a jingoistic and anti-German revue that he published with Paul Iribe during the war. Here he proposed "a depolarization" of the two antagonistic French cultures in the interest of the wartime call for union and for French moderation.[225] To establish his patriotic posture, Cocteau, together with Misia Sert, formed an "ambulance corps," but sporting uniforms designed by the patriotically suspect couturier, Paul Poiret. Before the war, Poiret's "modernism," and particularly his "orientalizing" influences, had earned him the wrath of the French nationalist Right, and the concomitant epithet of "boche." But Cocteau pushed the boundaries even further—he insinuated himself, unofficially, into a regiment of soldiers, but he was eventually discovered, arrested, and returned to civilian life.[226] His wartime efforts were henceforth artistic: now Cocteau would attempt to serve the French cause (and his own) by defining a wartime version of classicism that would justify French art of the present.

At the time that Cocteau turned to cubism, its cultural and political connotations remained ambiguous, for among cubist artists were those who did not support the nationalist myth. But painters such as Ozenfant invoked classic rhetoric by emphasizing the apparent "orderliness" of cubism, while other cubist artists rejected this tactic, simply ignoring the propaganda of the "classic." However, French cubists were inevitably forced to tread a fine line between practicing techniques considered "decadent" or "treasonous" and capitulation to the dominant aesthetic. For, as Christopher Green and Kenneth Silver have noted, both before and after 1917, when the new rhetoric of cubism appeared, the style, in general, was considered "boche," or dangerously close to Germanic modernism.[227] Cocteau apparently did not perceive that although cubism in visual art could be framed by a mitigating or exculpatory nationalist rhetoric, controlling the enunciation of the style in a collaborative theatrical work was far more difficult.

The other element of wartime propaganda to which the avant-garde now had to appeal was the discourse of France's mission to defend the "Latin," promoted as the oldest strain of pure Occidental culture. This argument would grow more significant when Italy, a purported "sister" Latin culture, joined the allied cause, in April 1915, to the joy and relief of the French.[228] However, there remained as much disagreement over what constituted authentic "Latin" traits as over French classicism, and indeed over what the French tradition itself comprised. All of these concepts were still ambiguous, and hence the inherent danger of an avant-garde interpretation that pushed their limits, especially at a moment of political and military crisis.

Compounding this risk, in *Parade*, was Cocteau's provocatively ambiguous scenario, which had undergone a complex evolution since its conception, for Diaghilev, in the spring of 1914. The ballet that Cocteau first planned, called *David*, was to center on the theme of the circus, thus bringing in elements from popular culture, and particularly the corporal or physical, by including acrobats and clowns. Cocteau, moreover, envisioned the visual dimension as including cubist set designs by Gleizes, with music that, he hoped, would be composed by the now famous "modernist," Igor Stravinsky. At first, Diaghilev rejected the project, but he was forced to reconsider upon his move to Switzerland during the war, and his subsequent artistic and financial problems. He had lost many of his former stars—including Nijinsky—which made Diaghilev necessarily more willing to experiment with an audaciously "modernist" approach in wartime.

In Cocteau's mature conception, the plot concerned a traveling theater, or "théâtre forain," which would present three music-hall numbers as the traditional alluring *parade*. A *parade* was the customary short spectacle presented outside the theater, which served as a dramatic enticement, intended to intrigue and thus lure the public inside. Hence, just as in Rouché's "matinées," the scenario of the work would focus on the fine line between reality and representation, although for substantially different artistic purposes.[229]

In his scenario for the work, Cocteau described the envisioned decor as simply "les maisons de Paris, un dimanche" (the houses of Paris on a Sunday); as we will see, Picasso would have quite different plans. Cocteau then specified that three "managers" proceed to organize the publicity around three short performances, given in succession by a Chinese magician, acrobats, and a little American girl. Here he was consciously attempting to employ the traditional language of French folk art in the work, and hence drew from a children's book, *Les cris de*

Paris, which illustrated the different street vendors of Paris in the manner of the folkloric *images d'Epinal*. It was from it that he chose several of the characters, which Picasso would illustrate or bring to life by crossing traditional French folk art with a still audacious cubism.[230]

In Cocteau's scenario, the public, however, does not respond to the continuing entreaties of the managers since they have mistakenly interpreted the preliminary, commercial *parade* as the performance itself. After the last number of the *parade*, the exhausted managers collapse in top of each other; the performers emerge from the theater and, perceiving their failure, attempt to explain that the performance takes place inside. For Cocteau, the work was allegorical: the real theme was the relation of the public to the artistic avant-garde, or the inherent inability of the general public to penetrate the psyche of the creator.[231]

In centering the scenario on the theme of a *parade* and the "managers," however, Cocteau was running a risk, for, given the historical connotations of these themes, other allegorical readings were possible. This was particularly true in wartime, and Cocteau's collaborators on "the artistic Left," Satie and Picasso, would seize the occasion to subvert and reorient the ballet's message. Cocteau may well have derived elements of his conception from articles written by conservative intellectuals before the war glorifying cabarets and music halls as innovative, but also honest and "safe." In 1913, for example, Louis Laloy published an article in the *Revue S.I.M.* in which he emphasized the latter's "actuality" but also, fortunately, the sense of social quietude they ultimately fostered:

> Elle n'exige pas la reforme de nos lois; elle ne flatte pas de jeter bas l'édifice social pour le reconstruire en principe. Elle se contente de signaler tous les excès de la vie, de l'ambition, et de la sottise; elle se réclame du bon sens; elle s'adresse à ce public d'honnêtes gens sans parti pris qui de tout temps a donné la plus juste mesure du goût français; elle est la revanche inoffensive de ce goût contre les charlatans de toute origine.[232]

> [It doesn't demand the reform of our laws; it doesn't flatter itself by debasing the social edifice in order to reconstruct it in principle. It is content to signal all the excesses of life, of ambition, and of stupidity; it calls on good sense; it addresses this public of honest people without prejudice who at all times have given the just measure of French taste; it is the inoffensive revenge of this taste against charlatans of all kinds.]

In wartime, as well, such traditional, collective popular French culture was considered a model, as inherently honest, shared by all, and "uncorrupted" by sophisticated ideologies. This was equally true of the traditional Italian equivalent, the commedia dell'arte, to which artists turned for inspiration, and with official encouragement, throughout the war.[233]

Such popular culture, however, carried another range of connotations of which not only Picasso, but Satie (who had often performed in cabarets) was well aware. It could, to the contrary, be subversive in its subtle, apparently inoffensive mocking of the official or political world, thus cleverly eluding censorship under the guise of farce. Cocteau was either oblivious to or simply ignored the darker connotations of *parades*, which those versed in traditional artistic imagery, like Picasso, could not escape. Given the premise of the scenario, Cocteau was at least apparently cognizant of the established identification in painting of the figure of the artist with that of the *saltimbanque*. In the nineteenth century, both were conventionally treated as martyrs to the public, thus making the clown or performer (as Debussy with Pierrot) the ultimate alter ego of the artist. Daumier, in particular, in such works as *Les saltimbanques*, depicting circus performers (artists), already allegorizes "the hopelessness of those struggling to attract an indifferent crowd."[234]

But added to this was yet another range of meanings, particularly in the nineteenth century, which linked the idea of a *parade* explicitly to both French politics and propaganda. By the 1860s, the emphasis had shifted to the image of the "charleton barker," or the modern "con man" (recalling Cocteau's "managers") who were actively promoting a "pitch." Indeed, appearance dominating essence, for many, was the metaphor for the Second Empire, or, as one scholar has put it, "the desperation of the regime to sell itself."[235] In addition, by the time of Rouault, one encounters the image of the "sacrificial clown," or the implicit association of the clown not only with the precarious, but specifically with death.

Finally, it is important to recall that the circus, as popular entertainment, inherently stood in cultural opposition to the "official" theater of the nineteenth century. For such popular theatrical genres evoked the association of immediate "democratic" appeal, or a theater which exhibited distrust of words, which it replaced with mime, or the visual. Moreover, it evoked the tradition of the carnival, with its physically transgressive aspects as well as its inherent confrontation with authoritative systems of social classification or control. And perhaps most important of all, the *parade* represented a liminal kind of drama, or one that was situated in the ambiguous realm midway between reality and representation. Picasso and Satie, in collusion, would subversively play upon all of these themes—propaganda, death, distrust of the word, and the nebulous realm between reality and the stage.

This may indeed help further explain that aspect of Picasso's design for the "red curtain" to which Steven Whiting has drawn attention: the paradoxical relation between exterior and interior. The "Rideau rouge," under the theater curtain depicts another parted curtain, which reveals what curtains are made to conceal—the performers in their backstage ambience. This curtain is subsequently raised to expose what generally takes place in front of the very first curtain, or the *parade*, meant to lure the public inside. This play of illusions is simultaneously a metaphor for the ambiguity we have noted between reality and representation so powerful in the conceit of a *parade*, and another means to break conceptual frames.[236] Indeed, both Picasso and Satie would thus be responsible for shifting the message, in the cultural context of wartime, from an allegory of the misunderstood artist to one of the control and propaganda of the war.

Pablo Picasso had originally met Cocteau through the composer Edgar Varèse, and it did not take Cocteau long to engage him in this theatrical project. Picasso, of course, had for some time been concerned with the traditional imagery of the circus, and was, like other avant-garde artists in Paris, now turning toward a neoclassic adaptation of cubism. In addition, a particular enticement for Picasso was that "Latin" subject matter was "à la mode" in Paris, being, as we have noted, promoted by the omnipresent wartime propaganda. Moreover, as a "neutral" foreign noncombatant, Picasso had, as Kenneth Silver has noted, "a special latitude, and thus could artistically bob and weave (with a soupçon of irony) through the wartime strictures."[237]

Given this "Latin" emphasis, Picasso found it appropriate to embrace the imagery of the commedia dell'arte, which, as we have noted, was now very much in vogue. And, as we have also observed, it here served as a model of "collective normal behavior," embodying a popular and healthy tradition, as opposed to the eccentric or "abnormal." In this context, the commedia dell'arte thus represented a world devoid of the "exceptional" or the "deviant"—a representation that Picasso and Satie would dexterously invert in *Parade*.[238]

It is also within this framework that we may, perhaps, most fully understand the iconographically complex curtain, as well as the decor and provocative costumes, that Picasso conceived for *Parade*. Like Satie, Picasso delivered the Latin or classical references that the dominant culture expected, but he cleverly wrung subtle subversive variations on their messages. His curtain, to begin with, was neoclassical, and on the surface appeared to be conformist, apparently representing a "sublimely Latin sentiment painted by a Latin artist."[239] The style indeed recalls Picasso's early and more classical depiction of circus performers, before the advent of his controversial cubist experimentation (see fig. 1).

The design consists of two groups of figures: the one on the right includes two harlequins (from the commedia dell'arte), two young peasant women (in *bergère* dress), an Italian sailor, a Spanish guitarist, a blackamoor, and a dog that is lying at their feet. Significantly, despite their association with "the Latin," these figures are either socially marginal or, within the dominant discourse of the period, considered to be "un-French." This is especially true of the harlequin, which, as Cocteau would articulate the next year in *Le coq et l'arlequin*, denoted the unfortunate "eclectic" mixture of foreign elements with the indigenously French.

Similarly significant is the fact that this group is being entertained by another on the left—a small circus act, including a contrived "winged" horse, suggesting the mythological Pegasus. Also present in this scene is a suckling foal, as well as a monkey climbing a ladder, which is painted unmistakably in the colors of the French national flag. In addition, on the horse there is an angel, who is apparently and ironically bestowing the "laurel wreath" on the monkey-artist, situated on the patriotic "tricolor" ladder. The grouping on the left thus suggests a kind of manipulative or "mock mythology," which would imply, given the nature of that on the right, the theme of reality versus myth, or the fine line between illusion and reality.[240]

Picasso thus appears to be making a trenchant comment not only on the myths of wartime, but on the role of certain artists (monkeys) climbing the patriotic ladder to official rewards, with a quasi-religious justification. But here Picasso could conveniently hide behind his authentic iconographic source, which he first saw reproduced on a postcard, when traveling in Naples with Stravinsky.

FIGURE 1—Picasso's curtain for *Parade*. © 2004 Estate of Pablo Picasso/Artists Rights Society (ARS), New York.

It depicts a drawing by the little-known artist Achille Vianelli, an early nineteenth-century genre painter who worked primarily in Naples. In this drawing, titled *Taverna*, the right side depicts a party scene, and the left side performers who, in Vianelli's depiction, are also being observed by the other group. But Picasso, in his rendering, transcends the local, picturesque element of his source and adroitly inflects the conventional image, transforming it into a trenchant statement about the sham character of wartime myth. In addition, he communicates an essential message about how to "read" the ballet to follow, thus making the curtain into a "frame" for perception, or a "hermeneutic window" onto the work.[241] As we will shortly see, Satie's contribution would cunningly do the rest, reinforcing symbolically, or in purely musical terms, Picasso's subversive metaphoric interpretation.

From the beginning, Picasso's and Cocteau's conceptions were clearly at odds, for Cocteau, even if manipulating propaganda for his own artistic interests, refused to sign the militant manifesto of the movement Art et Liberté, an association formed to defend artistic freedom in wartime France. Picasso, however, would soon find his ally in the person of Erik Satie, who had long manifest his distrust of cultural dogma as well as of the French official artistic world. Like his compatriots who were physically able, however, Satie made a gesture toward the defense of his country by enlisting, and became a corporal (at the age of forty-eight) in the militia stationed in his home suburb of Arcueil.242 Yet Satie had become a Socialist, and like his fellows in the party was initially opposed to the war, although once it was a fact, rallied, like they, to *l'union sacrée* and the nation's defense. But as we have already noted, by 1917 the tide was shifting: *l'union sacrée* broke apart, and Socialists again began to question the war and to combat its censorship.243

Again, Satie was not Cocteau's first choice for the project—originally he had sought out Stravinsky, but after the latter's refusal he turned to Satie as someone who could win Diaghilev's approbation. After already having attempted to collaborate with Satie, on the basis of his avant-garde reputation, Cocteau finally met him in 1915 though Valentine Gross, whose salon Satie attended. Satie did not decline, but he immediately felt a greater personal affinity with Picasso, which provoked Cocteau's complaint that Satie was ignoring him, believing Picasso's ideas to be far better.244 Satie and Picasso indeed colluded to extract a very different kind of message, one that confounded wartime ritual and propaganda, including its subtlest means of control. Platitude and myth would not only be exposed and ridiculed but confronted with "reality," and orthodox styles would be employed in unorthodox ways, together with materials that were considered "impure." For both artists were highly responsive to the atmosphere of disillusion and revolt against the war that, by 1917, was mounting in several sectors of the French population.245

Satie, always distrustful of conventional language and rigidity of meaning or perspective, was to manifest this even more clearly in *Parade*, abetted and emphatically seconded by Picasso. His tactics here were closely related to his stylistic tendencies in the years before the war, but now he turned from an exposure of the dogmatism of Scholism to the unmasking of that of French wartime culture. His specific target in *Parade* would be the prevailing dogma of wartime classicism, particularly as applied to dominant conceptions of its style and of appropriate musical form. Once again he relied on the potential of his musical language to say "something other," or to open up a new range of perceptions, while appearing naïvely to conform on the surface. His technique centers on the principle that the Dadaists (to whom he would grow close) were exploring: the breaking of conceptual expectations or conventional "frames" in order to attain new freedom of perception. By dislocating aesthetic norms, and demonstrating the irrelevance of existing "classification," art could prepare, or "release," the audience's cognitive capacities to adapt to "reality." Satie construed wartime classicism as obscurantist mystification, the premises of which had to be exposed, together with the social-political culture that sustained it.246

In *Parade* Satie thus consciously stresses the rigidity and limitations of the dominant conception of classicism, and reacts specifically to its myth regarding French classical hierarchy, proportions, and "order." In the strict formal plan, the score would appear to suggest the orthodox wartime ideal of the classic as consisting primarily of the qualities of symmetrical balance and logic. First, it is balanced by means of tonality, beginning and ending implacably (if abruptly) in the traditionally comforting or affirmative key of C major. Moreover, in each of the numbers the formal construction is rigidly symmetrical or "balanced" through Satie's literal use of a mechanical mirror-like procedure: after the first two sections in each number, the third, a kind of recapitulation, presents the material from the first section, but precisely in the reverse order.[247]

After this ridicule of balance or proportion, Satie turns next to "order" and "logic," thus further rendering absurd the wartime ideal of "true" French classicism. The "managers" have the most clearly defined and systematically recurrent material, which appears ominously in the opening chorale, although here it is adroitly disguised. Their theme, clearly, is not evocative of the nature of their characters as Cocteau conceived and described them explicitly in his original scenario for the ballet. Here they were "wild, uncivilized, vulgar, noisy creatures, harming whatever they praised and arousing the hatred, laughter, and scorn of the public by the strangeness of their appearance and behavior."[248]

In Satie's hands (as in Picasso's) the managers are rather senseless but rigid, mechanical "controllers," who gradually gain in momentum, and by the end loose all control. Their theme is not clearly major or minor, disassociated from the accompanying harmonies and meter, and is thus metrically ambiguous, although invoking the motor-like rhythms of Stravinsky's *Le sacre du printemps*. Indeed, its very character, as well as the relentless repetition, evokes not only the hopelessness, but the utter meaninglessness of mechanized martial combat. The theme is introduced clearly in the first section, or "number," and then appears briefly in the second; but from the middle of the third to the end it asserts itself obtrusively and with mounting fury. (see ex. 1)

From the general contour, intervallic, and rhythmic character of this theme Satie derives subsidiary motives, equally threatening, purposeless, and rigid. They frequently function as ostinati, forming a background against which the performers attempt to articulate a natural, truthful, or lyric utterance in a rhythmically and intervalically different style. But their characters cannot develop—they can only aspire to sustaining their lyricism, although the "little American girl" (in the key of C major and the idiom of ragtime) is the most successful in evading the managers' theme. As several scholars have noted, Satie modeled her "Ragtime du paquebot" after Irving Berlin's "That Mysterious Rag," parodying the orchestral arrangement of it, and preceding it with a bitonal cakewalk.[249] Her music falls symmetrically at the end of the first half of the work, and is followed by the dramatic entry of the stentorian, alarm-like sonority that occurs in the middle and serves to signal the formal and dramatic turning point of the work. Although the score contains the sounds of a typewriter, sirens, and a gun (suggestive of the war), Picasso successfully urged Satie to resist Cocteau's call for even more realistic sounds.[250]

After the central turning point, the managers' motives reappear, one by one, gradually overshadowing the lyric or human aspirations of the performers. The work concludes incongruously, however, with the return of the unmotivated and "comforting" chorale in C major, although in this context it does not sound as the tonic or conclusive.[251] The absurdity here is compounded by the fact that throughout the work there has been no real "development," which would have implied purposive movement in a logical direction—precisely what Satie avoids.

EXAMPLES 1—Satie, *Parade*.

Once exposed, the motivic units undergo no appreciable change, but are rather juxtaposed or layered, again recalling *Le sacre du printemps*, and the points of greatest tension are characterized by the greatest complexity of stratification. Satie, in effect, thus filled a facetious classic frame with unclassic procedures, and even with those that conservatives like d'Indy had repeatedly referred to as "boche." For d'Indy these qualities included the absence of a clear musical form or tonality, thus the use of bitonality, and the illogical repetition of short musical phrases.[252]

But Satie's satire of wartime pieties emerges through other aspects of style, including those that d'Indy himself continued to promote at the Schola. Again, the work opens, as it closes, with a mock "solemn chorale," and then proceeds with a perfunctory fugue, which soon "gives out," dissipating into a lethargic series of descending chords. This shift of rhetorical registers, stylistically, immediately renders the work ironic, or "brackets" it as a discourse intended to mock classical grammar, proportions, and themes. Satie himself wryly commented on the prelude of *Parade* in the following terms: "It is a fugal exposition, very restrained and solemn, and even dry, but short. . . . I like that sort of thing, slightly banal, pseudo-naive, blah, in fact."[253] This ironic invocation of a "pious" chorale, as we have noted, is reprised at the end of the work, suggesting that all the madness that intervened could be justified by "spiritualistic" rhetoric—as in the war.

That Satie's intent was seditious (thus reinforcing Picasso's bivocal message) is further suggested by the fact that over his music he wrote "Hommage à Picasso." Although Cocteau's intention may very well have been to win over his "elite" audience by surprising it without antagonizing it, this certainly was not the case with Satie and Picasso.[254] Like Picasso, Satie was disposed to a subtle kind of provocation that aimed to expose and ridicule the cultural orthodoxies imposed on artists during the war. In a period of controlled discourse, Satie and Picasso had access to nonverbal means: by manipulating classical components they could appear to conform yet simultaneously undermine.

Each, in his different way, exposed and ridiculed the preponderant wartime myth of a healthy, exclusive, classical, and Latin tradition as characterizing French art. Their goal was to awaken awareness; starting from Cocteau's scenario, they thus introduced the absurd or ironic in order to provoke a critical "reordering" in the midst of the war. Literalness, incongruity, and illogical juxtaposition were intellectual means to expose the assumptions of wartime culture that, because of vigilant censorship, remained invulnerable to attack through rhetoric.

The performative context of the premiere would only further reinforce the profoundly incendiary message wrung from Cocteau's scenario by Satie and Picasso. The work was to be premiered at the Théâtre du Châtelet on 18 May 1917, for the benefit of soldiers who had been wounded in the eastern Ardennes region.[255] The atmosphere in Paris was already tense, and not only because of the recent strikes by workers, but because of public awareness of the growing disillusionment of French soldiers in the trenches. Moreover, Diaghilev's company was quickly loosing favor among "patriotic" circles in Paris because the majority of the performers in it sympathized with the revolution in Russia, which had led to its withdrawal from the war as an ally. In addition, to the horror of the audience, already bitter over Russia's "defection" from the war, the troupe had unfurled a large red flag on the stage at the beginning of its season, two weeks before *Parade*'s premiere. By the time of Russia's default, the morale among the allies was already low, exacerbated by the mutinies and slaughter, most notably on the western front.[256]

The program notes, which discursively "framed" the performance, were by Guillaume Apollinaire, who, while close to Barrès, was, with Cocteau, among the advocates of the cubist painters, including Picasso.[257] In other words, although a "nationalist" like Cocteau, he positioned himself on the "liberal right," a daring position now within the dominant French wartime culture. Socially conservative but artistically progressive, and implacably promoting personal liberty, this faction, although suspect during the war, would become prominent in the postwar era.

But now, Apollinaire's assertions concerning Satie's music would reinforce the irony that, while adhering to certain classic traits, it was, in fact, an attack on wartime classicism. Specifically, according to Apollinaire's rhetoric, Satie's music was "so clear and simple that one will recognize the marvelously lucid spirit of France herself." He did, however, go on to see the interaction of the decor, music, and choreography in the work as a kind of "sur-réalisme," implicitly responding to Cocteau's reference to it as a "ballet réaliste." For him, it was thus "the point of departure for a series of manifestations of "l'esprit nouveau," a concept he had already developed several months before in the journal *Nord-Sud*.

Much of the elite audience present was indeed disposed to Apollinaire's "liberal" message, approving of a "restrained modernity" that was informed by classical values.[258] It included Diaghilev's supporters—the princesse de Polignac, the Etienne de Beaumonts, the comtesse de Chevigné, and the comtesse Greffulhe. Also present were major modernist literary and artistic figures, including not only the heroically wounded and bandaged Apollinaire, but the painter Juan Gris and the poet e. e. cummings. In addition, a group of rising young French composers were prominent at the premiere, including Georges Auric and Francis Poulenc, who would champion Satie's subversive message. Less inclined to do so, but notably in attendance for the occasion, were the poet and Italian nationalist politician Gabriele d'Annunzio and the conservative nationalist writers Maurice Barrès and Léon Daudet.[259]

The moment was decidedly wrong for an act of overt artistic provocation, or an attack on wartime pieties, which centrally included aesthetic values. Contemporary reports indeed attest that the "cautious" modernist message which Cocteau and Apollinaire intended was completely overshadowed by the impieties of Satie and Picasso. According to those present, most members of the audience perceived the ballet as antiwar and traitorous, or anti-French, thus provoking vociferous cries of "boche."[260] But other epithets were reportedly hurled, including (revealingly) "métèques" (half-breed or Jew), "trahison," "munichois," and "embusquées" (waiting in ambush)—all associated with unpatriotic behavior. As Kenneth Silver points out, these very same terms had earlier been used against Paul Poiret, the designer, whose modern German influences and orientalizing tendencies the prewar nationalists had viciously attacked. Particularly provocative in *Parade* was the appearance of a Chinaman on the stage, since all things "Oriental" were considered "un-French," especially with Turkey's entry into the war on the German side.[261]

As one might expect, *Parade* was immediately pilloried in the conservative press—Simone de Caellanet in *Le Gaulois* and Pierre Lalo in *Le temps*. Gaston Carraud summed it up aptly: *Parade*, for this group, appeared to be "a vivid illustration on the stage and in the audience of the war spirit characteristic of certain Parisian social spheres."[262] The furor that *Parade* elicited indeed reveals the consequences of transgressing classic strictures at a moment of insecurity, of strikes and mutinies, as in the spring of 1917. Further associating the ballet with wartime sedition and revolt was the subsequent behavior of Erik Satie, in response to one of the particularly unfavorable reviews. The critic, Jean Poueigh, a purported defender of the musical avant-garde but a member of the Ligue pour la Défense de la Musique Française, reviewed the ballet harshly in the *Carnet de la semaine*. In response, Poueigh received a postcard from the deeply insulted Satie, inscribed with the clever insult, "Monsieur et cher ami, vous êtes un cul, mais un cul sans musique." (Monsieur and dear friend, You are an asshole, but an asshole without music.)

Since the note was not in an envelope, Poueigh sued for defamation of character, and Satie was arraigned in civil court on 15 July 1917. In the context of wartime culture, the affair was perceived as one of patriotism and, by extension, an opportunity to judge the critical spirit of this avant-garde. Indeed, Jean Poueigh's lawyer here seized the occasion to denounce the entire French avant-garde as "boche," a belief that was widely shared by this point. In response, important "modernist" artists testified in Satie's defense, including the painters de la Fresange, Derain, Braque, Léger, and the poet Apollinaire.

Some even appeared in uniform, or prominently adorned with war decorations, and in the case of Apollinaire, with bandaged war wounds, to substantiate his ardent patriotism. But Satie nevertheless lost the case, and was fined one thousand francs, in addition to being forced, ignominiously, to serve an eight-day sentence in prison.[263] Modernism was indeed perceived as dangerous—as not only unpatriotic, but as socially seditious, associated with the foreign, the "enemy without," as well as with insidious elements within. French youth would confront this perception, not only in wartime, but throughout the twenties: in quest of innovation, they would necessarily be forced to develop their own tactics to legitimize a "new art."

THE BIRTH OF THE "NEXT GENERATION"

The lessons of *Parade* would not be lost on the next generation of French composers, which recognized the necessity of a patriotic discourse to defend artistic innovations. Their legitimization, aesthetically, would be entrusted to Cocteau, who appropriated Apollinaire's rhetoric and found a receptive public in the postwar period.

His new protégés, a generation in cultural rebellion, gradually became aware of the intellectual issues, and, like their elders during wartime, they eventually drew ideological conclusions in the 1930s. The paths they followed would differ, but their cultural point of origin was similar—a common rejection of wartime and postwar orthodoxies and a confrontation with attempted official cultural "control." Unlike many of their elders, who had acquiesced or willingly contributed to the project of national propaganda through culture, the next generation perceived this as bald cowardice.[264] Their message was one of reality, honesty, change, as well as cultural "inclusion," and it is not surprising in this context that their artistic idol was Erik Satie. If the war years indeed produced a "counterculture," or a counterdiscourse that called official dogma into question, as some have claimed, it is to this generation that we must turn to observe it.[265]

Les Six indeed went on to develop not only a new style, but a new "concert culture," one that was radically different from that of official French postwar culture. This group of young composers had begun their experiments in wartime Paris; still students, they sought out new venues, new means of publicity, and new sectors of support, which we will examine. Here, Cocteau was an invaluable ally, but he also did much to obfuscate the reality of the motivations, orientations, and interests of the very different members of this circle.

Intellectually complex, politically torn, aesthetically varied, they would all be cast in the press in a similar mold, one created by Cocteau in *Le coq et l'arlequin* (1918). In the following chapter we will analyze Cocteau's argument within the context of wartime and postwar culture, and the extent to which it mirrors, distorts, or obscures the realities of the new generation. But to understand their artistic innovations, we must once more begin with the hegemonic culture they faced—its values and its subtle mechanisms of symbolic control in the fragile postwar years.

2

The National or Universal in the Twenties

Part 1: Conservative Hegemony and Political-Cultural Conflict
Memory and the Nationalists' Agenda

COMMEMORATION, SPIRITUALISM, AND
THE CLASSIC IN MUSIC

The composer Gabriel Fauré passed away at a most inopportune moment politically—several months after the victory of the Cartel des Gauches, a left electoral alliance of Radicals and Socialists, over its adversaries to the right. Not having had time to define its policies on all cultural issues, the new government ceded to the pressures of an experienced, conservative functionary in the Ministry of Fine Arts, Paul Léon.[1] Having known the composer for years, and being a great advocate of Fauré's music, Léon insisted that he receive the full panoply of grandiose "obsèques nationales." This, after all, had been the case with Fauré's former teacher and mentor, Camille Saint-Saëns, for whom Léon had arranged a similar ceremony only three years before.[2]

But 1924 was a difficult, transitional moment to decide what to commemorate and to define what or who should become a national symbol, or a *lieu de mémoire*.[3] The political conjuncture was especially unfortunate since the nature of the ceremony being planned would enunciate a message about music and "the national" that was rather characteristic of the preceding regime. Through it, however, we may still glean much about those meanings, symbols, and "dominant" attitudes toward music that would characterize official French musical institutions throughout most of the 1920s. For not only had such attitudes dictated official policies up to this point, with the defeat of the Cartel des Gauches two years later, they would resurge and again dominate the decade.[4]

In this chapter we will trace the political progression of the 1920s together with its ideological-aesthetic battles over "the national," and the way in which both composers and intellectuals in other fields became implicated in them. We must thus begin by penetrating the nature and goals of that hegemonic culture which, apart form the hiatus of the Cartel, determined official policy, and to which political and cultural adversaries responded. Fauré's funeral may lead us not only into its themes and values in music, but into its subtle techniques, to which the avant-garde would respond with equal adroitness and subtlety.

Traditionally, republican funerals in France were freighted with ideological significance: carefully "orchestrated," they provided the regime with an occasion both to celebrate and propagate its values.[5] As part of the "culte des grands morts," the lives being consecrated were to become illustrations of republican virtues, their meaning "fixed," to provide an image for all future generations. Such funerals, however, contained not only communicative and cognitive elements, they also carried a socially unifying and affective dimension which was particularly crucial now.[6] Five years after the Versailles treaty, the atmosphere of mourning and commemoration persisted, especially among the older generation, which had witnessed the slaughter of its most able-bodied youth. And so, in Fauré's case, those religious elements that were generally avoided in traditional republican funerals could be incorporated as part of the mourning that hovered after the war.[7] Fauré's funeral, then, was both a religious and an artistic national ceremony, intended to thwart further "symbolic collapse" and thus to "shore up" existing symbols.[8]

Fauré's funeral, like Saint-Saëns's before, took place in the Madeleine, the prestigious church in central Paris where both had long served as principal organists. But Fauré's funeral included a performance of his own great *Requiem* mass, which could still be interpreted as—or conflated with—a requiem for the French dead of the war. The new government was thus present in force, represented by an impressively large official contingent that included the presidents of the Republic, the Senate, and the Chamber of Deputies, in addition to the archbishop of Paris.[9] The presence of the latter, unusual in a republican ceremony, was undoubtedly related both to Fauré's position at the Madeleine and to the greater republican tolerance of religion after the war. However, as Fauré's editor, Jacques Durand, who attended the ceremony, would later observe, none of the new officials appeared to be fully aware of the degree of Fauré's artistic importance.[10] But Léon had been free to arrange the kind of ritual that would enunciate the way in which he and others of centrist or conservative leanings construed Fauré's music and its cultural significance.

Although Fauré, if always evolving, was no longer considered "progressive" by the postwar period, he had continued to promote the nascent avant-garde and remained a member of both the conservative Société Nationale de Musique and the more innovative Société Musicale Indépendante. However, the work selected for performance, on the basis of its aptness, did not represent the more recent style of Fauré: his *Requiem*, begun in 1877, had been revised in the late 1880s, and then orchestrated at the turn of the century. Yet such a work, characteristic of the composer's later nineteenth-century style, was reassuring in 1924, spanning, as it did, late romantic and early twentieth-century innovations. For as Jean-Michel Nectoux has observed, although Fauré, in fact, never transgressed the limits of traditional tonality (and modality), he did broaden them considerably. Indeed, his use of "expanded tonality" and modality, as well as his long, rhythmically fluid and continually evolving melodies, were highly progressive at the turn of the century. Yet even if, to the approbation of conservatives, his early chamber works generally employed traditional forms, in his later works he did move beyond classical schemes and became not only more economical, but harmonically bold and more polyphonic.[11] Fauré, then, was by no means mired in the past, and yet through this ceremony conservative factions began to "construct" the composer in their image of a classical and traditionalist French culture.

Indeed, the funeral was eloquent for nationalists, still prominent even after their recent defeat, for the pacific composer's body (as a former member of the Académie) was carried past rows of bayonets, sabers, and canons. Durand, himself conservative, could not help but remark on the chauvinistic overtones now of such "militarism," observing that for many the prestige of Fauré's music and the victory over the Germans appeared to be linked.[12] Significantly, even after the war, the ideal of national "defense" through culture, and of the continuing threat of Germany, particularly in music, remained virulent in France. The idea of "defending" French culture had indeed been stressed by the preceding Bloc National, the conservative coalition of the Center and Right that had responded to postwar traumas and fears. These included the fear of both "invasion" and plots to undermine France politically and culturally, giving rise to the theme of "protecting" French culture through the continuing exclusion of anything "un-French." For many, still ardently chauvinistic, it continued to be a vitriolic "war of cultures," and with the exception of those on the Far Left, art and *patrie* remained irrefragably bound.

The symbols mobilized in Fauré's funeral were intended to reinforce the ideal of French "patriotism," as well as the orthodoxy that talent, like true "intelligence," was national, or "particular," as opposed to universal.[13] The funeral was therefore intended not to be socially "liminal," or ritually transformative, but rather, as in "ceremony" and celebration, to restrict and codify, or reify current meanings.[14] The sense of Fauré's music was specifically to be established as inherently "national" and thus classical: the author here "created" was entering the canon (like Debussy) through the process of distortion and selection within his style. And once again revealing the influence of Action Française, the performance of the *Requiem* was to evoke a religiosity that was not universal or transcendent, but rather rooted in the French national community.[15]

The meaning of Fauré's life and music, as symbolically defined in the ceremony, was soon thereafter cast into terms of discourse by his successor at the Académie des Beaux-Arts. In this prestigious site of cultural conservatism, the composer Alfred Bruneau, elected to Fauré's chair upon his death, paid the traditional tribute to his predecessor in his inaugural speech.[16] Bruneau here characterized Fauré's music as "simple, solid, severe, and strong," thus construing it as reflecting "true" French classicism, as understood since the time of the war. Classicism remained synonymous with "the French," although now, as we will shortly see, in the context of postwar polarization it would become a matrix for ideological contestation.

The Left and the liberal Right, now resurfacing, were articulating a modern or progressive interpretation of "the classic," hence promoting their own versions of the national culture and its canons. Within this contestatory context, Bruneau goes on, after lauding the "true" classicism of Fauré, to an increasingly common attack on the modern, or the "pseudo-destructors" of this great edifice.[17] Misrepresenting both Fauré's cosmopolitan style and his tolerance of or openness to the innovations of youth, Bruneau argued (quoting the composer out of context) that he had consistently pleaded "the cause of classicism."[18]

POLITICAL AND SYMBOLIC CONFRONTATIONS

All Bruneau's themes were already ensconced in the dominant musical discourse, one marked by an obsessive fear of anarchy or disorder, as well as of eclecticism or pollution from outside. This was closely related to the sense of France's weakness after the war, and particularly its devastating problems in the realms of both manpower and public finance.[19] In dissonant counterpoint to the projected myth of continuing French leadership in Europe and to official narratives of the glories of French identity and memory was the reality of France's weakened position after the war. And this was also a moment of pressing internal political and social problems, particularly the questioning and discontent on the part of both French workers and youth. The Left responded to their desire for a radical change or for a "new era," particularly after social expectations were not immediately met with the advent of peace.[20]

This was the context of the birth of the French Communist Party, which was precipitated initially by a split within factions of the French Socialist Party in 1920. The Communist press was soon active, and it attracted many new readers with its action-oriented, antimilitaristic, and forceful, nontheoretical approach.[21] But the gains of the Left soon led to even further polarization, or to more extreme positions on the right, and thus the reemergence of rival groupings within it. Tensions, in fact, became most acute during the two-year period of the Cartel des Gauches, as the political, cultural, and symbolic chasm between Right and Left began to grow. This chasm was deepened further shortly after Fauré's funeral by such symbolically aggressive acts as the reburial of the Socialist leader Jean Jaurès in the Panthéon.[22]

Also developing at about this time was a current of extreme political reaction on the right, among a more radical generation that had fought in the war, and manifest in the renewed formation of leagues that were "conservative, reactionary, and counter-revolutionary in spirit."[23] In 1924, Pierre Taittinger established the Jeunesses Patriotes, and Francis Coty, now owner of *Le Figaro*, also sought a position in the "counterrevolution." In 1925 the former Sorelian and member of Action Française, Georges Valois (with Coty's financial help), founded a fascist-oriented party, Le Faisceau, along with a paper, *Le nouveau siècle*. Coty also subsidized the Ligue de l'Action Française, and sponsored the Croix-de-Feu, a veteran's organization led by Colonel Count François de La Rocque. Meanwhile, Maurras's tactics grew so violent that in 1926 he was tried for threats made against republican politicians, which contributed to the condemnation of Action Française by the Vatican.[24]

The power of reactionary forces increased with the return of Poincaré under the government of "Union Nationale," which was founded in 1926.[25] With this conservative victory, as with that of the Bloc National in 1919, came a sense of return to the social order that had preceded the war. Poincaré's political tendencies were known to be not only strongly nationalist, but domestically they were decidedly conservative, as well as sometimes socially repressive. After the war, moreover, Poincaré was widely perceived as sympathetic to Action Française, which only further encouraged its growing popularity. With his return in 1926 came a period of financial prosperity and international peace that further neutralized the Left, already weakened by its internal divisions over Communism.[26]

Bruneau's discourse on Fauré was thus only one aspect of the conservative trend in French culture to which Maurice Agulhon has aptly referred as "le système politique et mental d'après guerre" (the political and mental system after the war).[27] As we have seen, through most of the decade, with a brief hiatus, official French culture was defensive and protectionist, traits we encounter in all institutions, including those concerned with music. Dangerous currents, both externally and internally, were to be combated through a concerted inculcation of classical values and French classical taste, construed as synonymous with the spiritual unity of the nation. Such classical "particularism" (as opposed to the universal) found its expression in other French cultural fields, as during the war, and continued to dominate within the French university system.[28]

This was the very situation that Julien Benda decried in his *La trahison des clercs*—the invasion of the intellectual realm by the political, and particularly by nationalist as opposed to universal values. In music his indictment was particularly apt, as we will see when examining the French musical world, or that sector of it that was dominated directly or indirectly by state institutions. Concern with the national informed not only the reclassification of French composers, but equally their canonization, as we may witness in the case of Fauré. In light of the stress on the national as classical, the emphasis remained on high art, as opposed to the popular, and on the past, as opposed to the idea of progress, new music or change. Attacks on "radical" young composers were thus frequent, as was the condemnation of German influence and "the modern," which included not only foreign music, but also its dangerous artistic influence in France. In sum, the dominant or official French musical culture in the decade that followed the war was far from our common image of *les années folles*, with which, in reality, it was in constant, hostile dialogue.[29]

The official conception of the classic was still linked to a holistic, conservative French community, as contraposed to the "anarchic," to a socially critical spirit, or any revolutionary break from the past.[30] Officials continued to enforce this conception through a subtly functioning network of institutional influences, not only by prescribing priorities in official institutions, but by pressuring the private sector, as during the war. Evidence of this, and of the now dominant mentality, led by the state, can be found in the many commemorative pieces that flooded the postwar period, the result of either official or related private commissions. Clemenceau himself patently fostered this tendency by having French school children sing Henry Février's "Hymne aux morts," with words by Péguy (a work written during the war), in 1918. And Saint-Saëns continued to produce such works, including his "fantaisie" for chorus, organ, and orchestra, titled

Cyprès et lauriers, in 1919, to celebrate the victory. Dedicated to the president of the Republic, Raymond Poincaré, it was performed at the Trocadéro, on 24 October 1920, by the celebrated Concerts Colonne. The first part, "Cyprès," for organ alone, was associated with funeral ceremonies, while "Lauriers" was a song of victory, and meant to be suggestive of a village fête and a triumphal march.

Many such works were commissioned to accompany the consecration of the numerous monuments constructed between 1918 and 1922, and then for the anniversary commemorations. All such official homages were meant to exalt national sacrifice, mourning, and memory, and thus they furthered the production of lamentations, as well as masses for the dead and other religious works. Among those in the commemorative genre were Noël Gallon's *Dormez en paix* and *Fantômes*, both of 1920, and Cécil Chauminade's *Au pays dévasté*, of 1919. Reynaldo Hahn's *A nos morts ignorés* is typical in its economy of means and search for an expressive style that incorporates learned archaisms, such as modal allusions and *ars antiqua* organum.

Other works include hymns to peace, often drawing on religious reference to the crucifixion and resurrection, such as Albert Roussel's *Pour une fête de printemps* (1922) and Nadia Boulanger's *Vers la vie nouvelle* (1919). André Caplet's *La croix douloureuse: Prière des âmes en deuil* (1918) also falls into this genre, and was performed on 14 May 1919, at the Société Nationale de Musique. André Messager's *La paix en blanc vêtue*, based on the Hugo poem "Ceux qui pieusement sont morts pour la patrie," dates from 1922, and Saint-Saëns's *Hymne à la paix* from 1920.

Despite cultural "demobilization," the official world still exerted indirect pressure on musical production, and applied the lessons learned during the war concerning the shaping of meaning and the orientation of taste. The state continued to occupy the intellectual and cultural terrain that it had carved out in wartime and to implement an agenda of national education through the arts. For unlike the contemporary Weimar Republic, the goal was not to employ the arts to foster renovation and social change, but rather to consolidate, "return," and protect. Moreover, there was a need to project a national image of continuing strength in the international order, where culture was an agent in the battle for French "presence" and influence.[31] The war was thus not a parenthesis in French culture but a school of experimentation in the control and redefinition of the nation's cultural priorities, from which the postwar nationalist government would learn. Again, during most of the twenties, aside from the two-year interlude of the Cartel des Gauches, the political and cultural center of gravity remained situated firmly to the right.[32]

CONSECRATION, CONCERTS, AND THE ORIENTATION OF TASTE

Fauré was by no means the only French composer who became implicated (and distorted) in the process of constructing a national memory and cultural identity, while also commemorating the dead of the war. For, in general, it was a period not only of mourning, but also of the creation of symbols—often embodied in individuals, like Foch and Clemenceau, who were subsequently "consecrated" in monuments.[33] In music, those musicians who died in the war were accorded an "archival consecration" by being inscribed in the "Archives littéraires des écrivains et des artistes morts pour la France" (the literary archives of those artists and writers who died for France). This occurred in March 1919, through the agency of a committee of French "intellectuals," who were placed officially under the sponsorship of the president of the Republic. This group, which made the decisions concerning whom to consecrate, included not only Jean Richepin and Léon Bonnat, but also the implacably nationalist Vincent d'Indy.[34]

Great French musicians who had recently died if not in but during the war were similarly commemorated and also consecrated through monuments, to establish the "national sense" of their art. This frequently occurred not as a result of fiats or direct intervention by officials, but as result of a collaborative effort with individual initiatives from outside the official sector. Public and private spheres interacted closely to establish cultural hegemony in the interests of tradition and of national propaganda in a weakened postwar France.

Indeed, this is how the hegemony of the dominant, conservative musical culture in France would function, in part, in the twenties—through state "suggestions" or approval of independent musical projects. The latter was, in fact, the case when plans were initiated to consecrate Debussy with a monument after his death, which was to be followed by a festival of his music. The project was the direct result of the initiative of three enterprising sculptors, first Antoine Bourdelle and after his death Jan and Noël Martel, who were aided in securing funds by a committee of "friends" of Debussy. But the project required official authorization in order to obtain the ground, as well as the presence of state officials at the unveiling and consecration of the monument for public legitimization. Ground was allotted in the square, which was named the Jardin Claude Debussy, located near Debussy's home, close to the Bois de Boulogne, in an elegant sector of Paris. But the project took over a decade, and the consecration did not take place until 15 July 1932, fourteen years after Debussy's death. When the monument was finally unveiled, present at the ceremony was not only Paul Léon, director of the Beaux-Arts, who delivered a speech, but the president of the Republic himself as well as the undersecretary of state and the president of the municipal council.[35] Debussy was at last consecrated in stone, if not as an "immortal" academician: the always unorthodox composer was now finally ensconced in official French cultural memory.

Constructing such a memory was not without problems. Despite concerted efforts to orient taste toward French music and toward its past, the general public often refused to comply. While the hall at the Opéra-Comique was only half full for performances of *Pelléas*, that of the Opéra would soon be overflowing for performances of Wagner's works.[36] The public's desires could not be ignored, but a gesture still had to be made to the ideological orthodoxies that emerged from the war, and particularly those concerning German music later than the classical period. Most problematic of all was Wagner, and one response was to leave the decision as to whether to perform him to the audience itself, thus encouraging it to reflect upon the issues involved. Hence on 30 October and 1 and 2 November 1919, the audience of the subsidized Pasdeloup Concerts, which specialized in more recent repertoire, was asked to vote on whether the performance of Wagner's works should resume.[37] Testifying to the continuing popularity of Wagner's music in France, despite the recent wartime propaganda against him, the vote was overwhelmingly in Wagner's favor.

Still, on 9 November, at the Concerts Lamoureux, which had specialized in Wagner before the war, their conductor, Camille Chevillard, felt obliged to defend his performance of excerpts from *Tristan und Isolde*. His argument was cunningly chauvinistic: he recalled that in spite of the rancor that had been caused by the war, it was important to remember that the French had, after all, defeated the Germans. By the following year both Beethoven and Wagner were again being frequently performed, but opposition persisted, with some even fearing a "renaissance wagnérienne."[38] Wagner had reappeared on the stage of the Opéra, on 5 January 1921, with *Die Walküre*, with *Siegfried* to follow in March, and *Lohengrin* in May 1922. Although figures like Cocteau would continue denouncing Wagner, as we will shortly see, he did have defenders, not only at the Schola, but also among those on the left. Included in the latter was the Socialist librarian of the Opéra, J.-G. Prod'homme, who staunchly defended the German composer in his *Richard Wagner et la France*(1921). Here he agrees with d'Indy that the only French composers whom Wagner forced out of the Paris opera were, in fact, those who were already well in decline. And he notes that so beloved were Wagner's works that they returned ineluctably to the French stage only a year after the Versailles treaty was signed.[39]

Although older works of the former "enemy nations" reappeared in the repertoire by 1919, anti-German sentiment remained strong, bestowed with intellectual legitimacy by academic circles that still stressed German atrocities, and thus attempted to ban German culture from the "civilized nations." This resulted in an exclusion of Germany from French intellectual exchanges, and a continuing emphasis on "national character," or "l'âme ancestrale," and the deep indigenous nature of a "race." As we will see later in this chapter, those on the left, like Jacques Rivière, in *La nouvelle revue française*, would argue, to the contrary, for the open "universalism" of the French nation.[40]

However, the official mentality was to remain suspect of contemporary Germans, as manifest in an incident of 1928, and recounted by the conductor, D.-E. Inghelbrecht. René Baton, now one of the two directors of the Pasdeloup Concerts, asked Felix Weingartner, director of the Conservatory in Basel, to conduct as a guest in the series. As soon as the posters went up, Inghelbrecht (Baton's assistant) was summoned by the prefect of police, who expressed his amazement that the Pasdeloup Concerts had invited a "boche" to conduct. Specifically, the prefect was concerned about a German wartime manifesto that Weingartner had signed; Inghelbrecht pointed out that the French were also forced to sign similar cultural documents. Yet the conductor was refused entry into France, only to have this decision ultimately reversed by the government, although suspicious police agents did attend the performance—of Beethoven symphonies.[41]

Continuing concern with whether or not to perform Wagner in postwar

France was also discernible among French composers, who remained as divided as ever over the issue. This emerges clearly in a survey published in "Wagner et la France," a special issue of *La revue musicale* (1923). D'Indy remained firm in his position, one that he had articulated for decades at the Schola Cantorum, and continued to employ the same anti-Semitic rhetoric as justification. As he put it: "J'estime que Wagner a rendu le plus grand service à la musique française, en ce qu'il l'a libérée du joug italo-judaïco-éclectique sous lequel elle se traînait péniblement et semblait même avoir renié ses qualités natives de clarté et de logique expressive."[42] (I assess that Wagner has rendered the greatest service to French music in that he liberated it from the Italo-Judaïc-eclectic yoke under which it was painfully pulled and seemed even to have renounced its qualities of clarity and expressive logic.) This, of course, was d'Indy's manner of reconciling his enduring admiration of Wagner with the wartime and continuing postwar rhetoric of French music as essentially "classic."

Alfred Bruneau, a former admirer and emulator of Wagner's innovations, was now more critical; while arguing that Wagner was a "classic" (in the tradition of Beethoven), he nevertheless pointed out the dangers. Wagner's irresistible attraction, he opined, had turned French composers away from their "path," obscuring their taste for clarity and measure—the characteristics of the "national genius."[43] Wartime rhetoric ostensibly persisted in light of the German and Wagnerian threat, even among former Dreyfusards like Bruneau, purportedly defenders of universal values.

Ravel, uncharacteristically, and perhaps here quoted out of context in the survey, asserted that the faults of Wagner are those of the Germans in general, and pointed out his pernicious effects on the French.[44] It is important to recall, however, that Ravel, while aesthetically opposed to Wagner, had been an outspoken defender of the performance of modern German and Austrian works in France during the war. While a "patriot," and clearly opposed to the German aggression during the war, he refused to go so far as to condemn the nation and its culture, regardless of context. Charles Koechlin went even further: while he had been similarly sympathetic to French wartime defense, as an admirer of Wagner's operas, he expressed the desire to hear one in full again in France.[45] Like Ravel, Koechlin had not been a member of the Ligue pour la Défense de la Musique Française, and he continued to defend the performance of contemporary German and Austrian works.

As one might expect, opinions concerning the performance of German and Austrian music, past and present, collided in the Société Nationale and the Société Musicale Indépendante. While the SMI did boldly present modern German and Austrian music in the twenties, the Société Nationale would not do so until the late 1930s. However, while generally more progressive, the SMI did count among its members those who would irascibly attack the "young" French music, or the "modern."[46] Both societies would find themselves increasingly bypassed by French youth, who were developing new repertoires and concert venues, more appropriate to their aesthetic.

The most innovative concert series were those independent of the state; they included the concerts given by Koussevitsky in the early twenties, with an orchestra composed of the best instrumentalists in Paris, often including famous soloists. Koussevitsky's concerts began in the spring of 1921, at the Salle Gaveau, with the initial goal of firmly establishing both older and newer Russian works in the repertory. In the autumn of 1921, and then in 1922, he rented the Opéra for his concerts, with enthusiastic public and press response. The press, in particular, noted the general backwardness of the officially subsidized French concert series and thus welcomed the innovation of a wider and more progressive repertoire.

The works that Koussevitsky presented included not only those of Skryabin, Prokofiev, and Stravinsky, but also the older and newer French school, in particular, Ravel, Roussel, Florent Schmitt, and Honegger. Although Prokofiev was generally overshadowed by his more famous compatriot Stravinsky, the press was beginning to note him as "more Russian," or picturesque, than the increasingly Occidental Stravinsky. José Bruyr, in particular, singled out Prokofiev for his "ardeur sauvage," which Bruyr associated with the Russian Revolution, as opposed to the "bourgeois," more Western Stravinsky. Prokofiev's *Suite scythe* was acclaimed in Paris in 1921, his *Chout*, in 1923, and his *Pas d'acier* (with Diaghilev), in 1928.

Equally outside the norm were the concerts sponsored by Walter Straram, which intrepidly featured international contemporary music. This even included Schoenberg, and Straram boldly performed his *Chamber* Symphony, despite the fact that clearly neither the musicians nor audience liked the work.[47] But aside from these isolated efforts, French concert culture was so parochial that the French section of the Société Internationale pour la Musique Contemporaine was created to promote the "penetration" of modern foreign music into France.[48]

Meantime, the government was multiplying the concert societies it subsidized in order to further its conservative conception of French music, and thus Fauré, still the president of the Société Nationale, faced the difficult task of justifying his request for a more adequate subsidy. By 1923 the societies supported included not only the older Société des Concerts du Conservatoire, but also newer ones, such as the Concerts Touche, the Concerts du Vieux Colombier, the Concerts Poulet, the Concerts Siohan, and the Orchestre Symphonique de Paris.[49] But Fauré, in defense of his society, patriotically pointed out in a letter of 9 July 1919, to the minister of public instruction and fine arts, that the Société Nationale was founded in 1871 to "defend" and assure the diffusion of French music. Despite this fact, it had received only the modest yearly subvention of two thousand francs before World War I, a sum that had not been renewed. Fauré was only partially successful, for despite his request for an annual subvention of six thousand francs, he received just two thousand, or that of the prewar period.[50]

In spite of Fauré's powerful rhetoric of the "defense" of French music, the interests of the government were no longer in small private elite or avant-garde societies, but in broad diffusion and "education" through music. The wartime emphasis on French music history and on national public pedagogy through concerts, often in association with lectures, ostensibly extended into the postwar era. The state-subsidized popular Pasdeloup Concerts, which specialized in the more recent repertoire, presented a series of "historical" concerts, accompanied by scholarly lectures, in 1920 and 1921. The lecturers included such eminent musical and academic figures as Maurice Emmanuel, Henri Expert, Henry Prunières, Julien Tiersot, Gaston Carraud, Vincent d'Indy, and Emile Vuillermoz. Although the concerts were historical, they centered on French music of the recent past, with d'Indy, for example, speaking on Chabrier and Dukas, and Vuillermoz on Debussy. But the Pasdeloup Concerts also attempted to be more progressive in repertoire, and in 1922 André Caplet programmed the French premiere of Schoenberg's *Five Pieces for Orchestra*. The event, however, created a scandal: the performance was greeted with whistles, catcalls, and, in particular, the cry of "boche." Not surprisingly, it was the open-minded *Revue musicale* that ardently defended the enterprise, as did the now Communist *L'humanité*, which supported artistic freedom.[51]

Along with the Pasdeloup Concerts, three other venerable symphonic associations continued to present concerts in Paris to enthusiastic audiences in the postwar era. The Société des Concerts du Conservatoire remained the guardian of the "classical repertoire," the Concerts Lamoureux (under Camille Chevillard and then Paul Paray) specialized in Wagner, Schumann, and Liszt, and the Concerts Colonne, under Gabriel Pierné, concentrated on more recent French masters. Pierné performed d'Indy's Symphony no. 2 and his *Jour d'été à la montagne*; Lamoureux now presented Roussel's *Evocations*, and the Conservatoire Concerts the symphonic work of Ernest Chausson.[52] The older generation of French composers thus found itself in a privileged position—presented as the most recent manifestations of a long tradition of "true" French and great music. For the same reason French youth in this period faced increasing resistance, their music attacked as not only dangerously "modernist," but concomitantly "un-French."

But there were those like Jacques Rouché, at the Opéra, who knew how to mediate the old and the seemingly innovative, presenting the works of a now "consecrated" older French generation (to balance Wagner) and selected premieres.[53] Successful in both business and politics, Rouché astutely balanced works that were "ideologically correct" with those that the audience wanted, particularly Wagner and lavish new ballets. And as Inghelbrecht perceptively noted, Rouché sagaciously introduced the more "modern" Ballets Russes, including older and more recent works of Stravinsky, into the prestigious Palais Garnier with beguiling splendor.[54] He also observed that Rouché allowed independent artists to "rent" the hall for ballet—a financially profitable policy in a period of fiscal crisis. Indeed, according to Piero Coppola, the hall was now filled with the French elite (as before the war), and with noted foreigners, or as he disdainfully puts it, with the greatest names in art, politics, and "cosmopolitan laziness."[55]

THE OPERA OF CONSERVATIVE IDEAS

If the Société Nationale de Musique was having difficulty soliciting official funds, the same was clearly less true for the Opéra under the guidance of Jacques Rouché. Just as during the war, Rouché knew that the Opéra should not only appeal to the public it sought to attract, but that it must serve current national interests as well.[56] Hence, even in a period of financial hardship, as in the early

1920s, Rouché succeeded, at least, in obtaining his prewar subvention of eight hundred thousand francs. Indeed, within the forty million francs budget of the Administration des Beaux-Arts, the Opéra was the institution that received by far the most substantial share.[57]

Perhaps one reason for the state's generosity was that it now became widely known that Rouché already had poured huge sums from his own private fortune into the Opéra. By 1924, at a parliamentary session, the official *rapporteur* of the budget claimed to be "scandalized" that the Opéra's subvention had remained the same despite the spiraling cost of living. As he put it succinctly, "M. Rouché subventionne l'Etat pour avoir l'honneur de diriger l'Opéra" (Mr. Rouché is subsidizing the state for the honor of directing the Opéra).[58]

The integrity of the state opera was a serious matter, for, just as in the contemporary Weimar Republic, it was to serve an educational role, although here it was one that was not progressive, but rather politically conservative and nationalist.[59] On the basis of his experience during the war, Rouché knew just what to stage, selecting works from the older and newer repertoire that would fulfill this pedagogical function. On 21 March 1918, in keeping with the still resonant doctrines of classicism and of the French tradition, he wisely revived Rameau's *Castor et Pollux*. As soon as the war was over, he turned to the ardently patriotic Camille Saint-Saëns, producing his historical opera, *Henry VIII*, in December 1918. Two years later Rouché presented the work of Saint-Saëns's antagonist, Vincent d'Indy, a composer who was equally venerable, prominent, and unimpeachably nationalist. Appropriately, it was during the Bloc National that d'Indy's opera, *La légende de Saint-Christophe* (which he had worked on since 1903 and referred to as his "drame anti-juif"), finally had its premiere.[60]

Perhaps one of the rationales for this choice on the part of Rouché and his scholarly secretary, Louis Laloy, was the belief that the myth evoked in the work would reinforce the ideology of the ruling coalition and engage with current intellectual issues. For as they were undoubtedly aware, this was the moment of a revival of "neomedievalism" and "neo-Scholasticism" among prominent Catholic circles in France. Hence it was also the period of the revival of the "miracle play," as promoted by fervent Catholics such as Henri Ghéon, who wrote a large number of them, to be performed by Catholic charity organizations. Similarly, the twenties saw a marked neomedieval revival in French Catholic architecture and sculpture, as well as in the omnipresent war monuments.[61]

Such an emphasis was also characteristic of figures such as Etienne Gilson and Jacques Maritain, the latter publishing his influential *Art et scolastique* (Art and scholasticism) in 1920. Moreover, other themes in d'Indy's opera could be interpreted as relating to the current tensions and issues in not only the intellectual and religious but also the political and social realms. This was the period when ecclesiastical authorities joined the Right in condemning political liberalism, together with the equally threatening "naturalism," socialism, and communism. D'Indy had combined these themes in his opera, along with the equally compelling issues of "traitors" and race—as resonant now as during the Dreyfus affair, when d'Indy was conceiving the work. Although I have already discussed this work in detail in a previous study, it is important here to review those elements that, together, helped shape its reception and its influence in the twenties.⁶²

The opera was based upon a thirteenth-century collection of the lives of saints, the *Legenda aurea*, the product of a Dominican monk known in France as Jacques de Voragine. In the wake of the Dreyfus affair, the ardently anti-Dreyfusard d'Indy had attempted to adapt the legend of Saint Christopher to the service of his nationalist ideological cause. As a great admirer of Wagner, he had already sought out the composer, who then urged him to recover his own national traditions and mythic sources, cleansed of the "contaminated" "Jewish style." For a French composer, the "légende dorée," as it became known in France, was perhaps the closest thing to a collective mythos or national legendary source.

In the tale of Saint Christophe, he is a giant who, in search of the greatest king in the world, encounters the devil; but upon seeing the devil avoid a cross, he decides the true king is Jesus Christ, for whom he now searches, while meanwhile seeking an appropriate way to serve him. He finds this in helping travelers across a dangerous river, and, one day, one traveler turns out to be Christ, who instructs him to help the Christians in Samos. Christophe immediately converts many to Christianity, causing the king to put him in prison and to send beautiful young girls to lure him to sin; but Christophe converts them. Christophe is to be shot by arrows, but one instead hits the king in the eye, upon which Christophe informs the king to moisten mud with his (Christophe's) blood, put it on his eye, and he will see again. Christophe is decapitated, the king is healed, and he too is subsequently converted.⁶³

D'Indy designed his version of the legend not as an opera, but as a "mystery play" which would demonstrate aspects of what he termed the "judeo-Dreyfusard influence," in particular "orgueil, jouissance," and "argent" (pride, pleasure, and money), which he wished to present in conflict with goodness, faith, hope, and charity.⁶⁴ He projected this opposition onto the story, emphasizing the section in which the giant seeks the greatest power on earth, but manipulating elements of the legend while fusing genres and theatrical conventions. D'Indy thus locates his story not in Canaan but in France (in the Cévennes), although his action begins in his own version of Venusberg, where the giant is being entertained by La Reine de Volupté. This idyllic existence is interrupted when the doors open and a sinister yellow light floods the room, revealing a small man whom d'Indy describes in the score as pudgy and jolly, with frizzy hair and a hooked nose. Behind him appear valets, whose leather sacks are filled with gold; those assembled comment on this strange man, who is "not one of us." He is Le Roi de l'Or, who has already "purchased" the Queen's ministers and her weapons, and proceeds to buy all her "beaux objets d'art." The giant then converts to his service.

The next scene reveals the "king's" ties to Germany and the fact that he has had traitors declared innocent; now he introduces his faithful ally, the Prince du Mal. D'Indy then presents his farcical "armée de l'erreur," which here serves both a dramatic and pragmatic function, as the operatic spectacle. It includes the "faux penseurs" (who denounce religion), the "faux savants" (who claim science to be infallible), and finally a crowd carrying a red banner inscribed with the word

Guerre and calling for the destruction of the "powerful" and the priests. They are followed by "les arrivistes orgueilleux" and finally by "les faux artistes" (the impressionists), who claim to make fashion, cherishing originality, and denouncing enthusiasm, the ideal, and all rules. But a cathedral now appears, followed by a large cross, and when it is clear that the Prince du Mal fears them, the giant seeks Jesus Christ.

The second act proceeds more or less according to the legend, with the giant, now named Christophe, helping travelers across a river. But the third act returns to Le Roi de l'Or, who has now become Le Grand Juge and has not only conquered all the chief deputies of state, but has condemned Christophe. Here the Grand Juge sends the Reine de Volupté into prison to corrupt Christophe, but, as in the legend, the latter instead succeeds in converting her. In the final scene Christophe is tortured and then shot with an arrow, which instead turns back and fatally pierces the eye of the Grand Juge. The latter proclaims that he is dying, and significantly, here receives no redemption. Christophe is decapitated offstage, as his "chant triomphale" continues ever higher, broken briefly by the fall of the axe. The Reine de Volupté, renamed Nicéa, who has witnessed the execution, reenters the stage, now dramatically and poignantly covered with blood. Light slowly pervades the stage and all sing praises to the glory of God, the chorus ending solemnly with the words "Saint Christopher, pray for us."

Although d'Indy's model was purportedly a "mystery play," in order to highlight the didactic elements he borrowed characteristics from the oratorio, in particular a narrator and a chorus. In keeping with d'Indy's moralistic, metaphoric approach to form, even the structure of the opera is didactic and symbolic. Apart from the prologues, he divided the work strictly into divisions of three—three acts, each with three scenes, which was meant to carry a symbolic resonance. In information circulated before the performance, d'Indy made it clear that this choice was dictated by ideology, the "triptych form" (representing the Trinity) being the only truly national one.[65]

And as always with d'Indy, the tonal structure of the work is equally symbolic, thus turning Wagner's associative use of tonalities into a rigid, didactic system. For d'Indy ardently admired what he stubbornly and reductively perceived to be Wagner's "usage méthodique des tonalités significatives" (Wagner's methodical use of significant, or symbolic, tonalities). Typical of his reading of Wagner, and in keeping with his own proclivities, he sought a more systematic and intellectual approach than Wagner ever actually intended. D'Indy thus employs keys not only in association with feelings and situations, but with individual characters and even specific objects.[66]

But perhaps the most symbolic and didactic element in this "drame mystère" lies in the choice and manipulation of Gregorian chant, which d'Indy carried to unprecedented extremes. Of the opera's twenty-four themes, seven are taken literally from the Gregorian repertoire, and probably intended (idealistically) to be recognized by the audience. D'Indy had employed Gregorian chant in his previous operas, but here the seven chants used bring with them specific liturgical associations—several, for example, are taken directly from the Common of Martyrs Who Are Not a Bishop.[67] But d'Indy deploys other stylistic resources, beyond just melodies, in the interest of exegesis, including allusions to the masters admired (and as interpreted) at the Schola, in particular Bach and Beethoven. These references, like the Renaissance motet style that d'Indy (and others) associated with "les primitifs," appear when the text refers to sincerity, spiritual probity, and the certitudes of faith.68

This rhetorical or strategic use of styles extends to the depiction of evil, probably the most trenchant and pervasive theme throughout the work. Not surprisingly, d'Indy reserves the most devastating devices in his stylistic arsenal for the Roi de l'Or, making him repugnant musically as well as morally. Significantly, he is accompanied by the same kind of jerky, uneven rhythms, suggesting physical deformity, as Alberich in *The Ring*. However, going far beyond Wagner's technique of equating moral shiftiness with tonal ambiguity, d'Indy associates his villain with the harshest of dissonances and the gravest of harmonic faults.

Along with this we find reference to the "Italo-Judaïque-eclectic" style, especially to the squareness and monotony of rhythm that d'Indy associated with Meyerbeer. Although used most consistently for the Roi de l'Or, and (slightly less so) for the Prince du Mal, some of these traits appear with other social groups that d'Indy wished to vilify: the bourgeoisie in the final act, the people whenever misled, and the Emperor's evil soldiers. Open stylistic parody is reserved for the comical "armée de l'erreur," with the "faux artistes" depicted visually and musically through a caricature of impressionism. All these techniques stand out against the background of a Wagnerian idiom, d'Indy's post-Wagnerian harmonies and fluid rhythms forming the stylistic "ground" of the work.69

What, then, was the message that d'Indy originally intended in the wake of the Dreyfus affair? It was antimaterialistic and antirepublican, directed at a world motivated by profit and a corrupt authority structure. Against such greed and corruption, he contraposed duty, sacrifice, and heroism, the purity of race and nation, and the primacy of collective values and social hierarchy. The latter themes were particularly resonant now, in the wake of the war, with the advent of the Bloc National and the current turn to spirituality and religion.

La légende de Saint-Christophe premiered on 6 June 1920, and was clearly meant to be the highlight of a less than triumphant operatic season.70 The other works that year, none of which received an enthusiastic response, included two other works with biblical themes—Florent Schmitt's *La tragédie de Salomé* and Mariotte's *Salomé*—as well as Ollone's *Retour*. Knowledge of *La légende de Saint-Christophe* had been circulating since before the war, arousing considerable curiosity in the press and among the French musical public. Awareness of the strongly anti-Semitic cast of d'Indy's libretto had caused him, as we have noted, to be dropped by Durand, the editor of most of his works to this point.71 But d'Indy's personal prestige was high, not only because of his patriotism during the war, but because his works had been frequently performed in concerts throughout its duration. Moreover, a selection from the opera, the "symphonie descriptive" that precedes the second act, the "Queste de Dieu," was presented at the Colonne-Lamoureux Concerts on 1 April 1917.

D'Indy's apparently religious work not only promised to comfort good Catholics, but it premiered in the midst of pervasive social anxiety, which even included the moderate Left. For together with the political polarization, there was a rapidly mounting fear of bolshevism, which worked to the advantage of the Right in the defensive postwar climate. Moreover, in 1919 Paris had been crippled by a series of strikes, and in 1920 they extended even to the capital's prestigious lyric theaters. All this, together with the continuing postwar trauma that we have observed, made the work appear appropriate as both theater and public ritual.[72]

The symbolic function of the opera, as Rouché defined it during the war—to help achieve national unity and ideological consensus—was still here firmly in place. The only factor militating against this Wagnerian-influenced work was the continuing hostility of many to Wagner, especially among stalwart nationalist groups such as Action Française. But d'Indy responded to such attacks in L'éclair and continued to defend his idol, although he did circulate notices defining his work as more a "mystère" than a "drame wagnérien."[73]

One further circumstance, however, was to have a decided impact on both audience and critics—the general consensus that Scholism had triumphed in its tenacious battle for "tradition" in music. But the reception of d'Indy's opera was affected not only by all these factors: equally important was the decor by Maurice Denis, which was substantially different from d'Indy's description in the score. As opposed to d'Indy's explicit and lavish nineteenth-century conception, Denis stressed the sacred and abstract nature of the drama, thus diverting attention from d'Indy's topical and controversial references.

For the prologue, Denis replaced the simple somber curtain described in the score with a greatly enlarged traditional iconographic image of the saint (see fig. 2). His scenery for the palace of the Reine de Volupté also disregards d'Indy's description of Byzantine mosaics, intended to suggest the "dangerous," sybaritic Orient, as opposed to the Occident. Instead he created the appropriate mood by means of sensuous shapes, but again at the expense of d'Indy's explicit realistic detail. Denis's designs for act 1, scene 2, "A Passage in the Mountains" and act 2, scene 2, "A Forest of Pine Trees," exhibit similar tendencies, suggesting a setting without time or place, rather than a specific region of France. The final scene is no exception: Denis's "Large Public Square" focuses less on the monuments d'Indy describes than on the emotional force of abstract shapes.[74] This abstraction, however, was counteracted by the combination of the costumes and makeup, particularly that of the Roi de l'Or, whose features, as specified in the sketches, and yellowish lighting, as described in the score, unmistakably suggest "the Jew" (see fig. 3).

Finally, the work's reception was affected by the cuts that the Opéra made for the first presentation. (It also made suggestions for a shortened, or expurgated version.) Certain omissions are not surprising: reference to those who think "librement," the phrases "la patrie n'est qu'un vain mot" (the homeland is but an empty word), and "la guerre est abolie" (war is abolished). All this was still too close to the war for comfort, or too overtly offensive to specific social groups. But also suppressed were references to those who want to destroy all, including their superiors ("le peuple trompé"), which invoked the menace of the strikes and ferment on the left. Aside from these isolated passages, the only sizable cut that was

FIGURE 2—Curtain for d' Indy's *La légende de Saint Christophe*, by Maurice Denis. © 2004 Artists Rights Society (ARS), New York; ADAGP (Société des auteurs dans les arts graphiques et plastiques), Paris.

made was of the extensive scene of the "armée de l'erreur"—again too overtly offensive.

What remained, however, was clearly reflective of a conservative ideological perspective, one that was highly exclusionary, authoritarian, or socially holistic and spiritualistic. Far from causing outrage in most circles, it won approbation, and less on the basis of its musical qualities than because of the "ideas" that it represented for different groups. *Bonsoir*, reporting on the standing ovation accorded d'Indy at the opera's dress rehearsal, commented explicitly, "on a l'air de libérer sa conscience" (one seems to set one's conscience free).[75] Sentiments that could not be stated openly elsewhere might be vented publicly here, veiled by the context of this unrealistic theatrical genre.

Almost all the reviews describe the work in quasi-religious terms—as an "oeuvre de foi," elevated in tone, sincere, and hence truly worthy of respect. *Le théâtre* remarked on its lofty aspirations, as well as on d'Indy's attempt to "liberate" the "drame lyrique," and his concomitant avoidance of "toute adultération théâtrale." *Le Figaro* similarly focused on the "elevated symbolism" of the text, so elegantly written that it could be classed "parmi les meilleures pages de la littéra-

FIGURE 3—Costumes for d' Indy's *La légende de Saint Christophe*, by Maurice Denis. © 2004 Artists Rights Society (ARS), New York; ADAGP (Société des auteurs dans les arts graphiques et plastiques), Paris.

ture française" (among the finest pages of French literature).[76] *Le journal des débats* wrote of its "succès éclatant," and *Le théâtre* marveled on how fully the work lived up to long-held public expectations.[77] But perhaps most surprisingly, several journals commented on how closely d'Indy's story followed the original "légende dorée," despite all the revisions we have seen.[78] D'Indy's attempt to "adjust" the legend seemed plausible to most reviewers, who frequently referred to the opera as synonymous with the legend itself.

In addition to press reports, the critic Adolphe Boschot, in his book *Chez les musiciens* (1922), provides a revealing and detailed discussion of *La légende de Saint-Christophe*. Reflecting the dominant conservative mentality, he first praises d'Indy and his teaching, referring to him eulogistically as "une des plus hautes figures de l'heure actuelle" (one of the most prominent figures of the present time). What Boschot admires in the opera is the sureness and variety of d'Indy's style, and the fact that the composer has invested himself personally in a work of such lofty aspirations. And he stresses d'Indy's view of art as something that is interior, like faith, the final goal of both being "l'enseignement des vérités éternelles" (the teaching of eternal truths). This, he points out, employing d'Indy's own rhetoric, is something that is not often found in the theater, but is realized more frequently in religious music, chamber music, and the symphony.[79]

Although Boschot cannot praise the opera without some reservations, he points out the way it has helped to liberate opera from mere theatrics and returned it to the serene grandeur of the oratorio. Moreover, he admires the way in which d'Indy has employed a legendary subject in order to incorporate his own highly personal social and religious convictions. In sum, his aspirations are noble, and the opera testifies to "les rares et hautes qualités d'un artiste qui aime son art plus que lui-même" (the rare and lofty qualities of an artist who loves his art more than himself).[80]

Negative reviews are difficult to find, except—not surprisingly—in the press associated with Action Française, well known for its reserve toward d'Indy's stalwart Wagnerism. The newspaper *L'action française* announced only the dress rehearsal, describing the work succinctly in the most cursory, perfunctory terms; and a review that appeared in a journal close to the league, *La revue critique des idées et des livres*, found the work's Wagnerian style to be the principal drawback. But as a product of the master of the Schola, the opera nevertheless commanded respect, and hence *La revue critique* pointed out that it never stooped to the "vulgarité ostentatoire" of Wagner. The message of the work was so multivalent in the context that even the Socialist *Le populaire de Paris* was highly laudatory of the opera, although certainly not of the libretto's content or its literary quality. As it notes ironically, despite the guarded approbation of *L'action française*, the work was palpably infiltrated by a kind of Marxist Socialism, or "bolshevism."[81] Perhaps this was in reference to the depiction of the bourgeoisie as materialistic and "misled"—although in d'Indy's conception, the hero was not "the people" but rather the aristocracy.

But despite generally favorable reviews and the multiple interpretations that the opera could accommodate, d'Indy's *La légende de Saint-Christophe* was only a "succès d'estime," eventually overshadowed by the lavish Ballets Russes.[82] As

Rouché foresaw, interpretation of the opera was closely linked to the political context, which, in large part, accounted for its broad appeal and ability to engage the audience. What had begun as a conservative, hostile reaction in the wake of the Dreyfus affair was now, in the postwar era, interpreted as a statement of French "defensiveness" and spiritualism or social justice. Moreover, the postwar social crisis had created a situation in which both the Right and the Left could see their social enemies in d'Indy's operatic villains. D'Indy's was an "opera of ideas," and the ideological element had a strong appeal, although this has made it inimical to a nuanced and thus satisfying artistic treatment. But this was an era of concern with ideologies, on the part of both the Left and the Right, reflected in a number of artistic genres, among which the opera was only one.

Another was the "novel of ideas," a novel in which the content was sociological and philosophical, and which flourished throughout the 1920s, as exemplified by writers like Roger Martin du Gard. Here we see the same tensions as in the operatic cognate in France between the hortatory and poetic elements, or between ideological certainty and human complexity. As Susan Suleiman has aptly expressed it, this is a genre inherently "divided against itself," for it is activated by the opposing tendencies of schematization and concrete human experience.[83] Maurice Barrès, who had practiced the genre since the later nineteenth century, and who would be acclaimed through a national funeral in 1923, was at the height of his popularity among nationalists. Now, not surprisingly, one of Barrès's most controversial novels, *Un jardin sur l'Oronte*, was being made into an opera by Alfred Bachelet, whom Barrès himself selected to be the composer.[84] But Barrès died before he could construct a libretto from the novel as he had planned, although, being an admirer of Wagner, he claimed to have projected a Wagnerian conception onto the work.[85]

The novel, Barrès's last, published in 1922, concerns the love of a Christian and a Sarrasin, an episode drawn from a long epic of the Crusades in the Middle Ages. Its topicality lay in that it dealt with the still highly charged theme of the Orient as opposed to the Occident, and concomitantly of the conflict of races and thus, purportedly, the "modes of feeling." Yet despite the widely known conservatism of Barrès, the novel created a scandal, particularly in the Catholic press, which perceived its sensuality as an outrage to religious morality.[86] It was perhaps this media attention that initially attracted Bachelet to the project, for he employed stylistic elements that heightened the racial conflict—music evocative of the Christian Middle Ages as opposed to sinuous Oriental vocalises.[87] But he also included conventional forms that are related both to serious opera and to opéra-comique, including recitatives, "airs," "chants," "proverbes" (evoking folk culture), and religious processions.

The scandal over the novel undoubtedly delayed the premiere, and the work, now ambiguous as to its political implications, was finally presented by Rouché at the Opéra on 7 November 1932, the year that a Leftist government came into power. Predictably, conservative journals seized the occasion to laud the opera, which, despite its ecclesiastical condemnation, represented the prestige and values of Maurice Barrès. René Dumesnil, in the *Mercure de France*, reported an "étonnante réussite" (astonishing success), both in terms of the libretto's adaptation of the novel and Bachelet's ability to capture its nuances. Yet he felt compelled to begin by addressing the continuing controversy over the novel, particularly among Catholic circles, and then quoted Barrès's own response to his critics: "Dans ce *Jardin sur l'Oronte*, je ne prétends pas plus mener le bon combat 'Catholique et Chrétien' que Racine dans ses tragédies, Fénélon dans son *Télémaque* ou le Tasse dans sa *Jérusalem*. . . ." (I don't claim to lead the same "Christian and Catholic" combat as Racine in his tragedies, Fénélon in his *Télémaque*, or Tasso in his *Jerusalem*).[88]

The goal, Dumesnil explains, is "art," and he then cites a quote by the abbé Brémond, who characterizes it as a "fantaisie," in order to justify Barrès's provocation. Dumesnil also notes the opera's apt adaptation of Wagnerian stylistic traits—for him, the supple and ingenious leitmotifs, the solid construction and well-developed plan. In short, it is characterized by (an implicitly d'Indyste) "natural nobility" and erudition as seen in its use of "Oriental folklore" as well as of music from the Middle Ages.[89] Here the conservative goal of separating the two cultures of Orient and Occident is, in effect, undermined or ignored in his discussion of the effective aesthetic results of their fusion. But Dumesnil predictably does laud Bachelet's "archaïsme charmant" in his use of old French dances such as a "pastourelle campagnarde," a "carole gracieuse," an "estompie," and a "gigue."[90]

The work, which transcended ideological lines, containing elements that appealed to Right and Left, became for some an embodiment of conservative values and for others a bold defiance of the church. Each position was therefore forced to accept those factors, ideological or stylistic, that it would otherwise have considered inimical if priority were given to either the work's content or its style. The opera's presentation (even at a politically transitional moment) was undoubtedly a result of the success of other operas based upon libretti concerning philosophical or social ideas that were of the moment. One was Georges Huë's *Dans l'ombre de la cathédrale* (1922), which centers on the opposition between "l'idéal religieux" and "l'idéal libertaire."[91] In light of the volatility of the issue in France, the action is judiciously set in Spain (traditionally associated by the French with fervent religiosity), at the Cathedral of Toledo, and was taken by the librettists M. Luna and H. Ferrare from a work of Blasco Ibáñez. It is significant here that Huë considered himself a conservative intellectual, and in 1935 would be one of the signers of the "Manifeste pour la paix en Europe et la défense de l'Occident," which supported Mussolini's aggression in Ethiopia.[92]

The vogue of the politically didactic opera continued in the early twenties, but when the Cartel des Gauches assumed power, Rouché made an ingenious adjustment at the Opéra, now screening a film with music by the Conservatoire's director, Henri Rabaud, the *Miracle des loups*. Rabaud was ensconced in official circles: having been conductor at the Opéra from 1908 to 1918, he was subsequently elected to the Institut and then made the Conservatoire's director after Fauré. The film, based on a novel by Dupuy-Mazuel, concerns a key episode from early French history: the story of Louis XI, Charles the Bold, and the siege of Beauvais, crowned by the heroism of Jeanne Hachette.[93] Perhaps because of its historical resonance and its association with heroism and patriotism, the film was presented before the head of state and members of the new government on 13 November 1924.

Not all politically didactic operas were performed without incident, however: the Opéra-Comique most probably accepted Marcel Delannoy's *Le poirier de misère* under the Cartel des Gauches, but it did not premiere (at the Opéra-Comique) until 21 February 1927, under the conservative Union Nationale. It had, according to reports, the effect of a bomb exploding in the hall.[94] Several important critics were explicit in their condemnation of the work, accusing the author of vulgarity and having been influenced by the increasingly threatening "bolshevist tendencies." This was undoubtedly a reference to continuing agitation on the French Left, which had been battling vitriolically with the Right over finances in the chamber throughout the previous year.[95]

In the tradition of the more "popular" works of the Left (intended for a working-class audience), the text, by André de la Tourrasse and Jean Limouzin, is allegorical, described alternately as based on the ancient myth of Sisyphus or on a Flemish folk tale. The characters include such abstract yet, in the context, politically charged and emblematic figures as Misère, Le Peuple, Le Saint, and La Mort. And the score, provocatively for a work that was clearly associated with the political Left, is titled (recalling d'Indy) a "Mystère en 3 actes," with one of the copies being dedicated to Maurice Ravel.[96] The tumult at the work's premiere was provoked, in part, by this bold effacement of ideological-stylistic divisions, which did engage, and enrage, the public. Not surprisingly, both Jean Marnold and his friend Ravel immediately leapt to the defense of the work when Pierre Lalo (Ravel's old nemesis in the press) unequivocally condemned it. Recalling the time when Lalo had attacked his own works, Ravel particularly took issue with Lalo's recommendation that the author follow Ravel's example.[97]

Far more acceptable to conservatives in the later 1920s was Joseph Canteloube's *Le mas*, which was premiered at the Opéra on 3 April 1929, at the urging of the reactionary Paul Bertrand, who was associated with *Le ménestrel*.[98] Canteloube, a biographer and supporter of d'Indy (and to become an important functionary during the Vichy regime) had selected a theme that once again recalls Maurice Barrès. For the title of the work, *Le mas*, refers to the traditional name of a family farm in southern France, thus immediately evoking both regionalist and nationalist associations within the context.

The action, as described in the score, takes place in Quercy, in southern Auvergne, "dans une famille de vieille souche terrienne" (of old stock of the earth).[99] The work was begun before the First World War (the dates given in the score are 1911–13), and, like so many works of this period, employs leitmotifs, although not systematically or symphonically, and boldly introduces bitonal passages for specific dramatic reasons.[100] But it was the theme of the story that was so compelling for conservatives; a contemporary scholar, highly sympathetic to the work, described it by employing terminology and concepts that make reference to Barrès's theme of "rootedness" in *Les déracinés*: "C'est le thème des ancêtres qui, plus fort que l'attrait des villes, reconquiert un jeune déraciné et le fixe définitivement au pays natal." (It is the theme of ancestors that, stronger than the attraction of cities, reconquers a young uprooted man and fixes him definitively in his native land).[101] Others stressed its roots in classic culture, describing it as a commentary, in three acts, on the fortunes of the ancient georgics, from Vergil, thus again ignoring the stylistic innovations in the work.[102]

As we have seen, in some cases it was the theme that determined the ideological interpretation, but in others it was the style employed, as construed within the current context. Yet perhaps because of this ambiguity, and the concomitant engagement that it fostered among the public, the Opéra persisted in the presentation of works with ideological or political themes. The tendency, of both the Right and the Left, to use the opera as a commentary on national themes or ideologies would continue into the early 1930s, as we have noted. Under a government of the Left, on 23 June 1933, for example, the Opéra presented Joseph Canteloube's *Vercingétorix*, despite the composer's conservative orientation. For, once more, the theme was one with which the Left could identify in light of the fascist threat—French patriotism, and appropriately with an emphasis not on soil and blood, but on nobility and sacrifice. Free of regional elements, this history of the ancient Gauls (to a libretto by Etienne Clément) led Canteloube to further innovations, such as the first use of the ondes Martenot in an opera orchestra.[103]

Hence the utterance was once more ambiguous, as had been the case in previous works we have seen, which did not dissuade the Opéra from persevering in its attempts to foster the genre. For, again, the Opéra's function, as had been reestablished during the war, was to diffuse ideas in the national interest that, even if contested, would "engage." The opera of ideas, then, was both a necessity and condemned to failure: while meeting expectations for a serious and hortatory art, if musically successful, it worked against its own end. But it did achieve cultural centrality, fusing cultural sectors and employing those themes that intrigued the audience, and forced established creeds to examine their ideological-aesthetic stances.

Hence now, more than ever, political ideas, generally of a conservative cast, were evident in the opera, but they appeared elsewhere, and most notably in both criticism and in musical scholarship. Julien Benda was indeed correct when, in *La trahison des clercs* (1927), he observed that all was becoming political, or tied to passions of race, nation, and class. Ideologies were contentiously opposing each other in literature, philosophy, and art, as political combat was implicating French culture, or invading the intellectual and aesthetic realms.[104]

RECLASSIFICATIONS IN SCHOLARSHIP AND CRITICISM

As we have seen, the official musical culture, against which more extreme positions on the right and the left would soon define themselves, was no exception to Benda's observation. Although subtly, its themes and policies, or principal preoccupations, were closely connected to the political concerns characteristic of the still traumatized postwar Republic. The immediate postwar government, of the moderate Right, now often referred to itself as "conservateur," or "modéré," as opposed to the more extremist nationalist position embodied by leagues like Action Française. The position of the "conservateurs," who sought "conservation" in culture, or "protection" as opposed to innovation, is manifest in several prominent cultural journals. Again, here we may observe what Maurice Agulhon refers to as "le système politique et mental d'après guerre," especially in prestigious publications such as *La revue de Paris* and *La revue des deux mondes*.[105]

Occupying a political middle ground, these journals assured the circulation of ideas that were common denominators for the Right, and particularly the necessary continuity of tradition. *La revue des deux mondes* incarnated the French academic and conservative position, or that of the "corps constitués"—academics, "maréchaux," cardinals, "savants," and influential writers and journalists.[106]

This position accordingly found its reflection in the dominant French musical world, or the tightly bound network of conservative academic, official, and journalistic figures. We find such a "mentality" manifest in numerous postwar publications, particularly in the many books on French music of the more recent past, several of which we will examine here. For just as in visual art, the postwar period saw a series of attempts to conceptualize the development of French music over the past several decades in terms of the development and triumph of the *âme nationale*. Such overviews of the more recent past—of French music between the defeat by Germany in 1870 and the victory of 1918—would lead to a series of "reclassifications."[107] The new French "cultural icons" would become those composers construed as incarnations of authentic French classicism, and concomitantly of the antiuniversalist and antimodern position.

A central question, at this point, was who should provide the model for postwar French youth—those who had been spared by the war, and who would go on to construct and to lead the "new France." There was thus a pervasive concern over certain tendencies among the more progressive young composers, all too ready to sacrifice the past and open themselves to dangerous new influences from outside. Hence, attacks on the direction of innovative young musicians would be frequent, as well as on those outside French culture who were thought to propagate maleficent new models. As Martha Hanna points out, cultural modernists, in general those who supported innovation and cosmopolitan values, became increasingly suspect in this period. They were "challenged with increasing efficacy by an emerging cultural conservatism that was comparable to and compatible with the political conservatism of the Bloc National government."[108]

The dominant response was to "reconstruct" the "old masters" in order to canonize them as "classic" exemplars, within a discourse infused with those political conceptions that were aligned closely with the conservative viewpoint. Specifically, in a period of the recruitment of immigrant labor to compensate for the extensive war losses, the theme of cultural tradition and insularity would be of primary concern.[109] So too would the theme of "race," now referring not only to a cultural unit, but to purity of "blood," which led, within the decade, to a new series of racist attacks.

Several of these themes appear in a book that was published in 1921 by the critic Gaston Carraud, titled *La vie, l'oeuvre et la mort d'Albéric Magnard*. Here Carraud undertakes the enshrinement or canonization of Albéric Magnard, who was "martyred" during the war while defending his home against the German enemy.[110] Carraud turns the biography into a topical attack on insidious foreign influences which he perceives as having undermined French music over the last hundred years. Like d'Indy he stresses the supposed superficiality and ostentation of the Italian school, which, he claims, invaded French music, thus suffocating the indigenous national art.

Again, like d'Indy, Carraud singles out Meyerbeer as a German-Jewish "parasite" in France, noting, with the subtle implication of treason, that he went on to become the "General-musikdirektor" for the king of Prussia. He thus blames Meyerbeer's nationality and "race" for the pollution of the "pure" French style, or for its contamination with traits that he refers to as "brutaux, pesants, fourbes" and "bas" (brutal, heavy, rascally, and lowly). Again building on the still painful memory of the war, he proceeds to equate Meyerbeer's music with the spirit of Prussian Germany, or "l'esprit boche," implying the Jewish, modernist, and the German.[111]

To these influences Carraud then contrasts the heroic and traditionalist style of Magnard who, although a romantic, insisted on subordinating feeling to the more classical laws of "order." Magnard's art, he continues, was therefore the opposite of the "cosmopolitan," with the implication that the composer, although a Dreyfusard, had no discernible Jewish influences in his style. To the contrary, only French elements—the "classic"—are present in Magnard's music, as manifest in the character, diversity, and truth of his feelings, the harmonious balance of his style, and his stress on melodic and rhythmic elements. His work is thus characterized stylistically by clarity, by his ability to invent new themes, which nevertheless suggest old *airs populaires*, and his unfailing propensity for equilibrium and measure. In sum, Carraud seeks to canonize Magnard as not only the incarnation of the "véritable esprit classique," but also, by extension, of the "véritable esprit national."[112]

Similar themes of purity, race, and "models" appear in a book by the conservative critic and writer on music, Adolphe Boschot, whose *Chez les musiciens* appeared in 1922. It too recalls wartime rhetoric, as well as d'Indy's specific argument that Wagner, although a German, had helped to "purify" French music of all the accretions (from Jewish composers) that had sullied it. Boschot, however, here praises not Wagner, but rather another German composer, Mozart, whose music he believes can serve a similar "hygienic function" in contemporary France.[113] For, according to Boschot, the postwar epoch is a period of trial for those intellectuals and artists who are less concerned with their own individual interests than with "le culte de l'idéal." Such altruistic idealists, he opines, will ultimately protect the French from the continuing threat of the foreign, and specifically the German influence, or "la barbarie qui nous menace" (the barbarism that menaces us). Boschot perceives the incarnation of the magnanimous individual pursuing the disinterested "cult of the ideal" in Mozart, who becomes for him the model of "good taste."[114] Just as during the war, the high classic Viennese style ironically provides the paradigm, being considered the stylistic embodiment of the most elevated and venerable "true" classic traits. The classical, once again, is here associated with the collectivity, with authority, and hierarchy, and thus with those qualities considered essential to the maintenance of social order. Mozart's music, Boschot thus continues, can help to "cure" the postwar

French of the philistinism and disorder caused by that arrogant upstart, "le caliban démocratique."

Boschot, like so many conservatives, perceived only anarchy in French politics as well as in art—a disorder caused by dangerous postwar social movements and infiltrations by the enemies outside. L'âme française, he asserts, must now reject these troublesome elements with vigor, elements he associates not only with foreigners, but also with "half-breeds," or "les demi-Français." The latter, since the time of the Dreyfus affair, had come to refer to Frenchmen of different racial origins, such as Jews, who nationalists claimed could never fully assimilate into French culture. Hence, as Boschot concludes, no figure more than Mozart, no longer considered "boche," but rather a "good German" of the classical past, can abet France in purging its cultural "bad blood."[115]

As opposed to d'Indy, Wagner, for Boschot, although not as dangerous as the more recent Germans, engenders only depression and "ennui," while Mozart radiates "light." But like d'Indy, Boschot proceeds to argue that "la musique post-wagnérienne d'outre Rhin était souvent une expression de la barbarie pangermaniste."[116] (Post-Wagnerian German music is often the expression of pan-Germanist barbarism.) For music, according to Boschot, remains the expression of a national culture, and closely bound to the nation, particularly within the more "realist," power-oriented nationalism of the period that Julien Benda so acutely observed.[117] Again, Benda's observation that the "mysticism of the nation" was infiltrating all sectors—that the âme collective had become the object of worship, supplanting universal values—here rings true.

Other writers on music who were as alarmed as Boschot by the direction being taken by French musical taste now turned to young French composers, and began a relentless attack on them. This even included members of the supposedly progressive Société Musicale Indépendante, who here broke away from confrères like Ravel to condemn certain newer directions. Such figures included Emile Vuillermoz, the former Debussyste, who continued to defend Debussy, now not from attacks of conservatives but rather from those of certain young composers and their "spokesman," Cocteau. Vuillermoz undertakes this defense in Musiques d'aujourd'hui (1923), typically stressing "l'élément national du génie de cet artiste de l'Ile de France" (the national element in the genius of this artist of the Ile de France). Hostile to the Schola's nationalism, Vuillermoz had nevertheless imbibed wartime orthodoxies and henceforth resembled Benda's nationalist "ideal type," just like Carraud and Boschot.[118]

Vuillermoz makes a point of noting the esteem in which French composers still hold Debussy, probably with the attacks against him by figures such as Jean Cocteau in mind. What clearly perturbed Vuillermoz, like other conservatives of his generation, is that younger French composers were decidedly rejecting, and even ridiculing, the venerable Debussy. In his 1920 book on Debussy, Vuillermoz thus underscores the irony that while youth now repudiate Debussy, it was he who taught them to liberate themselves from useless formulae. But again recalling wartime rhetoric, he now emphasizes that all that Debussy wrote was carefully balanced and solidly constructed, although each individual work had its own proper form.[119]

After deploring youths' rejection of "the master," Vuillermoz then proceeds to attack them aggressively, and particularly the group which became known as Les Six. In reality, Vuillermoz is attacking the unified and distorted image of this group that publicists and critics like Cocteau and Collet had created in the press. According to Vuillermoz, these young "so-called musicians" are not really interested in "écriture," and profess a "mépris absolu des vieilles règles du jour de l'écriture harmonique ou contrapuntique" (an absolute contempt for the old rules of harmonic and contrapuntal writing).[120] However, of the six composers, Vuillermoz, like other conservatives of his generation, is most drawn to Arthur Honegger, whose *Le roi David* he finds to be spontaneous as well as sincere.[121]

Similar arguments appear in a book by the composer and writer on music (and editor of *Le ménéstrel*) Robert Bernard, whose *Les tendances de la musique française moderne* was published in 1930. The book includes not only a particularly virulent condemnation of Les Six, but also a prominent attack on two composers whom they admired, Satie and Stravinsky. Significantly, the contents of this book were originally delivered as a series of lectures, followed, as so often in wartime (and at the Schola before) by illustrative or "pedagogical" concerts.

Equally significant is the fact that these lectures were originally intended for youth—perhaps as a reproach or a warning—having been initially delivered at both the Conservatoire and the Sorbonne. Before both these audiences Bernard had argued that what was lacking in current French music was a true "école musicale," with a unified aesthetic and a "chef de file."[122] Recalling not only wartime collectivism, but also d'Indy's arguments, he then asserts that since art progresses by gradual evolution, the results of radical modifications are destined to perish. And echoing others obsessed with chaos, anarchy, and the need for purification, he concludes that "schools" ought to govern artistic spirits as a kind of "intellectual hygiene."

Like many in his generation (and in Action Française), Bernard was convinced that the present disorder in thought and art stemmed from the irrational application of romantic principles. Indeed, he perceived the deleterious effects of intellectual anarchy in all domains, as did so many other conservatives writing in the postwar period. The connection of his argument with that of Action Française becomes explicit when Bernard cites Pierre Lasserre, the prominent denouncer of romanticism, formerly associated with the nationalist league.[123]

Paradoxically, it is in the name of classicism that Bernard then indicts the neoclassic Stravinsky for his insidious influence on the younger generation of French composers. Stravinsky, according to Bernard, has destroyed both classical construction and thematic development, preferring the distinctly unclassical technique of merely juxtaposing discrete ideas. He is thus by no means a true classic, despite his reference to past musical styles; rather, he is promoting an "artistic formula" that is the mere codification of "disorder." Although Stravinsky associated his ideal of historical objectivity with the temperate and the neutral, Bernard ascribes to it the ironic or critical distance, the aggressive attack on a suffocating tradition, characteristic of Les Six.[124] For Bernard, Stravinsky's bare and simplified technique stems not from a true classic aesthetic, but rather reveals the composer's disquieting hostility to both thought and expression.[125]

Satie, for Bernard, presents a mixed case, since Bernard, like Cocteau, perceives what he considers essentially classic elements informing Satie's unassuming work. These comprise bareness, simplicity, absence of the "extramusical," a propensity for the horizontal (or counterpoint), an interest in line, and the distrust of "les ambiances sonores floues et indéterminées" (vague and indeterminant sonorous ambiences).[126] However, he notes that what is missing not only in the work of Satie himself, but in that of Les Six, whom he directly influenced, is any sense of a "climat spirituel." As we have seen, for conservatives in the postwar era, the "spiritual" was primary, part of their quest for a different world, one whole and pure, to be born of the war.

Like Vuillermoz, however, Bernard considers Honegger to be the one member of the group who is capable of overcoming what Bernard perceives as an inevitable aesthetic impass.[127] But the composer in whom he places most hope is the more traditionally oriented Georges Migot, whose "esprit synthétique" has discerned the common elements in all manifestations of the "French genius." In conclusion, Bernard expresses his desire for a new leader, like Franck or Fauré before, to guide young composers away from the seduction of theories still penetrating France from "outside." For someone had to warn them against the excesses that avant-garde audiences now encouraged, someone who could intuitively touch the deepest fibers of "notre génie racial."[128] Again, Benda was correct in his analysis from the perspective of this sector of the French musical world: as in other fields, it was obsessed with the "mystique" of the nation and its effable "spirit."

NEW GOALS IN FRENCH MUSICAL EDUCATION

An obsession with the national and spiritual penetrated other domains of the musical world as well, including most prominently both musical education and cultural programs exported abroad. The early twenties, in general, was a period of reform in French education, one that was concerned with repudiating "modernist" orthodoxies and reaffirming the importance of Latin and of the classic tradition.[129] Accordingly, musical education, now following the lead of the Schola, was linked to national patrimony, spirit, and tradition, not only on the level of the Conservatoire, but in secondary and "popular" education.[130] As a result of the impetus of the war, when lectures and concerts became part of a "national education," instruction in music now burgeoned, often being tied to larger ideological and social programs. The resulting broader demand for education in music would accordingly generate new institutions, providing wider opportunities for students and for teachers previously excluded from the academic system. The education they propagated was conservative, not only on the lower but on the higher or professional levels, which would have distinct implications for the style of younger composers, who would mature in the 1930s.

Again, the Schola's emphasis on both spiritual values and tradition, particularly the great works of the past, was by now part of mainstream French musical culture, and was even, in large part, incorporated into the Conservatoire under the leadership of Henri Rabaud. D'Indy's presence at the Conservatoire during the war was undoubtedly an important factor in the denouement of the vitriolic battle between the institutions in the prewar years. In this respect it is significant that the monumental *Encyclopédie de la musique et dictionnaire du Conservatoire*, published in 1931, included an article on the Schola by d'Indy.[131] Equally significant is that Charles Tournemire, the "spiritualist" organist and composer, an advocate of Bach and Franck, was appointed professor at the Conservatoire in 1919. He, along with others who were part of the postwar spiritualist and traditionalist climate, would be highly influential on the pupils at the Conservatoire during this period, including Olivier Messiaen.[132] This generation of students would thus have a far different education and experience from that of their immediate predecessors, whose studies and paths to official consecration had been ruptured by the war.

Since the twenties was a decade of far-reaching reforms in French education, not surprisingly this included reforms in the teaching of music. Again its significance as a potential pedagogical instrument to help instill national values and tradition, as well as encourage social communion, had now been fully recognized. Not only did musical instruction become obligatory in *écoles primaires supérieures*, but an *arrêté ministériel* from Herriot instituted a commission charged with the renovation and development of musical studies in France.[133]

In addition, the instruction dispensed in the provincial conservatories became a subject of primary concern, and the issues they raised provide a further index of postwar priorities in French cultural politics. A questionnaire distributed to such conservatories poses a set of questions that reveal the desire to balance what had been the pedagogical priorities of the prewar Conservatoire with those of the Schola.[134] It asks, for example, how many times a week counterpoint and fugue (promoted by the Schola) are being taught, and how long the classes are in relation to those in harmony and solfège (emphasized traditionally by the Conservatoire).[135]

This, however, was not the only concern; several reports from this period reveal the larger cultural and political goals that officials envisaged for the provincial conservatories. One example is the report on a city in the department of the Pas-de-Calais by the *inspecteur de l'enseignement musical* (and professor at the Conservatoire) André Bloch. Bloch expresses his hope and desire that this school will serve as the seedbed for performers who can then go on to participate actively in the many musical societies of the region. This desire indeed resembles the goal for music in the contemporary Weimar Republic—to unite a divided society, although the means suggested here are distinct. Bloch recommends that the young now study the admirable canons of Gédalge, followed by "l'impérissable folklore des maîtres de la Renaissance" (the unperishable folklore of the masters of the Renaissance). For such "fresh" choral works can be performed in municipal festivals in the immediate future, imparting "un vif éclat sur la ville et sa nouvelle école nationale" (a lively brilliance on the city and its new national school).[136]

Here, as opposed to the Weimar Republic, the emphasis was not on simple folk music (among other types) as a means to achieve a new unity, but rather on the great French choral music that incorporated it.[137] Moreover, as we will shortly see, the social goals envisaged for such a fête were distinct from those being planned by both the Weimar Republic and the French Far Left. The official French musical world sought communal "elevation," and thus quietistic assimilation into a great indigenous tradition rooted in conservative conceptions of the national past.

We may observe precisely how this official "network" functioned by examining the composition of the Commission Consultative Chargée d'Examiner les Candidatures Vacantes d'Inspection de l'Enseignement Musical (the consultative committee charged with examining the vacant candidacies for the inspection of musical education). Just as in the state educational system, inspectors were sent to national conservatories in the provinces in order to ensure that they conformed to official regulations and authorized programs. By focusing on the commission to select inspectors for musical education we may specifically observe the close interaction of official figures with the most prestigious critics in the press. This was a primary means to co-opt key personalities from outside the state system, thus encouraging their participation in official agendas to guide musical taste in the desired direction.

The commission of 1920, for example, consisted of Paul Léon (director of the Beaux-Arts), Gabriel Fauré (soon to retire as director of the Conservatoire), Charles-Marie Widor (of the Institut), Théodore Dubois (former director of the Conservatoire), the composer Alfred Bruneau (now an academician and influential critic), Gustave Charpentier (much honored by the French state), Henri Rabaud (who replaced Fauré at the Conservatoire in 1920), Pierre Lalo (the powerful critic), Camille Chevillard (the conductor of the Concerts Lamoureux), Gaston Carraud (the critic and now member of the Conseil Supérieur d'Enseignement at the Conservatoire), and Georges Hüe (the politically conservative composer).

In the later twenties the composition of this important commission was not radically different: it remained conservative, despite the new directions and pronounced innovations in French music. It consisted of Paul Léon (still general director of the Beaux-Arts), Alfred Bruneau (now general inspector of music education), Adolphe Boschot (the conservative critic), Gustave Charpentier, Henri Rabaud (now director of the Conservatoire), André Bloch (still professor at the Conservatoire and inspector of musical education), Paul Vidal (the composer), Pierre Lalo (the critic and member of the Conseil Supérieur d'Enseignement du Conservatoire), in addition to the "sous-directeur" of the Beaux-Arts, chief of the theater bureau.[138] It was this network of prominent but aging, increasingly conservative figures that sought to direct the future of French music, and to determine "symbolic legitimacy," or that which could be accepted aesthetically.

As we have noted, choral singing became a point of emphasis for provincial conservatories, but its importance was yet to increase, growing particularly prominent by the later 1920s. Already a part of the ideological programs of the syndicalist Left, in official culture it was now designed ostensibly to serve a socially conservative end. Although only the universities of Paris and Strasbourg offered courses in music history, the teaching of choral singing was organized not just in lycées, but in the *écoles normales d'instituteurs et d'institutrices*.[139]

In addition to primary and secondary education, "popular" education in music, as well as in the arts in general, was an area of significant official concern. Societies like L'Art pour Tous, which had been founded privately in 1901, were still active, but now the *président d'honneur* was Paul Léon, director of the Beaux-Arts."[140] In addition, "popular" conservatories, such as Charpentier's Conservatoire Populaire de Mimi Pinson, continued, even in the 1920s, to receive a nominal or honorific subvention.[141]

The demand for musical education in the postwar period was growing in almost all sectors, stimulated, as we have seen, by the sense of national importance that it had assumed. In order to meet the needs of largely nonprofessional musicians, predominantly of the middle class, a new institution opened its doors in Paris, in 1919. The Ecole Normale de Musique filled a significant gap in French musical education, admitting students of all nationalities (unlike the Conservatoire) and (like the Schola Cantorum) with no age limit or competition for entry.[142] Its fees were relatively modest, and for those who could not afford them it provided limited scholarships, resulting in a socially broad student base. This may well be one of the reasons why the school received a subvention, even if a modest one, from the Ministère de l'Instruction Publique et des Beaux-Arts. Another reason was undoubtedly the fact that its founders were Adolphe Mangeot, Pablo Casals, and Alfred Cortot, the former director of musical propaganda during the war.

The school's faculty consisted largely of those associated with both the Schola and Conservatoire, with roots in wartime conceptions of the conservative classic French tradition. It included Paul Dukas, Georges Hüe, Vincent d'Indy, Max d'Ollone, Georges Witowski, Wanda Landowska, Marguerite Long, Reynaldo Hahn, Marcel Dupré, Jacques Thibaud, and Nadia Boulanger. The latter, as we will see, found herself forced to tread a fine and difficult line, both within her own aesthetic and within the school, between tradition and her embrace of innovation.[143] But the school itself did include innovations, and one of them was a series of master classes, modeled on the German *Meisterschule*, in which prominent international performers gave classes for both French and foreign students. Clearly, it met a need, and in doing so brought numerous important departures in French musical education, as indeed had the Schola Cantorum at the turn of the century.[144]

THE COMPLEX CASE OF NADIA BOULANGER

Another of the Ecole Normale's innovations was the inclusion on its faculty of a woman—Nadia Boulanger—who, despite her prominence, had long been excluded from the Conservatoire's faculty. This was also in spite of her political orientation and aesthetic rhetoric, which were now close to key points of the official perspective, although not without some tensions. The daughter of a French composer and (purportedly) a Russian princess, which made her a supporter of aristocracy and monarchy, Boulanger was drawn ideologically to the doctrines of Action Française. Moreover, she shared the anti-Semitism characteristic of the Church, the league, and many conservatives, even if she was careful to hide her feelings from her Jewish students. Believing Jews to be members of a different "race," as well as collectively responsible for the crucifixion of Christ, she attempted to limit the number of Jewish students she accepted into her class.[145]

Like d'Indy, she believed that, collectively, Jews were endemically destined to fail in all creative endeavors, even though they could excel as both performers and teachers. This indeed accorded well with the perspective of conservatives like Boschot, who considered Jews to be "demi-Français," and thus "polluters" of the national culture. And, again like d'Indy, Boulanger was not reticent to expound her political ideas to her students, considering these ideas, as did he, to be inseparable from her artistic beliefs. Hence she preached the virtues of monarchy, while condemning democracy (like many conservatives, such as Boschot), and continued to do so until the end of her life.[146]

In the twenties, Boulanger's aesthetic rhetoric remained close to nationalist orthodoxies, emphasizing the roots of French classicism in the Ancien Régime, and thus stressing proportion and balance. But, while many conservatives employed this rhetoric to attack Stravinsky, arguing that he was not truly classic, Boulanger would rather employ it to defend him. She would take considerable risks not only in attempting to justify the maligned Stravinsky as a "classic," but also in openly expressing interest in Arnold Schoenberg's music.

As we have seen, not only was the "establishment" still hostile to contemporary German and Austrian music, but to Jews in general, and particularly those who were Germanic. Yet by 1923 Boulanger, following her own musical interests and instincts, was analyzing Schoenberg's work in her classes, although this would end abruptly, and without explanation. It has been hypothesized that it was the pressure put upon her by Stravinsky, who considered Schoenberg to be a rival, that brought about this peremptory exclusion.[147] But an equally plausible explanation is an awareness of the political and racial issues surrounding Schoenberg's music, and thus the pressure applied by "establishment" circles.

If also suspicious to official circles, Boulanger's support for Stravinsky and for modernist neoclassicism paralleled (and helped form) the taste of the princesse de Polignac, her patron in these years. For despite her attempt to espouse aesthetic orthodoxies, Boulanger, excluded from the Paris Conservatoire, was forced to enter nominally funded, lower-status institutions, and to seek independent support. The institutions with which she became affiliated included not only the Ecole Normale de Musique, but the new Conservatoire Américain and private concert organizations such as the Cercle Interallié. But again, paradoxically, despite her support for Stravinsky and her exclusion as too "progressive" (as well as for being a woman), the aesthetic she expounded in such peripheral institutions was close to French conservative doctrine. Her aesthetic conceptions as well as the canon that she taught resembled those of the Schola, which she was known to have admired, having studied with one of its founders, Alexandre Guilmant.[148]

FORGING THE FRENCH IMAGE ABROAD

Despite her continuing exclusion from the highest of French academic circles, Boulanger was nevertheless active in postwar official propagandistic organizations. These were specifically designed to disseminate the orthodox image of French culture abroad—to reaffirm the strength and presence of France in a world order in which power was shifting.[149] If classicism, in domestic policy, was to foster consensus and bestow civic virtues, in foreign relations it was to project the image of French national order and strength. This image was to become an agent or a weapon to establish a strong French presence, and concomitantly a political influence in the still uncertain postwar era. In the sciences and social sciences as well, French propaganda, as initiated in wartime, was still being aimed not only at the international community, but specifically at America, now an unquestioned world power.[150]

Within this context, one primary goal of the Ministry of Fine Arts in the twenties was to export and vigorously promote French "classic" art, as well as French artists in America. Hence the constitution of a group affiliated with the ministry, the Committee for French Restoration, the goal of which was to further the French cultural presence and to foster exchange. It promptly formed a network of correspondents, whose charge was regularly to report to the Ministry of Fine Arts concerning the current character of cultural activities in the United States. A related organization was the Franco-American Musical Society, one of whose founders, E. Robert Schmitz, a former pupil of Debussy, and promoter of French music in America, worked together with the Committee for French Restoration. Both Nadia Boulanger and (until her premature death) her sister Lili, the composer, were active members of this society from its inception.

Schmitz, who headed the Pro Musica Society, was closely connected with an official of the French Ministry of Fine Arts, Robert Brussel, who was now specifically charged with the task of postwar "propagande musicale." Hence Schmitz's published rhetoric reveals a great deal about the content of such propaganda as it was disseminated throughout this period in the American press. In June 1919, in the New York periodical the *Literary Digest*, Schmitz denigrates German art (as had d'Indy) for its worship of the "Kolossal," as implicitly opposed to French classic proportion, precision, and measure. And since, as we have seen, anti-Semitism and anti-Germanism were closely bound in this rhetoric, it is not surprising that Schmitz here denigrates Mendelssohn and Schoenberg for their lack of creative power.[151] Such concepts, propagated during the war, were now widespread in France, having gradually become a part of the orthodox discourse in official circles.

The other organization associated with the postwar Ministry of Fine Arts, and conceived to advance similar national goals, was Action Artistique à l'Etranger. Here too the informing rationale was that French classic culture could now be a "weapon" in the battle to establish French intellectual and cultural power abroad. Just as during the war, the "myth" to be exported was that of a pure French culture, manifest in a series of great French works that embodied the "national genius." A similar rationale informed the foundation in 1921 of the Conservatoire Américain at Fontainebleau, which was partially subsidized by the French government, and in which Nadia Boulanger, who had been a founder of the Comité Franco-Américain during the war, taught traditional French compositional method to American students. Its founder and first director was Francis Casadesus, who had studied at the Conservatoire and had been associated with Gustave Charpentier's Conservatoire Populaire de Mimi Pinson.[152] The French were well aware that America, too, because of the war, felt compelled to repudiate Germanic influence, which had for so long been dominant in both the university and in musical education. But to conserve the "classic" French image, the avant-garde had again to be extruded, forcing composers like Edgar Varèse to seek a more hospitable environment as an expatriate in New York. Moreover, those French youth who were drawn to the new American culture, as well as to that of the former "enemy" countries, were forced to find new sources of support and new performance venues.

Cultural Responses of the Far Right and Left

POLITICS THROUGH CULTURE

Official hegemony provoked responses that were simultaneously political and cultural, for culture was now one of the most powerful languages of politics, as it had been at the turn of the century. Hence it is not only a battle of political principles that we encounter in the postwar period, but one of discourses and symbols, in which aesthetic values remained key agents in articulating sociopolitical aspirations. Music was accordingly in the field of struggle over ideology and symbolic relations of power, and the primary political issues inevitably penetrated French musical culture, if in refracted form. These included the questions of classicism, of national "intelligence," and of patriotism, which both the Left and the Right addressed through a discourse on music, as well as through other spheres of culture.

Unlike the contemporary Weimar Republic, here it was not political parties per se which sought to engage music in their political struggles, but rather politicized groupings on the Far Right and Left. The journals of such groupings included discussions of music that were not without influence on the French musical world, and by the end of the decade some of these groups would attract the allegiance of prominent French composers. This would be particularly true of the right-wing league, the Action Française, whose tactics had long included addressing political issues through the language of culture.

THE ACTION FRANÇAISE AND "INTELLIGENCE"

After the war, the position of Action Française could not have been stronger. The prestige and influence of the league was at its peak: politically and intellectually it appeared to be "the winner." It was now infiltrating or forming alliances with the more moderate Right, and despite the stridency of its tone, it would attract allied groupings, such as the venerable Fédération Républicaine.[153] Although the league was clearly to the right of the conservative Republic after the war, as we have noted, Poincaré was still sympathetic to it, even tolerating its occasional violence. Indeed, the league had been perceived as a useful "monitor" of wartime *union sacrée*, and despite its doctrinal monarchism had supported both republican leaders Clemenceau and Poincaré. Hence in 1919 it managed to penetrate the conservative Bloc National, with the election to the chamber of some thirty candidates who were close to or in the league, including the notoriously outspoken Léon Daudet. Now its power grew to the extent that many perceived it as simply the outer right wing of the conservative and nationalist center, behind Poincaré.[154]

Its influence on Catholic circles was considerable. The Action Française now managed to win over such prominent Catholic writers as Léon Bloy and the neo-Thomist philosopher and theologian Jacques Maritain.[155] The latter was a regular collaborator on the journal of Catholic intellectuals, *La revue universelle*, which was close to Action Française, and propounded both nationalist and anti-German sentiments.[156] The situation, however, was to change with the pope's condemnation of the movement in 1926, as a result of Daudet's reckless threats and the league's relentless application of its motto, "Politique d'abord" (Politics first). It was now inescapably clear that the movement was merely using the church "instrumentally," which prompted the intellectual response of Maritain—his *Primauté du spirituel* (1927).[157]

The eventual result would be a new political climate in French Catholic circles, including an openness to Christian Democracy, but the more immediate response of the league was to further infiltrate parties of the Right.[158] Consequently, the intellectual impact of the league would be felt throughout the decade, and its major postwar concerns and themes would penetrate the discourse of the Right. These we will see recurring implicitly or explicitly in conservative French musical discourse, which musicians imbibed, invoked, and addressed, or unequivocally rejected.

Perhaps the most prominent issue to appear in all French intellectual circles was that of "intelligence"—or whether the intellectual should still be subordinated to both national and political interests. On 26 June 1919, the (still) Socialist *L'humanité* published a manifesto by Romain Rolland repudiating servitude to the state, the polemic "Déclaration de l'indépendance de l'esprit," signed by, among intellectuals, Jean-Richard Bloch and Georges Duhamel.[159] The league responded dogmatically in the "Mainfeste pour un parti de l'intelligence" that Henri Massis (a prominent member) published in *Le Figaro* on 19 July 1919. Here the implicit enemy is the non-Christian, supranational, "bolshevist" intellectual Left, as opposed to "Occidental" Christianity and "pure" national values.[160] The assertion of universalist, as opposed to such "particularist" or nationalist priorities, was to become a cause célèbre among both intellectuals and artists on the Left.

But other points of contention that the league now raised would have ramifications for French musical circles, particularly in the case of Maurice Ravel, as we will see later in this chapter. These included attitudes toward wartime nationalism, Italian fascism, immigration into France, and the role of France in both its colonies and its protectorates. In particular, in the wake of the war, the right-wing xenophobia that had been responsible for its eruption and length was an object of opprobrium for the Left, now happier that the "butchery" was over than that the "boches" had been beaten. And while the Right was generally favorable to the "authoritarian" regime of Mussolini (Action Française openly praising him), the Left was opposed, perceiving the implications of fascism.[161] And as we have seen, in the face of massive and badly needed immigration, to perform essential labor after the war, the league still stressed "racial purity." Finally, it is important to emphasize that not only the Right but the Center believed in the legitimacy of colonialism and its continuation after the war. The Left would now start to question it, as articulated powerfully in Gide's indictment of the cruelty of European colonial policy, his *Voyage au Congo* (1927).[162]

The most prominent cultural concern of Action Française, however, was still "intelligence" as it was manifest in art, or the authentic French style that they believed to embody the fundamental essence of *l'esprit national*. Indeed, in aesthetic issues the league remained as central and strident as during the war, continuing to promote the conservative classic model as alone legitimate. According to this model all "foreign" elements (aside from German-Austrian high classicism) were to be vigorously excluded, and particularly those originating in a different "race." This continued to imply that the artistic influence of all Jews, even when French, should be systematically extirpated to preserve a "pristine" French culture. The aesthetic goal of Action Française thus continued to be homogeneity, or a purified national culture into which all complementary regional elements fed. Diversity was to be excluded: France was not to be governed by universal ideals, but rather by that which was indigenous to it, on the basis of French soil and blood.

These ideas were still being diffused not only by members of the league itself, but by critics who had imbibed its doctrine, and by those who, even after leaving the movement, remained highly influenced by it. The latter was the case of Pierre Lasserre, who was still prominent in both literary and musical circles, especially with the publication of his *Philosophie du goût musical* in 1922. Here he addresses the key issue of the classic—according to French conservative conceptions—and against which the Left would counterpose its own model, as we will shortly see.

Lasserre defines the classic in music as both perfect equilibrium and moderation in the means employed, which ensure that the work of art will withstand the attacks of time. He thus argues explicitly with the statement that was made by Anatole France (a proponent of the Left), in *La revue de Paris* in 1920, that music is the art most vulnerable to revolutions in taste and to the vicissitudes of feeling. Lasserre retorts that those who do not recognize the superiority of epochs of civilization that are capable of making a "general style" reign in the arts are, quite simply, "barbarians." Such epochs are, in fact, "classic," and they alone can give birth to lasting works, for their "divine harmony" exercises a controlling force on individual inspiration, necessary in a great culture.[163]

Such ideas found reflection in artistic journals allied with the Right, such as *L'art*, which railed against excessive foreign influence and supposed "complots étrangers." Between 1923 and 1928 *La peinture* crusaded for the restoration of moral order through the artistic means it believed necessary to effect it—pictorial order. Recalling wartime themes, its battle was still to save "form" in art, construed as not only integral to moral order, but as a source of true "French genius."[164] Other journals, like *Critique, art, philosophie,* thus attacked Jewish artists in the name of "ordre" and "puissance," or a "classical attitude" in politics and art. Less openly right-wing publications, even those associated with the French avant-garde, expounded similar ideas, espousing a conservative classicism in all the arts. *Après le cubisme,* by Amadée Ozenfant and Charles-Edouard Jeanneret (to become Le Corbusier), called for a "new purism," here associating classicism with the collectivity and with rigor.[165]

Critics associated with Action Française continued, as before the war, to pronounce on aesthetic matters, and to appropriate French composers of both past and present for their cause. This even involved the use of composers who were, in fact, hostile to the league, but whose music the critics in Action Française could "read" as orthodox, through their ideological screen. This was ostensibly the case with Ravel, when in 1923, the journal that was affiliated with the league, *La revue critique des idées et des livres* lavished praise on the composer. In his discussion of *L'heure espagnole*, Fernand-Georges Roquebrune extols its humor as well as what he perceives as "cette alliance du bon goût et la tradition libre" (this alliance of good taste and the free [nonacademic] tradition). He then proceeds to compare Ravel's classicism in the work to the operettas of (the Jewish) Jacques Offenbach, which are, to the contrary, characterized by "l'outrance, la vivacité parodique, alliée à toutes les invraisemblances du sujet" (excessiveness, parodic vivacity, allied to all the unlikelihood of the subject). Offenbach's operettas, he continues, are characterized by an absence of taste, and hence "ne sauraient être assimilés complètement en France pour s'incorporer à notre tempérament fait de tact et de mesure" (could not be completely assimilated in France to be incorporated in our temperament consisting of tact and measure).[166] Despite the fact that Offenbach had lived in France since his teenage years, and had become completely assimilated, from the league's perspective he could never produce true French art.

THE "SCHOLA D'ACTION FRANÇAISE"

The Action Française was not only active in the domain of art and music criticism: it promoted concerts, sedulously explaining their ideological significance in the league's publications. On 5 June 1920, the newspaper *L'action française* announced "un concert d'Action Française," followed by this elaboration: "Tel est le nom qui convient au concert que nous avons annoncé comme devra avoir lieu lundi 7 juin dans la grande salle de la Schola Cantorum" (such is the name that suits the concert that we announced as to take place in the large hall of the Schola Cantorum).[167] The paper then clarifies that it can be called a "concert d'Action Française" because of its forces: it consisted of "Schola d'Action Française, Orchestre d'Action Française, etc."

The concert was undoubtedly a collaborative effort between associates of the Schola who were sympathetic to the league (necessarily with d'Indy's approbation) and members of Action Française itself. But the performance was apparently postponed, for another was announced for 14 June 1920, with the following eclectic program, one related to both the interests of the Schola and the league: an anonymous "Vieille chanson de France," the *Cantate à Jeanne d'Arc* by the abbé Brun, the finale of Vierne's First Symphony, the *Psaume* for chorus and orchestra of César Franck (d'Indy's teacher), and, surprisingly, Saint-Saëns's *La princesse jaune*. The inclusion of the latter was clearly another case of appropriation, for Saint-Saëns, hostile to d'Indy, as we have seen, was always a loyal republican. But we must recall that Saint-Saëns's reputation had soared in nationalist circles during the war due to his public and uncompromising patriotism, which probably explains his being so honored. Such concert ventures were by no means isolated: concert promotion and the resultant appropriation of composers would continue, not only on the part of the French Extreme Right, but on the Left, as we will now see.

THE LEFT: UNIVERSALISM AND THE "CLASSIC"

The French Left was in a far less advantageous position than the Right in the wake of the war: not ideologically as coherent, it splintered badly over Communism, among other issues. The looming social problems and tumultuous strikes of 1919 had helped to foster growing sympathy for Russian Communism, and specifically for the Bolshevists.[168] The Congress of Tours, in December 1920, finalized the growing split between the more moderate republican Socialists and the French Communist Party, which was now born.[169] This rift, however, did not prevent agreement and cooperation on several points which the postwar French Left continued to hold in common, in opposition to the Right. Together it would boldly confront the postwar French political and aesthetic order, challenging its hegemony, both overt and subtle, through ideological responses as well as cultural programs. Entering into dialogue with the state, the Left articulated its social vision in aesthetic terms, making the arts into agents through which to communicate its conception of community. Indeed, as Martha Hanna has acutely observed, just as in the spheres of religion and labor relations, the war had actually "deepened the old cultural divide."[170]

Several cultural themes now become prominent in both the French Socialist and Communist Left, as well as in the many intermediate groupings and publications that soon arose. In addition to the attitudes toward patriotism we have noted, the Left now espoused a substantially different view from the Right with regard to German-French reconciliation, and thus to German culture. Now the Left, with various degrees of intensity and intransigence, was inclined toward pacifism, and was open to all that could avert further war, including Franco-German cultural exchanges.[171]

But even more aggressively in response to the Right, it took up the volatile issue of "intelligence," redefining it in accordance with its own universalist, antinationalist, antiracist perspective. In effect, the Left subverted the Right's ideological conception of intelligence by asserting its own definition—as synonymous with the universal, or the "truly human." This was part of a continuing rejection of still virulent French wartime propaganda, or nationalist "brainwashing" to which the Left implacably opposed an "esprit critique."[172] Hence, as we have seen, on 26 June 1919, the then Socialist *L'humanité* published Romain Rolland's "Déclaration de l'indépendance de l'esprit." Its force was amplified by the fact that its signers included prominent French, Austrian, and German intellectuals, such as Georges Duhamel, Albert Einstein, Heinrich Mann, and Stefan Zweig.

Opposed to conservative republican nationalism, as well as to bourgeois culture, was *Clarté*, a journal launched in 1919 that was close to the Communist Party but still independent.[173] Its associates included prominent writers as well as artists who ranged from the more moderate Anatole France, Henri Barbusse, and Romain Rolland to the revolutionary surrealists. The journal's very title was a provocation, for the sense in which it invoked "clarté" had nothing to do with conceptions of distinctly French qualities, but rather with intellectual rigor. In the spirit of the Left, *Clarté* was not only antimilitarist and stolidly pacifist but openly hostile to the conventional conservative discourse in both French politics and culture.[174]

In its opening statement in 1921, Henri Barbusse declared the journal's goals—to orient public opinion toward "les grandes vérités," to foster the spirit of revolt, and to oppose "established forces."[175] This program was particularly attractive to the surrealists, who shared the journal's intellectual liberalism and "European spirit," as well as its committed antinationalism and anticolonialism. By 1927, five French surrealists went even further and became Communists, but they encountered inevitable tensions upon the Communist rejection of the literary avant-garde in the later 1920s.[176]

However, *Clarté* attracted other figures associated with the artistic avant-garde, including Jean-Richard Bloch, a friend of Romain Rolland who was equally interested in music (and a fine pianist).[177] Bloch was a Socialist, with progressive artistic interests, and hence in 1925 he published a "Prolégomènes à toute chronique musicale" in the journal, in which he attempted to lay the groundwork for its music criticism. Only the previous year he had written an article in *Le monde musical* with the iconoclastic title "Une insurrection contre la sensibilité."[178]

The theories of the Left, however, were not yet coherent enough for clear critical criteria in music to emerge, and thus Bloch's ruminations were not followed by regular columns of music criticism. It would not be before the mid-1930s, during the Popular Front, that Bloch would gather progressive French musicians (Les Six) around him, in support of his ideas. But he does here make an important point: that parvenu and nouveau riche patrons can play an indispensable role in artistic evolution, being open to the new, as implicitly imposed to the conservatism of the state.[179] In the twenties, this would indeed be the case, for it was largely "new money" as well as the old libertine aristocracy that joined forces against the bourgeois Republic in support of Les Six.

But Bloch was involved in another journal that similarly promoted intellectual independence and articulated the major themes of the Left concerning both politics and culture—*La nouvelle revue française*. Founded in 1909 by Gide and Copeau, it resumed publication after the war, in June 1919, under the bold direction of Jacques Rivière.[180] Rivière laid out the goals of the journal on 1 June

1919, the first of which was to end the constraints that the war had exerted on "intelligence."[181]

Rivière here welcomes "the claims of intelligence," which is searching to "resume its rights" in art, in implicit contrast to the conception of "intelligence" that was currently being advanced on the Right. In September 1919, he was more explicit in an article on the right-wing Parti de l'Intelligence, in which he cites (and then denounces) their fundamental principles as follows: "L'intelligence nationale au service de l'intérêt national, tel est notre premier principe" (National intelligence in the service of national interest, such is our first principle).[182] Julien Benda, eight years later, would, as we have noted, make a point similar to Rivière's in four articles in the same journal, which were soon after published as *La trahison des clercs* (1927).

Although *La nouvelle revue française* initially sought to free art from worldly or "practical" ends, in keeping with Benda's conception of the "disinterested intellectual," it would ultimately fail in this endeavor. Indeed, it would eventually criticize Benda's *La trahison des clercs* for cutting off the dialogue between the "eternal" and "real" human affairs, or removing the intellectual from the "engaged" pursuit of morally just ends, in the name of intellectual autonomy.[183] For Benda, the "clerc," which included artists, was the champion of universal truths, untainted by the passions of race, class, or nation, and unconcerned with purely pragmatic ends.[184] But despite this difference, *La nouvelle revue française* did agree with Benda that manifestations of "spirit" or intelligence, be they in science, philosophy, or art, should not be construed as "national."[185]

Another major theme of the journal, once again in direct confrontation with Action Française, concerned aesthetics, specifically "the classic," and how it ought to be construed. *La nouvelle revue française*, claiming the universality of classic art, was in strong opposition to the "Maurrasian" conception of the classic as tied to national values.[186] Jacques Rivière, in *La nouvelle revue française*, did foresee a "Renaissance classique," but one that was "non textuelle et de pure imitation," in the manner of Moréas and *La revue critique*; its "Renaissance" was more profound, being rooted in the "authentic" claims of intelligence, now in the process of resuming its rights, or its ties to universal values after the war.[187] This was a classicism founded upon the "critical spirit," or untrammeled intellectual inquiry, as opposed to nationalist classicism based upon imposed and rigid models. Such "revolutionary classicism" was one of "regeneration," as opposed to "order," one of "revolt" unity, progress, and the universal, hence "le vrai classicisme."[188] Even during the war, some republican scholars had stolidly promoted classicism as incarnating "truth and justice, reason and liberty," as in ancient Greece.[189] But again, the Left espoused no rigid "model," rather advocating a set of values, primary among which, as we have seen, were not only the simple and essential, but the universal, the critical spirit, and independence.

Such was the classicism that was being promoted by the collaborators of *La nouvelle revue française*, who included, perhaps most prominently, the writers André Gide and Paul Claudel.[190] Claudel, however, now at the summit of his fame, was no longer the incarnation of "the new": the relay, ostensibly, was being assumed by Valéry, Gide, and Proust.[191] But as one might expect, most of the authors who were associated with the journal soon became targets for Action Française and its many powerful associated publications.[192]

Particularly provocative was the support of La nouvelle revue française not only for a "Greek," or universalist, as opposed to "Latin," or nationalist classicism, but also for modernist Dada.[193] For it perceived the movement as another mode (in addition to revolutionary or "critical" classicism) of confronting or critiquing the postwar order, and its artistic and nationalist pieties. Indeed, many members of the Dada movement were sympathetic to leftist politics, since most artistic journals prone to conventional classicism, as we have noted, were politically anchored to the Right.

All these conflicts would soon be refracted in the French musical world, where we will find not only contestatory classicisms but political confrontation within the avant-garde. Here it significant to note that one of the leading progressive French musical journals, La revue musicale (which we will soon examine) was taken over, after the war, by La nouvelle revue française. Indeed according to Francis Poulenc, in a letter to Stravinsky of 9 July 1922, the circle of La revue musicale was "normalien," or dominated by those who had attended the illustrious Ecole Normale Supérieure, as was the group at La nouvelle revue française.[194] La revue musicale, like its "parent journal," was decidedly internationalist: under the direction of its founder, Henry Prunières (a former student of Romain Rolland), it organized a series of concerts that promoted new European music from 1922 to 1924. The "Concerts de La revue musicale," held in the Théâtre du Vieux Colombier, presented French and foreign works of both past and present, with emphasis on those composers who were forgotten, unknown, or rarely played. This prominently included Arnold Schoenberg, who was also being promoted intrepidly by other innovative, independent performance societies, despite the dominant tide.[195] However, Jean Cocteau, while indisputably avant-garde, professed an aesthetic which contested such internationalism, being bound to the "liberal" or socially conservative but culturally progressive Right. Hence he would be frequently attacked in the pages of La nouvelle revue française, and in turn would be opposed not only to many of its authors, but to the musical ideals that its "sister journal" espoused.

SYNDICALISM, MUSIC, AND THE FÊTES DU PEUPLE

Confrontation with the postwar order occurred not only in composition and print, but also through politicized concerts that entered into dialogue with those of conservative republicans and Action Française. These too would become an integral part of the complex configuration of postwar musical culture, a political culture of which musicians were aware, and in which some actively participated.[196] Such overtly politicized concerts were not generally avant-garde, but they did play a central role in assigning new political significance to musical works of both French and foreign composers. Here too canonical works were being "framed" and thus appropriated in a manner substantially different from that which we have observed in the context of both the wartime and postwar Right.

The most prominent effort of the Left to arrive at a politically charged construction of great musical works through control of the performative context took place through the syndicalist Fêtes du Peuple. Formed shortly before the outbreak of war, in the spring of 1914, by Albert Doyen, a committed "man of the Left" and protégé of Gustave Charpentier, they then remained dormant until 1919. Their goal was patently universalist, and indeed the first performance, in 1914, sponsored by the Bataille Syndicaliste, had been intended as a fraternal, antiwar demonstration.[197]

After the war, one motto of the group, the heart of which was a large mixed chorus of about 250, continued to be "L'affranchissement des hommes" (The emancipation of men), meaning physical, intellectual, and spiritual freedom.[198] The other prominent motto, significantly borrowed from a key work of their repertoire, Wagner's *Die Meistersinger*, was, appropriately, "Art et peuple fleurissent ensemble" (Art and the people flourish together). Their social and political goal was to be attained through the combination of leisure, education, and culture, which would also provide access to the illustrious patrimony and thus to the political life of the nation.

Here it is important to remember that in France, as opposed to Germany, the belief endured that entry into the nation's political culture could be attained not only through education, but also through access to "high culture." For culture was less socially stratified in France: the fact that Socialists and Communists were less unified than in Germany had thwarted the development of a distinctive working-class culture. In addition, we must recall that the culture of Socialism in France traditionally owed far less to Marx than to the indigenous legacies of both Proudhon and Fourier. Although some historians have argued that its cultural proximity to other, more "bourgeois," groups is a sign of the quelling of social agitation and a return to "elitism," this is a misleading view.[199] The French working-class ideal of entering into traditional high culture did not necessarily imply that its manner of appropriating such culture was identical to that of the other classes. In the Fêtes, for example, the musical works were carefully framed—sometimes performed with substitute texts, and frequently juxtaposed with apt poetic or political readings. This, together with the presence of a vast working-class audience, served to mediate the experience of the works performed, inscribing them with specific social and political connotations or resonances. In the tradition of the Socialist leader Jean Jaurès, art was here a vehicle to transform the people, even if the art selected was not always in accordance with the current tastes of the audience.[200]

The first season of the Fêtes du Peuple, after the war, culminated grandiosely at the Trocadéro, with a Fête du Souvenir in memory of both Jaurès (assassinated in 1914) and those killed in the war. Significantly, the pieces performed included works of Richard Wagner, whose music, as we have seen, was now the subject of febrile controversy within the Right.[201] But the Fêtes had performed Wagner even before the war, when it had presented the last scene of *Die Meistersinger* at an antiwar rally; it here was meant to connote not nationalism, but the universal solidarity of workers.[202] The first Fête after the war included a performance of the funeral march from *Gotterdämmerung*, intended now to invoke the memory of all those killed in the war.

Since the dead included the former enemy, the rest of the program boldly incorporated German and Austrian works, as well as French compositions. At a time of continuing controversy over repertoire, the Left was taking the initiative symbolically, not only reintegrating Germanic works, but ascribing to them universal values. The compositions performed included a Bach prelude, Franck's *Redemption* and Third Chorale, as well as the symbolically protean choral finale of Beethoven's Ninth Symphony. Again, accompanying these works, to "frame" them, or to serve as "hermeneutic windows," were readings from the writings of (among others) Jean Jaurès, Anatole France, and the Austrian (and Jewish) Stephan Zweig.[203] These were intended to "illuminate" the topical meaning of the compositions performed, to imbue them with politically semantic qualities, even more powerfully than the preconcert lectures employed by the Right.

In order further to assert its presence in the midst of the dominant postwar conservatism, the Fêtes celebrated its founding, on 12 December 1919, under their banner "Art and the People Flourish Together."[204] Such a theme is indeed characteristic of the group's founder, Albert Doyen, and his circle, which included not only Gustave Charpentier, but leading French intellectuals and artists on the Left. Those who gathered in Doyen's studio in the Rue de Caulaincourt (in Montmartre) included the doctor and writer Georges Duhamel and the Swiss proponent of eurhythmics E. Jacques-Dalcroze.[205] The latter's message could be indeed construed ideologically in a diversity of ways, as could one of the principal conceptions associated with eurhythmics—"order." While the Right emphasized the collective, "orderly" community-forming potential of eurhythmics, the Left stressed its role in self-mastery, or the development of the individual person.[206]

The rational individual, with all his or her rights, yet still within the larger collectivity, had been a central concept of the Left in France since the time of the French Revolution. In *L'esprit nouveau*, in 1920, Jacques-Dalcroze published an article that undoubtedly pleased Doyen and the Left, "Un nouvel idéal musical." Here he stresses classic values, but not with the authoritarian connotation of the dominant discourse; rather he emphasizes feeling and "fantasy"—"une architecture satisfaisant à la fois aux besoins de la fantaisie émotive et aux exigences de l'ordre" (an architecture that satisfies at the same time the needs of emotive fantasy and the exigencies of order).[207] We find a similar dual emphasis on individuality and order in Doyen's Fêtes, in addition to his and the organization's stress on the memory of the French Revolution—still a resonant symbol for the French Left.

Despite the provocative beginnings of the Fêtes (in which the still politically suspect Free Masons also collaborated), from the period of the Cartel des Gauches on, they received official subventions, which steadily continued to mount.[208] One of the primary reasons that the Cartel may well have supported the Fêtes, in addition to their political connotations, was its interest in promoting "order"—to counteract the agitation of antiparliamentary leagues that began when it assumed power. Some of these leagues, as we noted earlier, were openly fascist, and there was ostensible fear that such groups could recruit among the French working class, as had occurred in Italy.

This may also have been the reason why the more moderate Right, when it returned to power with the government of National Union, in 1926, continued to support the Fêtes.[209] In fact, in 1926 it was considered to be a legitimate *société musicale* in the budget (like the Société Nationale) and received the relatively generous sum of four thousand francs. This was renewed for the next two years, and with the improving financial situation in France in 1929 and 1930, it was augmented to five thousand francs.[210] Indeed, it became so "legitimate" that now it was considered a part of the French musical world, and even socially conservative journals like *Comoedia* regularly reported on its concerts. This was true of the concert of 12 January 1923, when the group performed works of Berlioz, Rimsky-Korsakov, Chabrier, Saint-Saëns, Borodin, and Schumann, after a reading of poems by Paul Fort. Despite the dominant ideology of the French classic canon, there was clearly a desire to hear other repertoire, which the Left could easily justify performing, thus attracting a broad general audience.

There were, however, more radical interpretations of the Fêtes on the French Far Left, in journals such as the now Communist *L'humanité*, which stressed that part of its repertoire that was associated with the French Revolution. In January 1924, several months before the Cartel triumphed, the journal reported on the forthcoming program of 20 January, on which Gossec's "Hymne du 20 Prairial"— not heard since Robespierre's "Fête de l'Etre Suprême"—would be performed. The programming of such a work was ostensibly an attempt to liken the Fêtes du Peuple to the Revolutionary fête, thus reinforcing the association of the Left with the French Revolution. But apparently the attempt to impose musical taste on the basis of ideology proved as unsuccessful for the French Far Left as it had been for the Right. Despite the presence of romantic works on the program (including Schubert, Mendelssohn, and Schumann), on 24 January *L'humanité* reported the paltry attendance for the performance of Gossec's composition.

But *L'humanité* continued to support the Fêtes; indeed, one could buy tickets at the office of the paper, and for the relatively modest price, in the period, of around three francs. But by 4 February 1924, it was stressing the financial problems being faced by the Fêtes and requesting funds on its behalf—a request that would soon be met officially, following the election of the Cartel des Gauches.[211] In the meantime, the Fêtes du Peuple was forced to enter the commercial French musical world, presenting a concert of "modern" French music (centering on Saint-Saëns, Fauré, Debussy, and Ravel) at the Salle Pleyel on 16 February 1924.

The Fêtes du Peuple, like so many other musical organizations of this period in France, was here precariously situated on the border between the political and commercial musical worlds. As such, its choice of repertoire had to balance ideological concerns with concessions not only to public taste, but to the limited performing capacities of the participants. Unlike the Orphéons, however, its choral group was not "segregated" within the musical world, competing only against similar groups, under government supervision, and with a repertoire tailored to its amateur capacities. Yet the Fêtes were still part of the phenomenon that Benda observed—the politicization of all cultural spheres in the twenties, or the subordination of culture to the interests of race, nation, or class. Here the initiatives of the government and the Right were being met with a homologous program on the Left, which further assigned political significance to the respective repertoires that each performed.

The repertoire of the Fêtes du Peuple is particularly revealing in this respect, for in it we may discern which composers, periods, and works were symbolically resonant for the Left. Its focus was decidedly not on the seventeenth- and eighteenth-century French classic tradition, but rather on the revolutionary period, on composers who carried "populist" associations (due to previous ideological efforts) and the romantic repertoire, including both Austrian and German composers.[212] The group's taste was not yet "advanced" enough to include more contemporary French and foreign works—this would occur with the Popular Front and its more progressive programs in the 1930s, which would build on the foundations laid here and on the example of the Weimar Republic.

At the Fêtes du Peuple one could rather hear compositions such as Méhul's "Hymne à la raison" (now with particular resonance for the Left), excerpts from his opéra comique, *Joseph*, and a chorus from Handel's *Judas Macabeus*.[213] Also performed were Charpentier's *La vie du poète*, the "Spinning Chorus" from Wagner's *The Flying Dutchman*, Saint-Saëns's "Chanson du grand-père," and the nineteenth-century Russian repertoire, including Borodin's "Polivezian Dances" from *Prince Igor* and the Russian popular song, "The Vulga Boatmen." The contemporary Soviet composers would not be performed in such musical-social contexts before the more artistically advanced efforts of the Popular Front in the following decade.

The repertoire, however, did not neglect the distant French past and even included two chansons by the Renaissance composer, Clément Janequin. The significance of such works, once again, stems from the period before the war when the left-republican canon embraced the French secular Renaissance repertoire, as opposed to the emphasis on religious polyphony at the Schola Cantorum. But the Left, just as the Right, also reappropriated compositions from its political adversaries, attempting to reorient their meaning, or redefine their established ideological associations. The fêtes thus performed not only two choruses by Louis Bourgault-Ducoudray (professor of music history at the Conservatoire before the war and close to Action Française), but a work of Vincent d'Indy, his "Lied maritime."[214]

What, then, was the larger message intended by such a program and such a repertoire? The goal of the Fêtes du Peuple, like other similar organizations of the Left, was to form a new community, to project a France that was socially and culturally defined more broadly. In its concerts with readings it thus attempted to create or affect a liminal social realm, as opposed to the static, tautological ceremonies and performances of the conservative postwar Republic. And so the Left experimented with other projects as well, although in some cases with less success, as in that of the revival of Charpentier's *Le couronnement de la muse du peuple*, which dated from the later nineteenth century.[215] For Charpentier continued to be active and prominent with his syndicalist activities, as well as with his Oeuvre de Mimi Pinson, to which he added his charitable Oeuvre des Vieux Musiciens. His final opera, *Duthoit*, completed after the war, is, according to Manfred Kelkel, informed with a renewed belief in anarcho-syndicalism.[216]

Having been performed all over the country, Charpentier's fête, *Le couronnement de la muse*, was again presented in 1925 (during the Cartel des Gauches) through the efforts of the syndicalist Left. Here what had begun within the context of the musical world of the turn of the century was appropriated politically, first by the "Dreyfusard Republic," and now by the syndicalist movement. The performance itself was the result of the initiative of the syndicalists' Comité des Fêtes, for the profit of the wards of the nation (presumably the many orphans left by the war). Charpentier had become a prominent supporter of French syndicalism, and himself had prepared the music that was performed at Jaurès's reburial in the Panthéon in 1924.[217] A leading figure in the French musical world, serving on important committees, as we have seen, he was also a political celebrity, known for his support for leftist causes in general.

Charpentier, by now, was accustomed to the political use and misuse of his works: *Louise* had (wrongly) been interpreted as Dreyfusard at the time of the Dreyfus affair, and as "patriotic" during World War I.[218] Here its central spectacle was endowed with a syndicalist interpretation, as we may see in the "explication" of it in the syndicalist daily, *Le peuple*, on 15 July 1925. As the paper reports, the performance took place in the Tuileries gardens, with a stage that was dominated visually by a huge and grandiose throne. The author of the article, Marc Lap, proceeds to interpret the work in a manner that is far more serious and politically literal than Charpentier ever intended it. That which the composer originally conceived in an ironic tone, within the framework of a drama, here assumes another level of meaning, presented in this very different context.[219] Lap, for example, describes the sounds of trumpets and other brasses not as an ironic commentary, but as "l'espoir des temps nouveaux auxquels s'oppose l'implacable destin des hommes" (the hope of new times to which is opposed the implacable destiny of men). The facetious "Cortège" of the Muse that follows he interprets as the bringing of art to the people, with the theme here being "L'art est né pour le peuple. . . . A l'ouvrier de le reprendre" (Art was born for the people. . . . It is up to the worker to reclaim it).[220]

Recalling the disquieting implications of the circus performers in *Parade*, Lap describes the appearance of Pierrot—dressed in black, in the midst of all the movement, as an apparition, or the "le spectre de malheur" (the apparition of misfortune). Pierrot proceeds to mime "l'éternelle souffrance, le travail de l'esclave, la grande douleur humaine" (eternal suffering, the work of the slave, the great human pain), all clearly evocative of the working class. He then mounts the throne of the Muse and throws himself pathetically at her feet; but she lifts him up, symbolizing the reconciliation of the people and art, and the people sing: "Gloire à toi! Soeur de détresse / des innombrables opprimés! / Tendre promesse / d'une meilleure humanité" (Glory to you! Sister of distress / of the innumerable oppressed! / Tender promise / of a better humanity). Finally, at the conclusion of the work, and in the name of "la République de Montmartre," a noted chansonnier presents "des petits poulbots héroïques" (the heroic little street urchins) to the audience.[221]

Such a political appropriation of art by the Left was not rare in the 1920s, and it even extended, in subtler forms, to "pure music," or nontheatrical, untexted works. This we may observe in the review of "Les Grands Concerts" in *L'humanité*, on 28 February 1924, by Georges Chennevière. Here he discusses André Gédalge, the former Conservatoire professor, and his Symphony no. 3 (1905–6). It is perhaps significant that the work was one that Gédalge had pointedly defined against the Scholiste model by appending the motto "Ni littérature ni peinture."[222] Chennevière's review emphasizes the classical traits of Gédalge's work (although without using the term), stressing the qualities of "intelligence," workmanship, and discipline:

> A. [André] Gédalge, musicien, nous livre un travail fort de main ouvrier, une symphonie bien construite, dont les développements sont réglés par une intelligence lucide et nourrie par les sentiments d'une âme noble. . . . Son plan est net, facile à suivre. Son édifice tient debout. . . . Je ne sache pas que le génie ait jamais eu à souffrir de l'école, où de l'obéissance à un style. Bien au contraire, l'enseignement fait les miracles et la discipline l'aide à économiser ses forces."[223] (A. Gédalge, musician, delivers us a strong work from the hand of a worker, a well-constructed symphony, whose developments are regulated by a lucid intelligence and nourished by the feelings of a noble soul. . . . His plan is clear, easy to follow. His edifice stands up. . . . I do not think that genius ever had to suffer from school or from obeisance to a style. To the contrary, teaching can do miracles and discipline aids in economizing forces.)

Clearly important for Chennevière is access to public instruction, honest intellectual labor, and conscientious craftsmanship. The review concludes with praise of the efforts of other musicians, including Albert Doyen, and an explicit statement of the need for "discipline" in the present, or for the avoidance of "anarchy." This again recalls the themes of conservatives that we have examined, except that the implication here is the construction of a "new" social order as the goal. For the critic, it is discipline that "unifierait les efforts dispersés, leur donnerait un sens et substituerait à l'anarchie un régime d'autorité salutaire" (will unify the dispersed efforts, give them a meaning and will substitute a regime of healthy authority for anarchy).[224] As in the theories of Jacques-Dalcroze, music remains a means to achieve self-discipline, in the interests not only of the collectivity itself, but equally of the individual participating in it.

Because of this sense of the utility of music, performing organizations continued to pullulate on the Left, and as opposed to those on the right, were aimed at the amateur musician as participant. For music to them was less a means to "illustrate" ideology than to "participate" in it, and thus to aid in the realization of the new community now being sought. On 28 January 1924, for example, *L'humanité* announced a call for participants in an amateur instrumental ensemble that had recently been reborn. Created in 1910, with the name Harmonie Socialiste du 12e [Arrondissement], it was now an ensemble of forty, under the direction of M. Taglione. The announcement explicitly invites the participation in the ensemble of "les camarades musciens syndicalistes, communistes et sympathisants" (comrade musicians who are syndicalist, communist, or sympathizers). Clearly the nineteenth-century Fourierist metaphor of "harmony" was still in place, and music remained a powerful symbol and agent of unity for the French Left.[225]

For some composers this was a compelling image, but French composers responded to the political-cultural appeals of the government and of its adversaries diversely, on the basis of generation and their reactions to the issues. The cultural issues they faced all carried political implications in the context, for how to relate to the past and to define the national culture, and specifically "classicism," implied a political orientation. Members of the older generation would not skirt such questions—their political consciousness had been raised by the war, but they commented on them indirectly, through symbols, gestures, and style.

Part 2: French Composers as Intellectuals and the Issues

THE OLDER GENERATION AND ITS CHOICES

The wartime augmentation of state intervention in culture, as well as the concomitant application of techniques of inscribing political meaning in style, continued long after the war. This encouraged the political opposition's responses to the postwar government in kind, or through the language of aesthetics and cultural programs, including music. Hence, with the return of open political opposition after the war, despite continuing censorship, the options of composers, in their choice of cultural models or symbols, were broader: they could conform to official expectations or seek alternative styles and sponsors.[226] Those who were older would make their choices between ideological conformity or alliance with opposition groupings and their programs, while youth, rebelling culturally, would only gradually realize the full political implications of their gestures.

Few French composers of the older generation, or those who had experienced the war as adults, would have countered Julien Benda's observation that "all" in the postwar era had waxed political. As Benda perceived, it was not only within the political, moral, and intellectual fields that the "passions" of nation, race, and class now predominated, but in the realm of the aesthetic as well.[227] Contestatory political parties, unions, and leagues were belligerently confronting each other's political principles with the "weapons" of language, philosophy, literature, and the arts. Nationalists, Communists, and Fascist sympathizers had all energetically implicated culture, which, according to Benda, led many artists to perceive their interests at stake, and thus become consumed by such passions.[228] Already sensitized to French cultural propaganda, the older generation, which had lived through the war as adults, was indeed attuned to both the political issues and the manner in which they impacted aesthetic values in art.

Musicians were well aware that political groupings across the full spectrum had either elaborated an aesthetic of musical classicism, a cultural program involving music, or both. The older generation, which had experienced many of the projects born of wartime propaganda, knew the sophisticated manner in which music could be "mediated" to inscribe it obliquely with French nationalist values. For some, this experience of politics through culture was *the* politicizing experience itself, compelling them to join parties, make symbolic gestures, resist certain mediations, and even modify their style. The latter they did subtly, through meaningful inflections within the dominant neoclassicism, employing those elements, or rejecting those values most clearly inscribed with ideological significance. The challenge was both technical and ideological, for although most accepted what was considered to be the "national style," they had to find interest and meaning within it in both an ideologically and aesthetically honest manner.[229]

D'INDY: INNOVATION VERSUS DOGMA

For composers with political sympathies on the Right, the range of possibilities was capacious, extending from the "modernism" of the progressive or liberal Right (of Cocteau and Maritain) to the rigid classicism of traditionalist factions.[230] Saint-Saëns's political position had become centrist republican, which was, in essence, now to the Right, and may be seen in his acerbic reaction to the strikes by the Confédération Générale du Travail (CGT) in 1920. As reported in *Comoedia* on 21 January 1920, he prohibited striking artists at the Opéra from performing his works during their "représentations populaires" that took place at the seat of the CGT, just outside Paris. As Saint-Saëns himself asked rhetorically, would we have won the war if, before going into battle, officers and soldiers went on strike? For Saint-Saëns, the "system of strikes" was leading to universal ruin, and this, together with his traditionally classicizing style, led to his classification as "conservative."[231]

D'Indy, his nemesis in certain ideological issues, remained firmly within the traditionalist camp, and like other such conservatives frequently struck out against French youth and the "dangerous" new directions they were taking, to the neglect of both the distant and recent past. While admiring their commitment to their principles, he nevertheless expressed his deep concern that they were ignorant of the art of composition, believing that all that came before was now unequivocally "dead."[232]

Even more trenchant, however, was d'Indy's attack on the music of Arnold Schoenberg in his response to a survey on the current state of French music, in *Comoedia* in 1928. Speaking of Schoenberg and those whom he influenced, he writes: "Pour gagner de l'argent, pour attirer l'attention sur eux, ils font du bruit, non de la musique." (To earn money, to draw attention to themselves, they make noise, not music.)[233] His attack on Schoenberg is thus rhetorically similar to his earlier attack on Meyerbeer: their primary goal, as avaricious and uncreative Jews, is to attract publicity and thus make money from their art (an argument that had been employed by Wagner).

Yet d'Indy was game and open enough to attend a Dada session in Paris, although his response was pure bewilderment, as he described in a letter to Auguste Sérieyx: "J'en suis revenu sans avoir besoin d'être interné a Bicêtre, ce qui prouva en faveur de ma résistance intellectuelle" (I came back without having to be interned in Bicêtre [the psychiatric hospital just outside Paris], which proved in favor of my intellectual resistance).[234]

Resistant he was: throughout this period d'Indy continued implacably to defend Richard Wagner, and once again employed explicitly racial, anti-Semitic rhetoric to do so. To inaugurate a new collection by the publisher, Delagrave, "Les Grands musiciens par les maîtres d'aujourd'hui," d'Indy wrote a small volume titled *Richard Wagner et son influence sur l'art musical d'aujourd'hui*.[235] The book is, in a sense, the theoretical complement to *La légende de Saint Christophe*, for at its core is another extensive, thinly veiled anti-Semitic tract. Here, once more, d'Indy adamantly argues that Wagner "saved" French music from the Jews, who had invaded nineteenth-century opera, rerouting it from its own national tradition. Concomitantly, he again repeats that "la race hébraïque," which is otherwise unquestionably endowed with "serious qualities," has always been unable to be truly creative in art. The Jew, he continues (echoing Wagner) posses a gift for assimilation which allows him to produce amazing imitations, as evidenced by Auber, Hérold, Félicien David, and Offenbach.[236]

The implication, of course, is that the assimilation of Jews is, in fact, never "complete," for by their very racial nature they are inherently incapable of fully entering into French culture. A German genius like Wagner, whose "classic" model may be adapted to the traditions of French culture, can thus exercise a salubrious influence by counteracting the noxious traits of the French Jew. Anticipating the argument that became characteristic of the late 1930s and of the Vichy regime, he alleges, as evidence, that Debussy's art issued from Wagner's. While Cocteau would concur, although perceiving this as a fault, d'Indy, conversely, construes it as a merit, arguing that in *Pelléas* Debussy adapted Wagner's techniques in a French manner, stressing clarity and declamation.[237]

Now, more than ever, d'Indy expressed his opinions concerning matters that he perceived (correctly) as being simultaneously of political and of musical concern in France. One example is his article published in January 1923 in *Comoedia* on the subject of the still active working men's choral societies, or Orphéons.[238] Here d'Indy acutely perceives the way in which official support for such choral groups was unambiguously subtended by specific political or ideological agendas or interests.[239] In a paternal, hierarchical, and aristocratic manner, d'Indy still firmly believed that the goal of societies such as the Orphéons should be exclusively to help elevate the base "esprit populaire."

If d'Indy's political opinions had not changed, his position in the social world clearly had, as his personal fortune began to dwindle in the decade following the war. For the first time in his life, the proud, beneficent, and independent aristocrat now began, like so many others, to experience pressing financial difficulties. Moreover, long a widower, he now remarried, to a much younger woman from a substantially lower social class, to the dismay of his family and friends.[240] And as his popularity with the public began to decline in the course of the twenties, his musical style underwent an evident and surprising change. In keeping with the tendency of his time, his style was becoming more economical, and by the second half of the decade was even participating in more contemporary classic trends.[241]

But all were surprised even further when d'Indy decided to write an opéra bouffe—a genre recalling Offenbach and thus maligned as "impure" on the right. *Le Rêve de Cinyras*, with a text by Xavier de Courville, was an authentic comic opera that some nationalists vindicated as being animated by the traditional French sense of gaiety and parody.[242] Despite such justifications, in reality d'Indy was forced down from the lofty heights of idealism by the pragmatic necessity he once decried—of making money, or a living from his art.

Yet despite the fact that d'Indy's reactionary opinions increasingly were being ridiculed by youth, and his music was largely considered out of date, he was bestowed with official honors at the end of the decade. On the occasion of his seventy-eighth birthday, on 24 March 1929, Gabriel Pierné conducted a program composed entirely of d'Indy's works. Like Debussy, long a critic of the French official and academic worlds, he too grew closer to the more conservative Republic, and ended up accepting its honors. An official reception followed the performance, and, significantly, in attendance, as a tribute to d'Indy's position, prestige, and contribution, was the director of the Beaux-Arts.[243] Now reconciled with the Republic, d'Indy would die of a heart attack in 1931, his music neglected, but soon to be rediscovered by a new French Right at the end of the decade.

RAVEL: REASSERTING THE UNIVERSAL AND THE MODERN

If d'Indy was the most prominent French composer to espouse the dominant postwar order, then Ravel was precisely his opposite—its unremitting critic in practically every respect. Like d'Indy during the period of the Dreyfus affair, Ravel now sought ideological expression for the cultural position he gradually defined for himself in the course of the war. As we have seen, this was one that implacably rejected uncritical nationalism as well as the narrow official dogma concerning French culture and all that it excludes. Ravel's ideal of French patriotism was firmly rooted in the traditional republican, ultimately revolutionary conception of individual responsibility, founded unequivocally in human reason.[244]

While fellow members of the Société Musicale Indépendante, such as Emile Vuillermoz and Florent Schmitt, now rejected the political implications of their cultural independence before the war, Ravel unequivocally did not. His response to the postwar climate and to the cultural orthodoxies that we have examined was to assume the intellectually critical role that we have identified with the Left. Ravel became engaged with ideological issues, but subtly, on a symbolic level, and through gestures that can only be understood fully within the context that we have examined.

The fact that Ravel had Socialist sympathies, subscribing only to the Socialist *Le populaire de Paris*, and frequented Socialist politicians like Léon Blum and Paul Painlevé, reveals just one level of his engagement.[245] As Arbie Orenstein has observed, Ravel's social origins were in the lower middle class, but in the course of his career he gradually moved into the upper middle class, or "bourgeoisie."[246] It may have been his contact with the working class during the war, and under such dire conditions, that awakened his sense of his origins, and thus of social solidarity with workers. Manuel Rosenthal points out emphatically in his memoirs about Ravel, "Il était ce qu'on appellerait aujourd'hui un homme de gauche" (he was what one today would call a man of the Left).[247]

Ravel's cultural gestures, choices, and proclivities in the postwar period are as telling as his reading, and reveal a consistent consonance with the cultural ideals of the contemporary Left. To perceive this we must examine his reaction to "hypernationalism," "particularism," and his response to foreign cultural influences (especially those of Austria and Germany). We must also consider his reaction to racial issues and to French colonialism, in addition to the literary circles he frequented and the kind of classicism that he embraced. Ravel's choices in these areas were not arbitrary; rather, they were highly consistent ideologically and reveal some of the motivating forces behind his artistic decisions or tendencies throughout these years.

Ravel's political gestures were many. Not only did he assiduously read the French Socialist press, he frequented the salon of M. and Mme Paul Clemenceau, as did (among others) Albert Einstein, Paul Painlevé, and Stefan Zweig.[248] Significantly, Mme Clemenceau was born Sophie Szeps, daughter of a friend of the Archduke Francis-Ferdinand and thus close to Austrian and German intellectual and artistic circles. And in a period of widespread anti-Semitism he remained close friends with Mme Fernand Dreyfus, as well as with Ida Rubenstein, who extended her financial assistance to him whenever it was needed.[249] In fact, in 1920 (the year of the premiere of d'Indy's *La légende de Saint Christophe*) Ravel made an orchestral version of his *Mélodies hébraïques*, which were performed at the Concerts Pasdeloup on 17 April 1920.[250] Manuel Rosenthal noted that because Ravel was so frequently surrounded by Jewish friends that many came wrongly to assume that he himself was Jewish.[251]

Just as iconoclastic in this period was Ravel's acknowledged artistic interest in composers who were not only Jewish, but from the still proscribed "enemy nations," Austria and Germany. Ravel continued to admire Gustav Mahler, and even met his widow, Alma; indeed, works like *La valse*, of 1919 (inspired by the Viennese waltz) reveal Ravel's attraction to Mahler's poignant, ironic vision, and technique of powerfully distorting banal themes.[252] As Ravel put it, the project that he initially conceived in 1906 had taken a substantially different turn by the end of World War I: "J'ai conçu cette oeuvre comme une espèce d'apothéose de la valse viennoise à laquelle se mêle, dans mon esprit, l'impression d'un tournoiement fantastique et fatal. Je situe cette valse dans le cadre d'un palais impérial, environ 1855." (I conceived this work as a kind of apotheosis of the Viennese waltz with which was mingled, in my mind, the impression of a fantastic and fatal whirling. I situate this waltz in the context of an imperial palace, around 1855.)[253]

In 1918 Diaghilev accepted the idea of a ballet after Ravel's proposed "Wien"—originally a "poème symphonique," that would become *La valse* in 1919. Diaghilev, having commissioned the ballet, was undoubtedly wary of having the work named "Wien" in the still bellicose, xenophobic postwar climate.[254] If the work now assumed a tragic cast, it was most likely the tragedy of the recent war it reflected, as devastating and horrific for the former enemy, Austria, as it was for France. Carl Schorske's brilliant reading of the work as recording "the violent death of the nineteenth-century world" rings true, as does Ravel's statement about his association of it with "a fantastic whirl of destiny."[255]

Despite the "ban" on all things associated with the former Austro-Hungarian Empire, Ravel persisted in his interest in its musical culture of both past and present. In a letter of 3 October 1924, he not only requests a copy of Liszt's *Hungarian Rhapsodies*, but that one of his photographs be sent to a publisher in Vienna, who wanted it for a lexicon.[256] This was indeed a bold gesture at a time when all cultural communication was essentially cut off within official and conservative circles between France and its former wartime enemies. Of equal temerity in this bellicose climate was Ravel's completion, in 1925, of, as he put it, his own "rhapsodie hongroise," referring to *Tzigane*.[257]

But Ravel made even more aggressive gestures. At a time when contemporary German and Austrian music was still considered "boche" and dangerous, he openly championed the work of Arnold Schoenberg. In his autobiographical sketch, "Ma vie et ma musique," published in *La revue musicale* after his death, Ravel avows the influence of Schoenberg's *Pierrot Lunaire* on his *Trois poèmes de Mallarmé* (1913). Ravel retained his interest in Schoenberg, even after it was professionally dangerous to do so, as we noted with regard to his response to the Ligue pour la Défense de la Musique Française during the war. Later, in 1927, when conservative sentiment was still strongly against Schoenberg and his influence, Ravel pressed the SMI (of which he was a vice president) to invite Schoenberg to present his works at two concerts of the society.[258] This was at a time when the still nationalist Société Nationale de Musique would permit the presence of foreign composers only from formerly allied or neutral countries.[259]

Ravel was indeed patriotic, but his patriotism, once more, was clearly that of the French political Left, which identified France with the Enlightenment ideal of universality.[260] As we have seen, for the Left this implied a patriotism that was tempered by sympathy, and thus an attitude of sadness at the end of the war, as opposed to triumph at having beaten the "boches." These attitudes would ineluctably come into play in Ravel's perhaps most defiant gesture: his public refusal of the Légion d'Honneur, when he was nominated after the war. This act, of course, like Ravel's other decisions, must be construed within the dense texture of his experience in several interacting cultural spheres: its coherence emerges only from the perspective of such complexity.

In early 1920 Ravel received a notice from Léon Bérard, in the Ministère de l'Instruction Publique, who wished to nominate him to be a Chevalier de la Légion d'Honneur.[261] Several years earlier, Ravel had specifically asked his friends that his candidacy not be proposed "in the way that it was presented," which, at the time, was undoubtedly in a chauvinistic context.[262] Now, however, Ravel was sent papers to fill out, and since he did not reply immediately the minister assumed tacit acceptance, and the award was listed in the *Journal Officiel* on 15 January 1920.

Ravel, however, refused to accept the award, and instead of personally explaining his reasons left it to his brother, Edouard, to do so in *Le temps*, which only raised further speculation. Edouard Ravel here elliptically made reference to purported "personal reasons," which his brother noted bemusedly only further intrigued the press.²⁶³ But Edouard's other statement, a quotation from Baudelaire's *Mon coeur mis à nu*, is far more revealing of Ravel's perhaps most fundamental motivation: "Consentir à être décoré, c'est reconnaître à l'Etat ou au Prince le droit de vous juger" (to consent to be decorated is to recognize the right of the state or the Prince to judge you).²⁶⁴

Several explanations of Ravel's refusal have been offered by contemporaries and historians: according to Manuel Rosenthal it was because so many had been killed in the war, and Ravel had not actually fought.²⁶⁵ Another theory is that Ravel had asked Painlevé to make sure that he was accepted into the army, but that nothing be said to his elderly mother, who was ill; yet she was told, and Ravel felt betrayed. Others cite his brother's (untrue) statement that Ravel was opposed to decorations, as well as his supposed resentment for having been refused the Prix de Rome five times by the Institut.²⁶⁶ But the most probable explanation, within the context that we have examined, relates to the quotation from Baudelaire concerning the legitimacy of the state in judging the artist.

Ravel's assessment of the postwar government and its policies was well known, particularly to his close circle of friends to whom he expressed his now "dangerous" political opinions. In the postwar climate of heightened nationalism and fear of revolution and anarchy, open expression of politically far left–wing views would have been risky, particularly for an artist. As Ravel confided to Roland-Manuel, in a highly revealing jest (in a letter of 22 January 1920) "un légionnaire n'a pas le droit d'être bolchevik et leur triomphe n'est tout de même pas une raison pour les lâcher" (a legionnaire does not have the right to be a bolchevik, and their triumph is not a reason to let them go).²⁶⁷ "Bolchevik" being a term now applied not only to the Communist Left in Russia, but in general to dissenters on the French Left, Ravel was evidently referring to his own refusal of orthodox postwar nationalism.

Like others with sympathies to the Left, Ravel perceived the war as, although justified in the beginning, having lasted too long, and with too much slaughter, and now distastefully being exalted in the name of "patriotism." Hence, in a letter to Marnold of 13 April 1920, Ravel complains that *L'ordre public* said precisely what it shouldn't—probably a reference to the phrase about "a host of courageous men wearing a red ribbon in their buttonhole."²⁶⁸ For it was apparent to many that the huge number of nominations for the Légion d'Honneur in 1920—some 2,071 for all grades—was related to wartime service, as a kind of patriotic recompense. In the same letter Ravel then pointed out that *L'humanité* made an intelligent statement regarding his refusal, saying (on 8 April 1920) that "a red ribbon will not bleed on his buttonhole. This distinction deserves another one."²⁶⁹ Ravel, then, refused to be decorated, in part, on the basis of association with the devastating war, which he perceived, with those on the Left, less as a French victory than as bloody and tragic.

In his works and style in these years Ravel made other gestures that are telling in the context—gestures of refusal of orthodoxies that he considered as repellent in culture as he did in politics. This applied to his appreciation of Mahler and to the daring theme of Vienna in the xenophobic culture of the early twenties, as well as to other foreign influences and subjects. According to Ravel his "fantaisie lyrique en deux actes" (to a text of Colette), L'enfant et les sortilèges (completed in 1925), was composed in the spirit of "l'opérette américaine."[270] In an era when it had become provocative for a French composer to manifest the influence of American popular culture, Ravel boldly represented jazz onstage, playfully associating it with a black teapot.[271]

As Ravel put it in a letter to Colette, "What do you think of a cup and a teapot, in old black Wedgewood, singing a ragtime? I confess that the idea of having two Negroes singing a ragtime at our National Academy of Music fills me with great joy."[272] Ravel thus defied a pronounced current of anti-Americanism coming from both the nationalists and the conservative center, which were both economically and culturally protectionist.[273]

But Ravel's playfully provocative marshalling of styles in the work is not limited to jazz—at a time of stress on French "purity," he invokes the "Oriental," but here also mocks colonialist Orientalism. The solo aria of the Chinese cup, for example, facetiously employs the typical parallel fourths and pentatonicism of the common stylistic reference to the Oriental.[274] Moreover, at the beginning of the work, Ravel consciously employs Oriental clichés to evoke an atmosphere of fantasy, especially through the color of the oboe, the pentatonic pitch material, and the open sonorities of the fifths and fourths.[275] Perhaps most clever and incisive, however, is Ravel's ridicule, through trivialization, of those styles still associated with d'Indy and the Schola Cantorum, whose reactionary stance Ravel had long loathed.[276] Here it is important to note that d'Indy's nationalist, pedantic, and overtly anti-Semitic opera, La légende de Saint Christophe, premiered at the time that Ravel was composing his work. As we may recall, d'Indy here didactically "deployed" those styles that the Schola associated with its conservative social philosophy—medieval organum and Renaissance sacred choral music.

These are precisely the styles that Ravel employs gloriously and skillfully, but absurdly so within the dramatic context, as in the final sublime a cappella fugue of the animals. In d'Indy's work such a style is marshaled when the chorus in the opera sings of the power of the cross to prevent sinners from damnation: Ravel employs it when the animals praise the good child. As Jankélévitch noted, this final chorus, "with its canon-like imitations and its seething superimposed voices reveals a polyphonist worthy of the masters of the Renaissance."[277] But Ravel goes even further in inverting the meaning of the Schola's "sacred" styles, employing medieval organum and making reference to the French baroque.[278] In the former case Ravel refers to early organum, along with the "Oriental," in order to suggest the naive fairy world of the child, thus provocatively conflating, not opposing, East and West. Just as perversely (for conservatives) he combines medieval organum with modernist techniques condemned at the Schola, including Stravinskian changing meters and Schoenbergian vocal glissandi. This confrontational symbolism, or syncretism, extends to the use of French baroque elements which, as in Le tombeau de Couperin, Ravel combines with stylistic suggestions of the non-French Scarlatti.[279] Other stylistic references include composers condemned at the Schola, such as Offenbach, Puccini, and Massenet, who for d'Indy were the products of pernicious Jewish influences—even those who were not Jewish, such as the latter two.[280]

Ravel acknowledged his amusing, subversive stylistic intentions in a letter to Roland-Manuel of 30 August 1920: "I can still assure you that this work, in 2 parts, will be distinguished by a mixture of styles which will be severely criticized, which leaves Colette indifferent, and me not caring a damn."[281] Ravel was indeed correct: when the work premiered at the Opéra-Comique on 21 March 1925 (during the Cartel des Gauches), disruptions by those offended predictably broke out. Although some critics in more conservative journals (such as Henry Malherbe in *Le temps*) did praise it, seeing "classicism" and spirited sensuality in the work, others were far less sanguine. The critic for *La liberté*, Robert Dezarnaux (writing on 3 February 1926), was clearly not amused by Ravel's ironic stylistic manipulations.[282]

But Ravel was undaunted by the criticism and continued his provocation, both in terms of style and choice of text, as in the case of the *Chansons madécasses*. Perhaps not coincidentally, this work was composed in 1925–26, just as colonialism was becoming the subject of torrid debate in France. André Gide would publish his devastating *Voyage au Congo* in 1927, but it appeared first in several issues of *La nouvelle revue française*. Ravel's old friend, Léon Blum, wrote two articles about the work in the paper to which Ravel subscribed (exclusively), the Socialist *Le populaire*.[283]

In this context it is significant that the text Ravel selected relates to a major theme of the French Left: blacks' mistreatment and thus justified resentment of whites. Ravel was indeed free to chose his own text, according to the commission of Elizabeth Sprague Coolidge (in 1925), although she strongly encouraged him to set it to the accompaniment of cello, piano, and flute. Ravel decided upon the *Chansons madécasses* (1787), by Evariste-Désiré de Pamy, who never went to Madagascar, but was influenced by the popular model of "Malagasy" poetry. The poems range from the sensual to the dangerously erotic, but the middle one specifically concerns European treachery, and thus the resentment and distrust of the African natives (see ex. 2).

Even more provocative was Ravel's acknowledgement of the influence of Schoenberg on the work, in particular the counterpoint and independence of parts, as in *Pierrot Lunaire*. Hence it is not surprising that the premiere of the *Chansons madécasses* provoked immediate scandal, particularly at a time not only of intensified anti-Semitism but of a war in Africa. The style was also an element here, for Ravel matches the violent imagery of the text with a high degree of dissonance and a predominantly declamatory writing in the vocal part.[284]

When writing of the work in his autobiographical sketch, Ravel, characteristically, discussed only the style. As he put it: "C'est une sorte de quatuor où la voix joue le rôle d'instrument principal. La simplicité y domine. L'indépendance des parties s'y affine que l'on trouvera plus marquée que dans la *Sonate*." (It is a sort of quartet where the voice plays the role of the principal instrument. Simplicity dominates. The independence of the parts, which one will find more marked than in the Sonata [for violin and cello], is here refined).[285] The fact that

EXAMPLES 2—Ravel, *Chansons madécasses*.

Ravel did not mention content in his works may well have been related to the aversion (typical of *La nouvelle revue française*) to overtly political projects in art after the "brainwashing" of the war. This also applies to his tart retort to the pamphlet and letter of Tenroc's wartime league, which referred to the economic and social role of music, with clearly bellicose intent within the content.

But, again, while *La nouvelle revue française* called for aesthetic autonomy, it eventually found this impossible within the context of the intellectual battle that the Left was now waging against the Right. Ravel, who repudiated most wartime propaganda, and saw the deleterious effects of blatant politics on art, rather attempted to communicate his positions through telling stylistic manipulations as well as through choice of texts. However, when discussing the *Chansons madécasses* in his autobiographical sketch, Ravel does point out the erotic element in them, something also considered "dangerous" in art music of the period. Ravel's subversion was always subtle, taking place on the level of symbols and gestures, which, as he well knew, could be even more powerful than conventional discursive confrontation.

Privately, Ravel was known to protest injustices, as in the case of his letter concerning Vuillemin's complaint in *Le courrier musical* (of 1 November 1925) that foreign artists (such as the Polish-Jewish Marya Freund) were awarded the Legion of Honor, while French artists (such as Louis Aubert) were overlooked.[286] In this context it is also significant to note that Ravel made plans for, but did not complete, what he described as "a large lyric work based on Joseph Delteil's *Jeanne d'Arc*."[287] Delteil, a surrealist, who became a Communist (later one of the first to be "expelled" from the party) wrote a work about the saint that implicitly entered into dialogue with the Jeanne d'Arc of the Right. Had Ravel completed the work, this too would have been one of his boldest gestures, made once again through choice of text within the specific ideological and political context. As it turned out, it was Ravel's pupil, Manuel Rosenthal, who set Delteil's *Jeanne d'Arc* (as a "Suite symphonique") in 1936, when the Popular Front assumed power.[288]

Political gestures through style were indeed frequent in Ravel, as we observed with regard to the influences on him, particularly at a time when the composers he emulated were being attacked by the conservative press. And, as we might expect, Ravel made other implicit statements through his treatment of classicism, allying himself with the classic values associated with the postwar Left. As we have seen, its classic doctrine proposed no "mold," but rather a set of priorities and concepts that were diametrically opposed to those associated with dominant "prescriptions." Prominent among these concepts was individual "autonomy," as opposed to collectivism or established formulae, as well as universality, or an openness to the riches of other cultures.

An example of such classicism is the small *Duo* that Ravel composed in 1920 in response to an invitation from *La revue musicale* (again, now in the hands of *La nouvelle revue française*) to contribute to a special issue in honor of Debussy. Ravel's Duo apparently derived its inspiration from Debussy's project (left uncompleted at the time of his death) of composing six sonatas for various combinations of instruments.[289] But Ravel thereafter developed his Duo into a full-scale sonata, his Sonata for Violin and Cello (1920–22), which he claimed marked a turning point in his style and career.

As Ravel himself described it: "Le dépouillement y est poussé à l'extrême. Renoncement au charme harmonique; réaction de plus en plus marquée dans le sens de la mélodie." (The spareness is here pushed to the extreme. Renunciation of harmonic charm; reaction, more and more marked, in the sense of the melody.)[290] But in addition, the sonata adheres to Ravel's own interpretation of classic form—one far closer to the independent approach of the Left than to the rigid "mold" of the conservative Right. For while its weight is concentrated on the first movement (in the high classic tradition), which adheres to the outlines of sonata form, it is far from a *sonate d'école*, developing not in the classical manner, but through a kind of contrapuntal evolution. The "Scherzo" suggests the rhythm of a childish round (as in Debussy's "Rondes du printemps" in his orchestral *Images*), and it returns again in the final "Ronde," which resembles a classical rondo form.

The latter movement, moreover, again in the manner of Debussy's *Rondes du printemps*, makes a perceptible allusion to a number of old French popular chansons.[291] As we will recall, Ravel had gone out of his way bravely to defend Debussy's *Rondes* when it was attacked (because of its distortions and irony) in the press. Here Ravel is just as irreverent toward the Scholiste classic mold and its concomitant "seriousness" as the composer he so admired, and who had inspired the original Duo. As in Ravel's other work of this period, the sonata is also characterized not only by its economy of means but by its occasional harmonically harsh or violent "exclamations."[292]

Even more pertinacious in its stylistic innovations was Ravel's Sonata for Violin and Piano, which was publicly premiered at the Salle Erard in 1927. Notable here is the clear jazz influence, which even the younger composers, Les Six, had by now renounced: Ravel still makes unmistakable reference to jazz, especially in the second movement, marked "Blues."[293] Also unorthodox for the period in general (aside from the avant-garde) is Ravel's use of bitonality, as well as frequent reference in the themes to blues-like gestures.[294]

How, then, was Ravel "classic"? This was a central issue now in music (just as in literature), and one that Ravel's friends addressed, perceiving in him a classicism that was not that of the Right. His classic iconoclasm, however, as we have seen, did not prevent Action Française from attempting to appropriate his work (like Debussy's before) by projecting its model onto selected compositions. Apparently in response to such malevolent appropriations, *La revue musicale* brought out an issue on Ravel in 1925, during the government of the leftist coalition, the Cartel des Gauches. It is in this special issue, devoted to Ravel, that Roland-Manuel emphasized the following classic qualities in his work: "Héritier des classiques français, il pratique à leur exemple l'imitation des anciens. Discipline rigoureuse qui détourne le créateur des séductions de l'arbitraire, le préserve des entreprises de l'ange du bizarre." (Inheritor of the French classics, he practices after their example the imitation of the ancients. Rigorous discipline that diverts the creator from the seductions of the arbitrary, preserves him from the enterprises of the angel of the bizarre.)[295] For Roland-Manuel, Ravel's classicism lies in his critical intelligence as well as in his rigorous discipline, after the model of the "ancients," and not according to d'Indy's dogmatic high classic "rules."[296] According to Roland-Manuel, then, Ravel "manifests" his values in the music, asserting, through his compelling stylistic synthesis and independence, the truth of "revolutionary classicism."

Roland-Manuel proceeds to draw a revealing comparison between Ravel and Stravinsky, who "se plaisent l'un et l'autre à confondre le 'beau' et 'l'utile'" (who both like to mingle the beautiful and the useful).[297] Here he was probably defending Ravel against the charges of critics like Henri Collet (as well as Les Six, whom Collet championed) against the charge of being "overrefined."[298] He was also attempting to protect Ravel from appropriation as a model of the classic values of the Right, which similarly admired his music, but projected substantially different qualities onto it. As we have noted, Action Française perceived "pure" Frenchness of spirit in his music—the absence of those foreign or modern German elements that Ravel, in fact, sincerely emulated. Many "themes" concerning Ravel could be and were applied to his work in the context, but their diversity should not blind us to the fact that most carried a thinly or more profoundly concealed agenda.

Yet it was because of the possibility of these different constructions, in addition to the appeal of Ravel's art, that he was already one of the most popular and performed of the living composers in France.[299] Less widely performed, but still subject to a dual appropriation by both Right and Left, was another composer who, in fact, now shared Ravel's political orientation. Erik Satie similarly solidified his ideological stance in the wake of the war and positioned his classicism on what would soon become the side of *La nouvelle revue française*.

SATIE AND LEFTIST INDIVIDUALISM: *SOCRATE*

Satie's response to the political injunction of classicism during the war had been to inflect the values associated with it in an ironic or facetious manner. But later, at the end of the war, he anticipated the redefinition of classicism that would be associated with the French Left—the return to the critical "spirit" of the ancient Greeks. The theme that Satie now embraced was one to which the Left would turn soon after the war: the duty of the individual conscience in the wake of wartime anti-individualism and collectivism. In *Socrate*, completed in 1918, Satie would once again comment on "truth"; here not in the irreverent spirit of Dada—but, rather, subtly, through style and choice of text. He now defined yet another means to challenge the monologic "truth" of wartime, which had admitted no perspective, no dialogue or dissent, in either ideology or art. Once more, since the Left proposed no "model," but rather a set of concepts and values as being "classic," it is these that we may discern, translated creatively in *Socrate*, and above all the ideals of critical autonomy and dialogue.

In 1916 the princesse de Polignac had heard of Satie from several friends, including Debussy, Cocteau, Picasso, and the singer Jane Bathori. She asked Bathori to arrange a meeting, at which she found herself much amused by Satie's tales of his experiences as d'Indy's pupil at the Schola Cantorum. The princess then suggested a commission—a small work for chamber orchestra, but one related to her own current studies of the ancient Greek language and its literature. Since she was currently reading the *Dialogues* of Plato in the original Greek, she suggested that Satie develop a new dramatic form to set passages from the work. Satie had long been interested in ancient culture, and, in fact, had recently read Victor Cousin's nineteenth-century French translation of the *Dialogues*.[300] It has already been postulated that Satie identified personally with the figure of Socrates, seen as society's "gadfly," pungently noting its injustices and hypocrisies. But it is also important to note that nationalist thinkers, such as the later Georges Sorel, had condemned Socrates' intellectual independence, perceiving him not as a victim, but as justly punished.[301] This was particularly true during the war, when "conformity" was rigidly imposed, which imparts special meaning to Satie's selection of the poignant death of Socrates from the *Dialogues*.[302]

The princess's original idea was that she and her friends, who spoke Greek fluently, would recite passages from Plato over the background of the music to be composed by Satie. The two then collaborated closely, but Satie's ideas eventually won out: the reciters became singers, and the original Greek was replaced with the more comprehensible translation by Cousin.[303] The result was *Socrate*, a "drame symphonique" for four sopranos and a small orchestra, a work that Poulenc, however, later described as a kind of chamber cantata. In *Socrate* Satie would compliantly draw on certain aspects of the "French tradition," but as he understood and interpreted them, in accordance with his own personal conception of "the French."

These were indeed well suited to the literary genre of the text itself—Socratic dialogue, which, like the "mennipean discourse" that preceded it, challenges monologic truth.[304] The former, like the latter, is not rhetorical, but rather comprises a series of quotations, leading ultimately to a "decentered" or a "deconstructed" text. Socratic dialogue instead attempts to reveal truth "dialogically," by employing the structure of a supposedly recorded dialogue of speakers, framed by narrative. Such a genre (like Dada) is inherently opposed to "monologism" or discursive control, construing "truth" as arising from the dialogical relationship between the different speakers. Satie would thus define a musical style that was inherently suited to the absence of a strong "authorial" voice, or dominant perspective within the work.[305]

In *Socrate* Satie employs stylistic means to which he referred as "simple and familiar," for, like Debussy, despite wartime expectations, he continued to reject "la grande musique." Like *Parade*, *Socrate* is a highly unified composition, but here Satie relies not on symmetrical structure and repetition but on the force of rhythmic continuity. This, indeed, was another original interpretation of the wartime belief that a distinctive feature of French music was, traditionally, its rhythmic emphasis. But the work is also "classical" in the sense that certain rhythmic techniques it employs can be traced to the origins of the French tradition of musical drama in Lully (an Italian immigrant).

EXAMPLES 3—Satie, *Socrate*.

Satie's evocative rhythmic patters in the "Bords de l'Illissus" are indeed reminiscent of Lully's riverside scenes, in which a suggestive rhythmic figure is frequently dominant and establishes the mood (see ex. 3). In fact, each section of *Socrate* is characterized by a predominant rhythmic figure that runs consistently throughout it, both creating an appropriate atmosphere and supporting the text. Transformations of rhythmic patters are closely linked to the meaning of the text, and where appropriate, voice and orchestra proceed in a poignant, taught rhythmic tension. For the expression of heightened emotion Satie relies not only on this technique, as well as on orchestration, but on the gradual rise of the vocal tessitura. And, once more as in Lully, Satie is interpreting dramatic veracity primarily in terms of a scrupulous attention to the clarity of the incisive text. Here, like Ravel, he makes the "leap" from political discourse to "representation" through a stylistic articulation that subtly contests dogma and "insinuates" its message.

Perhaps the greatest irony of *Socrate* is that it premiered publicly after the war, on 7 June 1920, at the Société Nationale, an organization whose beliefs concerning French culture and "truth" were, on the whole, opposite those of Satie. Indeed, this may have been due in part to the personal influence of d'Indy, who had taught Satie at the Schola, and held Satie's "serious" efforts in high esteem. In a letter to Auguste Sérieyx, after the war, he wrote explicitly, "Seul Erik Satie reste sage et ne fait que ce qu'il sent pouvoir faire, il semble maintenant un ancêtre vénérable, et vraiment il y avait dans son *Socrate* des choses vraiment poétiques et musicalement senties." (Alone Erik Satie remains wise and does only what he feels he can do, he now seems to be a venerable ancestor, and really there were in his *Socrate* things truly poetic and musically felt.)[306]

Satie could no more prevent the conservative reception of his *Socrate*, which focused on superficial "classical" traits, than he could that of *Parade*, after the war. In both cases the dialogism of his message was being "flattened out" in the discourse around it: for Cocteau, as we will soon see, *Parade* became an example of the very discourse that Satie was critiquing in it. Both *Parade* and *Socrate* were revived several times shortly after the war, and with great success, now representing a contemporary classicism that had been impossible during the war. *Socrate* even won the praise of *L'action française* when performed on 4 January 1923, as noted by Francis Poulenc.[307] With this triumph both Satie and Picasso were "taken up" by Parisian high society, thus effecting the social-artistic alliance for which Cocteau had schemed during the war.[308] But while Picasso became decidedly more "bourgeois," in keeping with the social circle of his new wife, Satie maintained his resistance, clinging tenaciously to his former social identity.

Having already made the defiant gesture of joining the Socialist Party at the start of the war, Satie joined the French Communist Party in 1921 (just a year after its founding).[309] Now he (in part) facetiously referred to himself as "un vieux bolcheviste," and when introduced to a female aristocrat would incongruously effuse an obsequious greeting from "Erik Satie, du Soviet d'Arcueil."[310] One evening, when invited to a dinner in his honor by the princesse de Polignac, he arrived two hours late, long after her aristocratic guests were assembled. When announced by the footman as "le maître Erik Satie," he appeared in his usual garb of a *petit fonctionnaire*, but covered with dust, having walked from Arcueil to her home in Neuilly. To further accentuate the disparity between his social status and that of her guests, he halted, looked around, and exclaimed with wonderment, "Oh! Quel beau monde."[311]

Satie refused a new social status as recalcitrantly as he refused a simple "unique truth," or the dominant wartime and postwar political, cultural, and social orthodoxies. This may well have been a central reason why, although he flirted with surrealism (which would share his attraction for Communism) he rather remained true to the spirit of Dada.[312] Dada's conception of the political act as refusal of chauvinistic cultural orthodoxy, and its opening up of perception and consciousness through radical disorientation remained attractive to Satie, who participated in both Dada "events" and journals. Satie liked Tristan Tzara, and took part in the Dada soirée that the latter organized on 6 July 1922 at the Théâtre Michel. Here, along with performances of works by members of Les Six (together with Marcel Meyer), Satie performed his early *Trois morceaux en forme de poire*.[313]

Satie's participation in *Relâche* is further testimony to his commitment to Dada, for the scenario of the work—upon Satie's instigation—was conceived by Francis Picabia, the "prince of Dada."[314] As Martin Marks has pointed out, although the ballet, created for Rolph de Maré's Ballets Suédois (and premiered 5 December 1924), was not a success, the film inserted into the ballet (directed by René Clair) did survive. The twenty-minute film (with a central episode featuring a runaway hearse) consisted largely of Dadaist non sequiturs and nonsensical jokes in an antinarrative visual style. Accordingly, Satie's score is characterized by a concatenation of brief repetitive patterns in units of four and eight measures, explicitly invoking current musical-hall clichés.[315]

As we might expect, Satie gave no credence to the surrealist idea of a single "deeper truth," located through automatic writing, or in the subconscious. Moreover, unlike the Dadaists, the surrealists Breton and Aragon were opposed to music in principle, which, in part, elicited Satie's sobriquet for the movement as "faux-Dada."[316] In addition, Satie did not like Breton and was eventually to tangle with both him and Aragon in 1924, at the time of the premiere of their collaborative ballet, *Mercure*. In this collaboration—arranged by Diaghilev—Breton and Aragon (together with Auric and Poulenc) praised and supported Picasso at the expense of Satie, as he perceived it.[317]

This incident, together with Satie's continuing adherence to a Dadaist approach, would eventually bring about his rupture not only with Cocteau, but with Les Six. While the later, for reasons that we will now examine, allowed themselves to be "co-opted" by Cocteau and his nationalist neoclassic rhetoric, Satie pertinaciously refused. And although the younger generation's rejection of postwar orthodoxy was not yet accompanied by coherent political principles, for Satie and his generation, with their experience of wartime, the separation was no longer possible.

The Adversative Modernism of Youth

WIÉNER'S CHALLENGE THROUGH REPERTOIRE

A younger generation of composers, Les Six was marked from the start by contradiction—a trait that Cocteau attributed to all the new art, although his theories would be part of the paradox.[318] While they were less compromising than their elders in all they rejected of the dominant nationalist culture, they would still tolerate Cocteau's "new nationalist" rhetoric, in which he construed them as "classic" and purely French. Nowhere may we perceive this disjunction more clearly than in the "countercultural" concerts in which they participated in the early twenties, the implicit message of which was far different from that of their "publicist," Cocteau. From here we can proceed to consider both why they acquiesced to his distortion of them in the press, and then why most sought out alliances with intellectuals holding views of "the classic" substantially different from Cocteau's. Far from being frivolous products of *les années folles*, as they are often portrayed, Les Six soon progressed from cultural rejection to political awareness, and in the thirties to "engagement."

In December 1921, Jean Wiéner began a series of "concerts salades," in which he audaciously presented "la musique vivante," or "la musique de notre temps" (the music of our times).[319] A friend of Stravinsky and Milhaud, with whom he had attended the Paris Conservatoire, Wiéner had recently opened a chic new Parisian bar, the Gaya.[320] A former student of André Gédalge at the Conservatoire, he was a pianist and composer, of independent means, who could afford to experiment with the aesthetically unorthodox.[321] The musical style he developed (one supported in part by commissions from the princesse de Polignac) boldly mixed classical form with the influences of American popular music, and particularly its syncopation.

Significantly, Wiéner made it clear that he wished to give concerts of "the music of our times," embracing "all" contemporary music—both elite and popular—in opposition to the dominant traditionalist culture.[322] He thus made provocative statements in the press concerning his eclectic musical taste, such as the fact that he derived the same pleasure from hearing a jazz band and Viennese waltzes as from hearing symphonic works. This aesthetic of cultural leveling was immediately attacked in the conservative press: journals like *L'information* accused him of "snobisme," "futurisme," and even "cubisme musical."[323]

Fortunately, through his bar Wiéner could mobilize "le tout Paris," or those socially prominent and culturally open who could afford to deride the now "bourgeois" Republic and its official classic aesthetic.[324] Along with them came the nouveau riche merchants who provided them with the products of fashion, and particularly designers like Poiret and Chanel, now in search of a new means of social "distinction."[325] For even if wealthy, as manual laborers and merchants they had no place within bourgeois society, which preferred the company of those who had succeeded in traditional areas like banking or industry. But Wiéner also attracted artistic luminaries to his bar and concerts, including Gide, Diaghilev, Picasso, Picabia, Tzara, Cocteau, and Ravel.[326]

Wiéner thus found a place for "new music"—for all that official France had excluded, a place for young composers in aesthetic revolt, and in need of a new means of recognition. For the wartime generation of students had not only found their studies abruptly disrupted, but with the suspension of the Prix de Rome during the war, their traditional channels of professional consecration were cut off.[327] Hence this generation of composers, unlike those that preceded and followed it, faced entirely new rules, and at the same time unprecedented freedom to make a new statement. Wiéner described the atmosphere among them as one of revolt and contestation, or, as the young composer Georges Auric was to put it, a "new spirit," now free of all prejudice.[328]

This was the period when (in 1921) a young group of Dadaists (later surrealists) held a mock trial of the notoriously nationalist and bigoted Maurice Barrès.[329] As Maurice Agulhon has noted, the youth who came out of the war also harbored a violent hatred for "la France officielle" and translated their indignation into new aesthetic directions.[330] This rejection of the official emerged provocatively in Wiéner's concerts, intended to be—and immediately construed as—a challenge to the nationalist and "exclusive" aesthetic. For many avant-garde artists were communicating their growing alienation not only through derision of the dominant culture, but in the contentious exercise of artistic "liberties."[331]

Wiéner's provocation was inherent not only in the aesthetic nature of the works he selected, but in the mélange of music from different levels of culture, different national cultures, and even different races. Most challenging of all was the inclusion of jazz and modern German music, still shunned in most other concerts since, throughout much of the twenties, to perform it was widely considered unpatriotic. While Bakhtin, in Russia, was theoretically positing that cultural "unities" are constructions of monological power, as opposed to the reality of a creative dialogue of subcultures, Wiéner was intuitively manifesting awareness of this in practice.[332] In the postwar context these concerts were, in part, political enunciations, in that they called into question the very presuppositions of the official and dominant culture.

On 6 December 1921, Wiéner gave the first of his "countercultural" concerts, in which he boldly included the American jazz orchestra of Billy Arnold.[333] Jazz, to this point in Paris, had been performed primarily in music halls, as well as in popular dancing establishments and revues.[334] Here, juxtaposed with jazz was a performance of Stravinsky's iconoclastic Le sacre du printemps on player piano, as well as a sonata by Wiéner's good friend, Darius Milhaud. On 15 December he programmed Schoenberg's atonal Pierrot Lunaire, together with works of Stravinsky, Satie, and Milhaud, to which he added a quarter-tone piece of Habá. This was by no means the first performance of Arnold Schoenberg in France: avant-garde circles had discovered his music before the war, both performing it and writing articles about it. The Société Musicale Indépendante was particularly supportive, and continued to be so after the war, performing not only Schoenberg but other contemporary European composers from both former allied and "enemy" countries. Wiéner's concerts thus became part of the small but intrepid group of those who fostered contemporary music, regardless of the composers' ethnic, racial, or national origins.[335]

Other programs of Wiéner in 1922 included Webern, Schoenberg (conducted by Milhaud), and, in 1923, members of Les Six, to which he added works by Stravinsky and Satie, as well as Rossini, Gounod, and Mozart. The increasing incorporation of classical works was not without meaning within the context, for Wiéner was seeking not only the "shock effect" of juxtaposition, but also to reassert or reapproriate specific figures. Gounod, for Les Six, embodied the authentic French tradition (despite his love of German music), together with figures such as Chabrier and Bizet, who, in fact, had felt the impact of Wagner. But the majority of their music eschewed Wagnerian grandiloquence in favor of those qualities that Les Six wished to promote as French (against the norm), such as humor and grace.[336] And the inclusion of Rossini was, in part, an implicit response to the nationalist rhetoric according to which Rossini had "sullied" French music (having been emulated by a series of French Jewish composers), which was later "purified" by the influence of Mozart or Wagner. To understand the rationale of these concerts fully, however, we must first examine the audience at which they were aimed, the rhetoric that surrounded their presentation, and their cultural message within the context.

THE GENERATION OF 1914 IN MUSIC

The six young French composers whom Wiéner brought to greater public notice, and who were later christened Les Six, shared the traits generally ascribed to their generation—that of 1914. As Robert Wohl has pointed out, this was, in essence, the younger, or second war generation, one that went "directly from school examinations . . . to the front."[337] The young Frenchmen of this generation returned home with bitterness and irony, drained of patriotism, inclined toward nihilism, and devoid of respect for their elders.

For, unlike the preceding generation, they perceived the war less as an occasion for confirmation of the culture that existed before it than as an opportunity for radical cultural change. Unified not only by experience but by a sense of fate, they were by no means "carefree" but sought to articulate values that were different from that of the world that disappeared with the war.[338] This generation had been fully aware of the changes occurring around it in the social as well as the technological world throughout the war. Hence their inescapable sense that the new world to which they would soon belong would indeed be radically different from that experienced by all previous generations. As Wohl has also observed, artistically this was, in fact, the "fourth modernist generation," and included figures like Duchamp and Cocteau, whose full impact would be felt just after the war.[339] This was a generation, then, that had grown up exposed to modernist innovation, but often felt torn between this option and more traditional cultural values.[340]

This profile holds true for the six young composers, Georges Auric, Francis Poulenc, Darius Milhaud, Louis Durey, Arthur Honegger, and Germaine Tailleferre. They were all students during the war, and several were drafted for military service either in the course of the war, or, as with Auric and Poulenc, toward its end. They all pursued an artistic education in the "dominant" culture, while still attracted to modernist currents, and were marked in particular by *Le sacre du printemps* and *Parade*. And all rejected the moral idealism, narrow nationalism, and concomitant feticization of selected "great" musical figures or icons within the dominant musical culture. They were similarly repulsed by attempts to control the production of meaning in music during the war, as well as by the official conservative and exclusive conception of the classic. The conventions that they rejected, then, were, as for Satie, those associated with the artistic strictures applied during the war, as well as with the narrow sense of aesthetic legitimacy these sought to enforce.

They, therefore, did not reject the use of all traditional forms and techniques, but they utilized them with a new attitude that was both open to the popular and antiromantic. They could thus retain tradition but bring to it an entirely new content or meaning—one devoid of the conventional associations and practices adhering to "high art."[341] Most of the members of the group did share a common educational experience: they had attended the Conservatoire, and some the Schola as well, either before or during the war. This meant that they were well versed in music history, for not only was it stressed at the Schola, but this was the first generation to experience the required courses in music history introduced by Fauré in 1905.[342]

In addition, they shared a taste for the new, more experimental culture available outside the institution's walls, and not yet officially recognized as "legitimate." Again, not only had they been awakened by the "explosion" of *Le sacre du printemps*, they found a resonant model in Satie's disquieting and provocative use of style in *Parade*. His strategic "play" with established "serious" meanings and styles, or his modernist "critical" classicism that evaded controls and authority, now held an immense appeal for most. Their mocking of convention would have a similar source: a rejection of all the official pieties and a desire to enter into dialogue with, or to challenge, its dominant meanings. Incorporating popular elements within the classic became a means of both social commentary and trenchant cultural critique, but in a subtle manner, in a different register from the more overt satire in the Weimar Republic.

Their neoclassicism would thus be "cultural" and critical, unlike Stravinsky's, which they admired, but the motivation of which was more a formal and conservative exploration of styles. They rather sought a true "modernism," or "critical dismantling of inherited cultural languages" as ideological constructions, in the spirit of Satie and Dada. As a result they drew from several "oppositional" traditions—the popular (including the folk), the commercial, and the aristocratic—which they used to define themselves against the official or academic norm. All of these they would throw into new, experimental relations, creating both new meaning and awareness not only of the reality of experience itself, but how meaning construction occurred in the past within specific conventions.[343] Stravinsky's goal, unlike theirs, was to "reconstruct" a musical style— or to rediscover and extrapolate from the coherence that existed between elements within musical styles of the past. His search, like Boulanger's, was for the "laws" of good music in the great European tradition, one with which he, as a Russian émigré, was seeking ardently to identify.[344] Like Satie, Les Six rather challenged the cultural assumptions of "high art," construing the "popular" not as affirmative (in the manner of Adorno) but as a social challenge. Their quest, in the most integral sense, was for a culture more immediate and "real"—closer to experience—than the fossilized, reified "classic" culture being imposed by their elders.

Accordingly, their cultural message was to be one of reality, innovation, and inclusion, as opposed to the idealistic, mythic, retrogressive culture characteristic of "official France."[345] Not only were they rejecting the specific classicism promoted during the war, they were also reacting to characteristics of both the now "consecrated" classic style and the "impressionist" works that had preceded it. As Poulenc later observed, they shared "la réaction contre le flou, le retour à la mélodie, le retour du contrepoint, la précision," and "la simplification" (the reaction against the hazy, the return to melody, the return to counterpoint, precision and simplification).[346]

Some of the prewar ("impressionist") values were similarly rejected by the dominant musical culture, although it still promoted the "serious," traditional, large-scale works that youth now iconoclastically rejected. The "generation of 1914" rhetorically repudiated not only Debussy and Ravel, but also the wartime and postwar canonized "greats," in particular Beethoven, Wagner, and Franck. They rather sought a kind of creativity that was related to their own experiences in the modern world: while eschewing "romantic isolation," they sought a new subjectivity that was not individualistic but rooted in the "popular" collectivity. Hence their desire, in expressing "their" experience, to draw upon the music of other cultural groups, but through that music to evolve their own appropriate musical language. Inner reality, for them, was something shared by all human beings, in other words, something that, despite different articulations, was "universal," as opposed both to the unique romantic emotions of the heart and to the nationalist creed.[347]

THE COUNTERCULTURE AND ITS SUPPORTERS

Deprived of access to traditional "paths to success," and with no place in the official musical culture, these young composers needed a way to attract a new public's attention. They, and those who came to their aid, acting as promoters and sponsors, appealed to the taste and cultural tendencies of the more open, "elite" audience, which now provided a potential new infrastructure. The intermediaries here would be artists and writers, as opposed to the official "network" that, before the war, established a composer's career after his winning of the Prix de Rome.[348]

As Poulenc later explained, for those who were still left in Paris in wartime, there was the group around the (prewar) *Nouvelle revue française* (relaunched after the war), the "Apollinaire group," the "Cendrars group," and the "Cocteau group."[349] These groupings were not mutually exclusive: in fact, members of Les Six would participate in several, beginning with that of Blaise Cendrars, who proposed they give concerts, which Satie christened the "Concerts des Nouveaux

Jeunes."350 This label may well have implied a distinction from the conservative portraiture of French youth promoted by right-wing figures like Massis and de Tarde in the years preceding the war. For they had claimed that French youth admired such nationalist figures as Charles Maurras, Charles Péguy, Georges Sorel, and, above all, Maurice Barrès.351

The initial members of the group were Auric, Honegger, Tailleferre, and Durey, later joined by Poulenc and then Milhaud, upon his return from wartime administrative service in Brazil.352 Although having Cendrars as a "guide," Auric and Poulenc also approached Cocteau, who, in 1917, was already making provocative comments about music of the past and present.353 But it was, in fact, Cendrars who helped to initiate and advise the group's first concerts in 1917, together with the actor Pierre Bertin and the conductor Félix Delgrange.354

It was largely of necessity, at first, that these concerts assumed a novel format in new venues, and were consequently different in atmosphere and setting from other wartime concerts we have examined. The group had briefly borrowed the Théâtre du Vieux-Colombier for their concerts, through the help of their friend, the singer Jane Bathori. This was convenient while the theater's own troupe and its director, Jacques Copeau, were in America, but when the troupe returned the musicians had to seek another site.355 They finally found one with the help of Louis Durey's brother André, a painter, who located an atelier in Montparnasse, in the Rue Huyghens.

On the walls of the atelier were the works of young Parisian painters, in addition to those of such established masters as Matisse and Picasso.356 And so, as suggested by the setting, the concerts were combined with exhibitions of works of art, and hence appropriately endowed with the title of "Lyre et palette."357 It is significant that nothing could have been further removed from wartime didactic "lecture-concerts," presenting music of the past and framed by the verbal propaganda now distrusted by youth. The new visual framing was both immediate and suggestive, contemporary and semiotically "open," in marked distinction to the tautological wartime rhetoric and methods of intellectual "control."358

Eventually, however, Cendrars and Cocteau would come into personal conflict, for Cendrars did not like the small pamphlet Cocteau published in 1918, *Le coq et l'arlequin*.359 The reasons will become clear when we examine this work and the rhetoric through which Cocteau later "framed" the group, one that played to, while subtly manipulating, wartime assumptions and themes. It was thus Cocteau who now assumed the role of publicist or sponsor for the group, despite the fact that, as we have noted, he substantially misrepresented their cultural substance and complexity. But he provided a useful service, drawing attention to the young composers and protecting them with legitimizing rhetoric from the damning charge of being unpatriotic.

Cocteau publicized the group not only in the press (in papers such as *Paris-Midi*) but by making them collaborators in journals, together with prominent writers and intellectuals.360 They articulated their aesthetic ideals at first in a collective publication—a "broadsheet" titled *Le coq*, which lasted for only four issues. This innovative publication appeared between May and November 1920, with the third and fourth numbers being renamed *Le coq parisien*.361 In addition to Cocteau, other writers participated, including his protégé Raymond Radiguet, Paul Morand, Lucien Daudet, Max Jacob, and Blaise Cendrars. Provocative even in its format, it consisted of poems, articles, aphorisms, announcements, often employing different kinds of type, and even incorporating fragments of music. And it included iconoclastic aesthetic pronouncements, probably instigated by Cocteau, palpably intended to shock the conservative musical culture of their elders. These included, "The six musicians are no longer interested in harmonic counterpoint," and, in the midst of anti-German and anti-Semitic sentiment, "Arnold Schoenberg, the six musicians salute you."362

Significantly, *Le coq* appeared at the height of Dadaist agitation in Paris, as well as in the context of a general proliferation of antitraditionalist journals of art. The latter, on the whole, were not only antimilitarist but culturally antiexclusionary (although not without some notable inconsistencies). Moreover, Dadaist provocation in 1920 was characterized not by only unconventional statements and lectures, but also by challenging and bumptious "manifestos." Reaction against such gestures and acts may well have contributed to perceptions of Les Six as Dadistic provocateurs, especially when performances of works of Milhaud and Honegger caused a scuffle at the Concerts Colonne on 24 October 1920.363

Les Six, however, came to public attention not only through Dadaist techniques, but through two collective works that brought them to further prominence in the 1920s. One was *L'éventail de Jeanne*, of 1927, a suite of dances by ten composers (including the group), which, after its premiere at the salon of Mme Jeanne Dubost, Rouché decided to mount at the Paris Opéra. The work diplomatically drew on both the older and the younger generation, undoubtedly increasing its appeal to Rouché, who was aware of the conservatism of the audience at the Opéra. Hence, in addition to Milhaud, Poulenc, and Auric, it included Maurice Ravel, Albert Roussel, Florent Schmitt, Pierre-Octave Ferroud, Marcel Delannoy, Jacques Ibert, and Roland-Manuel.364

The new concerts often included performances of works by Roland-Manuel, whose real name was Roger Lévy, as well as by Les Six, who were his close friends. After having been "awakened" by the experience of *Pelléas et Mélisande* in 1905, he became a pupil of Roussel and Sérieyx at the Schola Cantorum. Perhaps it was, in part, the religious atmosphere predominant at the Schola that influenced his subsequent conversion to Catholicism. The other factor may have been the influence of his brother-in-law, who was said to be behind his conversion and his baptism at Solesmes. Roland-Manuel subsequently grew close to the monks at Solesmes and even became associated with the Benedictine order as an oblate.365 But he also allied himself with Satie, who introduced him to Ravel, and he subsequently became Ravel's loyal composition pupil and biographer. Hence, despite his close association with Les Six, Roland-Manuel was to remain apart, still aesthetically influenced by both Fauré and Ravel.366

The earlier collective work of Les Six (minus Durey) that first brought them to greater public attention was a ballet conceived by Cocteau, *Les mariés de la Tour Eiffel*. Said to be situated on the border between Cocteau's Dadaist and surrealist periods, the work was presented on 18 June 1921 at the Comédie des

Champs-Elysées and predictably created a scandal.[367] But it was this ballet, financially backed by the Swedish industrialist Rolf de Maré, that purportedly caught the attention and thus interest of Diaghilev in the group.[368] The work, which mocks the bourgeois ritual of marriage, parodies both traditional idioms (as in Honegger's Funeral March) as well as the modern (the high bassoons suggesting Stravinsky). Moreover, the genre is ambiguous, containing elements of opera and ballet, and thus inevitably recalling (and mocking) Rouché's more serious wartime invocation of French *opéra-ballet* (see fig. 4).

Those who fostered the unconventional experiments of the group were several, and here it is also important to remember the key role of the princesse de Polignac, who was close to Wiéner and Diaghilev, and influential in obtaining commissions for both Stravinsky and the young composers, as well as commissioning works herself. In the early twenties she commissioned Milhaud's *Les malheurs d'Orphée*, as well as works by Francis Poulenc and his friend Sauguet (a member of Satie's Ecole d'Arcueil). Her influence was undoubtedly central in Diaghilev's commissions for his "Soirées de Paris" (in 1924) of Poulenc's *Les biches*, Auric's *Les fâcheux*, Milhaud's *Le train bleu*, as well as Satie's *Mercure*.[369]

Yet other figures were central in helping to develop this new "concert cul-

FIGURE 4—Decor for *Les mariées de la Tour Eiffel*. Artist unknown. Bibliothèque nationale de France. Opéra.

ture": the comte Etienne de Beaumont financed the "Soirées de Paris" and commissioned Satie's ballet *Mercure*. The designer Coco Chanel also "saved" Diaghilev financially, in addition to doing the costumes for Cocteau and Honegger's *Antigone* and Milhaud's *Le train bleu*.[370] But again, perhaps the most important intermediary here was Jean Wiéner, who recruited wealthy patrons such as the princesse de Polignac, the Rothschilds, and the Paul Clemenceaus.[371]

This was a circle that had no need or desire for conservative postwar official culture, or for the social groups that supported it among the bourgeois middle and upper classes. It consisted largely of Parisian aristocrats, declining in social influence and in search of a new role, one which would allow them to reassert their traditional freedom to be both libertine and "above the rules." The princesse de Polignac, for example, née Winaretta Singer, was not only a homosexual (married to another homosexual) but an American, ready to mix social classes and groups. Indeed, as Proust revealed so evocatively in his last novel, *Le temps retrouvé*, the old social world, or *le monde*, was disappearing and a new elite was taking its place. The latter included designers like Chanel and Poiret, who were similarly wealthy but rejected by the bourgeoisie, and thus in search of a social position and role. This world mingled freely with progressive artists, just as Cocteau had "schemed" (if prematurely in wartime), but still with clairvoyance in view of the new elite that emerged from the war. Rejecting the historicist "culture of the past," being revived in the official theaters, the new elite chose to champion youth, particularly after the decimation of this generation in the war. Although the culture and style that they supported, a modernist neoclassicism, has been reduced by some to a manifestation of their purported quest to be stylish and urbane, the motivations were far more profound.

It was this circle that promoted Cocteau's precocious protégé, the writer Raymond Radiguet, and which, as Auric observed, often "ornamented" their grand dinners in the Faubourg Saint-Germain with progressive young musicians.[372] As he notes, the group specifically included those who sought "liberation" within their "caste," such as Etienne de Beaumont, the circle of Anna de Noailles, Paul Painlevé, and Robert de Montesquieu.[373] This was not only an elite group of sponsors: it similarly attracted a select new audience, referred to repeatedly in writings of the period as "snobs," or those seeking distinction through a "progressive" but cultivated taste. Significantly, after the group's wartime debut in the more marginal, avant-garde context of Montparnasse, the most important works of Les Six after the war would be performed in the elite arrondissements, home of the "upper class" theaters such as the Théâtre des Champs-Elysées. Auric observed acutely, for example, that present at this theater for the premiere of Milhaud's *Le boeuf sur le toit* was an audience ranging from the fashionable Faubourg Saint-Germain to the advanced artistic circles of Montparnasse and Montmartre.[374]

Like Cocteau, Wiéner knew precisely how to draw on this specific world, or to court a new progressive audience consisting of the Parisian social aristocracy and avant-garde artists. He pointed out that he was well aware of "a wind of revolt or contestation," one already being drawn upon actively by Dadaists and surrealists in art and literature.[375] But he also knew, like Cocteau, that first he needed to mobilize the new social group to support his musical venture, hence his opening of the bar Le Gaya, later renamed Le Boeuf sur le Toit. Here, in the early twenties, patrons consisting of the new "tout Paris," as well as progressive artists, could talk, drink, and listen to American jazz. This included figures such as Gide, Diaghilev, Picasso, Satie, René Clair, Picabia, Poiret, Tzara, Cocteau, Anna de Noailles, Auric, the princesse Murat, Fernand Léger, Poulenc, and Ravel. Wiéner himself, after his later conversion to communism, retrospectively described this elite as characterized by "snobisme."[376]

Wiéner's concerts were a logical extension of this culture, one both intellectual and *mondain* (worldly); they were designed for that small group in Paris now open to his iconoclastic mixing of cultural levels and national repertoires. As Wiéner himself later put it, his desire to organize concerts originally stemmed from the musical situation that he and others encountered in Paris by 1920. Nowhere else could one hear modern German and Austrian music together with that of young French composers, popular music of black Americans, and selected masters from the musical past. But Wiéner also presented established French masters like Debussy and Ravel, provocatively (for the period) mixed with others, such as Mussorgsky, Stravinsky, and members of Les Six.[377]

Progressive members of the French musical world enthusiastically embraced Wiéner's endeavor and his choices: Ravel (but not Roussel) praised the inclusion of jazz in his audacious "concerts salades." Roland-Manuel, writing in *L'éclair*, in 1922, claimed that it had been a long time since the Société Musicale Indépendante had offered such interesting concerts.[378] They clearly filled a gap, in addition to making an intrepid cultural statement, one that was to be viciously attacked by those who felt threatened by it. For Wiéner's supporters, the performance of works like Schoenberg's atonal *Pierrot Lunaire* (of 1912), on 15 October 1921, was both welcome and long overdue. The presentation of Schoenberg's song cycle even won the encomium of certain conservatives, such as (the Scholiste) Paul Le Flem, in *Comoedia*; Gustave Bret, in the nationalist *L'intransigeant*; and Emile Vuillermoz, in *Excelsior*. Here their musical interests apparently overrode the ideological "ban" so widely imposed in Paris on the performance of the former "enemies'" music.[379]

Wiéner was thus perhaps the most important French sponsor or promoter of Stravinsky and Les Six, leading Milhaud to refer to him explicitly as "notre mécène artiste."[380] He "created" a context for them, and thus also a mode of cultural construction, as part of a progressive configuration of culture for which a new, elite audience was ready. Ironically, it was this iconoclastic image of Les Six—one that was confrontational in the context—that Cocteau was counteracting in order to "legitimize" them in postwar French culture.

Since the time of *Le coq et l'arlequin*, written in the wake of attacks on *Parade*, Cocteau had been developing a rhetoric in which to construe the "new music" as both French and patriotic. This was not Wiéner's concern, yet despite the fact that his "message" was opposed to Cocteau's, he rather liked the iconoclastic spirit of *Le coq*, and considered Cocteau as part of his circle.[381] Although Jewish, Wiéner had been baptized a Catholic, believing himself fully assimilated, and thus did not object to (or even perhaps perceive) the racial implications of Cocteau's rhetoric, which we will now examine. Like Milhaud, Wiéner refused to acknowledge the reality of his cultural exclusion (if only in theory) until it was almost too late—both escaping Paris in the summer of 1940.

COCTEAU: PROTECTING MODERNISM WITH NATIONALISM

Cocteau was the self-appointed "theoretician" of Les Six, which provoked Emile Vuillermoz to refer to Wiéner's audacious "concerts salades" as essentially the "concerts Jean Cocteau." Vuillermoz went on to deprecate members of Les Six as not only sustained by "snobisme," but launched by "publicity agents," implying, first Wiéner, and then Cocteau.[382] Again, the latter had made himself the spokesman for the "new" French music in the pamphlet *Le coq et l'arlequin*, completed in the summer of 1918 and appearing soon after, shortly before the war's end. It was published by the new Editions de la Sirène, which Cocteau and Cendrars had founded the preceding spring as a result of their rejection by other publishers, including the circle of *La nouvelle revue française*.[383]

Le coq was stimulated both by Cocteau's reaction to the failure of *Parade* as well as by his conversations with Georges Auric, which took place before and after the "scandal."[384] Dedicated to Auric, it was thus perceived as the "manifesto" of the six young composers that Cocteau would sponsor after *Parade* and in the early twenties. Its appearance was apparently timely; the first edition immediately sold out, for as we will see, Cocteau astutely appealed to French chauvinists, as well as to restive youth.[385]

Le coq has been analyzed repeatedly, and scholars have noted not only its themes, but its aphoristic style that recalls both Nietzsche (the eventual enemy of Wagner) as well as the classic La Rochefoucauld.[386] Not adequately studied, however, are Cocteau's tactics within the context of the wartime discourse that we have examined, and the way his own rhetoric was perceived in the early 1920s. Moreover, careful analysis of the work reveals the extent to which Cocteau obscured the real motivations of the young composers in the interests of his own personal, professional strategy. In *Le coq* Cocteau, in reality, sought to legitimize the endeavor of the collaborators on *Parade* by providing a contemporary version of the wartime chauvinistic aesthetic discourse.

Here he built upon the argument that Apollinaire has already initiated in connection with Satie and *Parade*, as well as with the cubist painters whom he had supported preceding the war. Both Apollinaire and Cocteau attempted to make a place for the new music and art within traditionalist discourse by presenting them as "art vivant," the living incarnation of a still vital past, and thus "safe." For as we have noted, cubism could be construed as simultaneously traditional and patriotic and as oriented toward the future—the ideal continuity between modernity and tradition.[387] As we have also noted, although this discourse was greeted with skepticism during the war itself, it would find a far more responsive reception at its conclusion. For France would now need to prove not only her roots in the illustrious past, but also that it still had a vital and creative future, in the postwar order.

And so Cocteau's tactic, like Apollinaire's, was, essentially, to espouse wartime values—to invoke nationalist themes and clichés, while arguing for a more capacious, contemporary interpretation of them. He thus provocatively proclaimed the necessity of "reinventing French nationalism," opposing his conception to both conservative traditionalism and to nihilistic Dada.[388] We may witness this strategy in the opening paragraphs, his dedication to Georges Auric, in which he immediately condemns "eclecticism"—the "pollution" of French culture by non-French elements. The metaphoric harlequin, for Cocteau, with his "mask" and his multicolored costume, is, by insinuation (and in keeping with wartime dogma) inherently "unpatriotic": "Après avoir renié le chant du coq, il se cache. C'est un coq de la nuit." (After having renounced the song of the cock [the symbol of French patriotism] he hides. He is a cock of the night.)[389] The theme of anti-Germanism also appears when Cocteau praises the young Georges Auric for having, like his friend, the captive aviator Roland Garros, "escaped" from Germany, but in a different way. This then naturally leads Cocteau into repeated attacks on Wagner, as well as on musicians who felt his influence (and that of other countries), such as Claude Debussy.

Like so many others during the war, Cocteau here revels in Nietzsche's condemnation of Wagner and his concomitant praise of Bizet's *Carmen* in *The Case of Wagner*. But Cocteau goes even further in denouncing "impressionism," and specifically Debussy, as narrowly escaping the "German ambush" only to fall subsequently into the Russian "trap." Debussy and Wagner, for Cocteau, ostensibly shared certain dangerous qualities, including a tendency to "envelop" the listener, be it through the "Wagnerian fog" or the "impressionist mist."[390] Both artists are thus dishonest, thwarting not only clarity but "realism"–the very qualities praised in wartime and earlier by Nietzsche, who similarly connected them with French traits.[391]

As in so much wartime propaganda, Cocteau here presents Wagner as typically German in being both long and tedious, his music, in essence, a drug to "stupefy the faithful."[392] But while German music, especially Wagner, was particularly noxious, Cocteau considered all foreign infiltrations, even those of former allies such as Russia, to be insidious: "La musique russe est admirable parce qú elle est la musique russe. La musique française russe ou la musique française allemande est forcément bâtarde, même si elle s'inspire d'un Moussorgsky, d'un Strawinsky [sic], d'un Wagner, d'un Schoenberg. Je demande une musique française de France." (Russian music is admirable because it is Russian. French-Russian music or French-German music is necessarily bastard, even if it is inspired by a Mussorgsky, a Stravinsky, a Wagner, a Schoenberg. I ask for a French music of France.)[393]

As we have noted, such rhetoric was already standard French wartime propaganda, which consistently called for the immediate extirpation of all non-French elements within French culture. Also common was Cocteau's attack on "exoticism," here embracing the traditionally threatening "Oriental" elements (including the Jewish), as well as the romantic and the American.[394] Like Pierre Lasserre, Cocteau praises classicists like Ingres and then denigrates romantics such as Delacroix, derisively referring to the latter's "riche bazar." As an antidote to these "exotic" perturbations of French taste, Cocteau proposes (like Laloy before) the example of the *café-concert*, despite its recent Anglo-American influence. For here, as Cocteau argues, "On y conserve une certaine tradition qui, pour être crapuleuse, n'en est pas moins de race. C'est sans doute là qu'un jeune musicien pourrait reprendre le fil perdu." (Here one conserves a certain tradition that, to be villainous, is nothing less than race. It is undoubtedly here that a young musician could take up the lost thread.)[395]

However, Cocteau is careful to point out that the music hall, the circus, the American negro orchestras, are not "art" but rather inspire art—they are mere stimuli, symbols of modernity like machines or danger.[396] As he further implies, young French musicians, in returning to this immediate and honest tradition, can avoid the trap of their counterparts in Germany, who are now being "reacademicized."[397] Cocteau therefore accentuates the popular, modern exploration of "the real" in these genres, their search for simplicity and concision, abjuring the sentimental as the time demanded.[398]

Throughout *Le coq* Cocteau repeatedly advocates those wartime values considered distinctively "French"—line (or melody), simplicity, a human scale (as opposed to German titanism), and a balanced architecture. This leads, first, to his repudiation of the "wrong" classic models, and particularly those so highly prized by French conservatives in music: the German classics, and especially Beethoven. Here Cocteau (like Debussy before) audaciously counterposes the baroque example of Bach to that of Beethoven and the "high classic" style, which so many now lauded: "Beethoven est fastidieux lorsqu'il développe, Bach pas, parce que Beethoven fait du développement de forme, et Bach du développement d'idée. (Beethoven is fastidious when he develops, not Bach, because Beethoven develops form and Bach develops ideas.) [399] Already, before the war, members of the younger generation, the Debussystes, like their idol, had denigrated Beethoven in similar terms, introducing an argument that Cocteau here expands. He too opposes ideas to form, but goes on to seize the occasion to counteract wartime rhetoric concerning the necessity of an immediate return to the past.

Cocteau rather stresses the necessity that art—even one based on the classic tradition—be of "one's time," or lead the way forward, as opposed to turning retrospectively toward the past: "Lorsqu'une oeuvre semble en avance sur son époque, c'est simplement que son époque est en retard sur elle. . . . un artiste qui recule ne trahit pas. Il se trahit." (When a work seems in advance of its period, it is simply its period that is behind it. . . . an artist who retreats does not betray. He betrays himself.)[400] In this context Cocteau adulates Satie in *Parade* as both classic and honest, or of his time, exemplary in his simplicity and clarity, and a true "architect," in the best sense.[401]

As we have seen in his notes for *Parade*, Apollinaire had referred to Satie's score as "so clear and simple that one will recognize the marvelously lucid spirit of France herself." And in a subsequent lecture on "the new spirit" and the poets (published in the conservative *Mercure de France* on 1 December 1918), he argues that "the new spirit which we can already discern, claims above all to have inherited from the classics a solid spirit of criticism, a wide view of the world and the human mind, and that sense of duty which limits or rather controls displays of emotion." For Apollinaire, as for Cocteau, *Parade* provoked the beginning of a new era, "a classical and patriotic era of lucid, restrained modernity that would find the French elite among its audience."[402]

Clearly, Cocteau did not wish to perceive the perverse humor in *Parade*'s construction, even ignorantly accusing Stravinsky, in *Le sacre du printemps* (a true masterpiece of musical architecture), of not yet being of "the race of architects." Then, as opposed to the sense of "religious complicity" that he sees around Stravinsky's work (thus associating it illogically with Wagner and Bayreuth) he calls for a "musique de tous les jours." Again, the model implied is Satie, who, for both Cocteau and Les Six, insouciantly abjures "the sublime," creating a music that is "of this world," or one constructed "to the measure of man."[403]

However, as we will see when examining the actual tastes of the composers in Les Six, they also had an interest in the music of Schoenberg, which led to tensions within Cocteau's *Le coq et l'arlequin*. For in it we find statements concerning Schoenberg that are both positive and negative, in an attempt to satisfy orthodox opinion as well as the young composers who are clearly being courted: "Schoenberg est un maître; tous nos musiciens et Strawinsky [sic] lui doivent quelque chose, mais Schoenberg est surtout un musicien de tableau noir." (Schoenberg is a master; all our musicians and Stravinsky owe him something, but Schoenberg is above all a musician of the blackboard.)[404]

Such a statement, in effect, allows the author to acknowledge the contribution of Schoenberg, but also chauvinistically to proclaim the supremacy of French music: "Je vous annonce, la musique française va influencer le monde." (I announce to you, French music will influence the world.)[405] While Schoenberg would later patriotically claim this distinction rather for German music, Cocteau's proclamation was warmly greeted, accounting, in part, for the appeal of his pamphlet.

Cocteau's tactics were right on target. He would indeed go on to achieve his goal of becoming the spokesman not only for "new music" but for a contemporary nationalist classicism. Others, equally progressive, soon took note of his conceptual innovations here, thus further publicizing his work, and these included the theologian Jacques Maritain. In 1920, Maritain, a professor at the Institut Catholique, published his book *Art et scolastique*, in which he quoted several aphorisms from Cocteau's *Le coq et l'arlequin*. Although at this point orthodox and traditionalist, Maritain nevertheless maintained a firm conviction concerning the capacity for "good" in modern art, or its ability to deliver spiritual messages. He was therefore enthusiastic about the painters Rouault and Chagall, as well as about Cocteau's young literary protégé, the novelist Raymond Radiguet.[406]

In addition, Marcel Proust, although he did perceive the contradictions inherent in Cocteau's pamphlet, nevertheless, as an admirer of Cocteau, was indeed pleased by the work.[407] But in light of the postwar polarization of "nationalist" and "universalist" classicism, Cocteau would gradually grow more conservative, responding to his critics on the traditionalist Right. In the 1923 preface to *Le coq*, Cocteau makes it clear that he was not actually "praising" the circus and the music hall—the charm of the clowns and the negroes—but rather their lesson of equilibrium, discrete force, and grace.[408]

On 3 May of that same year, Cocteau, who had now "arrived" in the "established" world in France, further recanted his earlier audacities in a lecture that he delivered at the prestigious Collège de France. This lecture, "D'un ordre considéré comme une anarchie," would later become the third part of his *Le rappel à l'ordre* (together with *Le coq et l'arlequin*, "Le secret professionnel," and "Picasso"), published in 1926, during the conservative regime of Poincaré. Here Cocteau discusses Satie, Picasso, and Radiguet as exemplars of the innovative, "living" classicism that he still sought, if less iconoclastically. Moreover, this later edition of *Le coq* included a new appendix titled "Stravinsky dernière heure," written after Cocteau's reconciliation with the now neoclassic Stravinsky.[409] Here he observes with approbation that Stravinsky's earlier "romantisme oriental" has fortunately been replaced by the more praiseworthy "ordre latin."

The retrenchment we see here in Cocteau was occurring simultaneously among critics in the visual arts, for even progressive publications, associated with the avant-garde, were espousing a conservative classicism in both politics and art.[410] Hence Cocteau was now positioning himself squarely against the "leftist" classicism of *La nouvelle revue française*, which was currently in battle with the circle of Action Française in the Catholic *Revue universelle*. Here Jacques Maritain attempted to challenge the claim of Gide and his colleagues in *La nouvelle revue française* that they alone represented "modern" French classicism. Maritain enlisted the aid of his friend, the Catholic journalist Henri Massis, who refuted such assertions in an article on Raymond Radiguet in *La revue universelle* on 15 August 1924.[411]

In addition to this battle over classicism, Cocteau was explicitly referring to himself as an "anti-Dadaist," even though he had ostensibly participated in the Dadaist circle during the war. It was specifically their attack on the political and aesthetic "order" that issued from the war that Cocteau was now abjuring, as articulated most amply in *Le rappel à l'ordre*.[412] He was, in part, forced into this position by both his animosity toward André Breton and the harsh ridicule he himself encountered in *La nouvelle revue française*, which still supported Dada.[413] And since "the modern" had become synonymous with what Cocteau derisively labeled "le Suicide-Club Dada," he therefore equated his "esprit nouveau" with the "antimodern." He even went so far as to suggest, together with Raymond Radiguet, the foundation of an "antimodern league" to further a return to poetry, the disappearance of skyscrapers, and the "reappearance of the rose."[414]

Now both Cocteau and Stravinsky brashly referred to themselves as "antimodern," a repudiation that we must perceive in the context of their emphatic rejection of Dada.[415] Moreover, in the mid-1920s Cocteau abruptly decided to return to the church, a trend that included other writers such as Pierre Reverdy and Henri Ghéon. But this conversion was also partially prompted by Cocteau's growing and overt animosity toward those to whom he referred derogatorily as "the atheistic surrealists." Revealingly, Cocteau's play *Orphée* premiered on 15 June 1926, and in it Orpheus is a surrealist poet who, in the end, is finally "converted."[416]

COLLET AND THE MYTH OF LES SIX

Cocteau's original goals were unmistakable: he wished to become the aesthetic spokesman for the French liberal Right, resurfacing after the war, and the classic avant-garde that it promoted. This was as opposed not only to the orthodox classicism of the traditionalist Right, but equally to "universalist classicism," Dada, and surrealism, now associated with the French Left. Les Six, like Satie, were useful tools to illustrate Cocteau's points, although few of its members would be in accordance with all his dictums. But his role for them was pivotal: he brought recognition to obscure young composers in a period of institutional crisis, when traditional means of recognition ceased to function. As contemporaries noted, publicity was becoming essential to the postwar generation, for whom the professional "rules of the game" were in flux and rapidly changing. In place of slowly built careers, consecrated by a series of official awards, the new, independent concert life now arising rather demanded a constant quest for attention.[417] Here Cocteau made himself indispensable not only as a literary spokesman and sponsor, but as a purveyor of useful contacts in the press, primary among whom was Henri Collet.

Collet, a composer, critic, and musicologist, who would endow Les Six with their name in a celebrated article of 1920, was close to Cocteau both in terms of his circle and his political-aesthetic position.[418] An *agrégé* in Spanish and a *docteur ès lettres*, he contributed to the right-wing avant-garde journal *L'esprit nouveau*, in which, in 1920, he published an article on Satie that employed arguments resembling Cocteau's. In addition, he was a critic for *Comoedia* (to which Cocteau also contributed), perhaps the most important theatrical journal, avowedly nationalist and emphatically anti-German.[419] Cocteau thus recognized the utility of introducing his musical protégés to Collet, who had expressed the desire to write about them and their music in the journal.[420] He did so in a two-part article, published in *Comoedia* on 16 and 23 January 1920, titled "Un livre de Rimsky et un livre de Cocteau—Les cinq Russes, les six Français et Erik Satie" (A book of Rimsky [-Korsakov] and a book of Cocteau—the five Russians, the six Frenchmen, and Erik Satie). Here Collet compares Les Six, as he anoints them, with the celebrated "Russian Five," the nineteenth-century Russian nationalist composers who had won the encomium of the prewar French Right. Moreover, during the war, critics like Pierre Lasserre had singled out "the Five" as exemplars of composers who had rooted their style and inspiration in their "native soil."[421]

Collet therefore seized the opportunity to compare a phrase from Cocteau (in *Le coq et l'arlequin*), whom he presents as the spokesman for Les Six, with one by the Russian, Rimsky-Korsakov. Here he juxtaposes Cocteau's pithy dictum, "Je demande une musique française de France" (I ask for a French music of France), with the following sentence from Rimsky-Korsakov's autobiography, *Ma vie musi-*

cale: "En réalité, toute musique qu'on a l'habitude de considérer comme universelle est quand même nationale." (In reality, all music that we usually consider universal is, all the same, national.) This, as we may recall, had indeed become dogma during the war, as had the injunction that Collet now makes to young musicians—"la nécessité d'être de sa race" (the necessity of being of one's race). As we have noted, *race* was a term that appeared frequently in music criticism during the war to denote fundamentally "national" as opposed to more literally racial distinctions. But now, in the postwar period, the term was increasingly employed in conjunction with a concept of "purity" that implied clear reference not only to culture, but also to blood.

Collet here not only claims that Les Six have imbibed the precepts of Cocteau, but that they have heeded his advice to learn from Satie and his "magnifique et volontaire retour à la simplicité" (his magnificent and voluntary return to simplicity). While he admits that the individual personalities of the six composers are substantially different, Collet advances that they share a common conception of French art, the one exemplified, for Cocteau, in Satie. Here he invokes the metaphor that Cocteau employed in the dedication of *Le coq*, noting that all have managed to "escape" from Germany, and from Debussy, through the model of Satie. But as we will see when examining these composers, the former could not have been further from the truth, although Collet's and Cocteau's conception of them would stick in the minds of the group's supporters and antagonists.

Like most other postwar critics who praised *Parade*, Collet, in these articles, presents it in a very different light than that in which it was originally perceived. While acknowledging that some still consider it to be a "charivari et mystification de cubiste" (a charivari and cubist mystification), he argues, to the contrary, that it is rather thoroughly classic in its simplicity.[422] It represents an "authentic" classicism, which Collet here implicitly defines as one that evades the arbitrary rules of the past (recalling Cocteau) to discover "purity" anew.

From this he then extrapolates no less than the annunciation of another "golden age" in music, one comparable with that of the sixteenth century in the Netherlands, Italy, and Spain. A brilliant nationalist stratagem, this argument justifies the young composers' modernism as a new flowering of their own civilization. Collet therefore associates Les Six with the advent of the heroic new world being born of the war, and of a France assuming leadership among all of the civilized nations. His argument was indeed close to others now appearing in journals like the *Mercure de France* (similarly associated with the liberal Right), such as one in January 1919. Here the journal also projects the possibility of a "new Renaissance" of the arts in France, if artists can work together, just as Collet, Bernard, and others now argued.[423]

Collet's conception of a "progressive" neoclassicism (again resembling Cocteau's) emerges in his discussion of the young composers' techniques, as opposed to those characteristic of the past. Recalling Cocteau's discussion of Satie's compositional techniques in *Parade*, he stresses that Les Six no longer have an interest in formal development, in the traditional sense. But this, he qualifies, does not imply that they lack in compositional skill: rather, it is positive testimony to their admirable, healthy, and vigorous modernity. Such modernity, Collet explains, should not be construed as a repudiation of the past, but in terms of the metaphor of the phoenix, arising from the ashes of the recent war. This, of course, was a myth that postwar France wanted desperately to believe, and Collet here astutely applies it to his diplomatic argument to legitimize French modernity. This allows him to conclude that Les Six have heroically succeeded in bursting the boundaries of a seemingly limited horizon and that, if they remain together, the future is theirs.

Such arguments received support in other intellectual circles as well, including that of the Catholic theologian we have noted, Jacques Maritain. As we saw, in his *Art et scolastique*, of 1920, Maritain argues for a new, more modern Christian art, specifically inspired by the renewal of Thomism.[424] And so he expresses his desire that religious art turn to universal form and abstract "order," which was indeed the province of the artistic avant-garde. Moreover, like Cocteau, he appeals directly to French nationalist sentiments, asserting that French civilization and values are, when true to themselves, universal. Classical art, for Maritain, expresses a "general form," which has both imbued it with universal value and linked it naturally to the avant-garde.[425] For Collet, Cocteau, and Maritain, then, "avant-garde art dresses up eternal forms in the latest fashions, rendering eternal verities commensurable with exhaustingly ceaseless novelty."[426]

LEGITIMIZING MODERNITY THROUGH TRADITION: BOULANGER AND STRAVINSKY

Collet's, Cocteau's, and Maritain's attempts to justify innovative neoclassicism were far from isolated: others similarly sought rhetorical means to legitimize more "progressive" composers. Nadia Boulanger, in particular, was pushed to such tactics in the defense of Stravinsky, who, like Les Six, was being attacked in the conservative press, particularly after Wiéner's concerts. Despite the fact that Stravinsky's motivations were substantially different from those of Les Six and their generational cultural rebellion, his appearance along with them would have adverse effects. In 1922 his Symphony for Wind Instruments and his *Concertino* was met with hilarity and whistles, and his case was not abetted by the counterapplause of his supporters among Wiéner's circle. His *Mavra*, performed by the Ballets Russes in 1922 and 1923 (with *Renard*) similarly incited the wrath of conservatives in the audience as well as the press. But Stravinsky did have his defenders, including Koussevitsky, who continued to perform him, and Laloy, who supported him in *Comoedia* throughout the difficult years of 1922 and 1923.[427] Boulanger, who, as we have noted, was probably forced to abandon her interest in the music of Schoenberg in this conservative climate, now had to justify her support of Stravinsky. This she would do in articles such as one that appeared in *Le monde musical* in November 1923, after several of Stravinsky's public fiascos.

As Scott Messing has observed, here she praises Stravinsky's "constructivism," or his "architectural" approach (one noted by other supportive critics, in works such as his *Octet*).[428] It is important, moreover, to recall that since the period of wartime *union sacrée*, "architecture," along with "la France classique," were central constructive metaphors in artistic discourse.[429] But Boulanger also then argues that Stravinsky's precise, simple, and classic lines specifically recall "the old masters of the Renaissance and J. S. Bach."[430] Even if straining against conservative strictures, Boulanger employs the dominant rhetoric as a necessary or judicious means of "protecting" Stravinsky's innovations in postwar France.[431]

Rather than emphasizing innovations in counterpoint, as did Cocteau with regard to Les Six, Boulanger prefers to associate Stravinsky with ties to tradition and to Bach's place within it. Bach, of course, was currently being constructed in several different ways in France, ranging from a master of counterpoint and a proponent of the "objective" to a moralizing and spiritualistic composer. In an article, "The Esthetics of Contemporary Music," published in English translation in 1929, André Coeuroy cites Albert Roussel's apt observations on the multifaceted "return to Bach." As Koechlin pointed out to Coeuroy, for him (as for Cocteau) praise of Bach was aesthetically part of the quest for an art that is "clean, vigorous, not descriptive, and even non-expressive." Yet Koechlin acknowledged that thus making Bach into an austere cult, in reaction to Debussy (as did Cocteau), is to ignore his "inwardness," his sensibility, and the "moral character" of his work.[432] Coeuroy, however, stresses the nonemotional, technical aspects of Bach, observing that such "objective" art is an unquestionable necessity after a period of upheaval. However, we must recall that during this period "spiritualist" composers such as Charles Tournemire, now teaching at the Conservatoire, were emphasizing the mystic and spiritual side of Bach. Boulanger here took the middle path in her historical comparison of Stravinsky with Bach, presenting both as belonging to a technical tradition of workmanship that characterized the canon.[433]

"Modernist neoclassicism" clearly had two strains, both defined against the nostalgic and retrogressive classic norm: one was that professed by Boulanger and Stravinsky, and the other by Les Six. While the latter admired Stravinsky, their intent, culturally, was fundamentally different, a fact recognized by both them and Stravinsky, if not by hostile critics on the public. In choosing models in the past, the crucial issue was still, as in the period of Claude Debussy, which past was to serve as a paradigm, and how, or the spirit in which it was to be used.

As several scholars have noted, the original use of the term *neoclassic* in France was pejorative—applied in the late nineteenth century to composers perceived as epigonic, such as Brahms. The positive term was rather *classic*, and we have seen all that this could embrace: *neoclassic*, however, was first applied to Stravinsky, without deprecation, in 1923. As such it implied a certain subset of the classic—different from that of both Les Six and academic classicism, although it did share with them a stress on purity and objectivity, as opposed to the German. It was specifically associated with a restrained modernity, a socially conservative but aesthetically liberal stance, as in Boulanger and Stravinsky who, having "lost Russia" was now turning to a "reappropriation" of the West.

This was the sense in which Stravinsky was the "paragon of Frenchness" for figures such as Nadia Boulanger, and for himself, who basked in and reflected back the image of a conservative but progressive elite artist. Politically to the right (he was an open admirer of Mussolini), Stravinsky was not, in the French context, perceived as such by the hegemonic culture, and was suspect because of his many trips to Germany. Stravinsky's style and orientation, then, was not neo-classicism *tout court*, if we are to apply the term (now common practice) to Les Six, who did not abjure "modernism" (as Stravinsky did), and sought to "disorient" through Dadaist techniques. While admiring and learning from Stravinsky, they had little interest in his objective, modern reconstruction of Western styles; rather, they sought to "awaken" or provoke their own culture, and to incorporate that which it excluded.[434]

But Boulanger was not alone, and her stress on the ties of "progressive" composers such as Stravinsky to the precision and simplicity of "the classic" recurs in other members of the politically conservative avant-garde. One clear example is Henri Sauguet, who ironically found himself acting as the spokesman for the Ecole d'Arcueil when its mentor, Satie, lay on his deathbed. For after Satie's rupture with Les Six, he had gone on to sponsor another group, formed in 1922, with similar inclinations, and whose name referred to Satie's working-class suburb. It comprised the young composers Henri Sauguet, Henri Cliquet-Pleyel, Roger Desormière (later a conductor), and Maxime Jacob (later to become Dom Clément Jacob).

Several of the group's members went on to become important conductors and musical figures in the thirties, especially during the Popular Front, but perhaps its most prominent composer would be the maverick Henri Sauguet. Issuing from a humble background in Bordeaux, and devoutly religious, Sauguet had been forced by the war to end his (primary) education but later went on to study composition with the Scholiste Joseph Canteloube. Sauguet's great awakening, however, came when he discovered Satie and Cocteau (through Milhaud), which led to a prompt renunciation of his earlier interests in Debussy, d'Indy, and Wagner. He subsequently studied with Charles Koechlin and, greatly admiring Les Six, became good friends with Darius Milhaud, who then introduced him to Erik Satie.[435]

Despite his modest background and his association with figures like Satie and Koechlin, who were sympathetic to the Left, Sauguet became a monarchist, remaining so throughout the 1930s.[436] Sauguet's conservative position aesthetically and politically was, in fact, not characteristic of his group, as we may see in the context of a lecture that he delivered at the Sorbonne in 1925, filling in for the now dying Satie. In this address Sauguet attempts to frame the innovative compositions performed with a discourse that indeed resembles the liberal nationalism we have seen in Cocteau. Like Cocteau, Collet, and Boulanger, he stresses that French music, in essence, consists fundamentally of the qualities of clarity, reserve, grace, sobriety, and elegance.[437]

Satie would have rather emphasized honesty, directness, acuity, and universality, or the ability of French music to transcend the national and the "collective," as he had communicated so poignantly through *Socrate*. But this was a period when success was still predicated on such "framing" by conservative discourse, or a justification of the new in terms of national tradition or of French nationalist values. Composers in Les Six and the Ecole d'Arcueil would thus permit this, as a necessity, in the twenties—as a vital means of publicity as well as of protection, despite all it distorted. As we will now see, the motivations of the members of Les Six were far more complex, and in some cases even contrary to such nationalist rationales, an opposition that would eventually become more overt. Such nationalist rhetoric would both help and hinder, attracting publicity but distorting perceptions of their work, and eventually provoking critics to attack its members on the basis of Cocteau's claims.

LES SIX AND NEOCLASSICISM: REALITY VERSUS MYTH

The cultural reality of Les Six is substantially different from the picture that Cocteau painted in *Le coq et l'arlequin* and Collet in his article that gave them their name. Far from being insouciant, iconoclastic, or nationalist youth, sharing Cocteau's opinions, as was then (and has subsequently been) supposed, they were engaged with the major intellectual issues of their period. Not yet politically aligned, as were their elders, they were still cognizant of the cultural questions and addressed them in their works not only through stylistic oppositions but through choices of collaborators and texts.[438]

Primary among these questions was that of the national (or "particular") as opposed to the universal, which here centrally included the question of German and other foreign influence in France. Far from sharing Cocteau's nationalism, almost all felt an ineluctable fascination with contemporary German and Austrian music, and especially with that of Arnold Schoenberg. Moreover, as opposed to Cocteau, most did not flatly reject the music of their elders, but felt attraction as well as repulsion to it—an ambiguity that, as we noted, characterized their generation.[439]

Les Six were part of the postwar rebellion, but equally part of its subsequent search for answers to questions that had been posed by the war, as well as by the political polarization that followed. Almost all drew close to politically aware writers, entering into their intellectual circles, and were fully apprized of the ideological issues, which they too felt compelled to address. For as opposed to their friend Stravinsky, they were in a continual, tense dialogue with their culture, investing their works symbolically with a commentary that we must attempt to recreate within the context. Powerful cultural and intellectual tensions subtended their innovations in musical style, innovations that are not fully explicable in terms of the internal development of the musical language itself.

Although their responses were not yet politically articulate, Les Six nevertheless assumed the role of intellectuals by addressing the primary questions posed by the postwar order in France. But to understand their diverse responses we must examine the background of each individual, the positions each assumed during and after the war, and how these were translated into stylistic or artistic decisions. As Georges Auric himself observed, despite the collective success of the group, its members would follow their own paths, ones that would lead them, despite their friendship, in sometimes opposite directions.[440] This included both political and stylistic decisions, which grew increasingly intertwined in the polarized and febrile 1930s.

AURIC: THE NATIONAL OR THE UNIVERSAL?

Georges Auric was undoubtedly the most articulate member of the group, and the one who, despite Cocteau's pretensions, would become its "serious" aesthetic spokesman. Even though it was his initial conversations with Cocteau which led to *Le coq et l'arlequin*, Auric entered into relations with groups of politicized writers who opposed Cocteau. Throughout the twenties Auric experienced tensions between nationalist groups and their critics, being drawn in opposite directions, or caught between conflicting nationalist and universalist ideals. He would express these ideological tensions in the twenties primarily through the medium of print, confronting the major intellectual issues of the day in his incisive critical writings. In the thirties, however, this would change, as Auric, facing the decade's political polarities and questions, now became more firmly ideologically aligned. He would express his commitment not only in print, but through stylistic decisions, attempting to adhere to the aesthetic of the Popular Front, in which he became visibly active.

Auric, the son of a *notaire*, was from Montpellier, the home of one of the founders of the Schola Cantorum, Charles Bordes, who had organized concerts there that influenced Auric's early taste. Similarly in Montpellier, he met the Scholiste Déodat de Séverac, who subsequently put him in touch with the influential composer Florent Schmitt in Paris.[441] There Auric attended the Conservatoire, which he found did not meet all his needs, and hence upon the completion of his studies (and perhaps influenced by Séverac) he entered the Schola Cantorum. Here he joined Vincent d'Indy's class in composition, but was soon disillusioned, and after the war was to become d'Indy's harshest critic.[442]

Just as important as Auric's musical background was his equally intense intellectual formation, one highly unusual for a musician in the period, and which he owed to several key contacts. The first was Mme Menard-Dorian, whom he met through his childhood friend in Montpellier, her grandson, Jean Hugo. She later introduced Auric to her "salon" in Paris; here he met not only prominent artists, but writers and politicians who, like Mme Menard-Dorian, a Socialist, were associated with the Left. In 1917 he even met important figures involved with the revolution in Russia, and he later became "secretary" of her group during the period of their concern over Mussolini's rise. Among the leftist literary figures he also encountered here were the now famous Anatole France and the young winner of the Prix Goncourt, Georges Duhamel.[443]

At the same time, however, he met important personalities associated with very different tendencies—those connected with "spiritualist" circles, and clearly aligned with the Right. Auric met the Catholic writer Léon Bloy through Ricardo Viñes, the pianist and fervent Catholic, to whom, Poulenc, a pupil of his, was close.[444] Like Viñes, along with other figures such as Paul Valéry and Maurice Ravel, Auric also frequented the politically more mixed salon of Ida and Cipa Godebski. It was then through Bloy, whom Auric (a practicing Catholic) admired, that he met the innovative Catholic theologian Jacques Maritain, and thus once more came into contact with "spiritualist" circles.[445] But Auric would not be the only member of Les Six to be drawn to Maritain, who, as we have noted, was close to Action Française and believed in the spiritual force of modern art. Arthur Honegger, although a Protestant, would similarly be attracted to his circle and to the idea of a modern religious art, as he demonstrated in *Le roi David*.

But, Auric was simultaneously attracted to a very different variety of postwar spiritualism, although one equally innovative in spirit—that of the surrealist aesthetic. Indeed, Auric became part of their circle even before they officially formed as a group in 1922, after their final break from Dada the previous year.[446] Breton, their leader, had been drafted while a medical student, in 1915; it was during his service in the medical corps (when he discovered Freud) that he met Auric. After the war, those who would eventually become the major surrealists, Philippe Soupault, Louis Aragon, and André Breton, formed the journal *Littérature*. In its second issue, in April 1919, Auric published an article on Satie's *Socrate*, and in its new series, in 1922, Breton included Auric's name as one of the collaborators. Before the surrealists broke with the Dadaists, Auric moved in their common circles and, along with those of Milhaud, Duchamp, Cocteau, Tzara, Poulenc, and Poiret, his name was included in Picabia's Dadaist painting, *L'oeil cacodylate*.[447]

Tensions between the surrealists and Auric, however, ineluctably surfaced when Breton squared off with Cocteau in 1922 (in addition to disapproving of Auric's admiration for Léon Bloy). Breton now firmly defended "l'esprit moderne," which he confrontationally opposed to Cocteau's "retour à l'ordre," or the return to classic tradition and craft.[448] To this end, Breton wished to convene a "Congrès international pour la défense de l'esprit moderne," and formed an organizing committee consisting of four directors of journals, two painters and a musician. These included Ozenfant (for *L'esprit nouveau*), Paulhan (for *La nouvelle revue française*), Vitrac (for *Aventure*), Breton (for *Littérature*), along with the painters Delaunay and Léger, and the musician Georges Auric.[449]

Although tentative with regard to the surrealists, Auric was undoubtedly enticed into their circle because of their bracing emphasis on the new, on action, and on cultural subversion. This was similarly one primary factor in his deep interest in popular music—its natural impiety, which could counteract torpor, especially if humorously mixed with "high art."[450] Auric, even if caught between cultural currents, evinced acute awareness of the intellectual issues, frequently invoking them, as well as the major figures involved, in his music criticism for *Les nouvelles littéraires*. In fact, he used the journal (denounced by André Breton as "bourgeois") to articulate an aesthetic position more closely aligned with members of Les Six than that with Cocteau.

Les nouvelles littéraires had already veered toward an aesthetic similar to Auric's, since René Chalupt, its established critic, had taken up the defense of Erik Satie. For Chalupt, who was aesthetically progressive, even if construing Satie nationalistically, considered him to be the prescient "promoteur de l'esthétique de demain" (the prescient promoter of the aesthetic of tomorrow).[451] Chalupt, however, also held opinions that were favorable to the Schola Cantorum, and here Auric, who had experienced it, was forced to disagree vehemently with his colleague. Completely disillusioned with the musical training he had gained at the Schola, as well as with the institution's philosophy, he attacked it violently on 9 December 1922. Here Auric argues (in contradiction with Cocteau) that if the symphony did attain a new grandeur with Beethoven, it arrived at a kind of "hypertrophy" after Franck, and especially with Vincent d'Indy.[452]

As a former and disaffected student, Auric (like Debussy before) ridicules the Schola's stress on cyclic form, or its belief that a "generating theme" is the "raison expressive" of the entire cycle. And here he cites a line from Chabrier's comic opera, L'étoile, "Faisons nous petits, petits" (let us make ourselves small, small), noting d'Indy's derisory use of this phrase in La légende de Saint Christophe.[453]

In addition, Auric was aware of the political connotations of musical aesthetics and style in the circle of Action Française, which prominently included Pierre Lasserre. In discussing Lasserre's strongly nationalist Philosophie du goût musical, Auric similarly considers the still volatile issue of the "true" French tradition in music.[454] Specifically, Auric cites Lasserre's doctrinaire definition of this tradition as that which does not have an "air de travail" (like the German), but is rather "léger, gracieux, ou profond" (light, gracious, or profound). This then provides him with the occasion to raise the central intellectual issues of not only the manner in which to construe the French tradition, but the reasons why it still persists. Auric, like other members of Les Six, refused to accept Cocteau's definition as dogma, but rather sought strenuously and arduously to define for himself the essence of French tradition and its national or universal nature. As a result, he made often contradictory comments, including several concerning both nationalism and jazz, which are frequently taken out of context and seen as solid evidence of his nationalism.[455]

Auric's aesthetic independence emerges in his ballet, Les fâcheux, based on the Molière play, which, appropriately for the spirit of Les Six, ridiculed a series of social "types." Auric originally wrote the music for the 1922 revival of Molière's play at the Odéon, composing dances for the ends of the acts. Diaghilev subsequently commissioned a full-scale ballet, or an expanded version, with choreography by Nijinska and the decor and costumes by Braque.[456] The work, consisting of an "ouverture et scène," followed by nine dances and a "finale," display's Auric's strong feeling for tonality, if "peppered" with carefully placed "wrong notes." Although it makes reference to eighteenth-century French style, and particularly to the articulation and clarity of the clavecinistes, its melody is childlike, recalling Satie, as does its deliberate disjunction, or stylistic juxtaposition. The form is clear and traditionally balanced, although by no means as rigidly as at the Schola, and it is filled with both harmonic surprises and episodes recalling Stravinsky in rhythm, as well as in timbre and texture. Auric's French tradition was a highly personal blend, and always unorthodox, for even when invoking his impressive formal training, he often throws it into sharp relief against modernist influences, and especially that of Satie.

MILHAUD AND THE TRANSCENDENT COLLECTIVITY

Milhaud, even more so than Auric, was preoccupied with tradition for most of his life, but confronted a particular dilemma in defining it, as an assimilated French Jew from Provence. He considered his own tradition to be French, which for Milhaud was unquestionably universal, tolerating a variety of religions and races ever since the French Revolution. And so in introducing himself in his autobiography as a Frenchman from Provence and as an "israélite," Milhaud was defining himself as a Frenchman of the Jewish religion, and one long rooted in southern France.[457] Milhaud came from an old French-Jewish tradition which maintained that while essential elements of Jewish religious identity should be preserved, those ethnic features inimical to French civilization should be jettisoned.[458] At first glance, then, although Milhaud's stress on tradition seems surprisingly conservative and close to the Right, deeper examination reveals how he strategically inflected traditionalist rhetoric.

Milhaud was of the postwar generation that "questioned"—a true "clerc" in Julien Benda's sense—in search of truth and universal values in the new world that emerged from the war. His quest was to reconcile the inner tensions that he experienced, from the very start, between tradition and the contemporary world and between his Judaism and the dominant French Catholicism.[459] The lighthearted, worldly side of Milhaud indeed obscures this intellectual quest, which was that of a member of an advanced cultural elite, in which he was inherently "marginal." Like his friend Wiéner, Milhaud's full recognition of anti-Semitism in French society would not occur until the following decade, although in the twenties we may perceive subtle awareness. And while some of his compositions do appear to accord with Cocteau's pithy dictums in Le coq et l'arlequin, Milhaud, along with Honegger, was essentially impervious to Cocteau's intellectual influence.[460] He rather chose other French intellectuals to frequent, although still collaborating with Cocteau and employing his texts: it is the circle that Milhaud developed that is significant here, and the logic of the specific choices that he made.

From the very start of his career, Milhaud was engaged in an intellectual search for "roots" that could encompass his identity, both national and regional, as well as his religion, in a comprehensive totality. Coming from southern France (Provence), where Jews and other Frenchmen had long coexisted, Milhaud thus considered himself "Mediterranean," an appellation that could capaciously embrace both groups. Milhaud retained this identity, even while a student of Gédalge at the Conservatoire, as opposed to his fellow student, Jean Wiéner, who was both a native Parisian and a converted, Catholic Jew. Milhaud's dual identity as both French and Jewish emerges powerfully and immediately in his exquisite early set of songs, the Poèmes juifs, of 1916. Significantly, despite their content, they are set in the orthodox French wartime style, and in a manner recalling Debussy's scrupulous sense of appropriate, subtle French diction.

But Milhaud discovered another source that bound both Christians and Jews historically in a common civilization, as well as in a geographic identity. While he was at the Conservatoire, meeting other future members of Les Six, Milhaud was also developing what would become a lifelong passion for ancient Greek civilization and myth. As for Freud before him, both Greek and Roman civilization, for Milhaud, provided the model of a culture that was originally shared by Jews and non-Jews alike. Thus, in a sense, for both figures, their passion for the classical world and ancient history was one viable path toward an ardently desired assimilation within their own cultures. For Freud, in fin-de-siècle Vienna, as well as for

Milhaud, in twentieth-century France, ancient myths and culture provided the basis for the construction of a collective identity. Milhaud repeatedly propounded an idea previously been proposed by Freud—that classical culture was indeed the common ground originally uniting Christian and Jew. Indeed, this may have been a reason why Milhaud, unusually well educated for a musician (as were several of Les Six) obtained his *baccalauréat* in *latin-grec*.[461]

Milhaud's interest in Greek civilization was to be fostered further by his long collaboration with the writer Paul Claudel, which began in Milhaud's youth, before World War I. In the period extending between 1913 and 1924, Milhaud composed the music for Claudel's French adaptation of Aeschylus's trilogy, the *Oresteia*.[462] In the second work of the trilogy, *Les Choéphores* (1915–16), Milhaud attempts, in wartime, to set a text that Jeremy Drake has aptly described as "of savage intensity." Here the text is rhythmically declaimed over an accompaniment of percussion alone, and occasionally the chorus joins with the soloists in reciting the text, or then repeats it.[463] But here it is important to note that Milhaud's interest in the ancient world was not limited to his collaboration with Claudel: the princesse de Polignac, another lover of ancient Greece, commissioned Milhaud's opera *Les malheurs d'Orphée*.[464] Both during and after the war, then, as he was collaborating with Claudel and others, Milhaud maintained his belief in the deep connection between Greek mythology and Hebrew thought. Milhaud's profound faith became immediately evident to the equally devout Claudel, who, unlike Milhaud, did not come from a strongly religious background. He was therefore all the more impressed not only with Milhaud's intelligence, but with his unaffected religiosity, seeing him as a kind of "living presence" of the Bible itself.[465]

His bond with Claudel grew stronger when the latter was appointed *chargé d'affaires* for the French Legation in Brazil, in 1917, and took Milhaud along as his official secretary.[466] Already suffering from the poor health that would plague him for the rest of his life, Milhaud, unfit for combat, thus fulfilled his national service administratively, in Brazil. Since there were no "cultural attachés" in this period, Milhaud worked under a different rubric, and was now (ironically) put in charge of "propaganda" for the allied cause. He not only translated coded messages, but helped Claudel to organize receptions as well as concerts and lectures in aid of the French and English Red Crosses.[467] Milhaud thus had firsthand experience of wartime cultural propaganda for the French, which was to foster further tensions within him that would, for many years, penetrate his work. For he retained an ambiguous, tense relation with this conservative conception of French tradition, employing its rhetoric while, as we have noted, subtly refocusing its meaning.

This we may witness in a lecture that Milhaud was asked to deliver in Paris on 7 January 1917, at the prestigious intellectual venue of the Ecole des Hautes Etudes Sociales.[468] The lecture was specifically in commemoration of the French composer Albéric Magnard, who had been killed in the war—not in combat but "heroically" defending his home against the Germans. In spite of Cocteau's rhetoric, Milhaud would long continue to admire this former Scholiste composer and his music, a passion that he would soon pass on to his friend Arthur Honegger. For both composers, perhaps more so than any other members of the group, remained faithful to the traditional forms, despite their innovations in content—Milhaud mixing them with popular music, and Honegger with technological references.[469]

But as we may see in Milhaud's lecture, it was equally the man and the legend that attracted him, above all Magnard's outspoken defense of Alfred Dreyfus during the Dreyfus affair. In this progressive scholarly milieu, Milhaud stresses Magnard's "culture" and yet independence, while also acknowledging his debt to the Schola and to the Société Nationale, which promoted his music. He thus recognizes Magnard's strong debt to d'Indy, in fact sounding very much like d'Indy himself when he construes Magnard's musical ideas as the fruit of his concentrated "inner self." Moreover, as an anti-Debussyste youth, Milhaud emphasizes Magnard's obvious distance from the movement toward harmonic "overrefinement," supposedly characteristic of Debussy and his followers. As he trenchantly puts it, for both Magnard and for himself as well, "la recherche de l'harmonie savoureuse est un mensonge musical" (the search for a savory harmony is a musical lie). And here Milhaud notes the Scholiste understanding of harmony as the result of the convergence of lines, now a timely idea that he could accept from Magnard, but not from the rigid dogma of d'Indy.

Clearly, now, just as in the late 1930s, Milhaud maintained ideas about tradition far different from those of Cocteau and several members of Les Six. As a member of a marginalized group, Milhaud (like Honegger, a Swiss Protestant) felt a conflicting need to both root himself in tradition and to explore avant-garde alternatives to the dominant language. Even when writing articles in defense of modern music in the conservative musical culture of the early 1920s, Milhaud would continue to praise older French composers, most notably Magnard, but also Chabrier and Roussel.[470]

Again contrary to Cocteau, Milhaud ardently praises Magnard's symphonic works as fundamentally in the tradition of Beethoven, noting his use of fugue as well as the influence here of the Schola Cantorum. Evidently what Milhaud admired in Magnard, and so persistently sought for himself, was an authentic musical language capable of expressing basic human truths. But particularly poignant is Milhaud's observation of the importance for Magnard of "la Terre, la Terre de France, où il habite, où il chant son coeur sain et vigoreux" (the soil, the soil of France, where he lives, where he sings his healthy and vigorous heart). This encomium of the land by a member of a group long deprived of the right to own it in France was part of Milhaud's assimilation and identity with the post-revolutionary French Republic.

Also highly revealing in this context is the fact that Milhaud concludes by noting Magnard's role in the Dreyfus affair, and in memory of which he wrote his moving *Hymne à la justice*. Perhaps one reason for emphasizing this is that the work was reissued for piano-four-hands during the war, but with no mention of its original political context.[471] Since "justice" now implied reference to the war, Milhaud makes it unequivocally clear that Magnard was here referring to justice in a broader political sense. Yet Milhaud himself then conflates racial justice and wartime patriotism by affirming, in closing, "C'est pour la Justice . . . qu'Albéric Magnard est mort" (It is for justice . . . that Albéric Magnard died). Equally trenchant, in view of the antirevolutionary sentiments still expressed by many French nationalists, is Milhaud's equation of the death of André Chenier, during the French Revolution, with that of Magnard: "Ah! Combien nous nous sentons, à ce rapprochement, les lourds sacrifices qu'exigent les grands crises humaines—les révolutions et les guerres" (Oh! how much we feel, at this rapprochement, the heavy sacrifices demanded by the great human crises—revolutions and wars).[472] Again, the French Revolution was a defining moment for his identity as a Jew in France, to whom the nation had at last unequivocally brought full civil rights.

Milhaud's close collaboration with Claudel continued unabated after the war, when the latter became a prominent member of the circle at *La nouvelle revue française*. During this period Claudel was not only at the height of his fame, but consequently was now being consistently attacked by the nationalist French Far Right. Indeed, Pierre Lasserre's *Les chapelles littéraires*, which appeared in 1920, assaults Claudel as the leader of an intolerant, malevolent intellectual "clique." Sounding like Julien Benda later, although from the opposite ideological point of view, Lasserre excoriates "les tyrannies de clan et de secte, de ces organisations d'intolérance" (the tyrannies of clans and sects, of these organizations of intolerance).[473]

Such groups, Lasserre argues, exist only to promote what are unequivocally false values, while exaggerating their own virtues as much as possible before the public. And here he remarks on all the Jews, "littéraires ou gens du monde," who admire Claudel, as well as noting their attack on himself as "un demi-traître envers ma patrie" (a half-traitor to my country). For Lasserre had observed a connection—one extremely dangerous at the time—between Claudel and German romantic writers, for which he was immediately attacked.[474] But, Milhaud stuck with Claudel, as both probed the connections between the world's great religions, or those that bound Judaism and Christianity, as opposed to what drew them apart.

In works like *L'homme et son désir*, written in 1918 (for the Ballets Suédois), they together address the concept of humanity, as well as man's existential plight in the world. While Claudel was searching for literary themes that would cut across political, social, or national lines, Milhaud was seeking a universal language that would express man's elemental experience. For Milhaud, this language was to be that of traditional and urban popular music, which he considered capable of expressing primal being, from sadness to exultation. Though his friendship with Heitor Villa-Lobos in Brazil, Milhaud became acquainted with Brazilian Carnival music, and was also influenced by Villa-Lobos's *Amazon*, which similarly evokes "the primitive" through the use of percussion instruments.[475]

But Milhaud's collaboration with intellectuals in France was not limited to Paul Claudel: at the time of his discovery of the latter, he was also drawn to André Gide, and then to Francis Jammes. All three writers were, in fact, friends, and moved within the same circles, all having been collaborators on *La nouvelle revue française* before the war.[476] According to Madeleine Milhaud, her husband liked Francis Jammes's poetry as opposed to that of the symbolists, which he had already rejected in favor of Claudel's almost "prophet-like lyricism."[477]

Because of his broad cultural interests, Milhaud consciously cultivated connections with other intellectuals outside of music, including (partly because of family connections) those in philosophy.[478] Later, when Les Six met every Saturday night at Milhaud's home, they would characteristically find a broad circle of academics, painters, writers, composers, and performers. These included Dadaists such as Tzara, Picabia, and Duchamp, and surrealists, including the most prominent—Breton, Aragon, and Desnos.[479] The appeal of the Dadaists for Milhaud, and for other members of Les Six, was undoubtedly linked to this group's close association with the postwar generational rebellion. But the attraction to the surrealists for Milhaud and his colleagues was far more complex, and indeed was different in nature and degree for each member of the group.

One may speculate that, for Milhaud, the surrealists' political awareness and commitment to the pursuit of political and social justice was one of the most important elements. The surrealists would immediately speak out against Mussolini's invasion of Ethiopia, as opposed to the conservative claim that the "civilized" occident should indeed prevail. Milhaud was highly sensitive to issues of racial justice in any guise; in fact his interest in jazz was inseparable from his belief that Jews and blacks were similarly oppressed peoples. As he later put it (in 1938):

> Le coté primitif africain est resté profondément ancré chez les noirs des Etats-Unis, et c'est là qu'il faut voir la source de cette puissance rythmique formidable, ainsi que celle des mélodies si expressives, qui sont douées du lyrisme que seule des races opprimées peuvent produire. . . . C'est la même tendresse, la même tristesse, la même foi que celle qui animaient les esclaves qui, dans leurs chants, comparaient leur sort à celui des Juifs captifs en Egypte et qui appelaient de toute leur âme un Moïse qui les sauverait."[480]
>
> [The primitive African side has remained profoundly rooted in the blacks of the United States, and it is there that we can see the source of that formidable rhythmic power, as well as that of the melodies, which are so expressive, and which are endowed with a lyricism that only oppressed races can produce. . . . It is the same tenderness, the same sadness, the same faith as that which animated the slaves who, in their songs, compared their fate to that of the Jews captive in Egypt and who called, with all their souls, for a Moses who would save them.]

For Milhaud, as opposed to Cocteau, jazz did have a fundamental meaning: it was an expressive language, representative of a collective aspiration of another oppressed race, and as such a deeply felt articulation of the human condition.

We may see further manifestation of Milhaud's cultural and musical interest in jazz in his ballet, *La création du monde* (1923), again for Rolf de Maré's Ballet Suédois, with decor by Fernand Léger. Only the previous year Milhaud had heard authentic jazz in Harlem (including Harlem blues and New Orleans style jazz), during his first trip to the United States on a concert tour organized by E. Robert Schmitz. In the ballet, the scenario of which is based on an African myth of the creation of the world, Milhaud employs precisely those elements of jazz, as well as of other popular music, that, for him, best evoke the "profound soul of this race." He here uses not just the intervals and timbres of jazz (stressing the soulful saxophone) but its powerful rhythms and syncopations, although layering these polyrhythmically and introducing a moving blues-like quality. But we may also observe Milhaud's simultaneous repulsion for and attraction to the past, for he deftly combines these jazz elements with classical techniques of formal musical organization, including a fugue, if based on new materials. In spite of his interest in popular culture, Milhaud remained rooted in tradition, and indeed wanted to be perceived as such, and not as a "show-ground musician."[481]

Milhaud proclaimed his loss of interest in jazz in 1926, to surprised American journalists during a trip to the United States. He then argued that it was merely a phenomenon of cultural snobism, having been taken up by the "milieu mondain," from which he had distanced himself. Significantly, this was the same year as the publication of *Le jazz*, the first French scholarly work on the subject, by the ethnomusicologist André Schaeffner and the music critic André Coeuroy. The book stresses the African roots of jazz, tracing the use of certain instruments or timbres, as well as its connection to daily life, later including prayer. After analyzing the specific characteristics of this music, the authors then proceed to claim that these features were later united most powerfully by the white musicians who adapted them. Hence jazz, they claim, as Milhaud now did, if for different reasons, provided an essential "jolt" to French avant-garde composition, but the latter had since "found" itself.[482] Abjuring this racist argument, Milhaud had simply moved on in the continuing exploration of aspects of his heritage, and now to the specifically Jewish element.

Despite the fact that Wiéner and Milhaud held different conceptions of their identity as French Jews, they remained good friends, collaborating on important musical and intellectual endeavors. One of particular relevance here is a lecture that Milhaud gave for the Groupe d'Etudes Philosophiques et Scientifiques pour l'Examen des Idées Nouvelles (The Group for Philosophic and Scholarly Examination of New Ideas). Delivered at the Sorbonne, in the Amphithéâtre Descartes, on 22 May 1924, its subject was "Les ressources nouvelles de la musique." As with so many lectures both during the war and in the postwar period, it was followed by a concert, which prominently included works of Wiéner and Milhaud. The concert in effect legitimized Wiéner's originally iconoclastic endeavor through its intellectual framing by the lecture and the august institutional context.

Resembling the "concerts salades," it employed both a "jazz-band" as well as "instruments mécaniques," and included the playing of a recording of "disques nègres," *Trois blues* by Wiéner, harmonized "Bayou Ballades," and works of Stravinsky on player piano.[483] But Wiéner's mélange at the prestigious Sorbonne, just before the installation of the Cartel des Gauches, was presented not as an "affront" to conservative postwar culture, but now as an intellectually legitimate cultural enterprise. Its implicit justification lay unmistakably in the theories of the Far Left, to which both Milhaud and Wiéner would be drawn more overtly in the 1930s.

Milhaud, unlike Cocteau, although anti-Wagnerian, was not Germanophobic in the French nationalist sense, and thus did not shun either German or Austrian music, including their modernist avant-gardes. In 1921, in fact, Milhaud and Poulenc went to Vienna (a city, in effect, under "ban") to give several concerts of French music, along with the singer Marya Freund. During the trip they were able to meet not only Arnold Schoenberg but his pupils Berg and Webern, whose music they similarly admired. All of this was brave enough, but Milhaud defied the cultural "ban" once more by becoming the only French composer to be published by the Viennese Universal Editions. Milhaud returned to Vienna in 1922 to conduct a performance of *Pierrot Lunaire*, together with Schoenberg himself. Just as boldly, in 1920 Milhaud had already flouted postwar chauvinism by openly dedicating his String Quartet to Schoenberg. These gestures helped to spread his fame not only in Austria but in Germany as well, where (through his friendship with Hindemith and Stravinsky) he would participate in several of its avant-garde festivals.[484]

Milhaud and his colleagues could not help but see the difference between the new cultural ideals of the Weimar Republic, with its promotion of avant-garde culture, and those of conservative postwar France. Believing that cultural innovation would help to realize the new social order, both government and private organizations in Germany sponsored performance societies that encouraged "new," international music. And German musical education, as opposed to the French, was now on the cutting edge: the Berlin Hochschule für Musik included "radiophonic studies," the Prussian Academy boasted Schoenberg and Stravinsky on its faculty, and the Frankfurt Conservatory even offered a class in jazz.[485]

Hindemith was a prominent figure in this culture, not only through his Gemeinschaft für Musik in Frankfurt, but with the avant-garde festivals of Donaueschingen and then Baden-Baden. In 1927, the festival at Baden-Baden (which was initially financed by the government) was devoted to short chamber operas, in an implicitly anti-Wagnerian spirit. The performances included not only Hindemith's *Hin und zurück*, but Brecht and Weill's *Mahagonny-Songspiel* and the first of Milhaud's "opéra-minutes." The latter, *L'enlèvement d'Europe*, lasting all of nine minutes, pointedly ridicules the dominant French classicism as well as operatic conventions and genres, including the French "opera of ideas."

Just as in traditional French opera, the work begins and ends with a chorus, however here it makes humorous and mocking comments, in addition to narrating the action and participating in it. The opera, which employs Stravinsky-like rhythms, as well as Milhaud's beloved polytonality, so impressed the director of Universal Editions in Vienna that he requested two more, to make a facetious trilogy. But Milhaud would have other successful performances of his operas in Germany: the avant-garde Kroll Opera produced *Le pauvre matelot* (with a libretto by Cocteau) in 1929, and the more conservative Berlin State opera staged *Christophe Colomb* (with a libretto by Claudel) in 1930.

The later work, rejected at the Paris Opéra, is eclectic in its genre, containing elements from the oratorio, the medieval parable and mystery play, and even includes a film sequence. Central to the opera is the narrator, who reads from "the book of Columbus's life" (as in an Epistle or Gospel) according to Claudel's Catholic interpretation of story. As Jeremy Drake has noted, Milhaud employs a wide gamut of styles to bring the story alive—ranging from the historical to the modern—including both neoclassic simplicity and baroque grandeur.[486]

But Milhaud's vistas would extend beyond Austria and Germany, and in 1926 he and Wiéner were invited by the State Philharmonic to give several concerts in the Soviet Union.[487] While conservative French culture had been "exported" to the United States, especially during the Bloc National, under the Cartel des Gauches the avant-garde briefly became the cultural ambassador. This was especially appropriate in the mid-1920s, during the flourishing of the Soviet avant-garde, before the antimodernist reaction that would occur under Stalin. Milhaud and Wiéner were among the first foreign musicians to be invited by the Soviets, an experience that was undoubtedly influential for them in the thirties, when both supported the Popular Front.[488]

Upon his return from the Soviet Union, Milhaud, in fact, became a regular music critic for the major Communist paper, *L'humanité*.[489] Later, in the early thirties, he would also write for a conservative paper, *Le jour*, before he assumed a more clearly committed political stance in the mid-1930s. From this experience, writing for both papers, Milhaud grew aware that although a work may not itself be inherently political, it could be ascribed a political position, or "read" within different contexts. As he put it (in 1930):

> La preuve de l'absurdité de vouloir donner une couleur politique à la musique est qu'en Allemagne d'anciennes chansons révolutionnaires sont devenues nazies, en changeant les paroles. Bien des compositions sont interdites en Allemagne comme "culture bolchevique" et les mêmes sont supprimées en URSS comme "déliquescence bourgeoise!"[490]
>
> [The proof of the absurdity of wanting to give a political color to music is that in Germany former revolutionary songs have become Nazi, by changing the words. Indeed, even those compositions which are banned in Germany as "bolchevik culture" are suppressed in the Soviet Union as "bourgeois decay."]

These are the words of a composer who was neither politically naive nor unaware of the cultural politics characteristic of the 1920s and 1930s.[491] Although not yet firmly aligned, Milhaud was certainly apprised of the political situation, and when the time came for commitment, he would enthusiastically join the Popular Front in combating fascism. Nor was he unaware of the musical-political currents of the Weimar Republic, particularly after his travels there, and his contact with figures such as Hindemith.[492]

But Milhaud continued judiciously, at first, to promote moderation in questions such as tradition and nationality, always seeking the middle path, as opposed to the early Cocteau. As he wrote in an article, "L'évolution de la musique à Paris et à Vienne," in 1923:

> Toute oeuvre n'est qu'un chaînon d'une chaîne, et les apports nouveaux de la pensée ou de la technique ne font que se surajouter à tout un passé. . . . On dit que l'art n'avait pas de patrie. Cela ne me paraît signifier qu'une chose: c'est que, pour tout

coeur sensible, toute oeuvre humaine sera vivante si elle est pleinement réalisée, quelle que soit la patrie de son auteur. Mais chaque race, chaque pays apporte avec soi tout un passé qui pèse sur ses artistes, et les grandes oppositions de race se retrouvent chez tous les musiciens.493

[Any work is but a link in a chain, and the new contributions of thought or technique are only added on to a whole past. . . . One says that art does not have a country. That seems to indicate one thing, that is for any sensitive heart, all human works will be alive if they are fully realized, whatever the country of their author. But each race, each country contributes with it a whole past that weighs on its artists, and the great oppositions of race are found in all musicians.]

Patriotic but still universalist, Milhaud would implacably maintain this position, even against the looming political threat and divisions of the late 1930s.

HONEGGER AND THE DILEMMA OF THE "NATIONAL"

As we have observed, it is indeed a misconception to dismiss Auric and Milhaud as frivolous youth, as conservatives painted them in the twenties and the thirties, influencing many later sources on them. This "revision" applies equally to Arthur Honegger who, like Auric and Milhaud, was a true intellectual, an avid reader, seeking out writers who addressed issues of the day, as he himself would do in print in the thirties. Like Milhaud, the tensions within Honegger's identity would similarly permeate his work—tensions related both to religion (he was a Protestant) and to his dual French-Swiss identity.

Born of German-speaking Swiss parents in Le Havre, France, Honegger thereafter spent time in both countries, attending the conservatory in Zurich before entering the Paris Conservatoire in 1912. Only the previous year, having attained the age of nineteen, Honegger opted for Swiss nationality, and yet continued to reside in Paris.494 As we may recall, this was a period saturated with nationalist rhetoric concerning art and the national "soil," which created ambiguities within Honegger over nationalism that would long remain. This may well have been the driving factor behind his intellectual, and later his political, search for a doctrine or an ideological identity to which he could relate and thus endorse.

Honegger, then, was initially exposed to a very different educational background in music than his colleagues in Les Six, and this training would long have an impact on his taste and style. Already well formed aesthetically and technically when he entered the Paris Conservatoire, he studied there with Gédalge, Widor, and (during the war) d'Indy.495

Looking back later on his student years, Honegger himself recounted both his educational experience as well as his rapidly changing musical taste in this period: "I arrived in Paris at the age of 19, nourished on the classics and the romantics, enamored of Richard Strauss and Max Reger, the latter completely unknown in Paris. . . . I was introduced to d'Indy, Fauré . . . and Debussy, and Fauré made a useful counterbalance, in my aesthetic and feelings, to the classics and Wagner."496

Unlike Auric, Honegger did not reject the aesthetic philosophy of Vincent d'Indy, a fact of considerable significance to his career in the late 1930s.[497] Also important to his later career, and a determining factor in attracting more conservative supporters, was that Honegger, accordingly, did not reject the "grande musique" of Beethoven, Wagner, and Franck. Nor did he immediately repudiate the music of Debussy and Ravel, as opposed to several other members of Les Six, as well as to Cocteau.[498] And after Milhaud introduced Honegger to the music of Albéric Magnard, the work of this former Scholiste was to exert a strong influence upon his style. Honegger later would even be accused of having plagiarized passages from Magnard's *Hymne à la justice* in his musical score for the film *La roue* (1924).[499]

In sum, Honegger's music is one illustration of Jay Winter's point that the war, far from quelling romantic tendencies of expression, in fact reinforced them. Although now a "refashioned set of ideas and images derived from a range of older traditions," they provided badly needed expressions of emotional responses to the war. The result was a singular kind of modernism that, far from rejecting traditional languages, now "recast" them, as a means of "walking backwards into the future."[500] Honegger's music, as a result, is less concerned with ironic commentary or "disruption" and provocation than that of his colleagues, although he too resisted cultural restrictions and ardently embraced the modern. His starting point was tradition, but as freely enriched with contemporary techniques, and his gift was for conveying the modern within this framework, making it accessible to a broad public. Honegger, like his audience, had a sincere need to connect with history, with a "grand" tradition that comforted, and in which he still found beauty.

Honegger's distance from his colleagues, aesthetically, was clear by 1920, particularly in the opinions he expressed in a survey of composers that was conducted by Paul Landormy. His responses were reported in the conservative Right *Revue hebdomadaire* by André Coeuroy, who, reflecting the journal's perspective, pronounced Honegger the "model" of the modern musician. Coeuroy cites the composer's declaration of his abiding commitment to "musical architecture," as well as to chamber and symphonic music, in other words, to "la grande musique":

Je ne cherche pas, comme certains musiciens anti-impressionnistes, un retour à la simplicité harmonique. Je trouve, au contraire, que nous devons nous servir des matériaux harmoniques créés par cette école qui nous a précédée, mais dans un sens différent, comme base à des lignes et à des rythmes. . . . Je n'ai pas la culture de la foire et du music-hall, mais au contraire, celui de la musique de chambre et de la musique symphonique dans ce qu'elle a de plus grand et plus austère.[501]

[I do not seek, like certain anti-impressionist musicians, a return to harmonic simplicity. I find, to the contrary, that we must avail ourselves of the harmonic material created by that school that preceded us, but in a different sense, as a basis for lines and rhythms. . . . I do not have the culture of the fair and the music hall, but, to the contrary, that of chamber and symphonic music at its most grand and austere.]

Nothing could have been further from Cocteau's declarations in *Le coq*, and the tensions between the two men would only increase in the early 1920s. Given Honegger's orientation, it is certainly not surprising that, among traditionalists, he remained exempt from their general condemnation of innovation and of Les Six. As we may recall, d'Indy, who had briefly been a teacher of Honegger at the Conservatoire, found him to be one of the most gifted members of the younger generation of composers.[502] Honegger's style, like Ravel's, struck a balance between tendencies acceptable to progressives and those that pleased conservatives, although different works clearly appealed more strongly to the different publics.

This would become particularly clear in the case of the oratorio *Le roi David*, perceived as "treasonous" by Cocteau and Milhaud but warmly greeted by a more conservative audience.[503] Indeed, throughout his career Honegger found himself torn between an authentic desire to appeal to a "general public" and a more uncompromising stylistic exploration. He would eventually find an ideological justification for reaching out to "the masses" in the 1930s, while still attempting to lead his audience into the future.

In the case of *Le roi David*, Honegger received unflinching support from the religious milieu that had exercised an attraction for Georges Auric—that of Jacques Maritain. Honegger's "modern neoclassicism" in the work was indeed an apt exemplification of the modern, yet classic, religious art being called for by Maritain and his circle. This oratorio, ostensibly influenced by Honegger's study of Bach and Handel, premiered initially as a "psaume dramatique," with a text by René Morax, for the traditional "fêtes du Jorat" (in Switzerland) in June 1921.[504] Originally written for performance by amateurs, with an orchestra of only fifteen players, it was then recast as an oratorio for performance in Paris, through the assistance of a wealthy banker.

Certainly, the work was apt for the milieu of its patron—the conservative bourgeoisie, in a period of postwar spirituality and concern with reconstruction in the world emerging from the war.[505] The style is immediately accessible, in part due to its simple melodic structure and its use of repetition, despite its harmonic innovations. Honegger, counseled by Stravinsky, cleverly wrote in a relatively uncomplicated manner for his amateur soloists and chorus, but enlivened their material with a more sophisticated orchestral style. His blend of traditional styles (inspired by the Protestants Bach and Goudimel) within a contemporary idiom (including bitonality and atonality) powerfully expresses the text.

Those journals that praised the work, not surprisingly, were largely politically conservative—*Le temps*, *La revue hebdomadaire*, and *La revue de France*. Significantly, Jacques Maritain also supported *Le roi David* in *La revue des jeunes*, which, again, was entirely consistent with his ideal of a modern classic but spiritual expression.[506] Maritain praised the work for the very same reasons that he supported the paintings of Rouault—both were able to "recast" the message of the sacred in modern guise, in a period of postwar mourning.[507] Both could build a "bridge" between the old and the new, as well as between the world of the sacred and the dead and the new world of the future, the profane modern world which France now faced.[508] Yet *Le roi David* was also traditional and modern in other ways, since here Honegger updated the venerable oratorio by employing a "speaker," in addition to mixing tonality with newer atonal sections. Cocteau, again, was not pleased by this endeavor to invoke baroque traditions, as well as to appeal to a much broader public, rather than the elite he had courted since *Parade*.[509]

But Honegger would garner more popular success, and particularly with a work of 1923–24 that uses stylistically innovative techniques within the context of a traditional form to suggest a new technological world. Originally titled *Mouvement symphonique*, it became known as *Pacific 231*, thus referring to Honegger's own fascination with technology and particularly with trains. For Honegger, the work originated as a technical challenge—how to suggest the impression of speed or acceleration through mathematic, rhythmic means within a firm formal framework. While advocating modernity and innovation, Honegger, like d'Indy, maintained the importance of not rejecting tradition, but of rather constructively building upon it. Hence, suggesting the gradual accumulation of speed by increasing the rhythmic subdivisions while decreasing the tempo, he casts the work formally as a kind of "chorale prelude," after the model of Bach. Here the "chorale" proper is not stated integrally as a cantus firmus until almost the end of the work, after having been anticipated by fragments and different versions of it.[510] But despite his use of Bach-like techniques and his return to Beethovenian motivic development, Honegger blends this with the rhythmic influence of Stravinsky, and masks it with the modern imagery of a train.

The work premiered in the context of a series of concerts that Serge Koussevitsky gave at the Opéra, and was greeted with so much enthusiasm by the audience that it had to be repeated.[511] In the thirties Honegger would also find popular success in his many compositions for film, in which he would continue to reach a broad public while nevertheless innovating in form and technique. And throughout this decade, Honegger increasingly sought to justify his goal in ideological terms by seeking a new collectivity that was supranational, and to which he thus belonged.[512]

However, tensions still existed in the twenties, when Honegger characteristically alternated between those works conceived for a more general public and those opposed to such an end, aimed rather at an innovative, knowing elite. And so he also engaged in more politically controversial projects, again, at the very same time that he was writing works that pleased both broad and elite audiences simultaneously. In fact, the very year that he wrote the highly successful *Pacific 231*, he also wrote the incidental music for Romain Rolland's antiwar play, *Liluli*.[513] Ironically, the public that was so enthusiastic about *Le roi David* was the same conservative public that, in general, was bellicose and nationalistic. Yet Honegger would continue to collaborate with major intellectual figures on both sides of the political spectrum, including not only d'Annunzio but Claudel, Valéry, and Gide.[514] Most notably, Honegger wrote the scenic music for a play of Gide titled *Saul*, which premiered at the Théâtre du Vieux Colombier on 17 June 1922.[515]

In the later 1920s Honegger finally reconciled with Jean Cocteau when they collaborated on the audaciously innovative opera *Antigone*. Premiering in Brussels in 1927, *Antigone* also included sets designed by Picasso, and costumes by

Coco Chanel. Honegger labored over Cocteau's adaptation of Sophocles between 1924 and 1927, a work in which Cocteau, although asserting "classicism," employed a contemporary and colloquial diction as well as a concentrated or synoptic approach. Honegger's goal was therefore to avoid conventional French prosody and accentuation in a vocal line that was carefully molded to the word, and within an economic symphonic construction.[516] His desire, above all, was for clarity, not easy to achieve within a fast declamation, and so he frequently displaced the "correct" French accents, using not the spoken language (or Debussy) as his model, but rather theatrical declamation. The vocal line is thus largely syllabic, and centered on the middle range, except for points or words of emphasis on which the accent falls, and where the vocal inflection often rises. Moreover, despite the thematic, symphonic continuity, the style itself markedly shifts to highlight the action, and employs a tonal, polytonal, or atonal language. His ideal was thus both Germanic and French, in keeping with Honegger's own mixed identity, and as unequivocally opposed to the nationalist, exclusionary ideas Cocteau expressed in Le coq.

Despite its prominent collaborators, the work was not accepted for performance in France until 1943 (during the German Occupation), premiering rather in Brussels and then performed in Essen. The following year, in *Amphion*, a ballet written with Paul Valéry for Ida Rubenstein, Honegger would cede to Valéry's insistence that the music sound like that of Wagner.[517] Honegger's wavering between the accessible and the avant-garde, once again, would end in the thirties, when he was finally able to reconcile his conflicting propensities through an ideological orientation, which was close to that of his fellow Swiss artist, Le Corbusier.

POULENC: MODERNITY AND TRADITION

Francis Poulenc, like Arthur Honegger, was torn between tradition and "the modern," and for him as well, the reconciliation between these rival tendencies would occur through ideology in the later 1930s. However, here the most apt comparison would be with the poet Guillaume Apollinaire, who, as Jay Winter has eloquently put it, was an "iconoclast with a flair for tradition." For composer as well as poet, "paradox" was central to their stylistic approach, which was situated consciously and provocatively between the modern and the conventional.[518]

Of all the members of Les Six, Poulenc was closest in style as well as friendship to Stravinsky, who sought out the young Poulenc for opinions on his work in the early twenties. Yet Poulenc's attraction to postwar "innovative" neoclassicism was not only technical or musical: it was also cultural—he was indeed part of the generational rebellion against the conservative classic model. For this reason, in part, Poulenc was close to Cocteau, sharing his attraction to contemporary popular music, although his tastes were not identical to Cocteau's, diverging substantially from the pronouncements in Le coq.

Yet Poulenc's social background was not distant from Cocteau's: both were of the upper bourgeoisie, Poulenc's father coming from a wealthy Catholic family of pharmaceutical manufacturers.[519] Poulenc's educational background had certainly not prepared him for an artistic career, since his father was determined that he first pass his baccalaureate, which had precluded any study at the Conservatoire. Instead, he studied piano privately with the musically well-connected Ricardo Viñes, and it was at the latter's home that Poulenc met Satie as well as Stravinsky, Cocteau, and Auric.[520]

Having already been influenced by Chabrier, Ravel, and Stravinsky, through Viñes, Poulenc, upon meeting Satie (in 1916), immediately perceived him as the leader toward "a new path for French music."[521] Lacking academic training in music, Poulenc now applied to but was rejected by the Paris Conservatoire, and soon after, in the fall of 1917, he was drafted into the army. After the war, Poulenc continued his studies privately, now with Charles Koechlin, having been recommended to him by Ravel, upon the instigation of Viñes.[522]

Throughout the postwar period Poulenc remained particularly close to Jean Cocteau, setting his revolutionary Dadaist poems *Cocardes* in 1919. But significantly, as Keith Daniel observes, the poems of *Cocardes* were conceived aleatorically, thus lacking formal cohesion—the words and images can be placed on the page in any manner. Poulenc's musical setting, however, is rather tightly controlled, even if clearly imbued with an appropriate "popular" strain.[523] His classical proclivity resurfaces even more strongly in the ballet, *Les biches*, of 1924, commissioned by Serge Diaghilev, with sets and costumes by Marie Laurencin. Clearly influenced by Stravinsky's *Pulcinella*, of 1919 (also commissioned by Diaghilev, in keeping with neoclassic norms of the postwar period), each movement is in ABA form, with a regular phrase structure and a judicious use of dissonance for "spice."

Poulenc, like Honegger, made frequent reference to traditional forms, or balanced, closed structures, to articulate contemporary experience, but Honegger always took them seriously, even as he filled them with modern techniques. Poulenc, on the other hand, tended to use such forms as an external "molds," finding, like his ally Stravinsky (if less abstractly and more ironically) new means of development within them. For he sought to comment not on the music or the style of the eighteenth century, but rather on its cultural essence, its "spirit," as communicated through the language of the present. For Poulenc, as opposed to Stravinsky, the past was not a foreign object to appropriate, or a challenging technical construct, but rather a part of his own identity. Poulenc deftly captured the eighteenth century's ironic, cutting humor in order, incisively, to criticize his culture, often evoking the eighteenth century's greater freedom in sexual mores as a commentary on his own day. This also becomes clear in his *Concert Champêtre* of 1927, in which he seizes the wit and spirit of eighteenth-century France, as well as its harpsichord idioms, while jolting the listener back to the present with frequent harmonic surprises. Indeed, his work appealed to Wanda Landowska, for whom it was written, and far more than did de Falla's more serious Concerto for Harpsichord and Five Instruments, which she premiered the same year.

Les biches, clearly set in the contemporary world and based on a modern "house party," allowed the composer to experiment with the idea of an updated *fêtes galantes*, a context in which elite and popular culture could again mingle freely.[524] With a huge blue sofa around which the dancers cavort as the only piece of furniture, and with almost scandalous costumes by Laurencin, the work was inherently libertine and provocative. Like Satie, Poulenc here accordingly plays with both stylistic rhetoric and gestures that suggest the eighteenth century, while cleverly suggesting a hidden meaning or commentary, as well as erotic innuendos. Poulenc's interest in French popular culture, of both the past and present, was enduring, fostered originally by his experience of it in both Nogent-sur-Marne (his home) and Paris. For him, it was not only a counterthrust to the nineteenth-century "serious" tradition, but the embodiment of direct expression, or an honest, spontaneous, natural "voice." And in popular as well as in elite culture, Poulenc instinctively sought continuity across time, while his "universalist" colleague, Milhaud, rather sought it across races and cultures.[525]

Unlike Cocteau, Poulenc also frequented the circle of the surrealists (beginning in Monte Carlo in 1924), along with Auric, as we have noted.[526] Despite his friendship and intellectual exchange with the surrealists, however, Poulenc's own exploration of surrealism, in particular the poetry of Paul Eluard, would not occur until the following decade. And then, ironically, it was not the "revolutionary" aspects of the movement that attracted him, but rather its proclivity for the mystical and spiritual, which coincided with Poulenc's rediscovery of Catholicism and a more romantic style.[527] Still trying to come to terms with his own homosexuality in the thirties, he found the surrealists' stress on "the esoteric," inward vision, impotence, metamorphosis, and liberation profoundly appealing. His identity remained deeply conflicted despite his outward airs of a *grand seigneur*, with a conventional eighteenth-century château, landscaped and furnished in the traditional French manner.[528] Indeed, while the surrealists remained decisively to the Left, Poulenc, in the thirties, positioned himself, like his family before him, in the conservative republican Center.[529] Although drawn to the popular, raucous world of the *café-concert* and the music hall in the twenties, Poulenc would now rediscover his conservative social and religious roots.[530]

Even in the 1920s, however, tensions between Poulenc's two social worlds would surface, as Cocteau introduced him to prominent patrons (from their own social milieu), while they explored a more marginal Parisian nightlife together.[531] Poulenc now frequented the circle of the princesse Edmond de Polignac, the prince and princesse Jean and Marie-Blanche de Polignac, the vicomte and vicomtesse de Noailles, and the comte and comtesse Etienne de Beaumont.[532]

It was while he was experiencing these different social poles that Poulenc was discovering his own homosexuality, which would result in a feeling of marginality, although he took great pains to remain discreet. Already, he was torn between the conventions and social norms to which he deeply wanted to be able to adhere, and the realities of his gradually realized sexuality.[533] While often preferring men of the lower social classes, he would often nevertheless be accompanied by cultivated, upper-class women in the salons that he continued to frequent. It has already been postulated that his works of the later 1920s, such as *Le bal masqué* and *Aubade* relate, in terms of both program and style, to this inner crisis. *Aubade*, a "concerto choréographique," commissioned by the vicomte and vicomtesse Charles de Noailles, and premiered at one of their costume balls, is based on the theme of "Diana's eternal chastity."⁵³⁴ In deep depression over his lack of success in forming a heterosexual relationship and his rejected marriage proposal to Raymonde Linosier, Poulenc was drawn to the story of Diana, "who retreats to the forest, her eyes full of tears."⁵³⁵

It was also in this period that Poulenc was introduced to the noted harpsichordist and promoter of the music of the baroque, Wanda Landowska, at the home of the princesse de Polignac. It was through the financial assistance of the princess in 1927 that Landowska was able to commission Poulenc's *Concert champêtre* for harpsichord and orchestra.⁵³⁶ Again, this work is testimony to Poulenc's nostalgia for the eighteenth century, but here viewed from an ironic distance, as indicated by its disjointed harmonies and juxtaposition of unrelated sections, or "additive structure." But like *Aubade*, which would be completed soon after, it is nevertheless tinged with sadness, or unmistakably evocative of melancholy, especially at the end, with its minor tonal inflections.

Perhaps because of this moroseness, Poulenc, like Milhaud (and Ravel), was an admirer of Mahler and his tragic, ironic vision, as well as of the Second Viennese School. As we noted, in a time of rabid anti-Germanism, Poulenc and Milhaud not only visited Alma Mahler in Vienna, but, through her, met Berg and Webern, and finally Schoenberg.⁵³⁷ No more than the other members of Les Six, then, did Poulenc resemble the irreverently iconoclastic and nationalist young composers evoked by Cocteau in *Le coq et l'arlequin*. He too experienced tensions between the universal (or outside influences) and the national, the pull of the present and nostalgia for the past, and the attraction of popular and elite art. Like other young composers of this period, Poulenc was fully cognizant of all these contemporary intellectual conflicts, which informed his work in the twenties, and would help to determine his stylistic and political direction in the thirties.

DUREY: AESTHETIC AND POLITICAL INTEGRITY

Louis Durey would similarly be torn between his own cultural or intellectual proclivities and those associated with his privileged background, as the son of a partner in a printing business. Like Poulenc, he came to formal training in music somewhat late, despite his devotion to the art ever since hearing a performance of Debussy's *Pelléas et Mélisande* in 1907.⁵³⁸ Like others of his station, Durey was not educationally prepared for entrance into the Paris Conservatoire, and so he (like Auric, but having no alternative) studied instead at the Schola Cantorum from 1907 to 1914. Although he learned solfège, harmony, counterpoint, and fugue at the Schola, Durey also resisted its "doctrine," and particularly its nationalist, conservative aversion to new, "experimental" German music. His first song cycle, of 1914, *L'offrande lyrique*, set to Gide's translation of poems of the "panhumanist" Rabindranath Tagore, manifest considerable audacity for the period, being inspired by Arnold Schoenberg's *Book of the Hanging Garden*, which Durey discovered that same year.

Like Milhaud and Honegger, Durey was becoming enthusiastic about Schoenberg's music, and acquiring his scores, but for him this was also an enunciation of his antichauvinistic stance. During the war, Durey then turned to the poetry of Saint-John Perse, in his *Eloges*, and again to André Gide in his *Voyage d'Urien*. Also during the war Durey completed his first string quartet, dedicated to Georges Auric, and performed at a concert of the Nouveaux Jeunes in June 1917. Although influenced by Ravel's and Debussy's quartets, particularly in its lyricism, the work shocked the audience with its bold bitonal opening.[539]

Just as defiantly, Durey's *Images à Crusoë*, again to the poems of Saint-John Perse, fluctuate between tonal, polytonal, and atonal treatment, in order to communicate the themes of loneliness, regret, and lost horizons. No less iconoclastic was Durey's choice of other texts to set, which included the openly erotic, as in the case of his song cycle, *Poèmes de Pétrone*, composed in 1919. Yet despite his startling departures, Durey, who was slightly older than the others, continued to admire Ravel, and even dedicated his *Neige*, for piano-four-hand, to Ravel in 1918.[540]

But Durey was unusual in yet another respect: being older and more politically aware than the others, he, like Satie, was among the first composers in France to turn to Communism, becoming interested in it in the twenties. This is not surprising, given his critical reaction to the war when he was drafted as a soldier, serving for sixteen months, and less willingly than his chauvinistic colleagues.[541] As a defiant gesture during the war, when all things German were effectively banned, Durey intrepidly began to write an opera based upon a German play, *Judith*, by Hebbel. Moreover, he read Jaurès's antiwar articles in *L'humanité* until Jaurès's assassination, and went on to subscribe to both *Guerre sociale* and *Le bonnet rouge*. After the war Durey remained close to Les Six, setting all of Apollinaire's *Bestiaire* (before Poulenc began to set selected poems from it) as well as Cocteau's *Le printemps au fond de la mer*. His Second String Quartet, of 1919, is dedicated to Arthur Honegger, and in the spirit of the group the second movement begins with a quote from a Haydn piano sonata, which is then cleverly subverted and varied.[542]

Compelled by a need for uncompromising artistic integrity, Durey decided to leave Les Six in 1921, moving far from Paris, to Saint-Tropez, in the south of France. In a letter to Milhaud of 4 August 1920, Durey confessed to not liking Cocteau's "légèreté d'esprit," and increasingly he was repelled by the growing *milieu mondain* of Les Six.[543] At first as uncompromising stylistically as politically, Durey continued his "experiments," particularly with instrumental music, but eventually, in the thirties, he would renounce his more "advanced" style in the interest of his political commitment.[544] It was ostensibly not social background but intellectual convictions that drew Durey to the Left at a time when Communism was attracting many French artists, including, as we have noted, the surrealists. But Durey, like Wiéner, and unlike the surrealists, would implacably retain his belief in the party throughout the thirties, and continue to support it for the rest of his life.[545]

TAILLEFERRE AND DUAL MARGINALITY

Germaine Tailleferre, like Poulenc and Durey, came from a well-to-do French bourgeois family, which was similarly opposed to her studying at the Paris Conservatoire. But after having done so surreptitiously, and winning prestigious prizes, she finally obtained her father's consent, though not his financial support.[546] Like Honegger and Durey (and unlike the others) Tailleferre did not repudiate the music of Ravel (who was by no means hostile to the group), and, in fact, she became a frequent guest at his home. As the only woman in the group, her battle was less against her elders, as it was for the others, than for a simple professional acceptance as a composer. Hence she often wrote in the older or conventional musical forms, remained clearer in both formal structure and line, and was less inclined to satire than were her colleagues. Her relation to the dominant musical language was necessarily of a different kind: Tailleferre's combat was related to that of her colleagues, but it was unique at the same time.[547]

Tailleferre, just as Poulenc, moved quickly into the circles of the Parisian elite, including that of the princesse de Polignac and the comte Etienne de Beaumont. And so she received numerous commissions, including *Le marchand d'oiseaux*, for Rolf de Maré's Ballet Suédois, in which she manifest her knowledge of eighteenth-century harpsichord music, like Poulenc.[548] However, despite the traditional dances, which include a *valse*, a *forlane*, and a *pavanne*, the style recalls Stravinsky's *Petrushka*, as well as that of Prokofiev's *Classical* Symphony. But pastiche is also present—not only a reference to Bach's Brandenburg Concerto no. 2, as well as to Chopin in the Valse, but to children's rounds. When reproached for this "frivolity," she defended herself vigorously, claiming (in *L'intransigeant*, on 3 June 1920) that her desire was not to imitate or to make fun of past composers but rather to allude to the small humorous ballets of the eighteenth century—a savvy tactic in such a nationalist journal.[549]

Tailleferre was clearly part of the generational rebellion after the war, defiantly embracing the image so feared in the period of the young, independent, professional woman. But it was clear that sex roles had to change, with the catastrophic loss of so many young men, and a new population of "single women," with little hope of either marrying or having children. As a result, the young, single woman was inevitable and yet threatening, symbolizing "female identity apart from traditional domesticity," as well as "the war's impact on the social organization of gender."[550]

Tailleferre was therefore in two new categories—the young, independent, working single woman, and the composer, the female artist, claiming equality with her five male colleagues. This was reflected in her public persona, in which she was depicted as working with men, but being both feminine and "modern," with the latest stylish clothes, and fashionably bobbed hair. But Tailleferre would find herself caught in the contradictory gender conceptions of her period, which despite a certain postwar openness nevertheless clung to traditional expectations. And so she would rebel, but within necessary limits, pushing the boundaries of conventional images and playing slyly with historical styles and techniques, inflected in a clever new manner.

Aware of her dual marginality as both avant-garde and a woman, she mingled the formal experimentation of the former with a critique of female identity that we would today call "feminist." For Tailleferre realized that for her male colleagues such "transgression" or questioning of fixed meaning and "paternal authority" was a conscious choice, while for her it was inherent in her "otherness," or alterity. Her challenge was to escape "two sets of expectations," as Susan Suleiman has so aptly put it, to avoid both the standard "revolutionary point of view" and the conventional "woman's point of view." She thus had to define her own position as "subject," and she did this, in part, through mimicry, or through "inhabiting stereotypes," but consciously, ironically, and trenchantly adapting techniques of her colleagues to comment on them.[551]

This we may see in works like the *Six chansons françaises*, of 1929, where she both invokes and undermines the expected female persona, with a disquieting and yet humorous effect. Composed shortly after the breakup of her first marriage, these songs, to the poetry of Voltaire and of anonymous French authors from the sixteenth to the eighteenth centuries, both praise infidelity and evoke deep sadness. The opening song, the ebullient "Non, non, la fidélité," is superficially simple in both melody and form, yet the harmony constantly startles with its nonfunctional relations. The beginning, for example, outlines an A minor scale, while the accompaniment remains tonally ambiguous, in the manner of Satie, and is thereafter frequently dissonant, proceeding with sudden unexpected shifts. In the course of the song Tailleferre also employs ostinati that recall Stravinsky, as well as using conventional harmonies in an unconventional manner, suggesting and yet avoiding functional tonality, again recalling Satie.[552]

Indeed, throughout her career, Tailleferre simultaneously invoked and broke away from established conventions, as the first French woman avant-garde composer. Although her influences and tastes were similar to those of Francis Poulenc's, she nevertheless was charged by critics with being ineluctably "feminine" in her style. Just as with Marie Laurencin, the painter who worked closely with Poulenc, gender typecasting played both a positive and negative role in Tailleferre's career. It brought recognition, but with it dismissal as "feminine," "pastel," and "light," or as Cocteau himself put it, "a Marie Laurencin for the ear."[553] But like Laurencin, she was indeed the sole female member of a prominent avant-garde at a time when women were, in general, involved with music more peripherally—as amateurs or patrons.[554]

Tailleferre, however, like her male colleagues, was attracted to circles of prominent French writers, including that of the leftist Paul Fort, at the beginning of her career, and in the 1920s, to that of Paul Claudel.[555] In the thirties her political awareness would deepen, and she would be drawn toward and aid such progressive political figures as Gaston Bergery by organizing concerts and giving performances. Eventually Tailleferre, like Durey and Wiéner, would grow close to the Communist Party, composing works for its many events, festivals, and commemorations for the rest of her life. But, in the twenties, like her colleagues in Les Six, she was already aware of the larger issues, political as well as more narrowly intellectual, although her response was cast in cultural terms. Abjuring the restrictions on style and most of the influences that were characteristic of the dominant musical culture, she responded by forging an iconoclastic image, intrepidly breaking all molds.

NATIONALISM, XENOPHOBIA, AND REVENGE ON "THE MODERN"

As we have already seen, Les Six had been systematically attacked since its very inception, first on primarily musical grounds by older traditionalists, such as Vincent d'Indy. Instigated initially by Wiéner's concerts, d'Indy had launched an assult on the "modernist" tendencies of youth in two scathing articles in the strongly nationalist *Comoedia*.556 In the first, "Le public et son évolution" (The public and its evolution), he indicted the new musical procedures of youth as incapable of producing anything "substantial," and thus destined to self-destruct.557 In the second, "Matière et forme dans l'art musical moderne" (Matter and form in modern musical art), he accuses youth of sullying the beautiful "matter" of musical sound and thus giving birth only to "monsters."558 Wiéner replied with alacrity in polite defense of the "new music," which prompted a letter from d'Indy, published in *Comoedia* on 3 March 1924. This time, as noted earlier, d'Indy, while once more stressing the importance of studying the great works of the past, congratulates Wiéner on his defense of his own beliefs.559

Auric, like others, was far more aggressive in his response: even earlier he seized the occasion to castigate d'Indy and his nationalist generation. Writing in *Les nouvelles littéraires*, on 13 January 1923, Auric analyzes the reaction to the Wiéner concerts on the basis of generational confrontation. More specifically, he refers to a critic of the concerts as "un compositeur avorté et amer" (a frustrated and bitter composer), as opposed to those youth who are able to assimilate and appreciate the culturally foreign and new. Auric then proceeds intrepidly to point out that in the time of Debussy it was indeed a "noble" cause to defend French music from the incursion of foreign (meaning Wagnerian) tyranny. But now it was no longer necessary, for a new spirit was ineluctably imposing itself, and such nationalist organizations as the Société Nationale de Musique Française were essentially superannuated.560

But attacks on "the modern" persisted. They notably included the recent works of Stravinsky, whose *Mavra* was premiered (by the Ballets Russes) in June 1922, and to the composer's chagrin was roundly condemned.561 But Wiéner nevertheless performed Stravinsky, even giving a concert consisting exclusively of his works on 26 December 1922. Schoenberg was another target: attacked by Paul Le Flem in *Comoedia*, on 18 December 1922, Wiéner pertinaciously kept his works in the repertoire of his concerts.562 As we have noted, the reactionaries included Emile Vuillermoz, the former Debussyste, who now targeted Cocteau on the assumption that he had, in fact, influenced Les Six. Again, writing in *Excelsior* on 8 January 1923, in reference to Wiéner's concerts, Vuillermoz asserted that these "manifestations théâtrales et mondaines" should be called "Les concerts Jean Cocteau." Here Vuillermoz postulates the impact of Cocteau's ideas, and is quick to point out their inherent inappropriateness for music, as made clear in the case of Les Six. For according to Vuillermoz, the "resulting" works of Satie and Poulenc are no more than "pranks," played on a benighted French public by adroit publicity agents. He then observes the "historic error" of considering musicians like Wiéner, Poulenc, Tailleferre, or Auric as participants in an authentic musical "movement." Instead he dismisses the group as simply "le petit troupeau hétéroclite et bariolé d'étudiants en musique qui hante la bergerie Cocteau" (the little unusual and motley herd of music students who frequent Cocteau's pen).[563]

On 1 January 1923, *Le courrier musical* went further and published an article by Louis Vuillemin titled, provocatively, "Concerts métèques." This term, often connoting "half breed" or a foreigner of Mediterranean origin living in France, and often specifically a Jew, had been introduced by Charles Maurras and widely propagated by Action Française.[564] Here Vuillemin attacks Wiéner's concerts, employing concepts that would long endure in condemnations of the composers involved, resurfacing particularly in the later 1930s. For Vuillemin, the works performed at these concerts (including those of Les Six and Stravinsky) are products of "le mauvais goût international" (international bad taste) the spreading of which in France, Vuillemin implies, is a kind of treason.

Employing arrestingly violent language, made admissible during the war, he then claims that this "movement" is beginning "à vomir les métèques et leur coco pianistique, vocal, ou symphonique" (to vomit half-breeds (Jews) and their pianistic, vocal, or symphonic "commies").[565] They are, he continues, successful primarily among "cosmopolitan suckers"—*cosmopolitan* referring most often in such discourse, again, indirectly to Jews. Moreover, invoking the postwar notion of a German-Jewish-Communist plot, he describes them (with Wiéner in mind) as physically "minable" (seedy), and as wearing "lunettes à la boche" (German-style glasses). Vuillemin then invidiously poses a question that clearly implies a plot—"Commandé par qui? . . . par quelle machiavélique et empoisonnée propagande?" (Commanded by whom? . . . by what Machiavellian and poisoned propaganda?)

But Vuillemin goes even further: suggesting a distinctly political goal, he employs a lurid analogy, one used, in fact, by Debussy during the war. Such musicians, he claims, seek to "gangrener notre organisme; de démontrer aux étrangers curieux, présents en nombre dans la salle, l'affaissement de goût chez les Français d'après-guerre!" (to gangrene our organism; to show the curious foreigners present in large numbers in the hall the sinking of taste among the French after the war).[566] Attacking French taste in the postwar period was tantamount to attacking France herself, a country that Vuillemin implies (as did many others) was still vulnerable in the sphere of culture. Vuillemin (like Vuillermoz) asserts that these composers are no more than "Dadaistes de la musique," thus directly associating them with a dangerous lack of seriousness that could further harm the national culture. He ends, however, by asserting that, happily, the public has uncovered the "plot," or has exposed their "exotisme intégral, faisandé autant qu'impuissant" (integral exoticism, as decadent as it is impotent).

Such charges and associations were by no means isolated in the period: Jewish-German-Communist plots to weaken the nation were now routinely decried. For as Norbert Elias points out (ironically, in connection with the Germans stigmatizing the Jews), the identification of the "other" as the enemy is a means of reassurance, to reinforce a self-image.567 Indeed, such a language of exclusion had been common in France since the turn of the century, in connection with the Dreyfus affair, as we saw in the case of d'Indy's *La légende de Saint Christophe*.568 Now it was present not only in music and literature (as we noted with Lasserre) but also in connection with painting, where Jewish artists were similarly becoming targets. As Romy Golan and Kenneth Silver have established, there was ostensible hostility to Jewish artists in the so-called School of Paris on the part of those who defined themselves, in contradistinction, as "French."569 While anti-Semitism was less important than xenophobia during the war, the two sides met and insidiously fused in the climate of defensive nationalism that followed the armistice.

A similar rhetoric therefore appears in artistic journals associated with the Far Right in this period: *L'art*, for example, railed against excessive foreign influence and "complots étrangers" (foreign plots). Between 1923 and 1928, *La peinture* crusaded for the restoration of moral order through the artistic means that it believed necessary to effect it—pictorial order.570 Other journals, like *Critique, art, philosophie*, openly attacked Jewish artists in the name of order and "puissance," or a classical attitude in both politics and art.571 Again, in all these cases, the concern with preserving the purity of the "national organism" was, in part, related to the necessary recruitment of immigrant labor in France after the war.572

As we can see, the rhetoric and racist circumlocutions that Vuillemin so dexterously interwove to attack Wiéner, Stravinsky, and Les Six were not exceptional in art or music criticism in this period. The image of the insidious, avaricious "outsider," or the "exotic" and rootless Jew, who is not truly French, but bound to international or Germanic conspiracies against the nation was common. Moreover, this discourse directly links the image to the assault on French tradition, or to the "modernist" and cosmopolitan danger now posed to indigenous French cultural values. It is small wonder that several members of Les Six sought greater sympathy in both Germany and Austria, which warmly welcomed their stylistic innovations, as they did those of Stravinsky.573

But even in France, such xenophobic assaults on the group did not go unanswered: Vuillemin's elicited a plethora of responses, ultimately causing the startled editors of *Le courrier musical* no small concern. Specifically, they feared that such a dispute would eventuate in a bifurcation into two hostile camps of the (at least, theoretically) "harmonious" body of French composers.574 But their worst fears were indeed realized in the thirties, when these issues assumed political and cultural centrality, eventually polarizing prominent composers and musicians in France. For the moment, however, and not surprisingly, it was the group around Maurice Ravel—Albert Roussel, André Caplet, and Roland-Manuel—which responded to Vuillemin with address.

These four musicians wrote immediately to *Le courrier musical* in vigorous protest of Vuillemin's article, pointing out that all musicians in France by no means held similar distasteful opinions. In fact, they here expressed their gratitude to Wiéner for allowing them to hear these new foreign works, especially Schoenberg's innovative, atonal *Pierrot Lunaire*. In their conclusion they seized the occasion, as they diplomatically put it, "pour émettre le voeu que le patriotisme s'égare un peu moins sur un terrain où il n'y a rien à conquérir, mais tout à perdre" (to express the wish that patriotism go astray a bit less on a terrain where there is nothing to conquer, but all to lose).[575]

Vuillemin's retort was violent, and again employed lurid imagery from the war, preposterously claiming that the authors of this letter were undoubtedly "intoxiqués par le gaz." Belittling their sincere response as "traitorously hilarious," he proceeds to assert that "le rôle des musiciens de chez nous n'est pas de fabriquer à l'étranger le musicien national qu'il n'a plus et regretté tant de ne plus avoir" (the role of musicians of our homeland is not to fabricate abroad the national musician that is no longer and so regretted no longer having).[576] The exchange of letters continued, with Vuillemin finally commenting snidely that the success of German decadents like Schoenberg in Paris was certain to amuse Berlin.

As we have seen, such rhetoric endured throughout the 1920s in France, seemingly legitimized by the still precarious state of the nation after the war. In the following decade the issue of race would continue to gain in importance, but it would become more specific in context and meaning, as French political positions evolved. For with the rise of the profascist Right, the extirpation of all insidious elements in the national "organism" became even more important than excluding those foreign (Germanic) elements that they now believed to be "healthy." The thirties, then, would bring the eventual culmination of the racist rhetoric legitimized in wartime, and transformed in the 1920s to refer specifically to ethnicity and blood.

Indeed, many of the conservative currents of thought in the twenties—the resurgent spiritualism, the stress on race, on grandeur, and on tradition, would triumph by the end of the thirties. But these currents were temporarily arrested, or contested, with the hiatus of the Popular Front, which responded to the political, economic, and social traumas that plagued the 1930s. This leftist government actively recruited among musicians, including Les Six, who, as their elders before, were now faced with both a professional and a political choice.

3

The "Defense" of French Culture in the Thirties

Part 1: The Popular Front: Culture as Politics
Programs and Ideals of the Government

ANTIFASCISM AND THE POLITICS OF THE SPECTACLE

It was not without relief and relish that members of Les Six and the Ecole d'Arcueil embraced the scarce official commissions for the Universal Exposition of 1937, in Paris. Perhaps most compelling for these "modernist" composers in this extravaganza of the now leftist government was the class of fêtes, on which the ruling coalition, the Popular Front, lavished its resources.[1] The politically ambidextrous Jacques Rouché, still entrenched at the Opéra, and aptly placed in charge of the fêtes, had no problem in adapting to this government, and again proving his mastery of the politics of spectacle.[2]

However, the message now was different: instead of convincing the French public of its ties to the past, as during and after the war, the point was to embrace a modern, egalitarian mass culture. Music was again marshaled to the service of propaganda, but the goals were the opposite of Rouché's wartime matinées, and equally distant from the message intended in Fauré's funeral and in the "opera of ideas." Most vividly illustrative of this distance was the series of fêtes called "Jeu de la Lumière et de l'Eau sur la Seine," which involved the collaboration of modernist architects as well as the commissioning of some twenty "modern" scores.

As Darius Milhaud, one of the principal composers participating, later marveled, this *fête nocturne*, conceived by the architect Beaudouin, was an iridescent play of water, music, and light. Barges floating down the Seine (together with loudspeakers on buildings and trees) diffused recorded modern music, which was precisely coordinated with a play of lights controlled through a central keyboard.[3] This light show, which all could enjoy, and which was "sonorized" by contemporary French music, thus deftly linked the Republic's democratic mass culture with modernity, technology, and splendor.[4]

Also presented on this occasion was the *Fête des belles eaux*, by the young Olivier Messiaen, who now had the unusual opportunity to write a work using ondes Martenot.[5] Of course, conceptions involving water also evoked the past spectacles of the French baroque, undoubtedly one of the references, but now as appropriated by a left republican aesthetic. Here the glory and "magic" of the state, a link between the messages of fêtes present and past, was communicated through a democratic, modernist performance in central Paris, stressing sight and sound.[6] The past, however, was only one subtle reference: the fête (like Fauré's funeral) evoked French "defense"—but in this case the defense against a mounting fascist threat, which included festivals with a menacing message. Responding to, and occasionally emulating, contemporary spectacles in Soviet Russia, the French fêtes similarly confronted the hierarchical, disciplined, archaic models of Mussolini and Hitler.

As opposed to fascist spectacles, these fêtes were "liminoid"—they sought "transition"—and so, in contrast to totalitarian ceremonies, they were polythematic, even embodying contradiction.[7] The goal was ultimately to promote *unanimisme*, or the desire of the Left to join together, a posture of reconciliation that had been vigorously promoted by the French Communist Party. Like the fêtes of the French Revolution, their point was to mobilize and to convince the masses, employing both visual and musical rhetoric at a moment when ideological orientations clashed.[8] Addressed to several different publics, the fêtes could signify in a different manner to each, as indeed did the Popular Front, so broad a coalition as to be inherently ambiguous. The Radicals saw the government as a complete republican program, and hence not at all "revolutionary" in its goals, while the Socialists perceived it as a manifestation of the masses, and the Communists as a new "class action."[9] Hence the fêtes of the 1937 Exposition invoked all the government's contradictory themes—social justice, national unification, peace, freedom, modernity, and enlightenment.[10]

Such fêtes were by no means isolated in disseminating these particular political messages—they articulated closely with numerous projects that the government implemented through its cultural channels. The values that these fêtes enunciated suffused many musical organizations and publications that were bound by either complicity or through state "patronage" (official sponsorship) or subventions to the Popular Front. Enthusiasm for the leftist coalition thus infected large sectors of the French musical world, which, in keeping with the government's goals, sought to reorient taste as well as musical style.

For a time, it seemed possible that the most artistically progressive aims of the musical world could be encouraged by the government and would further its ambitious new social programs. Recalling the policies of the Weimar Republic, French music promised to foster broad social change, and particularly equality and modernity, a national future aware of its past.[11] This necessitated not only an aesthetic reordering, as we shall see, but the attempt to produce new meanings in music, or to fundamentally redefine the significations of both genres and styles. Once more, modes of presentation and conditions of access to music became crucial, inseparable from the message communicated by works past and present, which were politically to be redefined. Here again, style was not "innocent": the meanings it carried were now actively reinscribed through interacting institutions and publications, of which French composers could not help but be aware.

France would again be split into hostile political-aesthetic camps, which would become pronounced in music, as political and musical cultures further fused. For, more so than ever, music became an integral part of French political programs, not only those of the Popular Front, but those of its vociferous opposition. And, once again, style in effect became a political enunciation, as combative parties emphasized the political symbolism and thus the ideological "agency" of music. The aesthetic battle within the field, then, became inseparable from the encompassing political battle, and brought with it a heightened degree of political awareness among French musicians.

It is thus impossible fully to explain the direction that French music followed in the mid and later 1930s without perceiving this fundamental phenomenon and its impact. Moreover, as political hegemony finally shifted to the Right, so too did symbolic or artistic legitimacy, based upon contemporary meanings, and it elicited a specific range of responses. We must, then, first recall the political rhythm of the 1930s in France, which was so integrally to affect the dominant musical aesthetic and reactions to it. For politics became inescapable, and intellectual choices had to be made, as musicians were forced to embrace shifting orthodoxies or to find themselves professionally marginalized. Since rejection of the dominant aesthetic had ideological implications within this context, certain composers would seek backing from contestatory political groupings that espoused alternative values. In some cases this implied a true political adherence, and in others mere professional necessity; but in both, the consequences were decisive, and could lead to politicized support or to politically charged attacks. For, as Julian Jackson has summarized the larger cultural situation in France in the thirties, there was no difference now between the political culture and the "cultural practice of politics."[12]

THE POLITICAL AND CULTURAL BACKGROUND

The Popular Front arrived at the crest of a disquieting period in French politics—in the midst of renewed agitation of restive political leagues, and of dismaying governmental instability. The moderate Right had ruled France until 1932, a year after the effects of the great American Depression began strongly to be felt in Europe.[13] A series of ephemeral ministries of the Left followed, during a period of agitation and polarization that exploded in the riot of February 1934. Just previous had been the "Stavisky scandal," leading to the replacement of Prime Minister Camille Chautemps by Edouard Daladier.[14] Such political confrontation indeed recalls the situation at the turn of the century, after the Dreyfus affair, when hostile coalitions of the Left and Right had similarly squared off.[15] But other factors were decisively to influence the political climate in these years, not only the growing impact of the economic depression, but the resurgence of right-wing violence. The latter was stimulated further by the flood of Jewish refugees from Germany, beginning in the spring of 1933, which would soon lead to an anti-Semitic backlash.[16]

Throughout the thirties, culture became a target, just as it had been following the Dreyfus affair, and indeed the latter event was now being revived as a political reference. So resonant were the memories from the affair that in 1931, when former Dreyfusards produced a German play about it, demonstrations by the Ligue de l'Action Française forced it to close.[17] And now surrealists became a target as well: when the Dalí-Buñel film *L'âge d'or* was shown in November and December 1930, it provoked violent attacks, leading to the banning of the film by the censor.[18] Hence one of the greatest worries for those in the political center and on the left was resurgence of aggressive political leagues and their tactics of politics through culture. These included not only Action Française and its bellicose offspring, the Camelots du Roi, but other leagues and groupings associated with both the traditional and the profascist "new Right."[19]

Now active on the right as well was the Fédération Nationale Catholique, which had already organized large demonstrations against the Cartel des Gauches in the mid-twenties over its laws that promoted laicism. Also founded in the previous decade (in 1924), by the nationalist deputy Pierre Taittinger, was the Jeunesses Patriotes, intended originally to promote ideals of the defeated Bloc National while the Left was in power. Although it was basically both a traditionalist and nationalist organization, its paramilitary "mobile groups" and fascist accouterments alarmed many. Ardently antirepublican, it advocated replacing the deputies of the National Assembly with a Committee of Public Safety, as in the French Revolution.[20]

Even more disquieting had been the openly fascist league Le Faisceau, founded in 1925 (it lasted until 1928) and led by Georges Valois, a dissident from Action Française.[21] Valois's model for Le Faisceau was clearly Italian fascism, and, like the latter movement, his included menacing, even violent combat groups. With the help of business interests, Valois had also created an accompanying journal, *Le nouveau siècle*, but his political tenability ended with the defeat of the Cartel des Gauches.

Yet leagues had continued to proliferate: the Croix-de-Feu was created in 1927, with a large part of its membership being former combatants in World War I. Led by its "president," the colonel and count François de la Rocque, and following military models, it was by far the best organized league among those now proliferating on the Far Right. Other leagues had appeared slightly earlier, including Le Francisme, founded in 1922, with subsidies from the Italian fascists and the ideal of forming a corporative regime. And in the same year François Coty, who helped to finance a number of right-wing leagues, founded his Solidarité Française, with a membership consisting largely of the now unemployed.[22]

Other right-wing groups formed parties. These included the Parti Social Français, Jacques Doriot's Parti Populaire Français, the Parti Républicain National Social, and the fascist Parti Franciste. But the leagues nevertheless remained prominent, with the principle or most visible right-wing groupings in the 1930s being the Jeunesses Patriotes and the Croix-de-Feu. The older groups on the Right, such as the Fédération Républicaine, did not fear the leagues and their violence, seeing them as "a wave of genuine popular indignation against a corrupt government."[23]

The leagues, however, frightened many of those in the center and on the Left, particularly after the bloody debacle of 6 February 1934. On this date demonstrators from various right-wing groups—including many members of the leagues—assembled at the Place de la Concorde to protest the policies of the Daladier government. The latter was the fifth in twenty months, a fact that political malcontents perceived as a sign of unacceptable ministerial instability at the height of the economic crisis.[24] The tumult, however, was probably initiated by the group that had formed to protest the demonstration, inciting the police to open fire and resulting in 15 deaths and over 1,435 wounded. But the violence achieved its immediate goal: Daladier promptly resigned, thus graphically demonstrating the threat as well as the ultimate efficacy of such physical confrontation.[25]

Yet the effects of this day were dual. For those who would later become fascists, like Pierre Drieu La Rochelle, it represented the alliance of the Far Right and Left against a decrepit parliamentary capitalism.[26] For others it testified to the necessity of an immediate alliance of the Left and Center, including intellectuals within both groups, against the threat of extremist fascist violence. This led, in 1934, to the formation of the Comité de Vigilance des Intellectuels Anti-Fascistes, to be followed the next year by more concrete political cooperation.[27]

In 1935, at the time of the Franco-Soviet pact, Stalin was promoting "popular fronts"—or alliances of proletarians, socialists, and democrats all over the world. This would therefore become one name for the alliance of Radicals, Socialists, and Communists that formed in a giant demonstration on 14 July 1935, and was voted into power in May 1936.[28] On 6 June, the new government, consisting of 147 Socialists, 106 Radicals, 72 Communists, and 51 members of smaller leftist groups, assumed its duties, with the Socialist intellectual Léon Blum at its head.[29] Significantly, this government, as opposed to previous coalitions, such as the Cartel des Gauches, comprised not just parties, but many smaller organizations, some with principally cultural objectives.[30] Its themes were broad and ambiguous: not only did they include antifascism (the exact meaning of which was unclear), but the eventually contradictory goals of "Pain, Paix et Liberté."[31] The new government would thus encounter not only the problem of different interpretations of what it represented, but the hostility of the Senate, which was still dominated by conservatives as well as Radicals.[32] But the initial enthusiasm for the coalition was enormous,, perhaps because it was vague and engendered great hope, not only for economic recovery, but for a forceful response to fascist threats.

THE NEW ROLE OF FRENCH LEFT INTELLECTUALS

Since the time of the Dreyfus affair the Left had stressed the role of intellectuals and artists in thwarting the attempts of the radical Right to sway the masses toward its extremist ideology. Now, especially, it emphasized the importance of *engagement*, or the need to assume a position and to take the lead in defending both its cultural ideals and political values.[33] Hence, not surprisingly, in 1935 (the year after the formation of the Comité de Vigilance des Intellectuels Anti-Fascistes), French Communist intellectuals and sympathizers held a conference in Paris, titled the International Congress of Writers in Defense of Culture.[34]

Gide and Malraux played leading roles in the congress which, although a brilliant "Communist operation," did not succeed in retaining the loyalty of "revolutionary" artists such as the surrealists (with the exception of Aragon), several of whom had already been expelled from the party.[35] This congress, however, was not unique in its goals, but followed earlier French Communist attempts to marshal intellectuals and artists against the growing force and appeal of fascism. These included the foundation of the Association des Ecrivains et Artistes Révolutionnaires (Association of Revolutionary Artists and Writers) in 1932, followed in 1933 by the appearance of the association's journal, *Commune*.[36]

A further provocation for combating fascism and for a joining of left-intellectual forces was Mussolini's imperialistic invasion of Ethiopia in 1935. Although condemned by the League of Nations, the Italian annexation of Ethiopia prompted Henri Massis, on behalf of the Right, to publish his "Pour la défense de l'Occident" in October 1935. Some one thousand right-wing intellectuals signed this tract, which exalted Occidental superiority and argued for the "civilizing mission" of the West, thus presenting the invasion as justified. This led to a countermanifesto of the Left, "Pour la justice et la paix," drafted by Jules Romains, and signed by prominent figures such as Emmanuel Mounier.[37]

Similarly devoted to combating incipient French fascism were, journals like *Commune*, which attacked those publications that covertly disseminated Nazi propaganda, such as *Candide*. *Commune* accused the latter's editor, Léon Daudet, of attempting gradually to prepare his readers for the eventual advent of fascism in France.[38] Such a charge was resonant for French intellectuals who, horrified by the events of 6 February 1934, and the prospect of a powerful fascist movement in France, had looked to the Communist Party.[39] Now it was impossible for intellectuals or artists to remain isolated from such imminent threats: politics was clearly no longer just a matter for specialists, and French Communists proposed clear responses.[40]

Although considered dangerous revolutionaries in the twenties, French Communists, by the time of the Popular Front, had entered the political mainstream as antifascists, and thus as defenders of the Third Republic.[41] They now identified with the French Revolution and, as opposed to more conservative republicans, stressed the "social question" from within the new government, linking it closely to its cultural programs.[42] But despite the Communists' appeal to many intellectuals and artists, some on the Left remained anti-Communist, together with those in the conservative center, or the French republican bourgeoisie. The latter were reticent in their attitude toward the government and particularly toward its social programs, which shook traditional republican alignments and conceptions, including that of "no enemies to the Left."[43]

Indeed, the leftist coalition, as well as its intellectual and artistic collaborators, would divide over the political issues of the period, and over key questions of culture. As we shall see when examining Les Six, these differences included not only attitudes toward Communism under Stalin, but to the Spanish Civil War and to the position of the Catholic Church. Certain intellectuals, like Gide, after his "awakening" during his trip to the Soviet Union, would speak out against the crimes of Stalin, as opposed to others, like Malraux, who remained "in the fold."44 And some were for direct intervention after right-wing attacks on the Spanish Popular Front, while more moderate republicans remained aloof from this external conflict.45 Finally, while the Left considered Mussolini a dangerous fascist, along with Hitler and Franco, many moderates, as well as those to the right, saw him merely as "authoritarian."46 Again, divisions over Mussolini would crest upon his invasion of Ethiopia, with intellectuals to the left condemning both it and colonialism, while moderates and the Right stressed "Occidental values" and peace. In sum, French writers took the lead in confronting the crises of the mid-1930s as intellectuals, engaging with the issues of fascism and colonialism in their prose and in their art.47

THE IDEOLOGY OF CULTURE IN 1936

Just as during the period that immediately followed the Dreyfus affair, the Republic now sought to combat the attempts of its opponents to sway the masses through culture. Even its cultural response was similar—"to provide a new mystique for republican democracy," as Julian Jackson puts it, which was once more "to romanticize the shabby realities of Third Republic politics."48 And it was also to provide a "cultural defense," and so now, as at the turn of the century and during the war, the Republic cast points of political conflict as a confrontation of symbols.49 To this end, the government henceforth entered into an unprecedented range of cultural activities, including not only the arts, but also sport, as well as scholarly or "scientific" research.50

Sport was patently a means to counter totalitarian programs on their own terms, and scholarly research was still a symbol of "enlightenment," as it had been during the "Dreyfusard Republic."51 The "enlightenment of the masses" through the agency of intellectuals implied, first, the development of cultural institutions and organizations to occupy the "space" that fascists or groupings on the extreme Right might otherwise cunningly fill. And so no fewer than ninety-eight cultural organizations became affiliated with the Comité du Rassemblement Populaire, and the funding of the Ministry of Fine Arts now increased by 38 million francs.52 The republican ideal of a "cultural state," or one unified by cultural values, and in which all citizens had a "right" to culture, here achieved its logical culmination.53

Again, as after the Dreyfus affair, a major goal of republican politics was to bring the people and high culture together in order to combat a demagogic opposition. Now aware of the success of fascist regimes in the organization of leisure for the masses in order to achieve moral consent, it appeared imperative that democracy follow suit. Competition with fascist regimes was equally clear in the obvious new emphasis on youth, and on the need for the state to form it culturally and thus to harness its energies constructively.54 In addition, there was a palpable concern with filling the augmented leisure time that had resulted from the new forty-hour workweek and the paid vacations that the regime introduced for French workers.55

The "worker" was now central, and again, as in the period that followed the

Dreyfus affair, the government turned to the cultural needs of this group, and particularly to appropriate theater. It introduced agitprop theater, influenced by German and Communist models, with the goal of transporting theater directly to both the factory and to public streets. Stylistically, such theater emphasized ideas proposed earlier for "the People's Theater" by Romain Rolland, especially spoken choruses, which allowed the participation of amateur performers.[56] Popular theater flourished, and hence the Socialist cultural organization, Mai '36, established three new theatrical associations: the CGT's Theater of the People, the theatrical section of Mai '36, and the theater collective Art et Travail.[57]

The Minister of National Education, Jean Zay, provided generous subsidies to ensure low ticket prices for large theatrical productions of such works as Romain Rolland's populist *Le 14 juillet*. His colleague Léo Lagrange similarly supported the theater, including that of the CGT, and himself helped to organize a spectacular production of Rolland's *Danton* in July 1936. And once again recalling earlier such theatrical projects at the turn of the century, he helped to provide inexpensive seats for working-class groups at all the major state-subsidized theaters.[58]

But the Popular Front equally attempted to promulgate its populist vision of culture through grandiose spectacles, thought to be appropriate to a new mass audience. For one means of asserting the political presence of workers was to make politics into a "pageant"—clearly a fascist technique, but one here imbued with republican ideological principles. Such "manifestation," or demonstration was to be associated not with protest, or with the hierarchical and militaristic, but rather with the concept of popular "celebration."[59] Moreover, in such celebration or spectacle the ideal was not to achieve the "colossal," as in the dictatorships, but a grandeur that abjured totalitarianism—a new kind of "total art."[60] Here we may observe the two poles of the Wagnerian conception of the *Gesamtkunstwerk* in confrontation—that which stresses the pragmatic force of the "whole," as in Germany, versus the Platonic model of cooperation, as in France.

Other of Lagrange's cultural projects again recall the turn of the century, especially his attempt to bring "the people to the museums and the museums to the people."[61] Concomitantly, he sought to break down old cultural barriers between the people and the libraries, creating the innovative "association for the development of popular reading."[62] But a looming question was still what kind of culture to bring to the people—whether to foster a specifically working-class culture or disseminate traditional "high" cultural values. Indeed, this issue lay at the core of the inherent ambiguity of the Popular Front, with its broad appeal to several French social groups for a variety of ideological and pragmatic reasons.

In the field of visual art and in music, as we shall shortly see, one goal was to "democratize" traditional "high culture," or to make it more widely accessible. In both arts, the concern was to persuade, to engage emotions in the interest of democracy, using elements of "the modern," while limiting the vocabulary to the simple or to the immediately comprehensible.[63] And from the perspective of French workers, who had not yet developed their own artistic culture (as had the German working class) it was a question of reclaiming their "patrimony," or finally gaining access to the nation's cultural treasures.[64] Even the French Communist Party now not only embraced modern and traditional French "high culture" but appropriated the role of protecting its integrity from outside threats. For despite the doctrinal Communist internationalism, the party, in order to justify its new political role, claimed to "defend" French culture and stressed its own foundation in the French tradition.[65]

Moreover, the party ascribed to the republican belief that immersion in the nation's culture, including its education and art, would lead to full political participation, and to a unifying "Frenchness." Hence, as the Communists in the Weimar Republic, they joined together with the Socialist Party to use high or "classic" as well as modern culture as a medium through which to "teach."[66] This conviction led, for some, to a conservative view of culture, or to the belief that political recognition required an exposure to the classics as traditionally taught in the schools.[67] However, as we have seen, the results could be new, as in the case of the Fêtes du Peuple, which had appropriated and used such culture in a highly distinctive ideological manner. But despite this dual appropriation, the government maintained that culture was essentially indivisible, and thus refused to draw a clear line between "bourgeois" and "popular" modern art.[68]

THEMES, MYTHS, AND PROGRAMS OF THE POPULAR FRONT

Another means to valorize the "popular" was to recognize a body of culture that, to this point, the French Left had held in suspicion, since it was traditionally associated with the Right. This was indigenous French folklore, which now was to be appropriated and politically reinterpreted, provoking both Zay and Lagrange to sponsor an international conference on folklore in Paris.[69] In 1937 also they established a new museum, the Musée des Arts et Traditions Populaires, one codirector of which was a musician—the composer Georges-Henri Rivière. A former pupil at the Conservatoire, and subsequently a student of the now prominent Charles Koechlin, he was also already well integrated into the social and artistic world of Paris.[70] As we shall shortly see, his friendship with Darius Milhaud would lead to the latter's receiving a commission for a cantata specifically to celebrate the museum's opening. But the major ideological issue surrounding the museum, which several members of Les Six would also face, was what should and should not now be embraced under the rubric of "folklore."

Ever since the French Revolution, the political Right and Left had consistently disputed which group represented "true" France, or embodied its most essential "voice." This argument was fundamentally related to the doctrine of French "essentialism," or the belief that certain groups represented or inherently embodied "authentic" France. Charles Maurras (of Action Française) had challenged the Republic's version of the "essential France," based upon its conception of a "pays légal," as opposed to a "pays réel." Henceforth the polemic was over the question of whether "true" French popular culture was represented by workers—in the republican tradition—or, as the Right claimed, by indigenous peasants.

In the 1920s and 1930s the Right (like Vichy later) maintained that it was the peasants, above all, who most fully embodied authentic French popular culture. The Left, however, now riposted that it was workers and peasants together who represented different, but equally valid, aspects of the nation's "real" popular culture. This clash of conceptions would come to a head in the First International Congress of Folklore, held in Paris in August 1937, in conjunction with the opening of the new Musée National des Arts et Traditions Populaires. Here it is important to note that the organizers of the congress were also the directors of the museum, Paul Rivet and Georges-Henri Rivière.[71]

On behalf of the Popular Front, they consciously deemphasized the national element in folklore (as opposed to Nazi Germany), and stressed a scholarly, as differentiated from a nostalgic, attitude (the latter associated with the Right).[72] In keeping with this emphasis, the new Phonothèque Nationale, founded in 1937 under the direction of the ethnomusicologist Roger Devigne, undertook a "sonorous documentation" of regional musics, of which the various musical organizations of the Popular Front could avail themselves.[73] This more scholarly and commodious conception of the Left was clearly in keeping with its ideal of French culture as "syncretic," or an "evolving, cosmopolitan and multicultural synthesis of the diverse."[74]

Such a conception also informed the fête—again, another point of emphasis for the Popular Front, which, as we have noted, also linked its identity to the French Revolution.[75] The journal *Vendredi* (close to the government) saw it as incarnating the revolutionary themes of "solidarity, fraternity, communion, youth, joy, hope, and happiness."[76] The fête, moreover, was to serve the same purpose as during the French Revolution—to break "the confines of party politics by positing the existence of a new community."[77] Indeed, one goal of the Popular Front was to unite the people under a common culture in order to efface all cultural barriers, and thus usher in an egalitarian new order.

In the tradition of William Morris, then, art was to be integrated with everyday life, although there was little consensus on precisely how to do so. There was agreement, however, that the function of art was not simply to raise public morale in a time of economic depression, but rather to serve an ideological end.[78] Culture was not to be clothed in "mystique," but to have a clear purpose—a public utility—yet, again, there was little agreement as to what kind of culture was most suitable. Should one attempt to make traditional "high" culture more accessible, as the Socialists sought? Or should one rather try to elevate traditional popular forms artistically?[79] These issues were inevitably to face most musicians active in France, including the composers in the group Les Six, and their responses would be far from monolithic.

Finally, the other basic cultural belief maintained by the Popular Front, as we have already noted, was the necessity of intellectuals' working together or collaborating with "the people." Again, as at the turn of the century, the rubric "intellectual" included artists, a fact that would now have important repercussions for both the artistic and musical worlds.[80] A major influence here, of course, was that of the Communist Party, which, since the Seventh Congress of the Comintern, had urged party members to recruit among the intellectuals. And, once more, it played a key role in helping to define the cultural programs of the

Popular Front through its influential Association of Revolutionary Artists and Writers.[81]

REDIRECTING FRENCH MUSICAL CULTURE

All of these themes and concerns were to play a prominent role in the French musical world, as official institutions became necessarily responsive to the ideals of the Popular Front. Hence the new government provides a matrix from which to examine the evolution of musical culture within the decade, and the transformation of attitudes and responses to the principal issues. The question of musical associations, popular music, of style, genre, repertoire, recordings, scholarship, criticism, and aesthetics were all impacted by changing ideals before, during, and after the Popular Front. The latter considered music to be not only an agent of education but a means of enunciating values and articulating memory, within its system of political representation.[82] Again, as in the Weimar Republic, music was to be part of the government's educational and aesthetic program, and the musical world responded by helping, symbolically, to create and disseminate new meanings.[83]

Although regular official commissions for new works were not instituted until the government's decline (in 1938), it had other, equally efficacious means of affecting French musical production and taste. As we have already seen, the state could "orient" production through subsidies and prizes, and redefine symbolic legitimacy through the awarding of honorific positions and decorations.[84] For, just as at the turn of the century, French music was to play an ideological role through both the uses to which it was put and the discourse that was circulated around it. Once more French musical institutions were charged with mediating and thus refracting the new cultural and political priorities of the beleaguered Third Republic. As government leaders perceived, these institutions could play a key role by accomplishing what political discourse could not: forging a cultural image of the government, and thus synthesizing its ambiguous vision. Music now was to combat the fascist threat, to symbolize new democratic ideals, and to refract the major themes and concerns of the increasingly fragile Third Republic.

Again, the musical programs of the government were integrally to draw on earlier tendencies and cultural emphases of previous governments and the Left, but to develop and organize them more fully. From this perspective, the impact of the Popular Front on the musical world was not only far-reaching but subtle, and if seen as such, was indeed far from negligible.[85] The government was determined to "occupy" the same cultural, symbolic "space" that had been "annexed" in wartime, and thereafter filled by successive governments of both the Right and Left.

In music this meant not only utilizing the established official French musical institutions, but supporting or "patronizing" others in order to connect them explicitly with the goals of the government. For one of its principal ideals was now to make music accessible to all social classes, including through the use of radio, and thus to spread "musical culture" as widely as possible.[86] As in the Weimar Republic, the radio was a central tool to unite society, although organized far less systematically in France, which brought immediate attacks from the Right, as we shall see.[87] But in the interests of "popularization," the six major Parisian symphonic associations—the Concerts Colonne, du Conservatoire, Lamoureux, Pasdeloup, Poulet-Siohan (now fused), and the Orchestre Symphonique de Paris—did present broadcasts of classical music during the peak listening hours.[88]

The low quality of their performances, however, together with their choice of repertoire—concentrating on lesser known French composers, nineteenth-century Russian composers, symphonic excerpts, and lighter short works, would bring further criticism from the Right.[89] The public, as represented by listeners' associations, which voted on radio policies, in fact preferred a lighter programming, and emphatically opposed excessive emphasis on *la grande musique*. The new government thus stressed "popularization" of music, as we shall see in detail when examining the Fédération Musicale Populaire, the musical branch of the Maison de Culture. But it made other, even more direct efforts, such as the establishment of an annual grand prize to be awarded in alternation to "harmonies" (1937), "fanfares" (1938), and "chorales" (1939). Other plans were less successful, due to the recalcitrance of the more conservative Senate; these included Léo Lagrange's proposal for performances (with commentaries) by the large symphonic associations in working-class districts.[90]

Efforts to "popularize" embraced the Opéra as well as the Opéra-Comique, which now were to attract a broader public, including the French working class.[91] There was an attempt not only to lower ticket prices but also to sell blocks of tickets to specific groups, such as union members and Renault employees, for appropriate weekend performances.[92] Finally, officials developed a plan, publicly supported by Milhaud in *Europe*, to take performances of the Opéra-Comique to working-class Paris suburbs. This, however, did not succeed because of the unsuitability, from a technical perspective, of the suburban theaters, as well as the lack of local civic subventions.[93]

The redirection and concomitant "popularization" of French musical culture extended as well to the domain of education, in which the government undertook several major initiatives. One concern, as in the early 1930s, continued to be the provincial conservatories, which, although titled "national," with directors named by the state, received only meager subventions. As a result, state inspection had little effect on the curriculum or instruction, which was more responsive to local exigencies, as opposed to national "programs."[94] The new government now sought specifically to create choral groups in each of these twenty-three schools, beginning in the fall of 1936, in order to diffuse the new "spirit."

On the higher or professional level, symbolic gestures were made, but real change at the Paris Conservatoire was severely limited by institutional inertia and by the significant conservative resistance internally. Aware of the archaism of the Grand Prix de Rome, but also of the professional consecration that it still marked, the government now offered a parallel prize, which did not oblige a stay in fascist Italy. As of 10 April 1937, a new prize of 5,400 francs was instituted as a "bourse de voyage," with the destination left open.[95]

French Musicians as Intellectuals of the Left

ROUSSEL AND THE FÉDÉRATION MUSICALE POPULAIRE

Composers participated in the "redirection" of musical culture for a variety of reasons, some of which were pragmatic, for in a time of economic retrenchment, commissions for works, especially large-scale ones, were scarce. Composers were also well aware of their increasing marginalization in light of the current stress on recordings, performers, and radio, and the rising status of popular music. But there were those who became actively "engaged," having reconsidered their purpose, and now also became committed intellectuals who responded to the competing ideological choices, as well as to the concrete political and social issues. This they would do not only through cultural projects, but through their music, for, again, styles and genres were assuming political significance within the discourse of both the government and its opponents. Composers saw clearly that competing musical values were once more imbricated with the comprehensive conflict between hostile political visions that had brought about, but still threatened, the Popular Front. Some, however, could not embrace the new government and its musical aesthetic—a posture that becomes clear when we examine their styles and works in this period. Stylistic rejection of the now dominant aesthetic was telling within the context, at a time when most French musicians, as during the war, felt pressured to comply with expectations.

The matrix for the implementation of the musical goals of the Popular Front, as well as for the explication and diffusion of its aesthetic values and meanings, was the Fédération Musicale Populaire. A branch of the official Maison de Culture (developed from Communist precedents), it established 140 musical groups in the summer of 1936 alone.[96] With the Communists now in the government, their established cultural organizations and musical ideals were to play a seminal role in the musical politics of the Popular Front.[97] But just as integral and important were those existing organizations of the broader Left that could now become affiliated with the government and its new cultural programs. One of these was the Fêtes du Peuple, which with the premature death of Doyen in 1935 had been taken over by the noted composer and conductor Francis Casadesus.[98] Under Casadesus the fêtes clearly shared both the spirit and goals of the Popular Front, as reflected in its new motto, "art et culture populaire," and its choice of repertoire. It included, at this point, Gossec and Berlioz, both icons of the Left in the period because of their "gigantism" and iconoclasm, as well as other canonic composers, such as Beethoven and Wagner.[99] But the organization now, in many ways, seemed to be outdated, with its emphasis on selective recruitment, the great repertoire of the past, and its continuing ideology of pacifism.[100]

A similar situation existed with regard to the Orphéon choral societies, the huge associations of French workingmen that the government had sponsored since the early nineteenth century. Although more definitively amateur, and not at first favored financially by the Popular Front, their subvention was indeed reestablished and augmented in 1937. This permitted the organization of a Festival de Musiques Populaires, conceived under the rubric of the "fifth class" of the International Exposition of 1937.[101]

But the Fédération also had to innovate, to develop new programs in the government's spirit, while still incorporating organizations that existed, including those that were associated with the working-class professions.[102] Its emphasis was clearly on vocal music, although it included instrumental associations such as the "Harmonie Populaire de Paris" and the "Philharmonie Populaire de Paris." In all the new organizations the goal was to bring amateurs and artist-intellectuals together in order effectively to combat the menacing "reactionary spirit." And so it is not surprising to find that the annual congress of the Fédération included not only notable left-wing intellectuals but speeches by the most renowned contemporary French composers. The second congress, held in the context of the 1937 International Exposition, featured not only the intellectuals Aragon, J.-R. Bloch, and Vaillant-Couturier but also, among others, Georges Auric, André Jolivet, Charles Koechlin, Louis Durey, and Maurice Jaubert.[103]

The Fédération's musical groups participated in the large collective theatrical works of the period, centrally including *Le 14 juillet*, *Naissance d'une cité*, and *Liberté*. It also held frequent festivals that were devoted to specific timely themes, such as Musique Soviétique and Chants de la Liberté. But just as important was the Fédération's expansive program in general musical education, led by Henri Radiguer, a musicologist specializing in the music of the French Revolution. Hence it is not surprising that the program included music history, and that the Fédération's journal, *L'art musical populaire*, included a regular column on the subject.

As we shall see, a similar project had already been undertaken by the profascist Right, which was actively propagating its ideologically charged conception of music history. Since this latter included an interpretation of jazz, with unmistakable racial implications, as one might expect, the Fédération sought to diffuse its own conception of jazz. The unions developed associated jazz bands, and articles on jazz correspondingly appeared in *L'art musical populaire*, in order to draw attention to the democratic implications of the style.[104]

Again, the Fédération's goal was to spread "musical culture," in the most comprehensive sense, in order to encompass (as had Wiéner's concerts) all those musics that had an impact on human life and experience. It was, then, not a historicist musical culture, but one that incorporated historical works, together with styles of the present, that had immediate resonance for contemporary life. To this end the Fédération began to offer mass courses on musical culture, beginning in October 1937, when it rented two large halls for this purpose, with great success.[105]

But the Fédération went yet further in its effort to diffuse a new musical culture, becoming associated with a record firm called Le Chant du Monde. The company was founded in 1937 as a private enterprise, financed through the fortune of Renaud de Jouvenel, a Communist sympathizer, and directed by his wife, Arlette, and the composer Henry Sauveplane. They rightly sensed that records were now affordable to the upper sectors of the French working class, which wanted a new repertoire that combined both the popular and the classic, as well as works of folkloric inspiration.[106] Such endeavors, in which the economic and political worked together, were highly successful, and although an attempt at a "Cabaret Front Populaire" was to fail, contemporary vocal artists followed the Weimar Republic's example with pronounced success. Some sought to fuse the heritage of the popular *chanson de critique sociale* with the influence of composers like Weill and Eisler, or to incorporate contemporary "hot" jazz. But most successful of all was Marianne Oswald (Marianne Colin), who had performed in Berlin cabarets and introduced the style to France in 1934. Being highly politicized herself, she did not hesitate to use texts of Brecht for her songs, to the enthusiastic and consistent praise of the press of the Left.[107]

Given the spirit of the times, the Left had a commercial advantage, if briefly, and this included the Fédération, with all of its associated institutions and companies. But the Fédération had still other resources that would encourage the participation of musicians—not only those with clear political sympathies, but others with more pragmatic professional interests. It became associated with a Communist publishing house, the Editions Sociales Internationales, which issued both printed music and records, eventually overshadowing Le Chant du Monde. Financially, it was extremely successful, having exclusive rights to the "Internationale," which allowed it to open its own recoding studio in 1938. The enterprise published not only Communist songs, but French and foreign folklore, popular music, and works of the prominent composers of the Fédération.[108]

It also published the music of important contemporary Soviet composers, still little known in France, including Dmitri Shostakovich.[109] And it concentrated on works that could be performed by the Fédération's own chorale, including revolutionary chansons, political songs of Hans Eisler, and classic works (considered populist) like Handel's *Judas Maccabeus*. This was in keeping with the Fédération's ideal of works that embodied a "collective expression," or those works produced in what were supposedly "great epochs of communitarian spirit."[110] Hence it included Handel, whom Romain Rolland had already placed in this category in his book devoted to the composer, which had been published decades earlier. And, of course, it included Beethoven, whom Rolland had construed in a similar manner in his book on the composer earlier in the century, a subsequent volume of which finally appeared in 1937.[111] Similarly falling under this rubric, as we have noted, were the revolutionary composers Méhul, Gossec, and Grétry, as well as Berlioz, since he was associated with the collective, communitarian spirit because of his massive works.[112] But the repertoire printed for the group also included both traditional workers' songs as well as *chants de folklore*, again seen as embodying "les grands sentiments humains," and including French and foreign songs.

The Fédération's professional advantage lay not only in its considerable resources, but also in its astute and prestigious leadership, which included the most revered "progressive" musicians.[113] The organization's first guiding spirits were the now Communist sympathizer Romain Rolland, together with Paul Vaillant-Couturier, a firmly committed Communist Party member. The latter had not only been the editor of the Communist *L'humanité*, but the mayor of the largely Communist town of Villejuif. A promoter of French cultural modernism, being both an amateur artist and poet, he would denounce the government's scant support for modern art in the Chamber of Deputies.[114] The first active leader, however, was someone who was highly regarded in the French musical world, elected president of the Fédération in the final year of his life—the intrepid Albert Roussel.[115]

As we noted earlier, Roussel felt impelled to dissociate himself from both d'Indy and the Schola, as tensions between the two men inevitably escalated in the course of the war. After the war, Roussel's sympathy for Socialism became increasingly pronounced, as did his interest in younger French composers, including Les Six, as was the case with Maurice Ravel. Roussel became convinced that music must ineluctably change after the cataclysmic war, which led, despite the disapproval of conservative critics, to his turn to bitonality, complex counterpoint, and more vigorous rhythms.[116]

As a composer, Roussel was well aware of the battle between "conservatives" and "progressives" in the twenties, as well as the inherent ideological and political dimensions that would eventually become manifest. In January 1930, Roussel responded to the request of the Belgian musicologist and composer Arthur Hoérée to participate in an "advanced" new group, which included himself, Honegger, and Varèse. While Roussel was indeed sympathetic with the general idea of such a group, he warned against the possibility of forming another "nouvelle petite chapelle," and, as he went on to remark: "Il y a malheureusement trop de politique en musique et les moeurs parlementaires commencent à s'y introduire un peu trop ouvertement . . . Aujourd'hui il y a dans l'air une nervosité qui n'existait pas autrefois." (There is unfortunately too much politics in music and parliamentary manners are beginning to appear in it a little too overtly. Today there is an air of neurosis that did not exist before.)[117]

Indeed, Roussel himself was suffering from the overt intrusion of politics into music: as he pointed out in a letter to Guy Ropartz five years later, "Je continue à être la bête noire du critique de *l'Action française*." (I continue to be the bête noire of the critic of *L'action française* [Dominique Sordet, an admirer of Vincent d'Indy]).[118] This may, in fact, be one of the reasons that Roussel was "recruited" by the Fédération, in addition to his support for independence, innovation, and his open Socialist sympathies.[119] Moreover, he represented a staunch rejection of the old Scholiste ideals, still associated with d'Indy, and which now became a target of persistent attacks by the Left.

Roussel, an articulate spokesman, aptly translated the key ideals of the Popular Front into terms of musical priorities and policies in the journal *Le point* in 1936. Here he stresses the political ideal of *rassemblement*, or the cooperation of all social classes as realized through the medium of an egalitarian culture, opposite that of the fascists:

> La musique est partout. De la salle de concert, du théâtre, où elle se tenait autrefois, distante et respectée, elle est descendue dans la rue, elle s'est trouvée installé dans le salon du bourgeois, dans la chambre du travailleur, à la brasserie ou à l'atelier."[120]
>
> [Music is everywhere. From the concert hall to the theater, where it remained before, it has descended into the street, it has installed itself in the "salon" of the bourgeois, in the room of the worker, in the "brasserie" or in the workshop.]

Here, of course, Roussel represented the socially and aesthetically moderate interpretation of the Popular Front—that which construed it within the republican, not the more overtly revolutionary tradition. Elite, or "high" culture, according to this model, was to be diffused to the masses, as opposed to the creation of a new, socially equalizing revolutionary culture.

Such moderation was equally evident in Roussel's aesthetic and in his attitude toward musical innovation, which was not one that would necessarily frighten either the Radicals or the Communists in the government. For he goes on to consider the ties between the music of the present and that of the past, describing music, in fact, as the paradigm of the mysterious bond between the "revolutionary" spirit and tradition. Roussel similarly avoids the extremes in invoking the "spiritual" element within music, in a manner that would appeal to traditionalists yet was clearly differentiated from the contemporary fascist discourse. For here, he emphasizes the central element of the "spiritual" in any society, and hence music's role in binding the community, even a democratic and secular one, together. As he puts it: "le culte des valeurs spirituelles est à la base de toute société qui se prétend civilisée et . . . la musique, parmi les arts, est l'expression la plus sensible et la plus élevée." (The worship of spiritual values is at the base of all societies that claim to be civilized . . . music, among the arts, is its most sensitive and elevated expression.)[121]

But Roussel was not merely an advocate for the role of music within the culture of the Popular Front, he was a key figure in organizing several of its most important institutions and events. As we shall shortly see, he participated in planning the musical programs for the 1937 Exposition, which, however, he did not live to experience.[122] Moreover, as president of the French section of the Société Internationale pour la Musique Contemporaine, Roussel was instrumental in coordinating its fifteenth festival with the Exposition, both held in Paris.[123] Roussel thus helped to reinforce the emphasis of the Fédération on contemporary music, in keeping with the Popular Front's stress on cultural modernity, as opposed to reactionary German fascism.[124]

KOECHLIN: STYLE AND IDEOLOGICAL INVESTMENT

After Albert Roussel's death it was logical that Charles Koechlin would assume his place as the titular or honorific president of the Fédération Musicale Populaire. As one might expect, Koechlin's "artistic committee" included such noted and progressive or "engaged" composers as Honegger, , Jolivet, Milhaud, Auric, Desormière, and Daniel Lazarus.[125] A former Dreyfusard, Koechlin (like Dreyfus) had come from a wealthy Alsatian family, one with a long philanthropic tradition and utopian socialist tendencies.[126] Enrolled initially in the Ecole Polytechnique, he completed its two-year program of study, but then devoted himself entirely to music, subsequently studying at the Conservatoire with Gédalge, Massenet, and Fauré. Moreover, in 1909 Koechlin helped his friend and former classmate, Maurice Ravel, in forming the innovative performing society for new music, the Société Musicale Indépendante. During the First World War, due in part to financial difficulties, Koechlin began to teach and give a series of lectures on modern music that were bold in the context. The latter, of course, did not win the approbation of the wartime musical establishment, and Koechlin henceforth suffered professionally from the conservative faction's overt hositility.[127]

In the 1920s, as we have noted, Koechlin grew close to several members of Les Six, becoming Poulenc's teacher and thus an important influence on his work. He promptly introduced Poulenc to the music of Bach, being himself a leading force in the return to the study of Bach as a means to escape romantic or impressionist tendencies. But still Koechlin did not obtain a position at the Paris Conservatoire, again largely because of his reputation for "advanced" positions, and his association with avant-garde circles. Hence, ironically, his only teaching position was at the newly reorganized Schola Cantorum (which had split off from the d'Indyste Ecole César Franck) between 1935 and the war.[128]

More politically radical than Roussel, Koechlin grew close to the Communist Party, responding to its appeal to artist-intellectuals and sharing its cultural and aesthetic concerns.[129] Beginning in 1934, he wrote a number of politically committed works, including an orchestration of the mass song "Libérons Thälmann," to protest the incarceration of Ernest Thälmann, head of the German Communist Party, by the Nazis.[130] His engagement is further manifest in two publications which appeared in 1936, both of which espouse the more extreme leftist aesthetic ideals of the Popular Front.

One was the small book, *La musique et le peuple*, in which Koechlin argues for the aesthetic legitimacy and social necessity of combining stylistic features of "high" and "popular" art. This volume, which helped to define a new official aesthetic in music, was one of several books that were published in 1936 by the Fédération's own Editions Sociales Internationales.[131] In this book Koechlin both advocates and defends the need for a modern and popular musical art for aesthetic and social reasons, and then defines it in terms of style:

> Nous rêvons d'un art moderne, riche de toutes les conquêtes de l'harmonie, du contrepoint, et de l'orchestration . . . ou même fait de chants collectifs . . . simples et nus. . . . Tous ces moyens à tour de rôle pour que l'artiste, libre, les emploie pour un art réellement humain.[132]
>
> [We dream of a modern art, rich from all the conquests of harmony, of counterpoint, and of orchestration . . . or even from collective songs . . . simple and naked. . . . All these means in turn so that the artist, free, employs them for a truly human art.]

Such a goal of a modern art that draws on both "high" and popular elements, allowing the artist freedom while remaining "human," was clearly defined against fascist models. For it was not "targeted" to specific social groups, retrogressive, "colossal," superhuman, or wary of contemporary techniques, in the manner of much of the art music promoted in Nazi Germany.

The vocabulary and concepts that Koechlin employs throughout the book indeed recall certain arguments of Cocteau in *Le coq et l'arlequin*, but in a far different ideological context. Koechlin, being politically astute, clearly perceived their innate affinity for the rhetoric of the Popular Front, as in fact did certain members of Les Six. Auric had already sensed their application to the ideology of the political Left, having stressed along with it (in the twenties) the themes of progress, universality, and cultural synthesis. As we shall shortly see, this connection was to redound to the benefit of most members of the group, who were soon to find themselves becoming almost the equivalent of "official" composers.

But the other themes that Koechlin introduces relate to a far older tradition of aesthetic argument within the Left, one stressing (again, like Cocteau, if for different reasons) the necessary imbrication of art and life. For Koechlin goes on to argue that music is not an "art d'agrément," accessory, or superfluous, but rather it is a vital necessity; as any manifestation of beauty that translates or communicates elements of "life," music helps us to live, or it comforts and sustains us. Koechlin here in fact sounds like his predecessor on the Left, Gustave Charpentier, when he speaks of a "rehabilitation de la poésie dans son rêve le plus large—rêve, espoir, tendresse, enthousiasme" (rehabilitation of poetry in its largest dream—dream, hope, tenderness, enthusiasm).[133]

Koechlin goes on to declare (recalling Cocteau): "J'aime mieux une jolie musique naïvement faite, que n'importe quel faux sublime, même réputé." (I prefer a pretty music naively done than any false sublime [work], even well known.)[134] Concomitantly, he argues for the elimination of pretension (associated with *la grande musique*), the absence of which he links to those qualities suggesting "good faith," or sincerity and naïveté. Koechlin, however, had long been an advocate of naïveté in art, having praised this quality in Chabrier's music (as had Debussy before) in his article "Pour Chabrier," in *La revue musicale* in January 1930.[135] Here, in fact, we can trace the seeds of Koechlin's model to his former Debussyste ideal of a simple and pleasing music, although now it assumes a clear political significance. But it is important to note that naïveté was valued not only in music, but equally in visual art, particularly as seen at the 1937 Exposition. It included an exhibition titled "Les maîtres populaires de la réalité," which now consecrated those artists who had previously been demeaned, such as Le Douanier Rousseau and Utrillo.[136]

In his book Koechlin also praises the earlier ideals of Romain Rolland, specifically those concerning large popular ceremonies, here emphasizing their potential for mass education.[137] And he makes further reference to the situation at the turn of the century in discussing works that were initially ostracized by hostile critics because of their political subjects. He cites the case of *Messidor*, an opera by Emile Zola and Alfred Bruneau that had been boycotted at the Paris Opéra because sections of its text appeared to some to be "socialistic." But the fundamental reason, he continues, is that both Bruneau and his librettist, Zola, were Dreyfusards, which led to a persecution of them that Koechlin emphatically pronounces "odieux."[138] Clearly the Dreyfusard experience was strongly imprinted upon Koechlin, just as it was on others, some of whom were still active in the current political-cultural battle.

Finally, Koechlin discusses the kind of classical music that he believes to be best suited to a "popular" appropriation at present—works for wind ensembles or bands. He advocates the repertoire of the past—Bach, Mozart, and Rameau—but not the present concert staples; Beethoven, he argues, is already overrepresented in the current wind ensemble repertoire.[139] Here, in the French Socialist tradition, he presents "high" art or culture as a vital means of access not only to "elevation," or education, but indeed to the nation's great cultural patrimony. For Koechlin and the Popular Front, however, the "high" art to be diffused to the people should not be romantic, but classic, for the former was now increasingly considered dangerous in light of fascist romanticism. Although a man of the Left, Koechlin had clearly imbibed the French postwar orthodoxy that the classic was related to simplicity, clarity, and balance—a discourse here appropriated by the Popular Front.

When turning to artistic creativity and to the new or "modern" art that ought to be created, Koechlin considers the social role that should be assumed by the artist, as a responsible intellectual. Here he refers explicitly to Julien Benda's indictment of contemporary intellectuals for their failure to fulfill their true role in his stirring book, *La trahison des clercs*. For Koechlin similarly wishes to distinguish those artists who are rather devoted to the most fundamental human values, and who attempt to express them in their work—the qualities of honesty, truth, and love. These values, Koechlin argues, some artists have betrayed for political or personal reasons, seeking to serve a nefarious ideology or to achieve an immediate professional success. The ideal of truly "noble" music, he continues, can embrace a wide variety of styles, including even atonal music, which can indeed be rich in sensibility. And here, once more (again recalling Cocteau) he distinguishes such art from the search for "elevation," or for the supposed preparation for the other world of "eternal life," thus implicitly denigrating the Schola. Good music is without such pretension, for, once again, it is closely linked to "life"; it need not be cast in "ambitious symphonies" and indeed can remain "light."[140]

As an example of such goals, Koechlin here cites the "revolution" in music undertaken by Jean Wiéner, Erik Satie, and Les Six, as well as by members of the Ecole d'Arcueil. All of these composers, he argues, were instrumental in helping to develop the taste for works that are simply and unpretentiously "charming," as opposed to those considered "sublime."[141] Koechlin thus ascribes an ideological significance to the cultural rebellion that these composers undertook in the twenties, the political implications of which many now perceived within the current context.

Most members of both of these groups were hence becoming active in the Fédération Musicale Populaire, participating in its activities and contributing to its journal, which we shall shortly examine. They would similarly espouse the belief (anticipated in the Weimar Republic) that the "masses" could comprehend modern music, and that it was not necessary, as in Soviet Russia, to develop new genres and styles for the workers. Finally, they also shared Koechlin's conviction that intellectuals now had to work with the people, an idea that, as we have noted, was being vigorously promoted by the French Communist Party. But as Koechlin himself was to put it, it is not enough for intellectuals to go to the people: the people, conversely, must become receptive to interaction with intellectuals.[142]

Koechlin remained active as a composer in these years, and was tangibly rewarded for his efforts, winning the prestigious Prix Cressent in 1937 for his grandiose *Symphonie d'hymnes*. The hymns recall those of the French Revolution, with texts such as "Hymne au soleil, au jour, à la mort, à la vie," which he wrote himself. As Koechlin avowed, in this work for orchestra, double chorus, and organ, "j'ai mis le plus de mon sentiment et de ma pensée, mais dans un langage auquel il est nécessaire de s'habituer." (I most fully put my feelings and ideas [in it], but in a language that takes getting used to.)[143] Koechlin not only believed that "ideas" could and should be expressed in music, but that they could effectively be communicated in an uncompromising language that might still reach the masses. His goal in the work was to translate man's anguish in the face of the pain and seemingly insoluble problems of humanity, but at the same time to express his forceful and indomitable passion for life.[144]

THE "DEFENSE" OF MUSICAL CULTURE

The theme of bringing the intellectuals and the people together would soon become central in the endeavors of the Popular Front, and was manifest in several spectacles, particularly those of the 1937 Exposition. And it was undoubtedly in part because of this sense of duty toward the people that other French musicians, as engaged intellectuals, became involved in the Fédération Musicale Populaire. The *presidium d'honneur* included not only Romain Rolland, but Auric, Henri Cliquet-Pleyel, Louis Durey, André Jolivet, Koechlin, Daniel Lazarus, and Albert Roussel. Durey (who had returned to Paris from Saint-Tropez in 1930) joined the Communist Party in 1936 and thus was now close to the government. Listed as "collaborators" of the organization were, most prominently, Honegger, Milhaud, and Ibert, among many others now lesser known. Several of these major figures expressed themselves in the Fédération's official journal, *L'art musical populaire*, which published regularly between 1936 and 1939. In it, one primary concern was the "defense" of musical culture, meaning specifically the defense against current fascist political and cultural threats.

This was the subject of an article by Roger Desormière in the very first issue of the journal, which would consistently stress the theme in almost every number thereafter.[145] Desormière and others were preoccupied not only with the diffusion of music to the working classes in order to combat fascist influence, but with other more personal and professional issues. One was the attack on modern music now being waged by the Nazi regime, to which Desormière, as both conductor and composer, here draws public attention. He describes his trip to Germany, even before Hitler's ascension to power, during which he encountered an organization of at least a million people dedicated to combating Communism, Judaism, and modern music. He then points out that the battle against modern music continues under Hitler, making it all the more important for the Fédération Musicale Populaire to react with alacrity.[146]

However, Desormière does not explicitly recall that Judaism and modern music had already been connected by French critics like Vuillemin in the 1920s, and so the threat of a recrudescence of such rhetoric loomed. But now the target was not primarily Schoenberg, for, as the journal later pointed out, the Third Reich was rather equating specific members of Les Six with "Judeo-Marxism." This included Honegger, despite the composer's ambivalence toward democracy; Honegger, indeed, was being represented as inaccurately in Germany as he was in France.[147]

Another aspect of the "defense of musical culture" appeared in the Fédération's journal as well—the idea that the people not only "needed" music but in fact had an inherent "right" of access to it. As the composer Daniel Lazarus put it, sounding like French republicans at the turn of the century, "Le peuple a droit à la musique, comme il a droit aux musées, aux jardins, à l'architecture" (the people have a right to music, as they have a right to museums, to gardens, and to architecture).[148] The earliest issues of the journal articulate a similar belief, common to the Fédération, that the working class is not concerned only with material needs, but has ideals, as expressed through culture. These aspirations, it implies, must now be "protected" against fascist beguilements, and this can be accomplished in part, at least, by forging an appropriate musical culture. Once again this led inevitably to the issue of style, as well as to the place of modernity, which, as we saw, the Fédération maintained was not inimical to "mass" consumption. As Koechlin himself had put it, "It is not necessarily the case that the masses will not comprehend our music until it makes concessions to them. . . . The absence of musical culture in the masses is, on the contrary, a guarantee of their comprehension."[149] This fervent belief in both the power and "purity" of the modern, its ability to meet the needs of the masses who were unsullied by preconceptions, was a hallmark of the Popular Front, as it was of the Weimar Republic.

So too was the belief that the "popular," if it were denuded of false incrustations, or identified in its "pure essence," could serve an equally salubrious social end. For a return to such authentic expression was also a means to combat current fascist manipulations of a supposedly popular mass culture that was, in reality, being falsely imposed. The Fédération therefore imbued the postwar turn to the "popular" and the modern on the part of rebellious French youth with a political dimension—the combat against manipulation through a menacing "false culture." In an article of May 1937, "La vraie et la fausse musique populaire" (True and false popular music), Koechlin defines his conception of an "authentic" French popular music. It is one, he argues, that expresses the feelings of a people from within it—a true articulation of their hopes and dreams, and a genuine expression of their diurnal life.[150]

This, of course, posed a challenge for composers: How were they to write a contemporary, uncompromising music that drew on an authentic popular style, and would now appeal to the masses? One solution was proposed by the composer Daniel Lazarus, who was active in the programs of the Fédération, besides being the director of the Opéra-Comique during part of the period of the Popular Front. A former syndicalist delegate, now a Communist, Lazarus had powerful political backing and attempted to "popularize" the Opéra-Comique, without great success.[151] But as a composer, Lazarus logically proposed that the emphasis should now be on melody and rhythm, and that complicated architecture and complex harmonies should be emphatically avoided. Here we may see yet another clear parallel with certain conceptions of the Weimar Republic, with regard to a music that is "new," yet both monumental and natural, thus able to reach a broad public.[152] It was perhaps the success of the Weimar Republic's earlier endeavors in music that caused Lazarus, as well as so many French musicians, to be optimistic that they too would succeed.[153]

In the realm of music hopes remained high in 1936 and 1937, with many "modernist" composers now perceiving the ideal occasion for wide diffusion of their art. This aspiration was indeed generally shared within the Fédération Musicale Populaire, which became associated with the Editions Sociales Internationales in order to disseminate the works of composers associated with it.[154] Again, such goals were currently pervading the other arts in France as well: in the visual arts, in particular, the issues of modernity and accessibility were central. Just as in the theatrical experiments that we shall examine, there was a belief among many (as in the Soviet Union in the twenties) that modern art could aid in the social revolution. Disillusion, however, was inevitable, both with the public failure of such modernist works, and with the Communist rejection of "artistic revolution" and expulsion of the surrealists.[155]

ATTACKS ON TRADITION AND "LA GRANDE MUSIQUE"

It is not surprising that the musical qualities now to be avoided recall those elements that had been stressed at the Schola Cantorum, for, again, this institution became the Fédération's target. Memories of the Schola, as it existed under the leadership of Vincent d'Indy, were still vivid for composers like Georges Auric, who had, for a time, been his pupil. Now, just as at the turn of the century, the political connotations of the school and its teachings were made explicit by the Fédération, which attacked it in unambiguously political terms.[156] This becomes clear in, among other articles, the obituary of Albert Roussel, which appeared in *L'art musical populaire* upon his death in 1937. While it acknowledges that Roussel both attended and taught at the Schola, it stresses that he was not influenced by the "spirit" of the school and that he contributed to Rolland's *Le 14 juillet*. In addition, it argues that no matter what certain German journalists have recently insinuated (because of this earlier association), Roussel was always faithful to the democratic tradition.[157]

Equally anti-Scholiste and anti-d'Indyste is an article about Georges Auric, in the Fédération's journal in April 1939, which also seeks to dissociate him from the Schola. The fall of the Popular Front, however, would bring a resurgence of Scholisme, but not without a continuing symbolic and rhetorical battle against it on the part of the Left. The article points out that while Auric had indeed studied composition with Vincent d'Indy, he experienced the latter's "sectarianism" and henceforth "liberated" himself from that milieu. It then goes on to emphasize Auric's recent efforts to write a "musique populaire," including songs for children, the harmonization of *chants populaires*, and his work for the Chorale Populaire de Paris.[158]

Even more specific in its attack on Scholiste doctrine is the article by Henri Cliquet-Pleyel, who, as we have noted before, was a former member of Satie's Ecole d'Arcueil. "La bonne et la mauvaise musique" attacks "false" stylistic grandeur, particularly as manifest in the symphony, where bad taste often rivals technical poverty in construction. Once again aiming at the Schola, he observes that composers of such works, who are rigidly schooled in the music of the "masters," are obediently in quest of the qualities of the "pure" and "sublime." They have thus been consistently encouraged to scorn the simple and direct in music, or works of a "popular essence," which they disdainfully associate with bad taste.[159]

Recalling Satie and Cocteau, Cliquet-Pleyel then goes on to praise, to the contrary, the value placed on melody in the contemporary French popular chanson. And echoing Cocteau once more, if here for very different purposes, he then observes "Nous avons passé le temps ou l'on écoutait la musique la tête entre les mains, dans une pose absorbé et tragique." (We have passed the time when one listened to music with one's head in one's hands in an absorbed and tragic pose.)[160] This argument, formerly that of the liberal Right in the postwar period (and of the Debussystes before), is here appropriated by the Left, which aptly perceived its affinities for the ideology of the Popular Front.

Also borrowed from an earlier period by the Popular Front were ideas concerning the "masters," or which French composers to canonize, and what qualities to emphasize in their work. As we might expect because of its links with earlier Dreyfusard culture, the Fédération proposed a canon that recalls that of the Left at the turn of the century.[161] Still central are Beethoven and Handel, again construed as populist composers, to whom the problematic Berlioz is added— problematic because he combined romanticism (now of the extreme Right) with "independence" (traditionally of the Left). As Roussel put it earlier, in a survey concerning Berlioz's influence (in 1934), "Son art est . . . trop intimement lié au sort du romantisme pour qu'on puisse prédire de nouveau son influence." (His art is too intimately tied to the fate of romanticism for one to predict its influence again.)[162]

But Berlioz was "rescued" by the Popular Front through the ingenious application of an argument that we may ultimately trace back to Romain Rolland, in the first decade of the twentieth century. For the first issue of *L'art musical populaire* (recalling Rolland's books on Beethoven and Handel) enjoins composers to emulate these "giants" by attempting, just as they, to incarnate a great historical epoch in their art.[163] According to this argument, since Berlioz, French composers have abandoned true heroic subjects, but like Berlioz (as in his opera, *Les Troyens*) they should once more embrace them. As we shall see when examining the contributions of individual composers sympathetic to the Left, most did at least attempt to follow this injunction in some of their works.

Finally, again as at the turn of the century, we find concomitant attempts in the journal to present its version of a republican, or a secular music history. One of several such articles appeared in *L'art musical populaire* in February 1938, and it cites a passage from Henry Prunières's *Nouvelle histoire de la musique*, the rhetoric of which recalls the Dreyfusard spokesman Alfred Bruneau. For, like

Bruneau, Prunières here argues that religious music, far from being the inspiration for all music (as claimed by d'Indy and the Schola), sprung from the same "human" source as secular music.[164] Other histories of music sympathetic to the Left would consistently support this view, and none more so than the writings of Romain Rolland, which had done so since the turn of the century.

THE INFLUENCE OF ROMAIN ROLLAND

The influence of Romain Rolland on the Fédération's historical concepts was unmistakable, and so it is not surprising that he contributed an article to the journal on Beethoven and his art. Although Rolland had abruptly lost favor in France during the war because of his pacifism, now his populism, Communist sympathies, and earlier cultural achievements exonerated him for the Left.[165] We may see how influential Rolland's interpretation of Beethoven now was in an article on the composer published in *La revue musicale* in January 1936. The journal, as we may recall, was owned by *La nouvelle revue française*, and so it too, at first, clearly expressed sympathies for the Popular Front.

The article, by Emmanuel Buenzod, titled "Vues sur Beethoven," indeed recalls the position assumed by Rolland, as opposed to the Schola, at the turn of the century. For he too argues as did Rolland (and as opposed to d'Indy) that Beethoven's artistic motivations and inspiration had nothing to do with the religious element.[166] Rather, his stylistic departures in the period around 1803 were motivated by his hatred of tradition—his ineluctable need to break the ties that (figuratively) bound him in chains.[167] Undoubtedly because of such rhetoric, Beethoven was now inundating concert programs in France, with sixty-four performances of his works taking place in 1936 alone.[168] Most of the performances were of Beethoven's symphonies (ironically, considering contemporary denigrations of the symphony), especially numbers 2, 5, 7, and 9—those considered most accessible or "heroic" and inspiring.

But Rolland, of course, also inspired new interest in the music of the French Revolution, which would directly affect many of the composers writing for the fêtes, as we shall soon see. And so, appropriately, the Fêtes du Peuple, in collaboration with the French Communist Party, offered Rolland a tribute for his seventieth birthday, stressing the musical models of Cherubini and Méhul.[169]

LES SIX AS CULTURAL ADVISORS

As we have noted, the aesthetic associated with Les Six in the twenties now became almost "official," however it was given a political interpretation far different from that which Cocteau had implied. Several members of the group, although not all, were thus frequently solicited, commissioned, and consulted, becoming indeed almost omnipresent in concert programs and in the press. As we noted in chapter 2, most had made contacts with composers and projects in Germany during the Weimar Republic and could therefore apply lessons learned in this context to France. For now it was their role to guide and to direct a national avant-garde culture—to propose positive solutions to real social problems through the development of appropriate genres and styles. As a result, they would lead experiments similar to those applied earlier in Germany, in such areas as the use of the radio both to diffuse modern culture and to integrate it into everyday life.

The French government's cultural initiatives extended, as we have seen, to the nation's theaters, which, through chosen intermediaries, it similarly hoped to imbue with the ideals of the Popular Front. But this was a difficult enterprise in the lyric theaters, for the financial state of the Opéra and the Opéra-Comique was alarming: employees at the latter participated in the general strike that confronted the new government in June 1936. The Opéra-Comique was now under the direction of a lawyer, Pierre-Barthélemy Gheusi, who had run it earlier, during World War I, until he was removed by Clemenceau.[170] Reappointed in 1932, when his friend Mme François Coty was the theater's major financier, he had brought the theater to a parlous state in terms of equipment, budgets, and repertoire.[171] The strike occurred when Gheusi lowered the salaries of the *machinistes*, and fired other employees, which led the CGT to demand not only redress, but Gheusi's immediate departure.[172] Particularly embarrassing to the government was the fact that the theater was "occupied" by its own artists, who gave concerts just outside it—as a kind of "parade"—for passers-by, who threw them money.[173] This, together with the fact that Gheusi was an outspoken opponent of the government, as well as an admirer of Mussolini, led to his dismissal and to a reorganization.

Rouché himself had been personally financing the Opéra for over twenty years in order to compensate for its habitually inadequate subvention, an arrangement that now seemed inappropriate. The only answer appeared to be to end this so called "régime du mécénat" (regime of patronage) by grouping both lyric theaters together and supporting them entirely through funds from the state. As Zay himself remarked, many other countries, including Germany, had already adopted such a centralized system with great success.[174]

This would occur in 1939, with the Réunion des Théâtres Lyriques Nationaux; when the administration of both theaters was entrusted to Rouché, and the personnel were made interchangeable between the two. Rouché was to be assisted by a Consultative Committee of twelve—all composers who were named by the minister—although he was the final authority for any of the administrative decisions. Before this, at the Opéra-Comique the artistic direction was placed under the composer Daniel Lazarus and the general administrator of the theater, Antoine Mariotte.[175] Lazarus, who had won first prize as a pianist at the Paris Conservatoire, had been musical director at the Théâtre du Vieux Colombier and then of the Ballets Futuristes Italiens. He had gradually grown engaged politically, becoming a member of the Communist Association des Ecrivains et Artistes Révolutionnaires, perhaps under the influence of J.-R. Bloch, with whom he had collaborated.[176]

As a composer, Lazarus had written numerous ballets and theatrical works, including a three-act opera to his own libretto about the pioneer of the Zionist movement, *Trumpeldor*.[177] After being made *chef du chant* at the Opéra-Comique in 1933, Lazarus wrote many articles concerning the necessary reform of the theater.[178] He was, then, an obvious choice, although his tenure was filled with controversy over his often poor artistic decisions, leading to his dismissal in late August 1939. But both the Opéra-Comique and the Opéra were, in the meantime, accorded adequate funds: given the importance of the theaters to the government both symbolically and as a means to reach a large public, the Chamber was quick to vote the subventions. In 1936 the Opéra had received a yearly subvention of about 6 million francs; in 1937 this was raised to 12,561,000 francs, and in 1938 to 17,000,000 francs.[179] In addition, in 1936 the Chamber approved an additional funding of 450,000 francs to aid the Opéra's presentation of new works by French composers.[180] With the government's rivalry and mounting tensions with Nazi Germany, French chauvinism (in both politics and culture) was now moving to the Left, especially as certain groups on the Right found French Communists more menacing than the Germans.

Although Zay eventually placed Rouché at the head of the two lyric theaters, he already added a "comité consultatif" for both, as he had for the Comédie-Française.[181] According to Zay, the collaboration of four *metteurs en scène* from outside the Comédie-Française had infused it with new life, and thus he hoped that the same would transpire at the Opéra. Yet this was simultaneously a means to exert greater ideological, governmental influence, thereby making the lyric theaters inherently more responsive to the government's new goals.

For the Opéra, Zay sought to appoint those composers whom he associated with the progressive, with "modernity," or, as he put it, those generally considered to be the "jeunes maîtres" of the present day. For him this was the group "des Sept," meaning not only the members of Les Six, but also including the now prominent Daniel Lazarus.[182] Several composers of the older generation were summoned for advice as well, including Henri Rabaud, Reynaldo Hahn, and the politically conservative Jacques Ibert. For the Opéra-Comique, the Comité Consultatif consisted of Georges Auric, Gustave Charpentier, Reynaldo Hahn, Arthur Honegger, Jacques Ibert, Charles Koechlin, Daniel Lazarus, Darius Milhaud, Max d'Ollone, Gabriel Piérné, and Albert Roussel.[183]

Zay was thoroughly disappointed by the final results, however; as he pointed out, whether it was because musicians had less talent for organization than theater directors, or because their collegial spirit was less developed, the result was no significant plan, only some internal "intrigues."[184] Clearly the battles within the fractious French musical world were far from ended by the advent of the Popular Front, and they would grow even more intense with its decline. For as Zay points out, much traditionalism remained, although the salaries for artists in the theaters did improve, perhaps accounting for the enthusiasm for the new government that now became predominant.

Within the repertoire, it is hardly surprising to find that works by Les Six, or those among them that supported the government, as well as works of their friends and associates, were now being emphasized. The Opéra performed music of Ibert, Roussel, and Honegger, including the latter's *ballet avec chant*, the *Cantique des cantiques*, which employed ondes Martenot. But works by lesser-known figures were also frequent, such as Philippe Gaubert's *Alexandre le grand* (premiered 21 June 1937) and Vittorio Rieti's *David triomphant* (premiered 26 May 1937).[185]

At the Opéra-Comique there was more of an attempt to renew the repertoire, particularly with the presence of Roger Desormière, who became the conductor of the theater after Eugène Bichot. New works were added to the repertoire, and others, including those of Massenet, Chabrier, Offenbach, Grétry, and Monsigny, were now revived. The previously dominant Italian verismo works in the repertoire were purged as no longer appropriate, but pressure from the performers led to the reintegration of Mascagni's *Cavalleria rusticana* and Puccini's *Madame Butterfly*.[186] Ideology could not determine all choices, but as we shall now see, it would inevitably lead to ruptures between those composers who were sympathetic to, and favored by, the government and those who were hostile or aloof, and thus excluded.

AESTHETICS, STYLE, AND "ENGAGEMENT"

Tensions inevitably appeared within both Les Six and the Ecole d'Arcueil, for although most members of both groups supported the government's projects, some did not, and refused to participate. For the majority of Les Six (and for Jean Wiéner), the new Leftist government was appealing; they had not only matured in the thirties, but had become more politically as well as socially aligned, and indeed "engaged."[187] Moreover, they now perceived the political implications of their aesthetic within the new context, leading most of them openly to demonstrate their sympathies with the republican Left.[188] Jean Wiéner, the dapper bourgeois (if iconoclastic) man-about-town of the twenties, now grew close to the Communist Party, and would remain so for the rest of his life. As Wiéner later explained, it was in the early and mid-1930s that he finally became fully conscious of "the general misery" of the postwar period.[189]

It was apparently Roger Desormière who had "converted" him while Desormière was in close contact with Wiéner, both as a conductor and as one who recorded Wiéner's work between 1932 and 1939. As Wiéner put it, Desormière kept him "au courant" of the "grandes choses" that were currently taking place, and with which he now associated himself, as someone close the Popular Front. Desormière, he thus avowed, was the one who had helped him to "situate himself" in the "social-political position" where he would intractably remain. While not a member of the Communist Party, Wiéner, as a close collaborator, was asked to become a regular music critic for the Communist paper *Ce soir*.[190]

Beginning in 1934, the year that frightened so many into action, Wiéner became involved with the Fédération du Théâtre Ouvrier de France, collaborating in "revolutionary sketches" (which included "choeurs parlés") with Jacques Prévert and the group Octobre. Wiéner also pointed out that all his friends became involved with the Popular Front, and he, like they, wanted simply to work for "la bonne cause." Among other projects, Wiéner was one of the principal musical collaborators in Jean Renoir's grandiose film, *La marseillaise*, in 1937.[191]

While most of Wiéner's circle shared his political sincerity, some undoubtedly were also aware of the possibilities of important large-scale commissions, and of having greater professional influence. Although orchestral music was deemphasized, there was an immediate need for works that could be performed by the choruses, bands, and wind ensembles of the Fédération.[192] Their motivation was undoubtedly complex, and most participated for a variety of reasons, while some, like Poulenc, because of his convictions, largely desisted, as we shall shortly see. Aware that their styles and values now carried new political implications, some members of Les Six and the Ecole d'Arcueil remained happily in former styles, while others felt compelled to change for ideological reasons. Some would find (as before World War I) that they were immediately imputed a political position on the basis of the style they employed, which was, in some cases, counter to their actual convictions.[193] Indeed, we shall see how Poulenc responded to such political associations ascribed to him, on the basis of his earlier style, by transforming his stylistic approach.

The most enthusiastic participants in the musical programs of the Popular Front, as we have noted, were clearly Auric, Durey, Milhaud, and Tailleferre. Auric provides a case in point of a composer who, after abandoning the style that he had developed in the twenties, returned to it consciously within the new political context. In the early thirties Auric had begun to search for a more "serious" and expressive style, rejecting the aesthetic associated with Les Six, and in fact returning to his Scholiste background. He now sought to emulate Berg, whom several members of Les Six had admired (in spite of Cocteau) and adopted a consciously turbulent style that was distant from his earlier neoclassicism.

This becomes particularly evident in his Piano Sonata in F, written in Auric's stylistically transitional years, 1931 to 1932. After having ridiculed Scholiste training in the twenties, he here openly embraces it, only vehemently to reject it once more at the time of the Popular Front. The work, not really in F, is cast in four movements, the first of which employs the classical sonata contrast of themes, as well as the Scholiste emphasis on counterpoint. The second movement is a scherzo, again highly complex rhythmically, and in addition it layers two thematic ideas that are consistently varied throughout the movement. The third movement, alternates poignant recitative-like sections with a contrastingly calm theme, and the fourth movement, while once again lyric, is marked "Vif et violent." Although the work is not overtly cyclic in the Scholiste manner, as taught by d'Indy (again, based on Franck), there is nevertheless a strong resemblance between themes in the different movements.[194]

The composition, however, was not a public success: responses were far from enthusiastic, which may have encouraged Auric to turn to the now more politically "correct" approach.[195] We can observe Auric's stylistic transformation in his Sonata in G for Violin and Piano of 1936, a work imbued with the aesthetic and populist spirit of the Popular Front (ex. 4). Here Auric attempts to adopt a more "popular" or simple musical style, one that is disarmingly direct—limpid in harmony and texture, as well as in structure.[196] Appropriately, the work was published in 1937 by the house that became associated with the Fédération, the Communist Editions Sociales Internationales, and dedicated to Yvonne Astruc. Again, we may recall that this was the period when Auric also wrote songs for

EXAMPLES 4—Auric, Sonata for violin and piano.

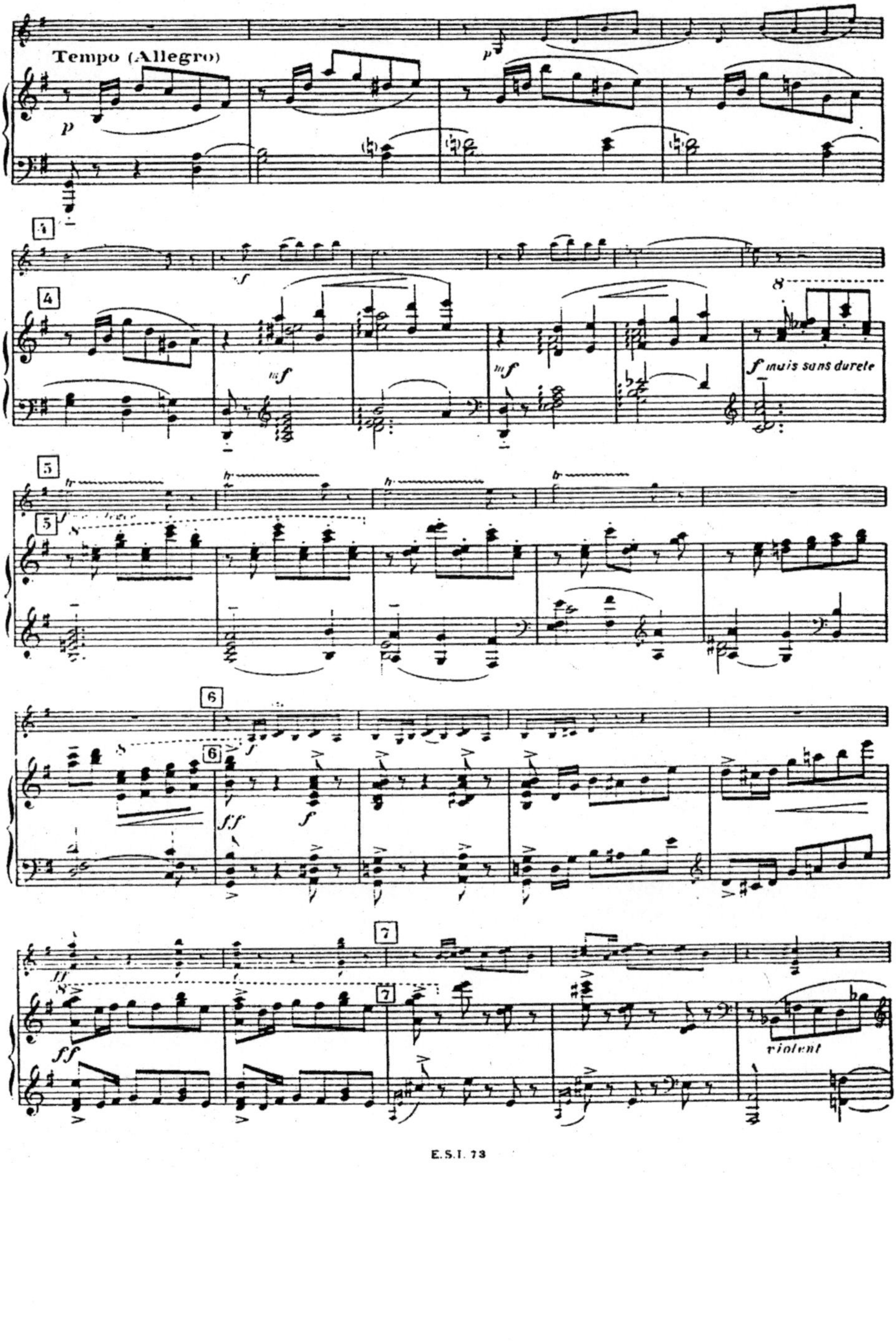
Tempo (Allegro)
p
4
mf
f mais sans dureté
5
6
ff
7
violent

children and harmonized folksongs, in addition to producing compositions for the Chorale Populaire de Paris. He similarly wrote works for organizations such as the Union des Jeunes de France, including "Chantons jeunes filles," to a text of Léon Moussinac. Also along these lines was his "Campeur en chocolat," part of the *Chants du campeur*, to texts of Paul Vaillant-Couturier, to be sung outdoors by various youth groups.[197]

Milhaud remained typically prolific and was engaged with the government's projects throughout these years, participating in many of its special events, as he enthusiastically describes in his memoirs. Already, in 1935, the year of the International Congress of Writers in Defense of Culture, Milhaud was caught up in the combative spirit of intellectuals in France. This was the year of his "scenic oratorio" with Claudel titled *La sagesse*, the theme of which was "the drama of man fighting against the forces that imprison him" and "man's awareness of the role assigned him."[198] At the end of this timely allegory about the state of humanity and man's conscience, wisdom is ultimately triumphant and forces man to follow its precepts.

The work, commissioned by Ida Rubenstein, was clearly attuned to the concerns of the day, but although suited to its period, did not premiere until another apt moment—in 1945. It employs the rhythmic declamation that Milhaud had explored earlier in his *Oresteia*, as well as melodies that for Milhaud were expressive of "l'âme populaire," including those suggesting Provençal origins. True to his beliefs, melody here continues to incarnate the "collective," for Milhaud, yet a collectivity that is not tied to a "place," but is rather representative of a universal humanity.[199] Milhaud's natural balance between harmonic modernity and an accessible melody, as well as his pronounced rhythm and supple forms were indeed well suited to the aesthetic of the Popular Front.

A collaborator, if not a member, of the Fédération, Milhaud participated in the collective score for Romain Rolland's *Le 14 juillet* in 1936, along with Auric, Ibert, Roussel, Koechlin, and Lazarus. As we have noted, he also contributed one of the twenty scores commissioned to accompany the fête, "Jeu de la Lumière et d'Eau sur la Seine" for the 1937 Exposition. Here again Milhaud was able to continue his collaboration with Paul Claudel, who, although more conservative than the government, wrote a poem for this occasion, as for others. Milhaud also participated in two other works for the 1937 Exposition—in the piece titled *Liberté*, and in the "modernist" extravaganza *La construction de la cité*. The former involved the collaboration of nine composers, including Ibert, Jaubert, Tailleferre, and Honegger, and in the latter spectacle, conceived by J.-R. Bloch, Milhaud again collaborated with Honegger.[200]

Here it is important to note that Milhaud also collaborated with J.-R. Bloch on the Communist paper *Ce soir*, of which Bloch was the codirector, along with Louis Aragon. Aimed at the "classes populaires," its contributors included both Communists and those who were not members but were sympathetic to the party, like Wiéner.[201] Undoubtedly, Milhaud's motivation for participation in such journalistic and musical projects was highly complex (again, he contributed simultaneously to conservative newspapers), but, in his later writings, he recalls the hovering menace of war. As he observes in *Notes sans musique*, after 1933 and the rise of Hitler to power in Germany, the general concern with possible war became almost obsessive.[202] Although not highly politicized, Milhaud was nevertheless sensitive to the events around him, particularly those that concerned fascist or totalitarian threats, not only in Europe, but also in France. His desire for peace, shared by many others in his circle, such as Claudel and the latter's friend Aristide Briand, the politician, did not imply acquiescence to Hitler, but their horror of the possibility of another war. Wanting to believe the best of France and of its national character and strength, Milhaud, like many assimilated French Jews, would face the political reality of the situation in his own country when it was almost too late.[203]

Believing, with idealism and enthusiasm, in the unity of the world's peoples and their religions, Milhaud helped to celebrate the inauguration of the new Musée de l'Homme with his *Cantate du Musée de l'Homme*. The work, set to a text of the prominent surrealist writer Robert Desnos, was a commission from two individuals who supported the government, the vicomte de Noailles and Henri Monnet.[204] Milhaud also received a commission for a work to be performed at the ceremony held by the government to commemorate the sixty-fifth birthday of Aristide Briand.[205] Here the pianist Marguerite Long, who was in charge of the project, proposed to her former pupil Milhaud that he write a work for the ceremony, to take place at the Sorbonne and in which speakers from several countries would participate. When he asked what forces would be available, Milhaud was told that he could make use of the Musique de la Garde Républicaine or the Manécanterie [choir school] des Petits Chanteurs à la Croix de Bois. Since Claudel had worked under Briand and admired his political principles, Milhaud made sure of the poet's collaboration in the work, which was to be for chorus. The result, appropriately for Briand, was the *Cantate de la paix*, performed by children of the *manécanterie*, to which a group of adult tenors and basses was added. Milhaud was so pleased with their performance that he wrote a second work for this choir of children from a popular quartier, under the direction of the abbé Maillet, his *Les deux cités*.[206]

Finally, Milhaud wrote another *pièce de circonstance*, of a different nature—one that related closely to his own identity and profound beliefs. It was a *hymne* for a cappella chorus, to a poem of Charles Vildrac, for the congress of the Ligue Internationale contre l'Antisémitisme, and premiered on 12 September 1937.[207] During this time Milhaud also became increasingly involved with youth, and with enlarging their access to music thorough a new organization that was tied to the Popular Front, the Loisirs Musicaux de la Jeunesse, of which he was president.[208] It was founded in 1937, at the time when further steps were being taken to make more musical instruction obligatory in the schools, which, as we may recall, was a theme of the early 1930s. Not only did the organization solicit works for youth, to be performed by instrumental and vocal ensembles, it opened music and record libraries, as well as offering a broad musical instruction.

Milhaud, who participated actively with the group until the time of the war, became its *président d'honneur* and attracted other notable contemporary composers, such as Arthur Honegger and Jean Wiéner. Milhaud had probably heard similar youth groups during his travels in Germany in the 1920s, and former related projects in central and eastern Europe did, in fact, provide models for the group, particularly in its use of folklore.[209] Also likely based on precedents that had been developed in the Weimar Republic, the organization introduced a "groupe de musique ancienne," as well as the first French recorder quartet.[210]

Milhaud, a noted critic for the leftist journal *Europe*, was also active in one of the journals associated with the Fédération Musicale Populaire, *Chansons au vent*, being its honorary president as well. Here he continued to preach his gospel of melody and its importance as representative of the most fundamentally human elements, thus lying above the divisions of both parties and other groups.[211] This is another context in which to understand the statement we noted from *Europe*: "Imaginez-vous un quatuor de gauche ou de droite?" (Can you imagine a quartet of the Left or the Right?)[212] By this, again, he did not mean that music is apolitical, or not subject to clearly political use—of which he was now well aware—but that the creative act was itself beyond the political. Significantly, it was for political reasons, during the Popular Front, that Milhaud was at last able to have his comic opera *Esther de Carpentras* performed. Although it was only in concert version, it is here important to note that it was broadcast on the radio, on 13 April 1937 (under Manuel Rosenthal), thus reaching a broad spectrum of the public. However, such programming of politically resonant works was perceived by the Right as a propagandistic use of the radio, and incited a backlash by the government's adversaries.[213]

Louis Durey, like Georges Auric, to whom he remained close, became similarly active in the Fédération Musicale Populaire and held the important office of its general secretary. But while Auric remained a Socialist, Durey, whose political commitment was always strong, moved even further to the Left, becoming a member of the Communist Party in 1936. Durey remained active creatively, entering into the spirit of the Popular Front by writing, among other works, a score for a small marionette play titled *L'intruse*. Although the play was based upon a work of the Belgian symbolist Maurice Maeterlinck, appropriately, the genre of the puppet play was rooted in a long tradition of popular entertainment.[214] Simultaneously, however, Durey was already engaged in various historical projects (which would occupy him throughout World War II), spending much of his time doing research in libraries and museums. Significantly, as a Communist, his interest now lay primarily in the French Revolution, and he accordingly undertook the reconstruction of works by Gossec and Blanchard for the Société Française de Musicologie.

Germaine Tailleferre similarly participated actively in the projects of the Popular Front, but this had been preceded by another political involvement with the Left in the early 1930s. Present in the audience of a concert in honor of the tenth anniversary of Les Six, at the Théâtre des Champs-Elysées in 1930, was the Radical-Socialist deputy Gaston Bergery.[215] A lover of music, Bergery apparently knew a good deal about it, thus impressing Tailleferre, who henceforth entered into regular contact with him. In her memoirs she revealingly describes what drew her toward Bergery in this period of increasing political anxiety which she, like Milhaud, could not help but perceive:

> Pour moi, qui ne comprenais absolument rien à la politique, dès qu'il prenait la parole, tous les problèmes du moment se clarifiaient. Je ne savais pas pourquoi tout était si embrouillé dans le gouvernement: il suffisait d'écouter Gaston Bergery et toutes les difficultés étaient résolues.[216]
>
> [For me, who understood absolutely nothing about politics, as soon as he spoke, all the problems of the moment were clarified. I didn't know why all was so muddled in the government: it sufficed to listen to Gaston Bergery and all the difficulties were resolved.]

Like so many other artists in the period, Tailleferre could not avoid being aware of the growing tensions within French politics, and in international relations with Germany as well as with Italy. But being unsophisticated politically, she, like others, would, for a time, be drawn ineluctably to charismatic, eloquent, and cultivated politicians like Gaston Bergery. So would Arthur Honegger, whom Bergery similarly courted in the thirties, and who remained his ally far longer, even after Bergery's growing criticism of the Third Republic.

In the early 1930s Bergery was perceived as a reformer within the Left, and, being a highly seductive individual, accrued a group of supporters who accompanied him on his electoral campaigns.[217] Tailleferre was regularly among them, and so was a young lawyer, Jean Lagéat, to whom she became romantically attracted, and whom she would marry in 1932. Lagéat was deeply engaged politically, and was among the counterdemonstrators in the riot of 6 February 1934, in which he was clubbed and sustained serious injuries.[218] Tailleferre and her husband together contributed actively to Bergery's electoral campaign—she by organizing small concerts with local amateur musicians during his tours. Her political involvement was later transferred to the cultural projects of the Popular Front, which Bergery initially supported, yet strongly criticized by 1937. But in 1933 Bergery had just left the Radical-Socialist Party to create his own Front Commun, an unambiguously antifascist political grouping.[219] His subsequent goals of fighting the excesses of both liberal democracy and Communism eventually led to the founding of his Parti Frontiste, born the same year as the Popular Front.[220]

Gradually disillusioned with the Popular Front, and with the French political system, by 1938 Bergery was denouncing all established political parties.[221] He also assumed an antiwar stance and a posture of isolationism specifically with regard to the threats of neighboring fascist regimes and authoritarian dictatorships in Germany, Italy, and Spain.[222] This was the period when Arthur Honegger, similarly unsatisfied by the orthodox ideological alternatives, drew close to Bergery, while Tailleferre began to take her distance. She went on to contribute to numerous works in the spirit and context of the Popular Front, including a commissioned cantata on "the state of man," the *Cantate de Narcisse*, to a text of Paul Valéry, in 1938. But she also contributed a more appropriately lighthearted opéra-bouffe, *Le marin de Bolivar*, for the 1937 Exposition in Paris.

LE 14 JUILLET: POLITICS AND REPRESENTATION

As we have seen, few French composers could resist participation in the government's lavish spectacles, which brought both public prominence as well as financial remuneration. Moreover, they offered composers the occasion to live up to the ideals that many of them now professed, of bringing a "high" yet accessible art to *le peuple*.[223] But they also provided the government with a means simultaneously to project and "represent" its ideals, thus manifesting its cultural vitality and establishing its political credibility.

The most immediate attempt to represent the grandeur envisioned by the Popular Front, or its conception of an *art total*, was the presentation of Romain Rolland's *Le 14 juillet*.[224] The play, or "action populaire," dated from the period of another leftist government (in 1902) and was the most advanced incarnation of Rolland's ideals concerning popular theater. In addition, it was his most expansive expression of social populism, its message being, in essence, that the masses are able to effect or to realize their own destiny.[225] This emphasis on the heroism of the masses, still considered to be the source of modern republicanism, was, as we might expect, highly resonant for the Popular Front.[226]

Appropriately, Rolland's play concludes grandiosely with a (supposedly) spontaneous "people's festival," Rolland perceiving this as a means to spread "the spirit of fraternalism" from the stage to the audience. Hence he employed the orchestra and chorus both dramatically and symbolically to bridge this gap, thereby making the work's dramatic action all the more "liminal," or on the border between the dramatic and the "real."[227] This technique of fusion was emphasized further by another means that had invaded the Parisian theaters in the revolutions of both 1789 and 1848. At the end of the performance, the actors and audience all join together in singing "La marseillaise," although now to be followed by the Communist anthem, "L'internationale." As a result, the work has often been described as less political theater than, in effect, simply a continuation of politics by other means.[228]

Indeed, this was a period when it seemed apparent to many that politics itself had, in short, become theater, the audience transformed into actors in an historical epoch, again recalling Rouché's matinées during World War I.[229] Rolland's play was now politically apt, and so despite the fact that it had not been performed since 1902 (during the "Dreyfusard Republic"), in 1936 the Maison de Culture decided to produce it. It did so lavishly, using, in part, a generous subvention from the new government, and soliciting the collaboration of important contemporary musicians and artists. Again, as during the First World War, the emphasis was clearly on collective endeavor, and on breaking down the barriers between the arts, recalling the communitarian conception of Wagner held by the Left in the twenties.

As with *Parade* before, Pablo Picasso designed the grandiose curtain, and the actors were drawn from the Comédie-Française, although some of the walk-on parts were performed by members of the CGT (union).[230] The composers involved were selected from both the older and younger generation, with, as one might expect, prominent representation of Les Six.[231] Unfortunately, they were limited by the forces made available—the musicians of the Fédération Musicale Populaire (consisting of a forty-five piece orchestra, without strings, as in the Revolution) as well as a small choir.[232]

The first piece, the "Ouverture," was by Jacques Ibert, a friend of several members of the group Les Six, but a composer who was still heavily influenced by both Debussy and Ravel. Although Ibert was politically conservative, in 1936 Jean Zay nevertheless wanted to offer him the position of director of the Conservatoire or of the Opéra-Comique. Perhaps this decision was the result of an attempt to balance innovation with conservation, so as to appease the more politically centrist members of the government. Zay was known for his political astuteness, which he managed to balance adeptly with both artistic and managerial criteria, as his memories indeed amply attest. Ibert, however, preferred to remain distant from Paris throughout this period, and therefore chose to direct the French Academy in Rome instead.[233]

But, again, Les Six were among the most prominent contributors to Rolland's work, with the prelude to the first act, "Le Palais Royal" (no. 2) by Georges Auric, and the finale to the first act, the "Introduction et marche funèbre" (no. 3) by Darius Milhaud. The latter, significantly, contains a *choeur parlé*, a technique with which Milhaud had been experimenting for years, ever since the *Oresteia*, his first collaboration with Paul Claudel. The "Prélude" to the second act was, appropriately, by Albert Roussel, and the finale to the second act, "Liberté" (no. 5) by Charles Koechlin. Honegger wrote the prelude to the third act, the "Marche sur la Bastille" (which included a "choeur à bouche fermée" [with mouths closed]), and Daniel Lazarus composed the finale to the third act, the "Interlude et fête populaire" (or Fête de la Liberté), which employs spoken lines.[234] Lazarus was already known as a composer on the basis of his politicized *Symphonie avec hymne*, of 1934, as we noted, intended to comprise a history of the Jewish people in five parts.[235] Most of the composers, therefore, were already associated with specific political sympathies, and particularly those connected with the ideals of the Popular Front.

Le 14 juillet was by far the most explicitly political work of the period, inciting immediate polarization in both the political and musical worlds. In some cases, the style itself was provocative, given the symbolic associations of the period, or the meanings now carried by styles within contemporary discourse. As Leslie Sprout has shown, Auric's contribution parodied an aristocratic gavotte, while Milhaud's made obvious reference to the marches of the revolutionary period by composers such as Gossec and Catel. Although he retains the stylistic "markers" of the genre, such as the drum rolls, the rhythms, and the fanfare, Milhaud combines this with contemporary harmonies and a contrapuntal combination of melodies, eloquently connecting past and present. Koechlin's contribution, in keeping with his theories, employs a popular song which is sung by a young girl and then taken up by the entire chorus.[236]

The work's reception was predictable: here the aesthetic and the political were ineluctably fused, with the Right systematically hostile, while journals of the Left were enthusiastic, and some even ebullient. *L'humanité* applauded the spectacle as an effort at a "collective musical art," which it perceived as indispensable to the development of a true "people's music."[237] As we have noted, such collective endeavors were a cultural theme of the Popular Front, which conceived them not as a negation of individuality but rather as "cooperation." Here the wartime "communal" values of the Right were reinscribed politically by the Left, now used metaphorically to signify the egalitarian fraternity that it envisioned.[238] The Socialist journal *Vendredi* was equally enthusiastic about *Le 14 juillet*, but here it was the theatrical fusion of artists and audience that prompted its encomium. For, as it observed, by the final spectacle "there were no longer actors playing roles": the attempted liminality was so successful that the theater had become reality.[239] Again, as opposed to the emphatic hierarchy and discipline of fascist ceremonies, the resulting "magical" effect was to produce the emotions that would help sustain an egalitarian order.

It was not the political press alone that waxed enthusiastic about Rolland's work; so too did journals in the French musical press, some of which were not overtly politicized. Not surprisingly, a highly positive review of the piece appeared in *La revue musicale*, which, again, reflected its close connections with *La nouvelle revue française*.[240] Here the author, Léon Kochnitzsky, immediately speaks of the work's noble intentions, referring to it as the "épopée républicaine" that is currently triumphing. He then proceeds to evaluate the individual musical contributions in terms of the function that the spectacle was meant to serve, both ideologically and socially. Notably in a musical journal, the criteria of evaluation were here not purely aesthetic, but now both political and social, in keeping with the spirit of the Popular Front. After praising not only Rolland, but Pablo Picasso's curtain, Kochnitzsky pronounces Koechlin's chorus, "La liberté, dans ce beau jour," the most successful of the musical contributions. But he equally admires the simple ingenuity of Ibert's overture, once more because of its effectiveness as a means to relate to the masses culturally. As he puts it, "sa musique veut être populaire au sens traditionnel—le compositeur épouse très adroitement les formes musicales qui passent encore pour faire les délires des foules." (His music attempts to be popular in the traditional sense—the composer very adroitly espouses the musical forms that still cause the delirium of the masses.)[241]

It is equally on the basis of its public effectiveness that the critic praises Honegger's overture, with its emphatic contrasts, its "violent" effects, and its arresting rhythms and timbres. But since Kochnitzsky's standard is quite clearly the "heroic," he criticizes Lazarus's finale, which he finds to be undramatic, and specifically reminiscent of the traditional dances of Opéra-Comique. However, for Kochnitzsky, the work, in general, met the aesthetic standards and needs of the day, since a "popular" audience could both understand and fully enjoy it. Yet he takes issue with a central element of the aesthetic doctrine of the Fédération Musicale Populaire—its unequivocal condemnation of "the sublime." For, as an admirer of the "heroic," he argues that this quality is not associated exclusively with the pretentious or the erudite, but with those works that are imbued with a universal and humanistic spirit. For him this includes, of course, Beethoven's *Egmont* Overture and *Fidelio*, as well as his Ninth Symphony, and even Bach's *Saint Matthew Passion*. These are works, he argues (recalling the rhetoric of the syndicalist Fêtes du Peuple) that even a popular audience could understand immediately, and thus be elevated, united, and inspired.[242]

PERFORMANCE AND IDEOLOGY: THE 1937 EXPOSITION

As noted at the beginning of this chapter, belief in the natural ability of the masses to comprehend great art, including the most contemporary, informed the programs of the 1937 Exposition. Planned by the previous government, the Exposition was inherited by that of Blum, which immediately perceived it as an appropriate opportunity to demonstrate its cultural and political success.[243] Here ideology was to emerge through "performance," or through the socially situated presentation of works of both past and present, which would imbue them with political connotations, making them ideological enunciations. They would be carefully placed within a schema of comprehension shaped by the government to ensure that the "interpretive frame" accorded closely with the ideology of the Popular Front. Theater, as we have seen, was central, and for the opening of the Exposition the government commissioned a collective play, *Vive la liberté*, which presented French history as leading teleologically to the Popular Front.[244]

Already, in May 1933, the Opéra's savvy director, Jacques Rouché, had been named a member of the Conseil Supérieur of the International Exposition. But, in addition, Rouché (also a member of the Institut) was later made president of the newly founded Commission des Fêtes et Spectacles de l'Exposition.[245] It was with the specific intent of reviving the tradition of grand civic fêtes that the Popular Front created a "classe supplémentaire," titled "L'art des fêtes."[246]

Enthusiasm for the Exposition was great, but, as contemporaries observed, it was prepared in the midst of both internal social turmoil and external political threats. Not only were strikes and the occupation of factories a constant concern of the government, but there was also the omnipresent shadow of a potential German annexation of Austria. As Milhaud later put it:

> Il y avait un Pavillon autrichien, mais les forces mauvaises de l'Anschluss n'en s'étaient jamais éloignées; la *Guernica* de Picasso s'étalait sur les murs du Pavillon espagnol, mais la République avait été assassinée; le Pavillon de l'Allemagne et celui de Russie Soviétique semblaient se défier face à face.[247]

> [There was an Austrian pavilion, but the evil forces of the Anschluss were never far away; Picasso's *Guernica* was displayed on the walls of the Spanish pavilion, but the Republic had been assassinated; the German and Soviet Russian pavilions seemed to challenge each other face to face.]

Milhaud was not isolated in an ivory tower but was well attuned to the political situation, and equally aware of the government's political goals in music by 1937. As he pointed out, the government seized upon the Exposition as a means to calm the ever-mounting fears of the public, while the political menace grew ominous.

Milhaud, as we have noted, was asked to contribute one of the twenty scores commissioned for the brilliant fête the "Jeu de la Lumière," with Claudel again writing the poem.[248] This fête was the conception of the architects Beaudouin and Lods, who envisaged a *fête nocturne* in which light, water, and music would merge in an incandescent, enchanting whole.[249] Other spectacles similarly celebrated modernity, as implicitly opposed to tradition, which was now being abused by the Nazi regime to celebrate totalitarian values. There was thus a concerted effort to renew or rejuvenate the official fête, to bring it up to date with the most "modernist" artistic currents that had developed in the twenties.[250]

The new spectacles included a ballet intended to glorify aviation, *L'oiseau bleu s'est envolé*, with the plot by Sacha Guitry, the choreography by Serge Lifar, and the music by Arthur Honegger. As we have noted, Honegger also participated in another collective spectacle titled *Liberté*, presented by the Socialist group Mai 1936 in conjunction with the 1937 Exposition.[251] Moreover, Honegger and Ibert's "drame musical," *L'Aiglon* (to libretto based on Edmond Rostand's play) was presented with great public success in the context of the Exposition, in September 1937.[252] Such events, then, were by no means peripheral to the French musical world of the period, but central vehicles for major composers, who embraced them for a variety of reasons.[253]

Rouché undertook other fêtes, one of which recalls not only Charpentier's *Couronnement de la muse*, but, once more, the now prominent theme of the joining of intellectuals with the people. This was the "Fête de la Pensée," in which, according to the explicatory text, "l'élite de la pensée française sera présentée au Peuple de Paris où chaque délégué fera le point sur ce que représente, au point de vue de l'art et les sciences, l'Exposition de 1937." (The elite of French thought will be presented to the People of Paris where each delegate will explain what the Exposition of 1937 represents from the point of view of art and the sciences.)[254] Here a dominant ideological theme was vividly "enacted," or represented through the vehicle of "performance," a means considered more appropriate than dry rhetoric for a "popular" audience. The organizers clearly perceived a notable gap between conceptions as stated discursively in prose and those that could be communicated figuratively, and more effectively, by means of the arts.[255]

Other fêtes similarly strove to "represent" those ideas now central to the government, including the Communist-influenced "Fête du Travail," involving a cortège conceived by Paul Cachin. Others, celebrating the seasons, recalled the original fêtes of the revolutionary period, as was the case with the Fête de l'Eté, with music by the composer Louis Aubert.[256] Some closely resembled the models of the revolutionary period itself, with theatrical floats carrying *tableaux vivants*, including actors in period costumes, and panels with giant portraits of revolutionary heroes or great intellectuals and artists of the past.[257] Not all the fêtes, however, were rooted in the French revolutionary past: the most daring and innovative, perhaps, was *La naissance d'une cité*, presented at the Grand Palais on 22 and 28 May 1937.[258] Conceived by Jean-Richard Bloch, it featured an architectural setting by E. Beaulouch, decors by Fernand Léger, and music by Arthur Honegger and Darius Milhaud.[259] An ostensible attempt to build on the momentum created by *Le 14 juillet*, it represented an even more far-reaching effort to incorporate the French artistic avant-garde—again recalling the Weimar Republic.[260]

As we have already noted, proponents of the Popular Front such as Charles Koechlin believed that the masses, unbiased in taste, could readily appreciate avant-garde art. One result of this belief in 1937 was that young French theatrical troupes, especially those that were avant-garde, were invited to perform in the Exposition. Indeed, Blum himself, who clearly appreciated the metaphor of brave exploration in both a new social art and in a "more beautiful" society, intervened on behalf of the participation of modern architects like Le Corbusier.[261]

The theme of *La naissance d'une cité* was man's alienation and revolt against the city, as a result of dehumanizing modern factory life, clearly in need of reform.[262] The production was correspondingly massive, with as many as seven hundred performers on stage at once, including acrobats, cyclists, mimes, dancers, and the now omnipresent spoken choruses.[263] This recalls not only previous experiments in workers' theater, but such avant-garde spectacles as *Parade*, which incorporated circus elements to invoke a "democratic" or immediate appeal. The fête also included such disparate musical works as Honegger's "Chanson de l'émigrant," Milhaud's "Java de la femme," an accordion interlude, fragments of national anthems, as well as fanfares and sirens.[264] Here these elements were incorporated within the context of a sophisticated, ironic scenario, one whose irony was far more overt than that of Charpentier's *Couronnement de la muse*. As a result, as opposed to Charpentier's earlier spectacle, it could not be easily construed on different cultural levels, thus simultaneously meeting the needs of diverse social groups. And so, despite the lavish effort, the work, in the end, was not a success, and such thoroughly modernist or "advanced" experiments were not undertaken again.

But daring steps were still being taken in visual arts at the Exposition; in the midst of escalating anti-Semitism, it sponsored an exhibition consisting largely of the "Ecole de Paris." Again, these were largely Jewish artists, and, in direct confrontation with right-wing rhetoric which denied that any Jews could become true Frenchmen, they were presented as "naturalized" French artists.[265] But of all the arts, film was most accessible to the masses, and thus was an area of strong interest to the Popular Front, which aggressively sought to employ it to convey its political message. Important musicians avidly participated: for example, in 1937 Jean Wiéner collaborated enthusiastically on Jean Renoir's film, *La marseillaise*.[266] And under the aegis of Ciné Liberté the government sponsored two substantial feature films, one of which was *Les bâtisseurs*, a documentary by Jean Epstein, after a text of the surrealist writer Robert Desnos, with music by Arthur Honegger and Arthur Hoérée. Made for the builder's union, it depicts the labor of two honest workers who are nobly and industriously attempting to restore the magnificent Chartres Cathedral.[267] But the ending waxes didactic, for here the architect Le Corbusier expands on his vision of a modern urbanism, followed to a hymn to "work" by his friend Arthur Honegger. The film, however, was not released until the beginning of 1938, by which time the ideology it espoused was in precipitous decline.[268]

But Honegger was involved in another such project—the film score for *Vis-

age de la France, a short Communist film written by Paul Nizan, R. Vigneau, and André Wurmser. Since the film was a gift to the Soviet Union, in honor of the twentieth anniversary of the October Revolution, at the end of the film Honegger aptly combined (in counterpoint) "La marseillaise" and "L'internationale." More powerful than any discourse concerning both the parallels and ideological affinities between the French and Russian Revolutions, Honegger's symbolic representation impressed many.[269] This, however, was not Honegger's only involvement with the Communist Party, for he also wrote several short *chants de masses* for the Communist publisher Le Chant du Monde. These included his "Jeunesse," of 1937, composed for the Fédération de la Jeunesse, with words by the prominent Communist writer Paul Vaillant-Couturier.[270]

Despite its emphasis on modernity, the Exposition of 1937, like its predecessor in 1900, did not neglect the history of French art.[271] For such an attempt to "preserve" French cultural patrimony was also a powerful means to articulate a conception of what was "French" by defining a canon of distinctively French "great works." Just as during the war, the issue of the French canon, as well as the discourse surrounding it, was, in the end, inseparable from the encompassing ideological and historical rhetoric. In fact, it was the idea of Blum himself, who was both aesthetically sophisticated and politically astute, to present a huge retrospective exhibition of French art at the 1937 Exposition. Once more, Blum, who undoubtedly recalled the 1900 Exposition in Paris, conceived the project specifically as furthering a distinctive republican conception of French cultural patrimony.[272] Of course, this project would include music, which was a vital political stake, as we have seen, ever since its presentation as French patrimony in the 1900 Exposition.

The political and musical worlds again touched when the historian and critic Paul Landormy (also active at the turn of the century) was placed in charge of a series of historical concerts.[273] One concert, in particular, which was planned to inaugurate the hall at the Trocadéro, was deemed important enough to warrant the attendance of the president of the Republic himself. This concert, just as the others, was intended to constitute a retrospective of French music, here over the last fifty years, thus manifesting "la vitalité de notre école moderne" (the vitality of our modern school). Six concerts, in fact, were devoted primarily to symphonic music and to chamber music, and some with the additional participation of choruses, drawn from the large Parisian musical associations.[274] The composers who were now in positions of honor were those who had emerged after World War I as the purest incarnations of the "true French spirit": Debussy, Ravel, and Fauré.[275] All great composers, belonging neither to the Left nor the Right, but interpreted ideologically by each in different ways, they now aroused the least opposition from different political groupings. But other concerts included symphonic works that were more provocative in nature, such as Daniel Lazarus's symphony recounting Jewish history, as discussed earlier.[276]

Lazarus's work, however, was not the only provocative composition presented at the Exposition—other such works, less expensive to perform, were selected, as a result of budget constraints. The limited funds supplied by the Commissariat Général for presentations of musical programs precluded the mounting of too many large-scale operas, spectacles, or ballets. Hence the decision to perform smaller, if daring "spectacles d'avant-garde," as well as musical comedies and opéras-bouffes at the Comédie des Champs-Elysées. These included three pieces by young musicians—Thiret's *La véridique histoire du docteur*, Manuel Rosenthal's *La poule noire*, and Jean Rivier's *Vénitienne*, to a text by René Kerdyk. Also performed in this context was an operetta by Marcel Delannoy (made famous by the "scandalous" *Le poirier de misère*), his *Philippine*, which was premiered at the Théâtre d'Essai in 1937.[277]

But the Exposition did not omit either foreign new music or programs aimed specifically at attracting the working class to the concerts, as the government's ideology enjoined. As noted earlier, under the leadership of Roussel, the Exposition helped to sponsor the festival of the Société Internationale pour la Musique Contemporaine in Paris in 1937. It also included what was termed a "festival permanent" of "musique populaire," which (in a long-established tradition) offered prizes for competing Orphéon choral societies.[278] Similarly well established was the government's attempt to increase the access of workers to theater in the interest of intellectual "emancipation," and undoubtedly (given earlier strikes) of social "guidance." Indeed, a passage from the budget of 1937, referring to official motivations, sounds revealingly like the rhetoric of the turn of the century, in the wake of the Dreyfus affair:

> Il apparaît indispensable de favoriser le développement intellectuel des masses en ajoutant une mesure qui aura pour effet de rendre plus accessible à l'ensemble des citoyens, en particulier, aux classes populaires, les représentations théâtrales. . . . L'émancipation intellectuelle n'étant pas moins nécessaire à une démocratie que l'amélioration de la condition sociale des travailleurs, il faut considérer l'art non comme un luxe, mais comme une chose indispensable.[279]
>
> [It would appear indispensable to favor the intellectual development of the masses by adding a measure that will have the effect of rendering theatrical performances accessible to all citizens, in particular, the "popular" classes. . . . Since intellectual emancipation is no less necessary to a democracy than amelioration of the social condition of the workers, it is necessary to consider art not as a luxury, but as something indispensable.]

Such rhetoric, of course, was rooted not only in nineteenth-century ideological sources but in awareness of programs for workers in contemporary Nazi Germany and in Soviet Russia. But typical of the consciously egalitarian goals of the Popular Front was the desire to integrate the entire social community within a common intellectual, cultural, and national community. As we have seen, because of its democratic and socially inclusive nature, the government attracted important musicians who often had no formulated political ideology, but who were taken with its projected new "spirit." Such was the case with figures like Wiéner, Durey, Tailleferre, Auric, and Milhaud, who responded to the emergent aesthetic and the atmosphere of social experimentation. But this was not uniformly the case; other prominent composers shared the reservations and symbolic opposition of the government's increasingly vociferous opponents.

Part 2: Political and Symbolic Challenges to the Government
The Conservative and Profascist "Defense" of Culture

POLITICAL DISSENSION AND THE SYMBOLIC BATTLE

While many in France held the aesthetic or cultural ideals and the social vision of the Popular Front, support was by no means uniform, and contestation surfaced almost immediately. Opponents ranged from those who, while generally sympathetic, did have some reservations, to those who were merely aloof, to those who were systematically, even violently, hostile. The government's triumphal assertion that it represented the true "rassemblement" of the French was indeed far more a rhetorical tactic or projected myth than a reflection of reality. There was continuous opposition to the government, particularly in the Senate, which in this period was dominated not by supporters of the leftist government, but by conservative Radicals. Thus both Zay and Lagrange had to cope with the latter's recalcitrance toward all the cultural and educational endeavors that they now so boldly undertook.[280]

This period, then, was one not of unity, but rather of a virtual "facing off" of priorities and sensibilities, stemming from fundamentally antagonistic social ideologies. Assaults on Blum, including physical violence, began immediately in February 1936 when members of Action Française's Camelots du Roi ambushed and brutally beat the prime minister.[281] This was accompanied by attacks in the press, which ranged from an "opposition de principe" in *Le temps, Le journal des débats*, and *L'illustration* to the overt hostility of the extreme right-wing press. The latter included, most prominently, *L'écho de Paris, L'ami du peuple, Le jour, L'action française, Candide, Je suis partout*, and *Gringoire*.[282]

Just as after the Dreyfus affair, those who were politically defeated and now outside power expressed their opposition in a number of ways, including the use of symbols. And once more they attempted to attack the regime in perhaps its most obviously vulnerable point, or to delegitimize it through vociferous condemnation of its vaunted cultural program. Again, the opponents of the regime identified a "cultural problem" that they perceived as fundamentally political, and thus a basis from which to launch a harsh political critique. Indeed, given the total politicization of culture by the Popular Front, its politics could be trenchantly contested and undermined through the cultural sphere, through an indictment of both its symbols and its artistic policies. So closely had the government bound its ideals to forms of cultural expression that the question of aesthetic legitimacy was here once again fundamentally political in nature.

Music was therefore an ostensible stake in the battle for symbolic domination, which was now assuming primary political importance, as it had at the turn of the century. Once more, as in the period following the Dreyfus affair, musical activity assumed new significance and intensity, being integrally imbricated with the acidulous political struggle between Right and Left. And, as thirty years earlier, the challenge to a musical culture thoroughly "colonized" by the government was to arise from the political nexus of the Republic's most intrepid opponents.[283] Two warring "chapelles" not only reappeared, but they made the deeper aesthetic and political premises upon which they were based explicitly, and thus impossible for French musicians to ignore.

For this reason it was only natural that, here too, political attitudes and conflicts would be brought to bear and expressed obliquely, or symbolically, through specific French musical debates. The major musical issues were thus inherently ideologically charged, and writers on music could not avoid connecting them to the larger question of French cultural politics. For those opposing the Republic, music was still a powerful symbol precisely because of all it could evoke or suggest when framed by an explicatory or exegetic discourse. Moreover, discussions of musical values could communicate aspects of a political vision and emotion that were central, but less easily articulated through more traditional discursive means.

PROFASCIST AND ROMANTIC CURRENTS

Again, the opposition varied, since the political resistance to the Popular Front assumed a number of different forms across the current ideological spectrum. All, however, were united by a "general rejection of liberal values and institutions" of the Third Republic and "an acute anxiety about the future of France." This tendency would eventually embrace such movements as communism, Christian democracy, and nonconformism, but it also included French fascism, now becoming a powerful intellectual current.[284] It was the press with fascist leanings or sympathies that most persistently and effectively attacked the musical aesthetic and culture associated with the Popular Front. The reasons for this, of course, are directly related to the nature of French fascist ideas, or to the nature of fascism as an ideological movement as it developed distinctively in France.

Much disagreement remains among scholars over whether we can properly label a larger sympathy or "mood," as opposed to a coherent political organization, as "fascist."[285] Equally at issue is the question of whether fascism as a movement was inherently French, or merely a foreign importation that lay outside the main French political traditions.[286] The latter question is central, since it has direct implications for our understanding of the political ideals and the cultural themes upon which French fascist sympathizers were to draw.

There is a general consensus among scholars concerning the distinctive character of the fascist "climate" as it developed in France, and finally crested in the later 1930s. First, most historians agree that fascist influence in France was spread by a small coterie of intellectuals, journalists, and men of letters—but one that wielded considerable influence. Hence fascism in France, despite the existence of small fascist parties, such as Jacques Doriot's, was more an intellectual and cultural than a coherent political movement.[287]

The ideology that French fascists espoused shared certain traits with other European fascisms—a revolt against liberal democracy and bourgeois society, and a systematic refusal of all materialism. They, too, believed that the state alone properly represented all the classes of society, and thus it was incumbent on the nation to realize a harmonious and organic collectivity. But the fascism of French intellectuals was far less *Völkish* in emphasis than the German variety, "less inclined to glorify a mystical Volk soul or the masses as its embodiment." And it emphasized an ethic—that of a "viril, pessimistic, and puritanical new world," or one that was founded upon an abiding sense of duty and sacrifice.[288]

Because of this emphasis on duty and "vision," French fascism promoted the sacred and subjective, and fused the ethical and aesthetic in a manner that recalls the romantic movement.[289] For fascist intellectuals like Pierre Drieu La Rochelle and Robert Brasillach, French fascism was synonymous with a new "mystique," or a new kind of social imagination. Like German "reactionary modernists," although proposing an industrial utopia, they were nevertheless regressive in spirit, emphasizing the theme of a cultural return to an imagined purity of origins.[290] But they were less concerned with political doctrine or a utilitarian aesthetic (as opposed to the German fascists) than with lyricism and affective themes, exalting emotional and moral values. French fascism thus addressed itself primarily to the imagination and feelings, its proponents seeking above all directly to affect the sensibility of their readers. In quest of a new "style" of collective life and a poeticization of the political world, they strove to confront a desacralized society with subjective moral and aesthetic conceptions.[291]

Figures like Pierre Drieu La Rochelle, perceiving a decadence in Christian Occidental society, idealized the Middle Ages (like Sorel and d'Indy before)—its saints, its simplicity, and its charity. Moreover, Drieu La Rochelle envisioned a "purification" dependant upon the destruction of a world in which such ideals were absent, to be followed by a "spiritual" renovation, together with the renewal of a truly "national" society.[292] Aesthetics, politics, and ideology were therefore fused in this quest for a new national "totality" in which the arts would play a Wagnerian role in effecting purification and "wholeness." But here the abandonment to the collectivity was not associated, as it had been by conservatives in the twenties, with consensual neoclassicism, rather, the paradigm now was emotional and romantic. The political valence of romanticism had changed: no longer associated with the individualistic or the egotistical—and thus inimical to society—it embodied a return to "spirit," a resacralization of the social.

As David Carroll has argued, such use of culture as a model of the French "spiritual" community had the noxious implication of excluding certain groups from this pure "aesthetic totality." Since the collective "subject" was inherently exclusionary, the ideal of an organic artwork that restored the community's "true" cultural values supported a baleful political ideology. French literary fascists couched their menacing ideology in aesthetic principles, as had Action Française before, thereby deceptively distancing themselves from overt politics.[293] That which they presented as a purely aesthetic goal was in reality an ideological weapon against "all national, ethnic, or cultural differences" that would pollute the "ideal" totality.[294] Political extremism was again inseparable from the aesthetic "defense" of literature, since the ideal aesthetic model, for French fascists, represented the very "truth of politics."[295] The political was concomitantly aestheticized, as fascism became a means to "restore" political and cultural values that expressed a "truer sense of man than that allowed by democracy, liberalism, and modernity."[296] For French fascist writers such literary ideals led directly to anti-Semitic politics, because these ideals, in their actual application, were intended to eliminate "all non-conforming elements."[297]

French fascism in the thirties, then, was primarily a literary movement, and therefore resembled early Italian fascism, which was more a kind of rhetoric than it was a clear political philosophy. Both movements consistently developed not only extant ideas and concepts, but also meanings and myths, as persuasive means to lure the public toward an ill-defined goal.[298] If the rhetoric of French fascism made consistent use of music, it was because, here especially, it could apply its nebulous spiritual and social values with special cogency and an emotional coherence. Far from being neglected, the imagery of music provided French fascist rhetoric with a powerful conceit—a language—and a legitimization through association with "high art." The appropriate vocabulary or aesthetic was indeed already extant in France: the Scholiste discourse had only to be adapted and explicitly related to French fascist ideals.

THE OPPOSITIONAL MUSICAL AESTHETIC

After the Popular Front banned the leagues, the press supportive of fascism appropriated their overtly propagandistic as well as their subtler cultural means.[299] Now the press, like the leagues before, co-opted critics as well as important French musicians, and sponsored concerts or formed cultural organizations that supported them. Given the generally perceived failure of the government to create a truly popularized but uncompromising modern culture, the profascist press was thus eager to claim the symbolic capital of traditional elite art. For, again, just as literature, music could be used to render fascist ideas more widely acceptable by making what was inherently political seem purely aesthetic. Here too aesthetic and political values could be imperceptibly fused and music criticism employed to imbue extremist ideology with a greater cultural credibility or "tone." We may see this not only in the attacks of critics against certain musical styles but in their definition of positive models and appropriation of specific French composers. It also emerges in the representation and refocusing of selected canonic works—often those that they claimed were "misused" by the government in their adaptation to the new social goal. This ineluctably led to critical "skirmishes" over composers like Maurice Ravel, as well as to a "reinvestment" in Wagner, who had previously been maligned by the classicist monarchist Right. And particularly useful here was the new public sphere of phonograph recordings which, as we shall see, the fascist press "invaded" by awarding prizes like the Prix Candide.

The profascist press in France consistently evinced a strong interest in music, just as did its political adversaries, with whom it now entered into an overt symbolic contestation. The discursive field having been opened by the government's prominent intervention and investment in music, its political antagonists were quick and avid to become interlocutors in the dialogue. They, just as the government, realized how powerful music could be as a symbol, and all that it could evoke when framed by an appropriate critical exegesis. This they accomplished, once more, through the canny mediation of those who could speak the language of "both worlds," and thus draw connections between them with subtlety and skill. And so now, more than ever, the political and musical press in France was effectively to fuse, since the very same critics frequently contributed to prominent publications in both areas.

Given the uniformity of values in profascist journals, and their recurring themes, innuendos, and references, agreement with and reinforcement of these was implied for their musical columnists. Indeed, the music criticism in profascist journals presents a coherent "family" of reception—one embedded essentially within the same discourse or web of references, associations, and meanings. And here, many of the same issues raised by the nationalists the turn of the century returned: "What is French?" "What is pure?" "What elements of German music are compatible with the French?" "What is 'great' or la grande musique?" In addition, this press again responded to the republican conceptualization of French tradition by proposing its own French canon, its interpretation of France's "master composers."

The profascist press was growing rapidly since gradually, as opposition to the government mounted, even organs of conservatism moved from support for parliamentary institutions to praise for the authoritarian regimes..[300] But the earliest and most explicitly and consistently profascist French journals in the mid-1930s were *Gringoire*, *Je suis partout*, and *La victoire*. This was an influential press with regard to the number of readers it reached, far exceeding that of either the Left or the "classic" Right. While the monarchist *Action française* and the Socialist *Vendredi* only obtained a circulation of 100,000 at their peaks in the thirties, by 1936 *Gringoire* had a circulation of 640,000 and *Candide* of 339,500.[301] This was a powerful incentive in attracting critics and writers on music who either adhered to, or could easily adopt, the appropriate political and aesthetic rhetoric.

Again, the discourse was already available—it did not have to be invented, only modified (like the Popular Front's) from earlier rhetorical models to meet the present political circumstance. If that of the Popular Front may be traced back not only to World War I but the turn of the century, that of the French fascist sympathizers had similar historical roots. While the Republic now adopted, or adapted, the discourse of the Dreyfusard Republic and the "liberal right," that of the French fascists built upon earlier anti-Dreyfusard and nationalist rhetoric. For here we may identify not only the themes of the conservative right in the twenties (and particularly anti-Semitism), but we may also perceive a marked return to Scholiste ideals.[302] Just as the journals of the Popular Front were attacking d'Indy and the Schola, those associated with its political opposition were praising the qualities that both had promoted. But now they made what for d'Indy was an implicit, if unmistakable, political stance far more explicit, aptly adapted to their journals' political values.

THE RETURN OF "D'INDYSME" AND "WAGNERISME"

Since d'Indy was an important connection between the earlier political and cultural opposition to the Republic and that of the mid-1930s, it is no coincidence that the profascist journals espoused his values. Moreover, d'Indy had also eventually become alienated from the circle of Action Française because of its rigid classic doctrine, and therefore its exclusion of German cultural influence. As a result, he sought out other political movements that, while nationalist and antidemocratic, recognized romantic elements, centrally including spiritual feelings or the emotions. His most substantial involvement was with that group that crystallized around Georges Sorel at the time when Sorel was attempting to join forces with the nationalist Far Right. Sorel's journal, *L'indépendance*, on which d'Indy collaborated, both through contributions and as a member of the editorial board, identified itself already as "National Socialist." Its themes were not only patriotism and the evils of parliamentary democracy and capitalism; it also included a persistent strain of virulent anti-Semitism.[303]

Looking back from the 1930s, the noted French writer Pierre Drieu La Rochelle, already a fascist sympathizer, made the following observation about the group:

> Sans doute, quand on se réfère à cette époque, on s'aperçoit que quelques éléments de l'atmosphère fasciste étaient réunis en France vers 1913, avant qu'ils le fussent ailleurs. Il avait des jeunes gens, sortie des divers classes de la société, qui étaient animés par l'amour de l'héroïsme et de la violence et qui rêvaient de combattre ce qu'ils appelaient le mal sur deux fronts: capitalisme et socialisme parlementaire.[304]
>
> [Without doubt, when one refers to this epoch, one perceives that several elements of the fascist atmosphere were joined in France toward 1913, before they were elsewhere. There were young men, from diverse classes of society, who were animated by a love of heroism and of violence and who dreamed of combating what they perceived as the evil on two fronts: capitalism and parliamentary socialism.]

It is highly significant that this statement appeared in an article by Pierre Andrieu in the politically and culturally "nonconformist" journal *Combat*, in February 1936. The article, revealingly titled "Fascisme 1913," attempts to draw a direct connection between Sorel's group and contemporary fascist ideals and values.[305]

Since D'Indy was part of this Sorelian circle, it is by no means surprising that the aesthetic which was linked to its emergent political philosophy now resurged within fascist circles in France. As we have seen, Scholiste values had not disappeared in the 1920s but were propagated specifically by the reactionary and conservative forces within French music. Now they were explicitly revived by French fascists because of the special resonance they carried within the larger "romantic" cultural discourse being propagated by the French Far Right. We may recall that rather than stressing harmony, as at the Paris Conservatoire, the Schola emphasized the more exalted "spiritual" (and Germanic) tradition of counterpoint. And while the Conservatoire had initiated performers in those works that were consecrated by popular success, the Schola taught them "masterpieces" from epochs that d'Indy considered morally healthy. This excluded most music associated with the "Protestant deviation," in addition to the works of all Jewish composers, believed to have tainted the art.[306]

It did not, however, exclude German music, despite d'Indy's rabid nationalism, for both he and the Schola placed special value on the work of Richard Wagner. Again, d'Indy justified this by arguing that the Germans had "seized" the classical spirit from France, but had ultimately betrayed it, leaving it to the French to "rescue" the true classical heritage. For d'Indy, this "rescue" had been made possible by Wagner, since he believed, like Maurice Barrès (a cofounder of the Ligue de la Patrie Française), that Wagner had helped "cleanse" French opera of its meretricious Jewish influences.[307] All good music, for d'Indy, was hortatory, or inspired by an intuited spiritual truth, which could naturally be realized in a multiplicity of manners, within the culture of different nations.[308]

Aesthetically, like the anti-Dreyfusard writers to whom he had once been close, d'Indy stressed the romantic qualities of heightened sensibility, intuition, and the inspired insight. This was as opposed to the "intellectual" Dreyfusard emphasis on reason or rationality, and was associated with certain genres believed to incarnate or demand such traits. Prominent here was the symphony which, for d'Indy, after Beethoven, had become a mirror of the composer's inner life, the vehicle of spiritual, moralizing messages, and the archetype of tradition and order.[309] And so it is not difficult to perceive the propinquity between d'Indy's aesthetic values in music and those that we have identified as characteristic of the romanticism of fascist writers in France. Nor is it difficult to understand why Scholiste rhetoric and terminology was now reprised in the burgeoning music criticism of the profascist French press.

As we have noted, given the imposing circulation of this press, it is not surprising that even the most extreme—*Gringoire*, *Candide*, and *La victoire*—could recruit prominent figures in music criticism.[310] Most of these critics now espoused values that were not only contrary to those of the Popular Front, and in keeping with broad tendencies in French fascist aesthetics, but fundamentally indebted to d'Indy. As we have seen, both of these currents were distant from the rationalist neoclassicism of the traditionalist Right (as well as the modernism of the Italian fascists), being inherently romantic, moralizing, and spiritualistic.[311]

In music as in literature, the cardinal cultural values for "elite" French fascist thinkers were emotion and lyricism, with a stress on the group (as opposed to the individual) and on the "pure" realm of the spirit. As we have noted, the Schola had associated these directly with symphonic music, with the German classics, Germanic forms, and with techniques and genres carrying religious associations. These are indeed the models promoted in *Gringoire*, *Candide*, and *Je suis partout* by prominent critics, some of whom who had attacked them decades before. Writing for such extreme journals, again, apparently required an espousal of their aesthetic ideologies, and this becomes evident in the articles of figures like Coeuroy, Vuillermoz, and Landormy.

All these critics, and others in such journals, were clearly well aware of their function within the larger ideological objectives of these militant publications.

The rhetoric, the paradigms of value and authority, the metaphors, concepts, and images deployed by music critics for these papers all have to be seen in this light. For their goal was not only to persuade by invoking the legitimacy associated with "high art" but inextricably to fuse an aesthetic and political or ideological frame of reference. In addition, they consistently sought to delegitimize the current government by impugning its artistic policies, as well as to form public opinion for the reception of certain works.

ATTACKS ON GOVERNMENT PROGRAMS AND ON LES SIX

As we might expect, condemnation of the spectacles that were sponsored by the Popular Front, as well as of the composers participating in them, were both frequent and venomous. Even Bergery's *La flèche* was quick to criticize *Le 14 juillet* through its regular and prominent music critic, André Boll. Undoubtedly because of its desire to court both intellectuals and artists and to give itself "tone," *La flèche* had regular columns on the arts, with music holding a central place. Here Boll waged an attack on the government's efforts in theater in general, and raised the still controversial issue of what a popular theater should be. Even more explicitly, he asserts that *Le 14 juillet*, as well as works such as *Liberté* and *Pas de ça chez nous*, are not art, but quite simply propaganda.[312] With the exception of Honegger, the members of Les Six (especially those who had participated in these fêtes), as well as Cocteau, were frequently condemned in the opposition press.

Milhaud, being Jewish, was, of course criticized in particular by the profascist press, as were other French Jewish composers involved in the government's projects, such as Jean Wiéner and Daniel Lazarus. This was especially true of the doctrinally anti-Semitic *Je suis partout*, which, like the other journals, took a strong and consistent interest in all of the arts. Founded in 1930, one of its goals was to follow the art world closely, and it moved even beyond *Candide* in covering the arts in the world at large. Created by the editor Arthème Fayard, a man of the Right and a nationalist (who also owned *Candide*), the journal, by 1936, was notable for its vehement fascist views, although it rarely qualified itself as "fascist" at the time. It was openly critical of Blum who, because he was a Jew, was (the paper implied) congenitally unable to think and feel properly "en français."[313]

Soon to become prominent was its critic of literature, art, and music, Lucien Rebatet, an ambitious young intellectual, hostile to both the bourgeoisie and to democracy, and previously associated with Action Française. A strong believer in the role of the arts in effecting genuine community, Rebatet, already knowledgeable in music, had been seized by the music of Wagner. Bored with his career in an insurance company, Rebatet had initially approached the most prominent music critic for *L'action française*, Dominique Sordet, for advice. It was Sordet who led him into journalism, giving him a column on music in *L'action française*, in addition to his other role as secretary for the literary section. It was here that Rebatet met several fellow collaborators with similar ideological inclinations, including Robert Brasillach, Thierry Maulnier, and Ralph Soupault.

Gradually, as Rebatet's ideas developed beyond those espoused by Action

Française, he, like Brasillach, found his natural intellectual "home" to be *Je suis partout*. Both writers, as well as the journal in general, were becoming less anti-German as their admiration for the Nazi regime (as they perceived it) began to grow. A rabid anti-Semite, Rebatet became publicly sympathetic to Germany after the German government's legislation against the Jews in 1938; but even earlier, in 1934, he made the first of many trips to Germany, and found a political culture by which he was deeply and permanently impressed.

By this point, *Je suis partout* was espousing not only corporatism and imperialism, but racism, xenophobia, anti-Semitism, the destruction of democracy, and the necessity of a "revolution." Although the journal itself did not openly employ the term "fascist" in print, several of its writers in private regularly referred to themselves as ideologically fascist. Whatever the label, it was open to a "new path"—one that promoted a rapprochement between antirepublican political "families" on the Far Left and Right that had traditionally been opposed.[314] Brasillach became the editor of the journal in June 1937, and henceforth it, like he, grew obsessed with Nazi Germany—with its romanticism and its deployment of resonant symbols.[315]

The major themes of *Je suis partout* found their way into Rebatet's discussions of musical issues, and as a result the spheres of politics and aesthetics continually crossed in his columns. As we might expect, he attacked the music of Schoenberg in 1934, and would thereafter systematically condemn both foreign and French Jewish composers.[316] But this also occurred in the writings of other critics in the journal, including Pierre Leclau, who regularly alternated a column on music with Rebatet. In 1939 Rebatet was busy editing a special anti-Semitic issue of *Je suis partout* titled "Les Juifs et la France."[317] And so it was Leclau who reviewed two of Milhaud's works, his *Fantaisie pastorale* and *Les éléments*, on 10 March 1939. Leclau peremptorily dismisses both, using fascist stereotypes of Jewish art as "incohérent, d'une écriture malpropre et outrancière, dont se dégage un mortel ennui" (incoherent, of a messy and extremist writing which results in mortal boredom).[318] This was indeed the very kind of critique to which French Jews like Offenbach had already been subjected for decades among anti-Semitic enclaves in France.

The previous month Leclau was harsh, if somewhat more cordial in tone, when reviewing the symphonic work of another French Jew, the flamboyant Daniel Lazarus. While he found the composer's Second Symphony to be technically a work of probity, it was still, for him, "scholastic," labored, and pretentious (implying "too intellectual"). In its contrapuntal sobriety and "bareness," it is (as the journal found most works of Les Six) "dry and devoid of feeling"—another stereotype of Jewish music, ever since Wagner's seminal *Judaism in Music*.[319]

Like *Je suis partout*, *Gringoire* carried a regular musical column, written by noted figures who published in exclusively musical journals as well. *Gringoire* was an important journal, launched in November 1928 by the Editions de France, at the same time that the Editions de la Nouvelle Revue Française created its leftist cognate, *Marianne*.[320] But by 1936 *Gringoire* had achieved a circulation of 640,000, while *Marianne* could only boast one of 120,000, even during the Popular Front. For while *Marianne*, on the Left, and *Candide*, on the Right, developed a tone appropriate to an intellectual elite, *Gringoire*, aiming at a broader audience, did not shy away from vulgarity.[321] It had gradually moved from a moderate to a more extreme ideological position, and by February 1934 was unequivocally situated on the Far Right. Significantly, while it referred to itself as a primarily political journal, it also employed the further qualification of "parisien et littéraire."[322]

As a profascist journal, *Gringoire* was quick to indict even the non-Jewish Francis Poulenc on the basis of his earlier musical style and participation in Les Six. In February 1938 René Kerdyk published what was supposedly a "portrait" of Francis Poulenc: as he summarized his view on the composer, "On a déjà entendu cette musique. C'est du Couperin le Petit" (We have already heard this music. It is by Couperin the Small).[323] Kerdyk denounces what he perceives as the element of pastiche in Poulenc's art—the fact that he appears to be inspired by French folklore, but that his reminiscences are too precise. As we may here recall, folklore remained a major political stake in France, being continually contested and claimed by proponents of both the Left and the Right. While Poulenc, in this work, employs not urban but rural folklore, as promoted by the Right, what disturbs Kerdyk is clearly his irreverent, humoristic treatment. Poulenc was thus caught between the criteria established by both the Left and the Right—condemned by the Right for his former style, and by the Left, as we shall soon see, for his new one.

The contradictory elements in Poulenc's life and personality, as expressed in his stylistic change, were now subjects of consistent criticism from one political extreme or the other. Here another concern emerges in Kerdyk's harsh critique—one related to the propaganda developed by Cocteau and Collet, but since appropriated by the Popular Front. The Left, as we may recall, had become the "protector" of French patriotism against Nazism, and for the Popular Front Les Six reincarnated the true French classical tradition. And so, according to Kerdyk, in using seventeenth- and eighteenth-century French models, Poulenc was stressing the importance of remembering the great French musicians of the past. Like *Je suis partout*, *Gringoire* was becoming more sympathetic to German art, while the Left was increasingly hostile both to Germany and to its culture of the present. The "new Right" was now making the fine distinction between a bad, former "Prussian" and anti-French Germany, and the supposedly "regenerated" Germany, which was the natural ally of France.[324]

The irony here is that Poulenc, who was in fact growing increasingly conservative, was politically more wary of the politics of the Popular Front than of that of its ideological opponents. But according to the operative stylistic code, and the association of Les Six with the Popular Front, he was branded as a man of the Left, and was thus open to attack by the opposition. Poulenc, as we shall see, was not only unsympathetic to the Popular Front, he professed to his close friends that he was an ardent admirer of Georges Clemenceau. Significantly, the "milieu Clemenceau," which included not only Léon Daudet, but Dominique Sordet, was now growing close to the profascist position in France.[325]

It was perhaps because of this avowal that in 1938 Poulenc was apparently approached by an activist group of proponents and zealous supporters of *Je suis partout.* They had organized a series of lectures titled "Conférences Rive Gauche," intended to provide a forum for speakers from the journal, or for those who were uncommitted but potentially sympathetic.[326] Poulenc may well have considered participating as a response to the politicized attacks against him, in order to differentiate his personal political inclinations from the implications of his former style. But his being solicited for such a series may also have been related to the fact that, with the bank failures of the thirties, Poulenc lost a large part of his financial security, and so was now relying on commissions, concerts, and lectures for income.[327]

But the profascist press did not limit itself to attacks on composers that it associated artistically with the Left: it also vituperated writers on music whom it found ideologically antipathetic. For *Gringoire*, perhaps one of the most serious misdemeanors was to consider Jewish composers, even those born and raised in France, as being "truly French." In 1937 an article titled "Musicologie amusante," by André Coeuroy attacked the recently deceased music historian Julien Tiersot. What apparently nettled Coeuroy was Tiersot's very assumption behind his collection titled *Lettres des musiciens écrits en français du XVe au XXe siècles* (Letters of musicians written in French from the fifteenth to the twentieth centuries). For Coeuroy it was an absurd idea to gather together the letters of Jewish composers like Auber and Hálevy, as well as their Italian idol, Rossini.[328]

Gringoire, like the other journals, targeted any foreign art that represented racial or social elements antithetic to its political doctrine. On 22 January 1937, Coeuroy denounced "Chostakovitsch" [sic] and "Miukovski" [sic] as gifted artists, but unfortunately hobbled by "des évangiles sociologiques" (sociological gospels).[329] Coeuroy was particularly perturbed by the nature of these "gospels," which were culturally populist, but not truly interested in art, and hence all too close in nature to the Popular Front. As we may recall, the Fédération Musicale Populaire was indeed allied with the Editions Sociales Internationales, which also published Russian revolutionary songs. The French fascist argument was purportedly against such a politicized use of art, in Russia as in France, although "great art," as they promoted it, was nevertheless inherently political. That which they denounced as "politics in art" was, in fact, the overt variety, and this denunciation further veiled their politicized uses of "pure" aesthetic models.

IDEOLOGICAL CONSTRUCTIONS OF RAVEL

As noted earlier, one goal of the profascist press was to delegitimize the Popular Front through an attack on its ideological core, or the government's "revolution" in culture, including music. It did so not only by attacking styles or composers associated with government programs, it assaulted the "official" interpretation or treatment of acknowledged "great composers" as well. One patent case of such an attempt to demean the Republic as "desacralized," and thus unworthy, was the profascist response to the official commemoration of Ravel. As with Beethoven at the turn of the century, Ravel belonged to no one faction; rather, both hostile perspectives interpreted his oeuvre in different ways.[330]

While this is not obvious in the musical press, when we examine the writings of the very same critics within the discursive frame of political journals, the ideological subtext is unmistakable. The goal of the profascist press was to present Ravel as a "magician" in music, or as a composer whose music possessed a depth and a "heart" that was impenetrable to the republican government. Praising Ravel was concomitantly another useful means to delegitimize Les Six, who had initially defined themselves (on the whole) against him, despite Ravel's support, to assert their identity. And so the press of the extreme Right now attempted to accuse the regime of consciously demeaning Ravel's art, the implication being that it was unworthy of protecting the nation's "true" cultural heritage.

Ironically, however, in the years before his death, in late 1937, Ravel had been victimized by the Nazi press, which had (like the American press) assumed, on circumstantial evidence, that he was of Jewish origin.[331] This was, in part, because, in addition to his works on Jewish texts, Ravel was a friend and supporter of Jewish musicians who were being persecuted by the fascist regimes. One case was that of Madeleine Grey, prevented by authorities from singing Ravel's *Chansons madécasses* at a festival in Florence because she was of the Jewish "race."[332] Once again Ravel seized the occasion to reject the concept that being Jewish automatically excluded anyone from either an international or a national community, including his native France. This he also made clear in his interview with the *Neue Freie Presse*, on 3 February 1932, in which he argued that the French are not a race but a cultural community, which is ultimately what unifies a people.[333] This was the aspect of Ravel that the profascist press clearly chose to ignore, representing him rather as someone who, through his art, implicitly shared their exclusionary ideals and "mysticism."

In the wake of Ravel's death, *Je suis partout* launched an immediate attack on the government through its critic, Lucien Rebatet, who, as we have noted, was a self-proclaimed fascist and integral anti-Semite. In an article titled "Le cercueil de Ravel," Rebatet presents Ravel as one of the greatest artists of the century, culminating the canon that runs from Berlioz to Bizet to Debussy. Clearly, Rebatet is attempting to make Ravel into a "modern romantic," thus implicitly arguing that romanticism is an integral part of the French tradition. Even earlier, in 1934, Dominique Sordet, in his book, *Maurice Ravel*, referred to Ravel as the man of "infaillible sortilèges" (infallible spell), and to Debussy as "l'homme des poétiques enchantements."[334] Already, before the Vichy regime, we see an attempt to revalorize the "impressionists" (so maligned in the postwar period) and to stress their connection to the romantic tradition, both German and French.

Like his allies, Rebatet makes Ravel into a symbol of the great musician with lofty or romantic goals, who is unfortunately mistreated by the pragmatic Popular Front. Moreover, he capitalizes on the lugubrious irony of the French morticians' strike the day after the composer's death, and thus the travail of his family in finding a coffin. Rebatet then proceeds to attack the government's minister, "Le Juif," Jean Zay, suggesting his impudence as a Jew in speaking of "our moral and artistic tradition."[335] And he observes that while radio stations all over the world immediately paid homage to Ravel, it took the French state eight days to respond, and with a mediocre program. The irony, of course, is that Ravel, who became a fervent Socialist after the war, would undoubtedly have supported not only the government, but also the morticians' strike.

These themes reappeared in *Candide*, in which René Bizet published an acidulous article with the gruesome and provocative title "Maurice Ravel, cadavre urgent."[336] Here he ridicules the funeral oration delivered by Jean Zay himself, and later published in a special "Ravel" commemorative issue of *La revue musicale*. Bizet was apparently inflamed by the minister's description of Ravel as "intellectual," a quality that, even worse, Zay went on to equate with the essential genius of France. Zay, moreover, refers explicitly to Ravel's intellectual heroism, to the "perpetual vigilance of his intelligence," and to his measured, analytical spirit as the very components of his grandeur. As we will recall, these were the qualities that the Left, since the 1920s, had consistently associated with its conception of authentic French classic culture. Now, in the context of the Popular Front, they had moved from the political opposition to the very center of political power, becoming, in effect, the new "official" position. All of these attributes here ascribed to Ravel were, of course, antithetical to the fundamentally romantic and anti-intellectual aesthetic of the French profascist journals. The fascist interest lay rather in the "performative" or ethical effects of music, achieved through a subconscious force, and thus able to develop prerational social "wholeness," as in Wagner. Moreover, fascism, once again, proposed a revolution in collective morals, considering other conceptions of "the political" as materialistic, and it sought the transcendental in art to buttress this goal.[337]

Themes similar to Bizet's recur in an article by Paul Landormy, who had been involved in the historical concerts of the 1937 Exposition, but now (as the Popular Front was declining) supported the interpretation of its adversaries.[338] His article, which appeared in *La victoire*, felicitously complemented Bizet's point by presenting Ravel unequivocally as a romantic, stressing his ability to "move profoundly."[339] *La victoire*, like the other journals, was one that had evolved politically, in this case from the syndicalist Left to growing support for the neighboring fascist regimes. By 1934 its director, Gustave Hervé, was identifying the journal on its masthead as "Quotidien révisionniste: Organe de la République autoritaire."[340]

The attack continued in *Candide*, the journal which aspired to the highest "tone," and consistently held the most sustained interest in both intellectual and cultural matters. Now part of its stable of notable critics was the former Debussyste Emile Vuillermoz, who published an impassioned article titled "Défendons Ravel."[341] Here he charges that the commemorative radio programs sponsored by the government conspired to sacrifice Ravel's greatest works in favor of lesser ones, thus attempting to minimize his genius.[342] It is important to note that radio programs were a new political stake, since by 1937 the government was making greater use of the radio for political purposes. Indeed, in 1937 a new heading had entered the budget of the Beaux-Arts titled "Subventions aux théâtres et concerts symphoniques pour l'organisation des manifestations artistiques et radiodiffusées" (subventions to theaters and symphonic concerts for the organization of radio-broadcast artistic manifestations). The more explicit political use of the radio was soon to lead to a campaign against it in the profascist press, of which the issue of Ravel's commemoration was clearly a part.[343] However, it was also related to the "radio elections" of February 1937, in which the public voted to elect representatives to the management councils of the state radio stations. Occurring nine months after the general elections, it provided an opportunity for opposing parties to continue to fight symbolically, with the Communists seeing it as yet another occasion to defeat the Far Right.[344] Right-wing forces were thus waiting to riposte, and Ravel's death and commemorative program offered a timely occasion to vent their spleen over the Left's aggressive cultural tactics.[345]

OTHER COMPOSERS APPROPRIATED

Ravel, of course, was not the only composer who now became a political stake, and was thus subject to a truculent battle of politicized aesthetic interpretations. This was equally true of great composers from the more distant past who, again as at the turn of the century, became ineluctably implicated in French cultural politics. Once more Beethoven was a central object of political-aesthetic contestation, and much in the same terms as he had been in the period immediately following the Dreyfus affair. Now profascist journals chose to emphasize Beethoven's "inner life" and its expression in his music, just as had Vincent d'Indy several decades before. And again recalling d'Indy, André Coeuroy, in *Gringoire*, assaulted Romain Rolland's interpretation of the composer as an artist who was motivated by social and humanitarian concerns.[346] Significantly, Coeuroy here identifies Beethoven's one weak work as *Fidelio*, which was currently being presented at the Opéra, as revived by Jacques Rouché. According to Coeuroy, the opera was not only marred by an imbecilic libretto: Beethoven's music for *Fidelio* was vitiated by his preoccupation with matters that properly lay outside of art.[347]

Candide reprised similar themes in January 1938, when Léon Daudet reviewed Adolphe Boschot's book suggestively titled *Musiciens-poètes*. Here Daudet praises the author's attempt to destroy the legend of Beethoven (who was performed so frequently during the Popular Front) as a partisan of democracy—or worse, of "L'internationale." It is primarily the Ninth Symphony to which Boschot is here referring, a work which had figured prominently not only in Rolland's interpretation, but in the syndicalist Fêtes du Peuple. Daudet underlines Boschot's emphasis (like d'Indy's) on Beethoven's "existence mystérieuse, insaisissable par les preuves de la raison et inhérent aux certitudes de foi" (mysterious existence, incapable of being grasped by the proofs of reason and inherent to the certitudes of faith).[348]

We see a similar attempt, slightly earlier, to "reclaim" the work of Bach from the neoclassic interpretation imposed upon it by "modernists" in the twenties, and to make it concomitantly more "spiritual." Even before the other journals, François Coty's *L'ami du peuple*, aimed at "les travailleurs de France," exhibited a sympathy for fascism. Also anticipating the others, it had promoted a contestatory romantic aesthetic, as seen in the review, in 1930, of a performance of the orchestral transcription of Bach's *Art of the Fugue*, by Wolfgang Graiser. To the question of whether Bach's work can please only the learned or professionals, the reviewer replies emphatically in the negative, and on the basis of the following romanticized rhetoric: "dès la première note et jusqu'à la dernière, vous vous sentez transposée et maintenue dans un monde d'émotions inépuisable, baignée d'un sublime qui ressemble continûment au premiers mouvement de la nature, pénétrée d'une voix haute . . . mais familière" (from the first note until the last, you feel transposed and maintained by something sublime, which continually resembles the first movement of nature, penetrated by a high but familiar voice).[349]

Even before this, in 1927, Valois's *Le nouveau siècle*, one of the first French fascist journals, praised Adolphe Boschot's book on the French romantic composer Hector Berlioz.[350] Although, as we saw, elements of Berlioz's style attracted the Left, and particularly his individuality, the Far Right could similarly project its values onto his work. Such reinterpretations extended even to canonized figures of the Left, including Gustave Charpentier and his now beloved opera *Louise*. Writing in *Candide* in February 1936 (shortly after the victory of the Popular Front) Dominique Sordet, now influential in the record industry, reviewed a new recoding of the opera.[351] After mentioning his own musical study with Gédalge (at the Conservatoire), Sordet goes on to note his special fondness for *Louise*, with all its distinctive weaknesses and strengths. As he puts it, the work is "anti-artistic," but nevertheless ineluctably captivating, and it is unmistakably clumsy yet ardent and full of cunningness at the same time.[352] Here it is both interesting and ironic that the one perspective which was finally able to perceive the profound irony and personal investment of Charpentier in his opera was that of the French profascists. Not blinded by the ideological goals of the turn-of-the-century Left and Right, it was this position that could appreciate both Charpentier's multivocal language and his profound personal ambiguity.[353]

Clearly, the profascist journals used music not only to delegitimize and criticize the Republic but to appropriate the symbolic capital of canonic composers to their own cause. They sought, accordingly, to legitimize themselves through association with the great cultural masterworks of the past, particularly those that could be convincingly presented as incarnating their cultural values. When examining what they praised or promoted, it is important, again, to recall that their musical perspective, terminology, and values owed much to the d'Indyste or Scholiste tradition. We find frequent and reverent reference to d'Indy, as well as support for composers perceived as embodying aspects of the "true" musical tradition that he had helped to revive. *Je suis partout*, for example, published an article on 21 October 1938, revealingly titled "Rentrée avec un collaborateur de Vincent d'Indy."[354]

But d'Indy is lauded most extensively in a collective volume on music history, one on which several prominent critics who would soon write for the profascist journals collaborated. This was *L'initiation à la musique, à l'usage des amateurs de radio*, edited by Dominique Sordet, with the participation, in the section on history, of Vuillermoz and Landormy.[355] Here we find overt adulation of the ideals of the Schola Cantorum, which (like César Franck's teaching) promoted moral elevation, respect for the "sacred" as well as for the secular classics, and disdain for the vagaries of current fashion. The book also notes d'Indy's qualities as a composer, especially the fact that his own compositions were far less rigorous or literal in applying his rigid pedagogical "prescriptions." The key point it makes, one integral to the aesthetic soon to appear in profascist journals, concerns d'Indy's reconciliation of his nationalism with his love of Wagner by means of anti-Semitism. This was to become an increasingly important argument before the war—that one could be a good Frenchman while absorbing German influences, now believed healthier than the "impure" ones at home.[356]

And here too, even before Sordet's article in *Candide*, we encounter praise of Gustave Charpentier and his interest in the social mission of music, although interpreted in a manner that distorts the composer's goal. As it is put in the volume, Charpentier intrepidly sought to capture in his works the collective "lyricism" of the society and civilization of his own time:

> Avec des moyens assez différents de ceux d'Alfred Bruneau, il chercha, lui aussi, à éveiller dans la coeur de la foule, cette exaltation latente qui n'a pas encore trouvé son expression mélodique et harmonique. Il le fit avec des moyens plus souples et une écriture plus séduisante.[357]
>
> [With these means so different from those of Alfred Bruneau, he also sought to awaken in the heart of the crowd this latent exaltation which had not yet found its melodic and harmonic expression. He did it with more supple means and more seductive writing.]

Here, in keeping with the profascist aesthetic, we see adulation of Charpentier's ability to evoke "mass ecstasy," although we do not encounter recognition of his irony, as in *Candide*. But, as opposed to Charpentier's own ideology, the emphasis here is decidedly not on social reality and justice but rather on exaltation of the "crowd."[358] As we also might expect in this volume, there is extensive praise of Richard Wagner, and particularly his goal of the "highest moral culture" and his condemnation of both Rossini and Meyerbeer for lacking it.[359]

But Debussy also receives a long and ardent encomium in the volume, one uncharacteristic of the Popular Front, but soon to be common throughout the Occupation. Specifically, we here encounter overt praise of Debussy's ability to express the conscious and unconscious (like Wagner), the most "secret" movements of the soul, and his ability (like Ravel) to suggest "magiques sortilèges." Ravel, of course, is praised as well, both for his antiacademicism and his "écriture véritablement magique," which leads us into unsuspected "zones" of emotion.[360] Indeed, all the composers who received the approbation of profascist publications were those considered capable of evoking the lofty, the emotional, or the "enchanted"—again an aestheticizing of the political. *Gringoire* praised the group Triton, which promoted the performance of foreign works, ironically, including the Second Viennese School, as well as composers such as Bartok and Martinu.[361] *Je suis partout* appreciated the more conservative Florent Schmitt, particularly his *Branle de sortie*, "étrangement évocatrice d'une foule en liesse avec son coloris chatoyant et ses contrastes" (strangely evocative of a crowd in jubilation with its shimmering colors and its contrasts).[362]

The profascist aesthetic ideal, in sum, was consistently defined against that of the Popular Front, which had publicly cast its left-republican values into resonant symbols. In music, the profascist aesthetic position, however, proved to be appealing to some, given the overall poverty and failure of many of the initiatives of the Popular Front. And, it drew on an established aesthetic stance that had defined itself convincingly against the Republic's since the turn of the century, and which it now seamlessly integrated into its rhetoric. No wonder, then, that those composers who were not politically inclined toward the Popular Front were attracted by this oppositional aesthetic, which further justified their own cultural resistance.

Political Tensions with the Government among Composers

POULENC AND SAUGUET: POLITICAL AND AESTHETIC RESISTANCE

Among those who either immediately resisted the politics and aesthetics of the Popular Front, or gradually felt themselves alienated from it, were members of Les Six and the Ecole d'Arcueil. While most of the composers in both of these groups were sympathetic to or cooperated with the cultural programs of the government, the notable exceptions were Francis Poulenc and Henri Sauguet. Particularly revealing in this context is Poulenc's correspondence with his friend Sauguet, who felt a similar tension between his politics and the associations of his earlier style. Despite the support for the Popular Front of other key members of the Ecole d'Arcueil, Sauguet remained steadfast in his right-wing, royalist beliefs.[363] In a letter to Poulenc of 10 August 1936, he tellingly reveals their common antipathies to the Popular Front and to its cultural programs:

> J'ai peu de nouvelles de Milhaud. Je ne sais rien de Georges [Auric]: et comme j'évite soigneusement les journaux de gauche pour ne pas avoir de colère ou de tristesse, je ne sais pas ce qui se passe de "son" côté. . . . Je pense, en effet, comme vous, cher Francis, que bien des ratés de notre profession vont profiter de la "politique" pour se tailler des parts de lion.[364]
>
> [I have little news from Milhaud. I know nothing of Georges [Auric]: and, since I carefully avoid the papers of the Left so as not to become angry or sad, I do not know what is happening on "his" side. . . . I think, in effect, like you, dear Francis, that the failures in our profession will profit from politics in order to carve out the lion's share.]

Sauguet also confided his opinion concerning the other political issue of the moment, one to become of particular concern to devout Catholics like himself and Poulenc. This was the Spanish Civil War, which would eventually divide the French Catholic world, particularly in 1938, with the publication of Georges Bernanos's *Les grandes cimetières sous la lune*.[365] Like many conservative Catholics such as Mauriac and Claudel, Bernanos had at first perceived the new, secular Spanish Republic as inherently the enemy of his faith. But his opinion was to change with the realization that many of the republicans were indeed good Catholics, as opposed to those supporters of Franco, who bombed the town of Guernica in 1937. This would pit Bernanos and Maritain against conservatives such as Charles Maurras, who, along with Paul Claudel, remained a loyal supporter of Franco. However, the more liberal, progressive Catholic journals such as *Esprit* (associated with the nonconformist movement) immediately rallied to Bernanos's point of view.[366]

Poulenc, as opposed to his current and future collaborators, Eluard and Bernanos, was not a supporter of the Spanish republicans, which now put him in an awkward position with regard to Eluard. As Poulenc noted in his journal in 1936, Eluard, who was spending January and February in Spain with Picasso, sent him his "Chanson espagnole," which Poulenc could not bring himself to set.[367] As of 1936, Sauguet, was also patently against the Spanish Republic, referred explicitly in the same letter to Poulenc to "l'horreur espagnole." This was in the context of his impassioned condemnation of the French government's sponsorship of the massive spectacle, *Le 14 juillet*, in which several of their friends, as we have seen, were involved. Similarly hostile to the Republic in Spain was the politically conservative, if artistically progressive, critic and scholar of modern Spanish music, as well as the "discoverer" of Les Six, Henri Collet. On 16 October 1936, he published an article in *Le ménestrel* expressing his concern for Spanish musicians suffering under the "barbarism of Marxist hordes."[368]

Although Poulenc did not publicly express his personal opinion on Spain at this point, he was aware of the issues, and did confide his general reservations concerning the politics of the Popular Front to his friends. He made his conflicted feelings explicit in a letter to Marie-Blanche, the comtesse Jean de Polignac, written on 15 August 1936. The apologetic tone of the letter would seem to indicate that she, one of his strong supporters, was not inherently hostile to the government of the Popular Front.[369] As Poulenc himself incisively puts it:

> Marie-Blanche, je ne suis pas Front Populaire, ai-je tort?
> Je suis un vieux républicain qui croyait dans la liberté. Je hais M. de la Rocque mais j'aimerais assez M. Loubet. Pour moi, la République, voyez-vous, c'était des hommes comme Clemenceau au testament duquel je pense souvent: Etre debout!!!
> Depuis hier, cependant je fais pouce avec le gouvernement et suis prêt à embrasser (pour une fois) Monsieur Zay car la nomination d'Edouard, si juste et intelligente me fait sauter de joie. Enfin un hommage à la compétence, au goût, à l'intelligence.
> Marie-Blanche, comme c'est mal me connaître que de croire que je n'ai pas de penchants populaires. Je croyais avoir donné longtemps la preuve que les fronts populaires me sont chers et j'avoue que ce qui m'a plu dans *14 juillet*, c'est vraiment la salle, tout cela est vraiment compliqué.[370]
>
> [Marie-Blanche, I am not Popular Front. Am I wrong? I hate Mr. de la Rocque but I would like M. Loubet well enough. For me, the Republic, you see, was those men like Clemenceau of whose testament I often think: Stand tall!!!
> Since yesterday I have called a truce with the government and am ready to embrace Mr. Zay (for once) because the nomination of Edouard [Bourdet], so right and

intelligent, makes me jump for joy. Finally, an homage to competence, to taste, to intelligence.

Marie-Blanche, it is to know me little to think that I don't have popular penchants. I think I have long given proof that popular fronts are dear to me and I avow that what pleased me in *14 juillet* was truly the hall, all this is very complicated.]

Poulenc's position was not unique: it was that of the center to right republicans, which included not only Clemenceau but Paul Reynaud (to become prime minister in the last government of the Third Republic) and Charles deGaulle.371 And it was one that was shared by many Catholic circles in general, who resented the political and cultural challenge of the Left in all its manifestations.372 This was also the position of those who were alienated by the militant spirit of the Popular Front, and the power that it granted to the workers, although they still defended the Republic and its humanist ideals.373

Poulenc did contribute two small works to an event of the 1937 Exposition, but this event, significantly, was both private and culturally elitist. Indeed, Poulenc himself admitted that his conception of "the popular" was substantially different from that of the Popular Front, and especially its definition of the "authentic" folklore of France. By 1936 both Poulenc and Honegger were turning not to the folklore of the workers and urban lower classes (that of the Left) but to that of the peasants (promoted by the conservatives and the Right). This was a resonant choice in the context, as were Poulenc's stylistic models, which we must consider from the perspective of his personal evolution and within the structure of symbolic confrontation.

Like Ravel in the twenties, if from a substantially different stance, Poulenc was now addressing current ideological issues both through gestures and through stylistic codes. Indeed, the fact that stylistic choices were politicized, or that an aesthetically oppositional stance had political implications, is something that we must consider in explaining Poulenc's stylistic change. The other element is his religious awakening, or Poulenc's return to the fervent Catholic faith of his father and his childhood, prompted, in part, by the tragic death of a close friend, Pierre-Octave Ferroud. Ferroud was a French admirer of Bartok, and a critic and concert organizer, who had founded the group Triton.374 Significantly, this was a period when political conversion to the French Right was frequently accompanied by a religious conversion, or explained by using this trope. But working together with all of these factors to influence Poulenc's stylistic evolution and subsequent turn to religious choral compositions was yet another major influence. In March 1936, Poulenc attended several performances of Monteverdi's motets, sung by Nadia Boulanger's vocal ensemble at the home of the princesse Edmond de Polignac. This led Poulenc to the study of choral works of the French and Flemish past, particularly those of the sixteenth-century composers Clément Janequin and Claude Le Jeune.375

It is not surprising that Poulenc would grow close to Nadia Boulanger in these years, for as a royalist she too was distant from the government, both politically and now aesthetically as well. Ignored by official institutions even when she espoused their classic ideals in the twenties, and now alienated from the Popular

Front, she emphasized the alternative stylistic tradition of the Schola. It had been the Schola, after all, which had originally revived the work of Monteverdi as part of its "alternative" musical culture, in confrontation with the government's Conservatoire. In addition, this was a period when private patronage became important for figures like Boulanger and Poulenc, who consciously rejected the new official aesthetic. Here, the princesse de Polignac, similarly distancing herself from the mainstream French republican culture, as she had in the twenties, supported Boulanger's and Poulenc's turn to tradition.

THE CASE OF POULENC'S *LITANIES À LA VIERGE NOIRE*

When the news of Ferroud's death in a car accident arrived, Poulenc was preparing, like his father before him, to visit the shrine of Rocamadour, which possessed a black wooden statue of the Virgin Mary.[376] For centuries these crude, simple statues had been central to local religious ceremonies: when religion was banned during the French Revolution, demonstrations occurred around them. Such statues henceforth incarnated popular resistance to the Revolution, for, in their own ineffable way, "black virgins insulted the Goddess of Liberty."[377] A return, like that of Poulenc, to traditional popular religious symbols was by no means isolated in France during the period of the Popular Front. As Eugen Weber has noted, beleaguered Catholics, now seeking to reinforce their faith in the face of the new government and the Spanish Civil War, again embraced pilgrimages and local traditions.[378]

It was upon his return from the shrine that Poulenc composed his *Litanies à la vierge noire*, for a chorus of women's voices (or children's), with only organ accompaniment. Given the political moment, the association of rustic folklore with the Right, and the current government's identifying with the French Revolution, Poulenc's gesture here was pregnant indeed. Poulenc himself later made the association of the work with the French peasantry explicit, as implicitly opposed to the Popular Front's more urban conception of popular culture: "In this work I tried to depict the mood of country devotion that so deeply struck me in this mountain locale." He also specifically explained that in the composition he was attempting to convey "the devotional tone and rustic simplicity of French peasant prayers."[379]

Stylistically, the work shares important features with Poulenc's other religious compositions at the height of the Popular Front and during its subsequent gradual decline. These include the *Messe en sol majeur* of 1937 (dedicated to the memory of his father) and the *Quatre motets pour un temps de pénitence* of 1938. Even the title of the latter is provocative in the context, for 1938 was a year of political penitence for many former supporters of the Popular Front.[380]

The style of Poulenc's motets is reminiscent of the French Renaissance composer Claude Le Jeune, with a dominant melodic line, full harmonic sonority, and careful, clear setting of the text.[381] But other stylistic influences in his religious works of the period carried meanings or associations that were telling within the context, given the musical aesthetics of the Popular Front. Poulenc's style in

EXAMPLES 5—Poulenc, *Litanies à la vierge noire.*

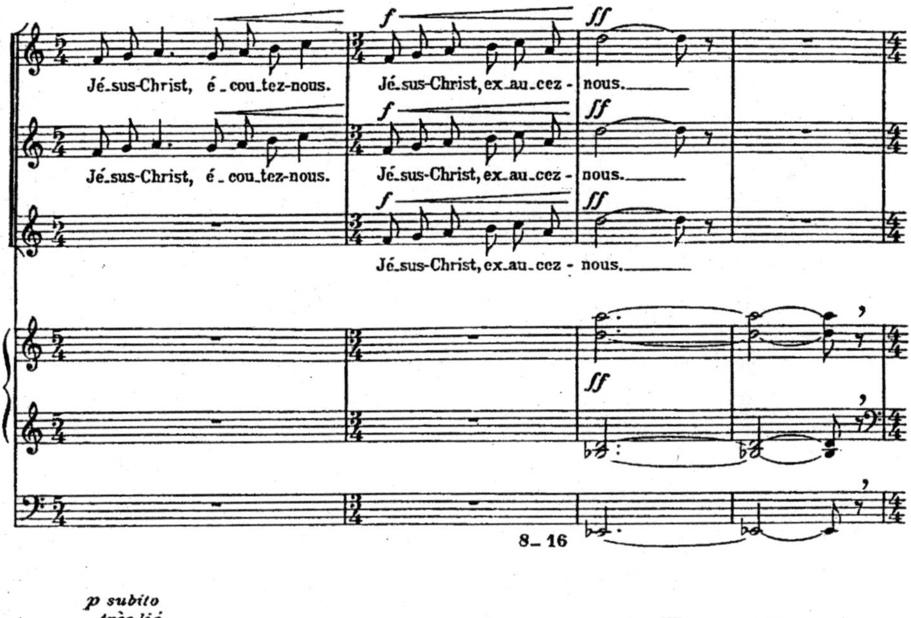

f
ff
Jé-sus-Christ, é-cou-tez-nous.
Jé-sus-Christ, ex-au-cez - nous.
Jé-sus-Christ, é-cou-tez-nous.
Jé-sus-Christ, ex-au-cez - nous.
Jé-sus-Christ, ex-au-cez - nous.
8-16
p subito
très lié
Dieu le pè-re, cré-a-teur, ay-ez pi-tié de nous.
pp
Dieu le fils, ré-demp-
2
pp très doux et aérien

these compositions has been described as of a "rustic flavor," or "rough-hewn," again suggesting the archaic, or a popular tradition outside of that promoted by the government. Following his ear, as opposed to the established conventions of proper voice-leading, Poulenc does not shy away from forbidden parallel and direct fifths and octaves.[382] Indeed, the *Litanies à la vierge noire* open boldly with an organ introduction that employs parallel fifths and an archaic sound, recalling a distant rustic past, when devotion was simple (ex. 5).[383]

In addition, Poulenc's religious works of this period bear the unmistakable imprint of Gregorian chant, and particularly the character of the melodies in the *Litanies à la vierge noire*. Moreover, as Keith Daniel has observed, Poulenc's religious choral music in these years often suggests a primitive organum, or is some cases the parallel 6/4 chords of "fauxbourdon." And yet these choral works employ little modality and are largely tonal, fulfilling Poulenc's goal of making them immediately accessible and tied to the present.[384] There are, however, frequent passages which are harshly dissonant, with unprepared and unresolved seventh and ninth chords, appoggiaturas, or nonharmonic tones, suggesting strong emotion. And in the *Litanies*, as in Poulenc's other choral works of the period, the declamation is largely syllabic, further imbuing the music with a directness and rustic ingenuousness.[385]

Many of Poulenc's stylistic elements not only lay outside the aesthetic now being promulgated by the Popular Front, but outside of the French republican tradition itself. For they were traditional and religious techniques associated with the Schola Cantorum and its earlier symbolic resistance to the culture of the Third Republic. Even Poulenc's two small contributions to the 1937 Exposition were equally distant from the Popular Front's expectations, in terms of their conception. For they were written not for a massive popular spectacle, but rather for private performance before an elite group of royalty and foreign intellectual figures. Poulenc's *Deux marches* and *Un intermède* were composed as accompaniments to a dinner at the Maison de la Chine, held by duc Francis d'Harcourt in honor of the writer Harold Nicholson and other English intellectuals. Stylistically, these works were also far from the popular manner promoted by the Fédération, rather being elegant, refined, and spirited, in the manner of Poulenc's idol, Emmanuel Chabrier.

Aside from this small commission, Poulenc sought private patronage throughout these years, primarily among those in his own social circle, such as the Noailles and the princesse Edmond de Polignac.[386] This was also the period of Poulenc's full immersion in surrealism, inspired by his turn to the poetry of Eluard, and his setting of the latter's poetic cycle *Tel jour telle nuit*.[387] Again, with its goal of revealing an internal truth through symbols and uncovering unconscious logic and essential human nature, surrealism unlocked Poulenc's deep emotional potential. His vocal writing now became more expressive, employing an extended range, projecting a sense of the poetry, often through manipulating its natural stress, and interacting with a more varied accompaniment. Indeed, this turn to both more emotional and spiritual expression would contribute to Poulenc's rising popularity among those ideological groups with which his affinity was greatest.[388] Previously marginalized because of his beliefs and style in the mid-1930s, his cultural and personal inclinations finally merged in his greater "romanticism," and he would soon find himself in the "center."[389]

HONEGGER'S AESTHETIC AND POLITICAL "NONCONFORMISM"

Arthur Honegger was scarcely more enthusiastic about the Popular Front than Poulenc, although he did participate in some of its projects, undoubtedly for pragmatic reasons. Honegger, like Poulenc, was sincerely attracted to "the popular" as a concept, and not in the narrowly ideological sense conceived by the current government. His search was for the right kind of relation between his aesthetic proclivities, which were both traditionalist and modern, and the broad audience that he wished to reach through his art. This would lead him to other movements that sought a different social and aesthetic future. As Honegger discovered, many of these groups, unlike most of his colleagues in Les Six, were not sympathetic to the republican tradition.

Honegger was well aware of the professional advantages of association with the Popular Front, although its aesthetic and political ideology was never fully consonant with his own. As we noted earlier, Honegger would become engaged with the movement of Gaston Bergery, which, in its later phases, more closely approximated his own inclinations. But even earlier, at the beginning of the decade, he had turned to a literary and philosophical circle associated with a new generation of French youth seeking a "spiritualist" solution to the political impasse. Referred to as the "nonconformist movement," some of its groupings would similarly attract younger French composers—however with a slight delay—as the Popular Front peaked and then declined. But Honegger was immediately drawn to specific aspects of this movement and particularly to one of its journals, the cultural concerns of which reflected his own. For Honegger was unquestionably an intellectual—an avid reader, aware of the implications of contemporary movements of thought, most of which, in this period, were responding to the political, social, and ideological crises. He did not hesitate to sign petitions, as, for example, one appealing for "justice" that appeared in *Le populaire* on 21 November 1936. Here he joined not only the musicians Louis Laloy and Maurice Jaubert, but also the philosopher Maurice Merleau-Ponty and the nonconformist Emmanuel Mounier.[390]

One of the many nonconformist journals founded in this period was *Plans*, directed by Philippe Lamour (a supporter of Mussolini), who would eventually attempt (unsuccessfully) to found a Parti Fasciste Révolutionnaire. Its spirit was one of both modernity and reform, which undoubtedly appealed to Honegger, as did its myth of the ideal "plan" for the technological state of the future. Ironically, given Honegger's background, *Plans* was a journal that also emphasized geographical and cultural regionalism, or the relation of man to the soil, to his "race," and to cultural tradition.[391] Honegger, as we will recall, though born in

France, was a Swiss national, raised by German-Swiss parents largely in France, and so perhaps it was in search of identity that he embraced the regional and racial ideals of the journal. As he later put it,

> Je dirai avec G. Jean-Aubry, . . . "en dépit de ceux qui assurent que la musique est un art universel, il est permis de penser que nul, peut-être, n'atteste mieux la race et que celle n'exclut en rien l'intérêt où l'attachement universel peut s'appliquer."[392]
>
> [I would say with G. Jean-Aubry, . . . "in spite of those who are sure that music is a universal art, it is permissible to think that none perhaps better attests to race and that this does not at all exclude the interest of cases where universal attachment is applicable."]

Honegger was attracted not only by *Plans*' conception of the national and of race, but by its attempt to provide a synthesis of the scientific, economic, political, and artistic advances of the period. Like other nonconformist journals, one of its essential themes was the necessity of the advent of a "new world," both progressive and spiritual, and the role of youth in its realization. Hence its editorial committee included members who were drawn not only from a variety of sympathetic social perspectives, but from different fields or cultural disciplines as well. On it, for example, was the Swiss architect (naturalized French) Le Corbusier, the artist Fernand Léger, the writer René Clair, and the composer Arthur Honegger.[393] The first issue of the journal, in fact, contained an article by Le Corbusier in which he presents his theory of a new kind of social order, or "la Ville Radieuse."[394] But it also included an article by Honegger which, like Le Corbusier's, advocates marshalling the latest techniques of his art in the interest of a new social vision.[395]

Honegger's essay "Du cinéma sonore à la musique réelle" (From sonorized cinema to real music) begins by addressing the problem of balancing cinematic exigencies with those of musical form. But it ends with a telling metaphor that reveals a great deal about Honegger's vision of the aesthetic and social goal of his art, and its ties to a certain trajectory within nonconformist thought:

> Le film sonore peut très bien . . . la compléter [la musique] en lui donnant un sens réel. . . . La musique peut . . . devenir elle-même, entrer dans la réalité, être comme le cinéma et avec lui, une force vraie, unanime, collective, non plus soumise aux révisions anarchiques des individualités, mais s'appliquant de toute sa force à une foule transportée.[396]
>
> [The sonorized film can very well complete [the music] in giving it a real sense. . . . Music can . . . become itself, enter into reality, be like the cinema and, with it, a true, unanimous, collective force, no longer subject to anarchic revisions of individualities but applying itself with all its force to a transported crowd.]

Honegger's stress on the collective, on the force and reality of the emotions that unite it, and on the use of technology toward such an antimaterialist end was by no means an isolated discourse. Rather, it ties into the journal's perspicacious adaptation of Sorelian rhetoric, and more specifically to its elaboration in the twenties by Sorel's follower, who became (in this decade) a fascist, Georges Valois. Both thinkers emphasized the importance of the spiritual, of resacralizing an atomized, materialistic society so that the classes would ultimately work together, fused through the force of a galvanizing collective myth. Tapping intuition, as opposed to reason, was thus paramount in realizing these values, as was altruism and sacrifice, which similarly demanded a myth that would both impress and unite.

Here the artist was central as a maker of myths; indeed, for Sorel the aesthetic dimension of myth was essential in inspiring and effecting political action. Aesthetic forces could "manifest" the new order as well as the new sensibility sustaining it so as not only to transform consciousness but to incite or inspire consequent acts. Artistic myths, then, did have criteria in order to arrive at the desired social end: they had to be attuned to the raw sensibility of the masses, which required dynamism, precision, and speed. Here one might immediately note the connection to the futurist strain in Italy, which is indeed no coincidence since Mussolini (as Valois noted) similarly traced his origins to the Sorelian circle. For Valois such imagery was also tied to violence, which was a necessary, vital, and regenerative force: spirituality, physically, and politically, it was a revolt against decadence and a source of creativity.

This, in turn, fostered the image of rebirth, but one based upon return to a past that was "pure" and more glorious—to healthy eras in national history as sources of regeneration. Again we find a parallel with fascism in Italy, with its cult of "Romanness," or reactionary nostalgia which could be convincingly combined with certain vital futurist elements. For Italian fascists (and French fascists in the twenties) cultural traditions were to form the basis of a new civilization that combined the revolutionary and conservative, addressing the future and the past at once. As a result, in both France and Italy, as opposed to Germany, such fascist aesthetics ran the gamut from abstract or "advanced" trends to various historicist and traditionalist styles. Sorel himself had idealized the medieval guilds as well as monastic communities, associating both with the art of the people, as did Ruskin and the pre-Raphaelites.

But the machine was also a resonant symbol, particularly for Georges Valois, who believed that rational, technological planning could be imbued with a creative and intuitive spirit. Technological modernism and vitalism were one, both part of the fascist mystique not only in Italy but also in France, and to a certain extent in German "reactionary modernism," as Jeffrey Herf has shown. Indeed, in Italian fascist futurism the machine became a model of social integration, of social and political organization, as well as of the functional harmonization of man and nature.

It is little surprise, then, that Valois's Faisceau, the first fascist party in France, founded in 1924, was quick to appropriate the urban ideals of Le Corbusier. In search of an organic order that was superior to democracy, they adapted his concepts to their Sorelian, antimaterialist, and corporatist social program. The architect was thus received with enthusiasm by the French fascist party, having been attracted to their circle in 1927, and giving a slide presentation at a fascist rally.

Valois eagerly allied Le Corbusier's conception of "la ville nouvelle" with his own ideal of the fascist "new city," again, a metaphor for the new social order. Accordingly, this affected the architect, who rejected his former modernism for curvilinear, organic structures, more in keeping with the aesthetics of the movement. This would also lead Le Corbusier, in the early thirties, to the circle of the Sorelian Hubert Lagardelle, who participated in the "planisme" movement, which found an expression in *Plans*.

Honegger was similarly drawn to these ideas, if at a later date, and as incorporated in "planisme," to which he could link his technological interests as well as his aesthetic. His simultaneous attraction to the past and the future was already clear in *Pacific 231*, in which he created the impression of increasing mechanical acceleration, thus masking the chorale prelude structure. It is similarly clear in his abiding interest in film, in which, as we have seen, his concern was to follow the necessities of the action or movement while balancing it with a coherent, controlled, or closed form. Moreover the cinema, like recordings, for Honegger and several of his colleagues, provided a way of reaching the masses, not exclusively for commercial purposes, but also for social goals. This motivation lay behind the efforts of composers like Jean Wiéner, as well as Honegger, both of whom participated in the large film projects of the Popular Front. As Honegger put it in another article, published in *Plans* in July 1931, opera is "dead"—one must therefore define and realize a new "lyric world," in which forms will be adapted to new needs, expressing new realities.[397] Honegger would long remain concerned with the nature of the new social collectivity, but unlike Wiéner, he was clearly not enthusiastic about the way the Popular Front envisioned it. The problem for Honegger was locating that ideological position which accorded with his aesthetic and his vision of the proper relation between the artist and the contemporary public.

And so both before and during the Popular Front, Honegger collaborated not only with various movements, but with highly engaged artists, most of whom were overtly politicized, which undoubtedly increased his own political awareness. These included the famous filmmaker Abel Gance, for whom he wrote the score for *Napoléon* in 1927; Romain Rolland, with whom he worked on the antiwar play *Liluli*; and Gabriele d'Annunzio, with whom he collaborated on *Phaedre*.[398] In the latter case, Honegger's cognizance of the political situation in Italy, and d'Annunzio's incendiary role within it, was clear in the early 1920s.[399] Honegger had originally been put in touch with the Italian poet, politician, and fascist sympathizer through the originally Russian dancer and entrepreneur Ida Rubenstein.[400] The first performance of their *Phaedre* in Rome led to violent protests and a near riot, when young fascists in the audience became enraged at the absence of their idol, d'Annunzio, who had been sent to prison.[401]

Honegger, however, now aware of d'Annunzio's fascist sympathies and actions, did not sever his relationship with the writer, and in fact later paid him a visit on his sumptuous Italian estate. But Honegger worked with other politically engaged artists on both the Left and the Right, such as Henry de Montherlant and Paul Claudel, which also raised his ideological awareness. He collaborated with Claudel on several works in these years, most of them concerning the relation of the individual to the collectivity, including *La danse des morts* and *Jeanne au* bûcher. But the years 1930–31 were also the period of Honegger's cantata, *Cris du monde*, which was closely related to the themes and issues raised by the nonconformist movement. For it concerns man's search for "significance" in a modern, highly mechanized world, with the chorus embodying the working masses, singing over the noise of machinery. But the cantata ends in a manner that recalls the nonconformist, spiritualist movement of youth, with "man" forsaking home and the masses in search of the salvation of his individual soul.[402]

Significantly, as we may recall, by the later 1930s, the work's librettist, René Bizet, was writing for the profascist journal *Candide* and espousing its "romantic" aesthetic. Bizet based the cantata's text upon Keats's romantic "Hymn to Solitude," with the theme of the libretto being the necessity of man's self-knowledge, and thus his solitude in the world. Some commentators have seen the theme's attraction for Honegger as lying not only in his Protestantism, but also in his continual concern in these years with the role of the artist in modern society.[403] But we may also see this proclivity in Honegger's strong attraction to the nonconformist movement and its preoccupation with "the person" as opposed to man as either part of "series" or as an independent "atom." Indeed, Honegger would collaborate with another nonconformist, the Swiss writer, naturalized French, Denis de Rougemont, on his oratorio *Nicolas de Flue* (1938–39). The story of a Swiss national hero, an advocate of neutrality, the work was intended to draw upon the performing forces of an entire local Swiss community, including chorus, orchestra, band, and brass ensemble.[404] The specific community originally involved was that of Neuchâtel, and the work was conceived for the National Exposition in Zurich, in the summer of 1939.

As we may recall, Honegger, despite his uncompromising works like *Antigone*, was never comfortable writing music for Cocteau's small avant-garde elite. Long before the others, Honegger had a sense of responsibility to a broad public, although his specific ideological orientation was not as yet defined. But ironically, in the case of *Jeanne au bûcher*, Honegger would find himself the victim of the populist spirit of the Popular Front, with which he had nevertheless collaborated. For Honegger never fully shared its ideals—its vision of the collective was clearly not his, and neither was its aesthetic, although he cooperated with it for professional reasons. And again, this cooperation was entirely natural for a composer like Honegger, who had always been genuinely interested in reaching out and communicating with a large audience. As he later put it, "My inclination and efforts have always been to write music which would be comprehensible to the great mass of listeners, and, at the same time, sufficiently free of banality to interest genuine music lovers."[405]

In 1936, as we saw, Honegger did attempt to relate to the goals of the Popular Front but, like Francis Poulenc, found that he imagined "the popular" in a substantially different way. Yet he obligingly espoused the regnant orthodoxy, however without compromising himself, in proclaiming that "la musique doit changer de public et s'adresser à la masse" (music should change its public and address itself to the masses).[406] And so Honegger did take part in several of the projects of the Popular Front, although, as we shall see, he quickly abandoned its goals as it declined.

As we have noted, he contributed to the grandiose production of Rolland's *Le 14 juillet* in 1936, composing the section "La prise de la Bastille." Honegger's active participation continued and expanded in 1937, when he contributed to the production of the collective work *Liberté*. For this spectacle, commissioned for the 1937 Exposition, Honegger wrote the "Prélude" to the section titled "La mort de Jaurès," to a text by Maurice Rostand.[407] And as we have also seen, for the Fête de la Lumière, which invoked "enlightenment," modernity, and state splendor, he composed the enticing music for "Mille et une nuits." Moreover, Honegger collaborated that same year on J.-R. Bloch's challenging modernist spectacle, *Construction d'une cité*, which unfortunately was a theatrical failure. Finally, for the Exposition's Pavillon des Arts et Techniques, Honegger wrote the score for a ballet, choreographed by Serge Lifar, titled *L'oiseau blanc s'est envolé*. The plot, conceived by Sacha Guitry, concerned a subject long of interest in France, and particularly since the First World War, the glories of modern aviation.[408]

Honegger's other contributions to spectacles in this period included the historical tableau *La bataille de Wagram*, which premiered in Monte Carlo on 10 May 1937. Here, in the spirit of the day, he included two chansons from the French Revolution, the "Chant du départ" (sung by the chorus) and the "Marseillaise" (performed by orchestra). Ironically, however, Honegger worked on the piece while traveling, including a trip to Nazi Germany, and he even composed part of it in a hotel in Bayreuth, sitting under a large portrait of Hitler.[409] Close to German culture through his background, Honegger never shared the anti-German sentiments attributed to Les Six by Cocteau, or those now expressed by the "patriotic" Popular Front. While not a proponent of Hitler, his antifascism was by no means as pronounced as that of other members of Les Six, particularly those on the Left, such as Tailleferre, Milhaud, and Auric.

FROM *JEANNE AU BÛCHER* TO FRONTISME

Even before his involvement with several of the projects of the Popular Front, Honegger had completed a work that embodied his distance from the aesthetic that it would espouse. The oratorio *Jeanne au bûcher* had been written to a text of Paul Claudel, who, although a supporter of pacifism and Franco-German reconciliation, was distanced from the Radical-Socialist Left by his fervent, if unorthodox Catholicism. Not a Catholic in the conservative or "classic Right" mold, his vision of Jeanne d'Arc, like Honegger's, was populist, and, like Honegger, he participated in some Popular Front programs but used them for his own personal ends.

Conceived in the ideologically more hospitable climate of the early 1930s, the work was stimulated by the fascination with the Middle Ages that had been developing in France since the 1920s. By 1933, public interest in medieval theater was at its peak, partly as a result of the persistent efforts of the Sorbonne professor Gustave Cohen. Together with his students, he had carefully reconstructed performances of medieval mystery plays for the first time in France, in the Salle des Thèses at the Sorbonne. In 1934 the dancer Ida Rubenstein conceived the idea of a "mystery play," after the medieval prototype, one with an authentically "popular" flavor. Specifically, it was modeled on those plays that originated in the period of the "wandering clerics," which were designed to take place before a general populace, and subsequently taken from city to city.

A conversation between Ida Rubenstein, Honegger, and the musicologist Jacques Chailley (who had participated in the Sorbonne project) led to the proposal of Jeanne d'Arc as a subject. Claudel was selected to provide the text, but he apparently hesitated because of the number of recent works written or in progress about Jeanne d'Arc in France. These included Paul Paray's *Messe de Jeanne d'Arc* and Manuel Rosenthal's work, based on the text of the surrealist Joseph Delteil (which Maurice Ravel had once planned to set). Again, while Ravel had envisioned Delteil's evocative text as a lyric drama, Rosenthal set it rather as a symphonic suite in five parts. As he avowed, it was both the peasant element and the sense of the "marvelous," or the resemblance to a "féerie française," that he wished to translate in his work. This, however, did not exclude an attempt to relate the story to the present day, and to the vision of the Left, by anachronistically incorporating the "Marseillaise."[410] Jeanne d'Arc, always resonant in a period of crisis, was here being claimed simultaneously by the Right and the Left, and thus the nature of her representation would be of key importance to how the work was interpreted.[411]

Claudel, wishing to distance himself from several contemporary settings of the story, avoided any reference to the present, preferring an elevated, sacred version.[412] In addition to this, the musical style became a central issue in interpretation, for although the work was not conceived within the framework of meanings propagated by the Popular Front, it would initially be construed within them. The score was completed by 1935, shortly before the advent of the new government (which would distance itself from it), and was later reworked as an oratorio, but not performed in France until 1939. In the tense, reactionary climate of the late 1930s, the work achieved immediate popularity, as had *Le roi David* in the traumatized postwar period.[413]

Honegger's goal was to write a simple but powerful kind of music that, in keeping with his professed aesthetic position, would not require technical knowledge on the part of the audience. Moreover, to bring the text alive he attempted to synthesize a diversity of styles and genres, including the traditional popular chanson, Gregorian chant, simple monophony, and polyphony.[414] Honegger thus integrated authentic folkloric elements into the score; inevitably in 1936, their rural associations caused ideological problems. Although Honegger profited more from his conservative stylistic inclinations in the postwar period, this clearly was not the case during the Popular Front. His use of traditional folkloric and religious references, although appropriate to the text, gave the work a conservative cast, which, predictably, militated against its production during the Popular Front government.

Created before the style employed was considered to be politically inimical to the government, *Jeanne d'Arc* was ready for production at a time when both religion and peasant folklore were associated with the Right. Again, Honegger's choices were based upon what he considered to be appropriate to the nature of

Claudel's text and, perhaps, to some of the values that he had imbibed in the circle of *Plans*.[415] For Honegger, the element of folklore was central to the full realization of the text, and so he attempted to incorporate folkloric elements, especially authentic popular chansons. He not only employed but emphasized these songs, as well as other relevant musical materials that were associated with those cities related to the text—Laon, Beaune, and Troyes.

But, in addition, Honegger utilized frequent references to older liturgical music, including Gregorian chant as well as early sacred polyphony.[416] These, however, were not the only stylistic references that would prove politically problematic under the secular and culturally militant government of the Popular Front. Although Honegger himself characterized the card scene in which Jeanne's fate is decided as a "ballet ironique," it has also been perceived as essentially an eighteenth-century pastiche. Irony is similarly evident in the court scene through the use of what is often described as, in effect, an exaggerated modern foxtrot style.[417] Here, perhaps making a personal commentary, Honegger employs styles associated with Les Six, but satirically, in a provocative synthesis of the archaic and the contemporary, to realize the incisive text.

The premiere was planned for the Paris Opéra in 1936, then pushed back to May 1937, and there are several explanations as to why neither performance occurred. Among these are lack of preparation and the financial constrictions being widely felt in France at the time, which made such a large-scale production difficult.[418] But here it is significant to note that in 1936 the Chamber of Deputies actually voted the opera an additional funding of 450,000 francs. This was intended to aid the presentation of new works by French composers and undoubtedly contributed to the lavish staging of Koechlin's more appropriate opera, *Oedipe*. It is therefore unlikely that the premiere of *Jeanne d'Arc* was cancelled due to lack of funds: a more plausible explanation is its stylistic and political inappropriateness in 1936 and 1937.[419]

Not surprisingly, when the work was finally presented in 1938 and 1939, the enthusiasm and support for it (despite the participation of Ida Rubenstein) came from politically conservative journals. And its eventual premiere took place not in France but in Basel, Switzerland, by the Basel Chamber Choir and Orchestra under Paul Sacher, on 12 May 1938. The French premiere did not occur until 8 May 1939, at Orléans, in conjunction with the annual festival of the saint, made a national holiday in 1922.[420]

There were clearly two Arthur Honeggers in the press—one that critics had seen as "heroic," and who pleased the proponents of the Popular Front, and the other who was "elevated," rather drawing praise from conservatives. But Honegger himself was divided, which perhaps accounts for his attachment in this period to a politically ambiguous movement that straddled the categories of Left and Right. By 1938, he had grown close to the circle around Gaston Bergery, whose politics, as we have noted, were by now increasingly contrary to the Popular Front's. As Bergery and his followers gradually perceived the political failures of the Popular Front, they started to criticize Blum and even to denounce all established political parties.[421] Already, in 1937, Bergery's discontent with Blum was mounting, and in May he addressed the Chamber, calling for a "rassemblement national," a kind of socialism that would be authentically French. Significantly, Bergery's proposal was applauded by both Right and Left at the time, the Right concurring with his attack on the "trusts," and the Left with his criticism of government policies concerning small industry and commerce.

When Blum's government began to loose support, Bergery was not unhappy: he started to join in the increasingly vocal critique, and broke with the Left's Ligue des Droits de l'Homme.[422] This rupture with the principal league of the Left was indeed a palpable political sign of the Frontistes' increasing alienation from the ideology of the Popular Front. Bergery, moreover, assumed an antiwar stance and concomitantly a posture of isolationism with regard to the fascist or authoritarian threats in Italy, Germany, and Spain.[423] Publicly, however, Bergery remained discreet, now avoiding any overt statement of his feelings with regard to the current fascist movements and regimes in Europe. Still, it was clear that Bergery valued certain aspects of the fascist regimes—their antiliberalism, their economic "dirigeance," and the state's organization of social life. In addition, he was anti-Semitic, although as Philippe Burrin has put it, "artfully so," blaming the Jews themselves for anti-Semitism, and stressing their comportment, as opposed to race.[424] (Bergery himself was Jewish.)

In January 1938 Bergery delivered a speech to the Chamber of Deputies in which he conclusively announced his refusal to support the government of the Popular Front.[425] His own movement, Frontisme, was still politically ambiguous in 1938 and 1939, since Bergery called for the reform but not abolition of the republican state. During this delicate period, he astutely continued to frequent society, being a member of the exclusive Golf de Paris and a frequent guest of Marie-Laure de Noailles. In addition, he was actively courting both intellectual and artistic circles, and in 1938 he formed a club to support his journal, called Les Amis de *La Flèche*. Among its *comité d'honneur* it counted not only André Gide but also Arthur Honegger, as well as Honegger's choreographic collaborator, Serge Lifar. At this point, the supporters of Bergery's journal came from both former members of the right-wing leagues as well as those who had been associated with the Left. But by 1938 Bergery's movement was clearly veering to the right—just ahead of the general defeat of republican values that would become manifest in the Munich accords.[426]

Frontisme, in retrospect, has historically been identified with the process of "fascization," for by 1938 it shared significant values with all of the major fascist movements. These included a desire for a homogeneous national body, achieved through exclusion, a sense of the necessity to take charge of the nation forcibly, and a belief in the integral role of the leader in doing so. Hence, having initially been a movement to combat fascism (when Tailleferre was attracted to it), Frontisme ended by, in fact, approving of certain fascist ideas.[427] This, as we have seen, was the moment when Arthur Honegger lent his name publicly in support of Bergery's journal, and by extension, or implication, to his ideas.[428] Even before, with *Plans*, as a believer in the social responsibility of the artist, Honegger, like d'Indy, sought out those intellectual movements that accorded most closely with his cultural values. Certainly, Honegger profited from his public association with *La flèche*: it strongly and consistently supported his music in a number of highly favorable reviews.[429] And it promoted Honegger not only in print, for *La flèche*, like *L'action française* before it, sponsored concerts, not only to obtain contributions but for "symbolic capital."[430]

On 1 January 1938, the journal advertised what it referred to as a "festival de *La flèche*," to be held at the elite, prestigiously located Salle Pleyel. Perhaps in an attempt to appear well apprised of contemporary musical and cultural trends, and to attract a varied elite musical audience, the program was highly diverse. One concert included not only Gluck, Bizet, and Liszt—all composers "approved" by the Right and Left, if construed differently by the two camps, but also Stravinsky (still promoted by the avant-garde and elite) and the Jewish Jacques Offenbach.[431] *La flèche*, unlike other opposition journals, did not publicly promote anti-Semitism, and thus was favorable to other Jewish composers like Milhaud.[432]

The tendency in all opposition journals was to underline Honegger's stylistic traditionalism, in order to further dissociate him from the antipathetic aesthetic of Les Six and the Popular Front. André Coeuroy, in *Gringoire*, asserted that Honegger would go down in history, but at the same time regretted his current proclivity to collaborate or work so often in "teams."[433] A great supporter of Honegger, Coeuroy, as one can see in his *La musique française moderne*, was a defender of German musical influence in France, even when it was most unfashionable.[434] And Lucien Rebatet, as we have noted, was a vocal supporter of Honegger's music, remaining faithful in his appreciation until his own death, over thirty years later. It is, in fact, in his post–World War II book on music history that Rebatet's striking image of Honegger and of his musical characteristics (which he had articulated earlier) emerges perhaps most clearly. Rebatet notes Honegger's earlier physical resemblance to the image of the romantic artist, as well as, in his vigorous youth, his love of fast cars, trains, and "speed" of all kinds. For Rebatet, Honegger was the quintessential young "athlete" of the 1920s, who flexed his muscles with calm assurance and wrote in a "virile" style, rooted in both tradition and his own time.[435]

Honegger was soon to benefit from such a construction of himself as an artist, for the aesthetic of the political opposition would triumph upon the failure and defeat of the Popular Front. A shift in aesthetic hegemony inevitably accompanied the change of government, although both cultural and political tensions would remain, even as France became mobilized for war. The new hegemonic position left only slight margins for resistance to its traditionalism and conservatism, but they would still be symbolically present within the French musical world. Now, stylistic inflections of the dominant spiritualist, romantic, and retrogressive aesthetic could articulate as subtle a range of responses as had those of "classicism" in the postwar period.

4

The Return to Spirit

Part 1: Redefinitions of Symbolic Legitimacy
The Decline of a Politics and an Aesthetics

RECONSTRUCTION OF RAVEL AND THE CONTEXT

On 6 January 1939, two months before France belatedly began preparations for an imminent war, Jacques Rouché astutely staged a work of Maurice Ravel. The choice of composition is revealing, for it was not one representative of the "less serious" Ravel that the Popular Front, according to its critics, hastily produced following his death. The work that Rouché now presented was Ravel's (choreographed) *Valses nobles et sentimentales*, a choice that articulated a changing mood and a process of symbolic reinvestment in his music.[1] Indeed, such reinterpretation of canonic French composers symbolically manifests a discernible shift in the state's priorities in music and in its criteria for aesthetic legitimacy. Rouché, heading the now united administration of the national lyric theaters (funded exclusively by the state), was here implementing the aesthetic agenda of a conservative government confronting certain crisis. The cultural "territory" that had been previously occupied and expanded by the Popular Front now was being reclaimed, invested with new meaning in light of the more conservative climate. This included the nation's lyric theaters, which were consolidated, just as the museums and libraries, in order both to improve efficiency and to better monitor their direction.[2]

Intellectuals promptly "registered" the conservative shift: Boris de Schloezer, in the vigilant *Nouvelle revue française*, was impelled to compare the "hommage" paid Ravel in *La revue musicale* in the mid-1920s and the one accorded him now.[3] In 1925 (during the Cartel des Gauches) contemporaries lauded Ravel in the journal as an "artisan," a master of form, recalling Stravinsky's clever sobriquet "the Swiss clockmaker."[4] Now, however, it was rather Ravel's lyricism, his sensibility, his richness of emotion, or the "pure humanity" of his art that overwhelmingly elicited French critical praise. The *Valses*, clearly inspired by Schubert, with graceful melodic lines and unambiguous tonality, are both romantic and contemporary, peppered with dissonance and characterized by a greater clarity of texture.[5] This too fit the predominant mood of the late 1930s, a kind of romantic irony which both longed for spiritual nobility and elevation and yet could not escape reality—the threat of a conflict that could prove disastrous for the nation. From this perspective, even the title of the work that Rouché mounted is telling,

...it resonated immediately with the dominant discourse, in which "nobility" was a central value. Seeking to rehabilitate "high art," its ideal was transcendence, spirituality, and the sublime—an art now freed of the "contagion" of politics that had vitiated the Popular Front's aesthetic, in the eyes of its critics. Not surprisingly, Jacques Rouché's decision won the immediate approbation of Pierre Leclau in *Je suis partout*, who pointed out that here Zay finally did the right thing.[6]

Politics, however, was still implicit: it inhered not only in what was rejected, but in the program of moral reform believed to be a prerequisite for artistic regeneration. For the ideal of "spirituality" implied not only a resacralization of collective, national life, but a distinct conception of the desired wholeness, and thus of what to extrude. Great art, which was fully human, sincere, and representative of the "whole person," could emerge only from a holistic society that was the antithesis of French liberal democracy.[7]

Similar reasoning would gradually inform official institutions of music in France and the manner in which they sought to mediate music, or select and present it to the French public. For them, music, on the eve of the war, was to provide a means to transcend harsh realities, to register national trauma, and to atone for the nation's collective sins. The way in which it could do so, however, was not entirely clear, and hence the concept of a "spiritual" art was highly nuanced, again splitting along ideological lines.[8]

The process of symbolic transformation was gradual, reflecting the trajectory of French politics in the thirties, as the balance of power shifted from Left to Right in the final years of the decade. Even then, superficial uniformity masked diversity, just as during World War I, but it is this subtle range of responses we must grasp to penetrate the late thirties and early forties more deeply.[9] As we have already noted, mounting opposition, of all shades, to the Popular Front both accompanied and furthered its political decline, which occurred in several distinct stages.[10] The first was Blum's resignation on 21 January 1937; the second was Chautemps's ministry, which lasted only three months, from January to March 1938. Now the government was deprived of the essential political support of the Radicals, although the Socialists remained in Chautemps's government and Léon Blum now became vice prime minister.[11] The third stage was Edouard Daladier's ascension to power in April 1938, which was to bring the government of the Popular Front to a definitive end by the following November.[12]

It was Daladier, therefore, who would sign the fateful "Munich agreement" in the supposed interest of maintaining peace in Europe on 30 September 1938.[13] This marked a new point of division for French intellectuals, some remaining implacably pacifist, perceiving the danger of Communism as greater than fascist aggression, and others determined to combat fascism.[14] Moreover, the Munich agreement was accompanied by an escalating fear among the French and, consequently, a more interventionist role on the part of the state in carrying out its conservative program.[15] In general, then, the period extending from 1938 to 1940 was one of greater centralized authority and mounting anxiety, with increasing concentration on several key themes.

One was anti-Semitism. Beginning in 1938, a notable wave of anti-Semitism

RETURN TO SPIRIT

swept through France, together with a stress on authoritarian values and the virtues of the soil.[16] And again, by 1938, when the failure of the Popular Front was patent, there was not only a discernible shift in French cultural values but a new emphasis on religion. However, as André Gide noted in his journal on 3 December 1938, the voices of a small number of honest Christians were being stifled by the clergy, whose interests were not spiritual but temporal.[17] The republican laws concerning the congregations were no longer being enforced, and in 1939 the pope lifted his ban on the Action Française.[18] Finally, attitudes toward Germany were changing: after noting Adolph Hitler's concerted antibolchevism, even many right-wing nationalists were growing less hostile to the "German enemy."[19]

DELEGITIMIZING MUSICAL NEOCLASSICISM

Along with the mounting force of the Right and its ever growing hegemony in culture, the shift in symbolic legitimacy became clear in the French musical world by 1938. Once again, critics were to play a key role in establishing what was now valued, not only in terms of musical aesthetics but implicitly in French culture as a whole. Now those critics who had formerly contributed to profascist journals became dominant voices not only in the general press but also in the French musical press. So consistently had the profascist press fused its political and musical values through symbols and codes that when the political climate waxed in its favor, so too did French musical policies and taste.

In musical journals, in criticism in the press, in institutions of official consecration, we may perceive manifestation of this victory in the evocative vocabulary of new honorific terms: the accolades omnipresent in the previous two years, or those of the Popular Front, were rare—in particular, "individual," "free," "audacious," "accessible," "life-like," and "heroic." In their place we encounter "elevated," "inspired," "idealistic," "noble," "subjective," "lyrical," and "spiritual," as well as such phrases as "rooted in collectivity and race." Scholisme was once more triumphant, and it is within this context that the heated combat against it that we encountered in *L'art musical populaire* in the later thirties becomes fully comprehensible.

Concurrent with the triumph of Scholism was the revalorization of German music, now once again being performed at the Société Nationale de Musique Française. Bravely, in 1938, the year of the Anschluss, the Société organized a concert dedicated to Austrian music that included Alban Berg's Four Pieces for Clarinet and Piano.[20] In 1939 it became even bolder in its performance of contemporary foreign works, presenting not only Hindemith's *Kammermusik*, no. 1, but Berg's *Lyric Suite* and Schoenberg's Quartet, op. 57. However, the inclusion of a work by a modernist Austrian Jew in this conservative context (probably on the instigation of Messiaen and Henri Martell) incited protest from the audience and harsh criticism in *Le ménestrel*.[21]

The new priorities were also to eventuate in a series of systematic "reclassifications" or rerankings of composers not only from the national past, but those who were currently active as well. And characteristic, once again, is reference to the political values associated with these figures in the musical press, and even direct articulation of political opinion in this context. For music was by now a central component of the political symbolic system, enunciating not only a conception of French national identity, but of French society itself. Accordingly, even musical journals such as the venerable *Le ménestrel* were ridiculing the previous government's cultural and musical endeavors. On 6 May 1938, for example, Paul Bertrand referred to the musical season that had been organized in conjunction with the 1937 International Exposition as a humiliating fiasco. As he pointedly remarks, the only art of the highest level that could be found in the Exposition's concerts was in connection with the "Semaine Allemande." He then goes on to accuse the former government of both favoritism and corruption, or of using public "organisms" to the advantage of a small clique, and not of French art as a whole.[22]

In addition, one can hardly open an issue of one of the most intellectually oriented musical journals of the period, *La revue musicale*, without being struck by the abruptness of its aesthetic shift. In taking this turn, it was following the path of its illustrious parent journal, *La nouvelle revue française*, which had preceded it in its political and cultural rejection of the previous government. Initially supportive of the Popular Front, and espousing an idealistic republicanism, the latter gradually recoiled from the Communist extremists, moving toward a decidedly more conservative stance. By 1938, not only did the journal favor the conservative government of "national unity," it even gave sympathetic treatment to the Republic's most implacable enemy, Charles Maurras.[23]

La revue musicale, formerly supportive of the aesthetic direction espoused by the Popular Front, now praised "d'Indysme," "tradition," and "la grande musique." Here we find many of the same themes and positions already articulated in the profascist press, and often by the very same writers, in particular, Coeuroy, Vuillermoz, and Landormy. In addition, we increasingly encounter condemnation of the postwar direction in music, or that associated with neoclassicism and "materialism," as opposed to the pure realm of "spirit." Indeed, the "national memory," as it had been articulated during the Popular Front, with reference to a musical tradition or canon, was now undergoing a fundamental revision. No longer was it centered on the consistent use of popular sources, or characterized by "charm, audacity," and "the actual," as in the preceding period: we rather encounter condemnation of that school now held responsible for the current misdirection or malaise: Les Six, and those believed to espouse their politically culpable aesthetic.

Typical is Alfred Cortot's biting indictment, revealingly titled "Le cas Satie," which appeared in *La revue musicale* in the issue of April–May 1938. Here Cortot begins by denouncing Jean Cocteau's "esprit frondeur" and the way in which he purportedly built a series of "jokes" into an aesthetic system.[24] The war and the turn from "Germanic sentimentality," he continues, only lent further credence to this school of young musicians that was basically founded upon "puerility." But here Cortot particularly deplores what he perceives as the vociferous aesthetic claims of the group in the mid-1920s to embody the essential traits of true French music. Confusing Cocteau's and Collet's publicity with the declarations and beliefs of the different members of Les Six themselves, Cortot remarks, with discernible indignation about their return to the so-called specific traits of French music:

> .... franchise du rythme, clarté quasi-élémentaire du contour mélodique, valeur intrinsèque de sonorité enfin libérées de toute signification idéologique ou sentimentale parasite.
> Ils participaient ainsi au présomptueux sentiment de la génération d'après-guerre . . . que toutes les valeurs spirituelles et artistiques allaient être mises en cause.[25]
>
> [freedom of rhythm, quasi-elementary clarity of melodic contour, the intrinsic value of sonority finally liberated from all ideological signification or parasitic sentimentalism.
> They thus participated in the presumptuous feeling of the postwar generation . . . that all artistic and spiritual values were going to be called into question.]

Ironically, as we will recall, Cortot, as "chief" of "musical propaganda," during the war had promoted the classical aesthetic and the view of France's past as classic. However, as we will also recall, this dominant or "official" neoclassicism had carried a spiritual dimension, which was now being projected onto other musical styles. Hence now, as in the twenties, Stravinsky once more comes under concerted attack, not in the general or political press, but in the specifically musical press. Apparently not being an indigenous French musician, or someone with public political opinions concerning France, he was not a real stake in the general press, which was concerned now with where "French" music should head. But in French musical journals he increasingly became a scapegoat, held responsible for leading French music astray, thus lessening the blame for native French musicians, who were reconsidering their pasts.

Those forces that were opposed to Stravinsky were already prominent by the mid-1930s, especially in the notorious bastion of cultural conservatism, the illustrious Institut de France. When the chair of Paul Dukas was to be filled, the painter Jacques-Emile Blanche persuaded Stravinsky to pose his candidacy; however, unfortunately his old friend, Florent Schmitt became a candidate as well. Inevitably, in the context, Stravinsky, although naturalized French since 1934, was defeated by the stylistically more conventional Schmitt, on 25 January 1936.

Yet Stravinsky was not without defenders. Still prominent among them was Darius Milhaud, who expressed his support as he had in the 1920s. But so controversial was Stravinsky at this point that *La revue musicale* was forced again to devote an issue to his defense, as it had in both 1921 and 1925. As we will recall, Stravinsky's neoclassicism in the twenties was different in its cultural motivation from that of Les Six, who nevertheless overlooked the difference. Coming from outside French culture, he naturally found a different, purely technical, challenge in the traditionalist expectations of the period. His conception of the neoclassic was, in fact, much closer to that of the composers of the Weimar Republic, where he had spent much time, to the public consternation of critics in France. Stravinsky's ideal, like that of his German confrères (whom he also influenced), was objectivity, as opposed to "barbarism"—a dispassionate analysis of past styles, or of the constructive principles at work within them.[26]

Les Six, as we have seen, were in search of a culture that was more immediate and "real" than the fossilized classical culture that had been propagated during the war. Critics, however, could not make the distinction; they melded Stravinsky's motivation and style with that of Les Six in the twenties and now they did so once again. Almost all of the articles in a 1939 issue of *La revue musicale* dedicated to Stravinsky concentrate on addressing the reproaches against him and Les Six, except that of Alfred Cortot, who assaults the neoclassic aesthetic.[27] Stravinsky's supporters included not only the faithful Darius Milhaud, but Roland-Manuel, Roger Desormière, Georges Auric, and, less enthusiastically, Arthur Honegger. The latter's brief tribute, titled "Strawinsky [sic], homme de métier," tellingly stresses not Stravinsky's aesthetic (from which Honegger was now distant) but rather his "craft."

This controversy over Stravinsky was immediately diffused to the larger French intellectual and artistic world through *La nouvelle revue française*. Boris de Schloezer's regular "Chronique musicale," in the issue of July–December 1939 (when France was bracing for Hitler's attack), was devoted to this very question.[28] De Schloezer notes the marked difference in tone in the 1939 issue of *La revue musicale* as compared to those appearing earlier on Stravinsky, and that Stravinsky's defenders were now necessarily more ardent. As he perceptively observes, it is here a question of fighting not only for a certain conception of music, but for the aesthetic ideology with which it is intimately associated.[29] He notes that in the article by André Schaeffner (the scholar of jazz and ethnomusicologist at the Musée des Arts et Traditions Populaires) it is a question now of defending Stravinsky's "objectivity."

By this he means Stravinsky's use of styles as consciously detached from their original historical contexts or connotations, and therefore devoid of traditional "signification." Stravinsky's art, for Schaeffner, is unquestionably one of "evocation," however with historical objectivity—styles are denuded of both nostalgia and emotional resonance.[30] As de Schloezer points out, it is this "divestment" of the emotional dimension that makes Stravinsky's art, for his detractors, a sign of the currently perceived failure of intellectual and moral values. But, as he continues, we may still define the "psychological" content of Stravinsky's art, for even if music does not express emotion, it can still communicate something else. True to the comprehensive spirit of *La nouvelle revue française*, he points out that Stravinsky's music can indeed be emotive in its own manner, in addition to being spiritual or otherwise "suggestive."[31]

Despite the defenses of Stravinsky in *La revue musicale*, the journal's tone continued to wax conservative, in keeping with the larger tendencies in French culture of the period.[32] It now even published articles that were openly laudatory of Vincent d'Indy, who had long been excluded from serious consideration in the journal for both musical and political reasons. In 1938 it published two articles by d'Indy's biographer, Léon Vallas, one comparing d'Indy's harmonies with those of the French (Jewish) composer Ernest Reyer and the other comparing d'Indy with Georges Bizet.[33]

Alignments were clearly shifting: by 1939 *La revue musicale*, formerly favorable to the aesthetic of the Popular Front, was defending the romantic tradition as authentically French. And concomitantly, a valorization of "spirit" was recurring, although now it assumed a wide range of connotations, or was construed in significantly different ways by different groups.[34] In early 1939 the prominent intellectual of the Left, Jean-Richard Bloch, published a revealing article in *La revue musicale* titled "Maurice Ravel ou les monstres domptés" (Maurice Ravel or the monsters tamed).[35] Although knowledgeable in music (and a fine pianist), Bloch was, as we have noted, primarily a writer who was politically engaged, as well as the founder of the Socialist journal *L'effort* (later *L'effort libre*). Bloch had subsequently gone on to be a collaborator on *La nouvelle revue française*, and finally in 1934 to become an active member of the French Communist Party.[36]

Here Bloch assumes an independent position, recalling the postwar Left, as opposed to the implacably anti-German, antiromantic stance of most French Communists of the period. As Bloch himself put it explicitly, "Je ne céderai pas au jeu puéril et vain de sacrifier le romantisme, l'expressionnisme germanique, à la pudeur française" (I will not give in to the vain and puerile game of sacrificing romanticism, German expressionism, to French prudery).[37] Sounding like Paul-Marie Masson, who shortly before World War I sought a similar political and aesthetic reconciliation, Bloch then argues that Ravel belongs to no one (meaning implicitly not just to French conservatives). Still implying that Ravel is essentially an "intellectual," or of the Left, Bloch also argues that a romantic tendency has long existed in France in figures such as Rabelais, Balzac, Berlioz, and Claudel. This conception of romanticism, however, is one that we encountered in the writings of the postwar Left—one that is characterized by both individualism and a spirituality that is not "mystical" but deeply "human."

REVALORIZING TRADITION AND "SPIRIT"

Other publications in this period made similar attempts at subtle aesthetic reconciliation, one being a volume that resulted from a 1938 congress in Italy. Several French figures participated (despite the Fascist government), including Darius Milhaud, Henry Prunières (the editor of *La revue musicale*), and the omnipresent Emile Vuillermoz. All of their presentations emphasized the current musical "crisis" (construed as intertwined with the political crisis) and endorse the recent French tendency to embrace tradition. Milhaud, like his friend Poulenc, may well have felt it necessary to defend himself in the new political climate by clarifying his position, as opposed to that ascribed to Les Six. Moreover, probably through the influence of the minister Jean Zay, he was now apparently under serious consideration as the next potential director of the Paris Conservatoire.[38]

Milhaud, in his article titled "La tradition," asserts that a sense of the force and necessity of tradition, in an art as "noble" as music, has always been dominant in his thought. This was indeed true, as we have seen, for despite the iconoclastic rhetoric of Cocteau, Milhaud had consistently admired traditionalist composers such as the uncompromising Magnard. Although the tradition to which he refers still lies along the lines established by the Left before World War I, he makes a point of praising d'Indy's *Symphonie montagnarde* for its use of folklore.[39] Yet absent from Milhaud's earlier rhetoric, and intrusively present here, is his assertion that tradition is the raison d'être of music today, as it has been at all times. Again as on the eve of World War I, another time of imminent upheaval and change, French artists like Milhaud sought the roots of their identity in a personal conception of French tradition. Milhaud here argues, moreover, that music, after all, is the expression of the "soul," or of a feeling deep in our hearts which he still believes is articulated most fully in melody.

Reflecting his experience with the Popular Front, Milhaud expresses his hope that future composers will be able to establish a better understanding, a more "profound confidence" with their audiences. But surprisingly, the former anti-Wagnerian now lists the name of Wagner, together with Berlioz, Bizet, Gounod, and Debussy (whom he had rejected) as those whose music had fortunately overcome initial resistance. And Milhaud, again in defense of Stravinsky, also emphasizes the latter's use of the past, but now construes it as sincere testimony to his love of the great composers.[40]

Vuillermoz's contribution "Le goût moderne et la musique du passé" (Modern taste and the music of the past) reverses his praise, before World War I, of innovation as opposed to tradition. Here he condemns those postwar youth (undoubtedly with Les Six in mind) who, unlike their elders, sought decisively to break with previous French musical tradition. Now Vuillermoz traces a musical tradition that is decisively opposed to the former nationalist and Debussyste rhetoric characteristic of his writings before 1914:[41] "De Bach à Beethoven, de Beethoven à Wagner, de Wagner à Debussy, de Debussy à Richard Strauss, de Richard Strauss à Maurice Ravel, il y a une évolution logique, une chaîne de continuité." (From Bach to Beethoven, from Beethoven to Wagner, from Wagner to Debussy, from Debussy to Richard Strauss, from Richard Strauss to Maurice Ravel, there is a logical evolution, a chain of continuity.)[42] Vuillermoz, perhaps influenced by the *Candide* circle, is here implying a natural cross-fertilization between French and German music, both part of one great encompassing tradition. And, as opposed to his earlier evolutionary, progressive views, he now argues firmly that all these artists respected the "natural laws" of harmony and the "traditional equilibrium" of modes and tones.

Prunières's article, revealingly titled "Que doit-il sortir de la crise qui traverse actuellement la musique?" (What will emerge from the crisis that is presently traversing music?), explicitly concerns music, yet makes clear that larger cultural causes underlie it. He particularly emphasizes the vast movement of artistic reaction throughout all of Europe, and that even Schoenberg, Stravinsky, and Bartok appear to have reassessed their goals. But Prunières's allegiance to progressive republican values is clear when he suggests a possible solution—to use the state radio to foster the development and propagation of new French works.[43]

Perhaps because of the menacing fascist involvement in the recording industry, the state did indeed use the radio, upon Zay's urging, to encourage French musical innovation.[44] As Zay himself put it, his major concern at the moment was to locate the necessary funds to diffuse both music and theater to the rest of the country, outside of Paris. For Parisian state theaters alone were included in the budget of the Beaux-Arts, and the Ministère des Finances refused to open a new rubric for funding other, new projects. Hence it appeared quite logical to Zay to turn, at this point, to the *ministre des postes*, under which the direction of "radiodiffusion" was currently subsumed.

As we saw, in 1937, funds had been appropriated for radio broadcast of concerts in France, in a chapter of the budget titled "Subventions aux théâtres et concerts symphoniques pour organisation des manifestations artistiques populaires radiodiffusées." Funding initially was generous: 7.4 million francs were allotted in 1937, but this was reduced to half a million in 1938 and 1939. Zay creatively saw this rubric as potentially a substitute source of funds, or, as he put it, "une sorte de succursale clandestine des Beaux-Arts" (a kind of clandestine branch of the Beaux-Arts).[45] Despite the shift in political climate, his cultural politics, centering on a wide diffusion of culture, remained the same, but now they were in subtle opposition.

RECLASSIFICATION OF GENRES

The shift in political hegemony from the Left to the Right, which was leading to redefinition of symbolic legitimacy, also affected commissions and other monetary awards. Commissions of musical works, to this point, had been associated either with a specific theater, with the Prix de Rome, or with special celebratory events, such as those of the Popular Front.[46] But now, while continuing the cultural expansion introduced by the Popular Front, the subsequent government was forced to address the pressing problem of unemployment among composers. Hence, upon the instigation of Zay, budget reporter Joanny Berlioz, and Georges Huisman (Directeur général des beaux-arts), new commissions were initiated, titled "Commandes exceptionnelles aux artistes vivants et compositeurs de musique en vue de lutter contre le chômage" (Exceptional commissions to living artists and composers of music for the purpose of battling unemployment). Despite the rationale given in the rubric, the attribution of a chapter in the budget for the regular commissioning of musical works is further evidence of the importance now being placed on music. Moreover, it is significant to note that Joanny Berlioz, reflected the growing anxiety over the continuity of French art in his argument for this innovation: "En réalité, le chômage des travailleurs intellectuels, des artistes de tous ordres en particulier . . . constitue un danger certain pour l'avenir du patrimoine culturel national." (In reality, the unemployment of intellectual workers, of artists of all kinds in particular . . . constitutes a certain danger for the future of the national patrimony.)[47] Artists here are now considered explicitly to be "intellectuals," but their primary charge is to continue to contribute to the nation's patrimony, to preserve the integrity of a great tradition.

In examining the decisions that were made concerning both the genres and the composers selected for the new official commissions, we should keep several different factors in mind. First, there was an element of pragmatism: the commissions had to reflect some attempt at compromise, since Zay remained in his position, although his priorities had to shift.[48] And so the composers selected included several former members of Les Six and those previously associated with the Popular Front, but the majority had more "spiritualistic" and traditionalist associations or tendencies. Yet, once more, the major concern was with combating unemployment, particularly among the country's most recognized contemporary composers, who belonged to both factions.[49] However, in the genres emphasized, as well as in certain choices of artists, we may see, within this context, an enunciation of specific shifting cultural values. Again, we cannot understand these decisions fully apart from the codes of meaning or signification that were, by now, implanted in the musical world. It was through these established associations of musical styles and forms that French institutions mediated or refracted the government's changing ideological orientation.

The new official commissions in music prominently included operatic and symphonic works, as well as ballets—genres de-emphasized by the Popular Front in favor of cantatas, theatrical spectacles, and fêtes.[50] As we have already noted, opera represented a more elite level of taste, while symphonic compositions continued to signify spiritual associations. Because of this, as well as of the possibility of performance by subsidized theaters and concert associations, the commissions for 1938 included an opera in three acts (by Marcel Delannoy), an opera in one act (by Georges Auric), a symphony (by Elsa Barraine), a cantata (by Germaine Tailleferre), and an opera in one act (by Darius Milhaud).[51] In addition, ballets were commissioned from Milhaud, Georges Migot, and Paul Le Flem, and symphonic works from Koechlin, Rivière, and several lesser known figures. It is not surprising, within this context that, as Leslie Sprout has noted, most of the commissions made reference to France's musical past, through quotation or through other stylistic references.[52]

A similar attempt at compromise is manifest in the choice of works to be performed in the major Parisian lyric theaters in the later 1930s. In 1938 the Opéra-Comique performed Milhaud's *Le pauvre matelot*, his *Suite provençale* (as a ballet), and, surprisingly in this climate, *Esther de Carpentras*. Milhaud was indeed now prominent, having been on the Conseil Supérieur of the State Radio since 1935, on the Consultative Committee of the Opéra-Comique since 1936, and on the Conseil Supérieur of the Conservatoire since 1937. *Le pauvre matelot* may well have appealed at this time because of its roots in French tradition, for Cocteau had originally modeled the libretto on the traditional *complainte*. And *Esther de Carpentras*, although about the Jews versus the Catholics, treated the subject with humor, and concerned religion and a "region," as well as compromise, all current points of emphasis.[53] It also represented a balance between the waning stylistic values of the Popular Front and the resurgent traditionalist stress on the importance of the "soil" and of spirit. A review in the conservative *Le temps*, of 5 February 1938, compliments Milhaud specifically for having remained true to his "pays natal." But, although praising the composer for his zeal, it expresses regret that the contrasts were not stronger, dismissing the subtle but trenchant work as "une amusante aventure judéo-méridionale."[54] Similarly, René Dumesnil's review in the equally conservative *Mercure de France* belittles the work as an "aimable farce," stressing not its now timely commentary, but rather its "fantaisie."[55]

In the principal concert societies a change of repertoire was particularly notable, as they responded to the now evident revalorization of "la grande musique." No longer concentrating on lesser known French composers, lighter works, or excerpts from larger compositions, they were increasingly centering on German music, particularly Wagner and Brahms, or those composers associated with "spirituality." A listing of the programs of the Concerts Colonne, Lamoureux, and Pasdeloup, as early as January 1938, reveals a preponderance of Wagner excerpts, entire symphonies of Brahms, and the works of Richard Strauss and Franz Liszt.[56]

Indeed, by the later 1930s the preoccupation with elevation and "spirit" was general, manifesting a psychological and emotional response to political failure, to uncertainty, and to crisis. But, once more, this does not imply a simple homogeneity of attitude in France, or evidence of a widespread cowardice and political retreat that would contribute to the French defeat. For "spirit," as a concept, was highly ramified, as we have seen in the case of "tradition," and it included not only the interpretations of the Left, the conservative Center, and the profascist Right, but a distinctive new one on the part of French youth.

Part 2: The Search for "Oppositionality"
French Youth and "Revolutionary Spiritualism"

THE NONCONFORMIST MOVEMENT AND ITS IMPACT

The innovative "spirituality" of French youth was already evident in the context of that movement of the early 1930s referred to as nonconformism, and in which we noted Honegger's involvement. Generally considered to be "over" in intellectual circles by the mid-1930s, its impact on young French musicians came later, when they learned of and appropriated it.[57] For this reason, although a return to the early 1930s is out of chronology, it is important to examine nonconformism in greater detail here, given its later effects on French music in the increasingly "spiritualist" climate.

The movement, which bore a complex relation to spiritualist currents in the 1920s, sought a "spiritual alternative" to the political impasse on both the Right and the Left. For, by the early 1930s, it was inescapably clear to many intellectuals that neither the traditional political Right nor Left could respond to the current French political crisis. On the right, the Action Française had been substantially weakened by its conflict with the pope, and the Left had been "neutralized" as a political force by the divisions engendered by Communism. And, as we have observed, the economic crisis of the 1930s, together with its political and financial scandals, led to increasingly antiparliamentarian sentiment. In light of the new political and cultural conflicts of the decade, then, the older positions, or points of ideological reference, no longer appeared to suffice.

One reaction on the part of the younger generation was simply to reject involvement in conventional politics and to shift the dialogue to the transcendent realms of philosophy and the "spirit." As a result, the 1930s saw a rapid proliferation of intellectual groupings and journals devoted to the utopian ideal of the construction of a radically different but nonfascist "new world."[58] These groups called for an end to the current political, economic, social, and spiritual "disorder," or "crisis" of civilization, through a constructive, organic, "spiritual revolution."[59] Man was no longer to be defined politically but rather spiritually, or as existing on a higher level of being or awareness, free of political rhetoric and of national boundaries. Some youth, of course, like certain members of the older generation, were drawn instead to Marxism, perceiving the major problems of the day as consisting primarily of joblessness, famine, and war. But both nonconformist and Marxist youth rejected the "old" society, sharing a general sense of crisis and a hatred of the "dehumanization" caused by capitalism.[60]

Their search was both for transcendence, like the Far Right's, and for renewal, like the current Left's, which led to inconsistencies and the tendency to cross political boundaries with apparent ease. Indeed, this generation strove to recast the very terms of the current French political debate, which no longer seemed to suffice in a world that was confronted by imminent crisis.[61] It was clearly a new generation, distinct from that of 1914—born after the turn of the century, reaching adolescence during the war and young adulthood in the 1920s. They were thus raised in, and bore a complex relation to, the conservative and spiritualistic dominant culture of the twenties, which had been characterized by the search for a world different from that which had engendered the war.[62] Despite this similarity, theirs was a generation that detested figures like Raymond Poincaré, perceived as the very personification of the now failing bourgeois Republic. They similarly shared a horror of the current parliamentary regime, as well as of economic liberalism and its approach to the individual as abstract, or as simply interchangeable. But they also gradually rejected the failing "neo-Maurrasian" monarchist Right, as well as the ideological solutions being proposed by both Marxism and fascism. All sought a future society in which the individual would be treated as a "person," as opposed explicitly to the "atom" of liberalism and to the "unit" within the totalitarian "series." As distinct from the latter, and from the liberal "aggregate" of discrete individuals, the "person" was a concrete being, tied by mutual responsibility to others, or with a "communitarian vocation." The "person," then, was not to be subordinated to race, nation, state, or history, or reduced to an elector or consumer, but seen as a socially responsible human being.[63]

This ideal, called "personalism," had a substantial impact on the entire span of nonconformist journals, which ranged in orientation from the Far Left to the Right. For despite their rejection of the panaceas of both the Left and Right, and their search for a new position of "oppositionality," some were slanted more toward one pole or the other.[64] The journal in which Arthur Honegger participated, *Plans*, as we have seen, was both reformist and modernist, however, it was more difficult to categorize in terms of Right or Left leanings.[65] For while it was technologically "progressive" and echoed many of the themes of other nonconformist journals, it also emphasized decentralization, or geographic and cultural regionalism, more characteristics of the Right. And like the "classic" Right, it advocated not only the relation of man to his native soil, but equally to his "race" and, concomitantly, to his own indigenous cultural tradition.⁶⁶

LEFTIST SPIRITUALISM AND YOUTH

More clearly oriented toward the Left, and attractive to younger artists, writers, and composers, was the far longer-lived nonconformist (and Catholic) journal *Esprit*. It was begun in 1932 by Emmanuel Mounier, a "spiritualist," but one of the Left, who would eventually be imprisoned by the Vichy government during the Occupation.[67] Mounier, like many in the movement, was an ardent admirer of Charles Péguy and his attacks on intellectualism, rationalism, and on the educational reforms of the "new" Sorbonne. He also promoted "personalism" which, for him, included antiliberalism, anticapitalism, antimaterialism, and a quest for "purification."[68] But Mounier, in addition, proclaimed the importance of ritual in society, and grew close to Jacques Maritain and his circle of Catholic intellectuals.[69] Maritain was thus a notable presence in *Esprit*, contributing articles such as "Religion et culture," in 1933, in which he stresses the suprarational, supranational, and supracultural nature of religion.[70] And, significantly, *Esprit* attracted a now converted, Catholic Cocteau in the thirties, as well as Louis Laloy, the former nationalist and supporter of Debussy, and then of modernism.[71]

Esprit, situated on the Left, was part of the larger Christian democratic current that had followed the condemnation of the Action Française in 1926, and which sought a more sincerely religious and a democratic Catholicism.[72] Even conservatives of the older generation who had distanced themselves from the Action Française after its condemnation by the pope (like Maritain), could feel comfortable within this new circle. Such a tendency in the Catholic world, away from the league and its politics as well as its aesthetics, was reflected in other journals such as *Sept* and *L'aube*.[73] The desire of all such journals was not only to rejuvenate and to reform the nation, but to modernize Christian expression, including that in the arts.[74] All were therefore in search of a new, more convincing Catholic aesthetic, more in keeping with their spiritual and social goals than the classicism of the Action Française.[75] One of the members of the older generation who now grew close to *Esprit*, drawn by the spiritual alternative proposed by youth, was the noted writer François Mauriac. A devout but independent Catholic, Mauriac fit immediately into the journal's intellectual circle, as well as into that of *Sept*, which openly supported the cause of French workers.[76]

In *Esprit* the emphasis of its youthful organizers and contributors of all ages was clear: it was on a cultural "revolution," as articulated in André Déléage's article in June 1933, "Littérature et révolution." Literature and the arts, he argued, should be nothing less than a veritable "call to combat," or an inspiration to all to remake themselves fundamentally. This "humanist" definition of revolutionary art was, of course, defined against those models already proposed not only by fascists but by Communists and surrealists (some of whom joined the Communist Party). The goal here was to prepare the revolution on a deep level by transforming man, or by disposing spirits to "transform the world": this was their activating, if utopian myth. It is also important to remember that their ideal of "humanism" was partly defined against the "neohumanism" being promoted by French fascist art critics like Waldemar George. His argument for a return to "the human subject" was part of his rejection of abstract modern art, and of his encomium of Italian fascism in his pamphlet *L'humanisme et l'idée de la patrie*. Others were promoting a "return to man" in a broader social and intellectual sense, as in the conference sponsored by the League of Nations on "New Humanism" in 1937. The nonconformists rather sought to redefine man in a philosophical, metaphysical sense, to consider his place in the cosmos—in a transcendent, or spiritual, order.[77]

Other articles in *Esprit* refer to a common desire to "refaire la Renaissance" (remake the Renaissance), for instance, the one bearing this title by Emmanuel Mounier in the October 1932 issue. Here he aptly stresses that the "spiritual" can indeed be socially progressive, and that it is therefore wrong to confuse it, as many still do, with simple political and cultural reaction.[78] Some nonconformist journals were indeed founded by those with clear origins on the Left, such as Arnaud Dandieu, who came from Socialism, and Robert Aron, who came from surrealism. Aron and Dandieu together started the journal *L'ordre nouveau*, one prominent theme of which was the condemnation of arid rationalism, previously associated with the Left by the Right. Against this and the abstract individualism that they, like other nonconformists, perceived as fostered by the state, they also espoused the doctrine of "personalism," or stress on the responsible "person."[79]

THE CONSERVATIVE CATHOLIC AVANT-GARDE

Other nonconformist journals were anchored quite clearly on the Right. Among these were *Réaction*, *Combat*, *La revue du siècle*, and *La revue française*. These journals, unlike those of the older French political and cultural Right, differed emphatically with regard to what should occur when the Republic is finally defeated. While the old Right, inspired by monarchism, advocated a return to a traditional order, the new "young Right" rather ardently wished for cataclysmic change—for a "national revolution." *Réaction*, for example, begun by Parisian students originally associated with Action Française, was, despite its title, motivated by modern social interests, and in search of a new "ordre chrétien."[80]

The response of Action Française to its ever-increasing marginalization was to insert itself into older, conservative currents, those against which French youth now reacted. The latter desired something "new," as opposed to the materialist individualism that they believed should have changed, but, in fact, did not, after all the sacrifices made in the war. The result was an enormous cultural gap, particularly evident on the Right, between those who were born circa 1885 and those who were born around the turn of the century.[81] Journals like *Combat*, begun in 1936 by youth within Action Française (led by Thierry Maulnier), called specifically for a "new idealism." Openly hostile to the government of the Popular Front, they were antidemocratic, anticapitalist, and strongly supportive of Franco. But their "ideal" was, in effect, an adaptation of the Maurrassian model of society, organized around communities that were to be arranged according to their natural hierarchies.

Although there were nonconformist journals that leaned more to the Left or to the Right, it is important to recall that for Catholic intellectuals the lines of division became increasingly blurred. Issues such as Mussolini's invasion of Ethiopia and the Spanish Civil War stirred those Catholics originally on the Right, like Maritain and Mauriac, to reconsider their allegiances and condemn Mussolini and Franco. Jolted out of their ethnocentrism both by Mussolini's actions and by the Colonial Exposition of 1931, all were interested in defining a new Catholic aesthetic, as well as in exploring non-Western modes of spirituality. The Catholic "prise de conscience" over such issues as Ethiopia and Spain accordingly brought a redefinition of the ideal of the "universal," now in distinction to the fascist conception of it. This we shall shortly see manifest in the context of the new musical grouping Jeune France, whose vocabulary, rhetoric, and preoccupations reflect the profound influence of the nonconformist movement.[82]

MUSIC IN NONCONFORMIST JOURNALS

All such publications were deeply interested in art, but perhaps the one most consistently concerned with music, to the point of including musicians among its collaborators, was the prominent journal *Esprit*. Not surprisingly, it took consistent interest in the more "spiritually oriented" modern musicians, particularly Arthur Lourié, a Russian émigré now active in France. Lourié had begun his career as a composer in Soviet Russia, but in 1921 he moved to Berlin, where he grew close to Busoni. In 1924 Lourié settled in France and at first became friends with Stravinsky, but unlike the latter he gradually turned from neoclassicism to "spiritualist" works, and their friendship ended. His later stylistic proclivities, in fact, relate closely to the tradition of the Schola Cantorum, being not only frequently modal, but also employing both chant and chorales. Not surprisingly, Jacques Maritain (with whom he became friends) discussed Lourié, in his *Intuition créatrice dans l'art et dans la poésie* (Creative intuition in art and poetry), as another example of a person who practiced a spiritualist yet modern art.[83]

In May 1936 (the month the Popular Front came to power), *Esprit* printed an extract from Lourié's *Sonata liturgica* (of 1928), along with extracts from an article on him that the journal had published in February 1935. The sonata, written for alto voices and chamber orchestra, employs melodies that recall Byzantine chant and is cast in a traditional suite-like form of four sections, here "chorales." In the article by Henri Davenson, "D'une musique nécessaire et d'Arthur Lourié," the emphasis is on what Lourié brought to music, which "we need so badly." For his music was not "light" or inconsequential, but at the same time it was "free" and devoid of antiquated romanticism, yet still imbued with a mystical orientation, the product of an "âme religieuse."[84]

A frequent writer on music for *Esprit* was the composer Maurice Jaubert, who was active in music for film, and worked for recording companies in Paris from 1925 to 1935. Jaubert was another figure who conveniently straddled the

Right and Left, being involved in some projects of the Popular Front, but retaining his spiritualism, encouraged in this by Arthur Honegger. Significantly, he wrote a *Symphonie concertante* for soprano and orchestra based upon Charles Péguy's *Jeanne d'Arc*, thoroughly in the spirit of the nonconformist movement. In 1938 Jaubert premiered two more traditionalist and spiritualist works, his *Cantate pour le temps pascal* and his *Ballade de Charles d'Orléans*, for mixed chorus a cappella.[85] But he also made statements in *Esprit* that would be resonant at the time of the Popular Front, such as that of October 1934 concerning the need to return to music "le sens du chant humain, et si possible, collectif" (the sense of the human and, if possible, collective song).[86] These ideals could relate to both the Left and Right, with different nuances of interpretation, as could those of Jolivet concerning the need to work in teams.[87]

It was Jaubert who reported on lectures given by both Poulenc and Milhaud, in the issues of March 1936 and May 1936, respectively. Poulenc's lecture was on "Erik Satie et notre jeunesse," and significantly one of Poulenc's main points is that one needs to combat the indifference to music of the current "pouvoirs publics."[88] Jaubert was predictably unfavorable to the music of both Poulenc (before his religious compositions) and Satie, seeing little substance in either, although he did praise Satie as a "non-conformiste-né," in both his life and his art. Milhaud's lecture, "Musique méditerranéenne," emphasized, as Jaubert reports, Milhaud's belief that Wagner's music was an "ancestor" to "le racisme hitlérien." But Jaubert's ambiguous position on race is here evident: he appreciates Milhaud's music because of its "vehement, tender, or tragic echoes" of "l'âme hébraïque," which, although "méditerranéenne," he finds "difficile à insérer dans une certain tradition française" (difficult to insert into a certain French tradition).

Writers for *Esprit* often shared opinions with those in *La nouvelle revue française*, as was the case with Schoenberg in the later 1930s. Boris de Schloezer, writing in the later, was highly enthusiastic about Schoenberg's Third String Quartet in 1938, despite the mounting tide of anti-Semitism in France. In 1939, when Schoenberg's Fourth String Quartet was performed at the Société Nationale, it won the praise of both de Schloezer and of René Leibowitz, in *Esprit*. The latter frequently disagreed with Jaubert, who defended Stravinsky (if not Poulenc); for Leibowitz, Stravinsky's music was devoid of the spiritual, while for Jaubert his traditional elements made his work accessible.[89]

Esprit, in general, did appreciate the music of Maurice Ravel, as seen in Henri Sauveplane's article of April 1933, "D'une audition du *Concerto pour Piano et Orchestre* de Maurice Ravel."[90] Here he notes that although many do not consider Ravel's music "profound," this is an error, for one cannot separate the "petite" from the "profonde." His position thus mediates those we have seen on the Left and the profascist Right through an argument that was characteristic of Ravel and his circle at the turn of the century. But *Esprit* was not alone in its progressive opinions concerning music: even more conservative nonconformist journals, or those "anchored" on the Right, maintained an interest in music, and shared similar musical tastes.

One illuminating case of such "progressivism" is that of the young jazz scholar Hugues Panassié, who was a member of Action Française but grew weary of its strict, retrogressive aesthetic. As Ludovic Tournès has observed, Panassié's interest in jazz must be seen within the context of the attempted "emancipation" of the young Maurrassians from the narrow aesthetic canon of the league.[91] In 1934, at the peak of nonconformist intellectual ferment in France, Panassié published a groundbreaking study of recent jazz currents titled *Le jazz hot*. Strongly influenced by, and frequently citing, Jacques Maritain in defense of new cultural values (if to buttress traditional beliefs), the book is both progressive and conservative at once.

Panassié uses the study to assert an emphatically anti-intellectual stance within the context of the conservative, corporatist social model that he still held.[92] Jazz here no longer represents rebellion or freedom, nor indigenous black music, as it had for Wiéner and Les Six: it rather becomes a model of sensitive, unwritten interaction between individuals. Moreover, in a specifically racial sense it serves as an argument to assert the superiority of whites, for according to Panassié white musicians took over and "perfected" the raw material of the blacks.[93] Performers such as Paul Whiteman, he argues, appropriated and refined the art of jazz by bringing to it the resources of their "superior" culture, and thus "improving" black music. Jazz, then, becomes a material of rejuvenation for a failing Western culture, or a means to combat decadence through infusion of a new current characterized by intuitive interaction.

NONCONFORMISM AND MUSICAL INNOVATION: RECONTEXTUALIZING JEUNE FRANCE

Among contemporary composers, who were producing the very kind of music called for so ardently in journals like *Esprit*, was the young Olivier Messiaen. He, along with three other young composers—André Jolivet, Yves Baudrier, and Jean Yves Daniel-Lesur—formed Jeune France, which was manifestly impregnated with the ideals, values, and rhetoric of the nonconformist movement. Again, although nonconformist ideals were waning in literature by 1936, because of the polarization triggered by the Popular Front, they were just now beginning to resonate in music.[94]

Jeune France neither overtly "practiced" nor negated politics, but, like nonconformists, asserted an implicit cultural opposition to established ideological-aesthetic stances. Defining itself against the narrow aesthetic ideals of the Popular Front, the group also opposed those of both the traditional Right and of French fascists. Their quest was not for "l'art pour l'art," but for a new kind of salutary "cultural force"—one that was, above all, spiritual, as that promoted by the nonconformist movement. It was, however, not a spirituality or ideal of transcendence that masked an exclusionary, purist vision like that of French fascists; rather, it was all-inclusive, or intended to be authentically universal. A very different "politics of spirit" and attempt to confront desacralization, it advocated spirituality, nobility, and romantic subjectivity, or *lyrisme*, but imbued these terms with new meaning. This applied equally to the vaunted *unanisme* being called for by the Popular Front, for Jeune France extended its significance to a truly universal dimension, or to those human qualities that unite all peoples. The sources of the group's innovations within tradition, then, were rooted in a spiritual and social ideal that shared its fundamental tenets with the intellectual tendencies of the nonconformist movement. Neither group, again, was narrowly "political," nor claimed an autonomy from political or social concerns: both were rather attempting to address the issues on philosophical and spiritual grounds.

Their generation faced concerns far different from those that confronted the generation that came of age immediately following the First World War, and which, as we have seen, confronted the political-cultural tensions of the thirties more overtly.[95] The nonconformist generation in music found their roots in spiritualist currents of the twenties, not only in philosophers such as Jacques Maritain, but in composers like Charles Tournemire. Maritain's appeal, once again, was related to his "universalizing" view of religion, particularly in the aftermath of Mussolini's invasion of Ethiopia. For some of the members of Jeune France, this would be complemented by the impact of ensembles from North Africa, French Equatorial Africa, and the Caribbean that they were able to hear at the Colonial Exposition of 1931.[96]

Both Maritain and Charles Tournemire were important links to this generation, for the latter produced his *L'orgue mystique* between 1927 and 1932. In this work he attempted, like Maritain, to join the medieval and the modern, in part through the creative paraphrasing of Gregorian chant, which would influence Olivier Messiaen, who himself discovered Maritain at the age of eighteen, after Maritain's rejection of the Action Française.[97] But the younger generation, only children in the twenties, as opposed to the "generation of 1914," found the established aesthetic-political choices of the thirties to be difficult, hence tensions with these choices activate their works. And like their elders during World War I, by the later 1930s they saw that the margins for opposition to the pervasive conservative hegemony in culture were small. Finally, just as Les Six originally, they had to make a place for themselves professionally, and elicit support initially (during the Popular Front) from those outside official circles.

The formation of Jeune France had been preceded by another group dedicated specifically to the performance of chamber music, and which had included three of its four members. Messiaen, Daniel-Lesur, and André Jolivet, along with Georges Migot (a pupil of Widor) and the older Scholiste Paul Le Flem, had formed the concert society called Spirale.[98] Not only did its name evoke d'Indy's favored image, a symbol of progress that builds upon tradition, it held its concerts in the Schola Cantorum. This, of course, was not the only independent concert society devoted to new music in the period—also prominent was Triton, founded by Pierre-Octave Ferroud, as well as the Serenade Concerts, founded by the princesse de Polignac and her friends. All three societies were open to international innovations, including those of the Second Viennese School: Webern's Five Pieces for Orchestra were performed by Spirale on 19 November 1936, and his Quartet for Violin, Clarinet, Tenor Saxophone and Piano by Triton on 10 May 1937. Prompted by Berg's death, Spirale gave a concert entirely dedicated to his works (on 5 May 1936), and by 1938 even the Société Nationale was performing Berg's Four Pieces for Clarinet and Piano. Despite Spirale's roots in tradition, its members (together with figures such as René Leibowitz) considered the music of the Second Viennese School as "spiritual," solidly constructed, and ultimately based upon the musical past.[99]

The idea for the group Jeune France originated when the composer Yves Baudrier heard a performance of Messiaen's *Les offrandes oubliées*, probably in 1931, at the Société des Concerts du Conservatoire. Baudrier decided that it was time to begin a movement to foster the development of symphonic music, which he and others perceived as being presently neglected in France. As we have seen, the major concerns of French officials involved in the arts in this period were social utility and combating fascist traditionalism and romanticism. According to Baudrier, however, there was another compelling reason to found the group: his attraction to the "mouvement spiritualiste" that was beginning to draw young composers.

In invoking this movement Baudrier was undoubtedly making reference to the nonconformist groupings in literature and philosophy of the early 1930s. And certainly, he was aware that the older generation, principally the Scholistes, including Paul Le Flem and d'Indy, associated symphonic music with the elevated and the spiritual. Baudrier himself had already written a provocative symphonic work—a "poème cinématographique" titled *Le musicien dans la cité*. Significantly, since the time of Sorel and Valois, "la cité française" denoted those common spiritual values as well as the political system that expressed the true French community.[100]

THE FRAMING MANIFESTO AND ITS DISCOURSE

It was in the midst of the clash of aesthetic models and associated ideologies as well as the call for a new spiritual art, rooted in tradition yet progressive, that Jeune France premiered, complete with manifesto, three days before the Popular Front officially assumed power. Defining itself provocatively against the two political-cultural extremes, it invoked and addressed their respective discourses in its manifesto as well as its program. Contrary to previous histories, which have placed its argument within a primarily musical context, I maintain that its sources were partly ideological, and that intertextual reference to the nonconformist movement is clear.

Indeed, the rhetoric of the nonconformist movement impregnated the group's public statements, including most prominently perhaps its motto: "retour au lyrisme, à l'humaine."[101] In addition, the group's manifesto, of 3 June 1936 (the date of their first public concert) is highly revealing of their intellectual sources. Significantly, it was drafted by one of its own members, Yves Baudrier, as opposed to being written by a promoter, as in the case of Jean Cocteau and Les Six. Again, appearing shortly before the government of the Popular Front was officially installed, it should be interpreted, at least in part, in light of this event. Baudrier saw that although no longer politically viable by 1936, given the polarization of Right and Left, the nonconformist movement of French youth was now resonant ideologically and aesthetically.

In this document, which "framed" their premiere, the group was already defining itself clearly against the artistic rhetoric characteristic of the established Left of the period. But it equally positioned itself with regard to the French traditional Right and the fascists, thus defining for the group, like the literary nonconformists, a new political-cultural "space."[102] Recalling the many manifestos of the earlier nonconformist journals, theirs employs an argument that stresses "the human" and an "aggressive spirituality." It was similarly a "call to combat," to confront the "crisis of civilization" and the dehumanizing forces of modernity, or to posit "the spiritual" as a progressive force. Although ostensibly discussing music, the discourse of this manifesto, like that of the nonconformists, was consistently bivocal—simultaneously invoking both ideology and aesthetics.[103]

The manifesto, although drafted by Baudrier, was approved by the other three members of the group, and thus, as a statement of their fundamental principles, should be here quoted in full:

> Les conditions de la vie devenant de plus en plus dures, mécaniques et impersonnelles, la musique doit d'apporter sans rejet, à ceux qui l'aiment, sa violence spirituelle et ses réactions généreuses. La Jeune France reprenant le titre que créa autrefois Berlioz, poursuit la route où durement chemina autrefois le maître: groupement musical de quatre jeunes compositeurs français, Olivier Messiaen, Daniel-Lesur, André Jolivet et Yves Baudrier, la "Jeune France" se propose la diffusion d'oeuvres jeunes, libres, aussi éloignés d'un poncif révolutionnaire que d'un poncif académique.
>
> Les tendances de ce groupement seront diverses, elles ne s'accordent que par le même désir de ne satisfaire que la sincérité, la générosité et la conscience artistique; son but est de créer et de faire créer une musique vivante.
>
> Dans chaque concert, la "Jeune France" forme un jury libre, pour faire exécuter, dans la mesure de ses moyens, une ou plusieurs oeuvres, caractéristiques d'une tendance intéressante dans le cadre de ses aspirations.
>
> Elle espère aussi encourager la jeune école française que l'indifférence ou la pénurie des pouvoirs officiels laisse mourir et continuer avec foi, l'oeuvre des grands aînés, qui firent de la musique française, dans ce siècle, l'un des purs joyaux de la civilisation.[104]
>
> [The conditions of life becoming harder and harder, mechanical and impersonal, music must bring without rejection, to those who love it, its spiritual violence and its generous reactions. Jeune France, taking up the title that Berlioz formerly created, pursues the route that the master formerly walked with difficulty: a musical grouping of four young French composers, Olivier Messiaen, Daniel-Lesur, André Jolivet, and Yves Baudrier, Jeune France proposes the diffusion of young, free works, as distant from a revolutionary stereotype as from an academic stereotype.
>
> The tendencies of this grouping are diverse, they only accord in the same desire to satisfy only sincerity, generosity and the artistic conscience; its goal is to create and to have created a living music.
>
> In each concert Jeune France [will] form a free jury to have executed, within the measure of its means, one or several works, characteristic of an interesting tendency within the framework of its aspirations. It also hopes to encourage the young French school that the indifference or penury of official powers are letting die and to continue with faith the work of the great predecessors who made French music, in this century, one of the pure jewels of civilization.]

Previous histories have stressed the nationalist implications of the group's chosen name, explaining it as largely a response to the Nazi reoccupation of the Rhineland in 1936. Or they frequently reduce the implicit intent of the text to the purely aesthetic desire to fight against the neoclassic aesthetic, and for the romantic movement.[105] However, we must also note that implicit in the opposition to neoclassicism (now being taken over by the Popular Front) was an opposition to the current aesthetic position of the French Left. Moreover, the stress on independence from both "revolutionary" as well as "academic" stereotypes or formulae was similarly a means of distinguishing themselves from both the Communists and the traditionalist Right. And here the invocation of "sincerity," or artistic conscience and "faith," subtly refers to the tradition of the Schola (with which two members of the group were associated) and to nonconformist discourse. But particularly daring in the context is the claim that the romantic aesthetic can indeed be "French," at a time when it was still associated closely with Germany and thus being promoted by French fascists. Like the nonconformists, then, Jeune France was seeking a new cultural ideological "place" which could not be aligned within the established French political-aesthetic positions.

THE CHOICE OF INTELLECTUAL SPONSORS

The group's desire to be neither Left nor Right, like their literary models, may also be seen in their choice of sponsors, or their intellectual "protectors," intended to legitimize their endeavor. Jeune France hence presented itself under the "patronage" of prominent writers of a slightly older generation who were similarly now located between Right and Left—Georges Duhamel, François Mauriac, and Marcel Prévost. Just as significant, Paul Valéry, whose daughter had studied at the Schola Cantorum, and who was now close to Nadia Boulanger, was present to lend support at Jeune France's première.[106] Such an intellectual presence also provided a means to recruit a new audience—one that was both "advanced" and elite, as that sought by Cocteau in the previous decade. Jeune France, like Les Six in the twenties, had to consider not only their authentic ideals, but a viable career "strategy" in order to find a "place," and here writers were a key.

Mauriac, now a major figure, having been elected to the Académie Française in 1933, had been politically conservative but was criticized by the Church for his frank depiction of sensuality and its "detrimental effect on youth." Like other formerly conservative Catholics, this, together with political events such as the invasion of Ethiopia, impelled him (as Maritain) to grow closer to left Catholicism, to Christian Democracy, and to *Esprit*.[107] Like the members of Jeune France itself, his position was characterized by inner contradiction and tensions—he was a Catholic but a former Dreyfusard, and a man of "order" who nevertheless remained culturally "progressive." Although a "spiritualist," rooted in the Right, he denounced not only Italy's invasion of Ethiopia but the bombing of Guernica in 1937, thus giving his support to the Spanish republicans.[108]

Georges Duhamel, who had frequented the leftist circle of the composer Albert Doyen in the twenties, was by now an ardent defender of an "individualist humanism." A doctor during the war, he thereafter devoted himself to literature, becoming associated with the progressive Left journal *Clarté* in the 1920s. He too, like Mauriac, was a major figure in letters by 1936, having also been recently elected to the Académie Française, in 1935. And under the political pressures of the 1930s, he too rejected the current alternatives, including Nazism and Communism, seeking rather an independent "third path."[109] Marcel Prévost was similarly a noted man of letters of the period—also a member of the Académie Française, and a star of the publishing house Flammarion.[110]

Close examination of the members of Jeune France reveals similar tensions and ambiguities of position, or a refusal to choose definitively among the existing ideological-aesthetic alternatives. Most were practicing Catholics but had decisively rejected both established conservative Catholic orthodoxies as well as the "Catholic" classic aesthetic of Action Française. Like their older colleague Poulenc, they lived through the crisis of Catholicism in the mid-1930s, and although approached by the Popular Front, most participated only sporadically, and not exclusively, in its projects. They too countered its modernist neoclassicism with an alternative stylistic direction, one that was ostensibly "spiritualistic" but, again, in the nonconformist and not the fascist sense. While Poulenc was more conservative or orthodox in his return to the Catholic past, both religiously and stylistically, they explored new styles that expressed an expansive, universal conception of "spirit."

Man, for them, as for the nonconformists (as well as for Maritain, Milhaud, and Claudel), was not part of a political or confessional collectivity but rather as part of the "universe" and shared basic human values with all other men and women. But this, paradoxically, they would express through concerted reassertion of "art music," as opposed to the Popular Front, but in their own version, in which its reputed loftiness was not disingenuous. Music, for them, as for the romantics, was to be a transcendent, authentically cosmic, universal art in which the human soul could find its most lyrical or expansive expression. Although members of the group did share certain traits, there are also important points of difference to note, particularly with regard to their stylistic proclivities, or the manner in which they chose to realize their ideals. All, unlike Les Six, admired Wagner, as well as Berlioz and Debussy, although they disagreed over the Second Viennese School—Baudrier and Daniel-Lesur being hostile, while Jolivet and Messiaen were attracted, with some reservations.[111] Moreover, Baudrier and Daniel-Lesur were still openly drawn to the neoclassical Stravinsky, whom Jolivet and Messiaen, in principle, rejected, while nevertheless being influenced by his style. Finally, the former two were more consistently traditional or Scholiste in their approach, while the latter two rather attempted to realize their humanistic ideal by invoking the non-Western and the "cosmic."

BEYOND MODERNISM: OLIVIER MESSIAEN

Olivier Messiaen, a devout young Catholic, was well prepared to become the group's leader stylistically, being perhaps the most thoroughly trained and professionally advanced of its members. The son of a poet (his mother), Cécile Sauvage, who was not religious, and a professor of English, Messiaen had entered the Conservatoire in the postwar period when the emphasis on music history was pronounced. Significantly, among other prizes he won the first prize in music history in 1924, in a competition that, as we may recall, was initiated by the French government during the war. His generation, unlike that of Les Six, had the benefit of an uninterrupted, if conservative education, in which the older prize system was once again in force as a means to establish careers.[112] Messiaen, however, tried twice, unsuccessfully, to win the Prix de Rome, his style, like that of Ravel, before, being considered too "advanced" by his conservative examiners.

When studying music history Messiaen became intrigued with both early Western music—including Gregorian chant (now taught at the Conservatoire)—and non-Western music, in particular Hindu rhythm.[113] In addition, he at first emulated Stravinsky, particularly his rhythmic innovations, while nevertheless continuing to adulate Debussy (whom he discovered in his youth), as did the generation previous to Les Six.[114] Paul Landormy points out that, according to Messiaen himself, his strongest influences were Debussy (especially *Pelléas et Mélisande*), Jean and Noël Gallon (for their rhythmic theories), Marcel Dupré (for his contrapuntal approach), Maurice Emmanuel (for his courses in music history), and his teacher, Paul Dukas, as well as Berg, Jolivet, Mussorgsky, and Rimsky-Korsakov. But it is also here significant again to note the influences of older Catholic composers, particularly Charles Tournemire, as well as of Russian émigré composers such as Obakhov and the now vaunted Arthur Lourié.[115]

As Messiaen himself later noted in his conversations with Claude Samuel, his literary and artistic influences included not only the poetry of his mother and brother, but also of Claudel, Reverdy, and Eluard, as well as the impressionist and then the cubist painters. Here it is important to recall that Claudel, an intrepid believer in Franco-German cultural reconciliation, was known to be a supporter of romantic tendencies as well as of Germanic influences.[116] Messiaen himself was a fervent supporter of Wagner, like Claudel, as opposed to Claudel's own musical protégé, the archly anti-Wagnerian Milhaud. And although surrealism was associated not only with atheism but with the Left, its exploration of an inner or spiritual realm deeply appealed to Messiaen, as to Poulenc. Here we may already see that Messiaen made little distinction between modes of spirituality, pointing out in an interview of 1931 that in his childhood "the spiritual climate was that of poetry itself."[117]

Yet despite these broad intellectual interests, many contemporaries then, as today, reductively labeled Messiaen as simply a "Catholic musician," inspired by his faith and by traditional Christian symbols.[118] However, Messiaen's "profound ambiguity between the personal and the universal," as a recent historian has put it, can be better explained in the light of a tension that was common to the nonconformist movement.[119] He was undoubtedly impelled by his faith, but it is important here to recognize the impact of the innovative intellectual directions within Catholicism, which blurred the boundaries between religion and politics. As we have seen, the more "progressive" or younger wing of French Catholics, that associated with the nonconformist movement, was aggressively embracing a new aesthetic as well as seeking a new ideological "third path" (Messiaen's artistic and religious clashes with Nadia Boulanger are well known). Messiaen was initially most successful in giving voice to these aspirations and thus to the newer trends within French Catholicism, as opposed to more mainstream contemporaries such as Maurice Duruflé, or his teachers, such as Marcel Duprès.

Drawn neither to the traditionalist Catholic Right nor to the fascist or Communist alternatives, Messiaen was similarly distant in ideological orientation from the Popular Front, although marginally participating in some of its fêtes.[120] Attempting to find a place in the French musical world, he accepted positions at both the Ecole Normale de Musique and the Schola Cantorum in 1936, in addition to his position as organist at La Trinité, which he held since 1931. Published by Durand, beginning in 1930, he was also elected to the committee of the Société Nationale, and had works performed in several independent concert societies, including the Concerts Servais and the Concerts Straram.[121] But despite his "progressive" connections, Messiaen was comfortable within the traditionalist atmosphere of the "new" Schola Cantorum, having studied d'Indy's *Cours de composition musicale* since childhood, as he openly avowed. It was accordingly within the context of tradition that Messiaen expressed his ideological contestation with the existing aesthetic-ideological paradigms, or through a style that provocatively mingled present and past.[122] Well aware of the consequences and of the way in which his style would be "read," he stubbornly persisted, always ready to defend his position to hostile critics.

The best known of his works from the early thirties are *Les offrandes oubliées* (1930), his organ cycle *La nativité du Seigneur* (1935), his *Poèmes pour Mi* (1936), and another organ cycle, *Les corps glorieux* (1939).[123] Written when he was only twenty-one years old, *Les offrandes oubliées* premiered in 1931, in the full flower of the nonconformist movement, at the Concerts Straram in the Théâtre des Champs-Elysées. As an expression of spirituality, the work, however, is distant from that of his Catholic contemporaries and from the culturally rooted devotion that Poulenc would soon seek in compositions like the *Litanies à la vierge noire*. Messiaen rather invokes the ineffable element inherent in all "religious mystery," employing techniques that inextricably combine tradition and modernity in a cosmic, atemporal synthesis. Called a "meditation symphonique," and carrying in the score an accompanying text by Messiaen himself, it may loosely be construed within the Scholiste or Franckiste tradition of the "symphony of ideas." As within this tradition, the idea of struggle or combat between the opposing forces of "good" and "evil" is central, as is reflected in the titles of the three movements: (1) "La croix," (2) "Le péché," and (3) "L'eucharistie." But the work similarly recalls Wagner's *Parsifal* in its quest to evoke mystical religious experience through music, as well as in its "bodiless," rhythmically expansive flexible melody, resembling Gregorian chant (ex. 6).[124]

Like his other idol, Claude Debussy, who was similarly influenced by *Parsifal*, Messiaen attempts to destroy the traditional Western notion of time, here employing (in the first and third movement) a slow tempo and irregular meters.[125] Similarly, as in Debussy's early work, the leading role is clearly being assigned to the melody, upon which the chord progressions depend, as does the larger shape of the movement. And, as in both Debussy and Wagner, the sound is voluptuously mystical and lush, for Messiaen similarly employs a large orchestra, with a strong emphasis on the warmth of the strings. Significantly, the only section of the work that approaches the neoclassical asperity and rhythmic articulation of Les Six and Stravinsky is the violent second movement, "Le péché" (Sin). Here we find fast-moving scalar passages and almost shrieking effects in the piccolo and upper strings, as well as certain rhythmic gestures by now closely associated with Igor Stravinsky.

Yet despite the traditionalist component, as William Austin has observed, it is important to recognize that Messiaen developed his own harmonic language, in addition to always writing his own texts. Already here he employs his "modes à transposition limitée," his own synthetic scales consisting of eight tones within the octave, which alternate whole and half steps, but are capable of transposition to a restricted number of pitches without duplication by enharmonic equivalents.[126] Messiaen uses these modes expressively, for each has a specific coloristic connotation: the "Eucharist," for example, employs his "second mode" in all of its transpositions. But Messiaen's innovations, as well as his traditionalism, served a purpose that was musical, ideological, and religious, for the nonconformist religious currents affecting him were, again, philosophical, aesthetic, and social.[127]

Like his colleague André Jolivet, Messiaen reflected the nonconformists' search for a spiritual expression of man's "essence," free of the established collectivities of race, nation, generation, or religion. This further encouraged both their interests in a variety of non-Western musics, which they were able to hear in performance at the Colonial Exposition, but which they now refused to treat as inferior, or as culturally "exotic." Paul Dukas, in particular, urged Messiaen to listen to the music of Bali, which had been such a stimulus to Claude Debussy, who remained one of Messiaen's models.[128] Messiaen, just as Jolivet in works like *Mana* or *Cinq incantations*, also rejects the Orientalist construction of the non-Western as hypersexual, irrational, or dangerous, rather seeking the East's authentic voice. But his philosophical interests also led Messiaen to a distinctive range of imagery in his work, particularly to the kind of apocalyptic imagery that Tyrus Miller associates not just with religion but with "late modernism." Rejecting the modernists' optimistic myth of an "aesthetically transformed world," late modernist writers between the World Wars characteristically oscillated between "despair and utopia." Like Louis-Ferdinand Céline (although not anti-Semitic, as he was), they questioned reason and plunged into a world in which its light had been "extinguished," one that could not be enunciated in neoclassic language. Reaction to or rejection of their society thus led to a radicalism in their art, despite its traditional components—to a refusal that was also the expression of a search for affirmation.[129] And so political crisis, for some, brought "renewed engagement with the world in which man lives, or with essential human dilemmas and emotional turmoil"—a "renegotiated connection of experience and values."[130] This we may similarly perceive in the nonconformists and in Messiaen, who can be understood further in such a light, as indeed may Messiaen's colleagues in Jeune France, including Jolivet.

EXAMPLES 6—Messiaen, *Les offrandes oubliees*.

Messiaen's *Poèmes pour Mi* reveals his engagement with emotions and with the world around him, as well as his resolute assertion of his oppositional aesthetic values. Written the year of the Popular Front's triumph (1936), and premiered by Spirale in 1937, the work displays a style that is almost diametrically opposite the one that was being currently promoted. Inspired by a text of Pierre Reverdy, it displays many of the same stylistic traits of Messiaen's other works in the early thirties—freedom from "the measure," the use of modal harmony, and an invocation of the style of chant. It also bears the mark of a continuing emulation of Claude Debussy, who, as we have noted, entered the canon at the Conservatoire in the conservative postwar period. The opening poem includes the harmonic parallelism that immediately suggests Debussy, as does the nonlinear, atmospheric approach, and the strongly sensual, almost physical effect of the whole. Like Debussy, Messiaen seeks a suspension of time as well as a play of colors, but the work also displays the influence of Wagner, especially the "romantic" ecstasy of the fourth poem.[131] As Paul Collaer has aptly put it, Messiaen was an innovator, not a "revolutionary": like his predecessors in Les Six, he drew on languages of the past, but instead of throwing them into a new experimental relation, he derived a new language from them.[132] For, like his colleague André Jolivet, Messiaen reflected the nonconformists' search for new ways to express man's existential "essence," and his endemic connection to a higher state of being.

Was nonconformism "in" his music? The inevitable question must here provoke a complex response; certainly, for contemporaries it was present in both his values and in his rejection of current Catholic exclusions. For Messiaen himself it was a guiding vision that provided him with direction and coherence; hermeneutically, perceiving such coherence is essential, and understanding this specific context helps us to do so most fully. Finally, was Messiaen then apolitical because he did not discuss politics explicitly, or was he contesting the ideological-aesthetic alternatives, as were those with whom he associated? Employing a style that was innovative yet rooted within tradition, he confronted the clashing ideologies of his period, their meanings and symbols, reinvesting them with a new significance, to say something "other."

BEYOND "ORIENTALISM" TO THE COSMIC: ANDRÉ JOLIVET

The background, interests, and aesthetic orientation of André Jolivet, the other prominent member of Jeune France, bear a complex relation to those of his friend and colleague Messiaen. Educated at the Ecole Normale d'Instituteurs in Auteuil to be a teacher, Jolivet had studied privately with the Scholiste Paul Le Flem, concentrating (predictably) on counterpoint, harmony, classical forms, and Renaissance polyphony.[133] But Jolivet also had more contemporary interests, and significantly was present at all three of the concerts of Schoenberg's music that Ravel had arranged through the Société Musicale Indépendante in 1927.[134] Le Flem, perceiving Jolivet's propensity for "daring experiment," entrusted him to the more progressive Edgar Varèse, who was back in Paris (from the United States) between 1927 to 1933.[135] Of a different generation aesthetically from Le Flem, Jolivet already had succeeded in scandalizing the habitués of the conservative Société Nationale, becoming its "enfant terrible."[136]

Jolivet studied with Varèse from 1930 to 1933, and was influenced by both his concept of "sound masses" and his Pythagorean stress on number ratios within the universe.[137] Music, for Jolivet, at this point, was to become a sonorous manifestation of the "cosmic universal system," just as it had been for the ancient Greeks. But Varèse also introduced Jolivet to the serial techniques of both Schoenberg and Berg, which would have a decided impact on his generation, as opposed to that of Les Six.[138] Jolivet went on to write an atonal (not yet serial) String Quartet in 1934, but also began to experiment with the "primitive" aspects of music, meaning, for him, its magical and incantatory powers.

Like Maritain in his writings in *Esprit*, Jolivet was interested in religion as something that was suprarational, supranational, and supracultural, or inherently cross-cultural. And just as the young nonconformist writer Emmanuel Mounier, Jolivet was deeply interested in the fundamental importance and function of ritual within society.[139] Both Messiaen and Jolivet, then, recalling nonconformist discourse, were seeking to "rehumanize" music by reintegrating it into a larger cosmic conception, making man once again united and meaningful within the "universe." Music was to be used to find the common link between all religions, cultures, and races, as well as between humanity and the unseen forces acting upon it.[140]

The fruits of these beliefs, as well as Varèse's Pythagorean theories, may be seen in Jolivet's *Mana*, of 1935, a work that attracted the attention of Messiaen, who wrote a highly laudatory review of it.[141] Both Jolivet and Messiaen were deeply interested in Eastern religiosity, as well as in its sense of ritual, which Jolivet attempted to incorporate into *Mana*, a set of six pieces for piano.[142] "Mana" refers to "that force which may connect a human being with some inanimate object," in other words his fetish, as in "primitive" conceptions of magic.[143] Each of the six pieces is thus devoted to an African totem, an object of wood or metal (gifts of Varèse) the "life force" or power of which is to be conveyed through the music. The performance of the music thus becomes a kind of ritual action in Jolivet's conception, since, as in African culture, it is inherently invested with magical, incantatory, powers.

Here it is important to recall the impact of the Colonial Exposition in Paris, which opened in 1931 to celebrate "the colonial achievement" and imperial future of France. In the Exposition, hired participants (including dance groups and musicians) in native dress were to "present" their culture to the French—to legitimize it by "wrapping" it in the context of French culture. The West Indian and African countries thus "staged" included Martinique, Réunion, and Guadeloupe, Algeria and North Africa; they also included French West and Equatorial Africa, comprising French Guinea, the Ivory Coast, Dahomey, Senegal, Mauritania, Sudan, Upper Volta, and Niger, as well as Togo and Cameroon. Despite the purported intent, the impact of these cultures was evidently profound on modern composers such as Jolivet, who "unwrapped" them, perceiving their indigenous vision as well as their power. Their "exposure" of such representations might well have been influenced by the "counterexposition," the "Exposition anti-impériale," which, with the collaboration of such noted surrealists as Aragon, Breton, and Eluard, and the sponsorship of the Communist Party, focused on colonialist exploitation and violence.[144]

As Messiaen pointed out in his article on *Mana*, which was later abstracted as a preface to the printed score, the work itself seems to exercise a "magic spell," and despite its various influences is stylistically "indefinable." The rhythm avoids repetition, proceeding by variation and "dislocation," and the melody, characterized by disjointed intervals and leaps of register, revolves around a pivot note, which acts as a sort of dominant (ex. 7). But the composition is still unequivocally atonal, employing a combination of perfect and augmented fourths, with both upper and lower resonances. According to Messiaen, the real originality of the composition, however, lies in its new conception of "soundspacing"—the low and high registers are opposed, blended, interpenetrated, or separated, in constant change. Yet Messiaen is at his most eloquent when describing Jolivet's innovative approach to silence, and indeed here reveals the emotional force he finds in Jolivet's style. For him, Jolivet "plays with silence: he allows it to spread freely round one line, then thickens it with heavy resonance, then cuts it up wildly with grating rhythms, and after whirling up through space its last remnants with angry drums on mysterious bells, kills it suddenly with a gigantic gong stroke."[145] Here we encounter not only description of a style, but a new manner of talking about music—its vocabulary, metaphors, and images radically different from that which preceded it. It rather resembles both poetic language and that of nonconformist writers, who similarly sought a new frame of reference, rooted in different world religions and in "the cosmic."

Similarly, Jolivet's *Cinq incantations*, of 1935, for solo flute, seek to evoke the primitive, "pure" emotions of humanity, free of historical contingencies and of everyday life. In an attempt to represent art as a natural force for primitive man, Jolivet strives to mesmerize his listeners, in fact, to make them unaware of the very passage of time. He thus repeats a simple chant-like melody with hypnotic effect, and achieves an ecstatic intensity through the use of extremes of range, repeated breath attacks, pitch-bending, and flutter-tonguing. Jolivet's goal here, as is all his works of the period, is to convince that art is not to be "understood" but "experienced" viscerally and mystically through faith, crossing boundaries of nation, race, and realms of existence. In many of his works, he similarly seeks the effect and power of religious "incantation," thus obscuring (like Debussy) the Western sense of ordinary, linear time.[146]

As we noted in *Mana* and *Cinq incantations*, Jolivet transcends "Orientalism," or a construal of the non-Western as "other," attempting, again like Debussy, to reintegrate the two cultures, or to penetrate authentically and therefore valorize the "East."[147] Again, non-Western art is no longer to be "wrapped" with the carapace of European high culture in order to provide it with colonialist legitimation; rather, it is to be "unwrapped," its language to become Jolivet's own.[148] For his goal is a "universal" language, attained through a true entry into other cultures and search for points of contact—a response that was triggered by his sense of civilization's current crisis.[149]

Even more so than Messiaen, Jolivet, like the nonconformists, was torn between political-aesthetic alternatives, for despite the iconoclasm of his aesthetic, so different from the Popular Front's, he did participate in some of its programs. Sometimes described in the musical press as being close to the Communist Party, or having the aura of a "leftist militant," the truth is indeed as complex as his generation. Like that of 1914, his was initially pulled between opposed political choices, but it found a new, more compatible orientation in the nonconformist proposition of a "third path." Just as other leftists, such as Emmanuel Mounier and Denis de Rougemont, Jolivet sought out various alternatives to a failing democracy—not only in Communism, but in "spirituality."[150] Hence his profound vacillation, like Jaubert's, even within the year 1936, between the answers proposed by the French Far Left and that of modern spiritualist circles.

In an article of 1939, Jolivet's rhetoric was now characteristically distant from that of the Popular Front, invoking both physics and the magical, and employing substantially different metaphors for "the crowd": "Une foule—une salle pleine d'auditeurs—c'est une conflagration de magnétismes individuels qui, le plus souvent, interfèrent, dont la musique doit provoquer l'intégration et l'amplification dans son champ de forces." (A hall full of listeners—it is a conflagration of individual magnetisms that, most often, interfere, of which the music must provoke the integration and amplification of its field of force.)[151] The vision is that, not of a Wagnerian "total art," but, in essence, of a mystical and spiritual fusion, a conception far closer to the new spirituality of nonconformist circles than to either Right or Left. Jolivet's modernism then, like Messiaen's, and like that of artists in fin-de-siècle Vienna, as Carl Schorske has so incisively shown, vacillated between avant-garde "rupture" and a "transmuted tradition."[152] Jolivet's political oscillations, once again, were not uncharacteristic; as Tony Judt has observed, with the advent of the Popular Front "many of the nonconformists of the early thirties placed their hope in the promise of radical social transformation from above."[153] Moreover, a simultaneous sympathy for nonconformism and Communism was thus also common, for both shared a concern with decay and corruption and hence a hope for renewal.[154]

The other members of Jeune France, Yves Baudrier and Jean Yves Daniel-Lesur, shared these tensions, although they were not as well known as composers at the time and would ultimately have less productive careers. Baudrier, who drafted the manifesto, had, in fact, published nothing before 1935, when he first met Messiaen, and was deeply attracted to both his work and his aesthetic.[155] Significantly, his background was in law and philosophy, and when he came, late, to music he studied with a former pupil of Vincent d'Indy, Georges Loth, the organist at the Sacré Coeur.[156] It was indeed because he worked outside of music that Baudrier felt a need for aesthetic sustenance, and decided to found the new group, having recognized his affinities with the other three composers. But more conservative than Messiaen, his style was closer to that of Honegger, and like the latter he went on to write a significant amount of music for the contemporary cinema.

Daniel-Lesur was an organist, like his Conservatoire classmate Messiaen, and a student of Charles Tournemire (among others), long remaining influenced by

EXAMPLES 7—Jolivet, *Mana*.

this "spiritualist" of the previous generation. While serving as Tournemire's assistant organist at Saint-Clotilde, he was, like Messiaen, appointed to the Schola Cantorum, but a year earlier, in 1935.[157] It was here, as a professor of counterpoint, that Daniel-Lesur organized the concerts of the group Spirale, which, as we have noted, directly preceded Jeune France, and was close to the Scholiste tradition.[158] Daniel-Lesur's style was, understandably, strongly influenced by that of Charles Tournemire, who had himself been a pupil of César Franck, a composer revered at the Schola.[159] Tournemire, in turn, had helped to disseminate aspects of the Schola's teaching at the Conservatoire after the war, when he was appointed, and would influence a new generation of students. Daniel-Lesur was among them, and was drawn to counterpoint as well as to the traditional Gregorian modes, as well as to the composers long in the Schola's canon—those of the Renaissance and the French "classics" like Rameau.[160]

CRITICAL READINGS ON THE RIGHT AND THE LEFT

The first orchestral concert of Jeune France took place on 3 June 1936, at the prestigious Salle Gaveau, with notable intellectual figures prominent in the audience.[161] Performed by the Orchestre Symphonique de Paris, under the direction of Roger Desormière, the program diplomatically included a piece by a member of the older generation—Germaine Tailleferre's *Ballade pour piano et orchestre*. Indeed, Tailleferre was given top billing, as was Ricardo Viñes, the dedicatee, who performed the work—a sure manner of attracting an audience for an unknown group. But to clarify its aims, the first concert began with a "commentaire" on both the authors and the works, or a kind of intellectual preparation intended to "initiate" the audience aesthetically.[162] The program itself was a subtle, indirect, yet implicit critique of the then official taste, one already clearly biased toward "the popular," the forthright and the immediately accessible. It began with Messiaen's "Hymne au Saint-Sacrement," followed by Baudrier's symphonic poem, *Raz de Sein*, Daniel-Lesur's *Suite française*, and Jolivet's *Danse incantatoire*. Desormière conducted the second concert as well, one also with orchestra and at the Salle Gaveau, on 4 June 1937; the third orchestral concert, however, did not occur until much later, in 1938, following the fall of the Popular Front, and thus in an aesthetically more propitious climate. It took place at the Ecole Normale de Musique, where, as we may recall, Messiaen was now a member of the school's faculty. The last of Jeune France's orchestral concerts was given at a moment of dire political crisis and anxiety—in 1939, just before its members were to be mobilized for war.[163]

But in addition to orchestral concerts the group held chamber music sessions, which were organized by a group of amateurs and patrons called Les Amis de la Jeune France. These concerts included works not only by members of the group itself but by other composers whom they wished to promote, including Georges Migot and (diplomatically) Jean Français. Migot, like Messiaen, was devoutly religious, and absorbed with philosophy and with medieval music, and similarly fascinated with ritual as well as with the "secret" spiritual power of music.164 Jean Français was, significantly, a student of Nadia Boulanger, who, as we may recall, was a colleague of Messiaen at the Ecole Normale and with whom he had tense relations.165

The group's concerts spanned several governments, in effect, the period of the Popular Front's rise and fall, but because Jeune France reflected the nonconformists' search for a "third path," it found supporters across the political spectrum. Its emotional resonance grew even stronger as the political crisis peaked, and France was threatened not only by an external menace but by an internal symbolic and moral collapse.

At first, of course, the praise of the Left was more limited, which is hardly surprising given the predominant aesthetic of the Popular Front, and the distance of the group's aesthetic from it. But Jolivet, as we may recall, was a visible supporter of the Popular Front, as well as being a participant in its projects and close politically to the Communist Party. Hence Auric did laud their first concert (which, again, included a work of Tailleferre) in the Socialist journal for which he was a critic, the now prominent *Marianne*.166 Yet the most consistently enthusiastic and supportive responses came from both the conservative and profascist press, particularly in the crisis-ridden years that followed, toward the end of the decade.

The politically conservative Sauguet, whose aesthetic and style, as we have noted, was distant, nevertheless enthusiastically praised the group and its concerts in the conservative Right paper *Le jour*. And *L'excelsior* specifically applauded them for not pursuing "la politique musicale," meaning, within this context, the openly engaged aesthetic of the current French Left. But as we have seen, they pursued a different "kind" of politics in stressing the "human" import of art, one with a "cosmic" sense, defying boundaries, as did the nonconformist movement.167 The more conservative members of Les Six perceived this—Poulenc was indeed impressed with their art, and Honegger, who shared certain stylistic proclivities and values, was a supporter of the young Messiaen.168

But it was the profascist press, in particular, that singled out Jeune France's "spirituality" and elevation of thought, its identification with the romantic movement, and its promotion of symphonic music. The profascists' conception of the spiritual, however, as we saw, was substantially different from that of Jeune France, for they conceived it as socially instrumental, or as a means to achieve collective cohesion. *Je suis partout* ardently praised Messiaen's *Les prismes* (or his *Chants de terre et de ciel*) not only for its "tendresse voilée" (veiled tenderness), but also for its "sentiment Chrétien," or, as the review continues, its "mysticisme."169 André Coeuroy perhaps best summed up the sentiments of Jeune France's supporters in both the conservative and profascist press, the aesthetics of which, as we have noted, were now converging: "On les aime bien, ces quatre petits frères spiritualistes. . . . Ils sont chefs de file de ce courant de haute pensée qui a régénéré avec bonheur la musique française." (We like them well, these four little spiritualist brothers. . . . They are leaders of the current of elevated thought that has happily regenerated French music.)170 Once more, elevation of thought and transcendence became cardinal values in French music, in consonance with shifting French political values and the pervasive sentiment of impending crisis. But, again, they carried different nuances: Jeune France, if now "legitimate," still retained its original sense of "oppositionality"—its search for a more viable, nonconformist "third path."

Part 3: Seeds of the Vichy and Resistance Aesthetics

REDEFINING "FRENCHNESS" IN MUSIC

As we have seen, with the fall of the Popular Front aesthetic legitimacy in French music had begun precipitously to shift, so closely had the government bound its politics to a specific aesthetic. By 1938 and 1939 the trend in French musical taste was unmistakably toward tradition and "spirit," even among the avant-garde, such as Jeune France. But again, the significance of both these values was highly diversified; shared terminology masked substantial ideological divergence, which would become evident in reactions to France's defeat. Now, moreover, with the increasing threat of war (as in the period preceding World War I), a general turn toward the past and toward "spirit" seemed to promise both unity and psychological comfort.

Hopes for peace were dashed with the conclusion of the pact between Stalin and Hitler in August 1939, followed in September by the outbreak of war.[171] As Francis Poulenc wrote in a letter of 17 August 1939, "Demandons à Dieu de garder la liberté de nos pays—qu'il les préserve aussi bien d'une croix gammée que d'une faucille." (Let us ask God to preserve the liberty of our countries and that he preserve them from the swastika as from the hammer and sickle.)[172] Only the preceding year Poulenc, who vividly remembered the First World War, had published his song, "Priez pour paix" (Pray for peace), to the poem of Charles d'Orléans, in *Le Figaro*. In December 1939, ostensibly in response to the advent of war, *La revue musicale* published a survey of leading musicians on the subject "Y aura t-il une musique de guerre?" (Will there be a music of war?). As one might expect, the general trend of opinion was that a "music of war" should be "spiritualistic," following the aesthetic model of groups like Jeune France.[173] For with French neoclassicism now "dishonored," it was no longer possible to return to the former model of "the French," and concomitantly of French nationalism as it developed during the previous war and in the twenties. Moreover, Action Française was no longer the dominant ideological force in articulating a conception of the quintessentially French—this role had passed to the "new" French Right. As we have seen, this Right (as d'Indy earlier) considered "good" German influence an acceptable means to cleanse the insidious cultural currents within France. Hence d'Indy's rhetoric was more influential than ever, and it would become increasingly so after the Germans finally attacked and invaded France in May and June 1940.[174] Religious ceremony immediately became resonant, and on the 26 May the relics of Saint Geneviève, the past "savior" of Paris, were carried in a solemn procession to the Sacré Coeur.[175]

In the midst of the trauma, in the fall of 1939, a reflective article appeared in

La revue musicale, the most intellectual of the musical journals, and it is aesthetically prescient in many ways. Resonantly titled "L'esprit de la musique française," it is not by a Frenchman, however, but by the close friend and associate of Milhaud and Les Six, the Belgian musicologist Paul Collaer. Again, the theme of defining French music was one that resurged in the later 1930s, as it had at previous moments when national identity was internally contested. And, as before, a primary concern was with defining it against "the other"—primarily modern Germany, but also the cultural forces considered "dangerous," or as infiltrations in France.[176] In Collaer's article, as in others that now proliferated in the French musical press, important Scholiste themes reappear, although in unique and innovative combinations. Collaer begins by reflecting (as did so many during World War I) on the distinctive traits that distinguish the supposedly indigenous French musical tradition. His observations here presage several of the principal themes soon to be developed during the Vichy Regime, which would palpably draw upon and expand the rhetoric characteristic of the late 1930s.[177] For Collaer observes that in the French tradition man is not considered to be independent; rather "l'homme est considéré en fonction de son association aux autres êtres" (man is considered in terms of his association with other beings).[178] Moreover, for Collaer, since the Frenchman has never really abandoned "La Terre," he is not an "artificial being"—he remains a peasant, maintaining instinctive relations with nature. Finally, according to Collaer, and recalling the rhetoric of the First World War (but here with more spiritualist connotations), French music is conceived on a "human" scale. Here Collaer is stressing not the contrast with German superhuman gigantism but the fact that all the arts in France humanely idealize the "noble" elements in man.

Equally distant from the discourse of classicism during the First World War and the twenties, and close to nonconformist and Scholiste concepts, is an article of March 1940. Charles Ribèyre published an extensive rumination in *La revue musicale* at this time, titled "Musiques d'hier et musique de demain," in which he develops similar themes.[179] He begins like so many other writers of the period by summarizing and then by evaluating the direction taken by French music between the World Wars from an overtly moral perspective. Just as writers of the early 1920s who examined the previous fifty years of the art, he assumes that French musical development is inextricably bound to national history and destiny. According to Ribèyre (recalling Robert Bernard in 1930), the limits imposed on musicians by the First World War led to the latter's hatred of all constraints, and to the desire for immediate pleasure. Over the next ten years, he continues, came "le règne de la bêtise et de la vulgarité" (the reign of stupidity and vulgarity), followed by a bitter "social war," all of which was to influence music.[180]

For Ribèyre, musically, the postwar period (for youth) was one of a frontal assault on impressionism and on "musique inspirée," with the goal of making French music more "robust." This led to an attempt to have a direct effect on the listener's "nerves," and therefore, technically, to an emphasis on rhythm above all the other musical elements. This Ribèyre calls "musical positivism," which was not only characteristic of the generation of the 1920s, but unfortunately has persisted, among certain circles, to the present. Again recalling the conservative discourse of the twenties, he asserts that this pernicious "positivism" is not at all synonymous with the classic, which he associates rather with a "return to Bach."[181]

But now, Ribèyre asserts, the situation is changing: the quest for a "healthy morale" is increasingly clear, as those on all levels of society are turning toward religious faith for comfort. He thus perceives the rejection of materialism as having direct implications for music, and expresses his hope that music in France will continue to follow this path. Citing a survey in the same journal the previous year, he notes those who here called for a general return to "le sens de la gravité, de la noblesse, de la grâce" (the sense of gravity, nobility, and grace). But this quest for "depth," for spirituality and for the "human" has specific musical implications for Ribèyre, which once again recall the meanings or associations that were established by the Schola. For he explicitly associates these qualities with symphonic music, above all else, which he links with the quest for the serious, the expressive, and the systematic, as had d'Indy before.

Ribèyre similarly remarks on the current popularity of music for organ, as well as of choral music, and especially traditional sacred genres like the oratorio.[182] Music, he concludes (again recalling d'Indy) must be motivated by "inner necessity"—it must reject the "objective" and reflect the soul, stressing lyricism and spirituality. But to protect himself from the charge of advocating a simple return to the "Scholiste system," he ends with a caveat that nevertheless reveals his basic Scholiste point of reference. It is not, he specifies, a simple question of recommending "Franckisme" or "d'Indysme," or of invoking a system that purports to "fabricate" nobility and elevation. It is rather a question of admitting the presence of certain aesthetic traits, and of recognizing that composers as diverse in style as the romantic Berlioz and the classic Couperin were indeed "bien français."[183] This preoccupation with redefining "the French" in music had a discernible impact not only in criticism in the musical and general press, as we have seen, but in public reception of new works. Here an illuminating case is the belated premiere of Claudel and Honegger's *Jeanne au bûcher* which, as *Le roi David* after the war, struck just the right chord.

JEANNE AU BÛCHER IN 1939

Not surprisingly, Honegger's star had been rising steadily in the late 1930s: now frequently performed, and with wide approbation, he was elected to the Institut de France.[184] But Honegger's greatest triumph of the period was unquestionably *Jeanne au bûcher*, which premiered in Basel in 1938, as we noted, and finally in France on 8 May 1939. The delayed French premiere, however, unlike most premieres of important new works, did not take place in Paris, but rather in connection with the annual festival of the saint in Orléans.[185] Although the event occurred outside Paris, it was nevertheless considered to be a national occasion, the yearly festival of the saint having become a national holiday in 1922.[186] Now the moment was right for Jeanne—indeed, it was perfect for a work that ritualistically celebrated a national saint, using material associated with religious and folk traditions. A transcendent, if contested symbol, Jeanne d'Arc could be linked once more with both resistance to foreign aggression, to traditional French values, and, by extension, to exclusion and anti-Semitism. Reception, again, was closely linked to shifting French cultural and political values, mediated by the press, which was consistently stressing those styles it associated, now, with "true France."

As we have noted, Honegger's choices with regard to the styles he employed were originally motivated, in the early thirties, both by his own values and by a desire to render Claudel's text as effectively as possible.[187] For Honegger, the element of folklore was central to the authentic realization of the text, and hence his attempt to incorporate folkloric elements, especially popular chansons drawn from the relevant regions. In the context of 1939, however, this was interpreted primarily as an ideological statement, or as an affirmation of solidarity with the now hegemonic conservative position. Indeed, the occasion of the performance was already construed as inherently political, for, exceptionally, this year the president of the Republic participated in the official cortège.[188]

Critics, in large part, were ecstatic: in the climate of mounting anxiety over the future of France, the work appeared to reflect the current plight of the nation, linking it to the past and sustaining new hopes. The enthusiastic reception and conservative interpretation may also have been influenced, in part, by Honegger's public association with Bergery, who was now espousing the same range of values.[189] Given the stylistic priorities of the period, most critics, predictably, praised Honegger's use of traditional popular chansons, of Gregorian chant, and of Renaissance polyphony.[190] But most fulsome of all was the article by André Coeuroy in the conservative *Mercure de France*, which focused on the way in which the composition responded to contemporary French emotional needs.[191] For Coeuroy, it was a "great" work—meaningful, noble, profound, and human— replete with "poésie populaire," and powerfully invoking those "shared memories and traditions that nourish us."[192] National memory is his point of reference, but now as constructed within a conservative framework that ties France's suffering, but inevitable victory, to a mythic interpretation of her religious, "heroic" past.

The theme of "the soil" is also prominent in the article, and is invoked in connection with the chansons employed in the work, which Coeuroy nostalgically associates with the healthy, authentic, and naive: "Des chansons passent— chansons des enfants de Lorraine, chansons de petites filles—et gardent cette fraîcheur naïve qui parfume l'ouvrage entier d'une saine et bonne odeur de campagne." (Chansons go by—chansons of the children of Lorraine, chansons of little girls—and retain that naive freshness that perfumes the entire work with a healthy and good odor of the countryside.)[193] Here too, it is the "elevation" of feelings, the ability of the work to uplift and inspire, or to effect a supposed transcendence, that so patently impresses Coeuroy in *Jeanne au bûcher*.[194]

Boris de Schloezer was predictably more temperate in his column in *La nouvelle revue française*, which reviewed the Parisian premiere of the work that took place shortly after, at the national Théâtre de Chaillot.[195] The Parisian premiere was unstaged, unlike the lavish production in Orléans, which had included the dramatic choreography of Ida Rubenstein and the decors of Alexandre Benoist.[196]

De Schloezer thus concentrates on Honegger's music, which he (in distinction to the majority of critics in France) frankly finds to be somewhat weak, and even troubling. For behind the "magnificent" orchestral clothing and impressive vocal writing de Schloezer perceives a "poverty of thought"—phrases are rarely significant in themselves, but rather rely on "effects." He especially singles out Honegger's attempt to depict vulgarity by simply "being vulgar," comparing it unfavorably with Stravinsky's work, from which he sees a clear influence, particularly *Oedipus Rex*. In his conclusion de Schloezer chooses to laud another of Honegger's compositions—his *Horace victorieux* (of 1921), advancing that here we may recognize a truly great musician.[197]

In addition to this honest criticism, another, openly biased, appeared—a "libelle," as Honegger described it, probably by a member of the Action Française, for it clearly employed the rhetoric of the league. It focuses upon the role of "the Jew" Ida Rubenstein, as well as the Freemason Jean Hervé, and of Honegger himself, here accused of being Jewish as he had sometimes been in the past, probably on the basis of his Germanic origins, his "modernism," and earlier criticism of his nonnative use of accentuation in *Le roi David*.[198] But such denunciations had little effect in the current romantic climate, so perfectly suited was the work, in style as well as content, to both the political and the emotional conjuncture.

RESISTANCE DESPITE THE ODDS

As we may also see, in spite of the appearance of unanimity, dissension persisted, under the cover of a shared vocabulary and themes, which masked fundamental differences of ideological vision. This we may perceive, once more, in the case of folklore and its divergent interpretations, which were still being contested as they had been during the Popular Front, although now more subtly. In 1938, with the Left in a defensive position, the Musée des Arts et Traditions Populaires nevertheless clung tenaciously to its previous broad interpretation of folklore. Still directed by Rivet and Rivière, it sponsored a series of scholarly radio programs with such invited guests as the prominent *Annales* historians Lucien Febvre and Marc Bloch. But the programs also included the participation of the museum's ethnomusicologist, André Schaeffner, coauthor of the first French scholarly study of jazz.[199] Their approach was decidedly not nostalgic, as it was on the Right, but rather "scientific," as well as inclusive, incorporating urban and rural life.

The contestation continued in 1939, when the leftist record company, Le Chant du Monde, assembled a vast collection of French rural chansons and commissioned leading French composers to harmonize them. Significantly, these included contemporary composers who were formerly associated with the Popular Front, and who undoubtedly had both practical and ideological motivations for participating in the project.[200] Just the previous year Le Chant du Monde had made another bold gesture within the increasingly conservative climate by performing and recording Koechlin's *Symphonies d'hymnes*.[201] But it was also at this time of rising national fear that L'Oiseau-Lyre was formed, recording both the music of the Middle Ages and classic French composers such as Couperin and Rameau.[202]

Given the shift toward conservative values, but with intrepid resistance on the Far Left, the issue of how to commemorate the 150th anniversary of the French Revolution was tense. Since the Revolution had originally given birth to the republican government, it was an obligatory republican celebration, despite the changing tenor of the Republic itself. Now, understandably, there was a notable reserve on the part of major French publications to celebrate the event, in particular the conservative but still superficially republican press. This included papers such as *Le temps* and such journals as *L'illustration* and *La revue des deux mondes*, all now responsive to the ideals of the counterrevolution.[203] But because of the centrality of the Revolution to the political identity of the more restive French Left, the issue of its meaning, and thus the mythology and symbols of its commemoration, could not be avoided.

It is within the framework of this tension that the Left continued to emphasize and to distribute revolutionary chansons, while the conservative republicans marshaled only general principles, or political abstractions. But the antirepublican press went even further: publications such as *L'action française*, *Gringoire*, and *Je suis partout* now spoke explicitly of "la barbarie révolutionnaire."[204] Against this background, the program for the celebration in 1939 took shape, organized by the Ministry of Education, a republican stronghold, still under the leadership of Jean Zay. But Zay was thwarted at every turn; indeed, the funds to organize the celebration were withheld until only several weeks before the event was to occur.[205]

Characteristically for Zay, the theme of the celebration this year was to be "The Revolution and Intellectual History," as realized in five large, historically oriented events. However, notably lacking here, as compared with the earlier celebrations of the Popular Front, was the element of "popular" participation, undoubtedly the result of a compromise with the conservative government. Performance of music of the French Revolution remained, but only in the context of specific occasions, such as a choreographed performance of the "Marseillaise," as orchestrated by Gossec.[206] Overt reference to republican symbolism was otherwise conscientiously avoided, and significantly, the official commission for the event in music was given to the conservative Florent Schmitt. In his work for the occasion, *L'arbre entre tous*, instead of emphasizing revolutionary symbolism, Schmitt predictably stressed patriotism, and even altered the text to this end.[207]

In sum, all domains of culture during the final years of the Third Republic were subject to subtle symbolic contestation, as the Right grew in strength and the Far Left continued its resistance.[208] As we have seen, this integrally included music where, although there was a decided shift in cultural hegemony, the Left implacably persisted in aesthetic and symbolic battle. The Fêtes du Peuple maintained performances in the interests of the ideological cause, as in the case of its fête for "Les enfants d'Espagne" (The children of Spain) on 26 December 1938.[209] The Communists similarly continued to stress and to practice "popular" celebrations, and to deploy revolutionary symbolism, even in the summer of 1939, despite the increasingly reactionary atmosphere.[210]

Contrary to their career interests and hopes for commissions, some composers, as intellectuals, resisted the inescapable hegemony of the Right, motivated by their beliefs or by their Communist sympathies. Jean Wiéner's first "political manifestation," as he phrased it, took place in 1938, in connection with a spectacle conceived by Jean-Richard Bloch, and held at the Vélodrome d'Hiver. The speakers at this event were committed Communists, and included such notable personalities in the French Communist Party as Maurice Thorez and Jacques Duclos. This and other involvements cemented Wiéner's friendship with Communist sympathizers and party members, including J.-R. Bloch, Louis Aragon, Marcel Cachin, and Georges Coginot.[211] According to Wiéner, it was this circle of friends that inevitably drew him toward the Communist Party, and for the rest of his life (although he did not formally join it). As the composer put it, it was their "communicative warmth," their "exceptional intelligence" and constant preoccupation with bettering the human condition that ineluctably attracted him to them. Charles Koechlin, also close to the Communist Party, although similarly not a member, continued to support its political causes after the fall of the Popular Front. In 1938, for example, he composed the music for Henri Cartier-Bresson's film about the Spanish Civil War, *Victoire de la vie*.[212] Such involvements became particularly risky with the pact between Stalin and Hitler in August 1939, when the Communists were considered "traitors," their press now banned, and the party dissolved in France.[213]

Clearly, not all musician-intellectuals were defeatist or morally "compromised" on the eve of the war, as some historians have argued with regard to French intellectuals in general. Nor were they uniformly disillusioned, "disengaged," or cynical by 1940; even members of the younger generation retained moral resources and envisioned a continuing French democracy.[214] Symbols here played a key role, ineffably articulating those values and ideals that could not be defended in rhetoric with impunity, and yet provided the resources of internal resistance.

Symbols also played a key role for the public. On 8 May 1940, Milhaud's opera, *Médée* (one of the commissions of 1938), premiered at the Paris Opéra. A story of high drama and vengeance, the opera—the last performed before the German occupation—was to a text of Madeleine Milhaud, who drew upon the Medea plays of Euripides, Seneca, and Corneille. The work itself is wrought with emotion, and, as differentiated from most of Milhaud's other stage works, the orchestra becomes more important, punctuating recitative and arioso passages, creating atmosphere and ensuring continuous musical development. Moreover, the style is provocatively varied in order to heighten the dramatic conflict: as Leslie Sprout has noted, the harmonic idioms include the octatonic and the polytonal as well as the modal. But, as she also observes, in important scenes featuring Médée and Créuse, Milhaud turns to a more classicizing language, using balanced phrase structure and a traditional diatonic language. Modern elements thus create a highly dramatic effect yet do not dominate Milhaud's score, which also contains a lyric style that critics related to composers from Gluck to Gounod and Saint-Saëns.

Presented before a full house, with many men already wearing uniforms, the music competed with the sound of anti-aircraft guns that could be heard outside the theater.[215] Although the music was by a Jewish and "modernist" composer, with strong ties to French republican circles, the audience was rapt—it clung to the work as a national symbol above contestation. Critics were more divided over Milhaud's eclectic if trenchant score while praising the sets by André Masson, the staging by Charles Dullin, and the choreography by Serge Lifar. Still, the work held the stage: Belgium and Holland were invaded on 10 May, yet the theater intrepidly repeated its performances of *Médée* on both 15 and 25 May 1940. Because of the imminence of invasion in France, the opera house slowly emptied, however the work survived, with continuing performances broadcast by the state radio.[216] Milhaud, with great pathos, heard the broadcast performance in Aix, on his route of escape from France, which subsequently took him to Spain, then to Portugal, where he left for safety in the United States.[217] But resonant symbols of resistance remained, both for him and for others, and indeed the battle of symbols would continue throughout the war, with particular potency in this nonsemantic realm.

On 10 June 1940, the French government ignominiously left Paris for the south of the country and German troops marched into the city soon after, without resistance, on 13 and 14 June.[218] On 16 June the majority of the cabinet voted to ask Germany for an immediate armistice: Reynaud, who advocated resistance, resigned, and recommended Pétain as the new leader.[219] De Gaulle made his heroic appeal for resistance from London on 18 June but was forced to invoke "legitimacy" as opposed to legality, for the new government was indeed "legal."[220] It was the elected French government that voted Léon Blum into power in June 1936, and which now accorded power to Maréchal Philippe Pétain on 10 July 1940.[221]

The new regime would soon deploy musical symbols, continuing, like its predecessor, to stress religious music, symphonic music, and music for organ, thus reinforcing the existing rhetoric of musical meaning and exclusion. Similarly, it continued to reassess what was "French" stylistically, and (as in painting) still criticized "laicism" and Parisian cosmopolitanism, revalorizing the regional and the communal.[222] With the accent on *la France profonde* and on both moral and educational reform, the interest in the *chanson populaire* resurged, along with attacks on neoclassicism as having promoted national decadence.[223] And given an escalating anti-Semitism, the emphasis in culture was on "purity" and "detoxification," especially of what were considered to be the most insidious forms of popular music. Still defined in racial terms, the targets no longer included the "German," but rather such styles as "black" American jazz, although French jazz was not excluded.[224]

Accordingly, the change in taste was not great, for already, by the later 1930s, the new aesthetic was in place: as Herman Lebovics has put it, the Popular Front's counterculture was now institutionalized.[225] Yet we must remain aware of the subtleties, for just as preceding the war there were still "apocalyptic" hopes, and "the apocalyptic imagination speaks resistance in a language halfway between hope and despair." Some religious imagery, such as that deployed by Jeune France, in the later 1930s, represented a battle with "symbolic collapse," and therefore retained an inherent "power for healing."[226] This power of hope remained latent in the oppressive climate characteristic of the Vichy regime, for here again, as during the previous war, in music there was room for subtle symbolic resistance. This we may also see in cases like that of Louis Durey, who, throughout the war, transcribed French Renaissance secular music, emphatically excluded by the Schola Cantorum as "pagan." As I shall examine in a subsequent study, there was a variegated "resistance culture" in music, which would finally triumph with the end of the war, although contestation would continue thereafter. But whatever position they supported, composers again chose to "register" it in terms of style, in the context of the stylistic meanings and symbolic battles that had gradually evolved in France. For they continued to be "intellectuals," assuming positions and accepting the consequences, yet by articulating these stances symbolically they opened new realms of vision and thus of "possibility."

CONCLUSION

THE SUBTLE SYMBOLIC DIALOGUE AND ITS IMPACT

Symbols play a prominent role in forging political perceptions and goals, and music served precisely these functions in interwar France, shaping images of the government and subtly enunciating opposition.[1] It provided a representation of national identity and culture for successive groups in power, and therefore a nexus for contestation by opponents of their political hegemony and the aesthetic expressing it. Aware that music was serving as a carrier of national memory and as a projection of identity, they pulled it into their battle of symbols, implicating it inextricably in the ideological struggle.

Music, then, was an agent in ideological persuasion and in mobilization, as well as in the formation of images, helping both to consolidate and to undermine political dominance. As such, it is part of the history not only of political symbols but of political behavior, for it possessed an enunciatory power that transcended discourse to "catch" public emotions and sentiments. Used as part of a network of ideological "impregnation," it thus had an impact on political perceptions, and not only the government and its opponents were cognizant of this fact, so too were composers in France.[2]

As we saw, the awareness that music could again serve as a national mobilizing force was developed most fully during World War I, in the state's attempt to use it to construct a unified image of French cultural identity. The wartime government here learned a great deal from prewar French nationalist leagues and the techniques they had developed to communicate their dogma of the indigenous "cultural essence" of France. As we have also observed, those cultural "spaces" that the state invested with the role of national self-representation in wartime were subsequently "reinvested" by successive postwar governments. In the interwar period, high culture, including music, became part of a comprehensive attempt to consolidate power and maintain hegemony, to impose representations that fused politics and aesthetics, as in France's royal and Republican past.

But such national representations provoked responses in kind from opponents when open dissension again became possible, and adversaries forged their own image of French values, as articulated or enunciated through culture. They perceived the hegemonic musical aesthetic as "symbolic violence," or as a means to maintain the status quo without physical violence—through classifications and representations.[3] Contemporaries could see that it was not just in Germany that music was now part of an ideological program, although in France this program was being implemented subtly, and often through indirect means, by the state. Here, as in Germany, political and aesthetic ideologies were imbricated tightly, which meant that the ideological or political dynamic of the government could provoke transformations of the dominant aesthetic. And so, in both of these countries where political ideals were cast symbolically, stylistic questions, as well as scholarship and aesthetics, ineluctably became part of the political conflict.[4]

Musicians were well aware of the fact that musical signification was affected by this process, and many, far from being apolitical, responded as intellectuals, taking a public stand through symbolic means. Several that we have examined underwent transformation, only gradually apprehending the stakes, and some, like Wiéner and Poulenc, threw their careers into jeopardy through their political choices. They responded artistically in various manners, depending on their own ideological proclivities—some by equivocating subtly with the dominant models, and others by undermining them, or embracing alternative values. But, as we have seen, their artistic responses differed substantially by generation, with youth characteristically developing avant-garde languages in dialogue with the dominant aesthetic models. However, these languages cannot easily be classified in terms of the politically progressive or conservative, and simple alignments of innovation or reaction with the French Left or Right do not hold. Those professing ideologies "outside" of power developed languages to express their contestation—in the case of the early twenties radically innovative or "modernist," and in the thirties still modern, yet rooted in tradition.

French youth in the twenties reacted critically to the conservative hegemony, primarily through cultural rebellion against those representations and meanings associated with its "exclusive" and retrogressive nationalism. Their elders responded more directly by inflecting or confronting the stylistic, classic, orthodoxies, or by making public gestures or statements that were immediately construed ideologically within the context. In the thirties we witnessed a similar situation: two generations of composers responded to the political-symbolic issues within the framework of their different styles, orientations, and experience. Now the youth of the twenties became the mature, "engaged" intellectuals of the thirties, participating in the clash of ideologies, which were polarized between Right and Left. The new generation of French youth reacted to the tensions of the decade differently—by proposing a new "path," like the nonconformist writers, one which was both religious or philosophical and aesthetic.

As we have seen, their apparent utopianism was, in fact, a form of ideological engagement—a refusal to accept existing ideological-aesthetic alternatives, and rather a conviction to define a new model. Choosing neither to "dislocate" their legacy nor to reject the past, they rather projected it, transformed, onto a transcendent plane, abjuring existing political and cultural visions. Their innovations, then, were tied to their universalist ideals, which illuminates the fact that one important vector of stylistic evolution emerged from this ideological-aesthetic response. Messiaen's stylistic "breakthrough," both modern and conservative, had its roots in these tensions, in conflicting conceptions of the "spiritual," and its national or universal nature, that pervaded these years. His innovations also illuminate the complexity of the French cultural-ideological situation on the eve of the war, in which idealism or optimism survived, if veiled by the shared emphasis on spirituality.

Perhaps it is this mode of representation that reveals most fully the highly ramified responses of the French on the eve of the war, containing both the seeds of Vichy and currents of resistance to it. While prominent writers decried the moral fiber of France, expressing collective self-doubt, French music, associated with a different, more idealistic topos, registers another range of emotions. Both hope and idealism remained, for some, although now obscured by the predominant rhetoric, which stressed tradition and "spirit," the need for firmer moral grounding, and repentance for past "sins." The collaborationist and resistance responses were both present here, if in embryonic form: the French had not lost all inner conviction, as some have argued, but it was now more subtly expressed. Indeed, if we are to "chart" the mood of a nation, we must see it as articulated through different cultural forms and means of representation, with their respective rhetorical traditions and tropes.

THE CONVERGENCE OF FRENCH MUSIC AND POLITICS

But was the music in itself political? As this book has argued, important French composers, acting as "intellectuals," did attempt to respond stylistically, within the framework of current meanings, to the major ideological questions of their period. The universal or the national, how to "defend" French culture from its "enemies," within and without, and how to reimbue culture with a spiritual dimension were issues that all French intellectuals successively faced. The ideas and values with which they responded were indeed factors in their artistic endeavors, as were the symbols and meanings to which they reacted, those defined in the political realm. Yet composers, as we have seen, did not just mirror the ideology expressed in discourse: there was no clear alignment of ideas or a specific ideology with the "the notes" themselves. They either translated sets of values through style, were guided partially by them, or commented stylistically on the models proposed by critics or institutions through inflections within shared stylistic codes.

We have also noted the transformative process of the collaborative and creative acts, and in the latter how the aesthetic logic—that of the mode of representation emerges, as does inner "dialogy" in the stronger works. There could, therefore, be a marked divergence or tension between intention and realization, or between the ideas that a composer expressed consciously in prose and those that emerged in his art. For another component of the self becomes manifest in the process of the aesthetic, creative act, one that interacts complexly with the conscious intellect, as we saw in the case of Debussy.[5] In the compositions, then, we find several modes of reasoning interacting in an eloquent "space"—the discursive or intellectual, and the aesthetic, as well as that of the unique language of the art.[6] It was in this evocative gap between discursive articulation and artistic "enunciation" that French composers created a new symbolic register through which they could express new possibilities.

Ideological forces thus affected French music in several distinctive yet related ways—in the "attempted" or manifest investment of meaning on the part of composers, in the "framing" or presentation of works, and in the interpretive act. But all of these phenomena must also be seen within the larger, more inclusive field of French political symbolism and discourse in these years of political trauma and crisis. For not only are texts inscribed within specific circumstances or modes of communication, they entered into dialogue with other texts of the period, which makes their intelligibility historically possible.[7] In this book I have attempted to identify those texts or cultural-political discourses, as well as the codes of ideological meaning, with which these works interacted in their day.

FROM POLITICAL UTTERANCE AND DISCOURSE BACK TO "TEXT"

My goal has thus been to recreate the world of public discourse, issues, and symbols that impinged upon music between the wars, making it a political "utterance" and galvanizing important French composers as intellectuals.[8] I have stressed the enunciative mechanisms involved, the historicity of the symbolic element, and how these symbols and contestatory discourses interacted with the formal characteristics of the works themselves. As a result, I have sought to recreate those symbolic meanings and discourses that explain the gestures, statements, and decisions of composers who attempted to serve an "intellectual function." While noting the stylistic influence of major foreign composers in France, my focus has been on how they impelled both composers and critics to define their own identities and cultural goals.

But the original significance of their statements and actions have vanished, together with the world of discourse and meaning that surrounded and interacted with these musical works in their period. For, as James Clifford has incisively observed, discourse does not transcend a specific dialogic or communicative situation: "there is no discursive meaning without interlocution or context."[9] The "discourse" has thus become "text" as these compositions have been abstracted from their historical nexus, gaining new autonomy, and with it susceptibility to different modalities of interpretation. The "great" works have survived the discursive context that originally imbued them with meaning, for they were simultaneously culturally "embedded" and the products of their authors' deep aesthetic integrity. They live on, beloved of both performers and audiences, and not because, as one musicologist has derogatorily asserted, they are "easy," or lack profundity, being devoid of all tensions or "shadows."[10] Rather, they retain the ability to engage, to disquiet, and to suggest both cultural and personal struggle, although these agonistic elements have now broken free from their original context. My aim here has been to recreate it, and thus to uncover the historical, hermeneutic dimension of these works, within their initial circumstances of performance and the discursive and symbolic context. In doing so, I have attempted to establish that all which we have largely relegated to the "background"—political, ideological, or cultural conflicts and intellectual responses—were significant forces in French musical evolution.

NOTES

INTRODUCTION

1. See Julien Benda, *La Trahison des clercs* (Paris: Grasset, 1927), and Edward Said, *Representations of the Intellectual* (New York: Pantheon, 1994), 4–5.

2. Said, *Representations of the Intellectual*, 22–23.

3. On the emergence of "the intellectual" as a social category as well as the specific traits associated with it see Christophe Charle, *Naissance des "intellectuels," 1880-1900* (Paris: Editions du Minuit, 1990).

4. Said, *Representations of the Intellectual*, p. xii and his *The World, the Text, and the Critic* (Cambridge, Mass.: Harvard University Press, 1983), 14.

5. Said, *The World, the Text, and the Critic*, 16 and 82.

6. See Jacques Julliard and Michel Winock, "Introduction" to their co-edited *Dictionnaire des intellectuels français* (Paris: Seuil, 1996).

7. See Benda, *La Trahison des clercs*, 118–120 and Said, *The World, the Text, and the Critic*, 83–84 and 87.

8. Said, *Representations of the Intellectual*, xv and 20.

9. Julliard and Winock, "Introduction," *Dictionnaire des intellectuels*, 12.

10. I was requested to contribute the entries on d'Indy, Satie, Ravel, and the group "Les Six." This is not to say that no other scholars have considered French composers as intellectuals, or recognized the role of ideas in their work; I simply mean that they have not extensively explored the implications. Annette Becker does refer to composers as intellectuals in "Musique et culture de guerre," in *Chefs-d'oeuvre et circonstances* (Archives

Départementales du Pas-de-Calais, 2000), 10. Rollo Myers notes the influence of ideas and writers on French composers in this period in *Modern French Music* (Oxford: Blackwell Press, 1971), 159, as does Paul Collaer in *A History of Modern Music*, trans. Sally Abeles (New York: The World Publishing Comp., 1961), 46.

Indeed, French contemporaries of these composers initially placed them in a cultural and political context—one that more recent historians have largely chosen to ignore. See, for example, René Dumesnil, *La Musique en France entre les deux guerres: 1919—1939* (Paris: Editions du Milieu du Monde, 1946) and Paul Landormy, *La Musique français après Debussy* (Paris: Gallimard, 1943).

My position concerning the importance of "reading" or interpreting the gestures and acts of composers, especially in politically tense situations, is opposed to the naïve tendency to rely only on verbal and public utterances, as well as on letters. For examples of the latter, see Tomi Mäkelä, "Towards a Theory of Internationalism, Europeanism, Nationalism, and 'Co-Nationalism' in Twentieth-Century Music," in *Music and Nationalism in Twentieth-Century Great Britain and Finland*, ed. By Tomi Mäkelä (Hamburg: Von Bockel, 1997), 12, and Carlo Caballero, "Patirotism or Nationalism? Fauré and the Great War," *Journal of the American Musicological Society* 52/3 (Fall 1999): 594.

11. See, for example, Christopher Williams, "Of Canons and Context: Toward a Historiography of Twentieth-Century Music," *Repercussions* 2/1 (Spring 1993): 31–74. This teleology of "the material" also appears in Adorno. See Peter U. Hohendahl, *Prismatic Thought: Theodor W. Adorno* (Lincoln: University of Nebraska Press, 1995), 193. Also see Richard Taruskin, "Back to Whom? Neoclassicism as Idelogy," *Nineteenth-Century Music* XVI/3 (Spring 1993): 287–88 and 299, which also indicts the false premises and determinism on which the historiography of twentieth-century music has rested, calling instead for a contextually informed music historiography as opposed to simple "style history."

12. See Theodor Adorno, *The Philosophy of Modern Music*, trans. Anne G. Mitchell and Wesley V. Bloomster (London: Sheed and Ward, 1973), 165–67, 204, 206, 212, and 215. Also see Hauke Brankhurst, "Irreconcilable Modernity: Adorno's Aesthetic Experimentalism and the Transgression Theorem," in *The Actuality of Adorno: Critical Essays on Adorno and the Postmodern*, ed. Max Pensky (Albany: State University of New York Press, 1977), 43–45 and 47, as well as Peter U. Hohendahl, *Prismatic Thought: Theodor W. Adorno*, 200.

The indictment of "Les Six" to which I here refer is in Michel Faure, *Du Néoclassicisme musical dans la France du premier XXe siècle* (Paris: Klinksieck, 1997). See especially pages 160–62, 240, 252, 259, 265, 305, and 337. Although Faure here cites Pierre Bourdieu in defense of his argument (252), in a conversation with me Bourdieu expressed his dismay over how Faure had misunderstood and misrepresented his ideas.

Other arguments dismissive of "Les Six" in terms similar to Faure's may be found in Marie-Claire Mussat, "La réception de Schoenberg en France avant la Second Guerre mondiale," *Revue de musicology* 87/1 (2001): 180, and Lucie Kayas and Laetitia Chassin-Dolliou, eds., *André Jolivet: Portraits* (Paris: Actes Sud, 1994). All the chapters that discuss "Les Six" dismiss them in such terms.

13. See Victoria Bonnell and Lynn Hunt, "Introduction" to *Beyond the Cultural Turn: New Directions in the Study of Society and Culture*, ed. by Victoria Bonnell and Lynn Hunt (Berkeley: University of California Press, 1999), 4–9. On Althusser and "post-modern Marxism" see J. K. Gibson-Graham, Stephen Resnick, and Richard D. Wolff, "Introduction" to *Re/Presenting Class: Essays in Post-Modern Marxism*, ed. by J. K. Gibson-Graham, Stephen Resnick, and Richard D. Wolff (Durham, NC: Duke University Press, 2001), 3–5 and 18–19.

For Bourdieu's perspective on symbolic meaning and its interactive context, see, for example, *Ce que parler veut dire. L'Economie des échanges linguistiques* (Paris: Fayard, 1982). Also see Niilo Kauppi, *The Politics of Embodiment: Habits, Power, and Pierre Bourdieu's Theory* (New York: Peter Lang, 2000), 66ff., and Pierre Bourdieu, "Penser la politique," *Actes de la recherche en sciences sociaels* March 1988: 2–3. For a perspective that reduces the motivations of the government to a quest for "gloire," thus ignoring the extensive historical literature and the relevant archival sources, see Roger Nichols, *The Harlequin Years: Music in Paris 1917–1929* (Berkeley: University of California Press, 2002). See, for example, 61. Nichols largely relies on notoriously biased second-hand press reports.

14. On ideology in the sense in which I use it here, see Karl Mannheim, *Ideology and Utopia: An Introduction to the Sociology of Knowledge,* trans. Louis White and Edward Shils (New York: Harcourt, Brace, and World Inc., 1953). On the "illocutionary force" of public discourse and journalism in defining musical meaning, see Taruskin, "Back to Whom?," 288.

For discussions of the two sides of the artist, see Friedrich Schiller, *Briefwechsel zwischen Schiller und Korner* (Stuttgart: Verlag der J. G. Cotta'schen Buchhandlung, 1892) Vol. I, and Robert Lewis Stevenson, *Across the Plains* (New York: Charles Scribner Sons, 1895).

15. On the movement from ideology into art, and specifically the novel, see Susan Suleiman, *Authoritarian Fictions: The Ideological Novel as a Literary Genre* (New York: Columbia University Press, 1983), 21–23, and Irving Howe, *Politics and the Novel* (New York: Avon, 1970: orig. ed., 1957), 20–21. The Spender quote came to my attention in Carl Schorske's discussion of its implications in his *Fin-de-Siècle Vienna: Politics and Culture* (New York: Alfred A. Knopf, 1980), 354.

16. See Jane F. Fulcher, *French Cultural Politics and Music from the Dreyfus Affair to the First World War* (New York: Oxford University Press, 1999), 17–20. On the implications of Bakhtin's conception of "dialogy," see Jane F. Fulcher, "Speaking the Truth to Power: The Dialogic Element in Debussy's Wartime Compositions," in Jane F. Fulcher, ed., *Debussy and his World* (Princeton, NJ: Princeton University Press, 2001). And on the situation in literature in this period and the theoretical issues involved, see David Carroll, *French Literary Fascism: Nationalism, Anti-Semitism, and the Ideology of Culture* (Princeton, NJ: Princeton University Press, 1995), 6–7, 35, and 73.

17. See Fulcher, *French Cultural Politics and Music,* 35–44.

18. Ibid., 24–35 and 48–55.

19. On the use of politically charged images during the Dreyfus affair, see Norman L. Kleeblat, ed., *The Dreyfus Affair: Art, Truth, and Justice* (Berkeley: University of California Press, 1988).

20. On the anthropological use of the Freudian concept of "primary process thought," see Myron J. Aronoff, ed., *Political Anthropology* Vol. 2 *Culture and Political Change* (New Brunswick, NJ: Transaction Books), 118ff.

21. See Fulcher, *French Cultural Politics,* 56–59.

22. On the pressures applied by the state in wartime and the response of French intellectuals, see Martha Hanna, *The Mobilization of Intellect: French Scholars and Writers during the Great War* (Cambridge, Mass.: Harvard University Press, 1996).

23. On Bakhtin and the subversion of "monologic consciousness" see Matei Calinescu, "Modernism and Ideology," in Monique Chefdor, Ricardo Quionones, and Albert Wachtel, eds., *Modernism: Challenges and Perspectives* (Urbana, Ill.: University of Illinois Press, 1986), 90.

24. Richard Taruskin, "Back to Whom?," 291–93, and Edward Said, *Representations of the Intellectual,* 23. On the revolutionary element in Dada, see Inez Hedges, *Languages of Revolt: Dada and Surrealist Literature and Film* (Durham, NC: Duke University Press,

1983), xi–xviii and 34–36. For an excellent discussion of Stravinsky's reaction to and commentary on the war, if not a consistent intellectual "prise de position," see Glenn Watkins, *Proof through the Night: Music and the Great War* (Berkeley: University of California Press, 2002), 143–53. While Stravinsky had strong anti-German sentiments during the war, as Watkins documents (133, 140), these did not survive into the twenties, when his works were better received in Germany than in France.

25. Even the most comprehensive study of the cultural programs of the Popular Front perceives only aesthetic pragmatism and eclecticism. See Pascal Ory, "La Politique culturelle du Front populaire français (1935–1938)." Thèse pour le doctorat d'état. Université de Paris X, Nanterre, 1990. Also see his subsequent book, *La Belle illusion: Culture et politique sous le signe du Front populaire 1935-1938* (Paris: Plon, 1994). As a result, few scholars have seen an official aesthetic shift in 1938. This is true not only of the work of historians like Ory, cited above, but also of that of musicologists. See, for example, Leslie Sprout, "Muse of the Révolution française or the Révolution nationale?" Music and National Celebration in France, 1936–1944," *Repercussions* 5/1 (Spring-Fall 1996): 69–127.

26. For studies that stress the pervasive sense of decline and inevitability of defeat, see Eugen Weber, *The Hollow Years: France in the 1930s* (New York: Norton, 1994); and Tony Judt, *Past Imperfect: French Intellectuals 1944–1956* (Berkeley: University of California Press, 1992).

27. Romy Golan, *Modernity and Nostalgia: Art and Politics in France between the Wars* (New Haven: Yale University Press, 1995), x.

CHAPTER 1

1. Rouché had owned and directed the "Théâtre des Arts," where, in 1913, he had begun to present a series of "concerts illustrés," with musicians in period costumes acting out concerts from the French historical past, while performing the music. Louis Laloy, the musical scholar and historian, who was assisting Rouché in the theater, undoubtedly had a major role in this venture. See Jane F. Fulcher, *French Cultural Politics and Music from the Dreyfus Affair to the First World War* (New York: Oxford University Press, 1999), 137. Rouché had been appointed director of the Paris Opera in 1914. Due to lack of funds from "commanditaires," he had to become his own source of finance. See D.-E. Inghelbrecht, *Mouvement contraire. Souvenirs d'un musicien* (Paris: Domat, 1947), 71.

Before the war Rouché had been attacked by the nationalists, as in *L'Action française* 1 Nov., 1913. Rouché had responded astutely, within the bellicose climate, by condemning modern German art and protesting its "invasion" in France, as in *La République française* 31 Oct., 1913. Léon Daudet, however, retorted in *L'Action française* on 22 Nov., 1913 by condemning the state of the Opéra over the past twenty years. See Charles Dupechez, *Histoire de l'Opéra de Paris: un siècle au Palais Garnier* (Paris: Perrin, 1984), 45–47.

2. On the popular song culture of wartime, see Regina Sweeney, *Singing Our Way to Victory: French Cultural Politics and Music during the Great War* (Middletown, CT: Wesleyan University Press, 2001), 10–12. On elite musical culture, see Jane F. Fulcher, "The Composer as Intellectual: Ideological Inscriptions in French Interwar Neoclassicism," *The Journal of Musicology* Vol. 17/2 (Spring 1999), 2. These productions were what anthropologists refer to as "cultural performances," or a kind of ritual that represents a dramatic encapsulation of one's culture in order to exhibit it to others, as well as to oneself. Distinctive of such performance is that the interaction between performers and audience in the theater is meant to reflect the various meanings assigned to the performance event and process. See Gerard Henri Béhague, "Musical Performance," in *Folklore, Cultural Perfor-*

mances, and Popular Entertainments, ed. Richard Bauman (New York: Oxford University Press, 1992), 176.

3. On the prewar influence of the Action Française and its doctrine, especially in music, see Jane F. Fulcher, *French Cultural Politics and Music*, 120–26.

4. See Regina Sweeney, *Singing Our Way to Victory*, 2. On the battle to impose "cultural representations" as a part of what propaganda referred to as a "war of cultures," see Christophe Prochasson and Anne Rasmussen, *Au nom de la patrie. Les intellectuels et la première guerre mondiale (1910–1919)* (Paris: La Découverte, 1996), 280. On the collaboration of leaders in education, religion, and the arts in wartime propaganda efforts, see Modris Eksteins, *Rites of Spring. The Great War and the Birth of the Modern Age* (Toronto: Lester and Orpen Dinnys, 1989), 223–36.

For a general overview of the cultural situation in France during the war, see the chapter by Marc Ferro, "Cultural Life in France 1914–1918," in *European Culture in the Great War. The Arts, Entertainment, and Propaganda, 1914–1918*, ed. Aviel Roschwald and Richard Stites (New York: Cambridge University Press, 1999), 295–307. Prochasson and Rasmussen also discuss the use of French historians to help mobilize national symbols and to combat doubt, 192–93. Also see Pascal Ory and Jean-François Sirinelli, *Les Intellectuels en France de l'Affair Dreyfus à nos jours* (Paris: Armand Colin, 1992), 62–66.

5. See Fulcher, *French Cultural Politics and Music*, 4–7.

6. On the necessity of intellectual and cultural mobilization during the war, see Prochasson and Rasmussen, *Au nom de la patrie*, 212, and Michel Winock, *Le Siècle des intellectuels* (Paris: Seuil, 1997), 139.

7. In the months preceding the outbreak of war—in August, 1914—the military authorities had squared off against the Socialists and Syndicalists. See Philippe Bernard, *Le Fin d'un monde 191–1929* (Paris: Seuil, 1975), 5 and Maurice Agulhon and André Nouschi, *La France de 1914 à 1940* (Paris: Fernand Nathan, 1974), p.2. On history and national identity see Modris Eksteins, *Rites of Spring*, 179, and Eric Hobsbawm and Terrence Ranger, eds., *The Invention of Tradition* (Cambridge, Eng.: Cambridge University Press, 1983), 12.

8. Eugen Weber, *Action Française: Royalism and Reaction in Twentieth-Century France* (Stanford: Stanford University Press, 1962), 10–11, and Herman Lebovics, *True France: The Wars Over Cultural Identity* (Ithaca, NY: Cornell University Press, 1992), 10. On the resurgence of classic doctrine in the period, after the challenges to it by Naturalism, Symbolism and modernism, see Martha Hanna, *The Mobilization of Intellect: French Scholars and Writers during the Great War* (Cambridge, Mass.: Harvard University Press, 1996), 11.

9. David Carroll, *French Literary Fascism: Nationalism, Anti-Semitism, and the Ideology of Culture* (Princeton, NJ: Princeton University Press, 1995), 16, 35, 40, 72–73, and 83.

10. Prochasson and Rasmussen, 280. On the role of Barrès now, as well as the increasing legitimacy of Maurras, see Michel Winock, *Le Siècle des intellectuels*, 137–38. On Barrès's theories of race and culture, see David Carroll, *French Literary Fascism*, 26. There was a similar national reaction among artists in Germany, where "high culture," in particular, felt the impact of war hysteria. See Peter Jelavich, "German Culture in the Great War," in *European Culture and the Great War*, 42.

11. See Pierre Lasserre, *L'Esprit de la musique française* (Paris: Payot, 1917), and Olivier Corpet, "La Revue," in *Histoire des Droites en France* Vol. 2, ed. Jean-François Sirinelli (Paris: Gallimard, 1992), 171.

12. Christopher Green, *Cubism and its Enemies: Modern Movements and Reaction in French Art, 1916–1928* (New Haven: Yale University Press, 1987), 14, 190, and 153, and Prochasson and Rasmussen, 180.

13. Martha Hanna, *The Mobilization of Intellect*, 9.

14. Jay Winter, *Sites of Memory, Sites of Mourning: The Great War in European Cultural History* (Cambridge, Eng.: Cambridge University Press, 1995), 54.

15. See Pierre Lasserre, *L'Esprit de la musique française*, 236. Also see Prochasson and Rasmussen, 72, on classicism as "the language of national defense."

16. On the concept of the "construction of the author" see Roland Barthes, "La Mort de l'auteur," in his *Le Bruissement de la langue* (Paris: Seuil, 1968) and Michel Foucault, "What Is an Author?" in *The Critical Tradition: Classic Texts and Contemporary Trends*, ed. David H. Richter (Boston: Bedford Books, 1998). On the "imagining" of a national community, see Benedict Anderson, *Imagined Communities: Reflections on the Origin and Spread of Nationalism* (London: Verso, 1983). A similar tendency to prefer national as opposed to foreign composers may be seen in England, as in other European countries. For the case of England, where Elgar replaced Beethoven on concert programs, see Jay Winter, in *European Culture and the Great War*, p. 345.

17. See Jane F. Fulcher, "The Concert as Political Propaganda in France and the Control of 'Performative Context'," *The Musical Quarterly* Vol. 82/1 (Spring 1998): 41–57. As I point out in this article, the anthropological concept of "performative context" hinges upon the awareness that a performance is a cultural presentation that is rendered meaningful through context, or that the way in which it is "situated" socially determines the connotations of that which is presented. I also posit there that a specific performance, to aid in the perception of such resonances, can be consciously "keyed" in order to place it within a particular schema of comprehension, or an "interpretive frame." Keys may include surrounding texts as well as nonverbal means that can interlock in mediating the musical experience, or in inscribing its significance within a culture.

18. See Jane F. Fulcher, *French Cultural Politics and Music*, pp. 15–35. The emphasis on classicism in France, however, does not mean that the war did not result in common stylistic tendencies in Europe and in particular a tendency toward simplicity and austerity. However, their cultural construction and connotations were substantially different, as a result of the political situation and background in each country. On the German variety of neoclassicism, or "neue Sachlichkeit," immediately after the war, in the context of the bold new cultural plan of the Weimar Republic, see Anton Kaes, Martin Jay, and Edward Dimendberg, *The Weimar Republic Sourcebook* (Berkeley: University of California Press, 1994), 474–76.

19. Contrary to previous interpretations, I have emphasized this diversity of response in "The Composer as Intellectual: Ideological Inscriptions Is French Interwar Neoclassicism," see especially 204–7.

20. Sweeney, 141. The Opéra re-opened in December 1915. On it, see Hanna, *The Mobilization of Intellect*, 142; and Prochasson and Rasmussen, 176. As the latter source points out, at first, the government decreed the closing of all the theaters, but there was a change of heart by November 1914. The Comédie Française gave many charity performances and presented works intended to edify—generally of mediocre quality.

21. See "Les Théâtres subventionnés pendant la guerre," *Bulletin de la Société de l'histoire des théatres*, no date. Pièce 96, Fonds Rouché, Bibliothèque de l'Opéra. After the Opéra re-opened in 1915, it maintained much of its activities throughout the war. On the Opéra in its larger context, see Michel Duchesneau, "La Musique française pendant la Guerre 1914–1918. Autour de la tentative de fusion de la Société Nationale de Musique et de la Société Musicale Indépendante," *Revue de musicologie* Vol. 82/1 (1996): 123–153.

22. On the world of culture away from the front, and its nationalistic goals, see Maurice Agulhon, *La République 1880–1990* Vol. 1 (Paris: Hachette, 1992), 267. Marcel Proust

also vividly evokes the wartime culture of Paris in the first part of *Le Temps retrouvé* (Paris: Gallimard, 1990).

23. The new conditions at the Opera are described in Charles Dupechez, *Histoire de l'Opéra de Paris: un siècle au Palais Garnier,* 152–56. On the formerly restrictive dress code, see Frédérique Patureau, *Le Palais Garnier dans la société parisienne* (Liège: Margada, 1991), 458. When the Opéra re-opened, the display of wealth caused such public protest that Dalamier prohibited evening dress in state theaters. Sweeney, 163.

24. Fonds Rouché, pièce 107A, Bibliothèque de l'Opéra. It should be noted that Rouché's plan was one way to make a virtue of the necessity, at first, of performing extracts of works from the repertoire. The presentation of complete works did not begin until 1916.

25. "Cahier des charges, 1915," Titre II, Art. 12: "Le Directeur sera tenu de faire jouer pendant la durée de son privilège dix-sept ouvrages nouveau, dont quatorze au moins de compositeurs français." Ministère de l'Instruction Publique et des Beaux-Arts. Archives Natinales, Paris F 21–4656.

26. Charles Dupechez, *Histoire de l'Opéra de Paris,* 150.

27. See Fulcher, *French Cultural Politics and Music,* 129–30.

28. "Les Théâtres subventionnés pendant la guerre": 41. As this article points out, many of the Opéra's employees had been drafted. As Inghelbrecht observes, in *Mouvement contraire,* 154, all the national theaters had to organize shorter performances as well as adopt a less formal dress code.

29. Dupechez, 152.

30. "Les Théâtres subventionnés pendant la guerre": 41.

31. The more contemporary French works produced included Zola and Bruneau's *Ouragan* (Act III) in 1916, d'Indy's *Le Chant de la cloche* (tableau 2) in 1916, Ravel's ballet, *Ma Mère l'Oye,* 1915, and Chausson's *Le Roi Arthus* (Act III) in 1916.

32. On these hostile factions, see Fulcher, *French Cultural Politics and Music,* 17–26.

33. Dupêchez, 156. As Roger Nichols notes in *The Harlequin Years: Music in Paris 1917–1929* (Berkeley: University of California Press, 2002), 62, "The 1916/17 season opened with the one complete act of Chabrier's opera *Biséis* . . ."

34. Ibid., 158. Gheusi and the Isola brothers had been named directors of the Opéra-Comique just before the war. See "Théâtres subventionnés pendant la guerre," 38. The Opéra-Comique re-opened in 1916. On it and the Opéra during the French Revolution, see Malcolm Boyd, ed., *Music and the French Revolution* (Cambridge, Eng.: Cambridge University Press, 1992; see Sophie-Anne Leterrier, "Culture de guerre et musique nationale," in *Chefs-d'oeuvre et circonstances* (Archives Départementales du Pas-de-Calais, 2000), 21. Other "pieces de circonstances" (not performed at the Opéra, but on other occasions) include Saint-Saëns's *Honneur à l'Amérique,* Fauré *C'est la paix,* Francis Casadesus's *Le Chant de guerre du paysan* (which evokes "the Hun," who kills and rapes), Saint-Saëns's *Victoire,* and Florent Schmitt's *Le Chant de guerre.* The latter premiered in 1915, at the front, where Schmitt was stationed. It depicts peace, a battle, and a village burned, and is set to a text of Léon Tonnelier. Ibid.

35. In the "military spirit," the Opéra-Comique also performed Donizetti's *La Fille du régiment,* as well as hymns and dances of the allied nations. Prochasson and Rasmussen, 177.

36. On the original ideological connotations of *Louise,* see Jane F. Fulcher, "Charpentier's Operatic 'Roman Musical' as Read in the Wake of the Dreyfus Affair," *19th-Century Music* Vol. 16/2 (Fall 1992): 161–80.

37. On the rival ideologically charged canons developed between 1900 and 1914, see Fulcher, *French Cultural Politics and Music,* 24–48.

38. On the resumption of both opera and concert activity, see Duchesneau, "La Musique Française pendant la Guerre 1914-1918," 126-27; and Inghelbrecht, *Mouvement contraire*, 153. Cortot was born in Switzerland, but attended the Paris Conservatoire.

39. Prochasson and Rasmussen, 177-78. Also Inghelbrecht, 153, and Albert Roussel, *Lettres et écrits*, ed. Nicole Labelle (Paris: Flammerion, 1987), 248. As Leterrier points out in "Culture de guerre et musique nationale," 21, participation in charity or solidarity concerts gave composers a means to have their music performed.

40. Prochasson and Rasmussen, 177-78. Also performed were works of Bizet, Widor, Pierné, Massenet, Charpentier, Bruneau, Chabrier, Chausson, and d'Indy. Also see Leterrier, 23.

41. See Jane F. Fulcher, "The Concert as Political Propaganda in France and the Control of 'Performative Context'": 41-47.

42. Inghelbrect, 153.

43. Ibid., 141. He also points out the problem of subsistence for musicians during the war.

44. Roussel, *Lettres et écrits*, 248.

45. Duchesneau, 126-27.

46. Prochasson and Rasmussen, 178 and Jacques Durand, *Quelques souvenirs d'un éditeur de musique* 2e série (1910-1924) (Paris: A. Durand et Fils, 1925), 100-101. See Leterrier, 23. The concerts Colonne et Lamoureux also performed other recent works, including Lili Boulanger's *Pour les funérailles d'un soldat* and Debussy's *Berçeuse héroïque*.

47. On the prewar situation and the question of Wagner then, see Fulcher, *French Cultural Politics and Music*, 104-109. On English attitudes to German music during World War I, see Jean Hoover, "Constructions of National Identities: Opera and Nationalism in the British Isles, Ph.D. dissertation, Indiana University, 1999, 514ff.

48. Inghelbrecht, 154; Leterrier, 22.

49. Prochasson and Rasmussen, 178.

50. On d'Indy's attitude toward Wagner, as opposed to that of the Action Française, see Fulcher, *French Cultural Politics and Music*, 23 -24, 32-33, and 123. On performances of Wagner and the concert societies, see Leterrier, 22. On Saint-Saëns's position, see Leterrier, 22-23.

51. Bernard Champigneulle, *Les Plus grands écrits des musiciens* (Paris: La Colombe, 1946), 346. And see Annette Becker, "Musique et culture de guerre," in *Chefs- d'oeuvre et circonstances*, 11–12. As she points out, letters from soldiers in the trenches indicate that they did not agree with Saint-Saëns about banning German music.

52. J.-G. Prod'homme, *Richard Wagner et la France* (Paris: Maurice Sénart, 1921), 32. Although d'Indy remained steadfast in his support for Wagner's music, the same was no longer true of his former colleague in the Ligue de la Patrie Française, Maurice Barrès. In a survey taken by *Le Correspondant* on August 25, 1914, Barrès denounced all German influence in every domain of French culture; see Jean Marnold, *Le Cas Wagner; La Musique pendant la guerre* (Paris: E. Demets, 1918), 104. And see Becker, 10.

53. See the brochure and statutes of the "Ligue Pour la Défense de la Musique Française," dated 10 March, 1916, and preserved in Maurice Ravel, Lettres Autographes, Bibliothèque Nationale de France Musique. Despite the league's claim to be aesthetically open, it too stressed the "racines Latines" of the French. And see Leterrier, (36–37) as she points out Tenroc was highly critical of foreign influences in the French national tradition in the second half of the nineteenth century, and stressed the need to affirm heredity.

54. Tenroc was not only editor of the *Courrier musical*, but would go on to write for *Comoedia* and the *Petite Parisien*. Piero Coppola, *Dix-sept ans de musique à Paris 1922–1939*

(Geneva: Slatkine, 1982; original edition Lausanne, 1944), 114. Also see Caballero, 645, who notes that the league's motto echoed the slogan of the "Ligue Anti-Sémitique de France," founded in 1887 by Edouard Drumont, "La France aux Français." Tenroc similarly emphasized "the artistic ascent of our Latin race."

55. The festivals were founded by the organizers of the journal, and assisted by members of the league. Duchesneau, 127–28. On Fauré's refusal to join the league, and on the concept of patriotism as opposed to nationalism, particularly in the case of Fauré, see Caballero, 594–96.

56. Caballero, 133, and Albert Roussel, *Lettres et écrits*, letter to Blanche Roussel of 6 November, 1916, 248. On Cortot's official functions and activities during World War I, see Bernard Gavoty, *Alfred Cortot* (Paris: Buchet/Chastel, 1977), 128ff.

57. Duchesneau, 137. And see Michel Duchesneau, *L'Avant-garde musicale à Paris de 1871 à 1939* (Liège: Mardaga, 1997), 41–43.

58. Here I disagree with Duchesneau's claim, in "La Musique française pendant la Guerre," 139, that despite his political terminology d'Indy had the "delicatesse" not to spread his political opinions to the public at large, as well as with his argument that d'Indy's nationalism was only a means to advance his aesthetic. See Fulcher, *French Cultural Politics and Music*, 24–35 and 206–07.

59. Roussel was skeptical that major figures in both the societies would agree to join in the union. Because of his ties to the Schola, although they were now gradually loosening, he remained in the "d'Indyste" camp, strongly opposing the idea of giving Saint-Saëns a place on the Directive Committee. See Roussel, *Lettre et écrits,* his letters to Blanche Roussel of 18 July and 22 November, 1916, 67 and 69.

60. As Duchesneau points out in *L'Avant-garde musicale à Paris*, 42, in 1917 the Société Nationale was given the free use of the concert hall at the old Conservatoire building, in order to further its "patriotic project." It used the hall until 1923, when it could no longer afford to pay for the maintenance and taxes.

61. Roussel, 67–69. As Caballero points out, 611, in January 1917, d'Indy published an article in the *Courrier musical* criticizing those in the SMI who refused the merger, and thus arousing the ire of Ravel.

62. For the programs, see Duchesneau, "La Musique française pendant la Guerre," 150–53. He notes the paucity of foreign works performed from 1915–1918 because of the problems of obtaining scores.

63. This is as differentiated from from Duchesneau's view, in "La Musique française pendant la Guerre," 147–48, that the orientation of both societies was similarly toward the classic tradition of the eighteenth century, and thus away from inherited Germanic forms. Debussy, however, acutely perceived, the orthodox model of d'Indy and his followers was essentially high classic Viennese.

64. J. Bach-Sisly, *Pour la musique française. Douze causeries* (Paris: Georges Grès, 1917).

65. On Debussy's opposition to sonata form as taught at the Schola, see Fulcher, *French Cultural Politics and Music*, 183–86.

66. Claude Debussy, "Préface" to *Pour la musique française*, v.

67. Ibid., vi.

68. This was also the position adopted by Debussy's unwanted followers, the "Debussystes." See Fulcher, *French Cultural Politics and Music*, 157–58.

69. Debussy, "Préface," vi–vii.

70. Jean Darnaudet, "La Musique française: Claude Debussy," *Action française* 1 and 15 August, 1915.

71. Ibid., 15 August, 1915.

72. See Jane F. Fulcher, "D'Indy's 'Drame anti-Juif' and its Meaning in Paris, 1920," *The Cambridge Opera Journal* 2/3 (Nov. 1990): 295-319.

73. Jean Darnaudet, "La Musique française," 15 August 1915.

74. See Jean Darnaudet, "L'Orchestre Wagnérien,"*Action française* 15 January, 1917.

75. Debussy, "Préface," vii. For another view of Debussy by a member of the Action Française, see Léon Daudet, *Ecrivains et artistes* vol. 7 (Paris: Editions du Capitole, 1929), 40.

76. See Henri Focillon, *La Peinture au XIXe siècle* (Paris: Flammarion, 1991).

77. See Bach-Sisly, ed., *Pour la musique française*, 175-76. D'Indy himself had served on the editorial board of the openly anti-Dreyfusard journal, *L'Occident*, before the war. See Fulcher, *French Cultural Politics and Music,* 48-50.

78. Jean Darnaudet, "L'Orchestre Wagnérien." Also see Pierre Lasserre, *L'Esprit de la musique française,* 236.

79. Bach-Sisly, ed., *Pour la musique française,* 295. For Debussy's prewar nationalist position, see Fulcher, *French Cultural Politics and Music,* 185-94.

80. Gabriel Fauré, "Préface," to Georges Jean-Aubry, *La Musique fraçaise d'aujourd'hui* (Paris: Librairie Académique Perrin, 1916), ix. On Jean-Aubry see Louis Laloy, *Louis Laloy (1874-1944) on Debussy, Ravel, and Stravinsky,* trans. and annotated by Deborah Priest (Aldershot: Ashgate, 1999) 312.

81. Ibid.

82. Ibid., ix-x.

83. Ibid., xii-xiii.

84. Georges Jean-Aubry, *La Musique française,* 206. The author attacks Romain Rolland (1) for his support of German music, and Camille Saint-Saëns (3) for his spirit of partisanship. Fauré's Second Violin Sonata, Op. 109, dedicated to Elizabeth, Queen of the Belgians, premiered at the Société Nationale on Nov. 10, 1917, the first concert of the society after the declaration of war. See Caballero, 609.

85. Martha Hanna, *The Mobilization of Intellect,* 16. On the parallel situation in Germany, see Peter Jelavich, "German Culture in the Great War," 46.

86. Prochasson and Rasmussen, 185-86.

87. Fulcher, *French Cultural Politics*, 56-59.

88. Paul-Marie Masson, *Rapport sur la musique française contemporaine* (Rome: Arman et Stein, 1913). And see Lionel de la Laurencie, "Le Mouvement musicographe," *Le Mercure musical* June 1907: 567.

89. Michel Brenet [Marie Bobilier], "Musicologie," in *Rapport sur la musique française contemporaine,* 17-18.

90. *Bulletin de la Société Française de Musicologie* No. 1 1917: 16.

91. Ibid.

92. Ibid., vi.

93. On the bureaucratic changes in the Ministère des Beaux-Arts in 1917, with the ascension on Clemenceau, see Paul Léon, *Du Palais-Royal au Palais-Bourbon* (Paris: Albin-Michel, 1947), 189. And see the letter to d'Estournelles de Constant, Director of the Beaux-Arts, from the Secrétaire-général of the Conseil d'Administration of the Société des Auteurs, Compositeurs, et Editeurs de Musique, dated 18 July, 1918, in F 21-4603, Archives Nationales, Paris.

94. Inghelbrecht, *Mouvement contraire,* 154, and Jacques Durand, *Quelques souvenirs,* 59-62. The French had also relied on Griepenkerl, Tausig, and Bülow for editions of the "classics."

95. Durand, *Quelques souvenirs,* 59. Durand points out that his father had conceived the idea of re-editing classic works to make them more available financially.

96. Ibid., 62–65. Durand was generally respectful of wartime standards of taste and form, rejecting works submitted to him for publication if they did not adhere, at least, superficially, to current dominant conceptions of the classic. See his letter to Charles Koechlin of 14 May, 1917, in Charles Koechlin, *Correspondance* (Paris: La Revue Musicale, 1982), 30.

97. Léon Vallas, *Claude Debussy et son temps* (Paris: Félix Alcan, 1932), 96.

98. Léon Vallas, *Vincent d'Indy* vol. 1, 96. D'Indy also participated in the classic editions of Rouart-Lerolle.

99. D'Indy, letter to Guy Ropartz of 28 December 1914, in d'Indy, Lettres Autographes, Bibliothèque Nationale de France. Musique.

100. Vallas, *Vincent d'Indy*, 96.

101. Durand, *Quelques souvenirs*, 70.

102. Ibid., 67.

103. Ibid., 68–70, and Jean Marnold, *Le Cas Wagner. La Musique pendant la guerre* (Paris: E. Demets, 1918), 48–49.

104. Inghelbrecht, 154. As Leterrier points out (24) in June 1918. Gaston Carraud, in the *Courrier musical,* was still calling for a popular "édition nationale" that extended from the classics through contemporary French composers.

105. Maurice Agulhon, *La République 1880-1990* vol. 1 (Paris: Hachette, 1990), 276. And as Martha Hanna points out in *The Mobilization of Intellect* (13) recent scholars have emphasized the extent to which pre-existent conflicts in French society continued during the war.

106. Agulhon, *La République,* 1: 261.

107. Modris Eksteins, *Rites of Spring,* 175–79. On the growing dissension over the war by 1917, see Michel Winock, *Le Siècle des intellectuels,* 309.

108. Agulhon, 1: 278, 310. As Agulhon points out, one can see the dissension in Socialist organs, such as *Le Populaire du centre.* The mutinies in the army began in May 1917, about the time that Russia left the war because of its internal Revolution. On sedition in popular song, see Sweeney, 10. As she also points out, conservatives responded by denigrating or devaluing the symbols and songs of the Left, such as "L'Internationale" and the "Carmagnole."

109. Eksteins, *Rites of Spring,* 210, 214. On Dada in Germany in the same period, see Peter Jelavich, "German Culture in the Great War," 49–54. On the dissent and rejection of the written word by soldiers at the front, see Hanna, 23.

110. Eksteins, 218-19 and 233.

111. David James Fisher, *Romain Rolland and the Politics of Intellectual Engagement* (Berkeley: University of California Press, 1988), 82.

112. Prochasson and Rasmussen, 218. Pacifism was also becoming prominent among intellectual and artistic circles in Germany. On the cases of Busoni and Hindemith, see Pascal Huynh, *La Musique sous la République de Weimar* (Paris: Fayard, 1998), 48–58. On other pacifist works, see 125.

113. See Fulcher, *French Cultural Politics,* 17–20. On the marked change in attitude among intellectuals in 1917 see Pascal Ory and Jean-Francois Sirinelli, *Les Intellectuels en France de l'Affaire Dreyfus à nos jours* (Paris: Armand Colin, 1992), 70–72.

114. See Marc Ferro, "Cultural Life in France, 1914–1918," in *European Culture in the Great War,* 297. As he here points out, "irrespective of official censorship, the wartime spirit of patriotism 'sealed off'...any possibility of intellectual dissent."

115. See Fulcher, "The Concert as Political Propaganda," 41–43.

116. Hanna, 8.

117. Nadia Boulanger, while contributing to the war effort through numerous pro-

jects, did express her view of the necessity of combating artistic restrictions that hampered the development of music. See her undated letter to Charles Koechlin in Charles Koechlin, *Correspondance*, 32–33.

118. See Prochasson and Rasmussen (140, 221) on how culture was placed under political constraints during the war, provoking a new kind of *art engagé* and a more critical relation of French artists to the state as their autonomy was challenged.

119. There was by no means "an intellectual and artistic vacuum," nor a loss of communication with the past, although Rollo Myers asserts there was in *Modern French Music* (Oxford: Blackwell Press, 1971), 123. See Marc Ferro, "Cultural Life in France," 304. My perspective on how to read the "meaning" of abstract works, in effect, provides an answer to the naive question posed by Caballero (620) on how to interpret Fauré's wartime sonatas—his Second Violin Sonata Op. 108 (1916–17) and his First Cello Sonata Op. 109 (1917). They should be seen less as a commentary on the war itself than on wartime stylistic restrictions and dominant models. Amazingly, Cabellero does not appear to be aware of the voluminous literature on style, classicism, and their meaning in this period, choosing to focus on one narrow issue. His research is clearly inadequate, as his ability to conceptualize the issues.

120. Aviel Roshwald and Richard Stites note perceptively in the "Introduction" in *European Culture in the Great War,* 1–2, that conventional images could be employed in sardonic new manners. This is as opposed to the perception of a general return to tradition as seen in Jay Winter's *Sites of Memory, Sites of Mourning.*

121. For d'Indy's perspective, as opposed to Saint-Saëns, see his article "Musique française et musique allemande," in *La Renaissance politique, littéraire, et artistique* 3 (12 June, 1915): 1–8.

122. For the prewar political positions of Satie and Charpentier, see Fulcher, *French Cultural Politics and Music,* 201–6.

123. Among the powerful "présidents d'honneurs" of the "Ligue pour la Défense de la Musique Française" were Vincent d'Indy, Camille Saint-Saëns, Théodore Dubois, Gustave Charpentier, Xavier Leroux, and Charles Lecoq. In addition, it included two politicians, both deputies and co-presidents of the "Groupe Parliamentaire de l'Art," Paul Meunier and Lucien Millerange. Besides a president, the league had an official secretary—a critic of music and composer, Jean Poueigh (who would have Satie sent to jail for libeling him on a postcard after his review of *Parade*). The league's list of adherents, probably actively recruited, relates closely to the tactics it proposed, for it includes the directors of the Opéra-Comique, the Odéon, the Trianon Lyrique, and the Maison Pleyel, among others.

On the Schola's Germanic (Viennese) conception of classicism (rooted in the eighteenth century), see Fulcher, *French Cultural Politics,* 30–31.

124. See Hanna, 166, on the dominant, conservative conception of classicism.

125. Vallas, *Vincent d'Indy,* 99.

126. Arthur Honegger, "La Classe de d'Indy au Conservatoire," *La Revue musicale* 1932: 40–41. On the "Comité franco-américain," see *Chefs-d'oeuvre et circonstances,* 105. Lili Boulanger, a pupil of Paul Vidal at the Conservatoire, won the Prix de Rome in 1914, and when the war broke out, returned from Rome to Paris. She died in March 1918, at age 24. On Saint-Saëns's "patriotic" works, see Leterrier, 22.

127. On d'Indy and "the symphony of ideas," see Brian Hart, "The Symphony in Theory and Practice in France 1900-1914" (Ph.D. dissertation, Indiana University, 1994), 82–103 and 433–434.

128. Vincent d'Indy, letter to Guy Ropartz, 17 October 1916. Lettres Autographes, Bibliothèque Nationale de France. Musique.

129. Vincent d'Indy, letter to Guy Ropartz, 4 January 1918. Lettres Autographes, Bibliothèque Nationale de France. Musique.

130. As Prochasson and Rasmussen point out, 176, in 1917 Jean Giraudoux went to the United States to give a series of lectures, one of the goals of which was to impart a sense of French gaiety and good humor, so that the French would not seem to be dazed by three years of war.

131. Vincent d'Indy, letter to Guy Ropartz, 4 January1918, Lettres Autographes, Bibliothèque Nationale de France. Musique. And see Vallas, *Vincent d'Indy,* 261–62. The score was published in 1919 by Rouart, Lerolle, and Cie., as his Op. 70.

132. On the romantic tendency to make the inner movements the "centers of gravity," see Friedrich Blume, *Classic and Romantic Music* (N.Y.: Norton, 1970), pp.155–56. And on the programmatic elements, see Glenn Watkins, *Proof through the Night: Music and the Great War* (Berkeley: University of California Press, 2002), 169.

On the perception of d'Indy's reliance on Hugo Riemann, see Duchesneau, "La Musique Française pendant la Guerre," 141.

133. On Charpentier's background and earlier career, including his series of popular "fêtes," see Fulcher, *French Cultural Politics and Music,* 77–97.

134. Ibid., 97–103.

135. For Debussy's dispeptic remarks on Charpentier's projects, Ibid., 196–97 and 103.

136. "La Cocarde de Mimi Pinson" eventually developed branches throughout France and abroad. See Gustave Charpentier, *Lettres inédites à ses parents,* ed. François Andrieux (Paris: Presses Universitaires de France, 1984), 115, and Gustave Charpentier, "Souvenirs, lettres, poésies," Bibliothèque Nationale de France. Musique, Réserve.

137. Charpentier prepared the music for the funeral of the Socialist leader Jean Jaurès, who was assassinated on July 31, 1914. See Avner Ben-Amos, "La Panthéonization de Jean Jaurès," *Terrain* vol. 15 (Oct. 1990): 49–64.

138. As reported (with irony) in *Action française* March 29, 1917.

139. Ibid.

140. Ibid. For previous attacks by the Right on Charpentier and on the naturalist aesthetic, see Fulcher, *French Cultural Politics,* 19–20 and 93–95.

141. See Fulcher, *French Cultural Politics,* 179–80 and 184–85.

142. On Debussy's belief, like Barrès, that the collectivity could produce individual freedom, and on his individualistic ideal of musical form, ibid., 180–94.

143. Claude Debussy, *Debussy on Music,* ed. François Lesure and Richard L. Smith (New York: Alfred A. Knopf, 1977), 322.

144. For the prewar attack on the "nouvelle Sorbonne" and the "German influences" on it see Agathon [Henri Massis and Gabriel de Tarde] *L'Esprit de la nouvelle Sorbonne. La Crise de la culture classique. La Crise du français* (Paris: Mercure de France, 1911), 144. If Debussy sounds more like writers such as Pierre Lasserre, there may well be a specific reason for it. Debussy's agenda, in which he recorded all his appointments in the period, appears to indicate that on December 14, 1916, he planned to attend a lecture by Lasserre. No longer officially in the Action Française, Lasserre's rhetoric nevertheless continued to reiterate its basic themes and concepts. See Debussy, "Agenda et carnet de notes, 1916–1917," Bibliothèque Nationale de France. Musique, Réserve.

145. Claude Debussy, *Claude Debussy: Lettres 1884–1918,* ed. François Lesure (Paris: Hermann, 1980), 265.

146. Ibid.

147. Barrès's concept of "rootedness" in the soil informs one of his most famous novels, *Les Déracinés* (Paris: Julien, n.d.) which is characteristic of his thought from 1897 on.

148. Debussy, *Lettres*, 264. Letter to Robert Godet of 14 October 1915.
149. See Fulcher, *French Cultural Politics*, 157.
150. Ibid., 186.
151. Debussy, *Lettres*, p. 264. Letter to Robert Godet of 14 October 1915. This is perhaps a reference to the fact that d'Indy was working on the Rameau edition (to which Debussy himself contributed), which has been launched by Saint-Saëns.
152. Ibid., 269. Letter to Igor Stravinsky of 24 October 1915.
153. Ibid., 265. Letter of October 23, 1915, to a purported Belgian music critic—in reality the young Francis Poulenc, seeking Debussy's autograph.
154. See Fulcher, *French Cultural Politics*, 43.
155. See Jurgen Vis, "Debussy and the War. Debussy, Luther, and Jannequin," *Cahiers Debussy* 5 (1991), 43. He dates the composition of the work as November 1914. As Letterier points out, 25, the *hommage* was a category of wartime music, and there were many dedicated to Belgium in 1914.
156. On images of the war, see Jay Winter, *Sites of Memory, Sites of Mourning*, 143–45.
157. Jurgen Vis, in "Debussy and the War," 44, also notes the presence of a slow soldier's march in the section marked "grave et soutenu." And see the editor's note by H. Suborensky in the Peter's Edition (London: 1975). On Debussy's use of the "Brabançonne," see Leterrier, 25, 30. It has also been noted that the opening melody of the work is then compressed as chords in the end, and that they recall Stravinsky's *Sacre du printemps*, which clearly continued to "haunt" Debussy. Also see Glenn Watkins, *Proof through the Night: Music and the Great War* (Berkeley: University of California Press, 2002), which observes that Debussy (88) cites the first two phrases of the anthem in C major before juxtaposing the opening motif against an accompaniment in D flat, to suggest it being heard from a distance.
158. Marc Ferro, "Cultural Life in France, 1914–1918," 298.
159. On the concept of "hermeneutic windows," see Lawrence Kramer, *Music as Cultural Practice 1800-1900* (Berkeley: University of California Press, 1990), 9–10. See Jonathan Dunsby on Debussy's *En blanc et noir*, in *Analytical Strategies and Musical Interpretation: Essays in Nineteenth and Twentieth-Century Music*, ed. by Craig Ayrey and Mark Everest (New York: Cambridge University Press, 1996), 152–53, 165, who notes the title had multiple resonances. Since the usual French idiom is rather "noir et blanc," the reversal perhaps refers to the white and black keys of the piano, or to a "chiaroscuro," a technique that Debussy admired in Velásquez. As he also notes, the third piece does contain "music snow-white and pitch-black music." Dunsby suggests, a bit more tenuously, that Debussy could here be invoking an analogy with cinema.
160. Vallas, *Claude Debussy et son temps*, 259. Dunsby, 167, also sees a reference to Gounod's music, noting that he was Debussy's symbol for the anti-German.
161. See Frank Dawes, *Debussy Piano Music* (Seattle: University of Washington Press, 1971), 55–56. Significantly, Gounod was a supporter of Debussy when Debussy won the Prix de Rome. The first and last pieces, ironically, are dedicated to foreigners—Serge Koussevitsky and Igor Stravinsky, respectively.
162. Charlot was a nephew of Debussy's editor, Durand, and had worked in his publishing house. As Vis points out, in "Debussy and the War" (32), in January 1914, when his uncle was ill, Charlot had temporarily taken over, and was in frequent contact with Debussy, who was very happy working with him. As Leterrier points out (29) it was common in the period to draw parallels with other enemies of France's past, such as England, as in the case of Charles d'Orléans.
163. Debussy was familiar with Jannequin's "Bataille de Marignan." See *Debussy on Music*, 35. Vis (45) points out Debussy's familiarity with Jannequin's compositions, includ-

NOTES TO PAGES 57–60   339

ing "La Guerre." He cites Debussy's review of a performance of "La Bataille de Marignon" in the *Revue S.I.M.*, in which he expresses his admiration for Jannequin. As Watkins notes (*Proof through the Night*, 172) the musicologist Henri Expert had edited "La Guerre," and d'Indy had performed it at the Schola, although he otherwise condemned the French secular Renaissance.

164. On the scandal caused by Barbusse's *Le Feu*, see Michel Winock, *Le Siècle des intellectuels*, 142. For a discussion of typical "war music" of the period, including Vermealen's, see Leterrier, 25.

165. Vallas, *Claude Debussy*, 255–56, and Vis, 36ff. Debussy had already made artful reference to the "Marseillaise" in his "Feu d'artifice" in book 2 of the *Preludes*, and in an equally abstract manner. And see Leterrier (27) who also points out the frequent models of military music, popular airs, and instruments with liturgical or "heavenly" associations, such as organ, harp, or bells. As Dunsby notes (164) Debussy's reference to the "Marseillaise" is so unclear that some scholars have questioned whether it is actually present. There was a long tradition of using such musical quotations to testify to patriotism, an example being Théodor Dubois's *Symphonie française*, of 1908. Also see Glenn Watkins, *Proof Through the Night: Music and the Great War* (Berkeley: University of California Press, 2002), 92. Roger Nichol's claim, in *The Harlequin Years: Music in Paris 1917–1929* (Berkeley: Univeristy of California Press, 2002), 21, that "Ein'feste Berg" and the "Marseillaise" "fight it out" is hardly credible.

166. On the sketches for the movement and its gradual evolution, see Vis, 33ff.

167. Inghelbrecht, 144. He also performed his Sonata for Violin and Piano. As Duchesneau points out in "La Musique pendant la Guerre," the performance took place on March 8, 1918. According to Laloy, 115–16, the "Noël" referred to Belgium being punished for its loyalty.

168. See Vallas, *Claude Debussy*, 264. On the traditional "popular" character of the "noël," see Leterrier, 32. Lerterrier argues that Debussy was certain that the work would enter "tout droit dans le coeur des citadins" (directly into the heart of urban dwellers), and it was indeed popular in Belgium. Debussy was not the only one to set a text that evokes war atrocities: Florent Schmitt's *Chant de guerre* denounces "le vampire de l'Europe," and its rage to oppress and kill; ibid., 27.

169. Ibid., 267. Watkins notes in *Proof through the Night* (117), that Debussy requested the text from Laloy following the battles of the Somme and Verdun.

170. Jacques Durand, *Quelques souvenirs*, 125. The work was later orchestrated from the sketch (dated 1917) by M.-F. Gaillard.

171. Inghelbrecht, 144.

172. The *Etudes* are, in fact, dedicated to the memory of Chopin. As Watkins points out in *Proof through the Night*, 99, Debussy was editing Chopin's waltzes and polonaises.

173. On it, see Dawes, *Debussy Piano Music*, 61.

174. Ibid., 62–63. Dawes also emphasizes the contrasting emotional registers of the work, or the way in which it alternates (perhaps autobiographically) between sadness and "unattainable" gaiety.

175. Debussy had already begun to experiment with the form in his string quartet of 1893, in which he made the necessary concessions to be accepted in the Société Nationale, but still avoided the orthodox "mold."

176. Jean Huré, *Dogmes musicaux (1904-1907)* (Paris: Editions du Monde Musicale, 1909), 165.

177. One of the original goals of the Société Nationale was to "meet and defeat" the Germans on their own grounds—in the large abstract forms. This meant adapting or "updating" the form to accommodate a new, imaginative French content. On the goals of the

early Société Nationale, see Martin Cooper, *French Music from the Death of Berlioz to the Death of Fauré* (Oxford: Oxford University Press, 1951), 1–54.

178. Durand, *Quelques souvenirs*, 78. Saint-Saëns's sonatas were published in 1921. On the other classicizing sonatas of the period, see Duchesneau, "La Musique française pendant la Guerre," 148–49.

179. Vallas, *Claude Debussy*, 259.

180. Wilfred Mellers, *François Couperin and the French Classical Tradition* (London: Faber and Faber, 1987), 144. See Kenneth Silver, *Esprit de Corps. The Art of the Parisian Avant-Garde and the First world War 1914–1925* (Princeton, NJ: Princeton University Press, 1989), 158–61, on the image of Pierrot in French modern art.

181. There is also an invocation of Pierrot in Debussy's settings of Théodore se Banville's poetry, of 1880–82; this identification with the ironic figure of Pierrot thus runs throughout Debussy's career.

182. Blanche Selva, *Quelques mots sur la sonate* (Paris: Delaplane, 1914), 56.

183. Edward Lockspeiser, *Debussy: His Life and Mind* (London: Cassel, 1965), 212. On the opening rhythm and its derivation from Rameau, see Watkins, *Proof through the Night*, 101. He also notes its "reasonably straightforward sonata-allegro design."

184. On Debussy's earlier denunciation of foreign influences, even as he himself continued to feel them, see Fulcher, *French Cultural Politics*, 179-81. On Debussy's earlier satirical use of academic (especially "scholiste") procedures in his Orchestral *Images* of 1909, see 187-88.

185. Edward Lockspeiser, *Debussy: His Life and Mind*, 180. Watkins, *Proof through the Night*, 107, notes that Debussy had organized a series of concerts for a war relief organization, the Aide Affectueuse aux Musiciens, and that this sonata was created for one of its performances.

186. Watkins, *Proof through the Night*, 179; and see Rollo Meyers, *Modern French Music* (Oxford: Blackwell Press, 1971), 101.

187. Charles-Marie Widor, *Fondations. Portraits de Massenet à Paladilhe* (Paris: Durand et Fils, 1927), 6–7.

188. Vallas, *Claude Debussy*, 250 and *Debussy on Music*, 148. Saint-Saëns, in so construing the nation aesthetically, was by no means alone in this period. See Prochasson and Rasmussen, 139. On Saint-Saëns's attempt to keep Debussy out of the Institut de France on the basis of his musical "atrocities," see Watkins, *Proof through the Night*, 93. As he points out (95) Widor had invited both Debussy and Rodin to present themselves as candidates.

189. See Matei Calinescu, "Modernism and Ideology," in *Modernism: Challenges and Perspectives*, eds., Monique Chefdor, Ricardo Quionones, and Albert Wachtel (Urbana, Ill.: University of Illinois Press, 1986), 89–91.

190. On discourse as opposed to text, see James Clifford, *The Predicament of Culture. Twentieth-Century Ethnography, Literature, and Art* (Cambridge, Mass.: Harvard University Press, 1988), 39. On Bakhtin and the concepts of "utterance" and the dialogic, see Michael Holquist and Katerina Clarck, *Mikhail Bakhtin: A Biography* (Cambridge, Mass.: Harvard University Press, 1984), 207, and Samuel Kinser, "Chrono-types and Catastrophes: The Cultural History of Mikhail Bakhtin," *The Journal of Modern History* June 1984: 301–10. The concept of "speaking the truth to power" is developed by Edward Said in *Representations of the Intellectual* (New York: Pantheon Books, 1994), xv, 20. On Bakhtin's concept of "internal dialogism," or reference to that which is absent but can be inferred from the response, see Susan Suleiman, *Subversive Intent: Gender, Politics, and the Avant-Garde* (Cambridge, Mass.: Harvard University Press, 1990), 27.

191. Durand, *Quelques souvenirs*, 67. As Laloy notes (14) several close friends accompanied his body from his home to Père Lachaise Cemetary, including the conductors Camille Chevillard and Gabriel Pierné. Only about thirty people were present at the cemetery.

192. See Maurice Agulhon, *Marianne au pouvoir. L'Imagerie et la symbolique républicaine de 1880 à 1914* (Paris: Flammarion, 1989), 317–19.

193. Hanna, 9, 11. As she points out (154) the French Republican tradition saw the values of truth, justice, reason, and liberty, as deriving from ancient Greece and transmitted to France via Rome.

194. Other "Apaches" included Manuel da Falla, Florent Schmitt, Roger Delage, D.-E. Inghelbrecht, and Emile Vuillermoz.

195. In a letter to Jean Marnold, of 1906, Ravel referred to the Scholistes as "morose followers of neo-Christianity," well aware of the political implications of this. See Arbie Orenstein, ed., *A Ravel Reader: Correspondence, Articles, Interviews* (New York: Columbia University Press, 1990), 80. On Ravel's "anti-scholisme" and his mocking of the Schola's "academic" techniques, see Marcel Marnat, *Maurice Ravel* (Paris: Fayard, 1986), 374–75.

196. On Ravel's attitude to the "scholiste" symphony, see Marnat, *Maurice Ravel*, 351–52, and Brian Hart, "The Symphony in Theory and Practice," 184–86.

197. Maurice Ravel, "A Propos des *Images* de Claude Debussy," *Les Cahiers d'aujourd'hui* 1913: 135–36.

198. Marnat, 539. This was also the year that Ravel completed his *Mélodies hébraiques*. Ravel's support for persecuted Jewish artists will be discussed further in Chapter Two.

199. Marnat, 406–10.

200. Ibid., 420.

201. Maurice Barrès, president of the "Ligue des Patriotes," wrote at least 269 articles that glorified the war in 1915. See Marc Ferro, "Cultural Life in France, 1914–1918," 301.

202. Albert Roussel, *Lettres et écrits*, 60. Roussel was a lieutenant in the army.

203. Marnat, 405. Or, as he put it, "...Vive la France! but, above all, down with Germany and Austria! or at least what these two nations represent at the present time." Watkins, *Proof through the Night*, 170.

204. Ibid., 418.

205. Société des Auteurs, Compositeurs, et Editeurs de Musique, *Maurice Ravel* (Paris: SACEM, 1975), 31–32.

206. See Marnold's review of the Trio in the *Mercure de France* 1 Nov., 1915, and Marnat, 394–97. On the *Trois chansons*, and their reception, see Leterrier, 2 and 51. And see Watkins, *Proof through the Night*, 171. He also notes the trumpet-like fanfare in the piano in the final movement.

207. Marnat, 409. As Watkins notes, *Proof through the Night*, 174, the Catholic Church had recently banned tangos as lascivious, and in 1914 the pope reportedly proposed that the forlana serve as a substitute.

208. Roland-Manuel, *Ravel* (Paris: Editions de la Nouvelle Revue Critique, 1938), 135. On the "tombeau," see Carolyn Abbate, "Outside Ravel's Tomb," *Journal of the American Musicological Society* 52/3 (Fall 1999): 469. As she notes (497) Ravel had transcribed a forlane by Couperin in 1914.

209. Manuel Rosenthal, *Ravel. Souvenirs* (Paris: Hazan, 1995), 145. As Rosenthal points out (172) we cannot be sure of how much Ravel knew of Scarlatti, but he did comment that Rameau, the other great exponent of harmonic effects and the expressive use of dissonance, was "trop raisonnable." Also, see Watkins, *Proof through the Night* 174.

210. Roland-Manuel, 136. And see Abbate, 470–73 and 498–504. The "Moorish" color that she notes in the *Toccata,* 522, was equally provocative. On Ravel's possible reference to aviation in the *Toccata,* see Watkins, *Proof through the Night,* 175–76.

211. Hanna, 143–45. As Abbate notes, the Republican stress on the cosmopolitan was also one way to win allies from other Latin nations. And as Marc Ferro points out, in "Cultural Life in France, 1914–1918," 299, for the Left, the war became a struggle for the victory of human rights, as incarnated in the Republic.

212. Satie's cleverness and ruses here recall the tradition of opposition to official culture begun during the Ancien Regime, and particularly the challenges of the fair theaters to official theater. On this, see Martin Cooper, *Opéra Comique* (London: M. Parrish, 1949), 9–43. My interpretation here is in clear disagreement with that of Michel Faure, who claims that neither Satie nor Picasso (in addition to Cocteau) were "subversive," 166. Dismissing Satie's socialism as "purement sentimental," and claiming that Picasso was here defending conservative values (167) he presents *Parade* (312) as a "nostalgic patchwork" and conciliation—in essence, a confirmation of *union sacrée.* As we may see, however, how the conventions to which he refers were, in fact, manipulated ironically and subversively by both Satie and Picasso.

213. See Frank Manning's chapter on "Spectacle," in *Folklore, Cultural Performances, and Popular Entertainments,* ed. Richard Bauman (New York: Oxford University Press, 1992), 27–28.

214. Ibid.

215. On assigning the "author function," see Michel Foucault, "What Is an Author?," in *The Critical Tradition: Classic Texts and Contemporary Trends,* ed. David Richter (Boston: Bedford Books, 1998), 70–74. In *Parade* Satie withholds a sense of "authorship" or "voice," of the "person," or identity, since the "author-function," as Foucault points out, neutralizes the contradictions within the work.

216. Prochasson and Rasmussen, 182–83. As Jay Winter has noted in *Sites of Memory, Sites of Mourning* (131–32) shortly after the war broke out, Cocteau crusaded against "exotic," dangerous, and particularly German influences in modern art, including cubism, until Picasso helped change his mind.

217. Prochasson and Rasmussen, 183.

218. Olivier Corpet, "La Revue," 171.

219. Douglass Cooper, *Picasso Theater* (New York: H. N. Abrams, 1987), 16; and Christopher Green, *Cubism and Its Enemies,* 141–45.

220. As cited by Kenneth Silver, *Esprit de Corps,* 92.

221. See Prochasson and Rasmussen, 276, on cultural *union sacrée.* On Satie's frequenting of Socialist circles, see Jean Wiéner, *Allegro appassionato* (Paris: Pierre Belfond, 1978), p.100; and Fulcher, *French Cultural Politics,* 204. Satie joined the French Socialist Party upon the assassination of Jean Jaurès, on July 31, 1914.

222. Green, *Cubism and Its Enemies,* 145.

223. Cocteau had initially made fun of the Cubists within the circle of *Montjoie!* See Francis Steegmuller, *Cocteau. A Biography* (Boston: Little, Brown, and Comp., 1970), 115.

224. See Kenneth Silver, *Esprit de Corps,* 108–15.

225. Ibid., 109.

226. Jean Cocteau, *Professional Secrets. An Autobiography of Jean Cocteau,* ed. Robert Phelps (New York: Farrar, Strauss, and Giroud, 1979), 67–68.

227. Camille Mauclair, for example, was quick to label cubism as a further sign of the unfortunate invasion of German culture in a beleaguered France. See Green, *Cubism Its Enemies,* 10–14, 190; and Silver, *Esprit de Corps,* 51, 80, 99.

228. Silver, 93.

229. On the cover of one of his notebooks, Cocteau wrote the Larousse definition of "parade": "a burlesque scene played outside a side-show booth to entice spectators inside." Steegmuller, *Cocteau*, 146. According to Nancy Perloff, in *Art and the Everyday: Popular Entertainment and the Circle of Erik Satie* (Oxford: Clarendon Press, 1991), 112, Cocteau based the scenario on the model of the "théâtre de magie-variété-music-hall," in a fairground setting. On the relationship between the scenarios of "David" and *Parade* see Nichols, *The Harlequin Years*, 34–35.

230. Winter, *Sites of Memory,* 132. See Steven Whiting, *Satie the Bohemian: from Cabaret to Concert Hall* (New York: Oxford University Press, 1999), 470. As he points out (479) it was Picasso and Satie who persuaded Cocteau to include the three managers, and dissuaded him from giving them a spoken text, as well as persuading him to take out some of the noises that he originally planned to use.

231. Green, 145.

232. Louis Laloy, "Cabarets et music-hall," *Revue S.I.M.* 13 (1913): 54.

233. Silver, 93–95.

234. Naomi Ritter, *Art as Spectacle: Images of the Entertainer Since Romanticism* (Columbia, MO: University of Missouri Press, 1984), 246, 252.

235. Ibid., 254–55.

236. Peter Stallybrass and Allon White, *The Politics and Poetics of Transgression* (Ithaca: Cornell University Press, 1986), 21–26. Their insights, of course, draw upon the work of Bakhtin and his study of carnival. And see Whiting, 474. Here, however, I disagree with Whiting that Satie mirrors this inversion through his fugal expositions at the beginning and end, which he construes as an "interiorized" musical style. There are other connotations of the fugal style in this context that, I believe, explain its significance here, especially its associations with the now prestigious Schola Cantorum.

237. Silver, 153–54. But as Marc Ferro points out (298) foreign-born artists such as Picasso did feel compelled to pay hommage to classic styles, being vulnerable to the charge of lack of patriotism.

238. On the dominant conception of the Commedia dell'arte, see Silver, 160–61.

239. Silver, 119. And see Douglass Cooper, *Picasso Theater,* 24.

240. Silver, 119 and Naomi Ritter, *Art as Spectacle,* 266.

241. Silver, 120–21. On "hermeneutic windows" see Lawrence Kramer, *Music as Cultural Performance,* 9–10.

242. Silver, 178–80; and James Harding, *The Ox on the Roof: Scenes from Musical Life in Paris in the Twenties* (New York: St. Martin's Press, 1972), 32. On Satie's distrust and mockery of official culture, see Fulcher, *French Cultural Politics,* 195–204; and Steven Whiting, ed., *Satie the Bohemian: from Cabaret to Concert Hall* (New York: Oxford University Press, 1999).

243. As Maurice Agulhon points out in *République* (1:260–62) Poincaré's term "union sacrée" was more myth than reality. On the continuing political divisions, despite "*l'union sacrée,*" see Winock, *Siècle des intellectuels,* 136–38. *Le Populaire,* a socialist and internationalist journal, was adamantly against censorship. See the article in it, "Prière à la censure," 15 September 1917, which defends liberty of thought.

244. Steegmuller, *Cocteau,* 167–68. See Whiting on the contact and meeting of Satie and Cocteau (461–63); and on the complicity of Satie and Picasso and their tensions with Cocteau (468).

245. On the transformations of *Parade* behind Cocteau's back, see W. D. Reis, *The Dance Theater of Jean Cocteau* (Ann Arbor: UMI Research Press, 1986), 40–41. The choreography was by Léonide Massine.

246. On Satie's earlier exposure and mockery of "scholisme," see Fulcher, *French Cul-*

tural Politics, 199–201. See Inez Hedges, *Languages of Revolt: Dada and Surrealist Literature and Film* (Durham, NC: Duke University Press, 1983), xv–xviii and 134–35 on Dada and "frame-breaking." My interpretation here, then, disagrees with Nancy Perloff's argument (143) that in stressing stylistic diversity Satie "wished to give his material a random quality and sense of surprise and the unexpected to simulate the diversity and juxtaposition of contemporary popular entertainment." This diversity, I contend, is overemphasized and made irrational in order to disorient and thwart expectations. But she does point out (150) that despite Cocteau's disclaimer, there are clearly strains of Dada in *Parade,* particularly in its emphasis on contradiction, the anti-academic, and its "life-celebrating elements."

247. Although many historians have noted the formal symmetries of *Parade,* it was Cocteau who first observed the "metronomical unity" that governs each of the dances in the work. See Martin Cooper, *French Music from the Death of Berlioz to the Death of Fauré,* 199. An extensive analysis of *Parade* may be found in Alan M. Gilmor, *Erik Satie* (Boston: Twayne, 1988). As he points out (207): "*Parade* is an elegant structure of mirrors within mirrors. Not only is the ballet framed by the music of the "Prélude du Rideau Rouge" and the Manager's theme, which functions like a frame within a frame, each of the central episodes—the "Prestidigateur chinois," the "Petite fille américaine," and the "acrobates"—is itself a mirror form, a series of ternary structures, whose recapitulations reflect the opening episodes in reverse order." Also see Whiting (475) on the "symmetrical framing," as he refers to it. On Satie's equally iconoclastic ridicule of eighteenth-century conventions in his *Sonatine bureaucratique,* also of 1917, see Watkins, *Proof through the Night,* 100.

248. Douglass Cooper, *Picasso Theater,* 26.

249. As has often been pointed out, the presence of the "little American girl" may well be a reference to the entry of the United States into the war in 1917. See Whiting, 476–79; and Nancy Perloff (132–43). Whiting also aptly notes the "disjointed waltz" that accompanies the acrobats and the circus-like fanfare that heralds the entrance and exit of the Chinese conjurer. Whiting perceptively discusses the Manager's theme and its treatment (479). He too notes that "they change only in intensity and never in substance." According to Perloff (113) the character of the little American girl was inspired by a "théâtre forain" act. Perloff also notes (118) the influence of *Le Sacre* on Satie's use of ostinati, as well as his use of modality in the work, and a pentatonic language for the Chinese conjurer. See her excellent analysis, 115–50.

250. Steegmuller, 168. As Whiting points out (481) Cocteau had specified the typewriter, revolvers, and sirens, seeing them as cubist flashes of reality, punctuating an abstract surface.

251. William Austin, in *Music in the Twentieth Century* (New York: Norton, 1966), 168, notes not only the framing and central use of the key of C (illogically) but also, within the work, Satie's use of pentatonic and whole-tone scales, as well as the polytonal effects.

252. See Duchesneau, "La Musique française pendant la Guerre," 139.

253. Steegmuller, 171.

254. Ibid., 170. Silver, in contrast, argues (119–20) that all of the collaborators shared Cocteau's intent—that all three sought to "insinuate themselves" in the heart of conservative French culture, a point with which I disagree.

255. Silver, 115.

256. Steegmuller, 175, 184; and Silver, 116. On the unfurling of the red flag at the Théâtre du Châtelet on May 11, 1917, together with performances of Stravinsky's new Russian anthem and of the "Marseillaise," preceding the performance for *Firebird,* see Watkins, *Proof through the Night,* 154.

257. Apollinaire was in the group at the *Mercure de France.* Steegmuller, 148.

258. Silver, 122–23; also see Whiting, 482. As Whiting points out, Apollinaire was competing with Cocteau for the leadership of the avant-garde, and thus practically ignored him.

259. See Michel de Cossart, *The Food of Love: Princesse Edmond de Polignac and her Salon (1895-1943)* (London: Hamish Hamilton, 1978), 125; Silver, 122; and Steegmuller, 184. As Whiting points out (482) Apollinaire wrote an article praising *Parade* in advance, and it was this article that was reprinted in the program booklet. Nancy Perloff notes (114) that this promotional article appeared in *Excelsior* on 1 May 1917, and that Apollinaire specifically claimed that "*Parade* will upset the ideas of quite a number of spectators."

260. Steegmuller, 186. See Paul Collaer, *A History of Modern Music,* trans. Sally Abeles (New York: The World Pub. Comp., 1961), 217, which points out that *Parade* was seen as "treasonous." On the cries of "sales boches," see Alan Gillmor, *Erik Satie*, 208, and Darius Milhaud, *Notes sans musique. Essais et chroniques,* ed. Jeremy Drake (Paris: Flammarion, 1982), 143.

261. Silver, 125. As we shall see, the conceptual fusion of the German, the Jew, and the traitor would continue in the postwar period.

262. Pierre-Daniel Templier, *Erik Satie,* (Orig. ed.: Paris: Rieder, 1932; trans., David F. French, Cambridge, MA: MIT Press, 1969), 38.

263. Silver, p, 120. Also see Nichols (38) on the support of the Princesses de Polignac for Satie and the comment by an official in the Ministry of the Interior that the Princesse was making a mistake "in concerning herself with those Boches." As Nichols also notes (39), *Parade* was performed only five times, between May 18 and 26, and then was revived nine times in Paris in the following seven years.

264. Pascal Ory and Jean-François Sirinelli, *Les intellectuels en France de l'Affaire Dreyfus à nos jours* (Paris: Armand Colin, 1992), 61.

265. Ferro, "Cultural Life in France, 1914–1918," 304.

CHAPTER 2

1. Fauré died on Nov. 4, 1924. The new government was elected in May, and assumed power in the Fall of 1924. Although the cabinet was all Radical (under Herriot) it had socialist support. On the preceeding conservative "Bloc National" and the "Cartel des Gauches" which replaced it, see Gordon Wright, *France in Modern Times* (New York: Rand McNally, 1974), 335–37, 347. The "Bloc National" had been voted into power in 1919, bringing the Radicals and the Right together to create a centrist majority opposed to Syndicalist activity. Paul Léon, a specialist on historical monuments, had been a Dreyfusard, although now politically he was not to the Left. He would finally loose his position under the next leftist coalition, in 1932, and then a position was created for him at Collège de France. I am grateful to Christophe Charle for pointing this out.

2. On Saint-Saëns's funeral, and how Léon managed to arrange it while the chamber, including the finance commission, which would have to vote the funds, was on vacation, see Paul Léon, *Du Palais-Royal au Palais-Bourbon* (Paris: Albin-Michel, 1947), 22–24. Léon may have been further motivated by the fact that Fauré had not been appropriately honored upon his retirement from the Conservatoire in 1920. Two years later, an "hommage national," was privately organized by Fauré's friend, Fernand Maillot. Léon's account of how the state funeral came about differs from that of Roger Nichols, in *The Harlequin Years: Music in Paris 1917–1929* (Berkeley: University of California Press, 2002), 60, who cites Jean-Michel Nectous's *Gabriel Fauré*. Whether or not Fauré's friends took the initiative, it was clearly Léon who was the essential intermediary.

On 28 Oct. 1922, *Les nouvelles littéraires* noted that the country's intellectual elite gathered on the occasion, at the Sorbonne, which was testimony to the composer's enduring prestige. Significantly, Barrès, who had rallied to the Republic during the war, was given a national funeral in 1923, as was Victor Hugo in 1885. See Michel Winock, *Le Siècle des intellectuels* (Paris: Seuil, 1997), 149–50.

3. This term has been made common parlance by the series of volumes edited by Pierre Nora, *Les Lieux de mémoire* 3 vols. (Paris: Gallimard, 1986).

4. On the reactionary cultural politics of the "retour à l'ordre" in the later twenties, see Romy Golan, *Modernity and Nostalgia: Art and Politics in France between the Wars* (New Haven: Yale University Press, 1995), viii; and see Maurice Agulhon, *La République 1880–1990* (Paris: Hachette, 1990), 1:42. He notes the muted patriotism of supporters of the Cartel was balanced by their desire for law and peace. They thus admired Aristide Briand and Jean Jaurès, who stood for peace, anti-nationalism, and anti-militarism, believing that war was to examined critically.

5. Avner Ben-Amos, "Les funérailles de gauche sous la IIIe République: deuil et contestation," in *Les Usages politiques des fêtes aux XIX-XXe siècles,* eds., Alain Corbin, Noëlle Gérome, and Danielle Tartakowsky (Paris: Publications de la Sorbonne, 1994), 200. Also see Ben-Amos's book on French state funerals, *Funerals, Politics, and Memory in Modern France, 1789–1996.* (Oxford and New York: Oxford University Press, 2000).

6. Ibid., "Funérailles," 199, 202.

7. Ibid., 202. The Versailles Treaty was signed on June 28, 1919. On the continuing emotional responses to the war, see Modris Eksteins, *Rites of Spring: The Great War and the Birth of the Modern Age* (Toronto: Lester and Orpen Dinnys, 1989), 261–65. And see Jay Winter, *Sites of Memory, Sites of Mourning: the Great War in European Cultural History* (Cambridge, Eng.: Cambridge University Press, 1995), 71. He points out the link between the spiritualist revival and the recent wartime experience, which is evident in much of the commemorative ritual of the postwar period. He too emphasizes the continuation of mourning in the twenties in France, as in the rest of Europe.

8. Winter, *Sites of Memory, Sites of Mourning,* 226. For his discussion of the difficult process of "breathing life" into the symbolic language of romantic, classical, and religious references after 1914, see 228. On the complex "vocabulary" of mourning now, see 223. Eric Hobsbawm, on the other hand, considers World War I as the "divide" in languages of symbolic discourse, introducing a new "idiom" that would be maintained between the wars in the context of a new mass politics. See Eric Hobsbawm and Terrence Rangers, eds., *The Invention of Tradition* (Cambridge, Eng.: Cambridge University Press, 1983).

Under the preceding "Bloc National" there was not only political conservativism but nostalgia for religion, as evidenced in the results of the elections of 1919, when many practicing Catholics entered the Chamber of Deputies, where they now formed a greater percentage than in the nation as a whole. And see Maurice Agulhon, *La République 1880–1900* (Paris: Hachette, 1990), 1: 332. As Agulhon observes, the Bloc National considered Republican anti-clericalism to be "passé." It was at this time that the "fête" of Jeanne d'Arc became a national holiday and diplomatic ties with the Vatican were re-established. See Yves Simon, *The Road to Vichy,* trans. James A. Corbett and George R. Morrow (New York: Sheed and Ward, 1942), 55; and Jean-Marie Mayeur, *La Vie politique sous la Troisième République* (Paris: Seuil, 1984), 253–54.

9. See Durand's discussion of the funeral in Jacques Durand, *Quelques souvenirs d'un éditeur de musique* 2e série (1910–1924) (Paris: A. Durand et Fils, 1925), 155–56.

10. Ibid., 155.

11. On Fauré's stylistic evolution, see Jean-Michel Nectoux, *Gabriel Fauré: les voix du clair-obscur* (Paris: Flammarion, 1990). On Fauré's judicious innovations while director of

the Paris Conservatoire, see Jane F. Fulcher, *French Cultural Politics and Music from the Dreyfus Affair to the First World War* (New York: Oxford University Press, 1999), 143–47; and see Gail Hilson Woldu, "Gabriel Fauré as Director of the Conservatoire National de Musique et de Déclamation, 1905–1920" (Ph.D. dissertation, Yale University, 1983).

12. Jacques Durand, *Quelques souvenirs,* 156.

13. On the general sense of allegiance to "la patrie," see Maurice Agulhon, *La République,* 350. On the concept of "intelligence" as national, see Christophe Prochasson and Anne Rasmussen, *Au nom de la patrie. Les intellectuels et la première guerre mondiale (1910–1919)* (Paris: Editions de la Découverte, 1996), 280 ff.

14. On Victor Turner's concept of "liminality" in ritual, see Bobby C. Alexander, *Victor Turner Revisted: Ritual and Social Change* (Atlanta: Scholars Press, 1991); and Victor Turner, *The Anthropology of Performance* (New York: PAJ Publications, 1986). And see Frank Manning's chapter on "Spectacle," in *Folklore, Cultural Performances, and Popular Entertainments,* ed., Richard Bauman (New York, Oxford University Press, 1992), 291-99. As Manning points out, "celebration," like ceremony, represents a closed and tautological structure of symbols; they employ "summarizing symbols," such as uniforms, flags, etc., as emblems of ideology or social structure. As he also notes, such "metonymy" (as opposed to metaphor) works to retard change, since it orders and restricts thought to the familiar.

15. The Catholic theologian, Jacques Maritain, was closely associated with the Action Française until 1926, when it was condemned by the pope, and he fully realized its "instrumental" use of religion for political ends. This realization prompted his book, *Primauté du spirituel* (Paris: Plon, 1927). The Catholic journal, *La Revue universelle,* was also associated with the Action Française until the league was condemned by the Vatican.

16. Bruneau was made "Commandeur de la Légion d'Honneur" in 1919. See Alfred Bruneau, "Souvenirs inédits," *Revue internationale de la musique française* vol. 7 (Feb. 1982): 8. On Bruneau's rapid ascent in official circles following the Dreyfus Affair, see Fulcher, *French Cultural Politics and Music,* 41. Bruneau remained close to Clemenceau after the Affair and followed his more conservative political trajectory. As he explains in his memoires, it was due to this connection that he was made Inspecteur Général des Beaux-Arts in 1911.

17. Alfred Bruneau, *La Vie et les oeuvres de Gabriel Fauré*. Notice lue par l'auteur à l'Académie des Beaux-Arts (Paris: Charpentier et Fasquelle, 1925), 30–31.

18. Ibid. Fauré was, in fact, not afraid to go against the current, including the cresting anti-Wagnerian tide. On the eve of the war, July 19, 1914, he praised Wagner's *Parsifal* in *Le Figaro.* See Gabriel Fauré, *Opinions musicales* (Paris: Rieder, 1930), 167.

After the war Fauré again went against the classical current in his encomium to Hector Berlioz, whose music, then being performed in a series of concerts at the Châtelet, was under attack by the nationalist Right. Fauré defended Berlioz against the charge of technical inadequacy by paraphrasing Clemenceau: "L'oeuvre de Berlioz dans sa totalité me semble devoir être considérée de la façon dont Georges Clemenceau a dit qu'il fallait considérer la Révolution française: comme un bloc." Ibid., 22. Also in Berlioz's defense, he pointed out that *Les Troyens* is an example of "musique méditerréene." Ibid., 23.

19. Agulhon, *La République,* 256. He also notes (324) the "affaiblissement moral," as a result of all the dead and wounded, as well as the physical ravaging of the countryside. Also see Gordon Wright, *France in Modern Times,* 314. And see Martha Hanna, *The Mobilization of Intellect: French Scholars and Writers during the Great War* (Cambridge, Mass.: Harvard University Press, 1996), 14. As she points out, "The First World War made the French nation more introspective, more suspicious of foreign influence, and more susceptible to calls for a 'return to French culture'."

20. Wright, *France in Modern Times,* 316, 349. On the necessity of recruitment of im-

migrants for labor after the war, and thus the reality of a "melting pot," as opposed to the myth of "purity," see 360. Also see Modris Eksteins, *Rites of Spring: The Great War and the Birth of the Modern Age* (Toronto: Lester and Orpen Dinnys, 1989), 255-57.

21. David James Fisher, *Romain Rolland and the Politics of Intellectual Engagement* (Berkeley: University of California Press, 1988), 80. Also see Robert Wohl, *French Communism in the Making* (Stanford, Calif.: Stanford University Press, 1966). Agulhon, in *La République*, 329, points out that it was because of the "revolutionary" threat that Clemenceau and the Bloc National won the legislative elections of November 1919. He also notes (332) that this was followed by the strikes of 1920, and that under a new law of 1920 (an ostensible response to the birth of French Communism), there were harsh penalties for antinational propaganda.

22. Jaurès was "Pantheonized" on Nov. 23, 1924. On the growing chasm between Right and Left, see Joel Blatt, "Relatives and Rivals. The Responses of the Action Française to Italian Fascism, 1919-26," *European Studies Review* 11/3 (July 1981): 274, 283. Herriot, a Radical, was Prime Minister under the Cartel des Gauches, and again in 1932. In June 1924, the economy began to recover, Alexandre Millerand was replaced as President of the Republic by the moderate Gaston Doumergue. The parliament, at this time, was predominantly anticlerical, and the French embassy to the Vatican was abolished in Feb. 1925. See Alastair Hamilton, *The Appeal of Fascism: A Study of Intellectuals and Fascism 1919-1945* (New York: Avon, 1973), 177-78.

23. Joel Blatt, "Relatives and Rivals": 275. Also see Pascal Ory and Jean-François Sirinelli, *Les Intellectuels en France de l'Affaire Dreyfus à nos jours* (Paris: Armand Colin, 1992), 83.

24. Ibid. And see Edward R. Tannenbaum, *The Action Française: Die-Hard Reactionaries in Twentieth-Century France* (New York: John Wiley and Sons, 1962), 113. Also see Hamilton, 181-84, 191-92.

25. Poincaré was president of the Republic until 1920, and then Prime Minister from 1922-24 and from 1926-29. See Wright, *France in Modern Times*, 348, 356. As Wright points out (363) Poincaré returned to power in 1926 partly as a result of the country's serious financial problems.

26. Blatt, "Relatives and Rivals": 264, and Yves Simon, *The Road to Vichy*, 40. And see Wright, 363. In 1919, given the mounting fear of social revolution, the alternatives, for many, appeared to be either socialism or monarchy, which further increased the nationalists's appeal. See Eugen Weber, *Action Française: Royalism and Reaction in Twentieth-Century France* (Stanford, Calif.: Stanford University Press, 1962), 124, 132. Also see Jean-Louis Loubet del Bayle, *Les Non-conformistes des années 30. Une tentative de la renouvellement de la pensée politique française* (Paris: Seuil, 1969), 12-14.

27. Agulhon, *La République*, 350.

28. Prochasson and Rasmussen, *Au nom de la patrie,* 212. And see Martha Hanna, *The Mobilization of Intellect,* 16-18.

29. Here the contrast with the ideals of the Weimar Republic could not have been stronger, for in Germany music provided a means both to "imagine" and to realize a new community, in keeping with the ideals of the social democratic regime. Traditionally a party of the masses, the Social Democratic Party, continued to emphasize both workers and youth. See Pascal Huynh, *La Musique sous la République de Weimar* (Paris: Fayard, 1998), 172-74.

And well before the French Popular Front, the Weimar Republic stressed the radio, including musical broadcasts, as a way of unifying a divided culture. See Karl Christian Fuhrer, "A Medium of Modernity? Broadcasting in Weimar Germany, 1923-1932," *The Journal of Modern History* 69/4 (Dec. 1999): 722-53.

The Kroll Opera promoted innovation (as opposed to the more conservative State Opera), and the Prussian Academy of Fine Arts stressed new music, and named the most important contemporary composers, including Schoenberg and Stravinsky, to its faculty. Moreover, the Frankfurt Conservatory offered a class in jazz, which stressed its technical innovations. See Huynh, 258–61. Also see John Willett, *Art and Politics in the Weimar Republic: the New Sobriety, 1917–1933* (New York: Pantheon, 1978), 164–67, and J. Bradford Robinson, "Jazz Reception in Weimar Germany: in Search of a Shimmy Figure," in Bryan Gilliam, ed., *Music and Performance during the Weimar Republic* (Cambridge, Eng.: Cambridge University Press, 1994), 107.

30. This was the position promoted by conservative publications like the *La revue des deux mondes* and the *La revue hebdomadaire*, which employed critics such as Pierre Lasserre and André Coeuroy.

31. On the social renovation attempted by the Weimar Repubic, see Peter Fritzsche, "Did Weimar Fail?," *The Journal of Modern History* 68 (Sept. 1996): 652. On the commemorative pieces, see Sophie-Anne Leterrier, "Culture de guerre et musique nationale," in *Chefs-d'oeuvre et circonstances* (Archives Départmentales du Pas-de-Calais, 2000), 26, 30–3, and subsequent discussions in the catalogue, 52, 102–4. Also see Bénédicte Grailles, "Chansons de marche, lamento funèbre, et hymne de la Renaissance: la production musicale imprimée entre 1918 et 1922," in the same collection, 44. As Leterrier and Grailles point out, Saint-Saëns also responded to private commissions, as in the case of "La Française," written for the *Petite Parisien*, as did Fauré with his song, "C'est la paix," the text of which celebrates the allied victory. The latter was to a poem of Georgette Delblandis, who had won a contest held by *Le Figaro*, with the winning poem to be set by Fauré who was a critic for the paper. Fauré did not like the poem, but was aware that commissions were few, and so agreed to set it anyway. See Leterrier, 26.

Noël Gallon would later be a teacher of Messiaen at the Conservatoire. André Caplet was a friend of Debussy, and had won the Prix de Rome in 1901, becoming both a composer and conductor.

32. Wright, *France in Modern Times*, 334.

33. See Agulhon, *La République*, 352–54, on all the monuments to the dead and their different "tonalities" or messages, depending on the symbols deployed, which ranged from mourning to "gloire nationale." Also see Prochasson and Rasmussen, 250, on the victory being "buried under mourning."

34. Prochasson and Rasmussen, 264.

35. D.-E. Inghelbrecht, *Mouvement contraire. Souvenirs d'un musicien* (Paris: Editions Domat, 1947), 11–12. The Ministry of Fine Arts in this period was under that of "Instruction Publique." The impressario, Gabriel Astruc, helped to raise the funds for the festival commemorating Debussy, which accompanied the statue's inauguration. And see Louis Laloy, *Louis Laloy (1874–1944) on Debussy, Ravel, and Stravinsky*, trans. and annotated by Deborah Priest (Aldershot: Ashgate, 1999), 114–18. The concert devoted to Debussy's works took place at the Théâtre des Champs-Elysées, and present in the audience were members of the government as well as foreign diplomats.

36. Piero Coppola, *Dix-sept ans de musique à Paris, 1922–1939* (Geneva: Slatkine, 1982. Original edition Lausanne, 1944), 17. On the tense state of Franco-German relations now, see Wright, 346.

37. Coppola, Ibid., 14. The Pasdeloup concerts, held at the Opéra, were conducted by René Baton.

38. See André Coeuroy, *La Musique française moderne* (Paris: Delagrave, 1924), 10–11. Also see Nichols, *The Harlequin Years*, 74. As he notes (71) other foreign composers performed at the Opéra in the postwar years included Malipiero, Verdi, Mozart,

Mussorgsky, Puccini, and, by 1927, Richard Strauss (*Der Rosenkavalier*). As he further notes (76), in 1928 the Vienna Opera came to the Palais Garnier to perform Mozart, Beethoven, and Wagner—all safely "classic" by now.

39. J.-G. Prod'homme, *Richard Wagner et la France* (Paris: Maurice Sénart, 1921), 44, 90.

40. See the *Nouvelle revue française* 1 June, 1919, and Prochasson and Rasmussen, 256.

41. Inghelbrecht, *Mouvement contraire*, 60. Inghelbrecht had been one of the "Apaches," or young musical "hooligans," grouped around Ravel between 1900 and 1905. He was a champion of Debussy and Ravel, and founded the Orchestre National de la radio-diffusion Française in 1934. See Laloy, 310.

42. D'Indy's response, in the survey on Wagner published in a special issue of the *Revue musicale* vol. IV, devoted to "Wagner et la France" in Oct. 1923, 271.

43. Ibid., 272.

44. Ibid.

45. Ibid.

46. See Darius Milhaud, *Notes sur la musique. Essais et chroniques*, ed. Jeremy Drake (Paris: Flammarion, 1982), 61. In 1921 the Société Musicale Indépendante performed Alban Berg's *Four Pieces for Piano and Clarinette*. And see Michel Duchesneau, *L'Avant garde musicale à Paris de 1871 à 1939* (Liège: Mardaga, 1997), 52.

47. Koussevitsky, however, did not remain in Paris, but left for the United States in 1923. See Arthur Lourié, *Sergei Koussevitsky and his Epoch: A Biographical Chronical*, trans. S. W. Pring (New York: AMS Press, 1971), 187–89, 206. Koussevitsky was even bold enough to perform works of the young Hindemith. See José Bruyr, *L'Ecran des musiciens*. Second série (Paris: Corti, 1933), 13, 20–26. On Straram's performance of Schoenberg, see Marie-Claire Mussat, "La réception de Schoenberg en France avant la Seconde Guerre mondiale," *Revue de musicologie* 87/1(2001): 175. He also performed Milhaud, notably his *Agamemnon* in 1927. See François Porcile, *La Belle époque de la musique française: le temps de Maurice Ravel, 1871–1940* (Paris: Fayard, 1999), 240.

48. See Francis Poulenc, *Correspondance 1915-1963*, ed. Myriam Chimènes (Paris: Fayard, 1994), 189. The board of the society included Fauré, Dukas, Ravel, Roussel, Satie, Koechlin, Stravinsky, Milhaud, Honegger, and Roland-Manuel. Significantly, it had its headquarters at the *La revue musicale*, which was now allied with the leftist *Nouvelle revue française*.

49. Myriam Chimènes, "Le Budget de la Musique sous la IIIe République," in *La Musique du théorique au politique*, eds., Hugues Dufourt and Joel-Marie Fauquet (Paris: Aux Amateurs de Livres, 1991), 288.

50. See Fauré's letter to the ministre de l'instruction publique et des beaux-arts of July 9, 1919 in F 21-4552, Number 3. Fauré proceeds to request the subvention be reestablished and augmented to the more adequate sum of six thousand francs. As Duchesneau points out, (*Avant-garde musicale*, 49), the subvention was cut during the war.

51. Undoubtedly due to the postwar financial situation, the subvention for the concert society now was small, not exceeding two thousand francs. See F 21–4652. On the performance of Schoeberg, see Mussat, 173–74.

52. Piero Coppola, *Dix-sept and de musique à Paris*, 14–17.

53. Rouché's continuing astuteness is in sharp contrast with the qualities of the director of the Opéra-Comique in this period, Albert Carré. On Carré's lack of knowledge of the repertoire and poor choice of singers see Inghelbrecht (his former assistant) *Mouvement contraire*, 13. And on the state of the Opéra-Comique, see Coppola, 18–21.

54. Inghelbrecht, 83.

55. Coppola, 21. According to Coppola, the level went down when Diaghilev became influenced by a "coterie of snobs"—habitués of the cafés and taverns of Montparnasse (where avant-garde artists congregated), who tempted him with "experiments."

56. Rouché continued to have Louis Laloy, who was always in touch with the latest intellectual and political developments, as his secretary. As Roger Nichols points out in *The Harlequin Years* (64), Rouché had to please, in particular, the powerful group of "abonnés des trois soirs," as well as the government and those individuals who provided additional financial backing.

57. The Opéra-Comique received 300,000 francs, the Paris Conservatoire 279,523, and the regional branches of the Conservatoire, as well as the "école départementales," 156,500 francs.

58. Myrian Chimènes, "Le Budget de la musique," 277.

59. On opera in the Weimar Republic see Pascal Huynh, *La Musique sous la République de Weimar,* 258–61; and Susan Cook, *Opera for a New Republic: The Zeitopern of Krenek, Weill, and Hindemith* (Ann Arbor: University of Michigan Press, 1988).

60. D'Indy referred to his opera as such in a letter of Sept. 17, 1903, to Pierre de Bréville, as cited by Léon Vallas, *Vincent d'Indy* 2 vols. (Paris: Albin Michel, 1950), 2: 327. For a complete listing of the older and new works that Rouché staged in the twenties, see Nichols, *The Harlequin Years*, 66–70. As one might expect, they included operas of Saint-Saëns, Massenet, and such contemporary conservative or established figures (many now serving official functions, pedagogic or administrative) as Max d'Ollone, Albert Roussel, Charles Tournemire, Charle-Marie Widor, Alfred Bruneau, André Bloch, Jacques Ibert, and Maurice Emmanuel. Works imported from the Opéra-Comique included those of Ravel, Rabaud, Massenet, and Bizet.

61. Dorothy Knowles, *French Drama of the Inter-War Years, 1918–1939* (London: George G. Harrap, 1967), 299; and Romy Golan, *Modernity and Nostalgia: Art and Politics in France between the Wars* (New Haven: Yale University Press, 1995), 30.

62. See Fulcher, *French Cultural Politics and Music*, 66–72, and Jane F. Fulcher, "D'Indy's 'Drame anti-Juif' and its Meaning in Paris, 1920," *The Cambridge Opera Journal*, Nov. 1990: 295–319.

63. Fulcher, "D'Indy's Drame 'Anti-Juif'": 303–04.

64. Léon Vallas, *Vincent d'Indy*, 2: 327.

65. Ibid., 328.

66. See Vincent d'Indy, *Richard Wagner et son influence sur l'art musical français* (Paris: Delagrave, 1930), 48. On the tonal plan of the work see Fernand Biron, *Le Chant grégorien dans l'enseignement et les oeuvres de Vincent d'Indy* (Ottowa: Les Editions de l'Université d'Ottowa, 1941), 166.

67. Vallas, *Vincent d'Indy*, 2: 336–38; and Biron, *Le Chant grégorien*, 171–72. Gregorian themes are used to symbolize the cross (through a chant that makes reference to it), as well as "Prière," "Grace," and "la Mort Chrétienne."

68. As Vallas, among others, (*Vincent d'Indy*, 2: 335) notes, d'Indy made musical reference to Bach's Passions and to Beethoven's *Missa Solemnis*.

69. See Vallas, *Vincent d'Indy*, 2: 335–36.

70. June 6 was actually the date of the open dress rehearsal, or the *répétition générale*, to which the press was invited, and so was treated as the premiere. The printed score gives June 9th as the date of the premiere, which indicates that it had to be changed, since the press reviews appeared on the 8th. Because of a series of strikes, the first commercial performance, or *création*, did not take place until 8 Dec.

71. Vallas, *Vincent d'Indy*, 2: 336.

72. On the emotional "trauma" of this period, see Maurice Denis, *Nouvelles theories*

sur l'art moderne. Sur l'art sacré (Paris: Rouart et Watelin, 1921), 194. On the strikes at the Opéra of 1919–20, see Michel Faure, *Du néoclassicisme musical dans la France du premier XXe siècle* (Paris: Klinksieck, 1997), 32. As he points out, in January 1920, they lasted eighteen days, and beginning in October, for fifty-one days. The musicians meanwhile gave free concerts at the Bourse de Travail, and were later joined by the Concerts Pasdeloup for free concerts at the Trocadero. On the strikes in other sectors, see Hamilton, 177. Also see Nichols, *The Harlequin Years*, 64.

73. Vallas, *Vincent d'Indy*, 2: 335.

74. On Denis's relation to d'Indy and the Schola Cantorum, see Fulcher, *French Cultural Politics and Music*, 49, 113–14, 134. Denis's political position was close to the Action Française. See Martha Hanna, *The Mobilization of Intellect*, 168. Significantly, several of Denis's costume designs are of modern dress, such as that for the "Dactylo," or typist, of the *Le roi de l'or*, and for the "King" himself (in evening dress), thus encouraging parallels with the present situation in France. The costume designs are preserved in the Bibliothèque de l'Opéra. On the position of the postware Right concerning the fundamental opposition of "Orient" and "Occident" see Gisèle Sapiro, *La guerre des écrivains 1940–1953* (Paris: Fayard, 1999), 150–153. She goes into considerable detail on this debate during the interwar period.

75. *Bonsoir* 8 June, 1920.

76. *Le théâtre* June 1920, 384; and *Le Figaro* 8 June 1920.

77. *Le journal des débats* 8 June 1920; and *Le théâtre* June 1920, 384.

78. See *La petite Marseillaise* 8 June 1920; and Vallas, *Vincent d'Indy*, 2: 235.

79. Adolphe Boschot, *Chez les musiciens* (Paris: Plon, 1922), 212.

80. Ibid., 214.

81. *Le populaire de Paris* 8 June 1920; and *La revue critique des idées et des livres* July 1920: 105–08.

82. Only the "symphonie descriptive" that serves as the prelude to act 2 remained in the concert repertoire beyond the autumn season of 1920.

83. Prochasson and Rasmussen, 155. I am indebted to my colleague, Gilbert Chaitin, the Department of French and Italian, for his information on the background to the *roman à thèse* in the earlier nineteenth century, and on the *drame à thèse*, as practiced by figures like Dumas fils. On the "roman à these" in the later nineteenth and early twentieth centuries, see Susan Suleiman, *Authorization Fictions: The Ideological Novel as a Literary Genre* (New York: Columbia University Press, 1983), 21–23. Also see Irving Howe, *Politics and the Novel* (New York: Avon, 1970; orig. ed. 1957), 20–22.

84. Alfred Bachelet was the *chef du chant* and then the conductor at the Opéra-Comique under Messager and Broussan, and later became the director of the Conservatoire at Nancy.

85. On Barrès's attraction to Wagner, see Fulcher, *French Cultural Politics*, 33. Barrès's novel was thus adapted as a libretto by Franc-Nohain.

86. Michel Winock, *Le Siècle des intelletuels* (Paris: Seuil, 1997), 195. Equally concerned with the opposition between Orient and Occident was the composer Florent Schmitt. See Faure, 85, on his *Psaume XLVIII*, of 1904, and its representation of the "lasciviousness" of the Orient though its serpentine lines.

87. See René Dumesnil, *La Musique en France entre les deux guerres: 1919–1939* (Paris: Editions du Milieu du Monde, 1946), 131.

88. Review of Bachelet's *Un Jardin sue l'Oronte* by René Dumesnil in the *Mercure de France* 15 Nov. 1932: 444–45.

89. Ibid., 446–50. As Dumesnil points out (450), this includes the use of ancient Arab modes.

90. Ibid., 451. Dumesnil ends, however, by praising Rouché for having "honored French art" in presenting this work, and then expresses his dismay that the Opéra's subvention had just been reduced to four hundred thousand francs (453).

91. Dumesnil, *La Musique en France entre deux guerres*, 134. The score at the Bibliothèque Nationale de France (hereafter BNF), Musique (Départment de la Musique hereafter, Musique), published in 1922, indicates cuts for performance at the Opéra-Comique.

92. Winock, *Le Siècle des intellectuels*, 625–27.

93. See Dumesnil, *Musique en France*, 134. Also see Porcile, *Belle èpoque*, 341. Contrary to Roger Nichols's claim (*The Harlequin Years*, 69), not all of the government's of the 1920s were afraid of the new medium of film. Nichols fails, throughout his book, to note the significance of the changes of government, and ignores the extensive literature on their changing cultural policies.

94. Nichols, *The Harlequin Years*, 199. The review in *Télérama* of 1 Aug. 1927, also notes the polemics that the work—which it describes as severe and powerful, influenced by folklore—inspired at its premiere. See Leslie Sprout, "Music for a 'New Era': Composers and National identity in France, 1936–1946," Ph.D. dissertation, Universty of California, Berkeley, 2000, 59. As she points out, Delannoy was only 29 when the work premiered and established his reputation. As Nichols notes (*The Harlequin Years*, 82), in 1925, the Isola brothers were replaced by a former pupil of Fauré, Louis Masson, at the Opéra-Comique, along with George Ricou. As he also notes (83), the 1926–27 season included *Louise, Madame Butterfly, Manon,* and *Carmen.* Delannoy's work was thus quite a shock. For the foreign works performed at the Opéra-Comique, see 80. They included works of Rossini, Verdi, Mascagni, and Puccini, and Falla.

95. Agulhon, *La République*, 434; and Sprout, 59. On the opera also see André Boll, *Marcel Delannoy* (Paris: Ventadour, n.d.), 14ff.

96. The review in *Telerama,* of 1 Aug. 1927, recounts the legend on which the work is based: Misery, an old lady, has nothing but a cabin and a pear tree. She welcomes and comforts a vagabond, who turns out to be Saint Denis. He allows her a wish, and she asks that her pear tree hold the thieves that have appeared as prisoner, but she thus imprisons Death. Humanity is happy until the sick, weak, and desperate come to implore her to release death. Then, all returns to order. The fact that it is an allegory of the present and that it uses religious references, of course, relates it to d'Indy's *La Légende de Saint Christophe.* Also see Sprout, "Music for a 'New Era,'" 59.

97. Significantly, the copy of the score at the BNF, Musique, published in Paris by Heugel, in 1926, is dedicated to Maurice Ravel.

98. Paul Bertrand, *Le Monde de la musique* (Geneva: La Palatine, 1947), 199.

99. See the score, *Le mas: Pièce lyrique en trois actes* (Paris: Au Ménestrel, Heugel, 1927).

100. I am grateful to Andrea Musk for discussing the work with me. See her "Aspects of Regionalism in French Music during the Third Republic: The Schola Cantorum, d'Indy, Sevérac, and Canteloube," Ph.D. dissertation, Oxford University, 1999.

101. Dumesnil, *Musique en France*, 103. A review by Dominique Sordet, in *Action française* on April 5, 1929, notes the regionalism in the work, and specifically the use of themes from the Auvergne, the composer's home region. But Sordet criticizes the music and the "mise en scène." Another review, by Roland-Manuel, in *Le ménestrel,* of 5 April 1929, similaryl notes its use of regional melodies, which here, he argues, accord well with the harmonic advances of the beginning of the century. And so, despite the conservative message of the libretto, Sordet is not enthusiastic about the work because of its "advanced" Wagnerian harmonic language , and Roland-Manuel, politically to the Left, defends it on the basis of its innovations for its period.

102. Dumesnil, *Musique en France*, 103.

103. Ibid., 104.

104. Julien Benda, *La Trahison des clercs* (Paris: Grasset, 1975. Original edition, 1927), 107, 116–118, 122. While I agree with Roger Nichols that Rouché was always ready to try new things (*The Harlequin Years*, 69), it was consistently within carefully circumscribed limits, determined by state expectations. As Nichols again fails to note, these changed substantially with successive governments, especially during the period of the Cartel des Gauches, on which there is abundant information in the major historical texts.

105. Agulhon, *République*, 1: 338.

106. Olivier Corpet, "La Revue," in *Histoire des Droites en France*, ed. Jean-François Sirinelli (Paris: Gallimard, 1992), 174–177.

107. See Christopher Green, *Cubism and its Enemies: Modern Movements and Reaction in French Art, 1916–1928* (New Haven: Yale University Press, 1987), 123. As he points out, this was a period when many writers on art attempted to draw "a clear all-embracing shape of the history of the preceding quarter century." He cites, as an example, André Salmon's *L'Art vivant*, of 1920. The same is true in music history, with works such as Julien Tiersot's *Un demi-siècle de musique française 1870–1919* (Paris: Félix Alcan, 1924).

108. Martha Hanna, *The Mobilization of Intellect*, 14.

109. On immigrant labor in this period, see Wright, *France in Modern Times*,. 360.

110. On Magnard's background and position in the Dreyfus Affair, see Fulcher, *French Cultural Politics*, 74–77.

111. Gaston Carraud, *La Vie, l'oeuvre, et la mort d'Albéric Magnard* (Paris: Rouart, Lerolle, et Cie., 1921), 8–9.

112. Ibid., 178, 197.

113. Adolphe Boschot, *Chez les musiciens* (Paris: Plon, 1922), 3.

114. Ibid., 4–7.

115. Surprisingly enough, as other positive models, Boschot praises not only d'Indy's *La légende de Saint Christophe,* but Gustave Charpentier and his sequel to Louise, *Julien,* of 1913. Although *Julien* is a complex work, reflecting both Charpentier's cynicism and disillusion, Boschot perceives only a simplicity and directness of expression that ties it to the French tradition. This is a tradition that, for Boschot, can be seen not only in Berlioz—now perceived as "direct," and thus French (as opposed to Wagner)—but in Charpentier's own teacher, Jules Massenet. See Boschot, *Chez les musiciens*, 178–81.

116. Ibid., 3.

117. Benda, *La Trahison des clercs*, 119, 126, 143.

118. See Emile Vuillermoz, *Musiques d'aujourd'hui* (Paris: G. Crès, 1923).

119. Emile Vuillermoz, *Claude Debussy* (Paris: Heugel, 1920), 20–21.

120. Vuillermoz, *Musiques d'aujourd'hui*, 76.

121. Ibid., 132.

122. Robert Bernard, *Les Tendances de la musique française moderne* (Paris: Durand et Fils, 1930), 119.

123. Ibid., 121 131.

124. Stravinsky's bitterness over such jaundiced, politicized readings would emerge blatantly in his diatribe on musical meaning and criticism in his *An Autobiography* (New York: Norton, 1962. Orig. edition, 1936), 174–76. Ironically, Stravinsky himself was a social and political conservative. See Richard Taruskin, *Stravinsky and the Russian Traditions: a Biography of the Works through Mavra* (Berkeley: University of California Press, 1996), 1514–16. For earlier attacks on Stravinsky in similar terms, especially in the context of *Mavra*, see 591–98. As he points out, even Boris de Schloezer in the *La nouvelle revue*

française, attacked the work as a pastiche. It was, of course, defended by Cocteau, Satie, and Les Six.

125. Bernard, *Les Tendances,* 124.
126. Ibid., 125–26.
127. Ibid., 127–28.
128. Ibid., 130.
129. Hanna, 146.
130. Significantly, this was also a period of emphasis on "popular theater." In 1920 the French government created the Théâtre National Populaire in the old theater of the Trocadero, with Firmin Gémier as director. It was meant for all classes, as a means to further collective communion. See Dorothy Knowles, *French Drama of the Interwar Years,* 294. At the Conservatoire, the influence of the Schola in the program of instruction was clear. As Nichols points out (*The Harlequin Years,* 183), the Conservatoire's new director, Henri Rabaud, "made the three chamber music classes obligatory for prize winners in paino, strings, and woodwinds," and in order to insure a higher quality of repertoire, he himself selected the test pieces for examinations. He also notes (187) that Rabaud instituted examinations in the music history classes the attendance at which had been made mandatory by Fauré. Rabaud took over the directorship upon Fauré's retirement in 1920.
131. See *Encyclopédie de la musique et dictionnaire du Conservatoire,* pt. 2, *Pédagogie, Ecoles, Concerts-Théatres,* ed. Albert Lavignac and Lionel de la Laurencie (Paris: Delagrave, 1931).
132. Tournemire would be highly influential on the next generation of organists and composers, which included not only Messiaen, but Duruflé amd Daniel-Lesure. Robert S. Lord, "Liturgy and Gregorian Chant in *L'Orgue mystique* of Charles Tournemire," Organ Yearbook 1984, 108.
133. Myriam Chimènes, "Le Budget de la musique sous la IIIe République," 179. Significantly, Herriot himself was an accomplished musician and highly knowledgeable about music. As Nichols observes (*The Harlequin Years,* 176), on 18 August, 1920 an *arrêté* decreed a compulsory hour of musical instruction (and one optional) per week for Ecoles Primaires Supérieures (for ages eleven to thirteen) and in 1922 two hours per week from the age of thirteen. Also see Yannick Simon, "Les Jeunesses musicales de France," in *La Vie musicale sous Vichy,* ed. Myriam Chimènes (Paris: Éditions Complexe, 2001), 206. He notes the formation of the "Comité national de propaganda pour la musique" in the later twenties.
134. For the different educational priorities of the prewar Schola Cantorum and Conservatoire, see Fulcher, *French Cultural Politics,* 26–31 and 143–45.
135. See the questionnaire distributed to the regional conservatories in the Archives Nationales F21–4588.
136. See the report by the *inspecteur de l'enseignement musical,* André Bloch, on the conservatory in the city of Hénin-Liétard, in the Archives Nationales F21–4588.
137. On choral music in the Weimar Republic see Pascal Huynh, *La Musique sous la République de Weimar,* 172–74. Large choral associations were encouraged by the Social Democrats to give concerts in various traditional and nontraditional venues both in Berlin and in the provinces. Bloch's reference to the Renaissance masters and folklore undoubtedly included Jannequin and Josquin, who were seen in this light in Republican circles at the turn of the century. See Fulcher, *French Cultural Politics,* 42–43.
138. See the list of the "Commission Consultative chargée d'examiner les candidatures vacantes d'inspection de l'enseignement musical" in the Archives Nationales F21–4588.

139. See the *Encyclopédie de la musique et dictionnaire du Conservatoire,* pt. 2, *Pédagogie, Ecoles, Concerts-Théatres,* 34–53.

140. See F21–4552, "Allocations exceptionnelles aux Ecoles des départements: Subventions aux théâtres et sociétés musicales," Archives Nationales, Paris.

141. Ibid. Charpentier's Conservatoire Populaire now received only the honorific sum of two hundred francs. On the Conservatoire Populaire, see Fulcher, *French Cultural Politics,* 97–103.

142. See Auguste Mangeot, "L'Ecole Normale de Musique," in *Encyclopédie de la musique et dictionnaire du Conservatoire* pt. 2, 36. As Nichols notes (*The Harlequin Years,* 180), the Schola's enrollment continued to grow in this period. It thus became clear that there was room for another unofficial school of music. The Ecole Niedermeyer continued to be active, but its goal was still to train professional church musicians. For more information of the Ecole Normale, see Bernard Gavoty, *Alfred Cortot* (Paris: Editions Buchet/Chastel, 1977), 132ff.

143. See Léonie Rosentiel, *Nadia Boulanger: A Life in Music* (New York: Norton, 1982), 145; and Leonard Isaacs, "Paris in 1930: the Ecole Normale de Musique," *Journal of the American Liszt Society* vol. 38 (July–Dec. 1995): 23. Also see Faure, 79. Nichols points out (*The Harlequin Years,* 187), that the Conservatoire admitted only two foreign students per class. On the diplomas it granted, see ibid., 187–88.

144. See Cecilia Dunoyer, *Marguerite Long. A Life in French Music 1874–1966* (Bloomington, Ind.: Indiana University Press, 1993), 110–111. Cortot and Casals were originally allied in the Casals Trio. Cortot had been a professor of piano at the Paris Conservatoire from 1907–1917, but his heavy teaching responsibilities there inevitably conflicted with his activities as a performer. See *The New Grove Dictionary of Music and Musicians* 1980 edition, s.v. "Cortot, Alfred," by Martin Cooper, 811–12.

145. Léonie Rosentiel, *Nadia Boulanger,* 197–99. As Rosentiel points out, although Boulanger did conceal her anti-Semitism from her students, she did not hide it from her Catholic friends. Also see Bruno Monsaignon, *Mademoiselle. Conversations with Nadia Boulanger,* trans. Robyn Marsack (Exeter, Eng.: Carcanet, 1985), 34; and Alan Kendell, *The Tender Tyrant: Nadia Boulanger. A Life Devoted to Music* (London: Macdonald and Jane's, 1976), 42–43.

146. Ibid. And on Maritain's changing position with regard to the Jews, see Jacques Maritain, *Impossible antisémitisme* (Paris: Desclée de Broawer, 1994).

147. Rosentiel, *Nadia Boulanger,* 168–70, 183–86.

148. On this canon, see Kendall, *The Tender Tyrant,* 420–43. D'Indy's canon, like Boulanger's, prominently included Bach, Rameau, and Monteverdi. See Fulcher, *French Cultural Politics,* 30–31.

149. See Wright, *France in Modern Times,* 343, on international relations after the war; also see 349 on France's postwar position in Europe in the twenties, and 346 on Franco-German relations specifically.

150. Numerous cultural organizations sought to spread French influence and an image of French cultural grandeur to America. These included the Conservatoire Américain and the Franco-American Musical Society.

151. Ronald Wiecki, "A Chronical of Pro Musica in the United States (1920-1944) with a Biographical Sketch of its Founder," E. Robert Schmitz," Ph.D. dissertation, University of Wisconsin, Madison, 1992, 119. On Schmitz, see Nancy Perloff, *Art and the Everyday: Popular Entertainment and the Circle of Erik Satie* (Oxford: Clarendon Press, 1991), 94.

152. Here it is important to note that a common French image of America was that of a "mass society," lacking individualism and refinement. See Michel Winock, *Nationalism, antisémitisme, et fascisme en France* (Paris: Seuil, 1990), 39. On Casadesus see *Chefs-*

d'oeuvre et circonstances, 84. On Boulanger's American students see Porcile, *Belle époque*, 387–89. They included Aaron Copland, Walter Piston, Elliot Carter, Roy Harris, Virgil Thomson, and George Antheil. This helped further exchanges between the French and American avant-gardes—for example, between Gide, Hemingway, Copland, Gertrude Stein, Thomson, and Henri Cliquet-Pleyel. For more information on the Conservatoire Americain, see Nichols, *The Harlequin Years*, 190. As Nichols points out, it originated during the war with General Pershing's need to train bandsmen. After the war it led to a special summer school for Americans, who paid tuition. Walter Damrosh represented the Americans in its administration. Nichols ignores the key role of Casadesus, rather emphasizing Widor, who also served as director.

153. See Michel Winock, *Siècle des intellectuels*, 143. Also see Herman Lebovics, *True France. The Wars Over Cultural Identity 1900–1945* (Ithaca: Cornell University Press, 1992), 38. As he points out, the Fédération Républicaine collaborated with the Action Française in the late twenties.

154. Winock, *Siècle des intellectuels*, 186–88. And see Hamilton, 177. As he points out (178), during the war the circulation of *Action française* grew several times over, and its readers now included Proust and Rodin. Among Maurras's admirers were Gide and Apollinaire.

155. Hamilton, 163, 188–89.

156. Olivier Corpet, "La Revue" in *Histoire des Droites en France*, ed. Jean-François Sirinelli (Paris: Gallimard, 1992), 178–80. As Prochasson and Rasmussen point out, p. 267, the *Revue universelle* was born in 1920, as part of the "Maurrassian program," and called for writers to rally to the "Renaissance intellectuelle et nationale," as opposed to the "Internationale" and "Révolution." Until the Action Française was condemned by the Vatican in 1921, Jacques Maritain wrote a philosophical column in its the journal.

157. Winock, *Siècle des intellectuels*, 189; and Wright, 340.

158. Olivier Corpet, "La Revue," 178; and Winock, *Siècle des intellectuels*, 193.

159. Prochasson and Rasmussen, 269. On intellectual nationalism, see Hanna, *The Mobilization of Intellect*, 14.

160. Corpet, "La Revue," 179–80.

161. Agulhon, *République*, 1:323–25, Wright, 351, and Winock, *Siècle des intellectuels* 144.

162. Agulhon, *République*, 364–66.

163. Pierre Lasserre, *Philosophie du goût musical* (Paris: Bernard Grasset, 1922), 61–62. Lasserre was now a prominent figure, having given a series of public lectures sponsored by the *La revue hebdomadaire*, in which he affirmed that he had strengthened his allegiance to the classic tradition. For more information on Lasserre see Sapiro, *La guerre des écrivains*, 115. On the larger politicization of literature in this period see 72ff. As she points out (132), Pierre Lasserre won the grand prize from the Académie française in 1922.

164. Corpet, 173. On the association of a "return to order" after the war with a classicism that valued "construction and rigor," but without academicism, on the part of factions of both the Left and the Right, see Matthew Affron, "Waldemar George: A Parisian Art Critic on Modernism and Fascism," in *Fascist Visions: Art and Ideology in France and Italy*, ed. By Matthew Affron and Mark Antliff (Princeton, NJ: Princeton University Press, 1997), 174.

165. Ibid., 174; and Prochasson and Rasmussen, 271.

166. See Fernand-Georges Roquebrune, review of *L'heure espagnole* in *La revue critique des idées et des livres*, 1923: 184–85.

167. "Un concert d'Action française," *L'action française* 5 June, 1920.

168. On France's social problems and strikes, see Wright, 360; on the Communists and "Bolshevism," see 339.//
169. Agulhon, République, 326.
170. Hanna, 20.
171. Agulhon, République, 356.
172. Ibid., 345. In the two years after the war many (including Romain Rolland) reflected on how to resolve the tension between universalism and particularism, especially in light of the concentration on the country's immediate advantage in this period, as opposed to the republican ideal of the universalism of French culture (Prochasson and Rasmussen, 253).
173. Winock, Siècle des intellectuels, 166–67; and 170. Henri Barbusse, who became a Communist in 1923, founded Clarté. See Pascal Ory and Jean-François Sirinelli, Les Intellectuels en France de l'Affaire Dreyfus à nos jours (Paris: Armand Colin, 1992), 85. On exchanges between the French and German Left over the Russian model, see Huynh, 76; and Willett, Art and Politics, 172. On the artistic and modernist journals of the Left that preceded Clarté, such as La caravane, Les cahiers idéalistes français, and La Forge, see Affron, 172. La Forge sought to bring intellectuals and workers together (173). In 1920 it founded a short-lived "Université du Peuple," which included instruction in politics, social questions, and dramatic, musical, and visual arts. It became involved with modern culture in Austria, Germany, and Russia as well.
174. Agulhon, République, 1:350.
175. See Barbusse's opening statement in Clarté 1921, 1.
176. Winock, Siècle des intellectuels, 182–83. As he points out (212, 214–16, 221), Joseph Delteil was among the first to be excluded by the Party, and the Surrealists were officially denounced in 1930, although Aragon remained a Communist after 1932. The definitive break between Surrealists and Communists would come in the years 1934–36.
177. Jean-Richard Bloch, Romain Rolland, and other pacifist intellectuals helped to found L'Europe in 1923. Bloch had previously collaborated on the journals L'effort and L'effort libre. Winock, 173.
178. Jean-Richard Bloch, "Une insurrection contre la sensibilité," as cited in Le Monde musical 17 (18 Sept. 1924). See Francis Poulenc, Correspondance 1910–1963, ed. Myriam Chimènes (Paris: Fayard, 1994), 240.
179. See Jean-Richard Bloch, "Prolégomènes à toute chronique musicale," Clarté 1925: 129.
180. See Jean Lacouture, Une Adolescence du siècle. Jacques Rivière et la Nouvelle revue française (Paris: Seuil, 1994), 564. As he points out, Rivière turned the journal away from the influence of Maurras.
181. Ibid., 4. Significantly, the Revue musicale passed into the hands of the Nouvelle revue française after the war.
182. Jacques Rivière, "Parti de l'intelligence," La Nouvelle revue française Sept. 1919: 613.
183. Prochasson and Rasmussen, 262; and Winock, 200. On the question of "pure art" in the La nouvelle revue française, also see Sapiro, Guerro des écrivains, 137–39.
184. Winock, Siècle des intellectuels, 195-97; and Benda, La Trahison des clercs, 131.
185. Benda, 142; and Jacques Rivière, editor's "Introduction" to La Nouvelle revue française June, 1919: 9.
186. Prochasson and Rasmussen, 212, 278.
187. Jacques Rivière, editor's "Introduction" to La Nouvelle revue française 1 June 1919: 8. Rivière condemned the Action Française as "pagan" in the journal in 1920. See Winock, Siècle des intellectuels 190.

188. Prochasson and Rasmussen, 270. During the war republican scholars had defined classical tradition as intrinsically cosmopolitan (Hanna, 145). On the "corruption" of classicism in the university in the nineteenth century, see Sapiro, *Guerre des écrivains,* 121.

189. Hanna, 154. The vice-president of the Ligue des Droits de l'Homme, Victor Basch, defined classicism as both universal and cosmopolitan (ibid., 159). On the classicism of the Left as opposed to that of the Right, see Affron, 174.

190. Winock, *Siècle des intellectuels,* 160. He points out that many collaborators on the journal became practicing Catholics. Winock also notes (157) that Gide, who became famous during the war, was friends with Claudel, but the latter saw himself a guardian of the moral order, which, inevitably led to a conflict with Gide over homosexuality.

191. Prochasson and Rasmussen, 278.

192. Winock, *Siècle des intellectuels,* 162. Also see Jean Lacouture, *Une Adolescence du siècle,* 571.

193. Winock, *Siècle des intellectuels,* 160.

194. Poulenc, *Correspondance,* ed. Myriam Chimènes, 163–64. André Coeuroy, one editor of the *La revue musicale,* was a "normalien," as was Louis Laloy, who also contributed to it..

195. Ibid., 175. On Prunières see Laloy, *Louis Laloy,* 314. On the concerts of the *La revue musicale* see Mussat, "Réception de Schoenberg,"155. André Coeuroy took over as editor after Prunières. On the concerts also see Nichols, *The Harlequin Years,* 197.

196. See Pascale Ory, in *Belle illusion: Culture et politique sous le signe du Front populaire 1935–1938* (Paris: Plon, 1994), 295. He notes the integration of this group into the musical life of Paris, as opposed to the Orphéon choral societies, composed of working men. But it is also important to be aware of the implications of this integration for the character and political dimension of French musical culture.

197. On the prewar genesis of the group, see Fulcher, *French Cultural Politics,* 30–33. Ory notes (*Belle illusion,* 295), that throughout his career Doyen remained a part of the political Left. Close not only to Charpentier, but also to Bruneau and Zola, he dedicated his own *Symphonie funèbre et triomphale,* modeled after Berlioz, to Emile Zola. After having assisted Charpentier with his Conservatoire Populaire de Mimi Pinson, he became, in 1906, a founding member of the group of artists and intellectuals at the Abbaye de Créteil. He was also close to the writer Georges Duhamel who, after Doyen's premature death in October 1935, published his "Thrène pour un ami, Albert Doyen."

198. See Jean Marguerite, *Les Fêtes du Peuple: l'Oeuvre, les moyens, le but* (Paris: Les Fêtes du Peuple, 1921), 3. The group consisted of a mixed chorus and amateur orchestra. See Ory, *La Belle illusion,* 295.

199. Herman Lebovics, *True France:The Wars Over Cultural Identity 1900–1945* (Ithaca: Cornell University Press, 1992), 158. For a view of the Fêtes as increasingly "bourgeois," see Michael Faure, *Néoclassicisme musical,* 224-25

200. See Jane F. Fulcher, "The Concert as Political Propaganda in France and the Control of Performative Context," *The Musical Quarterly* 82/1 (Spring 1998): 41–67.

201. This "fête" was organized by the "Conseil National et la Fédération de la Seine du Parti Socialiste et les Amis de Jaurès," and included a speech my Marcel Cachin.

202. On the changing and conflicting perceptions of Wagner's political implications in France, see Jane F. Fulcher, "A Political Barometer of Twentieth-Century France: Wagner as Jew or Anti-Semite," *The Musical Quarterly* 84/1 (Spring 2000): 41–57. As Faure points out (*Néoclassicisme musical,* 224), the group performed in a variety of venues and for groups that included unions, clerical employees, the *universités populaires,* masonic lodges, Socialist youth and Communist groups. Faure does not, however, take note of how

the significance of the works could be inflected or "radicalized" by such contexts, and rather sees the message communicated as being that taste was a bourgeois privilege, which the people could adopt.

203. On the repertoire of the "Fêtes du Peuple" before the war, see Fulcher, *French Cultural Politics*, 130–33. On the concept of "hermeneutic windows," see Lawrence Kramer, *Music as Cultural Practice 1800-1900* (Berkeley: University of California Press, 1990), 9–10. Michael Faure claims (*Néoclassicisme musical,* 225) that the readings became less militant with the turn to figures such as Laforgue, Verlaine, or Mallarmé. This is again misleading since it ignores the performative context, which affected the understanding of these texts.

204. See Jean Marguerite, *Les Fêtes du Peuple,* 3.

205. Georges Duhamel organized an intellectual circle that included Jules Romain, Albert Doyen, and Maurice Vlaminck. See Prochasson and Rasmussen, 278.

206. For an example of the interpretation of eurythmics in terms of "self-mastery" see the advertisement for it in *L'esprit nouveau* 1920, 184: "La rythmique donne à l'individu une connaissance plus fertile de soi-même et fait un individu mieux organisé, mieux armé pour la vie moderne, plus maître de soi."

207. Jacques-Dalcroze, "Une nouvelle idéale musicale," *L'esprit nouveau* 1920, 311.

208. The Cartel des Gauches, which lasted from 1924 to 1926, was a coalition of Radicals and Socialists, under the leadership of the Radical, Herriot, and opposed to postwar clericalism and nationalist politics. See Agulhon, *République,* 1: 358–59. The early postwar programs of the "Fêtes du Peuple" include the "Soirée organisée par la 9e section socialiste de la Seine à la Salle du Grand-Orient" (the Masonic Temple), 23 March 1919; the "matinée organisée par le Syndicat de la voiture-aviation à la Salle de l'Union des syndicats de la Seine," May 31, 1919; the "Commémeration solenelle du centenaire de la naissance de Walt Whitman," 18 June, 1919; the "Fête de la fraternité, organisée par les Fêtes du peuple à la Salle de l'Union de la Seine, 31 July, 1919; and the "fête" for Jaurès and the war dead, already mentioned. See Marguerite, 53. And as Prochasson and Rasmussen point out (234), in Oct. 1919 the "Fêtes du Peuple" organized a festival called "Offrande à la Russie."

209. On Poincaré's return to power, amidst the financial problems of 1926, see Wright, 348, 356.

210. Archives Nationales, F21–4552, "Subventions aux théatres et sociétés musicales."

211. The Cartel des Gauches was elected on May 11, 1924.

212. On the repertoire of the "Fêtes du Peuple," see Fulcher, *French Cultural Politics,* 132–33. On the repoliticization of romanticism and classicism after the war, see Sapiro, *Guerre des écrivains,* 123–24.

213. Handel carried populist associations in France ever since Romain Rolland's book on him of 1908, which emphasized the "popular" qualitites of his oratorios; Fulcher, *French Cultural Politics,* 58–59.

214. On Bourgault-Ducoudray and the Action Française, see Jane F. Fulcher, "The Concert as Political Propaganda in France and the Control of Performative Context," 41–42.

215. On Charpentier's *Couronnement de la muse du peuple,* see Fulcher, *French Cultural Politics,* 89–92.

216. See Manfred Kelkel, *Naturalisme, vérisme, et réalisme dans l'opéra de 1890 à 1930* (Paris: Librairie Philosophique J. Vrin, 1984), 205; and Paul Bertrand, *Le Monde de la musique* (Geneva: La Palatine, 1947), 76.

217. On Charpentier's political sympathies as they developed before the war, see Fulcher, *French Cultural Politics,* 204–6.

218. Ibid., 93–97.

219. On Charpentier's original intentions, Ibid., 82–93.

220. See Marc Lap, review of *Charpentier's Couronnement de la muse* in *Le peuple* 15 July, 1925.

221. Ibid.

222. On Gédalge's Third Symphony see Brian Hart, "The Symphony in Theory and Practice in France 1900-1914" (Ph.D. dissertation, Indiana University, 1994), 114–124.

223. Georges Chennevière, "Les grands concerts," *L'humanité* 28 Feb., 1924.

224. Ibid.

225. On the impact of Fourierist ideas on French musical aesthetics, see Jane F. Fulcher, *The Nation's Image: French Grand Opera as Politics and Politicized Art* (New York: Cambridge University Press, 1987), 114, 128, and 129–30.

226. See Jane F. Fulcher, "The Composer as Intellectual: Ideological Inscriptions In French Interwar Neoclassicism," *The Journal of Musicology* 17/2 (Spring 1999): 197–230.

227. Julien Benda, *La Trahison des clercs*, 199–20.

228. Ibid., 118, 120.

229. On the relation of political and intellectual trends to French cultural life in this period, see Agulhon, *République*, 1:370.

230. On the different Rights in this period, see Jean-François Sirinelli, ed., *Histoire des droites en France* vol. 2 (Paris: Gallimard, 1992), 513–26.

231. See *Comoedia*, 21 Jan. 1920.

232. Léon Vallas, *Vincent d'Indy*, 110. The letter from d'Indy to Jean Wiéner was published in *Comoedia* on 3 March 1924.

233. Vallas, *Vincent d'Indy*, 2: 110.

234. Vincent d'Indy, *Lettres à Auguste Sérieyx*, ed. M. L. Sérieyx (Lausanne: Editions du Cerrin, 1961), 26.

235. Vincent d'Indy, *Richard Wagner et son Influence sur l'art musical français* (Paris: Delagrave, 1930).

236. Ibid., 13.

237. Ibid., 84. This is in contrast to d'Indy's first review of *Pelléas*, in which he compared the declamation with that of Monteverdi, although he condemned other aspects of the opera. See Fulcher, *French Cultural Politics*, 178. It is also significant to note, in this connection, that d'Indy returns to a related preoccupation in his book on Wagner: He castigated "l'enseignement officiel" as incapable of assimilating the benefits of the Wagnerian reform. Here he again points out that Wagner's influence was absorbed through the efforts of the Société Nationale and the pupils of César Franck.

238. See Jane F. Fulcher, "The Orphéon Societies: 'Music for the Workers' in Second-Empire France," *International Review of the Aesthetics and Sociology of Music* X/1 (1979).

239. For further background on the Orphéon societies and their context, see Philippe Gumplowicz, *Les Travaus d'Orphé: 150 ans de vie musicale amateur en France: harmonies—chorales—fanfares* (Paris: Aubier, 1987).

240. Vallas, *Vincent d'Indy*, 103.

241. *The New Grove Dictionary of Music and Musicians* 1st edition, s.v. "Indy, Vincent d'," by Robert Orledge.

242. Paul Bertrand, *Le Monde de la musique*, 26.

243. Vallas, *Vincent d'Indy*, 118.

244. See Hanna, 9.

245. Arbie Orenstein, ed., *A Ravel Reader: Correspondence, Articles, Interviews* (New York: Columbia University Press), 113. As Orenstein points out (29), Ravel had known Léon Blum since the turn of the century, in the circle of the *Revue blanche*. Ravel continued

to admire Blum and Paul Painlevé, who had been Minister of Finance during the war. Also see Manuel Rosenthal, *Ravel, Souvenirs* (Paris: Hazan, 1995), 15, 127, on Ravel's dedication to *Le populaire* and his ties to Léon Blum. As Rosenthal also points out, it was an inherent sympathy for the poor that helped determine Ravel's political choices. See Dominique Saudinos, *Manual Rosenthal: une vie* (Paris: Mercure de France, 1992), 95, who also notes Raven's great friendship with Léon Blum and the fact that he read *Le populaire* attentively every day.

246. Orenstein, ed., *A Ravel Reader*, 181; and Rosenthal, *Rave, Souvenirs,*. 128.

247. Rosenthal, *Ravel*, 127.

248. Paul Painlevé went on to become a founder of the Cartel des Gauches. On Mme Clemenceau's salon and the composers and artist who gathered there, see Nichols, *The Harlequin Years*, 198.

249. Marcel Marnat, *Maurice Ravel* (Paris: Fayard, 1986), 460, 464.

250. Ibid., 418.

251. Rosenthal, *Ravel*, 88. Ravel also professed to like the music of the Jewish composer Meyerbeer, which had been consistently attacked by the anti-Semitic Right. In fact, Ravel claimed that he preferred Meyerbeer to Wagner. (ibid, 157).

252. Marnat, *Maurice Ravel*, 489. As Marnat points out (472), the work was dedicated to Misia Sert and premiered in her salon. On the Clemenceau salon, see Mussat, "Réception de Schoenberg," 151.

253. Maurice Ravel, "Esquisse autobiographique," *La revue musicale* 1938: 214.

254. Rosenthal, (*Ravel*, 32), points out that it was Ravel's good friend, Ida Rubenstein, who finally staged it.

255. Ibid., 170. As he points out, Ravel referred to the "valse" as "un rhythme qui hante l'humanité parce que c'est la 'danse du diable'." See Carl E. Schorske, *Fin-de-Siècle Vienna: Politics and Culture* (New York: Alfred A. Knopf, 1980), 3–4.

256. See Lettres autographes, Ravel. BNF, Musique, letter dated 10 March 1924. In this letter Ravel also indicates his plans to go to a performance of Honegger's *Le roi David*.

257. It was written between 1922 and 1924 for a Hungarian violinist. Rosenthal, *Ravel*, 20.

258. Marnat, 401. Here Ravel was seconded in his belief in the importance of hearing the contemporary music of all countries by Charles Koechlin. See Caballero, 614. Ravel had visited Vienna with Casella in 1920 for a series of concerts sponsored by the French embassy. Among the works they performed was the two-piano version of *La Valse*. Schoenberg had already made a gesture of cultural openness in his Society for Private Musical Performance in Vienna, in 1918, and which included the performance of modern French works not yet heard in Vienna, such as those by Debussy, Satie, Ravel. See Mussat, "Réception de Schoenberg," 157. On Schoenberg's performances at the SMI, see ibid, 161. As she points out, the first concert included the chorales of Bach, thus establishing Schoenberg's "serious" lineage. He was also invited to speak at the Ecole Normale de Musique, and was appropriately fêted by the Austrian ambassador and by those artists, aristocrats, and diplomats who were promoting French-Austrian "rapprochement," including Henirich Mann, the Duchesse de Clermont-Tonnerre, and the Paul Clemenceaus. Ibid, 163–69.

259. Michel Duchesneau, "La Musique française pendant la Guerre 1914–1918. Autour de la tentative de fusion de la Société Nationale de Musique et de la Société Musicale Indépendante," *Revue de Musicologie* 82/1 (1996): 144.

260. See Robert Morrissen's review of Gerd Kruleich's *Jeanne d'Arc in der Geschichte: Historiographie-Politik-Kultur* in *Journal of Modern History*, vol. 64, Dec. 1992: 800. As he points out, nineteenth-century patriotism originated in Jacobin thought, derived from the

Enlightenment and its universalist ideals. French nationalism thus belonged to the Left and was associated with universalism until the 1880s, when it shifted over to a "new" Right that combined traditionalist and populist thought.

261. Orenstein, ed., *A Ravel Reader,* 195, 198. Ravel later discerned that the nomination had been initiated by Lucien Gabor and Jacques Durand.

262. Ibid.

263. Ibid., 201.

264. Marnat, 486.

265. Ibid.

266. Orenstein, *A Ravel Reader,* 196.

267. Marnat, 486.

268. Orenstein, *A Ravel Reader,* 201.

269. Ibid. Significantly, Ravel was not the only artist to refuse the Légion d' Honneur for political reasons: Georges Bernanos, holding almost opposite political views, refused this honor from the Republic in 1927, 1938, and 1946. See Hamilton, 179.

270. Ravel, "Esquisse autobiographique," as published in the *La revue musicale* 1938: 214–15. The original manuscript is in the BNF, Musique, Réserve.

271. Ravel was uniquely bold among French composers in the twenties, being the only one to employ jazz on the operatic stage. On Ravel's enthusiasm for Billy Arnold's jazz orchestra, see Goeffrey J. Haydon, "A Study of the Exchange of Influence between the Music of Early Twentieth-Century Parisian Composers and Ragtime, Blues, and Early Jazz." (DMA Document, University of Texas at Austin, 1992), 58.

272. Orenstein, *A Ravel Reader,* 188. I am indebted to Gary Laycock, who brought many of the observations that follow concerning Ravel's stylistic manipulations in the work to my attention in his excellent seminar paper. As he and others have noted, a trombone "snear" announces the entrance of the English teapot and Chinese cup, followed by a bass clarinette playing a blues motive. The brassy orchestration and the rhythm further suggest both the foxtrot and ragtime.

273. See Eugen Weber, *The Hollow Years: France in the 1930s* (New York: Norton, 1994), 94–95.

274. On colonialist "orientalism" in France and its images, see Herman Lebovics, *True France: The Wars Over Cultural Identity 1900–1945* (Ithaca: Cornell University Press, 1992), 51–83.

275. See Glenn Watkins, *Soundings: Music in the Twentieth Century* (New York: Schirmer, 1988), 279–83. Here Watkins discusses the various styles used in the work.

276. On Ravel's aversion to the Schola, see Fulcher, *French Cultural Politics,* 209–210.

277. See Vladimir Jankelevitch, *Ravel,* trans. Margaret Crosland (New York: Grove Press, 1959), 127–28.

278. Laycock notes the specific similarity with Act I scene 3 of d'Indy's work.

279. Jankélévitch, *Ravel,* 127–28. Nichols (*The Harlequin Years,* 94), point out the stylisitc reference to Massenet, and notes in the aria for the fire, "Arrière! Je rechauffe les bons," a reference to the tradition of Delibe's *Lakmé,* in which fire is associated with "the exotic, dangerous other." Ravel was clearly a master of both evoking and distancing himself from convention, together with all the associations it carried.

280. The utterances of the clock suggest Offenbach, and there is, as Laycock also notes, a parody of Puccini as well. D'Indy, in fact, condemned Massenet in his treatise as the product of the "école judaique." See Fulcher, *French Cultural Politics,* 32. Here it is important to note that one of Ravel's primary supporters was the Russian Jewish dancer Ida Rubenstein, formerly of Diaghilev's Ballets Russes, and then independent. See Porcile, *Belle époque,* 137–38.

281. Orenstein, *A Ravel Reader*, 204. And see Carolyn Abbate, "Outside Ravel's Tomb," *Journal of the American Musicological Society* 52/3 (Fall 1999): 468, 473, 494, 507, 520. As Nichols points out (*The Harlequin Years*, 91), the work premiered in Monte Carlo in 1925, and it was probably, in part, the praise of influential figures, like Henry Prunières, editors of the *La revue musicale*, that influenced its acceptance at the Opéra-Comique.

282. Abbate, 204.

283. The articles appeared on 5 and 7 July 1927. See Winock *Le Siècle des intellectuels*, 223.

284. Rosenthal, *Ravel*, 119.

285. Maurice Ravel, "Ma vie et ma musique.Esquisse autobiographique," BNF, Musique, Reserve.

286. Marnat, 501–02.

287. Ravel, "Ma vie et ma musique."

288. See Manuel Rosenthal, *Jeanne d'Arc. Suite symphonique en 5 parties. Après le "Jeanne d'Arc" de Joseph Delteil* (Paris: Jean Jobert, Editeurs, 1936).

289. Marnat, 501. As previously mentioned, the works contributed to the issue were published as "Le tombeau de Debussy." Ravel's sonata was written between 1920 and 1922.

290. Ravel, "Esquisse autobiographique," as published in the *La revue musicale* 1938, 214.

291. Marnat, 502–05.

292. Paul Collaer, *A History of Modern Music*, trans. Sally Abeles (New York: The World Publishing Comp., 1961), 173–74.

293. See Rosenthal, *Ravel. Souvenirs,* 83–85; and Ludovic Tournes, *New Orleans sur Seine. Histoire du jazz en France* (Paris: Fayard, 1999), 21. Tournès also discusses Ravel's use of jazz in his *Concerto pour la main gauche*, as well as in several other works. As Rosenthal points out (*Ravel*, 86–87), Ravel often went to hear jazz in Paris, and like Milhaud was particularly drawn to its long, melancholy melodies, as in the blues. Rosenthal, again like Milhaud, perceives jazz as a common form of resistance among oppressed peoples, such as Jews and blacks. Ravel was also attracted, like Wiéner, by the rhythmic component of jazz, to its syncopations and characteristic assymetries. Ravel continued to praise jazz as late as 1932, arguing that "It is not a passing phase, but has come to stay. It is thrilling and inspiring" (Rosenthan, *A Ravel Reader*, 490).

294. On Ravel's bitonality, verging at times on the atonal, in the Duo Sonata of 1922, see H. H. Stuckenschmidt, *Maurice Ravel*, trans. Samuel R. Rosenbaum (Philadelphia: Chiton, 1968), 195. Ravel would continue to make references to jazz in the 1930s, most notably, perhaps, in the first and last movements of his Piano Concerto in G, of 1932.

295. As cited by Marnat, 529.

296. This conception of classicism was shared by their mutual friend, Charles Koechlin, who described it in a letter to Max d'Ollone, of 10 Feb., 1920, as follows: "Pour moi, Fauré et Debussy sont essentiellement classiques à cause de la pureté de l'écriture, de la réalisation de la pensée, parce que tout est dit nettement. . ." Charles Koechlin, *Correspondance* (Paris: La Revue Musicale, 1982), 43. It is significant to note that the *La revue musicale* encouraged the interaction of composers and aritsts from other countries at its weekly, salon-like meetings, which included the performance of music. See Nichols, *The Harlequin Years*, 206.

297. As cited in Marnat, 529. Roland-Manuel clearly perceived Ravel's evolution concerning this issue. Although his epigraph to the *Valses nobles* of 1911, from Henri de Regnier, referred to "le plaisir délicieux et toujours nouveau d'une occupation inutile," this did not apply to Ravel's postwar compositions, imbued with a different spirit.

298. Ibid., 492.

299. We may see a conservative appropriation of Ravel in the musical press as well, one example being the *Le monde musical* in May 1919. Here Ravel's art, as exemplified in *Le tombeau de Couperin*, is described as "measured" in taste and balance, like a tragedy by Racine, a fable by La Fontaine or "L'embarquement pour Cythère" by Watteau; as quoted in Cecilia Dunoyer, *Marguerite Long, A Life in French Music, 1874–1966* (Bloomington, Ind.: Indiana University Press, 1993), 80. Ravel, then, appealed to both ends of the political spectrum, which similarly saw him as a "classic," but for different reasons. As Marnat point out, 495, Ravel's work was being increasingly recorded on both player piano and on records.

300. On Satie's unconventional education, and his study of ancient Greek as a child, see Fulcher, *French Cultural Politics*, 195.

301. Benda, *La Trahison des clercs*, 170.

302. According to Milhaud, Satie told him that *Socrate* was "un pamphlet contre la magistrature. C'est une histoire si injuste." Darius Milhaud, *Notes sur la musique. Essais et chroniques*, ed. Jeremy Drake (Paris: Flammarion, 1982), 144. This was perhaps in reference to his own condemnation for libel, as recounted in the previous chapter. The "Mort de Socrate," from *Phaedo*, is the third section of thr work, following the opening "Portrait de Socrate," from *Symposium*, and the middle section, "Bords de l'Illissus," from *Phaedrus*. Satie was concerned not only with the purely philosophical passages, but rather with those depicting Socrate's personality and life. According to Satie, the work was a kind of hommage to Socrates" : "En écrivant cette oeuvre. . . . je n'ai nullement voulu ajouter à la beauté des Dialogues de Platon . . . ce n'est qu'une rêverie d'artiste . . . qu'un humble hommage." As cited in Ornella Volta, *L'Imagier d'Erik Satie* (Paris: Francis de Velde, 1977), 65.

303. Michel Crossart, *The Food of Love: Princesse Edmonde de Polignac and her Salon (1895–1943)* (London: Hamisch Hamilton, 1978), 123–25.

304. On the similarity between Satie's technique in earlier works and ancient "mennipean discourse" see Fulcher, *French Cultural Politics*, 198–99; and on "mennipean discourse" itself see Julia Kristeva, *Desire in Language: A Semiotic Approach to Literature* (New York: Columbia University Press, 1980), 81.

305. Kristeva, *Desire in Language*, 81. My argument here is thus strongly opposed to that of Faure (*Néoclassicisme musical*, 245), who not only construes Plato's dialogue as "bien-pensant," but claims that Satie's "blancheur tonale" confers a message of stoic resignation, and not a denunciation of injustice. The meaning of Satie's style, I contend, has to be read within the context of the discursive situation or dialogue, as well as of the meanings of the period.

306. Vincent d'Indy, *Lettres à Auguste Sérieyx* (Lausanne: Editions du Cerrin, 1961), 26. And on the public premiere, conducted by Félix Delgrange, see Porcile, *Bélle epoque*, 244. As Porcile points out, Jean Marnold was not favorable to the work, stressing what he saw as the work's "impuissance," stylistically.

307. Francis Poulenc, *Correspondance 1910–1963*, ed. Myriam Chimènes (Paris: Fayard, 1994), 184, letter from Poulenc to Milhaud of Jan. 1923. The first performance of *Socrate*, on June 24, 1918, was at the home of the comte Etienne de Beaumont, and was followed by another private performance on 21 March 1919, at Sylvia Beach's bookstore, Shakespeare and Company, with such notable intellectuals as Gide, Claudel, and Francis Jammes in attendance. The first public performance, at the Société Nationale de Musique, took place in Jan. 1920. Ibid., 88. The first performance of *Parade* (in concert version) after the war was on 11 May 1919, at the Salle Gaveau, under Felix Delgrange.

308. Francis Steegmuller, *Cocteau. A Biography* (Boston: Little, Brown, and Comp., 1970), 188, 191.

309. On the birth and appeal of Communism in France the early twenties, see Gordon Wright, *France in Modern Times* (New York: Rand McNally, 1974), 338–39.

310. Ornella Volta, *Erik Satie* (Paris: Seghers, 1979), 109.

311. Ibid., 120.

312. Moreover, Surrealism had a strongly spiritualist component with which Satie could not identify. See Jay Winter, *Sites of Memory. Sites of Mourning,* 143.

313. Robert Orledge, *Satie the Composer* (New York: Cambridge University Press, 1990), 234. As Orledge points out (235), Satie contributed to such Dadaist journals as *Action, Le mouvement accéléré,* and *Création.* On Dada's attack on existing artistic traditions as incapable of expressing the new awareness that came with the disruptions of wartime, see Inez Hedges, *Languages of Revolt: Dada and Surrealist Literature and Film* (Durham, NC: Duke University Pree, 1983), xi. As she stresses (xiii), Dada questions both the content and basis of language itself, aiming for a politics of radical disorientation which is to act as the prelude to a new consciousness. Man, the Dadaists believed, could renew himself through a firsthand contact with life forces, unmediated by all cultural conventions. Both Dada and Surrealism, as she points out (34), emphasize the role of art in activating the perceiver's cognitive adaptation to reality and question the function of art in terms of its relation to the world (41).

314. See Martin Marks, "Film Music of the Silent Period 1895–1924 (Ph.D. dissertation, Harvard University, 1990), 448–49. As he notes, the invitation for Picabia to collaborate on the work came from Satie.

315. Ibid., 451–54. As Hedges points out (75), ironically, the first performance of *Relâche* did have to be cancelled. When it finally premiered, it was attacked in the conservative *Mercure de France* and *Eclair* but praised in both *Bonsoir* and the *Journal littéraire.*

316. Robert Orledge, *Satie the Composer,* 234–35. Breton, Aragon, and Soupault first championed Dada in France, but rebelled against it in 1922 and founded Surrealism. See Steegmuller, *Cocteau,* 238.

317. Orledge, *Satie the Composer,* 235. *Mercure* was written for the comte de Beaumont, with decor by Picasso and choreography by Massine. At the end of the ballet the surrealists cried "Vive Picasso, à bas Satie"; Milhaud, *Notes sur la musique,* 145.

318. See Jann Pasler, "Paris: Conflicting Notions of Progress," in *Music and Society: The Late Romantic Era,* ed. Jim Samson (Englewood Cliffs, NJ: Prentice Hall, 1991), 408. As she here points out, according to Cocteau in 1919, "One could say that the spirit of the new in every period is the highest form of the spirit of contradiction."

319. Jean Wiéner, *Allegro appassionato* (Paris: Pierre Belfond, 1978), 47, 49, and 116. The first of these concerts was held at the Salle des Agriculteurs, on the rue d'Athène, on 6 Dec. 1921. The concerts continued until 1925. See Ludovic Tournès, *New Orleans-sur-Seine,* 19–20. On Wiéner, also see Denise Pilmer-Taylor, "*La Musique pour tout le monde:* Jean Wiéner and the Dawn of French Jazz" (Ph.D. dissertation, University of Michigan, 1998).

320. Wiéner, *Allegro appassionata,* 43–44. The bar later moved and was renamed Le Boeuf sur le Toit. Tournès, *New Orleans-sur- Seine,* 19. As Michael Faure notes (*Néoclassicisme musical,* 226), Wiéner came from "la grande bourgeoisie d'affaires," but as we shall see, his gradual integration of more classical music in his "concerts salades" between 1922 and 1925 was not an indication, as Faure argues, of a conservative trajectory, analogous to that of Poincaré. On the opening of the Bar Gaya, upon Milhaud's suggestion, and with the collaboration of Cocteau, see Nancy Perloff, 92.

321. Steegmuller, *Cocteau,* 264; and Marnat, 453.

322. Georges Auric, *Quand j'étais là* (Paris: Bernard Grasset, 1979), 163.

323. Wiéner, 66.

324. On his supporters, see ibid., 43–44, 53.

325. Ibid., 53. On the concept of social "distinction" through taste, see Pierre Bourdieu, *La distinction: Critique sociale du jugement* (Paris: Minuit, 1979). Among the patrons of the Gaya were Diaghilev, Misia Sert, René Clair, Jane Bathori, Maurice Chevalier, and Fernand Léger. See Perloff, 92.

326. Tournès, *New Orleans-sur-Seine*, 19. On the rage for jazz among the social elite, see 21. Tournès also notes, 24, the social heterogeneity of jazz fans in Paris, which ranged from social elites to the frequenters of music halls (24).

327. In other words, educational "reproduction" was temporarily suspended. On the concept of educational reproduction see Pierre Bourdieu and Jean-Claude Passeron, *Reproduction in Society and Culture*, trans. Richard Nice (Beverly Hills: Sage Publications, 1970).

328. Wiéner, 47, 75–77.

329. On the trial of Barrès as "the symbol of all that was shallow, dishonest, and stifling in the older generation," see Robert Soucy, "Barrès and French Fascism," *French Historical Studies* Spring 1967: 68. On the attack of youth on the blind moral idealism of their elders during the war, see Modris Eksteins, *Rites of Spring: The Great War and the Birth of the Modern Age* (Toronto: Lester and Orpen Dinnys, 1989), 257–58.

330. Agulhon, *République*, 351.

331. Ibid.

332. On Bakhtin's conception of monological power, see James Clifford, *The Predicament of Culture: Twentieth-Century Ethnography, Literature, and Art* (Cambridge, Mass.: Harvard University Press, 1988), 46.

333. Wiéner, 49–52. As Jeremy Drake points out, Wiéner played jazz with Vince Lowry at the Gaya. See Darius Milhaud, *Notes sur la musique*, 32.

334. Tournès, *New Orleans-sur-Seine*, 115. Also see Nancy Perloff, 92. On jazz in Paris in this period, and the place of Jean Wiéner, see Jeffrey H. Jackson, *Making Jazz French: Music and Modern Life in Interwar Paris* (Durham, NC: Duke University Press, 2003), 119.

335. Appearance in such a context soon proved dangerous to Stravinsky. In 1922 (in another concert venue) a performance of his Symphony for Wind Instruments and his Concertino provoked audience hilarity and whistles, and his case was not abetted by the counterapplause of Wiéner's circle. See Wiéner, 66. A similar reaction occurred at the premiere of *Mavra* in 1924. On it see Richard Taruskin, *Stravinsky and the Russian Traditions* (Berkeley: University of California Press, 1996), 591–96. Such responses may have been compounded by the fact that Stravinsky, who now advocated cosmopolitanism, was traveling continually, including trips to former "enemy countries."

On performances of and writings on Schoenberg in Paris both before and after the war, see Mussat, "Réception de Schoenberg," 145–47, 152–55. As Mussat notes, both Milhaud and Honegger were enthusiasts of his music by 1915, and Ravel by 1914. Schoenberg soon became a symbol of anti-chauvinism for young composers, if not for Cocteau. By 1920 Les Six were including his works in the concerts, as well as those of other contemporary foreign composers. Among the latter were Casella, Lourié, and Bartok. As she also points out, the Directive Committee of the SMI was open to foreign composers from 1921, and would include Schoenberg, Bartok, de Falla, Turina, and Szymanowski.

336. For the programs of the concerts, see Wiéner, 49–52. As Wiéner points out (47), his knowledge of Schoenberg's music came through the Polish singer (and friend of Milhaud) Marya Freund. Wiéner henceforth accumulated many scores of Schoenberg and Webern. On Milhaud's conception of the French tradition (and his anti-Wagnerism), see his *Notes sur la musique*, 42. As Sprout points out ("Music for a 'New Era'," 46), Diaghilev organized a production of Gounod's *Médecin malgré lui* and *Colombe* in 1924, with the spoken dialogue set to music by Satie and Poulenc.

337. Robert Wohl, *The Generation of 1914* (Cambridge, Mass.: Harvard University Press, 1979), 24.

338. Ibid., 2; and Eksteins, *Rites of Spring*, xv. Here again my interpretation differs substantially from that of Michael Faure who dismisses the wartime and postwar context of these composers, or the conservative culture with which they were in dialogue, stressing rather their purported emphasis on "pleasure" (*Néoclassicisme musical*, 160-61). Although they were questioning the "absolute," as he puts it, it was not simply in the interest of an "easy," accessible music and "good humor." Faure apparently misses the irony of the title of Milhaud's "mémoires," *Ma vie heureuse*, which he associates with their purported quest simply for "happiness" (164). On the impact of the war in discrediting bourgeois institutions and academies see Robert Wohl, "Heart of Darkness: Modernism and its Historians," *Journal of Modern History* vol. 74, no. 3 (Sept. 2002): 614.

339. On the different modernist generations see Robert Wohl, "The Generation of 1914 and Modernism," in *Modernism: Challenges and Perspectives*, eds., Monique Chefdor, Ricardo Quionones, and Albert Wachtel (Urbana, Ill.: University of Illinois Press, 1986), 374.

340. Ibid., 71–73. According to Tyrus Miller in *Late Modernism: Politics, Fiction, and the Arts between the World Wars* (Berkeley: University of California Press, 1999), 17, one of the characteristics of high modernist fiction (in writers such as Proust and Gide) is a focus on "the problem of mastering a chaotic modernity by means of formal techniques." He also notes an "ironic detachment" and self-referentiality—qualities that, as we shall see, appear in Les Six as well.

341. On modernism also see John E. Toews, "Intellectual History after the Linguistic Turn: The Autonomy of Meaning and the Irreducibility of Experience," *The American Historical Review* 92/4 (Oct. 1987), 87. As he points out, modernism may be seen as a "critical dismantling" of inherited cultural languages as ideological constructions. Accordingly, modernism transforms elements from oppositional traditions to official and academic culture: In modernist culture these elements are put into experimental relations, creating new patterns of meaning and self-consciousness about the way in which meaning construction occurs.

342. On Fauré's reforms at the Conservatoire, see Fulcher, *French Cultural Politics*, 143–47; and Gail Hilson Woldu, "Gabriel Fauré as Director of the Conservatoire National de Musique et de Déclamation, 1905–1920" (Ph.D. dissertation, Yale University, 1983).

343. On Stravinsky's neoclassicism within its broader context, see Scott Messing, *Neoclassicism in Music: From the Genesis of the Concept through the Schoenberg-Stravinsky Polemic* (Ann Arbor: UMI Research Press, 1988). On "modernism," as I use it here, see John E. Toews, "Intellectual History after the Linguistic Turn: the Autonomy of Meaning and the Irreducibility of Experience," 87.

344. On Stravinsky and the European past, the best source is still Eric Walter White, *Stravinsky: the Composer and His Works* (Berkeley: University of California Press, 1966).

345. Although neither Durey nor Wiéner were yet Communists, a Left political orientation gradually emerged in both, for, as Herman Lebovics points out in *True France* (163), the cultural vision of the Left (as opposed to the Right) was syncretic, and this clearly attracted them.

346. Paul Landormy, *Musique française après Debussy* (Paris: Gallimard, 1943), 115.

347. This is as opposed to the more common view, as expressed by Geoffrey Spratt in *The Music of Arthur Honegger* (Cork: Cork University Press, 1987), 221: "The external problems and forces whose spirit they chose to incorporate into their music were, to a large extent, only those that symbolized the Montmartre life they loved. They conveniently avoided all the harsh realities of life, but these were the very facts that meant more

to the socially aware Honegger"(221). The other members of the group were indeed equally "socially aware."

348. On the old "network" of official culture, see Frédérique Patureau, *Le Palais Garnier dans la société parisienne 1975–1914* (Liège: Mardaga, 1991), 212–21.

349. Francis Poulenc, *My Friends and Myself*, ed., Stéphane Audel, trans. James Harding (London: Dobson, 1978), 98.

350. Landormy, *Musique française après Debussy*, 41. And see Jean Roy, *Le Groupe des Six* (Paris: Seuil, 1994), 72. As Roy points out, in an article of 1914 Cocteau indeed referred to them as "Les Nouveau Jeunes."

351. See Robert Wohl, *The Generation of 1914*, 9. Massis and de Tarde had argued that the admiration of youth for Barrès was based upon his affirmation of the "ultimate reality" of the nation and his commitment to tradition. On Cocteau's role see Whiting, 493.

352. Satie was at first closely associated with the group, but after a year he left it with no explanation. Significantly, perhaps, the all-too-sensitive Satie was never again to speak to Durey. Ornella Volta, *Erik Satie*, 125–26.

353. Steegmuller, *Cocteau*, 202.

354. Ornella Volta, "Le Rideau se lève sur un os," *Revue internationale de musique française* vol. 23 (June 1987): 87.

355. See James Harding, *The Ox on the Roof: Scenes from Musical Life in Paris in the Twenties* (New York: St. Martin's Press, 1972), 60. Jane Bathori was the pseudonym for Jeanne-Marie Berthier, who had participated in the "universités populaires."

356. Georges Auric, *Quand j'étais là* (Paris: Bernard Grasset, 1979), 132.

357. Keith Daniel, *Francis Poulenc: His Artistic Development and Musical Style* (Ann Arbor: UMI Research Press, 1982), 14. As he points out, later they were able to move to the more capacious Théâtre du Vieux Colombier, and would include the works of friends such as Roland-Manuel on their programs. The "Lyre et Palette" concerts took place in Montparnasse. See Francis Poulenc, *Correspondance*, ed. Myriam Chimènes, 45.

358. Auric and Poulenc also experimented with "conférence-concerts," a prominent wartime genre, as we have seen. Here they had the valuable participation of Guillaume Apollinaire, as an "apologist." Auric, *Quand j'étais là*, 131.

359. Ibid., 132.

360. Ibid.

361. The journal was published by Cocteau's Editions de la Sirène. See Roy, *Le Group des Six*, 248.

362. Daniel, *Francis Poulenc*, 1. See Mussat, "Réception de Schoenberg," 145–47, 153. Just as provocative was Milhaud's dedication of his Fifth String Quartet to Schoenberg (in 1920). See Milhaud, 33. Schoenberg had already influenced Milhaud's Third Quartet, of 1916; Milhaud had heard Schoenberg's Second Quartet in Switzerland in 1913.

363. See Olivier Corpet, "La Revue," in *Histoire des Droites en France*, ed. Jean-François Sirinelli (Paris: Gallimard, 1992), 172. See Michel Winock, *Siècle des intellectuels*, 177–78. See Michael Faure, *Néoclassicisme musical*, 167. He also notes (118–22) Paul Dukas's denigration of Milhaud's *Le boeuf sur le toit*, which Dukas referred to as "une révolution pour faire du bruit," as well as the phrase in the *Guide du concert* of 18 October 1929, "le petit Soviet des Six." Clearly, in the general climate, while Dadaist humor was associated with revolution in a jocular sense, there were still undertones of the more deeply subversive element. On Dada's techniques of "frame breaking," see Hedges, xi–xii, 34–35. Significantly, Messiaen, in the thirties, noted the proximity of Les Six, in this period to Dada. See Nigel Simeone, "Offrandes oubliées: Messaien in the 1930s," *The Musical Times* 141 (2000): 35.

364. Paul Bertrand, *Le Monde de la musique* (Geneva: La Palatine, 1947), 22.

365. Ibid., 94.
366. Landormy, *Musique française après Debussy,* 293–94; and Keith Daniel, *Francis Poulenc,* 14.
367. Auric, 175.
368. Daniel, 18; and Louis Laloy, *Musique retrouvée* (Paris: Plon, 1928), 267.
369. Myriam Chimènes, "La Princesse Edmond de Polignac et la création musicale," in *Musique et le pouvoir,* eds., Hugues Dufourt and Joel-Marie Fauquet (Paris: Aux Amateurs de Livres, 1987), 131–32. Among the Ecole d'Arcueil, she also supported Roger Desormières. And see Porcile, *Bélle epoque,* 132–33. As Porcile points out, among the conductors who promoted contemporary music were Roger Desormières and Pierre Monteux. Of course, the Princesse de Polignac also commissioned works by Tailleferre, Kurt Weil, and Jean Francais, and came to the aid of Stravinsky on numerous occasions. See Nichols, *The Harlequin Years,* 291. Also see Chimènes, *Mécènes et musiciens,* 624–39; and Kahan, *Music's Modern Muse.*
370. Marnat, *Ravel,* 515; and Auric, 210. On the role of Coco Chanel, see Harding, *The Ox on the Roof,* 139. And on the circle that supported the new music, see Poulenc, *Correspondence,* ed. Myriam Chimènes, 156, the letter from Poulenc to Milhaud of 22 June, 1922, in which he mentions the circle at the home of the Princesse de Polignac, which included Barrès, the Noailles, Picasso, and Stravinsky.
371. Chimènes, "La Princesse Edmond de Polignac," 140. As she also points out, the Princesse de Polignac was on the supporting committee of the Concerts Wiéner (134).
372. Auric, 205.
373. The artists they frequented included Picasso, Cocteau, Satie, Reynaldo Hahn, and Les Six. Ibid., 206-07.
374. Ibid., 158
375. Wiéner, *Allegro appassionata,* 47.
376. Ibid., 43–44.
377. Ibid., 40, 49. The composers from the past who were performed also included Rossini, Gounod, and Mozart.
378. Ibid., 49. Roland-Manuel also asserted that Wiéner's concerts had done more for chamber music than the Société Nationale and the Société Musicale Indépendante together. Ibid., 14, Les Six also had the support of Charles Koechlin, whom they respected as a teacher. See Bertrand, *Le Monde de la musique,* 44. They similarly benefited from the support of Roussel, who wrote an article about them for the British journal, *The Chesterian* vol. 1 no. 2 (Oct. 1919): 33–37. See Albert Roussel, *Lettres et écrits,* ed. Nicole Labelle (Paris: Flammarion, 1987), 81.
379. Vuillermoz, however, did acerbically note the audience of "snobs," who were shocked at nothing, including a mélange of genres designed to shock. Wiéner, 57.
380. Chimènes, "La Princesse Edmond de Polignac," 140.
381. Wiéner, 40.
382. Wiéner, 74–75. Wiéner argues that Cocteau would "prend[re] la direction des opérations intellectuelle de l'après-guerre" (101).
383. Steegmuller, 205–7. It also published the score of *Parade.*
384. Auric, 78.
385. Jean Cocteau, *Romans, poésies, oeuvres diverses,* ed. Bernard Benech (Paris: La Pochothèque, 1996), 418–19.
386. Steegmuller, 205–07; and Daniel, 16.
387. Christopher Green, *Cubism and Its Enemies: Modern Movements and Reaction in French Art, 1916–1928* (New Haven: Yale University Press, 1987), 193. As Green points out (202), this provided the means for legitimizing cubism both during and after the war.

On the role of Apollinaire in the nationalist-classic discourse, see Christophe Prochasson and Anne Rasmussen, *Au nom de la patrie. Les intellectuels et la première guerre mondiale (1910–1919)* (Paris: Editions de la Découverte, 1996), 130. As Winock points out (138), Apollinaire was now impressed by the Action Française. On "reactionary modernism" see Rémy Golan, *Modernity and Nostalgia: Art and Politics in France between the Wars* (New Haven: Yale University Press, 1995), xiii. And on the forward-looking and backward-looking elements in Cocteau, see Jay Winter, *Sites of Memory, Sites of Mourning: The Great War in European Cultural History* (Cambridge, Eng.: Cambridge Unibersity Press, 1995), 131. Winter points out Cocteau's conservative, nationalist, and progressive tendencies.

388. Steegmuller, 257–59.

389. Jean Cocteau, *Le coq et l'arlequin*, in *Romans, poéstes, oeuvres diverses*, 427.

390. Ibid., 435.

391. As Cocteau puts it, "un rêveur est toujours un poète"; ibid., 432.

392. Ibid., 434.

393. Ibid., 436.

394. On the complex relation of Cocteau and Les Six to American culture, see Nancy Perloff, *Art and the Everyday: Popular Entertainment and the Circle of Erik Satie* (Oxford: Clarendon Press, 1991). On the fear of Taylorism and "Fordism in the twenties as by both Right and Left, as enslavement and subordination of creativity, see Harvey Levenstein, *Seductive Journey: American Tourists in France from Jefferson to the Jazz Age* (Chicago: University of Chicago Press, 1988), 258–59.

395. Cocteau, *Le coq et l'arlequin*, 438.

396. Ibid.

397. Ibid., 434. These points are emphasized by Paul Bertrand in *Le Monde de la musique*, 89.

398. As Christopher Green notes (190) in *Cubism and its Enemies*, "before, during, and after the war, the dominant notion of French tradition was one of reason, limitation, and order."

399. Cocteau, *Le coq et l'arlequin*, in *Romans, poésies*, 431. For Debussy's opinions on Beethoven, see Claude Debussy, *Debussy on Music*, eds. François Lesure and Richard L. Smith (New York: Alfred A. Knopf, 1977), 233.

400. Cocteau, *Le coq et l'arlequin*, in *Romans, poésies*, 430.

401. Ibid., 440.

402. See Kenneth Silver, *Esprit de Corps: The Art of the Parisian Avant-Garde and the First World War 1914–1925* (Princeton, NJ: Princeton University Press, 1989), 122–23. As Silver notes, Apollinaire added "the new spirit [is] a partisan and lyric expression of the French nation, just as the classical spirit is a sublime expression par excellence of that nation."

403. Cocteau, *Le coq et l'arlequin*, in *Romans, poési*, 437.

404. Ibid., 434.

405. Ibid., 439.

406. Steegmuller, 336–37. Steegmuller postulates that Maritain's quotations from *Le coq* brought him to the attention of Cocteau, who would soon return to the Catholic faith himself. Maritain thus provided a link between the avant-garde of the late twenties and the early thirties.

407. Steegmuller, 208.

408. Cocteau, preface to the 1924 edition of *Le coq et l'arlequin*, in *Romans, poésies, oeuvres divers*, 424.

409. Cocteau's reconciliation with Stravinsky after their break over *David* occurred in 1925, with their collaboration on *Oedipus Rex*. See Steegmuller, 110. Significantly, by 1925,

André Salmon was specifically to denounce the tendency of assertions of Frenchness in painting to justify racist attacks, in particular the attack on Jewish art in the *Mercure de France*. See Christopher Green, *Cubism and its Enemies*, 188–89.

410. Prochasson and Rasmussen, *Au nom de la patrie*, 27.

411. Steegmuller, 336–37. Massis and the Royalist, Jacques Banville, had together founded the *La revue universelle*. Maritain, who was close to the Action Française until 1926, had as we noted, quoted several aphorisms from *Le coq* in his *Art et scolastique*.

412. On Cocteau's "Dadaism," see Prochasson and Rasmussen, 273. The "retour à l'ordre esthétique" included the visual arts as well: Picasso, Derain, and Braque paid hommage to Claude Lorrain, Corot, David, and Ingres; ibid., 165. As they also point out (272, citing Kenneth Silver), the idea of classicism as the language of national defense was restated in 1919 in association with the "retour à l'ordre," or the call for regeneration. Once more, Romantic art, as well as impressionism, was read as a metaphor for the individualist fragmentation of society, as opposed to classicism, which stood for spiritual unity, order, and regeneration.

413. Breton, Aragon, and Soupault had first championed Dada in France, but rebelled against it in 1922, and founded surrealism. See Steegmuller, 238.

414. Paul Collaer, *A History of Modern Music*, 225.

415. Steegmuller, 257–59. Significantly, in the 1924 edition of *Le coq*, Cocteau "rehabilitates" Stravinsky, associating him no longer with "oriental Romanticism" but, in his neoclassic style, with "Latin order." See Steve Schloesser, "Mystic Realists: Sacrimental Modernism in French Catholic Revival, 1918–1928" (Ph.D. dissertation, Stanford University), 1998, 292.

416. Steegmuller, 346–48, 363–64.

417. Landormy, *Musique française après Debussy*, 41.

418. Collet, as a composer, had studied with Déodat de Séverac. Roy, *Groupe des Six*, 6. On Collet, also see Michael Faure, *Néoclassicisme musical*, 113–16. Collet in addition, wrote a book on modern Spanish music, *L'essor de la musique espagnole au XXe siècle* (Paris: Max Esching, 1929). After Cocteau contacted Collet, Milhaud invited him to one of the group's regular gatherings at his home.

419. Directed by Georges Casella, its editors also included Louis Laloy, Raymond Charpentier, and "Willy." Beate Kraus emphasizes Collet's nationalism and especially his desire for French music to triumph over all the others. See her article, "Henri Collet et Comoedia," *Revue internationale de musique française* June 1989: 31–32.

420. Auric, *Quand j'étais là*, 132.

421. See Fulcher, *French Cultural Politics and Music*, 123.

422. Henri Collet, "Un livre de Rimsky et un livre de Cocteau: Les cinq Russes, les six Français, et Erik Satie," *Comoedia* 16 and 23 Jan., 1920. *Charivari* was a traditional French peasant custom of publicly mocking (with noise) those who violate the norms of the community.

423. On the similar arguments in other journals, see Prochasson and Rasmussen, 277.

424. Ibid.

425. Schloesser, "Mystic Realists," 268–70, 273–74. As Schloesser points out (27), Maritain became friends with Cocteau in the twenties.

426. Ibid., 279, 294–95.

427. Wiéner (66), cites Charles Montclair's criticism of Stravinsky in *L'information* in 1922. And see Laloy, *Louis Laloy*, 294–98; and Richard Taruskin, *Stravinsky and the Russian Traditions* (Berkley: University of California Press, 1996). In her defense of the "progressive" within neoclassicism, Boulanger was not simply "la tradition faite femme," as

Faure claims (*Néoclassicisme musical*, 81). The true conservatives were figures such as Joseph Canteloube, who, as Faure notes (168), referred to Stravinsky's "hallucinations."

428. See Nadia Boulanger in *Le monde musical* 1923: 365, as cited by Scott Messing, "Polemic as History: The Case of Neoclassicism." *The Journal of Musicology* Fall 1991: 490–91. As Messing points out, reviews of Stravinsky's Octet similarly stressed its "objective, constructivist," and "architectural" qualities. Stravinsky did not object to such interpretations of his music, claiming counterpoint as "the architectural base of all music" (491).

429. See Silver, *Esprit de Corps*. This argument is made through the book. See 109ff., especially.

430. Messing, "Polemic as History," 490–91.

431. See the letter of Nadia Boulanger to Charles Koechlin of 1917, in which she points out the necessity of combating wartime strictures, but the difficulty in doing so. Charles Koechlin, *Correspondance* (Paris: La Revue Musicale, 1982), 33–35.

432. Coeuroy, "The Esthetics of Contemporary Music," *The Musical Quarterly* 1929: 248. The works of Stravinsky that are generally associated with the "return to Bach" include the Octet and the Concerto for Piano and Wind Instruments, of 1923–24.

433. Others defended "modern music" at the Ecole Normale, including the pianist Marguerite Long, who lectured there on contemporary composers, including Ravel, in 1921. As she bravely put it, "Let us study this music and, solidly armed, we will be able to defend it." See Cecilia Dunoyer, *Marguerite Long: A Life in French Music 1874–1966* (Bloomington, Ind: Indiana University Press, 1993), 83–84. As we can see, given all the nuances of the interpretation of Bach, it is somewhat of an oversimplification to say, as Taruskin does, (in "Back to Whom?," 295), that French Bachianism emanates purity and allusion to universal values. In the French context, this "Bachianism" was an appropriation or reinterpretation of the Schola's model. On this model, see Fulcher, *French Cultural Politics and Music*, 57, 71. It was, then, not simply an appropriation from Germany, as Taruskin argues (in "Back to Whom?," 297). The "French Bach," he curiously concludes was a Bach of the Right, as opposed to that of the Left, as in Weimar; however, this is clearly not true of figures such as Koechlin.

434. See Taruskin, "Back to Whom?," 489–92, 297, and Messing (*Neoclassicism*) whom he discussess. On different uses of the past, as opposed to Taruskin's more unified concept of French neoclassicm, see my discussion of the later Debussy in *French Cultural Politics and Music*, 179–94. And on the different uses of Stravinsky in France before as opposed to after the war (a distinction that Taruskin does not make), first by aesthetic-political "progressives," then by conservative modernists of the "liberal Right," see 216–19. Although both Taruskin's and Messing's insights are considerable, they fail to see how complex, multifaceted, and evolving what Taruskin refers to as "the French aesthetic program" actually was ("Back to Whom?," 291).

Taruskin correctly perceives *Pulcinella* as an exception in Stravinsky's neoclassic oeuvre, closer to the ironic tone of Les Six (to whom he was close at the time). It was indeed a commission from Diaghilev, accepted for the money. The latter wished to repeat the success of Tomasini's *Les femmes de bonne humeur* (based on Scarlatti), in the midst of wartime classicism, in 1917. Diaghliev astutely sensed the continuing postwar "classic" climate.

For Taruskin's discussion of Stravinsky's politics and his praise of Mussolini, see "Back to Whom?," 297; as well as "The Dark Side of Modern Music," *The New Republic* Sept. 5, 1988: 28–34. Taruskin sees evidence of this not only in the anti-egalitarian message of *Oedipus Rex*, but in the "white ballet," *Apollon Musagete*, of 1928. Ironically, however, *Apollon* premiered at the avant-garde Kroll Opera, in Berlin, which made it "boche" for French conservatives. It is also significant to note here that Stravinsky's politics would cause tensions in his collaboration with André Gide in the thirties. As Michael Faure notes (*Néoclassicisme musical*, 235), this came to a head around *Perséphone,* composed in 1933–34, when Stravinsky's sympathy for Mussolini aroused the ire of Gide, then a Communist. Moreover, Gide did not understand Stravinsky's music and detested his hierarchial attitude and refusal to see social reality.

Taruskin ("Back to Whom"?, 287) sees a position similar to Stravinsky's in that of Arthur Lourié; however, it is important to note Lourié's stylistic and ideological evolution, as we shall see in chapter 4. On Stravinsky's move from the Left to the Right flank of the modernists, see Lourié, 169–67. While Stravinsky eventually expressed his reaction against "the anarchy" into which modernism had degenerated, Les Six (as opposed to Cocteau) never did, although most of them remained friends with Stravinsky.

435. He also independently studied the works of Bach, Wagner, d'Indy, and Debussy. On his evolution, see Henri Sauguet, *Ma Musique, ma vie* (Paris: Séguier, 1990). On Sauguet see Marc Wood, "Henri Sauguet: Springing Surprises," *The Musical Times* Spring 2001: 22–25. The Ecole d'Arcueil gave their first concert in 1923, at the Sorbonne. Sauguet went on to write *La chatte* for Diaghilev in 1927, and began his opera, *La chartreuse de Parme,* which he finished in the mid-thirties. He also received commissions from the Princesse de Polignac and the comte Etienne de Beaumont.

436. On his politics, see his correspondence with Poulenc, especially in 1936, in Poulenc, *Correspondance,* ed. Myriam Chimènes, 418, 423–24.

437. Landormy, *Musique française après Debussy,* 331. Here, specifically recalling wartime discourse, he points out that, fortunately, France doesn't have "musical titans" like Beethoven or Wagner. Sauguet was later taken up by Diaghilev, who began his Paris season of 1927 with a performance of Sauguet's *Le chat,* with decor by Naum Gabo, at the Théâtre Sarah Bernhardt. Eksteins, *Rites of Spring* (272). A position similar to that of Sauguet may be seen in figures like Jean Français, a favored pupil of Nadia Boulanger and, like Stravinsky, an admirer of Mussolini. See Michael Faure, *Néoclassicisme musical,* 82.

438. This is as opposed to the position taken by many, including Rollo Myers, in *Modern French Music* (Oxford: Blackwell, 1971), 137, where he argues that the sponsors of Les Six were "more likely to be social than intellectual celebrities." It is also as opposed to that of Michael Faure, (*Néoclassicisme musical,* 141), who sees the group as representative of the spectrum of the "dominant class" in every sense. Although some of them moved in the same circles as their aristocratic supporters, this was a period when they were seeking alternatives to the official norm in both popular and aristocratic culture, or the two "extremes," as opposed to the "center." As we shall see, when they did move in political circles, their choices were carefully made and individualistic.

439. As Honegger pointed out explicitly in his article, "Petit historique nécessaire" (*Le courier musical* 1 Feb., 1922: 36), "Il n'y a pas d'esthétique du groupe." Moreover, he adds that Cocteau's *Le coq et l'arlequin* was never their gospel.

440. See Milhaud, *Notes sur la musique,* 110; and Auric, *Quand j'étais là,* 134.

441. On Déodat de Séverac, see Fulcher, *French Cultural Politics and Music,* 165–68.

442. Harding, *The Ox on the Roof,* 41–42; and Landormy, *La Musique française après Debussy,* 166.

443. Auric, 199–202. As we shall later see, certain groups on the Right viewed Mussolini favorably.

444. Ibid., 43. Bloy's daughter was a student of d'Indy at the Schola Cantorum. See Poulenc, *Correspondance,* ed. Myriam Chimènes, 87. Bloy was also associated with the artist Rouault, who similarly admired medieval poetry. See Winter, *Sites of Memory, Sites of Mourning,* 172.

445. Auric, 60.
446. Winock, *Siècle des intellectuels,* 178.
447. Auric, 114. The painting also included provocative declarations.
448. Winock, *Siècle des intellectuels,* 178.
449. Auric, 118. Auric would write music for surrealist films, during Cocteau's later surrealist phase, including for his *Le sang d'un poète* (1930). It was financed by Charles de Noailles who, as Eugen Weber has noted, was thereafter "drummed out of the Jockey Club." See Eugen Weber, *The Hollow Years: France in the 1930s* (New York: W.W. Norton, 1994), 221.
450. Weber, *The Hollow Years,* 220. And see Nancy Perloff, 101, 108. Here I disagree with Mussat, "Réception de Schoenberg," 180, who argues that Auric's praise for Stravinsky over Schoenberg in 1922 was evidence of "recentrage." For Auric, they were equally suggestive, daring, options. Significantly, Auric appeared in an "entr'acte" in the film that was inserted into Satie, Picabia, and Clair's ballet, *Relâche,* along with cameos by Man Ray, Marcel Duchamp, and Fancis Picabia.
451. René Chalupt, in *Les nouvelles littéraires,* 28 Oct. 1922. *Nouvelles littéraires,* a weekly devoted to "la vie artistique et scientifique," was born in October 1922. It was intended to be affordable for a broad public, as well as "impartial," and to follow all the tendencies in artistic life, audacious as well as traditional. It indeed became popular, attracting 150,000 readers by 1926. See Anne Simonin, "Les Nouvelles littéraires," in the *Dictionnaire des intellectuels français* (Paris: Seuil, 1996), 843; also see Sapiro, *Guerre des écrivains,* 73.
452. Auric repeats this attack on the Schola (for too meticulous good taste) on 6 Jan. 6 1923: 273. Here he denounces a "franckisme évolué, auquel l'autorité de Vincent d'Indy ne pouvait communiquer la vitalité qui lui avait toujours manqué" (a developed Franckisme to which d'Indy's authority could not communicate the vitality that it always lacked).
453. This quotation comes from the "Choeur des faux artistes." Since this section was cut from the 1920 performance, it is likely that Auric had seen the published score.
454. See Pierre Lasserre, *Philosophie du gout musical* (Paris: Bernard Grasset, 1992).
455. For Auric's related statement on the necessity of "reinventing nationalism," see Collaer, *A History of Modern Music,* 225. On his attitude toward jazz, see Nancy Perloff, 109.
456. Harding, *The Ox on the Roof,* 205. Diaghilev also commissioned Auric to do *Les Matelots,* with choreography by Massine, and *La pastorale,* with choreography by Balanchine, in 1926.
457. Significantly, Milhaud states at the beginning of his *Notes Without Music,* trans. Donald Evans (New York: Da Capo Press, 1970), 3: "I am a Frenchman from Provence, and by religion a Jew" (3). His great-grandfather, Joseph Milhaud, had delivered the inaugural speech of the Aix Temple in 1840, as President of the Consistory and Administration of the Temple (5). On Milhaud's background and self-conception see Jeremy Drake, *The Operas of Darius Milhaud* (New York: Garland, 1989), 14–17. Milhaud referred to himself as "israélite," signifying a Frenchman of the Jewish religion.
458. On this assimilationist concept, see Jay R. Berkovitz, *The Shaping of Jewish Identity in Nineteenth-Century France* (Detroit: Wayne State University Press, 1989).
459. Paul Collaer, *Darius Milhaud,* trans. Jane Galante (San Francisco: San Francisco Press, 1988), 11. Collaer describes Milhaud's sense of identity as a Jewish artist in the following terms: "His voice rises above everything that is narrowly individual and celebrates the most powerful of all human emotions, the struggle of conscience. . . ."
460. Roger Nichols, *Conversations with Madeleine Milhaud* (London: Faber and Faber, 1996), 26.

461. Carl E. Schorske, "Freud's Egyptian Dig," *The New York Review of Books* 27 May 1993: 35–37. Also see the more extended version in Carl E. Schorske, *Thinking with History: Explorations in the Passage to Moernism* (Princeton, N.J.: Princeton University Press, 1998), 191–215. On Milhaud's education, see Michael Faure, *Néoclassicisme musical*, 246.

462. On Aeschylus's *Oresteia*, which Wagner emulated in *The Ring*, see Herbert Lindenberger, *Opera in History: From Monteverdi to Cage* (Stanford, Calif: Stanford University Press, 1998), 148–49. Milhaud composed *Agamemnon* in 1913, *Les Choéphores* in 1915–16, and *Les Euménides* between 1917 and 1924. On Milhaud's trilogy, see Darius Milhaud, *Notes sans musique* (Paris: Julliard, 1949), 80; and Paul Collaer, *Darius Milhaud*, 109–11. As Jeremy Drake notes (25) in *The Operas of Darius Milhaud*, *Les Choéphores* was Milhaud's "first rigorously polytonal score," and it was dedicated to Charles Koechlin, a pioneer in polytonality.

463. Drake, 73. As he notes, elsewhere the setting is polytonal.

464. Harding, 183. Faure (*Néoclassicisme musical*, 199), notes the provincial and rustic element in this work, as well as in others of Milhaud, and does consider the idea that this attachment to the "soil" was related to the situation of the Jews in France before the French Revolution. But then, contrary to the evidence, he claims that it is also a protest against industrialization and capitalism, and that (201), Milhaud thus helped to nourish the current of feeling that would be exploited by the Revolution Nationale. This is profoundly to misread the nature of Milhaud's universalist, all-encomposing attraction to "the popular." As we shall see in chapter 3, it was not just the rural folklore, associated with the Right, that he embraced, but the broader, more synthetic conception that was held by the Left.

465. Collaer, *Darius Milhaud*, 243; and see Louis Chaigne, *Paul Claudel: The Man and the Mystic*, trans. By Pierre de Fontnouvelle (Westport, Conn.: Greenwood Press, 1978), 36.

466. During the war, Milhaud worked first in the Foyer Franco Belge and then in the "Maison de la Presse"; Roy, *Groupe des Six*, 117.

467. Nichols, *Conversations with Madeleine Milhaud*, 1; and see Drake, 9.

468. On the Ecole des Hautes Etudes Sociales, see Fulcher, *French Cultural Politics and Music*, 59–63. And see Milhaud, *Notes sur la musique*, ed. Jeremy Drake, 14. Drake (in his notes) postulates that the invitation for the lecture came through Milhaud's cousin, Xavier Léon, who was a part of the institution's circle.

469. Harding, *Ox on the Roof*, 143. Satie claimed to have steered Milhaud away from his other, more traditional style. Clearly, this was only temporary. Milhaud had introduced Honegger, as well as Auric and Tailleferre, to the music of Stravinsky, Magnard, and Debussy during the war. Ibid., 50.

470. Drake, 34.

471. See Albéric Magnard, *Hymne à la justice*, as transcribed by the "Scholiste," Gustave Samazeuilh, and published by Rouart, Lerolle, et cie., 1917.

472. Darius Milhaud, "Albéric Magnard." Conférence faite à l'Ecole des Hautes Etudes Sociales, 5 Jan. 1917. BNF, Musique, Réserve.

473. See Pierre Lasserre, *Les Chapelles littéraires. Claudel, Jammes, Péguy* (Paris: Garnier Frères, 1920), x.

474. Ibid., xi-xxv. Ironically, it appears to have been the more romantic elements in Claudel that attracted Milhaud. As Milhaud explained in 1927: "Je me trouvais au seuil d'un art vivant et sain, disposé à subir l'influence de cette force, qui secoue le coeur comme un élément de la nature" (Milhaud, *Notes sur la musique*, 19).

475. See Glenn Watkins, *Pyramids at the Louvre: Music, Culture, and Collage from Stravinsky to the Postmodernists* (Cambridge, Mass.: The Belknap Press of Harvard university, 1994), 112–13.

476. Winock, *Siécle des intellectuels*, 118. And see Collaer, *A History of Modern Music*, 233–34. Milhaud, like Claudel and Jammes, saw the individual as representative of "an ensemble of things and events." As Collaer points out, "Claudel's poetry rises above individual sensibilities": it is "the song of the human mind," concerned with depicting "states of consciousness." Ibid.

477. Nichols, *The Harlequin Years*, 9. Milhaud's first opera, *Le brebis égarée*, of 1910–14, was set to a libretto of Francis Jammes.

478. Ibid., 6–9. On traditon in Milhaud, see Barbara L. Kelly, *Tradition and Style in the Works of Darius Milhaud*, forthcoming from Ashgate. Unfortunately, this book was not yet available at the time of the final revisions of the present study.

479. Wiéner, *Allegro appassionata*, 42.

480. Milhaud, *Notes sur la musique*, 103–04.

481. Ludovic Tournès, *New Orleans-sur-Seine*, 22–23; and Drake, *The Operas of Darius Milhaud*, 36. On Milhaud's experience of jazz in the United States, see Nancy Perloff, 95. As she notes (96), Milhaud brought back some Black Swan labels records. She also discusses Milhaud's concern with perceptions of himself (110). On the popular sources that Milhaud employed, as well as on Léger's costumes and on the choreography, see Watkins, *Pyramids at the Louvre*, 157–58.

482. Tournès, *New Orleans-sur-Seine*, 23, 29–31.

483. Wiéner, 160.

484. Drake, 34, 243. And see Milhaud, *Notes sur la musique*, 132. On their trip, see Mussat, "Réception de Schoenberg," 157–58. As Mussant points out, they also met Egon Wellesz and Hugo von Hofmansthal, and attended the salon of Alma Mahler-Werfel.

485. Drake, 34; and Milhaud, *Notes sur la musique*, 132.

486. Drake, 39, 248–50. The other two operas were *L'abandon d'Ariane* and *La délivrance de Thésée*. The libretto is by Henri Hoppenot, a diplomat and friend of Milhaud

487. Ibid., 124. Milhaud went to Italy in the early twenties and played his pieces for piano and orchestra, resulting in a fiasco. See Harvey Sachs, *Music in Fascist Italy* (New York: Norton, 1988), 140. Milhaud wrote of his experience in the Soviet Union in an article, "La vie musicale au URSS" in *Le ménestrel* 88/2 (1924): 266–67.

488. Drake, 33; and Milhaud, *Notes sur la musique*, 28.

489. Milhaud, *Notes sur la musique*, 124.

490. Ibid. Drake rather sees this as proof that Milhaud was apolitical.

491. Again, this is as opposed to Drake's interpretation.

492. On Milhaud's work for the festival, including his "Opéra-minute," *L'enlèvement d'Europe*, see Pascal Huynh, *La Musique sous la République de Weimar* (Paris: Fayard, 1998), 234.

493. Milhaud, *Notes sur la musique*, 194–95.

494. This decision conveniently kept Honegger safe from combat during World War I. See Harry Halbereich, *Arthur Honegger, Un musicien dans la cité des hommes* (Paris: Fayard, 1992), 699–700. Honegger attended the Conservatory in Zurich from 1909–12. See Roy, *Group des Six*, 84. On Honegger's reading in psychology, philosophy, and literature, among other areas, see Harding, *Ox on the Roof*, 122.

495. Landormy, *Musique française après Debussy*, 168.

496. Arthur Honegger, *I Am a Composer*, trans. Wilson O. Clough (New York: St. Martin's Press, 1966), 91.

497. Ibid., 71. Honegger sounds very much like d'Indy when discussing the "logical construction" and the "rules" that have come down from the masters. And like d'Indy, he needed an ideology to which to relate his goals, and finally found it in the course of the thirties.

498. Harding, *The Ox on the Roof*, 122, 128. Since Honegger was the only member of the group Les Six who liked Beethoven, his colleagues playfully referred to him as Beethoven. Poulenc, *Correspondance*, ed., Myriam Chimènes, 155.

499. F. Porcile, *Présence de la musique à l'écran* (Paris: Editions du Cerf, 1969), 93. Honegger notes (in *I am a Composer*, 92), that Milhaud introduced him to the music of Magnard and Séverac. *La roue* is based upon the myth of Sisyphus, set in the modern age.

500. Jay Winter, *Sites of Memory. Sites of Mourning*, 221–22.

501. André Coeuroy, "Un musicien moderne: Arthur Honegger," *Revue hebdomadaire* 1928: 67.

502. Gustave Samazeuilh, *Musiciens de mon temps. Chroniques et souvenirs* (Paris: Editions Marcel Daubin, 1947), 69.

503. Poulenc speaks of the work in a letter to Paul Collaer of 8 April 1924, as "une oeuvre stérile, sans portée, conventionnelle, pauvre de mélodie, en un mot, une réussite à la d'Indy." Poulenc, *Correspondance*, ed. Myriam Chimènes, 226. On its triumph in Paris, see Poulenc's letter to Durey of May 1924, 228.

504. Harding, *Ox on the Roof*, 128–29; René Dumesnil, *La musique en France entre deux guerres: 1919–1939* (Paris: Editions du Milieu du Monde, 1996), 165. Several scholars have posited that the fact that Honegger was a Protestant may also explain his attraction to and familiarity with Bach and Handel, as well as his desire to make contact with the public. It was Stravinsky who, approached about the project, recommended Honegger to Ansermet. The work had its Paris premiere in 1924.

505. Harding, *Ox on the Roof*, 127–29. He is partially correct here in pointing out (127), that the work had a particular appeal for those "still exhausted and confused by the experience of war—and repelled by much of the new music." But it was ostensibly the lower classes who were more exhausted and confused by the war; the bourgeoisie, in political power, retained a firm belief in its justification, yet, given their conservative tastes, they were in fact "repelled by much of the new music."

506. Geoffrey Spratt, *The Music of Arthur Honegger*, 57–58.

507. On the related appeal of artists such as Rouault, who also attempted to "recast" the message of the sacred in a time of universal mourning, see Winter, *Sites of Memory*, 145. Although politically conservative journals, in general praised *Le roi David*, one exception was *La revue des deux mondes*, its critic being the reactionary partisan of the Action Française, Camille Bellaigue. For him, the work ignored the "principles" of music and the natural relation between the musical elements. See his review of the work, as presented at the Opéra, in the *La revue des deux mondes* 20/4 (15 April, 1924): 936–42.

508. Winter, 217.

509. See Harding, *Ox on the Roof*, 127–29. He points out Cocteau's sense of betrayal.

510. Spratt, 63–64. Honegger's fascination with the technological does not accord with Michael Faure's assertion (*Néoclassicisme musical*, 147), that as a lover of nature, he hated mass industrial society. As we shall see in the following chapter, Honegger would become involved with groups that were attempting to reform and to harnass technology. He was, however, as Faure points out (148) concerned with the condition of the workers in industry.

511. Piero Coppola, *Dix-sept ans de musique à Paris 1922–1939* (Geneva: Slatkine, 1982. Original edition Lausanne, 1922), 26. Honegger's second large symphonic work, his Mouvement symphonique #2, was similarly given a modern descriptive title, *Rugby*. Hence despite its traditional elements, it also helped consolidate his reputation as a "modernist" composer.

512. This would take him into the intellectual milieu of his fellow Swiss, residing in France, Le Corbusier.

513. Spratt, 74.

514. Harding, *Ox on the Roof*, 122–23. Gide was an amateur pianist, who wrote a book on Chopin. On Gide and music, see Rollo Myers, *Modern French Music*, 129.

515. See Poulenc, *Correspondance*, ed. Myriam Chimènes, 159.

516. Spratt, 93, 100, 129–33. Honegger himself acknowledged his admiration for and debt to Richard Strauss, which is immediately audible, especially Strauss's *Elektra*.

517. See Roy, *Groupe des Six*, 47, on *Antigone*'s premiere in Brussels. Harding, *Ox on the Roof*, 64, notes the influence of both Schoenberg and Stravinsky in Honegger's *Dit des jeux de monde*, which was also attacked by critics. On *Amphion*, see Sprout, "Music for a 'New Era'," (56). Mussat, "Réception de Schoenberg," (179), notes that Honegger acknowledged Schoenberg's influence on him.

518. Winter, 216.

519. See Poulenc, *Correspondance*, ed. Myriam Chimènes (45), on how he was able to cultivate ties to this social "network." Also see Chimènes's chapter, "Poulenc and his Patrons: Social Convergences," in *Francis Poulenc. Music, Art, and Literature*, ed. Sidney Buckland and Myriam Chimènes (Aldershot: Ashgate, 1999), 210–51.

520. Daniel, *Poulenc*, 9.

521. Poulenc, *My Friends and Myself*, 63–64. On Poulenc's love of Ravel's music, see the undated letter (probably from 1921) from Milhaud to Poulenc, in Poulenc, *Correspondance*, ed. Myriam Chimènes, 121.

522. Daniel, 14–15.

523. Ibid., 71. And see Collaer, *A History of Modern Music*, 267, on Cocteau's poem, which also gave Poulenc the opportunity to evoke the sadness of the crowded suburbs, "that Sabbath melancholy which seeks relief in artificial gaiety."

524. Poulenc, *My Friends and Myself*, 43. I am indebted to Carol Hess for her observations concerning the reception of de Falla in postwar France in a paper that she delivered at Indiana University in April 2002, "The Death of 'Guilty Sensuality': de Falla's Harpsichord Concento, Spanish Mysticism, and the Rhetoric of Neoclassicism." As she noted, de Falla was praised by Collet, Vuillermoz, and Delannoy, and (not surprisingly) he too was in contact with Jacques Maritain. On de Falla's concerto and Landowska's reaction to its "hieratic nature," see Porcile, *Belle époque*, 379.

525. See Poulenc, *Correspondance*, 45, on how Poulenc was able to cultivate useful ties within his own social circle. On Poulenc and French popular culture, see Nancy Perloff, 98–100. As she points out (104), French popular culture also mocked the "serious" romantic tradition, as in the "cello parody" of the Pompoff Clowns, which ridiculed Romantic melodies and performance style.

526. Daniel, 12–13.

527. See Poulenc, *Correspondance*, 40, on Poulenc and the Surrealists.

528. Collaer (*History*, 268), sees a connection between Poulenc's attraction to Apollinaire and to the surrealists in the technique of "unlocking" hidden truths. In Apollinaire, the voice of the poet poses enigmas, yet always seems to be simple. But Poulenc was equally attracted to Apollinaire's classical form, with its careful balance and structure. See Daniel (17), on the close links of surrealism to postwar spiritualism.

529. The five principal surrealists joined the Communist Party in 1927.

530. Poulenc sometimes referred to the conflict between these two cultures as related to the two different backgrounds of his parent—his father, a devout Catholic from the conservative provinces, and his mother from wordly Paris. See Poulenc, *My Friends and Myself*, 29.

531. On Poulenc's upper-class circle, see Chimènes, "Poulenc and his Patrons: Social Convergences." On his experience of popular culture and Parisian night life, see Perloff, 86ff.

532. See Chimènes, "Poulenc": and Daniel, 24.

533. On Poulenc's homosexuality, see Poulenc, *Correspondance*, ed. Myriam Chimènes, 27 ff.

534. Daniel, 29.

535. Poulenc, *Correspondance*, 27–28, 300. Also see the letter of August 1929 to Claire Croiza (309). Poulenc notes the resignation at the end of the work. On the plot, see 316.

536. Daniel, 24.

537. Ibid., 26, and Poulenc, *Correspondance*, 157. Poulenc also went to Salzburg in August 1922 for a chamber music festival, in which he performed with Marya Freund. On Webern, see the letter to Milhaud, of 16 August 1922, in which Poulenc refers to him as "un garçon exquis et plein de talent," and to Hindemith as "assez bien, dans le style brute"; ibid., 170.

538. Harding, *Ox on the Roof*, 54. As Roy points out, Durey began his studies at the Ecole des Hautes Etudes Commerciales (*Groupe des Six*, 68).

539. Roy, 68. Durey set Gide's *Voyage d'Urien* in 1916. On performance of and information on Schoenberg in France before the war, and on the attraction of Les Six to his music during and after it, see Mussat, "Réception de Schoenberg," 145–46, 152–53. And see Marc Wood, "Louis Durey: Homme de Tête," *The Musical Times* Winter 2000: 42. As he points out, Durey had heard only short extracts from Schoenberg's song cycle.

540. Roy, *Groupe des Six*, 70–71. It was, in fact, Ravel who recommended Durey to the publisher Jacques Durand. Like Ravel, Durey admired both Stravinsky and Schoenberg.

541. Harding, *Ox on the Roof*, 55. And see Wood, "Louis Durey," 42. Michael Faure, (*Néoclassicisme musical*, 192), posits that he may have come into contact with workers through his family business, which could have troubled his social conscience. But he then goes on to dismiss the sincerity of Durey's beliefs, observing that he had a bourgoie lifestyle in St. Tropez.

542. Ibid. On Durey's political involvements, see Harding, *Ox on the Roof*, 98.

543. Roy, *Groupe des Six*, 73. As Roy points out, he also disliked Satie's comments on Ravel in the journal *Le coq* in May 1920. And see Poulenc, *Correspondance*, 121, for Durey's letter to Poulenc of 25 March, 1921, in which he declares his desire to "continuer ma route à l'écart."

544. Further challenging the "establishment," Durey chose a scandalous story for his one-act opera, *L'ocassion*, based on Merimée, and which he wrote between 1923 and 1925. The story, which takes place in Havana, concerns a priest who becomes the lover of one of the young girls in the convent, leading to tragedy. The story also tempted Roland-Manuel who, however, realistically realized that no opera house would accept a work on such a subject. Durey, however, intrepidly proposed it to the directors of the Opéra-Comique, who, of course, in the postwar climate, rejected it. Roy, *Groupe des Six*, 75. Durey's *Dix inventions*, of 1924–27, are generally related to the "return to Bach," as is his *Concerto for Piano and Orchestra* of 1925, commissioned by the Princess de Polignac. See Michael Faure (*Néoclassicisme musical*, 293).

545. Durey returned to Paris in 1930. Roy, *Groupe des Six*, 79.

546. See Germaine Tailleferre, "Mémoires à l'emporte-pièce," ed. Frédéric Robert, *Revue internationale de musique française* 19 (Feb. 1986): 7–82, and Roy, *Groupe des Six*, 168.

547. See Roy, *Groupe des Six*, 173. Not only did Ravel advise her, but she also worked with Koechlin. Tailleferre wrote in both conventionally "male"genres—opera, concerto, quartet, sonata, etc.—as well as in traditionally "female" genres—songs and solo piano

pieces. Like her colleagues, she hated the conservative atmosphere of the Conservatoire, but she perservered to win several top prizes.

548. Harding, *Ox on the Roof*, 43.

549. Roy, *Groupe des Six*, 172. Here I disagree with Sprout ("Music for a 'New Era'," 56), who argues that Tailleferre needed "the reassurance of a given style" to "face the blank page when granted the prestige of a high-profile request." Like her colleagues, she was not using but defining herself against the past.

550. Mary Louise Roberts, *Civilization Without Sexes: Reconstructing Gender in Postwar France 1917–1927* (Chicago: University of Chicago Press, 1994), 11. As she also notes, many middle-class young women now "broke with family tradition to enter the labor force because of depleted fortunes and inflation" (ibid).

551. See Marc Ferro, "Cultural Life in France, 1914–1918," in *European Culture in the Great War: The Arts, Entertainment, and Propaganda 1914–1918*, ed. Aviel Roshwald and Richard Stites (New York: Cambridge University Press, 1999), 307. He notes the fact that veterans groups were now strongly antifeminist, and indeed French women could not vote until after World War II. Roberts, in *Civilization without Sexes* (14), points out the conflicting manners of imagining the female self in the postwar period. See Susan Suleiman, *Subversive Intent: Gender, Politics, and the Avant-Garde* (Cambridge, Mass.: Harvard University Press, 1990), xvii, 13, 15, 26–27. And see Mireille Rosello, *Declining the Stereotype: Ethnicity and Representation in French Culture* (Hanover, NH: University Press of New England, 1998) on the simultaneous participation in and refusal of stereotypes.

552. Here I am grateful to Jennifer Smull, who brought many of these insights to my attention in her excellent seminar paper on Tailleferre. My position here is again clearly opposed to that of Michale Faure (*Néoclassicisme musical*, 121), who claims that her function in the group was largely "decorative," and that she accepted "de ne faire que de la musique de femme." Her stylistic relation to Satie is no accident, for as Bruyr point out (*Ecran*, 94), it was thanks to Satie that her *Sonatina à cordes* was performed in one of the concerts of the Nouveau Jeunes in 1917. As Roberts notes (36–37), the issue of female sexual infidelity was prominent during the war, and became the subject of popular novels in the postwar period.

553. See *The New Grove Dictionary of Music and Musicians*, 1980 edition, s.v. Tailleferre, Germaine," by Arthur Hoérée. For the insight into deeper parallels between Tailleferre and Marie Laurencin, I am indebted to Mitra Sadeghpour.

554. She was, however, widely respected; Claudel , for example, asked her to write the music for *Sous les remparts d'Albenès*. Roy, *Groupe des Six*, 178.

555. Ibid.

556. "Modernist" was still often used synonymously with undesirable cultural change and with "the Jewish" in this period.

557. Vincent d'Indy, "Le Public et son évolution," *Comoedia* 1 Oct. 1923.

558. Vincent d'Indy, "Matière et forme dans l'art musical moderne," *Comoedia* 28 Jan. 1924.

559. See Wiéner, *Allegro appassionata*, 78–81.

560. Georges Auric in *Les nouvelles littéraires* 13 Jan., 1923. As cited in Wiéner, 75–76.

561. See Igor Stravinsky, *An Autobiography* (New York: Norton, 1962, original edition 1936), 103.

562. Ibid, 110. On Schoenberg, see Mussat, "Réception de Schoenberg," 171.

563. Emile Vuillermoz in *Excelsior* 8 Jan. 1923. See Wiéner, 75.

564. For similar attacks in the field of painting, see Eugen Weber, *The Hollow Years*, 88. As he points out, the former Dreyfusard, Camille Mauclair, now converted to anti-

Semitism, published *Les métèques contre l'art français* in 1930. He observes that "metic" was a term coined by the ancient Greeks "to designate aliens with no citizenship or other rights in the Greek city." Maurras adapted it in 1898 as a pejorative term for "aliens" in France.

565. Such charges, implying cultural bolshevism, did have their counterpart in the Weimar Republic, but on the part of the nationalist minority, which mounted in force in the course of the decade. Here it is important to note that Jews were also often associated with American culture and thus with jazz. See David Strauss, *Menace in the West: The Rise of French Anti-Americanism in Modern Times* (Westport, Conn.: Greenwood Press, 1978), 170.

566. As cited in Wiéner, 66.

567. See Norbert Elias, *The Germans: Power Struggles and the Development of Habitus in the Nineteenth and Twentieth Centuries*, ed. Michael Schroter, trans., Eric Dunning and Stephen Mennell (New York: Columbia University Press, 1996).

568. See Fulcher, *French Cultural Politics and Music*, 66–74, and Jane F. Fulcher, "The Preparation for Vichy: Anti-Semitism in French Musical Culture between the Two World Wars," *The Musical Quarterly* 71/2 (Fall 1995): 458–475.

569. Romy Golan, *Modernity and Nostalgia: Art and Politics in France between the Wars* (New Haven: Yale University Press, 1995), 137.

570. Jean-François Sirinelli, ed., *Histoire des droites en France* vol. 2 (Paris: Gallimard, 1992), 173.

571. Ibid., 174. On the evolution of Waldemar George's art criticism toward nationalism and racism, see Affron, 172.

572. Gordon Wright, *France in Modern Times* (New York: Rand McNally, 1974), 360.

573. As we will recall, Milhaud and Poulenc went to Vienna in 1921 to give several concerts with the Polish singer, Marya Freund. Milhaud, already impressed with Schoenberg, dedicated his String Quartet of 1920 to him. Milhaud went on to become the only French composer to be regularly published by the Universal Editions in Vienna. See Milhaud, *Notes sur la musique*, 30, and Huynh, 67. Les Six had its strongest impact in Berlin in the first half of the twenties, or the period of social instability and rising inflation in the Weimar Republic. The popularity of satire in Berlin cabarets certainly contributed to many Germans's receptivity to them, as did the battle against the older generation on the part of youth. See Huynh, 61.

574. Wiéner, 67.

575. Ibid.

576. Ibid., 71.

CHAPTER 3

1. The class of "fêtes" was class seventy-one. The Popular Front took over the Exposition from its predecessor, and then reshaped it to its own ends. See Pascal Ory, *Les Expositions Universelles de Paris* (Paris: Ramsay, 1982), on previous expositions in relation to this one.

2. On the role of Rouché, see Pascal Ory, "Théorie et pratique de l'art des fêtes sous le Front populaire," in Noëlle Gérome and Danielle Tartakowski, eds., *Les Usages politiques des fêtes aux XIX-XXe siècles* (Paris: Publications de la Sorbonne, 1994), 281. The full name of the exposition was "Exposition Internationale des Arts et des Techniques appliqués à la Vie Moderne." Se Nigel Simeone, "Music at the 1937 Paris Exposition: the Science of Enchantment," *The Musical Times* Spring 2002: 9–17.

3. Other composers who participated included Ibert, Milhaud, Messiaen, Louis Aubert, and Paul LeFlem.

4. See Manuel Rosenthal, *Ravel, Souvenirs* (Paris: Hazan, 1995), 185. As he points out, every country represented presented a ballet of multicolored lights on a barge, each of which lasted about twenty minutes. It was organized by the architect, Beaudouin, with the participation of eleven musicians (including Rosenthal), each of whom was given the "theme" of the spectacle. The text and scenario was by the doctor, Jean-Claude Mardus, a well-known translator of "oriental" tales. The spectacle took place in front of the Palais de Chaillot on 9 July 1937. See Harry Halbereich, *Arthur Honegge: Un musicien dans la cité des hommes* (Paris: Fayard, 1992), 175. See François Porcile, *La Belle époque de la musique française: le temps de Maurice Ravel, 1871–1940* (Paris: Fugard, 1999), 317, on the French composers who participated. They included several generations—Florent Schmitt, Elsa Barraine, Marcel Delannoy, Paul Le Flem, D.-E. Inghelbrecht, Olivier Messiaen, Charles Koechlin, Jean Rivier, Manuel Rosenthal, Arthur Honegger, and Darius Milhaud. Several used the "Ondes Martenot" in their scores. As Simeone observes ("Science of Enchantment, 10) the works for the fête were commissioned by the Paris city government. He provides a complete listing of all the composers who participated, as well as the title of each "event." He refers to the fêtes by the shortened title (also used), the "Fêtes de la lumière."

5. Halbereich, *Arthur Honegger*, 175. As Simeone notes ("Science of Enchantment, 10), eight of the works performed used from one to six ondes Martenot.

6. On the association of popular and democratic theater with the physical and the visual, as opposed to the textual, see Naomi Ritter, *Art as Spectacle: Images of the Entertainer Since Romanticism* (Columbia, Missouri: University of Missouri Press, 1984), 246–55.

7. On spectacle as polythematic and polyphonic, see Frank Manning's chapter on "Spectacle," in Richard Bauman, ed., *Folklore, Cultural Performance, and Popular Entertainments* (New York: Oxford University Press, 1992), 291–99. For a description of the ominous Italian and German pavilions, both overtly displaying fascist imagery, see Simeone, "Science of Enchantment, 9.

8. Pascal Ory, "Théorie et pratique de l'art des fêtes," 277.

9. Maurice Agulhon, *La République 1880–1990* vol. 2 (Paris: Hachette, 1990), 31.

10. Michel Winock, *Siècle des intellectuels* (Paris: Seuil, 1997), 250. Winock points out that antifascism did not in itself provide a clear concept of what the Popular Front represented. Also see Gordon Wright, *France in Modern Times* (New York: Rand McNally, 1974), 373, on the tensions between Socialists, Communists, and Radicals.

11. On the musical policies of the Weimar Republic, see Pascal Huynh, *La Musique sous la République de Weimar* (Paris: Fayard, 1998); and Bryan Gilliam, ed., *Music and Performance during the Weimar Republic* (Cambridge, Eng.: Cambridge University Press, 1994).

12. Julian Jackson, *The Popular Front in France: Defending Democracy 1934–38* (Cambridge, Eng.: Cambridge University Press, 1988), 26–27. Writers, in particular, noted the necessity of now making political choices. See Eugen Weber, *The Hollow Years: France in the 1930s* (New York: W.W. Norton, 1994), chapter VI, 147–81.

13. Agulhon, *République*, 2:371–72, and Herman Lebovics, *True France: The Wars Over Cultural Identity 1900–1945* (Ithaca: Cornell University Press, 1992), 35. In 1932 the parties of the Left won a majority in the chamber, leading to the ministry of Herriot, who was strongly interested in education. On Herriot, see Agulhon, *République*, 375.

14. Pierre-Marie Dioudonnat, *Je suis partout 1930–1944. Les Maurrassiens devant la tentation fasciste* (Paris: La Table Ronde, 1973), 41, 61.

15. On the polarization triggered by the Dreyfus Affair, see Douglas Johnson, *France and the Dreyfus Affair* (London: Blanford, 1966). See Alistair Hamilton, *The Appeal of Fascism: A Study of Intellectuals and Fascism 1919–1945* (New York: Avon, 1973), 190. Three ministries succeeded each other in 1932–33.

16. Vicki Caron, "The Anti-Semitic Revival in France in the 1930s: The Socioeconomic Dimension Reconsidered," *The Journal of Modern History* 70/1 (March 1998):24.

17. Robert Hoffman, *More Than a Trial: The Struggle for Captain Dreyfus* (New York: Free Press, 1980), 157.

18. Francis Steegmuller, *Cocteau, A Biography* (Boston: Little, Brown, and Com, 1970), 410.

19. See Gordon Wright, *France in Modern Times*, 367–69, on the leagues in the 1930s.

20. William Irvine, "French Conservatives and the 'New Right' during the 1930s," *French Historical Studies* 8 (1974): 535.

21. Before the war, Valois, an autodidact typographical worker from a "popular" background, had collaborated with the aristocratic d'Indy on the journal *L'indépendance*, which sought the fusion of nationalist and socialist doctrines. See Jane F. Fulcher, *French Cultural Politics and Music from the Dreyfus Affair to the First World War* (New York: Oxford University Press, 1999), 134–35. Also see Serge Berstein, *La France des années 30* (Paris: Armand Colin, 1988), 62–63. On Valois and art, see Mark Antliff, "La Cité française: Georges Valois, Le Corbusier, and Fascist Theories of Urbanism," in *Fascist Visions: Art and Ideology in France and Italy*, ed. Matthew Affron and Mark Antliff (Princeton, NJ: Princeton University Press, 1997): 134–70.

22. Berstein, *La France des années 30*, 63–64. On Col. de la Rocque, see Hamilton, 204. Although the Popular Front saw him as fascist, he did not think of himself as such, and criticized Mussolini and Hitler.

23. Irvine, "French Conservatives and the 'New Right'," 534 and 539–40. On Marcel Bucard, formerly of Valois's Faisceau, and the fascist Parti Franciste, see Hamilton, 192. On Doriot, see ibid., 215.

24. Julian Jackson, *The Popular Front*, 1–2. From 1932 on, many ephemeral ministries of the Left succeeded each other. Ibid., 61. By 1934 there was a clear polarization between Right and Left. Just before the Feb. 1934 riots, the government of Chautemps was replaced by that of Daladier, which was then followed by Domergue's also oriented to the Left. By 1935, most internal French conflicts assumed ideological significance, and the victory of a Left coalition seemed certain. See Dioudonnat, *Je suis partout*, 95.

25. On this event, also see Eugen Weber, *The Hollow Years*, 140; and see Hamilton, 191.

26. Winock, *Siècle des intellectuels*, 236; and Pascal Ory and Jean-François Sirinelli, *Les Intellectuels en France*, 96.

27. The Comité had been preceeded by a move within the Communist Party, beginning in 1932, to mobilize intellectuals and artistes, and the concomitant formation of the Association des Ecrivains et Artistes Rrévolutionnaires. Ory and Sirinelli, *Les Intellectuels en France*, 96. This was also the period of concern with the role of the state in culture. See Matthew Affron, "Waldemar George: A Parisian Art Critic on Modernism and Fascism," in *Fascist Visions: Art and Ideology in France and Italy*, ed. by Matthew Affron and Mark Antliff (Princeton, NJ: Princeton University Press, 1997), 192. As he points out, in 1934 the League of Nations sponsored a conference in conjunction with the Venice Biennale on "The Arts and Contemporary Reality—Art and the State."

28. Winock, *Siècle des intellectuels*, 244. On the "Rassemblement" see Ory and Sirinelli, 93–94.

29. Agulhon, *République* 2: 25. On the formation of the government, see Weber, *The Hollow Years*, 149.

30. Ory and Sirinelli, 106.

31. Winock, *Siècle des intellectuels*, 250; and Agulhon, *République* 1, 23.

32. Agulhon, *République*, 2: 16, 30. The only group within the Popular Front that would resist the new aesthetic directions being proposed were the Radicals, or more properly, the Radical-Socialists. Although they were firmly anticlerical, as indeed were the Socialists as well as the Communists, they alone continued to associate themselves clearly with the interests of the middle class. They had been allied with the Socialists during the period of the Cartel des Gauches, but this ended in 1926, when the Cartel was displaced by the government of "National Union," under Poincaré. The Radical-Socialists, under their leader Herroit, then joined this politically conservative alliance. See Julian Jackson, *The Popular Front*, 21.

33. On the initial enthusiasm for the Popular Front, including among intellectuals, see Jules Moch, *Le Front populaire, grande espérance* (Paris: Librairie Académique Perrin, 1971), 202–03.

34. This, together with a manifesto of Romain Rolland, led to another riposte on the Right—the proclamation of the "Parti de l'Intelligence," which published the manifesto, "Pour la Défense de l'Occident et de la paix en Europe," supporting Mussolini's invasion of Ethiopia. See Jacques Julliard and Michel Winock, "Introduction," *Dictionnaire des intellectuels français*, eds. Jacques Julliard and Michel Winock (Paris: Seuil, 1996), 15. As Affron points out (189), already in 1933, at a meeting of French antifascist writers and artists, the painter, Amédée Ozenfant, stressed the persecution of modern art in Nazi Germany and fascist Italy, as a warning to French intellectuals and artists. Affron also notes that the question of state support for modern art was already being raised.

35. On the antifascist reflex of French artists and intellectuals since 1933, and their subsequent role in the cultural projects of the Popular Front, see Pascal Ory, "Théorie et pratique de l' "art des fêtes," 277. On the expulsion of Breton and others from the Communist Part, see Ory and Sirinelli, 87.

36. The initial directive committee included Gide, Barbusse, Vaillant-Coutourier, and Romain Rolland. The *secrétaires de rédaction* were Louis Aragon and Paul Nizan. Julian Jackson, 74, 119.

37. Ory and Sirinelli, 111. This conservative position was also supported by Maritain and Mauriac. Ibid., 112.

38. Julian Jackson, 74.

39. Winock, *Siècle des intellectuels*, 226.

40. Agulhon, *République*, 39.

41. Ibid., 55.

42. Ibid., 18, 55. As René Rémond points out, the French Revolution was a critical point of reference for the Popular Front, "au sein de sa mythologie…au coeur de son fonctionnement idéologique." See René Rémond and Janine Bourdin, eds., *La France et les Français en 1938 et 1939* (Paris: Presses de la Fondation Nationale des Sciences Politiques, 1978), 127.

43. Agulhon, *République*, 56.

44. Winock, *Siècle des intellectuels*, 285. Gide's explosive *Retour de l'URSS* was published in 1936. On the Communist move from pacifism to overt hostility to the Nazis, see Wright, 382–83.

45. As Agulhon observes (*République*, 2: 46), the Right could now accuse the Left of bellicosity. See Wright, 387; and Agulhon, *République*, 2:32; on the Popular Front's response to the Spanish Civil War. As Agulhon points out, Blum was forced into nonintervention, but some on the Left did fight for the Spanish Republicans.

46. Agulhon, *République*, 1–8.

47. Ibid., 5; and Winock, *Siècle des intellectuels*, 275–78. Also see Gisèle Sapiro, *Guerre des écrivains 1940–1953* (Paris: Fayard), 144–50.

48. Julian Jackson, 285. But as he points out, Blum's government was not overtly anticlerical, as opposed to the Left Republican government at the turn of the century.

49. Julian Jackson, 287. Now, however, the opposing symbols were already established, and in a more coherent opposition than they had been at the turn of the century.

50. This was the period of the founding of the Centre National de la Recherche Scientifique (CNRS), through the minister of education, Jean Zay, and the under-secretary of state for "scientific" (scholarly) research, Irène Joliot-Curie, who was followed by Jean Perrin. I am grateful to Christophe Charles for this clarification.

51. Bernard Comte also sees a continuity with the early Third Republic, or the so-called "République Athénienne," and its republican emphasis on a humanistic education, intended to achieve "intellectual emancipation" for all. This implied an emphasis on classic taste as well as a cautious appropriation of "the modern." See Bernard Comte, "Pamphlet, histoire, et fantaisie. A propos de Mounier, Ministre de Culture de Vichy," *Le Débat* May–Aug. 1992: 49.

52. Julian Jackson, 113, 123. And see Wright (377), on the strikes of 1936, which may also have played a role in the immediate emphasis on culture. On the sense of the possibility of saving European culture without war, and of assimilating the Soviet revolution into the Western tradition, see Roger Shattuck, *The Innocent Eye: On Modern Literature and the Arts* (New York: Washington Square Press, 1986), 8.

53. On the Republican concept of a "cultural state," see Marie-Claude Gênet-Delacroix, "Esthétique officielle et art national sous la Troisième République," *Le Mouvement social* April–June 1985: 105–120.

54. Julian Jackson, 134.

55. Ibid., 114.

56. Ibid., 129. Indeed, as we shall see, Rolland's ideas were now to be powerful, not only in popular theater, but also in the domain of the fête.

57. This stress on the theater is related to the Communist ideal of a "fully liberated and inherently aesthetic world." See Matei Calinescu, "Modernism and Ideology," in *Modernism: Challenges and Perspectives*, eds. Monique Chefdor, Ricardo Quionones, and Albert Wachtel (Urbana, Ill.: University of Illinois Press, 1986): 80. And on Communist precedents, see Pascal Ory, *La Belle illusion: Culture et politique sous le signe du Front populaire 1935–1938* (Paris: Plon, 1994), 835. As he points out, the Communist Party had already begun to respond to working-class demands for cultural integration by forming a well-structured program.

58. On Gustave Charpentier's project to distribute free or low-priced tickets to the theater for the working class at the turn of the century, see Fulcher, *French Cultural Politics and Music*, 101–02. And on the efforts of the Popular Front, see Julian Jackson, 124–25.

59. Julian Jackson, 119.

60. Pascal Ory, "Le Front populaire et la création artistique," *Bulletin de la Société d'Histoire moderne* 8/3 (1974): 16.

61. On precedents in the attempt to bring art to "the people" at the turn of the century, see Fulcher, *French Cultural Politics and Music*, 130–33.

62. Julian Jackson, 124–25.

63. On the attempt to widen access to the museums and "bring them to the people," see Ory and Sirinelli, 102.

64. For precedents in the 19th century, see Jane F. Fulcher, *The Nation's Image: French Grand Opera as Politics and Politicized Art* (New York: Cambridge University Press, 1987), 197–200.

65. Julian Jackson, 119–20.
66. On the Weimar Republic's cultural projects, see Huynh, *La Musique sous la République de Weimar*, 295–96.
67. Lebovics, *True France*, 156–58
68. Julian Jackson, 128–29.
69. Ibid., 129.
70. Lebovics, 150. The codirector was Paul Rivet. See Ory and Sirinelli, 102.
71. On Rivière, see Ory and Sirinelli, 102.
72. Catherine Veley Vallantin, "Le Congrès internationale de folkore de 1937," *Annales: Histoire, sciences sociale* 54/2 (March–April 1999): 482; and Romy Golan, *Modernity and Nostalgia: Art and Politics in France between the Wars* (New Haven: Yale University Press, 1995), 120–22.
73. Pascal Ory, *La Belle illusion*, 308–09. Also see Florence Gétreau, "Le patriomoine musical de deux musées parisiens," in *La Vie musicale sous Vichy*, ed. Myriam Chimènes (Brussels: Editions Complexe, 2001), 190–191. As she points out, during the congress Claudie Marcel-Dubois called for a music that employed folklore, which was related to the appeal by Lucien Febvre to safeguard folklore. As she also notes, German fascists were represented in the congress by the future Ambassador during the Occupation, Otto Abetz.
74. Lebovics, *True France*, 136–39. As he points out, in addition to Maurras, the search for the "pays réel" in the early twentieth century was launched by Maurice Barrès and his friend, Fréderic Mistral, to name the most prominent. Here it is important to note that both the Right and Left, although embracing the same rural themes and regional traditions, were doing so with different meanings and in fundamentally different ways. Unfortunately, studies such as Romy Golan's *Modernity and Nostalgia: Art and Politics between the Wars*, tend to ignore this distinction, thus identifying uniform reactionary tendencies. Golan does, however, note the difference between Right and Left in the appropriation of folklore, or the Left's "more progressive version of regionalism" as seen in the Musée des Arts et Traditions Populaires." See Golan, 121–22. As she points out, the Left's conception was more commodious, embracing all aspects of life, including that of the workers.
75. Ory, "Théorie et pratique de l' "art des fêtes," 287. He notes that the folkloric element also entered into the "festive repertoire" in spectacles such as the Fête du Folklore, organized at the Mutualité 9 May 1936.
76. Winock, *Siècle des intellectuels*, 271 and 274.
77. This included breaking the barriers between "audience and performer, between creator and cultural consumer, between past and present, between science and art." See Julian Jackson, 116, 130–31. On the revolutionary fête, see Lynn Hunt, *Politics, Culture, and Class in the French Revolution* (Berkeley: University of California Press, 1984), 49; and Mona Ozouf, *La Fête révolutionnaire 1789–1799* (Paris: Gallimard, 1976).
78. This was as opposed to the more pragmatic goals of the contemporary Works Progress Administration in the United States.
79. These same issues were being faced by composers such as Gershwin and Copland in the United States.
80. See Fulcher, *French Cultural Politics and Music*, 17–18.
81. Julian Jackson, 118–20. As we will recall, several surrealists joined the Party in 1927, but, with the exception of Aragon, were expelled in 1933.
82. For other means of enunciating values and articulating memory, see Alain Corbin's chapter on "La Fête souveraineté," in *Les Usages politiques des fêtes*, 25–38.
83. On the use of music to further democratic national goals in the Weimar Republic, see Huynh, 292. My position is as opposed to that of Pascal Ory, who sees no clear aesthetic. Ory, *La Belle illusion*, 291. Indeed, there are many parallels with the musical pro-

grams of the Weimar Republic, which, as noted in chapter 2, several members of Les Six had seen firsthand. Milhaud's didactic cantatas of the mid-thirties recall the Weimar *Lehrstuck*. The French government's efforts to find new "popular" venues for music, to employ the radio to diffuse "high culture," to find a model of culture that would cut across the classes, linking aesthetic values to sociopolitical aspirations, similarly parallel those of the German government in the twenties.

84. On the way in which the state is able to "orient" cultural production, see Pierre Bourdieu, "The Market of Symbolic Goods," *Poetics* 14 (1985): 13–44.

85. Again, this is as opposed to the position presented by Pascal Ory in *La Belle illusion* and by Leslie Sprout in "Music of the Révolution française or the Révolution nationale? Music and National Celebration in France, 1936–1944," *Repercussions* V/1–2 (Spring–Fall 1996): 88.

86. Ory, *Belle illusion*, 293.

87. On the use of radio in the Weimar Republic, see Karl Christian Fuhrer, "A Medium of Modernity? Broadcasting in Weimar Germany, 1923–1932," *The Journal of Modern History* 69/4 (Dec. 1999): 722–753.

88. Ory, *Belle illusion*, 304.

89. For a comprehensive listing of the orchestral repertoire in the period, see the regular rubric, "Concerts," in *Le ménestrel*, which published the programs of the large concert societies.

90. Ory, *Belle illusion*, 305.

91. Ibid. He cites a letter to this effect from Léo Lagrange to Jacques Rouché, of December 1937.

92. The Opéra-Comique was traditionally less expensive. One example of such a "popular" performance was that of Bizet's *Les pêcheurs de perles*, for the 1937 Congress of the Union des Syndicats de Région Parisienne. Ibid., 306.

93. Ibid.

94. Ibid., 307–08.

95. Ibid., 308.

96. On the evolution of the Maison de Culture from the "Association des Ecrivains et Artistes Révolutionnaires," see Ory and Sirinelli, 102; and Ory, *Belle illusion*, 298–99. On the other cultural institutions tied to the Popular Front, see Ory, *Belle illusion*, 296.

97. Ory, *Belle illusion*, 298. He points out that Communist precedents were poorly organized and disparate.

98. Casadesus had been the first director of the Conservatoire Américain at Fontainebleau. See Ory, *Belle illusion*, 295. The Fêtes du Peuple became associated with the Maison de Culture. Ibid., 296.

99. Ibid., 295–96. They also continued to perform Charpentier and Bruneau. Not surprisingly, Beethoven was similarly a cultural icon in Republican Spain. On the situation in Germany, see David Dennis, *Beethoven in German Politics, 1870–1989* (New Haven, Conn.: Yale University Press, 1996).

100. Ibid., 296.

101. On the Orphéon choral societies, see Jane F. Fulcher, "The Orphéon Societies: 'Music for the Workers' in Second-Empire France," *International Review of the Aesthetics and Sociology of Music* X/1 (1979). Also see Philippe Gumplowicz, *Les Travaux d'Orphée. 150 ans de vie musicale amateur en France: harmonies-chorales-fanfares* (Paris: Aubier, 1987); and Ory, *Belle illusion*, 304–05.

102. Ory, *Belle illusion*, 299.

103. Ibid., 299–300. Durey spoke about the radio and Jaubert, who did many film scores, about the cinema.

104. Ibid., 301.

105. Ibid., 301–02. The Fédération's efforts to diffuse musical culture recall the Left-wing "Composer's Collective" in the United States in the thirties, which similarly sought to encourage a progressive yet accessible music and to educate its audience. Its members included Aron Copland, Henry Cowell, Marc Blitzstein, and Charles and Ruth Crawford Seeger.

106. Ibid., 303. Significantly, this was also the period when Soviet and American governments were stressing the use of folksong as a link to "the masses."

107. Ibid., 335. On the related tensions in the Weimar Republic between diffusing the "classic" tradition and the new "revolutionary" culture, see Huynh, 73–74.

108. Ibid., 303. This included Milhaud, Auric, and Koechlin, among others. It published Milhaud's "Pastorale," Auric's "Ouverture," and Koechlin's *Symphonie d'hymnes*, as well as works such as Shostakovich's Fifth Symphony. Although such works would undoubtedly sell few copies, they were balanced by more profitable works. Ibid., 323.

109. Ibid., 323.

110. Ibid., 320, 324.

111. This was part of his ultimately seven-volume *Beethoven. Les grandes époques créatrices*.

112. Ory, *Belle illusion*, 324.

113. It is significant to note that in the Weimar Republic one finds the same tensions in the repertoire of the choral societies—that between classical works and the revolutionary chansons that were encouraged by the Communists.

114. Louis Durey became the general secretary. Rolland was again in the public eye, now writing many articles on "popular theater," one of which was published in *Comoedia* on 14 July 1936. See Dorothy Knowles, *French Drama of the Inter-War Years* (London: George G. Harrup, 1967), 292. On Vaillant-Couturier see Affron, 182–83.

115. Ory, *Belle illusion*, 299. Rolland was its *président d'honneur* and Roussel president of the "Comité Executif."

116. As Manuel Rosenthal observed, because of his example and his support for innovation, Roussel was now generally considered to be the leader of the "jeune école française"; Manuel Rosenthal, *Ravel, Souvenirs*, 23. Ory (*Belle illusion*, 292), sees the choice of Roussel as based upon his lack of precise political affiliation and on his desire to conciliate those promoting more serious or "classical" music and those in favor of "the popular."

117. Albert Roussel, *Lettres et écrits*, ed. Nicole Labelle (Paris: Flammarion, 1989), 149–50. Letter to Arthur Hoérée, 9 June, 1930.

118. Ibid., 168. Letter to Guy Ropartz, 29 October, 1935.

119. Ory, *Belle illusion*, 299. Roussel had already accepted the *présidence d'honneur* of the Fédération des Sociétés Musicales du Nord-Pas-de-Calais, the center of the Orpheonic movement.

120. Roussel, *Lettres et écrits*, 282. Excerpt from "Savoir choisir," *Le point* 1936.

121. Ibid.

122. Ibid., 169.

123. Ory, *Belle illusion*, 292, notes the participation in the Popular Front programs of several major figures in the Société Internationale de Musique Contemporaine. The directive committee of the French section included Honegger, Milhaud, Marcel Delannoy, Koechlin, and Roland-Manuel. Poulenc, significantly, was not a member. This Ory attributes to his religious awakening, but, as we shall see, there were other factors as well. For a description of the music performed at the festival, see Simeone, ("Science of En-

chantment, 10). As he notes, it included concerts of quarter-tone music, as well as a series of lectures.

124. The last work of Roussel to be premiered during his lifetime was his *Rhapsodie flamande*, of 1936, based on five "chants populaires," including a particularly trenchant "Chant des gueux" (Beggars's Song). Ory, *Belle illusion*, 326.

125. Ibid., 900 (note). It also included Elsa Barraine amd Henry Sauveplane.

126. Robert Orledge, *Charles Koechlin: His Life and Work* (London: Harwood Academic Publishers, 1989), 3. As Orledge points out, Koechlin's maternal grandfather, Jean Dolfus, had constructed one of the first "cités ouvrières."

127. On the formation of the Société Musicale Indépendante, see Fulcher, *French Cultural Politics*, 161.

128. Orledge, *Charles Koechlin*, 3–11.

129. Koechlin was now regularly reading the Communist *L'humanité*, for which he wrote a musical column. See his letter to Romain Rolland of 4 April, 1937, in Charles Koechlin, *Correspondance* (Paris: La Revue Musicale, 1982), 99.

130. Ory, *Belle illusion*, 331.

131. Other volumes published include *Chants révolutionnaires français* and *Chants des peuples soviétiques*. Ory (*Belle illusion*, 292), points out that Koechlin's book was the first work of the Editions Sociales Internationales's "Petite Bibliothèque Musicale." He notes the significance of a workers's party devoting such attention to music, and the fact that now the press associated with the Popular Front all developed musical columns, with Pierre Kaldor in *Commune,* Luc Decaunes in *Regards,* Daniel Lazarus in *Europe,* and Koechlin and Sauveplane in *L'humanité.*

132. Charles Koechlin, *La Musique et le peuple* (Paris: Editions Sociales Internationales, 1936), 5.

133. As Ory notes (*Belle illusion*, 293), those associated with the Popular Front now saw music as a "service public." Koechlin thus argued, in *Musique et peuple* (16), that a "culture musicale de la nation" must be put in place. Significantly, many of the themes of the early 1930s now reappear, such as the use of regional conservatories to develop the musical organizations of their areas.

134. Koechlin, *Musique et peuple*, 6. Here he is indeed inverting the rhetoric of d'Indy and the Schola Cantorum, which associated the naive and simple with "the good," or "sincerity" with "good faith."

135. Charles Koechlin, "Pour Chabrier," *Revue musicale* Jan. 1930: 8.

136. Golan, *Modernity and Nostalgia*, 123.

137. Koechlin, *Musique et le peuple*, 13, 21.

138. Ibid., 21. On Zola and Bruneau during the Dreyfus Affair, see Fulcher, *French Cultural Politics and Music*, 15–20.

139. Koechlin, *Musique et peuple*, 24. Here we may see a parallel with England in the thirties, when the "classics" were employed to bring musical culture to wider social groups.

140. Again, we find the earlier Debussyste argument, although now redirected. On the aesthetic of this group (in which Koechlin had participated), see Fulcher, *French Cultural Politics*, 154–58.

141. Julian Jackson, 14. He cites *L'art musical populaire* of 1 May, 1937.

142. Ibid.

143. Koechlin, *Correspondance*, 102. Letter to Romain Rolland of 9 Jan., 1938.

144. Ibid.

145. See Ory, *Belle illusion*, 292. As he points out, Desormière helped to coordinate the concerts, fêtes, and musical programs of the Popular Front. On Durey now, see Marc

Wood, "Louis Durey: Homme de Tête," *The Musical Times*, Winter 2000: 45. As he points out, in the thirties Durey began editing not only the work of the French revolutionary composer, Gossec, but also the Renaissance composers Josquin de Prez and Lassus.

146. Roger Desormières, "La Défense de la culture musicale," *L'art musical populaire* 15 May 1937.

147. *L'art musical populaire* March 1939: 1 and 5. The journal points out Honegger's attraction to the "fêtes populaires," and uses *Jeanne au bûcher* as an example of this, thus misrepresenting Honegger's goals in the work, as we shall see.

148. Pascal Ory, "Le Front populaire et la création artistique," 9; and *L'art musicale populaire*, 15 May 1937.

149. Julian Jackson, 127. He cites *L'art musical populaire*, Nov.–May, 1937.

150. Charles Koechlin, "La Vraie et la fausse musique populaire," *L'art musical populare* May 1937: 19. These were precisely the qualities that Cocteau had perceived in authentic popular culture in *Le coq et l'arlequin*—an immunity to propaganda and an instinctive ability to express truth.

151. D.-E. Inghelbrecht, *Mouvement contraire. Souvenirs d'un musicien* (Paris: Editions Domat, 1947), 23. According to Inghelbrecht, Lazarus had made the Opéra-Comique an "opera-de-quatre-sous," and thus finally lost his position.

152. See Huynh, *La Musique sous la République de Weimar*, 67. He cites the arguments in the first issue of *Melos* in 1920.

153. Ibid., 76 ff., on the conception of "high" and popular music for the masses in the Weimar Republic.

154. Ory, "Le Front populaire et la création artistique," 9. And see *L'art musical populaire* 15 May, 1937. It was the Editions Sociales Internationales that published Milhaud's *Mort d'un tyran* (for chorus and orchestra) and the seven musical portions of Rolland's *Le 14 juillet*, in addition to several of Auric's works, which were deliberately in "the popular" style.

155. Eugen Weber, *The Hollow Years*, 220–23.

156. On the political associations of the Schola, see Fulcher, *French Cultural Politics*, 24–26.

157. Obituary of Roussel, in *L'art musical populaire* May 1937.

158. *L'art musical populaire* 1 April 1939, 3.

159. *L'art musical populaire* 15 May, 1937, 18.

160. Ibid.

161. On this canon, see Fulcher, *French Cultural Politics*, 41–44.

162. Roussel, *Lettres et écrits*, 15, 260.

163. On Rolland's earlier interpretations of Beethoven and Handel, see Fulcher, *French Cultural Politics*, 58–59.

164. *L'Art musical populaire*, Feb. 1938. On Republican music history at the turn of the century, see Fulcher, *French Cultural Politics*, 41–44.

165. See *L'art musical populaire* Dec. 1937; and Esteban Buch, *La Neuvième de Beethoven: Une histoire politique* (Paris: Gallimard, 1999), 212–13, on the use of Beethoven earlier, in 1922, under Poincaré. Also see David James Fisher, *Romain Rolland and the Politics of Intellectual Engagement* (Berkeley: University of California Press, 1988), 81.

166. Emmanuel Buenzod, "Vues sur Beethoven," *La revue musicale* Jan. 1936, 14. On d'Indy's contrasting argument concerning Beethoven, see Fulcher, *French Cultural Politics*, 59.

167. Ibid.

168. See Danièle Pistone, "Beethoven et Paris: Repères et évocations contemporaines,

Revue internationale de musique française vol. 12 (Feb. 1987): 21. The great, recently deceased French musicologist, François Lesure, personally recounted to me his memories as a boy in Paris, during the Popular Front, of being "innundated" by performances of Beethoven. Significantly, a similar phenomenon was occurring in Republican Spain.

169. Pascal Ory, "Théorie et pratique de 'l'art des fêtes' sous le Front populaire," in *Les Usages politiques des fêtes*, 284.

170. Ory, *Belle illusion*, 309.

171. Ibid., 30. Gheusi had been a critic for *Le Figaro*, which François Coty owned until his death.

172. Ibid.

173. Ibid., 311–12.

174. Jean Zay, *Souvenirs et solitude* (Paris: Talus d'Approche, 1987), 91. Rouché, married to a perfume heiress, was nominally to the Left, being the former owner of the "leftist" *Grande revue*, although he was not particularly enthusiastic about the Popular Front. Ory, *Belle illusion*, 313.

175. Ory, *Belle illusion*, 314. As Ory notes (319), this administrative reorganization would lead logically to a formalization of the structure in January 1939, with the creation of the "Réunion des théatres lyriques nationaux," under Rouché's direction.

176. Ibid., 315. Lazarus did the music to Bloch's libretto, inspired by Gobineau's *L'Illustre magicien*, which was produced in 1937.

177. Ibid. Although it was finished in 1935, it was not performed until 1936. As we have noted, Lazarus's *Symphonie avec hymne* was an hommage to the Jewish people, and construed more generally as about "collective emancipation," it won critical praise.

178. Lazarus wrote in both the *Courrier musical* and *Europe*.

179. Ory, *Belle illusion*, 315. As he notes, ten years before, the subvention had been only eight hundred thousand francs.

180. An equivalent amount was given to the Opéra-Comique. See Zay, *Souvenirs*, 191; and Myriam Chimènes, "Le Budget de la musique sous la IIIe République," in *La Musique du théorique au politique*, eds. Hugues Dufourt and Joel-Marie Fauquet (Paris: Aux Amateurs de Livres, 1991), 268.

181. Pascal Ory, "La Politique culturelle du premier gouvernement Blum," *Nouvelle revue sociale* 10–11 (1975): 75–80.

182. This, of course, excluded Poulenc, who, as Myriam Chimènes has observed, was paying the price for his known political sympathies, having been passed over for a commission in *Le 14 juillet*. As she observes, Poulenc's attitude was mixed—partially critical, he was nevertheless envious of the official roles of Milhaud and Auric. See Francis Poulenc, *Correspondance 1910-1963*, ed. Myriam Chimènes (Paris: Fayard, 1994), 43.

183. Ibid., 422.

184. Zay, *Souvenirs*, 172.

185. Ory, *Belle illusion*, 316. The works were examined and selected by the committee, which saw about forty to fifty per year.

186. Ibid., 316–17.

187. Agulhon, *République*, 2: 44. He sees less political influence on artists than on writers, but does cite the case of Picasso's *Guernica*, exhibited at the Spanish pavilion of the 1937 Exposition. Many sources ignore or dismiss the political engagement of Les Six. Significantly, several members of Les Six, as well as members of the less politically oriented groups Triton and La Sérénade joined together, despite tensions among them, to contribute a series of piano pieces in the "popular spirit" for an album entitled *A l'Exposition*, dedicated to the pianist and teacher (now close to the government), Marguerite Long. It was published by Esching in 1937. On it, see Porcile, *Belle époque*, 394. On the political

engagement of the "generation of 1914" in the 1930s, see Gisèle Sapiro, *La guerre des écrivains 1940-1953* (Paris: Fayard, 1999), 79.

188. See Ory, *Belle illusion*, 295. He notes the "remarkably high" level of political awareness of musicians in this period, but here it is important to recognize their growing consciousness of the political-cultural situation in the course of the previous decade, as well as the example of the older generation in the twenties.

189. Jean Wiéner, *Allegro appassionato* (Paris: Pierre Belfond, 1978), 47.

190. Ibid., 145, 148. Again, we may recall his trip to the Soviet Union in 1926, with Milhaud, who would also henceforth write for *L'humanité*. Wiéner became associated with the "Maison de Culture." See Ory, *Belle illusion*, 292.

191. Wiéner, *Allegro appassionata*, 154-55.

192. Ory, *Belle illusion*, 327. Among such works were Koechlin's *Quelques chorales pour les fêtes populaires*.

193. For the situation in the prewar period, see Fulcher, *French Cultural Politics and Music*, 153-58.

194. Antoine Goléa, *Georges Auric* (Paris: Ventadour, no date), 26-27. And see Jean Roy, *Le Groupe des Six* (Paris: Seuil, 1994), 60, who notes Auric's indebtedness, here, to his training at the Schola. Significantly, this was the period of Auric's scores for surrealist films, with Cocteau, which demanded a more serious style. With Cocteau, he did the music to *Le sang d'un poète*, in 1930, a film produced by the vicomte de Noailles, and on which René Clair collaborated. In 1931 Auric did the score to Clair's *A nous la liberté*. As opposed to Honegger, who sought to harmonize a coherent musical structure with the action of the film, Auric rather sought to follow its unpredictable action. Auric was also drawn to the music of Berg and Skryabin in this period.

195. On the cool reception of the work at the Concerts de la Sérénade in December, 1932, see Poulenc, *Correspondance, 1910-1963*, ed. Myrian Chimènes, 383.

196. On Auric's style see *The New Grove Dictionary of Music and Musicians* 1980 ed., s.v. "Auric, Georges," by André Boucourechliev. On the Editions Sociales Internationales, see Ory and Sirinelli, *Les intellectuels en France*, 101. Auric also contributed to the set of piano pieces published in 1937 with the title *A l'exposition*, and dedicated to Marguerite Long. On the other contributors see Simone, 16. As he points out, it was performed at the inauguration of the "Pavillon de la Femme, de l'Enfant, et de la Famille."

197. The collection also included Auric's "La Corvée d'eau" and Jolivet's "Jeu du camp fou."

198. Paul Collaer, *A History of Modern Music*, trans. Sally Abeles (New York: The World Publishing Co., 1961), 244, 247.

199. Ibid., 248.

200. Darius Milhaud, *Notes sans musique* (Paris: Julliard, 1949), 285. As Porcile points out (*Belle époque*, 335), Milhaud was not pleased with *Liberté*, finding it lacking in unity and in some parts "pompier."

201. Ory and Sirinelli, 108.

202. Milhaud, *Notes sans musique*, 240. In the midst of rising anti-Semitism, Milhaud continued to write on Jewish themes, prominently including his *Liturgie contadine* of 1933. On anti-Semitism in this period, see Martyn Cornick, *Intellectuals in History: The Nouvelle revue française* (Atlanta: Rodopi, 1995), 150 ff.

203. Significantly, Milhaud contributed music criticism to the conservative paper *Le jour* from October 1933 to March 1937. See Darius Milhaud, *Notes sur la musique. Essais et chroniques*, ed. Jeremy Drake (Paris: Flammarion, 1982), 27.

204. The work premiered on 4 Oct. 1937 on Radio Paris, under Manuel Rosenthal's

direction. It was written for speaker, flute, oboe, saxophone, bassoon, percussion, and piano.

205. On Aristide Briand, see Wright, 236.

206. "Paix" in this period referred to the motto of the Popular Front, "Pain, Paix, Liberté." Milhaud's *Cantate de la Paix* premiered in June 1937 at the Sorbonne. Ory, *Belle illusion*, 331. Also see Darius Milhaud, *Ma vie heureuse* (Paris: Editions Belfond, 1973), 205-07; and *Notes sans musique*, 284-85.

207. It was published by the Le Chant du Monde in 1938. Ory, *Belle illusion*, 331.

208. Ibid., 296. The Loisirs Musicaux de la Jeunesse was tied to the Ligue de l'Enseignement." Also see Yannick Simon, "Les Jeunesses Musicales de France," in *La Vie musicale sous Vichy*, 205–206.

209. Ory, *Belle illusion*, 297.

210. Ibid. On precedents in the Weimar Republic, see Bryan Gilliam, ed., *Music and Performance during the Weimar Republic*.

211. See *Chansons au vent*, April 1938.

212. See *Europe*, June 1938; and Ory, *Belle illusion*, 320.

213. On the radio broadcast of *Esther de Carpentras*, see Jeremy Drake, *The Operas of Darius Milhaud* (New York: Garland, 1989), 15. And see Poulenc, *Correspondance*, ed. Myriam Chimènes, 442. Although I agree with Michel Faure that Milhaud was not a political "revolutionary," he was in fact "progressive," and one cannot take his claim to admire Fascist Italy (after a trip there) seriously. All his other actions and statements attest to the contrary. Perhaps he was impressed by the fact that the trains did "run on time." See Michel Faure, *Du néoclassicisme musical dans la France du premier XXe siècle* (Paris: Klinksieck, 1997), 247.

214. See Frédéric Robert, "Louis Durey," *Cahiers Jean Cocteau* 9 (1981): 408. It is significant that Hindemith had written a piece for marionettes during the Weimar Republic, his *Nush-Nushi*. See Huynh, *La Musique sous la République de Weimar*, 139.

215. Bergery was a deputy from Mantes-la-Jollie. See Winock, *Siècle des intellectuels*, 237. He discusses Bergery in the early thirties on 235.

216. Germaine Tailleferre, "Mémoires à l'emporte-pièce," ed. Frédéric Robert, *Revue internationale de musique française* 19 (Feb. 1986): 7–82.

217. Winock, *Siècle des intellectuels*, 235. Bergery, like the nonconformist, Bertrand de Jouvenal, and Jean Zay, the Popular Front Minister, began in the Radical Party, but gradually moved closer to the Socialist position. See Weber, *The Hollow Years*, 117.

218. Also among the counterdemonstrators was Jean Wiéner's future mistress, and later second wife, of whose involvement in the event, and political judgment and engagement, he remained particularly proud. Wiéner, 157.

219. Winock, *Siècle des intellectuels*, 235. Michael Faure (*Néoclassicisme*, 249), makes the unsubstantiated and theoretically unfounded assumption that after her contact with Bergery, Tailleferre's music took on the color of "radicalisme élégant," translating its conciliatory character. He similarly explains, or reduces, her Communist commitment by seeing it as a laicized and politicized version of Christian values, and claims that her style betrayed her progressive attitude—again with no substantiation.

220. Zeev Sternhell, *Neither Right nor Left: Fascist Ideology in France*, trans. David Maisel (Berkeley: University of California Press, 1986), 17; and Philippe Burrin, *La Dérive fasciste: Doriot, Déat, Bergery, 1933–1945* (Paris: Seuil, 1986), 219–21.

221. Burrin, *La Dérive fasciste*, 218.

222. The Frontistes broke with the principal political league of the Left, one closely associated with the Popular Front, the "Ligue des Droits de l'Homme," in 1937. See Burrin, 219–21.

223. Julian Jackson, 120, argues that the Popular Front was less concerned with creating new cultural forms than with "democratizing" those which existed.

224. The performance of *Le 14 juillet* was organized by the Maison de Culture to commemorate the formation of the government of the Popular Front. It was performed at the Alhambra Theater and was extended to early August because of its success. See Leslie Sprout, "Music of the Révolution française or the Révolution nationale?," 85.

225. David J. Fisher, *Romain Rolland*, 91.

226. On Rolland's influnce and ability to attract musicians to the cause of the Popular Front, see Ory, *Belle illusion*, 328. This included Daniel Lazarus, who was a friend of Rolland.

227. Fisher, *Romain Rolland*, 91.

228. The technique here, of course, was less ritualistic and formal than in the fascist regimes, which frequently began theatrical performances with either a national or political anthem.

229. Julian Jackson, 126-27.

230. Ibid., 120-27.

231. On the rationale for the choice of composers. See Ory, *Belle illusion*, 328 ff.

232. Sprout, "Music of the Révolution," 75; and Ory, *Belle illusion*, 328. They had only three weeks to write it, and the total time for the seven pieces was only a little over half an hour.

233. Ibert indeed became traditionalist in the years preceding World War II. He did, however, resist the Vichy regime, being strongly anti-German, and was, in turn, persecuted by the Vichy government. See Halbereich, *Arthur Honegger*, 195. On Zay's many political-artistic decisions as minister, see his *Souvenirs et solitude* (Paris: Talus d'Approche, 1987). On the politician-ministers of the Third Republic, see Robert O. Paxton, *Vichy France: Old Guard and New Order* (New York: Norton, 1972), 159.

234. See the score of *Le 14 juillet* in the Bibliothèque Nationale de France, Musique, Autographes, MS. 15012.

235. René Dumesnil, *Musique en France entre les deux guerres: 1919-1939* (Paris: Editions du Milieu du Monde, 1946), 85. Lazarus's work was not an isolated gesture. See Jane F. Fulcher, "The Preparation for Vichy: Anti-Semitism in French Musical Culture between the Two World Wars," *The Musical Quarterly* 71/2 (Fall 1995): 458-75.

236. Sprout, "Music of the Révolution," 76-82.

237. Ibid.

238. Julian Jackson, 125. And see Christopher Green, *Cubism and Its Enemies: Modern Movements and Reaction in French Art, 1916-1928* (New Haven: Yale University Press, 1987), 147, 153. He points out how artists like Gleize idealized the collective endeavor of the medieval studio workshop. He thus held a view of the social function of mural art that was shared by Léger and Delaunoy.

239. Julian Jackson, 126-27.

240. On the *La nouvelle revue française* and its aesthetic, see Jane F. Fulcher, "The Composer as Intellectual: Ideological Inscriptions in French Interwar Neoclassicism," *The Journal of Musicology* 17/2 (Spring 1999): 197-230.

241. Revue of *Le 14 juillet* by Léon Kochnitzsky, *La revue musicale* 167 (July–August 1936): 43.

242. The "parent" journal of the *La revue musicale*, the *La nouvelle revue française*, also had some reservations, its critic noting that the audience was, in fact, bourgeois, and that the style was propagandistic or didactic, something that "the people" did not require. See Sprout, "Music of the Révolution," 85.

243. Julian Jackson, 11. As he points out (124), it also provided an occasion to clarify

further the cultural ideals that had resulted from the interaction of the government, its cultural organizations, and the political parties. Significantly, in June 1937 a new cabinet was formed, now with Radical leadership, and without Blum. See Wright, 380. It is also important to note that, as Romy Golan points out (19-20), Edmond Labbé, who was close to the prime minister (Gaston Doumergue) was named as the Exposition's general director in 1934, and was allowed to retain his office after the change of government in 1936. In some aspects, he preserved a more conservative perspective in the Exposition. On the "takeover" of the Exposition by the new government, and its last-minute budgetary "rescue," see Ory, "Théorie et pratique de l'art des fêtes," 277. For further information on the music at the Exposition, see Nigel Simeone, "Music at the 1937 Exposition: The Science of Enchantment," 13–16.

244. Well-known playwrights and directors received commissions, including Jean-Richard Bloch. The audience, again, turned out to be middle class. See Knowles, *French Drama of the Inter-War Years*, 293.

245. Letter of 25 May, 1933 to Rouché from the Ministère de Commerce et de l'Industrie, Direction du Personnel de l'Exposition. Bibliothèque Nationale de France, Opéra, Fonds Rouché, Pièce 116.

246. As president of the commission, Rouché received many letters, accompanied by résumés and references, requesting a seat on the panel. Bibliothèque Nationale de France, Opéra, Fonds Rouché, item 116. And see Ory, *Les Expositions Universelles de Paris*, 126; and Ory, "Théorie et pratique de l'art des fêtes," 281. As Ory points out ("Théorie," 282), the "politique festive" was coordinated by the "délégué général artistique du Commissariat des fêtes de Paris," Georges Wissant.

247. Milhaud discusses the Exposition and its musical programs in Darius Milhaud, *Notes Without Music* (New York: Knopf, 1953), 255–77.

248. Milhaud, *Ma vie heureuse*, 205–06.

249. Ory, "Théorie et pratique de l'art des fêtes," 281. As he also notes (283), one principal aim was to get away from Rouché's more posh and stilted conceptions and turn to "fêtes en plein air" that were free and thus available to all. This was accomplished with the help of Lagrange and the collaboration of various cultural associations connected to the government.

250. Ibid., 282. These new trends included a stress on the colossal, on geometric forms, and on new lighting techniques.

251. Ory, *Belle illusion*, 329–30. The work had 12 composers collaborating, each of whom wrote a piece associated with an historical epoch in France's past, and many incorporating "chansons populaires." The participants included Ibert, Jaubert, Milhaud, Delannoy, Rosenthal, Landowski, Hoérée, Lazarus, Siohan, Rolland-Manuel, and Tailleferre. See Marcel Delannoy, *Honegger* (Geneva: Slatkine, 1986), 163. It premiered at the Théatre des Champs-Elysées on May 2, 1937, at the opening of the Exposition. Honegger did the "Prélude à la mort de Jaurès." The scenario was by Maurice Rostand. See Halbereich, *Arthur Honegger*, 175.

252. Halbereich, 176. As he points out (170), it was originally commissioned for the Opéra de Monte-Carlo. Ibert composed the first and fifth acts, and Honegger the other three.

253. As we noted earlier, a group of French composers, primarily Les Six and the Ecole d'Arcueil, contributed a collection of piano pieces entitled *A l'Exposition*, and dedicated to the former teacher of many of them, Marguerite Long. The contributors included Auric, Delannoy, Ibert, Milhaud, Poullenc, Sauguet, Schmitt, and Tailleferre. The set was premiered by two of Long's younger pupils for the inauguration of the "Pavillon de l'en-

fant." See Cecilia Dunoyer, *Marguérite Long: A Life in French Music, 1874-1966* (Bloomington, Ind.: Indiana University Press, 1993), 103.

254. Bibliothèque Nationale de France, Opéra. Fonds Rouché, item 118, "Programmes, fêtes, et spectacles de l'Exposition de 1937. And see Ory, "Théorie et pratique de l'art des fêtes," 283. As he points out, it was planned to close the Exposition.

255. On the different "registers" of representation in the different arts, see Roger Chartier, *On the Edge of the Cliff: History, Language, and Practices*, trans. Lydia G. Cochrane (Baltimore: Johns Hopkins Press, 1997), 90–103.

256. Dumesnil, *La Musique en France entre les deux guerres*, 148.

257. See Ory, "Théorie et pratique de l'art des fêtes," 285. He also notes the use of Soviet models here. In some of the fêtes, there were projections into the sky, or onto giant screens.

258. It was also performed at the more "popular" Vélodrome d'Hiver in 1937. See Knowles, 294. The work is alternately referred to as *La Construction d'une cité*. See Halbereich, 176.

259. On Jean-Richard Bloch, see Ory and Sirinelli, *Les Intellectuels en France*, 10. Fernand Léger claimed to have discovered "le peuple français" during the war, and thereafter became not only an enthusiastic supporter of the Popular Front, but a member of the Communist Party. See Laurence Bertrand Dorléac, "Fernand Léger," in the *Dictionnaire des intellectuels français*, 697. The work consisted of forty musical pieces and was written and performed in less than two months, under the direction of Roger Desormière, with the assistance of Jean Wiéner. See Ory, *Belle illusion*, 330.

260. On related efforts, such as Leo Rostenberg's innovations in the Kroll Opera, see Huynh, 259.

261. Ory, *Les Expositions universelles*, 12, 32.

262. See Knowles, 294.

263. Julian Jackson, 129. J.-R. Bloch grew close to the Communist Party as early as 1934, and helped to found the Comité de Vigilance des Intellectuels anti-Fascistes. In 1937, still faithful to the Communists, he became director of the paper, *Le soir*, together with Louis Aragon and, in 1938, he officially became a member of the Communist Party. See Christophe Prochasson, "Bloch, Jean-Richard," in the *Dictionnaire des intellectuels français*, 155–57.

264. Ory, *Belle illusion*, 330. It used a juxtaposition of orchestral pieces, songs, and choruses.

265. Ibid.; and Julian Jackson, 129.

266. Wiéner, 155. And see Golan, 154.

267. Honegger contributed two *chansons*, and Arthur Hoérée did the rest. Halbereich, 178. He argues (169), that Honegger was resolutely to the Left.

268. Julian Jackson, 142–43. Able Gance adapted *Louise* for film in 1938.

269. Halbereich, 176. On the relation between the French and Russian revolutions see Arno J. Mayer, *The Furies: Violence and Terror in the French and Russian Revolutions* (Princeton, NJ: Princeton University Press, 2000).

270. Halbereich, 169.

271. On music history as presented at the 1900 Exposition, see Fulcher, *French Cultural Politics and Music*, 35–44.

272. Julian Jackson, 126. Of course, the Exposition did not neglect contemporary art. As Affron points out (192), Waldemar George was appointed an inspector with the Department of Works of Art at the Exposition, and worked together with agents of the Popular Front to oversee the murals by Léger for the Palais de la Découverte.

273. Paul Landormy (1869–1943) had given courses at the Ecole des Hautes Etudes Sociales before the war, and was a critic for *La Victoire, Le Figaro,* and *Le Temps*. At the 1937 Exposition he was in charge of the "fifth class." It is significant to note that in 1937 there was also official support for the Société des Concerts de Versailles, which performed seventeenth- and eighteenth-century French works. It was undoubtedly subsidized as part of the attempt to stress the French classic tradition, as opposed to the German romanticism currently being advocated as model by the pro-fascist Right. It was probably on the basis of this that major French composers similarly supported it, including Ravel, Roussel, Roland-Manuel, Honegger, and the writer, Paul Valéry.

274. Roussel, *Lettres et écrits,* 284–85.

275. Letter from Paul Landormy, sécrétaire de la classe 5, to the Ministère de Commerce et de l'Industrie, Exposition Internationale, Paris, 1937, dated 4 Oct. 1937. Bibliothèque Nationale de France, Opéra. Fonds Rouché, item 116.

276. Dumesnil, *Musique en France,* 212. Again, Lazarus's symphony was named after "the pioneer of modern Palestine," and attempted to trace the history of the Jewish people in five movements: (1) Voyage millénaire; (2) Mission d'Israel; (3) Pogrom; (4) Marche funèbre; and (5) Hymne. In 1937, Lazarus's opera, *L'illustre magicien,* was performed in Paris, bringing him to further prominence.

277. Jean Rivier, born in 1896, was highly influenced by Roussel. See Roussel, *Lettres et écrits,* 328. Although both Kerdyk and Rivier abetted the Republic here, politically, they were to the Right of it. On Delannoy's work see Leslie A. Sprout, "Music for a 'New Era': Composers and national Identity in France, 1936–1946," Ph.D. dissertation, University of California, Berkeley, 2000, 59. As Sprout also notes, in the intervening years Delannoy had produced a cantata-ballet, *La jour de la Dame,* which provocatively mixed diverse styles (including French folk song, blues, and jazz), and it was performed at the Opéra-Comique in 1930. In 1935 he wrote a ballet based upon the "Cinderella" of Perrault.

278. Ibid., 286. Again on the Orphéon choral societies and their history, see Jane F. Fulcher, "The Orphéon Societies: 'Music for the Workers' in Second-Empire France," *International Review of the Aesthetics and Sociology of Music* X/1 (1979): 47–56.

279. F21–4552 #2, Budget de 1937. Ammendement à la Loi de Finance présenté par M. Gabriel Lafarge, deputé-artiste: La taxe d'Etat sur le spectacle est supprimée à partir du premier janvier, 1937. Archives Nationales, Paris

280. Julian Jackson, 257–58. As Wright points out (385), in 1936 pro-Nazi and pro-appeasement sentiment was growing.

281. Julian Jackson, 8. On the unprecedented violence, both verbal and physical, on the part of the adversaries of the Popular Front, see Jules Moch, *Front populaire,* 202. He also notes (213–15), the eruption of immediate demonstrations on the part of the Croix-de-Feu and the Jeunesses Patriotes.

282. Louis Bodin and Jean Touchard, *Front populaire 1936* (Paris: Armand Colin, 1961), 2. The press in favor of the government included *L'humanité, Le populaire, L'oeuvre* (which was Radical), *Vendredi,* and *Marianne*.

283. On the situation thirty years earlier, see Fulcher, *French Cultural Politics,* 24–35. French readers were well aware of Hitler's ideas, for, as Hamilton points out (205), Hitler gave interviews to admirers in *Le matin* (in 1934), *Paris-soir* (in 1936), and *Le journal* (in 1938).

284. See Robert Wohl, "Fascism both Right and Left," *Journal of Modern History* vol. 63 (March 1991): 91–98.

285. Ibid. Wohl concludes that we must distinguish between a mood or mentality and the translation of feelings and ideas into political realities. As Hamilton notes (192), after Valois's Faisceau in the twenties, Marcel Bucard's Parti Franciste, founded in 1933,

was the most intransigent, if the least popular, fascist party in France. For a useful summary of the historical perspectives on French fascism see Matthew Affron and Mark Antliff, "Art and Fascist Ideology in France and Italy: An Introduction," in *Fascist Visions: Art and Ideology in France and Italy*, 3–10.

286. See Robert Soucy, "Barrès and French Fascism," *French Historical Studies* Spring 1967: 67. As he points out, some, like René Rémond, argue that fascism was a foreign importation, while Zeev Sternhell maintains that the seeds of fascism were, in fact, sown in France. Raoul Girardet, like Rémond, holds that fascism was inherently alien to French political traditions, and entered only as an infiltration of established ideologies. Also see Robert Soucy, "French Press Reactions to Hitler's First Two Years in Power," *Contemporary European History* 7/1 (1998): 21–22; and his book, *French Fascism: The Second Wave, 1933–1939* (New Haven: Yale University Press, 1995).

287. See Serge Berstein, *La France des années 30* (Paris: Armand Colin, 1988), 98 ff. Also see Soucy, "Barrès and French Fascism," 72; and Sternhell, *Neither Right nor Left*, 23. See Hamilton (198–200), on Céline and his admiration for fascism. As Hamilton points out (203), among the admirers of Mussolini in the thirties were Edouard Schuré and Guy de Pourtalès. Both were ardent Wagnerians.

288. Sternhell, *Neither Right nor Left*, 21–27; and Soucy, "Barrès and French Fascism," 67 ff.

289. Robert Brasillach, Drieu La Rochelle, and Lucien Rebatet all exhibit strong affinities with the romantic movement and its focus on the sacred and subjective.

290. Although the fascist "utopia" was an industrial society, dominated by the state, it was spiritually reactionary, questing for a return to an imagined purity of origins. See Jane F. Fulcher, "Musical Style, Meaning, and Politics in France on the Eve of the Second World War," *The Journal of Musicology* vol. 13 (Fall 1995): 425–453. On the related situation in Germany, see Jeffrey Herf, *Reactionary Modernism: Technology, Culture, and Politics in Weimar and the Third Reich* (New York: Cambridge University Press, 1986).

291. On those aspects of Hiter and German fascism that French fascists did not like, see Soucy, "French Press Reactions to Hitler's First Two Years in Power," 22.

292. Julian Jackson, 253. And see Paul Serant, *Le Romantisme fasciste: ou l'oeuvre politique de quelques écrivains français* (Paris: Fasquelle, 1959), 94–95, 122. Also see Soucy, "Barrès and French Fascism." As he point out (272), French fascism was "less taken with the Führer prinzip," and less attached to the principles of totalitarianism. Berstein, in *La France des années 30* (97–98), stresses French fascism's activating "mystique" and exaltation of vitalist values.

293. David Carroll, *French Literary Fascism: Nationalism, Anti-Semitism, and the Ideology of Culture* (Princeton, NJ: Princeton University Press, 1995), 8.

294. Ibid.

295. Ibid., 9.

296. Ibid., 3.

297. Ibid., 7. On the application of fascist ideas to the visual arts in France, see Affron, 185-90. As he notes, Waldemar George praised those artists who employed "Magic Realist or naturalistic idioms and classicizing vocabularies," including such figures as Giorgio de Chirico, Derain, and Maillot.

298. Walter L. Adamson, "The Language of Opposition in Early Twentieth-Century Italy: Rhetorical Continuities between Prewar Florentine Avant-gardism and Mussolini's Fascism," *The Journal of Modern History* March 1992: 22. The French were well aware of Italian fascism, with Italian fascists being "implanted" in more than twenty French towns, and the presence of twenty-four hundred of Mussolini's secret police, unofficial agents, and "provocateurs." See Weber, *The Hollow Years*, 89.

299. Dioudonnat, *Je suis partout*, 91. The leagues were dissolved on 10 June 1936, beginning with the Action Française.

300. See René Rémond, *Les Droites en France* (Paris: Aubier Montaigne, 1982), 219–20. As he points out, even the most important organs of conservative opinion began to move from their moderate attachment to parliamentary institutions to support for the neighboring authoritarian regimes. This he perceives not only in the case of journals like *Gringoire* and *Candide*, but also in *La revue universelle*, *La revue hebdomadaire*, *La revue de Paris*, and *La revue de France*. As journals of the moderate Right, he includes *L'echo de Paris*, *Le jour*, *Le figaro*, *Le matin*, and *Le journal*.

Also see Soucy, "French Press reactions," 24, on the spectrum of the Right-wing press. Among those on the moderate Right he includes *Le petit journal*, *La croix*, *L'information*, *Le petit parisien*, *Le temps*, and *L'intransigeante*. The center Left included *Paris-soir*, *La République*, *L'oeuvre*, and *Le populaire*. *Paris-soir*, the largest of the French newspapers in 1933, was sympathetic to the Radical Party, and also on the moderate Left. As Weber points out (*The Hollow Years*, 130,) "the vast majority of the Paris press was on the Right," which had no small implications for music criticism, since papers on the far Right, did expect their critics to echo their viewpoints. As Weber also points out, most papers were dependent on subsidies from banks, industry, and French or foreign governments.

301. See Agulhon, *République*, 2: 41–42, on the cultural image of the weeklies like *Gringoire*, and *Candide*, which had larger circulations than *Marianne*. On the more "popular" tone of *Gringoire*, as opposed to *Candide*, see Ory and Sirinelli, 95. Also see Claude Bellanger, Jacques Godechot, Pierre Guiral, and Fernand Terron, eds., *Histoire générale de la presse française* (Paris: Presses Universitaires de France, 1969) 3: 580–591.

302. On "Scholiste" ideals, see Fulcher, *French Cultural Politics*, 28–31. On the recrudescence of anti-Semitism in France in the thirties, see Vicki Caron, "The Anti-Semitic Revival in France in the 1930s."

303. See Fulcher, *French Cultural Politics*, 134–35. Also see Mark Antliff, "La Cité française: Georges Valois, Le Corbusier, and Fascist Theories of Urbanism," in *Fascist Visions: Art and Ideology in France and Italy*, eds. Matthew Affron and Mark Antliff (Princeton, NJ: Princeton University Press, 1997), 144–45.

304. Pierre Andrieu, "Fascisme 1913," *Combat* Feb. 1936: 25–26.

305. On the connection between *Combat* and the "nonconformist" movement, see Jean-Louis Loubet del Bayle, *Les Non-conformistes des années 30. Une tentative de la renouvellement de la pensée politique française* (Paris: Seuil, 1969), 75. He also discusses Brasillach's connection with its antidemocratic tendencies. Zeev Sternhell sees the birth of fascism in a grouping closely related to that of *L'indépendance*, the "Cercle Proudhon," a similar synthesis of the nationalist, antiliberal Right and the Sorelian Left against parliamentary democracy. See his *Ni droite ni gauche. L'Idéologie fasciste en France* (Paris: Seuil, 1983), 10–15.

306. See Fulcher, *French Cultural Politics*, 31–35.

307. See Jane F. Fulcher, "A Political Barometer of Twentieth-Century France: Wagner as Jew or Anti-Semite," *The Musical Quarterly* 84/1 (Spring 2000): 42–47. It is important to remember that d'Indy's virulently anti-Semitic book on Wagner, *Richard Wagner et son influence sur l'art musical français* (Paris: Delagrave, 1930), was published at the beginning of the decade.

308. See Fulcher, *French Cultural Politics*, 32–33. Significantly, figures like Alfredo Casella, in Italy, tried to reconcile the national and international in a similar manner. See Harvey Sachs, *Music in Fascist Italy* (New York: Norton, 1988), 138.

309. See Brian Hart, "The Symphony in Debussy's World: A Context for His Views on

the Genre and Early Interpretations of La Mer", in Debussy and His World, ed. Jane F. Fulcher (Princeton, NJ: Princeton University Press, 2001), 183–86.

310. Emile Vuillermoz, for example, was critic not only for L'excelsior and L'Illustration, but also for Candide. He, together with the former music critic for L'action française, the increasingly profascist Dominique Sordet, became allies in the effort to influence the direction of record companies. See Piero Coppola, Dix-sept ans de musique à Paris 1922–1939 (Geneva: Slatkine, 1982. Original edition, Lausanne, 1944), 171.

311. On the modernism of the Italian fascists, see Fanette Roche-Pézard, "Création artistique et idéologie politique: futurisme et fascisme," Cahiers d'histoire de l'art contemporain, May 1974: 4–11.

312. See André Boll, review of Le 14 juillet, La Flèche, July 1936: 4.

313. Dioudonnat, Je suis partout, 7–8, 12, 27, 34. The journal openly admired Mussolini (ibid., 29). Even the more moderate press of the Right attacked Milhaud. As Faure points out (Néoclassicisme, 86), Florent Schmitt, in a review of Bolivar in Le temps, 9 May 1936, condemned Milhaud's polytonality as well as his use of "chants nègres, tangos, shimmies," etc.

314. Dioudonnat, 69–83. On the political evolution of Je suis partout, see Ory and Sirinelli, 106.

315. Brasillach idolized Hitler's romantic, "poetic" appeal.

316. Rebatet eventually became a collaborator, and, like Brasillach, was sentenced to death, but unlike Brasillach, his sentence was commuted. Many years later, in 1969, shortly before his death, Rebatet felt free to state his still implicitly politicized opinions concerning music, which essentially had not changed. See his Une histoire de la musique (Paris: Robert Laffont, 1969), especially his attack on Cocteau and Les Six (564). His conception of nationalism was clearly that of d'Indy, as opposed to the post-World War I striving for French artistic "purity." As we might expect, the longest section of the book is devoted to Wagner, whom he sees as the precursor of the most fecund innovations of contemporary music. Implicit here is the argument made explicit by d'Indy in his book on Wagner of 1930—that Wagner had helped "save" French music from the malevolent influence of French Jewish composers. Equally revealing is his subtle paraphrasing of Wagner's Judaism in Music. On Rebatet's attack on Schoenberg see Maie-Claire Mussat, "La réception de Schoenberg en France avant la Seconde Guerre Mondiale," Revue de musicologie 87/1 (2001): 172. Oddly, she goes on to claim (173), that fortunately such attacks were rare in French music criticism. As we have seen in both here and in chapter 2, this was far from the case. And, as Porcile points out (Belle époque, 384), when three of Kurt Weill's songs were performed at the Salle Pleyel in Nov. 1933, the noted composer and critic Florent Schmitt stood up, amidst the booing and shouted "Vive Hitler." He was praised for this act by Rebatet in Action française on 2 Dec. 1933, in an article entitled "Une apostrophe de M. Florent Schmitt."

317. This issue appeared in February 1939.

318. Pierre Leclau, "Premières auditions," Je suis partout 10 March 1939.

319. Pierre Leclau, "Premières auditions," Je suis partout 3 Feb. 1939.

320. On Marianne see Ory and Sirinelli, 104. Gringoire was hostile to the La nouvelle revue française, accusing Gide, Rivière, and other members of its circle of being "contre l'esprit de chez nous." See Dioudonnat, 18.

321. Dioudonnat, 15.

322. Ibid., 19.

323. This is as opposed to the famous sobriquet "Couperin le Grand." See René Kerdyk, "Portrait de Francis Poulenc," Gringoire 11 Feb. 1938.

324. Ibid. And see Dioudonnat, 14, 23. On the Communists's support for French tradition by 1936, see Sapiro, *Guerre des écrivains*, 152.

325. Ibid., 70. Léon Daudet, in fact, wrote several books on Clemenceau.

326. Eugen Weber, *Action Française: Royalism and Reaction in Twentieth-Century France* (Stanford, Calif.: Stanford University Press, 1962), 508. Other speakers announced for the 1937–38 season included important men of letters and journalists, such as Montherlant, Maulnier, Brasillach, and Rebatet. On the "Conférences Rive Gauche," also see Ory, *Belle illusion*, 20.

327. On Poulenc's financial situation in these years, see Poulenc, *Correspondance*, ed. Myriam Chimènes, 30, 33. As she points out (29), his financial situation was never really in serious difficulty; he was giving lecture-concerts primarily for reasons of money and publicity, and even had an agent for this purpose. See his letter to André Latarjet, dated "Automne 1934," *Correspondence, 1910–1963*, 400. Chimènes observes (36) that Poulenc was always sensitive to press opinions of him.

328. André Coeuroy, "Musicologie amusante," *Gringoire* 8 Jan. 1937.

329. Ironically, this was after Shostakovich had already been denounced in the Soviet Union for "formalism."

330. On ideologically conflicting interpretations of Beethoven at the turn of the century, see Fulcher, *French Cultural Politics*, 58–59. By the time of the Popular Front, France's intellectual and cultural life had become as polarized as its politics. See Lebovics, *True France*, 36.

331. Ravel himself wrote to the German author who had included him in *Judentum und Musik*, threatening legal action. In addition, the French ambassador to Germany himself asked Goebbels if, because of this misunderstanding, Ravel's works were being boycotted in Germany. Goebells claimed that this was not the case. See Arbie Orenstein, *A Ravel Reader: Correspondence, Articles, Interviews* (New York: Columbia University Press, 1990), 325–26. As Orenstein points out (488), the American press assumed that Ravel was Jewish both because he championed Jewish artists and because his name was Maurice, which was thought to be Jewish.

332. Ibid., 313. Ravel, despite his own financial limitations, generously invited musicians who were being persecuted by Hitler to stay temporarily with him at his home in Monfort-Émaury. See Rosenthal, *Ravel*, 14. As Eugen Weber points out in *The Hollow Years* (103–04), by 1933 more than twenty thousand Germans sought refuge in France, but were often treated as associated with the German enemy. As he also points out (91), this was a period when, in response to increased immigration, French musicians, as early as 1931, were picketing to keep foreign orchestras out, perceiving them as unfair competition. He further notes (93–96), that this response extended into industry, where there were frequent complaints about Jewish and American "invaders."

333. Orenstein, *A Ravel Reader*, 487–88.

334. See Rebatet, "Le cercueil de Ravel," *Je suis partout* 7 Jan. 1938; and Dominique Sordet, *Maurice Ravel* (Paris: Editions de Tambourinaire, 1939), 1, 11.

335. Rebatet, "Le cerceuil de Ravel." Rebatet here refers to Zay as "un Juif entre les Juifs," and comments on the "impudence moral et artistique" of such a person daring to speak of "our" moral and artistic tradition.

336. René Bizet, "Maurice Ravel, cadavre urgent," *Candide* 6 Jan., 1938.

337. Ibid. In 1936 and 1937 Vuillermoz, Sordet, and Rebatet were all contributing to *Candide*, a period when the journal was openly favorable to both Mussolini and Hitler. See, for example, the article of 30 Jan. 1936, "Les Soirées musicales d'Hitler." The special issue of the *La revue musicale* devoted to Ravel appeared in December 1938. In this issue (225), Romain Rolland expresses his admiration for Ravel as well as for Rameau and Debussy.

Significantly, Guy de Portalès, a Socialist, refers pointedly (227) to Ravel's cosmopolitanism in a positive sense, noting his Savoisien and Swiss origins. The only negative article is by Cocteau, who dismisses Ravel as "le chef des petit-*maîtres* de l'impressionisme," thus ignoring Ravel's stylistic evolution (396-97).

338. See Paul Landormy in *La victoire* 4 Jan. 1938. Landormy had been pro-Scholiste, however he aided Roussel (who had been associated with and then distanced himself from the Schola) with the organization of the historical concerts for the 1937 Exposition.

339. As Landormy put it, "Voilà un musicien le plus discret qui sait nous émouvoir profondément." (Here, the most discreet musician who knows how to move us profoundly.) Ibid.

340. Sternhell, *Neither Right nor Left*, 16. Landormy had remained with the journal since the immediate postwar period.

341. Vuillermoz was now a critic for *L'excelsior, Candide,* and *L'Illustration,* which ranged from conservative to further Right.

342. Vuillermoz's article appeared on 13 Jan. 1938, in *Candide*. Here he notes that "Ce n'est qu'à la suite des protestations énergiques élevées par l'entourage immédiat de Maurice Ravel qu'on a pu obtenir un récent festival à la radio. Puis des modifications hatives enlevant au programme cette tendance à "minimiser" la génie de Ravel." (It was only following the energetic protestations raised by Maurice Ravel's immediate circle that one was able to obtain a recent festival on the radio. Then [there were] hasty modifications removing from the program this tendency to "minimize" Ravel's genius.)

343. On the political use of the radio now, see André-Jean Tudesq, "Utilisation gouvernementale de la radio," in *Edouard Daladier: Chef du gouvernement*, eds. René Rémond and Janine Bourdin (Paris: Presses de la Fondation des Sciences Politiques, 1977), 255–264. Also see Chimènes, "Le Budget de la musique," 297–98.

344. Eugen Weber, *The Hollow Years*, 198-91.

345. On precedents for the use of the radio in the Weimar Republic, see Huynh, 191.

346. On Rolland's interpretation of Beethoven, see Fulcher, *French Cultural Politics*, 58–59.

347. André Coeuroy, "Autour de *Fidelio*," *Gringoire* 22 Jan. 1937. Significantly, this was the period of the politically conservative Stravinsky's diatribe, in his autobiography, against the leftist political appropriation of Beethoven in both Russia and France. His argument concerning "pure" musical values closely resembles that of French fascist writers. See Igor Stravinsky, *An Autobiography* (New York: Norton, 1962), 116.

348. Léon Daudet, review of Adolphe Boschot's *Musiciens-poètes* in *Candide* 20 June 1938. On the larger context for the political use of Beethoven's Ninth Symphony, see Esteban Buch, *La Neuvième de Beethoven: Une histoire politique* (Paris: Gallimard, 1999).

349. See *L'ami du peuple* 7 Jan. 1930.

350. *Le nouveau siècle* 30 Jan. 1927.

351. On Sordet's influence in the recording industry, as well as as a critic, see Coppola, *Dix-sept ans de musique à Paris*, 71. It is also significant that Nadia Boulanger's recording of Monteverdi won the prize of the Fondation Candide. The influence of *Candide* extended to popular music, for there was a Prix Candide for popular chansons as well as for art music.

352. Sordet concludes that the work is not as bad as one thought. See Dominique Sordet, "*Louise* au phonographe," *Candide* 6 Feb. 1936. On the opera and its original ideological readings, see Fulcher, *French Cultural Politics*, 77–97.

353. See Jane F. Fulcher, "Charpentier's Operatic 'Roman Musical' as Read in the Wake of the Dreyfus Affair," *19th-Century Music* 16/2 (Fall 1992): 161–80.

354. Henri Poulain, "Rentrée avec un collaborateur de Vincent d'Indy," *Je suis partout* 21 Oct. 1938.

355. Dominique Sordet, ed., *L'initiation à la musique à l'usage des amateurs de radio* (Paris: Editions du Tambourinaire, 1935). Also collaborating on the volume, among others, was Reynaldo Hahn. The book was commissioned by the French company Thomson Hoester and by the Société des Etablissements Ducretet.

356. This position is implied in *L'initiation à la musique*, 74–77.

357. Ibid., 85.

358. The book goes on to emphasize his organization of outdoor performances before crowds of workers—seen as testimony to his generosity, in distinction to so many artists of the present. Ibid.

359. Ibid., 41–45 and 49.

360. Ibid., 92–94.

361. André Coeuroy, "Aidez-les," *Gringoire*, 15 Jan. 1937. *Gringoire* also approved of Jacques Ibert, who, although he had participated in some fêtes of the Popular Front, was not enthusiastic about the government. See René Kerdyk, "Portrait—Jacques Ibert," *Gringoire* 26 Feb. 1937.

362. Pierre Leclau, "Premières auditions," *Je suis partout*, 3 Feb. 1939.

363. See Rollo Myers, *Modern French Music* (Oxford: Blackwell, 1971), 143. As he points out, like Poulenc, Sauguet studied with Koechlin, but unlike Poulenc he also studied with the Scholiste Joseph Canteloube.

364. Poulenc, *Correspondance*, ed. Myriam Chimènes, 101. Letter from Henri Sauguet to Poulenc, 10 Aug. 1936.

365. On other works stimulated by the Spanish Civil War, including Picasso's *Guernica* and André Malraux's *L'espoir*, see Ory and Sirinelli, 113. On the division that was caused among French intellectuals, see Sapiro, *Guerre des écrivains*, 153–159.

366. Winock, *Siécle des intellectuels*, 297–304.

367. Poulenc, *Correspondance*, ed. Myriam Chimènes, 410.

368. Ibid., 101. Letter from Sauguet to Poulenc, 18 Aug. 1936. On the attitude of the French Right toward fascism, see Weber, *The Hollow Years*, 166–67. And see Henri Collet, "Où sont les musiciens espagnols?," *Le ménestrel* 16 Oct. 1936.

369. Although aristocratic, the Polignacs, like the Noailles, were apparently not against the Republic. For they were among the aristocracy that were successfully reintegrated into the Republic's elite. On this, this Christophe Charle, "Noblesses et élites en France au début du XXe siècle," in *Noblesses européens au XIX siècle*, 407–33 (Paris: Collection de l'Ecole Française de Rome 107, 1988).

370. Francis Poulenc, *Correspondance 1915-1963*, ed. Hélène de Wendel (Paris: Seuil, 1967), 98–99. Letter to the comtesse de Polignac, 15 Aug. 1936. On Poulenc and the Popular Front, see Poulenc, *Correspondance*, ed. Myriam Chimènes, 43. It is significant to note that Poulenc was already aware of public political issues, having responded to the tumultuous events of 6 Feb. 1934, in a letter to Jacques Lerolle of Feb. 9, 1934 as follows: "Je travaille beaucoup en tâchant d'oublier les laideurs et tristesses de la vie actuelle tant publique que personelles." Poulenc, *Correspondance, 1910–1936*, ed. Myriam Chimènes, 392. Poulenc wrote of his dislike for Léon Blum in a letter to Sauguet of 5 Aug.1936. Ibid., 420. But in a letter to Sauguet of 17 Aug. 1936, Poulenc did point out that Auric and Koechlin could now be helpful to him (Sauguet), apropos of his opera, *Le Chartreuse de Parme*, because of their official positions. He also ruefully observes that his own family is sorry that he is no longer in the papers, remarking that "les bourgeois sont si officiels même quand il s'agit du Front populaire." Ibid., 421–22. Marie-Blanche de Polignac was

the daughter of the couturier Jeanne Lanvin, and originally come from a "milieu modest." See Michael Faure, *Néoclassicisme*, 146.

371. Wright, 312.

372. Ory, *Belle illusion*, 814.

373. Agulhon, *République*, 2: 50. Here it is significant to point out, with regard to Poulenc's fervent Catholicism, that the Catholic Church, in general, opposed the Popular Front. See Weber, *The Hollow Years*, 147.

374. Paul Griffiths, *Olivier Messiaen and the Music of Time* (Ithaca: Cornell University Press, 1985), 74.

375. Keith Daniel, *Francis Poulenc: His Artistic Development and Musical Style* (Ann Arbor: UMI Research Press, 1982), 217. On Poulenc's turn to choral music, see Poulenc, *Correspondance, 1910–1963*, ed. Myriam Chimènes, 29.

376. Rocamadour is a site of annual Catholic pilgrimage.

377. Lynn Hunt, *Politics, Culture, and Class in the French Revolution* (Berkeley: University of California Press, 1984), 61.

378. Weber, *The Hollow Years*, 198.

379. Daniel, *Francis Poulenc*, 19–20. And see Poulenc, *Correspondance, 1910–1963*, ed. Myriam Chimènes, 426. According to Poulenc, with his visit to Rocamadour, the blood of his father's side of the family (which was from the neighboring department of Aveyronnais) triumphed over his Mother's Nogentais blood. Ibid., 428.

380. This included Gaston Bergery. Ironically, Poulenc later claimed that the motets were influenced by Milhaud's *Cantate de la paix*: perhaps they were an "answer" to it. Daniel, 225.

381. Collaer, *A History of Modern Music*, 270. The work, for mixed a capella chorus, was a commission from the abbé Maillet for the Petits Chanteurs à la Croix de Bois. It premiered in February 1939 at the Eglise Saint-Etienne-du-Mont in Paris. As Eugen Weber points out (*Hollow Years*, 205), just a year later, in 1940, Catholic and national penitents were indeed united in the annual pilgrimage to Rocamadour, which was "dedicated to accepting the country's harsh ordeal in a spirit of reparation."

382. Daniel, 203. Eschewing academic rules of voice leading, he composed what sounded good to him, which resulted in numerous parallel and direct fifths and octaves, unresolved seventh and ninth chords, and wide, disjunct inner voices.

383. Poulenc pointed out in a letter to Nadia Boulanger, of Sept. 1936: "Elle commence par quelques mesures d'introduction en ré majeur-mineur, ensuite nombreuses modulations dans des tons éloignés et puis conclusion, longuement, en sol mineur. C'est très spécial, humble, et je crois saisissant." Poulenc, *Correspondance 1910–1936*, ed. Myriam Chimènes, 428.

384. Daniel, 203–8, 221.

385. The *Litanies* premiered not in Paris, but in Lyon, on May 3, 1937, and the performance was broadcast on the radio. Poulenc asked Sauguet the day before the premiere to write about it in the moderate Right paper to which he contributed criticism, *Le jour*. Poulenc, *Correspondance 1910–1936*, ed. Myriam Chimènes, 441.

386. Henri Hell, *Francis Poulenc* (Paris: Fayard, 1978), 144, and Poulenc, *Correspondance 1910–1936*, ed. Myriam Chimènes, 30, 365. And see Myriam Chimènes, "Poulenc and His Patrons: Social Convergences," in *Francis Poulenc: Music, Art, and Literature*, eds. Sidney Buckland and Myriam Chimènes (Aldershot: Ashgate, 1999), 210–51. On Poulenc's "Marche 1889" and his "Marche 1937," as his "Intermède Champêtre," see Simeone, "Music at the 1937 Paris Exposition," 16. He also discusses Auric's contribution to the dinner.

387. Poulenc's *Cinq poèmes d'Eluard* were premiered at the Ecole Normale de Musique in 1935.

388. Keith Daniel sees Poulenc's "third period" (for Daniel, 1936–59) as marked by a greater romantic coloring and sustained lyricism, as required by the more lyric poetry he now set. He too notes Poulenc's attraction to the surrealist proclivity for the mystical, the religious, the esoteric, and the inward vision. See Daniel, *Poulenc*, 225–27. On surrealism and its ultimate goal of modifying society, see Inez Hedges, *Languages of Revolt: Dada and Surrealist Literature and Film* (Durham, NC: Duke University Press, 1983), xvi.

389. As Myriam Chimènes points out, Poulenc was introduced to the surrealist circle by his friend, Raymonde Linossier, which led, inevitably, to tensions with Cocteau. Poulenc, *Correspondance 1910–1936*, ed. Myriam Chimènes, 40.

390. Honegger may well have been introduced to nonconformist ideas by one of his literary collaborators of the period, a fellow Swiss, Denis de Rougemont [author of Love in the Western World (*L'amour et l'occident* (Paris: Plon, 1939))]. Rougemont, who moved to Paris in 1930, became involved with the nonconformist journals *L'ordre nouveau* and *Esprit*, while also collaborating on the *La nouvelle revue française*. It was he who would do the libretto for Honegger's *Nicolas de Flue*, based on the story of one of Switzerland's heroes. See the article on Denis de Rougemont by Pascal Belmand, 1006–07 in the *Dictionnaire des intellectuels français*. On the petition Honegger signed, see Porcile (*Belle époque*, 336).

391. See Loubet del Bayle, *Les Non-conformistes des années 30*, 92–96. *Plans* was considered "moderniste" and "réformateur," as was *L'Ordre nouveau*, which was edited by Robert Aron and Armand Dandrieu. See Olivier Corpet, "La Revue," in *Histoire des Droites en France*, ed. by Jean-François Sirinelli (Paris: Gallimard, 1992), 178. On the "planisme" of *Plans* and Philippe Lamour's myth of the ideal plan of the "Etat technicien" (which included Le Corbusier's model) see Golan, *Modernity and Nostalgia*, 76 ff. Also see Zeev Sternhell, *Ni Droite ni Gauche: l'idéologie fasciste en France* (Paris: Seuil, 1983), 163–64. He argues that "planisme" contained the seeds of National Socialism since it predicated social justice on national unity. As he points out, 165, national socialism similarly sought a "new order" that would express an organic ensemble of aspirations and ideals, and in which the technology of the middle class would be incorporated.

392. Arthur Honegger, *Incantation aux fossiles* (Lausanne: Editions d'Ouchy, 1948), 84.

393. Loubet del Bayle, 94–96.

394. Le Corbusier, "Invite à l'action," *Plans* Jan. 1931: 5. And see Golan, 76. As she notes, all the editors of the journal criticized "l'homme économique" of the Marxists and "l'homme abstrait" of the democrats, promoting rather "l'homme réel," or "concret." As the opening editorial of *Plans* was to put it, their goal was "the blossoming of a more human civilization, where man, dominating the tyranny of the machine . . . would retrieve his place in the universe." Ibid. On Le Corbusier's "new city" and its use by Valois, see Mark Antliff, "Cité française: Georges Valois, Le Corbusier, and Fascist Theories of Urbanism," in *Fascist Visions*, 137. Again, on the connection between "planisme" and national socialism, see Sternhell, *Ni droite ni gauche*, 163–64.

395. Le Corbusier moved definitively to Paris in 1917, and unlike Honegger was naturalized French in 1930. Politically, Le Corbusier tended to support those governments that were willing to use their authority in the interest of the "masses," and particularly by creating an architecture for them. On Le Corbusier see Mark Antliff, "La Cité française: Georges Valois, Le Corbusier, and Fascist Theories of Urbanism," in *Fascist Visions: Art and Ideology in France and Italy* (Princeton, NJ: Princeton University Press, 1997), 134–70.

396. Arthur Honegger, "Du cinéma sonore à la musique réelle," *Plans* Jan. 1931: 74–78.

397. Arthur Honegger, "Pour prendre congé," Plans July 1931, reproduced in Arthur Honegger, Ecrits, ed. Huguette Calmen (Paris: Honoré Champion, 1992), 111. On Le Corbusier's affiliation with the Sorelian Hubert Lagardelle and his "planisme," see Affron and Antliff, "Art and Fascist Ideology," 15; and Affron, "Waldemar George," 134. And see Antliff, "Cité française," 135-37. Le Corbusier was attracted to French fascist circles by 1927, but eventually turned to the technocratic Redressement Français and maintained his belief in the Republic. On Sorel see Affron and Antliff, 5-7; and see Antliff, 140, 145-46, 151, 156-58. Antliff notes the shared conceptions of Sorel and Valois, and points out that Valois used Le Corbusier's ideas selectively. Many of these ideas, including those on opera and film, were shared by Italian fascism, which also traced its roots to Sorelian circles. See Affron and Antliff, 10-18 and Antliff, 131-35, 149-51. Also see Andrew Hewitt, *Fascist Modernism: Aesthetics, Politics, and the Avant-garde* (Stanford, Calif.: Stanford University Press, 1993), 133, 147. On Lagardelle and his ties to Mussolini, see Robert O. Paxton, *Vichy France: Old Guard and New Order, 1940–1944*, 275.

398. The incidental music for *Liluli* was for orchestra, solo voice, and chorus. It premiered in March 1923. D'Annunzio's *Phaedra*, later translated by André Jodevet, with incidental music by Honegger and choreography by Ida Rubenstein, premiered in Rome in April 1926.

399. Honegger also collaborated with Paul Valéry, a believer in the necessity of return to traditional values, in *Amphion*. On the connection between French and Italian fascism in the twenties, see Antliff, 152.

400. Arthur Honegger, *I Am a Composer*, 107; and see James Harding, *The Ox on the Roof: Scenes from Musical Life in Paris in the Twenties* (New York: St. Martin's Press, 1972), 124.

401. Harding, 124.

402. Honegger, *I Am a Composer*, 110.

403. Geoffrey Spratt, *The Music of Arthur Honegger* (Cork: Cork University Press, 1987), 201-02. On *Cris du monde*, see 221.

404. Halbereich, 185, 701. Michael Faure (*Néoclassicisme*, 260) reads the work as, in effect, an expression of approbation for the Munich agreement and eventually for Pétain. As he does explain, however, this was the period when the Vatican was considering his canonization.

405. Honegger, *I am a Composer*, 92.

406. Delannoy, *Honegger*, 163.

407. Ibid. Honegger's *L'Aiglon* was premiered at the Paris Opera during the Popular Front, in 1937.

408. Ibid., 164. On the enthusiasm for aviation in France, see Robert Wohl, *A Passion for Wings: Aviation and the Western Imagination 1908–1918* (New Haven: Yale University Press, 1994), 33–66. *L'oiseau blanc* was performed at a gala of the Ecole des Hautes Etudes Commerciales, which took place at the Théâtre des Champs-Elysées on 24 May 1937.

409. Delannoy, *Honegger*, 171. Honegger remained in Bayreuth from 17 to 31 July 1936, when he left for the Olympics in Berlin. Ibid., 170.

410. See Manuel Rosenthal, *Jeanne d'Arc. Suite symphonique en 5 parties*. Après la "Jeanne d'Arc" de Joseph Delteil. Paris: Jean Jobert, Editeur, 1936. The work is dedicated to "Mon très cher maitre, Maurice Ravel." Written for large orchestra, it is in five movements: (1) Les Copines du ciel; (2) Le Camp de Blois; (3) Le Roi de Coeur; (4) Le Sacre de Charles VII; and (5) La Mort. On it see José Bruyr, *L'écran des musiciens. Seconde série* (Paris: Corti, 1933), 139. And see Dominique Saudinos, *Manuel Rosenthal: Une Vie* (Paris: Mercure de France, 1992), 88. As Saudinos points out, when it was premiered in 1936, at the Salle Pleyel, it was not well received.

411. On the other works about Jeanne d'Arc, see Delannoy, 175. The far Right began to celebrate the feast of Jeanne d'Arc in 1893, as a kind of countercelebration to the Republic's Fête Nationale, 14 July (known in English as "Bastille Day), which had been celebrated since 1880. On changing perceptions of Jeanne d'Arc in France in the postwar period, see Gerd Krumeich, *Jeanne d'Arc in der Geschichte: Historiographie, Politik, Kultur* (Sigmaringen: J. Thorbecke, 1989), 216–24.

412. Halbereich, 701.

413. Delannoy, 175. As we shall see, it was performed not only in Paris, but for the annual fête of Jeanne d'Arc in Orléans.

414. Ibid., 181–83. Despite these traditional elements, the score employs saxophones and ondes Martenots.

415. Spratt, 251–52. As he explains, the work was originally conceived by the Russian Jewish dancer Ida Rubenstein, who, since the early 1930s had been developing an interest in medieval theater. Inspired by the productions of the Sorbonne professor, Gustave Cohen, and the musicologist Jacques Chailley, she conceived the idea in 1933 of a creating a kind of "mystery play." Honegger completed the score for the work by 1935. See Honegger, *Ecrits*, ; and José Bruyr, *Honegger et son oeuvre* (Paris: Correa, 1947), 182.

416. On the nature of Honegger's collaboration with Claudel and the folkloric elements employed, see Honegger, *Ecrits*, 246; and Delannoy, 181–83.

417. Spratt, 258; and Bruyr, 184.

418. Honegger, *Ecrits*, 331; Halbereich, 172; Bruyr, 186; and Spratt, 253.

419. Chimènes, "Le Budget de la musique," 268 and Jean Zay, *Souvenirs et solitude*, 191.

420. Spratt, 253-54.

421. Burrin, *La Dérive fasciste*, 216. On Bergery's complex relation to the Popular Front, see Ory and Sirinelli, *Les Intellectuels en France*, 110. My view of Honegger as conflicted again differs from that of Michael Faure (*Néoclassicisme*, 240), who sees, in this work a compromise on the part of a "bourgeois"—an attempt to cross social classes. He even argues (260) that this work helped prepare for the collaboration and that Honegger was demagogic.

422. The Frontistes broke with the Ligue des Droits de l'Homme in 1937. Burrin, 219-21.

423. By this point, Bergery's journal, *La flèche*, was enjoying a certain measure of success: Its subscribers grew regularly from forty-five hundred in 1936 to ten thousand in 1938. In the interim, Bergery made a trip to Italy (in the summer of 1937) and, according to Georges Izard, was highly impressed with the fascist regime there. Burrin, 223–25.

424. Bergery was Jewish, but perhaps seeing himself as different, culturally, from Jews in other countries, apparently did not feel threatened by the racial laws of the fascist regimes. On his anti-Semitism, see Burrin, 238.

425. Burrin, 226–28. This was the moment of the formation of Chautemps's second government. When Blum briefly returned to power, Bergery did lend his support.

426. Ibid., 243–44. On Bergery's "frontisme" and anticommunism, see Robert O. Paxton, *Vichy France: Old Guard and New Order,* 273–74. As Paxton points out (243), for French conservatives by 1936 the main enemy was no longer Germany but Russia. Also see 214 on Bergery's anticapitalist rhetoric.

427. Ibid., 245.

428. The notorious French fascist, Lucien Rebatet, in his book, *Une Histoire de la musique* (Paris: Robert Laffont, 1969), later attempted to "vindicate" Honegger from his association with Ida Rubenstein in *Jeanne au bûcher* as well as from his ties to the Popular Front. As he puts it, his contribution to *Le 14 juillet* and to works for the 1937 Exposition

were done out of financial necessity, and goes on to remark that his heart was clearly not in them. Ibid., 574.

429. See the review of Honegger's *L'Aiglon* in *La flèche* 12 Sept. 1938. In the years before World War II, *La flèche* was one of the most widely read political journals, particularly among those who oscillated between the extremes of Communism and the Action Française. See Pierre Andreu, *Révoltées de l'esprit. Les revue des années 1930* (Paris: Kimé, 1991), 91.

430. I am here using "symbolic capital" in the sense made current by the sociologist Pierre Bourdieu. On Bergery's leftist supporters in the early 1930s and in *La flèche* see Winock, *Siécle des intellectuels*, 235–37.

431. The works performed were to be choreographed by Serge Lifar. On Milhaud, see *La flèche* 12 Feb. 1938, which praises the performance at the Opéra-Comique of *Le pauvre matelot*, *Esther de Carpentras*, and his *Suite provençale*. André Coeuroy, in *Gringoire*, also praised the revival of Cocteau and Milhaud's *Le pauvre matelot* at the Opéra-Comique, on 4 Feb. 1938.

432. Again, since Bergery was Jewish, it was perhaps in an attempt to distance himself from Jews of other countries and from newer Jewish immigrants that, according to contemporaries, he made anti-Semitic remarks. The inclusion of Offenbach may have been an attempt not to alienate more wealthy, educated, and assimilated Jews.

433. André Coeuroy, *Gringoire*, 18 Feb. 1938.

434. André Coeuroy, *La Musique française moderne,* (Paris: Delagrave, 1924).

435. Rebatet, *Une Histoire de la musique*, 570–73.

CHAPTER 4

1. Pierre Leclau, writing in *Je suis partout* on Jan. 6, 1939, approved the choice. The work was written for piano in 1911, with an homage to Schubert on the title page. It was transcribed for orchestra in 1912, at the request of Mme Trauhanova, for performance at the Châtelet as a ballet, with the new title *Adelaide ou le langage des fleurs*. It was performed briefly in 1916, in the context of Rouché's Thursday and Sunday matinees at the Opera. The new production was choreographed by Serge Lifar, with great critical success. See Louis Laloy, *Louis Laloy on Debussy, Ravel, and Stravinsky*, trans. and annotated by Deborah Priest (Aldershot: Ashgate, 1999), 264.

2. The theaters were reorganized in 1939. The president of the Republic, Albert Lebrun, signed a decree creating the Réunion des Théâtres Lyriques Nationaux and naming Rouché as administrator. Charles Dupêchez, *Histoire de l'Opéra de Paris: un siècle au Palais Garnier* (Paris: Perrin, 1984), 321–33; and Frédérique Patureau, *Le Palais Garnier dans la société parisienne 1875–1914* (Liège: Mardaga, 1991), 456. As Patureau points out, this marked the end of the directeur-entrepreneur: From this point on, the Opéra was financed fully by the state. It was now under the direction of Rouché, under the administration of the ministre des beaux-arts, affaires culturelles, within the Ministère de l'Education Nationale. And see Pascal Ory, *La Belle illusion: Culture et politique sous le signe du Front populaire 1935–1938* (Paris: Plon, 1994), 319. As Ory points out, this act, in January 1939, consolidated the transformation of the lyric theaters into "public organisms" with financial autonomy. Also see Leslie A. Sprout, "Music for a 'New Era': Composers and National Identity in France, 1936–1946," Ph.D. dissertation, University of California, Berkeley, 2000, 70. Sprout observes that now the personnel of the two theaters could be interchanged. On the role of both Zay and Rouché in bringing about the new arrangement, see Sandrine Grandgambe, "La Réunion des Théâtres Lyriques Nationaux," in *La Vie musicale sous Vichy*, ed. Myriam Chimènes (Brussels: Editions Complexe, 2001), 109–110.

3. Once again, the *La revue musicale* was published by the *La nouvelle revue française*.

4. Boris de Schloezer, *La nouvelle revue française* vol. 52 (Jan.–June 1939): 501–2.

5. The work was written in 1911. See Paul Collaer, *A History of Modern Music*, trans. Sally Abeles (New York: The World Pub. Company, 1961), 172. On Ravel's own characterization of his "tougher" style in the work, or his movement beyond the "impressionistic," see Roger Nichols, *The Harlequin Years: Music in Paris 1917–1929* (Berkeley: University of California Press, 2002), 22.

6. Pierre Leclau, *Je suis partout* 6 Jan. 1939. Zay remained in his position, even after the fall of the Popular Front.

7. See David Carroll, *French Literary Fascism: Nationalism, Anti-Semitism, and the Ideology of Culture* (Princeton, NJ: Princeton University Press, 1995), 16, 40, 72, 83. See Alastair Hamilton, *The Appeal of Fascism: A Study of Intellectuals and Fascism 1919-1945* (New York: Avon, 1973), 197. As Hamilton points out, Charles Maurras was elected to the Académie Française in 1938. As he also notes (201), in 1939 Jean Giraudoux, the playwrite and future minister of information under Daladier, expressed his concern with "foreigners" overrunning France in his *Pleins pouvoirs*.

8. Eugen Weber presents a different perspective on the late thirties in *The Hollow Years: France in the 1930s* (New York: W.W. Norton, 1994). Significantly, Jean Zay echoed the current conservative praise of Ravel in his contribution to a commemorative issue for Claude Debussy in the *La revue musicale* 83 (April–May 1938): 24, 43. He rather stresses Debussy's "depth," his ability to capture the elemental power of nature, as opposed to fleeting sensations. This, for Zay, makes Debussy a mirror of "l'âme française," and a source of both glory and pride.

9. This view is as opposed to that of Romy Golan in *Modernity and Nostalgia: Art and Politics in France between the Wars* (New Haven: Yale University Press, 1995); and by Pascal Ory in *La belle illusion*, 291–92. Ory does not see aesthetic oppositions during the Popular Front, or a clear shift in aesthetic values upon its decline.

10. See Maurice Agulhon, *La République 1880–1990* vol. 2 (Paris: Hachette, 1990), 55. As he notes, some saw the ministerial instability of the Popular Front as a handicap, which made it open to conservative discourse on the weakness of republican institutions.

11. Ibid., 2: 60, on the Radicals's break with the Popular Front and the sense of revenge of some bourgeois against "l'esprit social." In 1938, under Daladier, the Radicals moved to the Right. See Gordon Wright, *France in Modern Times* (New York: Rand McNally, 1974), 381.

12. Wright, 380; on the second, brief, Blum cabinet.

13. See Julian Jackson, *The Popular Front in France: Defending Democracy* (Cambridge, Eng.: Cambridge University Press, 1988), 12-13; and Louis Bodin and Jean Touchard, *Front Populaire 1936* (Paris: Armand Colin, 1961), 2. Also see Serge Berstein, *La France des années 30* (Paris: Armand Colin, 1988), 417. On the Right's attempt at accommodation with Mussolini and Hitler, see Wright, 382; and on the British pressure on Daladier in 1938 for a settlement at Munich, 388–89.

14. Pascal Ory and Jean-François Sirinelli, *Les Intellectuels en France de l'Affaire Dreyfus à nos jours* (Paris: Armand Colin, 1992), 115.

15. Gilles le Béguec, "L'Evolution de la politique gouvernementale et les problèmes instituionnels," in *Edouard Daladier. Chef du gouvernement*, eds. René Rémond and Janine Bourdin (Paris: Presses de la Fondation Nationale des Sciences Politiques, 1977), 55–56. And see Hamilton (223) who points out the government enacted a "family code" to boost the birth rate.

16. See Vicki Caron, "The Antisemitic Revival in France in the 1930s: The Socio-

economic Dimension Reconsidered," *The Journal of Modern History* 70/1 (March 1988): 27; and Eugen Weber, *The Hollow Years*, 108–09. Also see Gisèle Sapiro, *La guerre des écrivains 1940–1953* (Paris: Rayard, 1999), 160; and Ory, *Belle illusion*, 25.

17. André Gide, *Journal 1889–1939* (Paris: Gallimard, 1951), 1326.

18. The Action Française had printed a letter retracting its former threats and its placing the political over the spritual. See Yves R. Simon, *The Road to Vichy 1918–1938*, trans. James A. Corbett and George J. Morrow (New York: Sheed and Ward, 1942), 11.

19. Herman Lebovics, *True France: The Wars Over Cultural Identity* (Ithaca: Cornell University Press, 1992), 39. And see Agulhon, *République* vol. 2, 61. As Agulhon points out, despite the purported weakening of national energy against the German "enemy," Daladier did attempt to improve the military. After the signing of the Nazi-Soviet pact, in August 1939, the government banned the Communist Party. As Hamilton points out (224), many were arrested in 1939 as "dangerous pacifists."

20. Michel Duchesneau, *L'Avant-garde musicale à Paris de 1871 à 1939* (Liège: Mardaga, 1997), 52.

21. Ibid. Duchesneau cites the critique of Michel-Léon Hirsch in *Le ménestrel* 101.8 (24 Feb. 1939).

22. Paul Bertrand, "La Question du Salzbourg français," *Le ménestrel* 100.18 (6 May 1938), 128.

23. Martyn Cornick, *Intellectuals In History: The Nouvelle revue française* (Atlanta: Rodopi, 1995), 94–95.

24. Cocteau was now being attacked for different reasons by both the Left and the Right. By 1940 he was being castigated again in the *La nouvelle revue française* (the "parent" journal of the *La revue musicale*) for his "post-Maritain" career. And now Claude Mauriac, the son of François Mauriac, treated him as a "punster, trickster, and a publicity hound." Francis Steegmuller, *Cocteau. A Biography* (Boston: Little, Brown, and Comp., 1970), 437.

25. Alfred Cortot, "Le Cas Satie," *Revue musicale* April–May, 1938.

26. Georges Auric, *Quand j'étais là* (Paris: Bernard Grasset, 1979), 55. If the Académie des Beaux-Arts had admitted him, Stravinsky perhaps would have stayed in France, having been naturalized French in 1934. On the relation of Stravinsky's ideas and goals to those of composers in the Weimar Republic, see Pascal Huynh, *La Musique sous la République de Weimar* (Paris: Fayard, 1998), 174–78, 222–23. On the election at the Académie see François Porcile, *La Belle époque de la musique française: le temps de Maurice Ravel, 1871–1940* (Paris: Fayard, 1999), 384. As Porcile points out (385), Schmitt had continued his attacks on Kurt Weill in *Le temps*. Weill had previously been performed at the Sérénade concerts in 1932, and was given a commission by the princess de Polignac; but upon his return to Paris as a refugee, he did not find a warm welcome. Others who returned, such as Hans Eisler, were able to write for the French cinema, but Weill chose not to, and decided to leave France in 1935, first for London, and then for New York.

27. Alfred Cortot, "Stravinsky, le piano et les pianistes," *La revue musicale* May-June 1939: 241–54.

28. Boris de Schloezer, "Chronique musicale," *La nouvelle revue française* 53 (July–Dec., 1939): 630–35.

29. Ibid.: 632.

30. Ibid.: 633.

31. Ibid.: 635.

32. The formerly left-leaning *Revue musicale* was now even accepting advertisements for the politically conservative *Revue hebdomadaire* as well as for the Conférences de Rive Gauche, which, as we noted, were associated wuth *Je suis partout*. Not only were political

boundaries thus being obscured, but now, even moreso than before, those between the musical world and the larger political-cultural world were as well.

33. *La revue musicale* of August-September 1937 is devoted to the theme "Autour de Vincent d'Indy," and includes Gustave Samazeuil's "Le théâtre lyrique de Vincent d'Indy" and Arthur Hoérée's "Vincent d'Indy et son temps: souvenirs de la classe d'orchestre."

34. Already, in Sept. 1937, both the *La revue musicale* and its parent journal, the *Nouvelle revue fraçaise* were turning against the Popular Front. On the transformations in the *La nouvelle revue française* in this period, see Cornick, *Intellectuals in History*, 94ff.

35. Jean-Richard Bloch, "Maurice Ravel ou les monstres domptés," *La revue musicale* Jan.–Feb. 1939: 9.

36. Christophe Prochasson, "Bloch, Jean-Richard," in *Dictionnaire des intellectuals français*, eds. Jacques Julliard and Michel Winock (Paris: Seuil, 1996), 155–57.

37. Jean-Richard Bloch, "Maurice Ravel ou les monstres domptés": 9. On André Masson and his attempt at reconciliation before World War I, see Jane F. Fulcher, *French Cultural Politics and Music from the Dreyfus Affair to the First World War* (New York: Oxford University Press, 1999), 213–14.

38. See the interview with Olivier Messiaen, who was not enthusiastic about the possibility, in *L'art musical populaire* April 1939. The presence of Milhaud and his French colleagues at the conference in Italy was probably due to their old friend Casella, who had been organizing international festivals and conferences in Italy throughout the thirties. He had helped to organize the meeting of the International Music Society in Florence in 1935, together with his musicologist colleague Massimo Mila, as well as with Emile Vuillermoz, Alban Berg, and Alfred Einstein. Casella was a fascist, but was allowed to continue to promote modern music, as well as to invite Jewish colleagues to participate in most of the events. Modern music helped to give the regime a progressive image.

39. On Milhaud's continuing enthusiasm for Magnard, see Darius Milhaud, *Notes sur la musique. Essais et chroniques*, ed. Jeremy Drake (Paris: Flammarion, 1982), 114. On the sense of tradition and the canon established by the Left before World War I, see Fulcher, *French Cultural Politics and Music*, 147–50.

40. See Milhaud, *Notes sur la musique*, 93 ff.; and Milhaud, "La Tradition," *Atti del Terzo Congresso Internationale de Musica* Florence, April 1938: 89–91.

41. On Vuillermoz's earlier "Debussyste" rhetoric, see Fulcher, *French Cultural Politics and Music*, 147–50.

42. Emile Vuillermoz, "Le Goût moderne et la musique du passé," *Atti del Terzo Congresso Internationale di Musica*: 21.

43. Henry Prunières, "Que doit-il sortir de la crise que traverse actuellement la musique?" Ibid.: 79.

44. *Candide* not only offered a prize for the best recording of classical music, as we have noted, but also one for popular music.

45. See Jean Zay, *Souvenirs et solitude* (Paris: Talus d'Approche, 1987), 193; and Myriam Chimènes, "Le Budget de la musique sous la IIIe République," in *La Musique du théorique au politique*, eds. Hugues Dufourt and Joel-Marie Fauquet (Paris: Aux Amateurs de Livres, 1991), 266, 297.

46. Ory, *Belle illusion*, 307.

47. As cited in Chimènes, "Le Budget de la musique," 264–66, 299. As Chimènes observes, to this point the chapter in the budget titled "Acquisitions et commandes d'oeuvres d'art à des artistes vivantes" was exclusively devoted to the plastic arts. She notes that two hundred thousand francs were now allocated for musical compositions. And see Sprout, "Music for a 'New Era'," 34. As she notes, the commissions were initiated on 5 May 1938.

48. See Zay, *Souvenirs et solitude*, 193 ff; and Chimènes, "Le Budget de la musique," 266 ff. This perspective on the constraints on composers is as opposed to the view of Pascal Ory (*Belle illusion*, 327), who assumes the creative autonomy of those commissioned and thus the risks undertaken by the state. Here I disagree with Sprout's contention, (Music for a 'New Era'," 32), that the basic principle of selection was diversity, or the representation of those with different institutional affiliations and stylistic approaches, and that the goal was "maximum return on the investment." These choices have to be seen within the context of the larger evolution of French cultural politics and of musical meanings in these years.

49. Chimènes, "Le Budget," 300. Of the twenty-four composers receiving commissions, many had won the Prix de Rome, were professors at the Conservatoire or Schola, or well-known conductors or composers. Poulenc was conspicuously left out. As Sprout notes (Music for a 'New Era'," 32), the list of composers commissioned was dominated by those trained traditionally at the Conservatoire, and included three Prix de Rome winners. But it also included former Scholistes like Le Flem, and the majority had not participated in the Popular Front's cultural efforts.

50. Here again, I disagree with Sprout's contention that the choice of genres was dictated by a pragmatic concern with the possibilities of performance at existing venues, such as the Opéra and the Opéra-Comique or the subsidized symphonic associations. As she does note (Music for a 'New Era,'" 33), although they were required to perform a minimum number of new French works per season, the state did not guarantee performance of the works commissioned and offered no assistance to facilitate it, such as subsidies for copying, etc. Symphonic works were given ten thousand francs, ballets or lyric works in one act twenty thousand francs, and lyric pieces in three acts twenty-five thousand francs (34). Again, I disagree with her contention (51), that another motivation for choice of genres was concern about the viability of French music abroad. Clearly, internal French cultural politics here were just as important.

51. Auric was appropriately returning to a more traditionalist style, as may be seen in works such as his *Ouverture* of 1938. It is in G major, in a conventional rounded form, but with more complex, layered rhythms and a full orchestration, although elements of his earlier style remain. Auric was here responding to the stylistic compromises necessary by 1938. And see Darius Milhaud, *Ma vie heureuse* (Paris: Editions Belfond, 1973), 290. Also see the French Archives Nationales F21–5305. Arrêté. Ministre de l'Education Nationale. Beaux-Arts. Musique, Spectacles, Radio-diffusion. Budget 1938. 5 mars 1938. It includes "Commandes, 1939." See Chimènes, "Le Budget de la musique," 266. As Sprout observes (Music for a 'New Era,'" 53), it was Tailleferre's close association with Valéry that led her to collaborate with him on her cantata; the text was adapted from his two Narcissus poems. He specifically wanted "airs" and choruses in the style of Gluck.

52. The lesser-known figures included Ladmirault (a pupil of Fauré) and Leleu. Koechlin and Rivière had participated in the Popular Front, which may explain their inclusion. Tailleferre's cantata was her *Cantate de Narcisse*, to a text of the conservative Paul Valéry. See Jean Roy, *Groupe les Six* (Paris: Seuil, 1994), 180; and Ory, *Belle illusion*, 327; and Sprout, Music for a 'New Era,'" 60. And as Sprout observes (35), the works of the most prominent composers, with international reputations—Milhaud, Tailleferre, and Delannoy—were selected for performance first. Although I agree that the works commissioned made reference to the past, I disagree that the primary reason for this was accessibility, although this may have been a factor. The Popular Front had also encouraged the accessible, but not reference to tradition, which was considered ideologically "conservative."

The commissions continued in 1939, as Sprout discusses, (Music for a 'New Era,'" 69-70); the same amounts were awarded, but the number was affected by the Réunion des

Théâtres Lyriques Nationaux, and fell from twleve to eight. Sprout also observes (80) that a ballet, commissioned from Buzza in 1939 included "a whole range of popular expression," and sees this as evidence of an absorption of styles associated with Cocteau in "the strongholds of classical music in France." But it is significant that the premiere of the ballet, *Jeux de plage*, as she notes, wasn't scheduled for performance until 1943, and then was cancelled. This is not evidence that the commissions were pragmatic, as she argues, reflecting a desire that the works be liked. As we have seen, taste was generally moving in the opposite direction, and not all the works accorded with this.

53. See Sprout, Music for a 'New Era'" 36. *Esther de Carpentras* was finally performed in a staged version on 3 Feb. 1938. See Jeremy Drake, *The Operas of Darius Milhaud* (New York: Garland, 1989), 153. As Sprout observes, Milhaud's three-act opera, *Maximillien*, had been performed at the Opéra in January 1932.

54. See the review of Milhaud's *Le pauvre matelot*, *Esther de Carpentras*, and *Suite provençale* at the Opéra-Comique, by "C.T.," in *Le temps* 5 Feb. 1938.

55. René Dumesnil, "Revue de la quinzaine," *Mercure de France*, 1 March 1938.

56. Also prominent now were the French Wagnerians, such as Lalo, Franck, and Chabrier. There was a continuing emphasis on Beethoven and Berlioz.

57. According to Winock, the movement was essentially over in intellectual and literary circles by 1934–35. See Michel Winock, *Siècle des intellectuels* (Paris: Seuil, 1997), 205. Also see his book *Histoire politique de la revue Esprit 1930-1950* (Paris: Seuil, 1975).

58. Jean-Louis Loubet del Bayle, *Les Non-conformistes des années 30. Une tentative de la renouvellement de la pensée politique française* (Paris: Seuil, 1969), 16, 23, 29, 40.

59. Olivier Corpet, "La Revue," in *Histoire des Droites en France*, ed. Jean-François Sirinelli (Paris: Gallimard, 1992), 188. Significantly, Maritain left the Action Française in 1926.

60. Winock, *Siècle des intellectuels*, 209–11. On their search for renewal and "ease of communication across political barriers" see Tony Judt, *Past Imperfect: French Intellectuals 1944–1956* (Berkeley: University of California Press, 1992), 19. As Agulhon notes, (*République* 2: 38–39), nonconformism lay at the origins of several important currents of the future, including Communism, Christian Democracy, and Pétainism in France.

61. Ory and Sirinelli, *Les Intellectuels en France*, 89.

62. See Agulhon (*République*, 2: 337–38) on their consequent climate of innovation. Also see Winock, *Siècle des intellectuels*, 203, on this generation, born shortly after the turn of the century.

63. Winock, *Siècle des intellectuels*, 204–207.

64. Corpet, "La Revue," 178.

65. Ibid.

66. Ibid.

67. This was because of Mounier's ties to *Combat*. See Bernard Comte, "Pamphlet, histoire, et fantaisie. A propos de Mounier, Ministre de la Culture de Vichy," *Le Débat* May-Aug. 1992: 41–42 and 62. Although to the Left, this was the journal that coined the slogan "Ni droite ni gauche," later taken over by *L'ordre nouveau*. Mounier's original collaborators were Georges Izard and André Déléage. See Hamilton, 186.

68. Loubet del Bayle, 154; and Berstein, 89.

69. Begun in 1932, *Esprit* was close to Maritain by 1934, in its quest for a "third path" as opposed to those of Communism and liberalism, and for its desire for a new "spiritual order." Winock, *Siècle des intellectuels*, 268.

70. On *Esprit* see Weber, *The Hollow Years*, 201.

71. See Pierre de Senarclens, *Le Mouvement "Esprit" 1932–41* (Lausanne: Editions l'Age d'Homme, 1974), 9, 12, 15–16.

72. Agulhon, *République*, 2: 48; and Winock, *Siècle des intellectuels*, 210. As Eugen Weber points out (*The Hollow Years*, 200), as of 1931, the church tolerated and even encouraged democratic activists, and hence "progressives" gained a new foothold. See Michel Winock, *Histoire politique de la revue Esprit 1930–1950* (Paris: Seuil, 1993), 96–100. As he points out, *Esprit* participated in the renewal of socialist thought, and its founders were admirers of Pierre-Joseph Proudhon. They were thus able to rally vital currents in the "monde ouvrier." Although Mounier originally wanted to maintain a distance from politics, he slowly grew closer to it. And see Philippe Burrin, *La Dérive Fasciste: Doriot, Déat, Bergery, 1933–1945* (Paris: Seuil, 1986), 88. Burrin argues that Mounier gradually became a "compagnon de route" of the Left, while critical of elements of the Popular Front. Also see Pierre de Senarclens, *Le mouvement "Esprit" 1932–1942* (Lausanne: Editions l'Age d'Homme, 1974), 14. He points out that *Esprit* promoted the primacy of the spiritual, as did Maritain, but it also acknowledged a sense of responsibility to the world. Although it had no clear ideological contours, it rejected all rigid systems (52). This included Communism, although the journal remained sympathetic to "the people."

73. Ibid. Among those contributing to *Sept* and *L'aube* were François Mauriac and Paul Claudel. Weber, 203.

74. Agulhon, *République*, 2: 38–39. Agulhon also sees this tendency as at the origin of several currents of the future, including Communism, Christian Democracy, and Pétainism.

75. Winock, *Siècle des intellectuels*, 203.

76. Mauriac was also praised by the *La revue du siècle* in 1933. Corpet, 183.

77. André Déléage, "Littérature et révolution," *Esprit* June 1933: 346. And see Winock, *Siècle des intellectuels*, 93. Also see Matthew Affron, "Waldemar George: A Parisian Art Critic on Modernism and Fascism," in *Fascist Visions: Art and Ideology in France and Italy* (Princeton: NJ: Princeton University Press, 1997, 184–85, 190–91.

78. Emmanuel Mounier, "Refaire la Renaissance," *Esprit*, Oct. 1932: 7.

79. Loubet del Bayle, 86–88, 92. On *L'ordre nouveau* see Berstein, 95. Hamilton, 186, places *L'odre nouveau* in the "center."

80. Corpet, 181–82. *Réaction* (subtitled *Pour l'ordre*) ended in 1932, but was reborn as the *La revue du siècle* in 1933–34.

81. Ibid., 178–79.

82. Ibid., 184. In his *Au delà du nationalisme*, of 1934, Thierry Maulnier calls for a revolution of the nation. In 1942 he would go on to write *Révolution nationale: l'Avenir de la France*. Journals such as Henry de Jouvenel's *La revue des vivants* and Georges Radite's *L'homme nouveau* also wishes to "refound" the national community. Ibid., 178. As Hamilton points out (187), not only *Esprit* but also *L'ordre nouveau*, as well as *Jeune Droite*, spurned nationalism, calling instead for a federation of European regions, with economic cooperation. Another theme was the freedom of man from the machine—from capitalism as well as liberalism on the American model. Although Mounier was opposed to Mussolini in principle, *Jeune droite* admired him, and *L'ordre nouveau* admired aspects of German national socialism, but both within limits. As Winock points out (*Histoire politique de la revue "Espirit,"* 113), *Esprit* did explicitly condemn Mussolini's invasion of Ethiopia, but as Senarclens observes (232), after Munich, Mounier expressed his admiration for certain aspects of fascism, especially its total engagement of "being." On the response of writers such as Maritain and Maurriac to the Spanish civil war and to other contemporary crises see Jacques Duquesne, *Les Catholiques français sous l'Occupations* (Paris: Bernard Grasset, 1996; orig. ed., 1966), 121. He provides the background to later Catholic responses during Vichy.

83. On Lourié and his period in Berlin see Huynh, 77, 117. Also see the article,

"Lourié, Arthur Vincent," by Giovanni Caumajani and Detleff Gojowy in the *New Grove Dictionary of Music and Musicians* 2nd edition vol. 15, 223. Lourié left for the United States in 1941. And see Porcile, *Belle époque*, 376-77.

84. Henri Davenson, "D'une musique nécessaire et Arthur Lourié," *Esprit* May 1936: 220–21. Henri Davenson was the pseudonym of Henri-Irénée Marrou, an historian of antiquity, a *normalien*, and later professor at the Sorbonne (appointed 1946). See Marie-Claire Mussat, "La réception de Schoenberg en France avant la Seconde Guerre mondiale," *Revue de Musicologie* 87/1 (2001): 181. Davenson was also not taken with Schoenberg. On *the Sonata Liturgica* see Caumajani and Detleff, 223; and on Lourié's other "spiritualist" works see Porcile, *Belle époque*, 377. His compositions were performed by both "Triton" and by the Société Philharmonique.

85. Rollo Myers, *Modern French Music* (Oxford: Blackwell, 1971), 145-46. Jaubert was killed in World War II. On his works see Porcile, *Belle époque*, 354. Jaubert's *Cantate pour le temps pascal* was premiered in 1938 by Charles Munch and the Société Philharmonique, along with Lourié's First Symphony. Porcile, *Belle époque*, 336, points out that during the Popular Front Jaubert spoke out for a popular, human, and collective music.

86. Ory, *Belle illusion*, 321.

87. Maurice Jaubert, in *Comoedia* 6 Sept. 1936, as cited by Ory, *Belle illusion*, 320.

88. See Jaubert in *Esprit* May 1936: 72–73, 220–21.

89. Jaubert in *Esprit* May 1936: 250–51. On Schoenberg, see Mussat, "Réception de Schoenberg," 176; and see René Leibowitz, "Musique," in *Esprit* 1 April 1939: 141. Also see Michel Faure, *Néoclassicisme musical dans la France du premier XXe siècle* (Paris: Klinksieck, 1997), 308, who cites Jaubert's defense of the past but not in the context of his continuing belief in accessibility, and rather stresses his statement concerning the re-use of older materials. Leibowitz's condemnation of Stravinsky must also be seen in the context of the more generalized attack on him for lack of "the spiritual." For Leibowitz, Schoenberg represented solid construction—even a return to the Middle Ages and Renaissance, as well as melodic beauty, as Mussat points out (182-83). As she also notes, he similarly defended Webern in *Esprit* in 1939 when Webern's *Variations* op. 27 were performed at a concert at the Schola Cantorum. Leibowitz saw Webern as an ascetic, returning to the "sources" of music.

Not all the nonconformists defended Schoenberg (Mussat, "Réception de Schoenberg," 170–71). Gabriel Marcel, who wrote first for *Esprit* and then for *Jeune droite*, condemned *Pierrot Lunaire* when it was performed at a concert of Triton in 1934. For him, the music was not spiritual (as for Leibowitz), but rather "morbid," lacking in melody. As an explanation of the presence of figures like Leibowitz in *Esprit*, Mussat ("Réception de Schoenberg," 181) notes that it was a gathering point not only for Christian Left intellectuals, but for Protestants, Jews, and agnostics as well, or all those who were critical of capitalism, but still anticommunist. Leibowitz remained associated with *Esprit* until 1940. Boris de Schloezer, of the *La nouvelle revue française*, a Russian émigré, like Stravinsky and Lourié, reproached French music criticism, as a whole, for ignoring the "luttes d'idées" that alone give value and dignity to the profession. As we can see, the gap was being filled by the nonmusical journals we have examined, in the period before the Popular Front.

90. Ibid. 263–66.

91. Ludovic Tournès, *New Orléans-sur-Seine. Histoire du jazz en France* (Paris: Fayard, 1999), 36.

92. Ibid., 38–40.

93. Ibid., 37.

94. On the decline of the nonconformist movement in politics, as a result of the polarization of Right and Left, see Ory and Sirinelli, 92.

95. This is as opposed to Rollo Myers's assertion that Jeune France was responding to the older generation, which had ignored deeper human and spiritual values. As we have seen, the generation of 1914 did respond, but construed these values differently.

96. On the Colonial Exposition, see Lebovics, *True France*, 54–62. Also see Weber, *The Hollow Years*, 180. As Weber points out, the Exposition celebrated France's "generosity" in bringing "civilization" to the colonial realm. By the following year (1932), intellectual denunciations of French policy would escalate and the reality of financial exploitation would be further revealed. Tournemire, who taught Duruflé, Langlais, and Daniel-Lesur, was professor of instrumental ensembles at the Conservatoire from 1919 to 1939. His connection to those associated with the Catholic literary revival, such as Josephin Péladon and Joris-Karl Huysmans is explored in a paper by Robert Sholl, "Tournemire, Messiaen, and the Culture of Modernity," presented at the "Messiaen International Conference," held at the University of Sheffield, England, 20–23 June, 2002.

97. On Messiaen's first exposure to the writings of Maritain, see Brigitte Massin, *Olivier Messiaen: une poétique du merveilleux* (Aix-en-Provence: Alinéa, 1989), 170. Tournemire's *L'orgue mystique* is a set of Preludes, Offertoires, Elevations, Communions, and Finales for each Sunday of the Year. See Roger Nichols, *The Harlequin Years*, 193.

98. Le Flem was the successor of Roussel for the class in counterpoint at the Schola. See Serge Gut, *Le Groupe Jeune France* (Paris: Honoré Champion, 1977), 16. Daniel-Lesur and Baudrier had been friends since childhood at the Conservatoire. Jolivet's work came to their attention in 1930, when they saw a piece that he submitted to the Comité de Lecture of the Société Nationale de Musique. They then heard Messiaen's *Offrandes oubliées* performed in 1931. Georges Migot was similarly interested in medieval music as well as in sacred and secret messages in it. See Myers, 141.

99. On d'Indy's conception of tradition, see Fulcher, *French Cultural Politics and Music*, 30–31; and Gail Hilson Woldu, "Debussy, Fauré, and d'Indy and Conceptions of the Artist: The Institutions, the Dialogues, the Conflicts," in *Debussy and his World*, ed. Jane F. Fulcher (Princeton, NJ: Princeton University Press, 2001), 236–38. On "Triton," see Sprout, "Music for a 'New Era,'" 63. Triton performed composers as diverse as Jean Rivier and Schoenberg. On performances of "Triton" and "Spirale," see Mussat, "Réception de Schoenberg," 183–84, who also discusses their conceptions of the Second Viennese School as both traditionalist and spiritualist. She notes (185) that the Société Nationale finally performed Schoenberg in 1939, and (147) that Schoenberg was on the Comité d'Honneur of Triton from 1932 to 39. (He was, in addition, a member of the directive committee of the SMI when it was opened to foreign composers in 1921, as were Bartok and de Falla, among other). As she also points out (154), Triton had performed *Pierrot Lunaire* in 1934.

Berg's music was not always greeted with enthusiasm (Mussat, "Réception de Schoenberg," 184): His *Chamber Concerto* for piano, violin, and thirteen wind instruments caused a scandal when it was performed at the Concerts Straram in 1931, but the Sérénade Concerts still performed the Suite from *Wozzeck* in 1933. On the repetoire of Triton and the Sérénade concerts, as well as on their competition, see Porcile, *Belle époque*, 138–44. As he points out, Triton was named after the tritone—"the Devil" in music—and was intended to be provocative. It emphasized foreign composers, as opposed to the Société Nationale, and was more eclectic than the Sérénade concerts (although Milhaud was on the directive committee of both). Also on Triton's committee were Honegger and Prokofiev. Straram's innovative concerts continued until his death in 1933.

100. Gut, *Le Groupe Jeune France*, 16; and Paul Landormy, *Musique française après Debussy* (Paris: Gallimard, 1943), 39. Also see Paul Bertrand, *Le Monde de la musique* (Geneva: La Palatine, 1947), 109. However, it was not until after the war that the group consistently stressed symphonic music. See Jean Maillard and Jacques Nohoum, *Les Sym-*

phonies d'Arthur Honegger (Paris: Alphonse Leduc, 1974), 23. And see Porcile, *Belle époque*, 167; and Mark Antliff, "La Cité française: George Valois, Le Corbusier, and Fascist Theories of Urbanism," in *Fascist Visions: Art and Ideology in France and Italy*, ed. by Matthew Affron; and Mark Antliff (Princeton, NJ: Princeton University Press, 1997), 145.

101. Antliff, Cité française, 145.

102. This is as opposed to the interpretation of Pascal Ory (*Belle illusion*, 292) who sees Jeune France within the current of the Popular Front and the broad aesthetic with which he associates it.

103. It is thus a misinterpretation to read their stress on a "living music, having the impetus of sincerity, generosity, and artistic conscientiousness" as only an implicit attack on "the thread of frivolity always associated with Parisian neoclassicism" (Griffiths, *Olivier Messiaen*, 72). Griffiths, as many others, see Messiaen's religious impetous only in a narrow sense, or devoid of its implicit politics within the context.

104. As cited in Danièle Pistone, "Manifeste et musique en France," *Revue internationale de musique française* 20 (June 1986): 7–40.

105. See Gut, 17, 20. Gut notes the implications of the name chosen by the group, which he sees as expressing their approval not only for the romantic movement (of Hugo), but for both Wagner and Debussy, as opposed to their elders. The group also admired Berlioz, to whom it referred in its manifesto, when explaining the title it chose.

106. Griffiths, *Olivier Messiaen*, 72. Valéry was also close to Stravinsky. Poulenc, *Correspondance, 1910–1963*, ed. Myriam Chimènes, 40. A member of the Académie française since 1925, Valéry, who had collaborated with both Ravel and Honegger, as an internationalist, was close to the circle of the *La nouvelle revue française*. As a member of the International Commission for Intellectual Cooperation of the League of Nations since 1925, he presided over the permanent committee on arts and letters from 1936 to 1939, when this was no longer a "progressive" position. See "Valéry, Paul," by Daniel Oster, *Dictionnaire des intellectuels français*, 1142. His implicit support was highly valuable for Jeune France, since he was still a prominent intellectual.

107. Winock, *Siècle des intellectuels*, 268. As we have noted, Maritain was similarly in search of a new "spiritual order."

108. See "Mauriac, François," by Delphine Bouffartique, *Dictionnaire des intellectuels français*, 771. Also see Gisèle Sapiro, *La guerre des écrivains 1940–1953*, 229ff. On Mauriac's adamant antifascism in 1935, see Sapiro, 80.

109. See "Duhamel, Georges," by Giselle Sapiro, ibid., 400–1.

110. Jean-François Sirinelli, ed., *Histoire des droites en France* vol. 2 (Paris: Gallimard, 1992), 260, 269. As Eugen Weber points out, 217, Duhamel, like Valéry, Claudel, and now the younger generation, was condemning the mechanized modern world (Eugen Weber, *The Hollow Years*, 217).

111. Gut, 21–22. And see Bridget Conrad, "Le langage musical d'André Jolivet," in *André Jolivet. Portraits*, eds. Lucie Kayas and Laetitia Chassain-Dolliou (Paris: Actes Sud, 1994), 89.

112. Roger Nichols claims in *Harlequin Years* (9) that Messiaen failed the preliminary examination for the Prix de Rome in 1929; and that in 1930 he did pass the preliminaries, but failed to win the prize with his cantata. Nigel Simeone pointed out to me that he entered once more in 1931 but again failed to win. As Gary Laycock, after extensive press and archival research informed me, that he failed in 1930 (not 1929). In 1931, he was one of the six finalists, with his cantata "L'ensorceleuse."

113. Griffiths, (*Oliver Messiaen*, 17), has postulated the influences of Romain Rolland and Paul Claudel in the group's interest in non-Western music. He also points out that Messiaen learned Hindu rhythms, Greek modes, and plainsong from his teachers.

114. Messiaen also studied counterpoint and fugue with Caussade. Gut (77) sees the influence of Debussy in Messiaen's *Banquet céleste* of 1926, which was presented in Dukas's composition class. Dukas was an admirer of, and influenced by, Debussy, his near contemporary at the Conservatoire, although he also got along well with d'Indy and his more traditionationalist approach.

115. Griffiths, *Oliver Messiaen*, 24.

116. "Claudel, Paul," by Jacques Julliard, *Dictionnaire des intellectuels français*, 268–70. Also see Claude Samuel, ed. *Olivier Messiaen:. Conversations with Claude Samuel* (Portland: Amadeus Press, 1994). Alain Messiaen was already publishing "spiritual" poetry by 1936. See his *L'âme dévorée: nouvelles suppliques, nouvelles prières* (Paris: Editions Les Cahiers des Jeunes, 1936).

117. Griffiths (*Oliver Messiaen*, 25) sees the influence of the surrealists in their perception of how art might penetrate beyond the material world. And see Nigel Simeone, "Offrandes oubliées II. Messian, Boulanger, and José Bruyr," *The Musicial Times* 142 (2001): 20.

118. See Paul Landormy, *Musique française après Debussy*, 364–65; and Paul Bertrand, *Le Monde de la musique*, 109.

119. On the style of Messiaen's early works, see Nichols, *Harlequin Years*, 9.

120. As we will recall, Messiaen participated in the *Fête de la lumière et de l'eau* on 9 July, contributing the *Fête des belles eaux*, for a sextet of ondes Martenots. See Harry Halbereich, *Arthur Honegge: Un musicien dans la cité des hommes* (Paris: Fayard, 1992), 175.

121. Nichols, *Harlequin Years*, 9. In 1941, when there were many vacancies at the Conservatoire, Messiaen would be named Professor of Harmony. On Messiaen's troubled relations with Nadia Boulanger (who disapproved of his music) and his interaction with her both at La Trinité and at the Ecole Normale see Michael Faure, *Néoclassicisme*, 81; and Simeone, "Offrandes Oubliés II," 17. As Simeone points out in "Offrandes Oubliées: Messiaen in the 1930s," *The Musical Times* 141 (2000): 35, Messiaen had taught part-time at the Ecole Normale since 1934. Durand published three of Messiaen's works in 1930, and Messiaen attempted to promote the work of his friends with Durand (ibid., 33–34). On the difficulty of this generation in finding independent financial support, see ibid., 34. Although a member of the Société Nationale, Messiaen did have a premiere at the SMI, and was in touch with Boulanger about it ("Offrandes Oubliées II, 17). The SMI finally collapsed in 1935, but Messiaen was influenced by its more international tastes. On his attempt to convince the Curé at the Trinité that he would not disturb the piety of the faithful with his innovations in the organ works, and would place the liturgy first, see Catherine Massip, ed., *Portrait(s) d'Olivier Messiaen* (Paris: Bibliothèque national de France, 1996), 11. On his interest in theater, especially Shakespeare (his father's specialty) since his youth, see 8.

122. Olivier Messiaen, *Music and Color: Conversations with Claude Samuel*, trans. E. Thomas Glasgow (Portland, Oregon: Amadeus Press, 1986), 175.

123. Messiaen wrote *Les Offrandes oubliées* in 1930 when he was only twenty-one. On his admiration of Tournemire, see Simeone, "Offrandes Oubliées II," 21-22. (*L'orgue mystique* was written 1927-32.) On Messiaen's other works of this period, see Simeone, "Offrandes Oubliées: Messiaen in the 1930s," 36. Like Collet before him, Messiaen admired de Falla and the way in which he was able to use Spanish popular song to "rediscover the depths of the soul—the mystical soul and faith." See Simeone, "Offrandes Oubliées II," 22. Apparently, Messiaen was able to ignore or accept the neoclassic element in de Falla. Messiaen continued to see Paul Dukas (his teacher) and Florent Schmitt as great composers. See José Bruyr, *L'écran des musiciens, Seconde série* (Paris: Corti, 1933), 128.

124. On the invocation of chant in Messiaen's melody and rhythm, see William Austin, *Music In the Twentieth Century* (New York: Norton, 1966), 391. As Simeone points

out in "Offrandes oubliées II," 18, in a letter to Nadia Boulanger of 25 March, 1931, Messiaen refers to *Les Offrandes oubliées* as a symphonic poem. In an interview with the Belgian poet and musicologist, José Bruyr in 1931, Messiaen observed the importance of enriching tonality and noted "we have terribly neglected Gregorian chant" (ibid., 21).

125. See Collaer (*History*, 279) who observes that Messiaen here discards the sense of duration to impart the feeling that the work has neither a beginning nor an end.

126. Austin, *Music in the Twentieth Century*, 391–92. As Simeone points out in "Offrandes Oubliées: Messiaen in the 1930s," 40, Messiaen was experimenting with his "modes of limited transposition" since he was a student. And in "Offrandes Oubliées II," 21, he cites from the interview with Bruyr in 1931, demonstrating that Messiaen was highly critical of the neoclassic Stravinsky and of neoclassicism in general. On the harmonic influence of Skryabin on Messiaen, see Collaer, *History*, 279.

127. On the larger "recasting" of tradition after the war, see Jay Winter, *Sites of Memory, Sites of Mourning: The Great War in European Cultural History* (Cambridge, Eng.: Cambridge University Press, 1995), 222.

128. On the influence of non-Western music and of Debussy on Jolivet, see Conrad, "Le Langage musical d'André Jolivet," 94.

129. Tyrus Miller, *Late Modernism: Politics, Fiction, and the Arts between the World Wars* (Berkeley: University of California Press, 1999), 14. On Céline see Charles Krance, *L.-F. Céline: The I of the Storm* (Lexington, Ky.: French Forum Publishers, 1992), 18–19. He discusses how Céline's language captures "the chaotic jolts of a tumultuous existence." Also see Robert Wohl, "The Generation of 1914 and Modernism," in *Modernism: Challenges and Perspectives*, ed. by Monique Chefdor, Ricardo Quionones and Albert Wachtel (Urbana, Ill.: University of Illinois Press, 1986), 66-78. As Wohl points out, the generation of 1930 saw the limits of modernism and rejected its full implications.

130. Miller, 33.

131. Collaer, *History*, 278. Collaer also sees a connection to Milhaud's *Oresteia* as well as to Dukas's *La Péri*. See Simeone, "Offrandes Oubliées [I]" 36, on the premier of the *Poemes pour Mi* on 28 April 1937.

132. Collaer, *History*, 278. As Simeone points out ("Offrandes oubliées [I]," 40), Messiaen published three articles on his works in *Le monde musical* in 1935, 1936, and 1939. In the first, on *L'Ascension*, he stresses his innovations in harmony and rhythm.

133. David Fuller and Bruce Gustafson, "Jolivet, André," *The New Grove Dictionary of Music and Musicians*, 2001 ed., sv., 13-174–75.

134. Gut, 49.

135. Varèse had studied with Roussel and d'Indy at the Schola, and with Widor at the Conservatoire. He then studied with Busoni, while in Berlin, and left for the United States in 1916. Myers, 148.

136. Jean-Jacques Brothier, ed., *La Jeune France. Yves Baudrier, André Jolivet, Daniel-Lesur, Olivier Messiaen* (Paris: Association des Amis de la Jeune France, 1954), 6.

137. On Jolivet's use of "the golden section," like Bartok, see Conrad, "Language musical," 121. Jolivet studied with Varèse while he was in Paris in the late 1920s and early 1930s. Porcile, *Belle époque*, 390.

138. Myers, 148.

139. On Jolivet's earlier, more conventional works, such as his *Chorale et fugue* of 1930, see Lucie Kayas, "De Découverte en découverte. Le fonds André Jolivet," in *André Jolivet: Portraits*, eds. Lucie Kayas and Laetitia Chassain-Dollion, 80.

140. On Jolivet's relation to Messiaen, see Griffiths, *Olivier Messiaen*, 71. Like Messiaen, Jolivet wrote some Catholic works in the thirties, but he was far more attracted to "the magical power attributed music in certain Eastern and primitive religions" (72).

141. On Varèse's influence on *Mana*, see Griffiths, *Olivier Messiaen*, 71.

142. Messiaen credited Jolivet with "restoring magic to music." See Messiaen, *Music and Color*, 161 ff. And see Austin, 393, on how Jolivet broadened Messiaen's horizons. Also see Collaer (*History*, 284), on the impact of the "Moscow school" and Scriabin on philosophical concerns in music in France and the belief in the magical powers of music.

143. Myers, 139.

144. Ibid., 140–41. Again, on the Colonial Exposition see Lebovics, especially 54–57, 62–76. Here I disagree with his argument (94), that the Exposition, together with the presence of African American and African students in Paris, created a craze for *négritude* which, in effect, participated in furthering European hegemony. See the article by Charles-Robert Ageron, "L'Exposition Colonial de 1931," in *Les Lieux de mémoire*, vol. 1 ed, Pierre Nora (Paris: Gallimard, 1984), 561–591. On the "counterexposition," see 571–572. On the attitude of the Surrealists to the Orient, see Gisèle Sapiro, *La guerre des écrivains 1940–1953* (Paris: Fayard, 1999), 147.

145. See André Jolivet, *Mana: 6 pièces pour piano* (Paris: Editions Costallat, 1946). Introduction by Olivier Messiaen, trans. Pierre Messiaen and Rollo Myers.

146. On Jolivet's turn away from traditional Western conceptions of time, see Conrad, 89–90, 115. On Jolivet's frequent use of characteristically non-European melodic techniques, such as repetition of formulae, rhythmic and melodic ostinati, and his rhythms based on prime numbers, see ibid., 90. On Debussy's influence on his innovations in musical time, melodic structures, and use of natural resonances, as well as on his colors and timbres, see ibid, 99.

147. On the transformation of "Orientalism" from nineteenth- to twentieth-century models, see Herbert Lindenberger, *Opera in History: From Monteverdi to Cage* (Stanford, Calif.: Stanford University Press, 1998), 18.

148. Stephen Schloesser, "Mystic Realists: Sacramental Modernism in French Catholic Revival, 1918–1928" (Ph.D. dissertation, Stanford University, 1998), 292. And see Herbert Lindenberger, *Opera in History: From Monteverdi to Cage*, 161, on "orientalist" stereotypes as backward and hypersexual, etc.

149. Edward Said, *Orientalism* (New York: Pantheon, 1978), 3.

150. Judt, *Past Imperfect*, 17.

151. Conrad, "Language musical," 100.

152. Carl E. Schorske, *Thinking with History: Explorations in the Passage to Modernism* (Princeton, NJ: Princeton University Press, 1998), 12.

153. Judt, *Past Imperfect*, 20. Maurice Jaubert was in a similar position, writing for *Esprit*, but also growing increasingly close to the French Communist Party by 1936. See Ory and Sirinelli, 103. Jolivet was associated with the Maison de Culture. Ory, *Belle illusion*, 292.

154. Ibid., 22. In 1935 and 1936 Communists were courting Catholics, particularly in working-class communities (Eugen Weber, *The Hollow Years*, 202). On Jolivet's affinities with Communism, see Ory, *Belle illusion*, 294.

155. Griffiths, *Olivier Messiaen*, 71.

156. Gut, 25.

157. Maurice Duruflé was also their classmate. In 1927, he became Tournemire's assistant at Saint-Clotilde, and remained there until 1937, when he became organist for the Benedictine Abby in Paris. Gut, 33–34.

158. Poulenc, *Correspondance, 1910–1963*, ed. Myriam Chimènes, 1019. He became director of the Schola in 1957.

159. Gut, 34.

160. Ibid., 35.

161. Griffiths, *Olivier Messiaen*, 72. Honegger was in the audience as well, and, although a Protestant, thereafter supported Messiaen. Halbereich, 169; and Gut, 17.

162. Gut, 19. He also provides a list of the works performed.

163. Brothier, *La Jeune France*, 10-11. The second concert included the music of Messiaen's friend and fellow pupil in Dukas's composition class, Claude Arrieu (Simeone, "Offrandes Oubliées [I],"36).

164. Myers, 140–41. As Myers points out, Migot's style was based on an architectural conception of form, as well as on continuously unfolding, chant-like lines, thus placing him in the tradition of the Schola Cantorum. Jean Français was, in fact, not a supporter of Messiaen, and shared Nadia Boulanger's hostility to his music. See Simeone, "Offrandes Oubliées [II]," 12.

165. Poulenc, *Correspondance 1910–1963*, ed. Myriam Chimènes, 1025.

166. Ory (*Belle illusion*, 292), notes the praise of Messiaen by some of those associated with the Popular Front, such as Jacques Duclos.

167. Brothier, 8. On the blurring of boundaries between politics and art, see L. C. Knights, *Public Voices: Literature and Politics with Special Reference to the Seventeenth Century* (London: Chatto and Winders, 1971), 13.

168. Poulenc, *Correspondance 1910–1963*, ed. Myriam Chimènes, 38; and James Harding, *The Ox on the Roof: Scenes from Musical Life in Paris in the Twenties* (New York: St. Martin's Press, 1972), 230.

169. Pierre Leclau, "Premières auditions," *Je suis partout* 3 Feb. 1939. See Simeone ("Offrandes Oubliées [I]," 41) who points out that Messiaen's *Chants de terre et de ciel* premiered at the Concerts Triton on 23 Jan. 1939, as *Prismes*. Messiaen himself was certain that the work would be attacked, and defended it in his article on it in *Le monde musical* of 30 April 1939, 126, arguing that "every subject can be a religious one on condition that it is viewed through the eyes of one who believes." As Simeone points out, by now Messiaen was defensive about his musical language, asserting that "no–it isn't crazy."

170. As cited by Gut, 17.

171. See Agulhon, *République* 2: 62, on the division of opinion over what to do about Poland, and then the entry of England and France in the war in 1939.

172. Poulenc, *Correspondance 1910–1963*, ed. Myrian Chimènes, 43.

173. "Une enquête: Y aurait-il une musique de guerre?," *La revue musicale* Dec. 1939: 146-52. Poulenc's song was published in *Le Figaro* on 28 Sept. 1938. On it see Sophie-Anne Leterrier, "Culture de guerre et musique nationale," in *Chefs-d'oeuvers et circonstances* (Archives Départementales du Pas-de-Calais, 2000), 32. On similar surveys in literature by Sept. 1930, see Gisèle Sapiro, *La guerre des écrivains 1940–1953*, 165.

174. Agulhon, *République*, 2: 68. Having already invaded Belgium, Holland, and Luxembourg, Hitler invaded France on 10 May 1940. Also see Weber, *The Hollow Years*, 272. The Germans entered Paris on 14 June 1940. Before the invasion of France there had been a cabinet crisis in March 1940, when Daladier was replaced by Paul Reynaud. Another cabinet collapse occured on 4 May, when Hitler entered the Low Countries. Wright, 394.

175. Weber, *The Hollow Years*, 274.

176. Paul Collaer, "L'Esprit de la musique française," *La revue musicale* Feb. 1940. Collaer remained close to Poulenc in this period. See Poulenc, *Correspondance 1910–1963*, ed. Myriam Chimènes, 489. Sprout ("Music for a 'New Era,'" 48), cites Koechlin's article of 1938, "The Current Situation of Music in France," in the context of the debate over what was "French"; but it is important to note Koechlin's oppositional position here, as he continued to defend the simplicity of language promoted by the Popular Front. Poulenc continued to read and exchange letters with Paul Valéry. Ibid., 483. Milhaud left Paris after the first performance of his opera, *Médée* on 27 May. See Milhaud, *Notes sur la musique*, 148.

He then left France for Spain, and then Portugal, where he finally departed for the United States on 6 July 1940. Ibid., 501.

177. This was in fact occurring in the culture at large. See Agulhon, *République*, 2: 61. Already, there were measures in favor of the family in France. Pétain was made ambassador to Franco's Spain.

178. Collaer, "L'Esprit de la musique française," 83.

179. Charles Ribèyre, "Musiques d'hier et de demain," *Revue musicale* Feb. 1940: 66–75.

180. Ibid., 66 Ribèyre's points are often echoed in contemporary attacks on neoclassicism.

181. Ibid., 72. He also notes (75), that those who formerly encouraged "positivism," especially Stravinsky, Milhaud, and Ravel, are indeed not the last of those to renounce it.

182. Significantly, Poulenc's *Concerto pour orgue*, of 1938, had its first public premiere in June of 1939, at the Salle Gaveau, performed by Duruflé.

183. Ribèyre, 70.

184. Honegger was elected to the Institut de France in 1938. His melodrama, *Le cantique des cantiques* (1926) was presented at the Opéra, choreographed by Serge Lifar, on 12 Feb. 1938. See Halbereich, 178.

185. Appropriately, it was performed in a theater built on the foundations of an early church.

186. See Antoine Prost, "Jeanne d'Arc à la fête. Identité collective et mémoire à Orléans depuis la Révolution française," in *La France démocratique. Mélanges offerts à Maurice Agulhon*, eds. Christophe Charle, Jacqueline Lalouette, Michel Pigenet, and Anne-Marie Sohn (Paris: Publications de la Sorbonne, 1998), 398. The work was performed in Orléans as a result of the initiative of both the mayor and the archbishop Halbereich, 188.

187. See Geoffrey Spratt, *The Music of Arthur Honegger* (Cork: Cork University Press, 1987), 251, on the original collaboration.

188. Prost, "Jeanne d'Arc à la fête," 389.

189. Marcel Delannoy, *Honegger* (Geneva: Slatkine, 1986), 175–76.

190. Ibid., 182–84.

191. Review of *Jeanne au bûcher* by André Coeuroy, *Mercure de France* vol. 293 (1 July, 1939): 194–99.

192. Ibid., 194–95.

193. Ibid., 197.

194. Ibid., 198.

195. Boris de Schloezer, review of *Jeanne au bûcher* in *La nouvelle revue française* vol. 53 (July–Dec. 1939): 153–55.

196. It was performed by the Orchestra Philharmonique de Paris, under the direction of Louis Fourestier. Halbereich, 188.

197. Boris de Schloezer, review of *Jeanne au bûcher*, 155.

198. Halbereich, 188.

199. Lebovics, *True France*, 170. On the programs organized by Rivière and broadcast by Radio-Paris between 25 Jan. and 15 April 1938, see Catherine Veley Vallantin, "Le Congrès international de folklore de 1937," *Annales. Histoire, Sciences sociales* vol. 54/2 (March–April 1999): 506.

200. As Milhaud recalls, it also brought out an "admirable" series, one quite daring for the period, which included "Chants des armées républicaines espagnoles." The composers participating in the collection of chansons included Koechlin, Auric, Jaubert, Delannoy, Honegger, Desormières, Hoérée, and Milhaud. Milhaud harmonized those from his native Provence. 1939 was also the year of the first French ethnological mission, under the

aegis of the Ministère de l'Education Nationale, in the region of the Alpes and Provence. See Ory, *Belle illusion*, 308. Ory notes the emphasis placed on ethnomusicological collections of folklore by figures such as Charles Koechlin. See Ory, 321–24; and Milhaud, *Ma vie heureuse*, 212.

201. Ory, *Belle illusion*, 331. The performance and recording were in the Spring of 1938.

202. Not surprisingly, it also recorded Milhaud's *Suite après Corette*.

203. The change of heart even included some former Dreyfusards, such as Daniel Halévy. In fact, not a few of those who had been ardent Dreyfusards at the turn of the century now espoused conservative values, as in the case of Camille Mauclair.

204. Pascal Ory, "La Commémoration révolutionnaire en 1939," in *La France et les Français en 1938 et 1939*, eds. René Rémond and Janine Bourdin (Paris: Presses de la Fondation Nationale des Sciences Politiques, 1978), 115–23.

205. One triumph, however, was that Romain Rolland's *Le Jeu de l'amour et de la mort* was staged at the Comédie-Française on 5 July 1939, as part of the celebration. On the debate and funding, see Sprout, "Music for a 'New Era,'" 89.

206. Ibid., 89–90.

207. Ibid., 95–96. The performance of the work was postponed until March 1940, and took place not in the Place de la Nation, but in a concert hall, by the Concerts Pasdelou Ibid., 104.

208. Under Daladier's government, Zay tried to continue his programs and ideals, but found himself increasingly isolated among a majority that was moving to the Right, and had no sympathy with "popularization" (Ory, *La Belle illusion*, 81).

209. Ibid., 296.

210. Sprout, "Music for a 'New Era,'" 98.

211. See Pascal Ory, "Théorie et pratique de l'art des fêtes sous le Front populaire," in *Les Usages politiques des fêtes aux XIX–XXe siècles*, eds. Alain Corbin, Noëlle Gérome, and Danielle Tartakowsky (Paris: Publications de la Sorbonne, 1994), 289. As he points out, by 1938 it was the Communist Party alone, which retained the ideal of the fête, although the audience for such events had declined.

212. Robert Orledge, *Charles Koechlin: His Life and Works* (London: Harwood Academic Publishers, 1989), 160. The film was shown in Paris on 3 June, 27 Nov., and 8 Dec. 1938. And see Porcile, *Belle époque*, 33, who also points out that Milhaud composed the music for Malraux's film *L'espoir*.

213. Agulhon, *République*, 2: 65. When the Communists sought neutrality, the hostility was even greater. See Wright, 390–92; and Sprout, "Music for a 'New Era,'" 60–62.

214. See Judt, *Past Imperfect*, 21–23, for a view of the French as disillusioned and disengaged. "Those who did remain loyal to the Republic were a disproportionate number of intellectuals from an older generation" (23).

215. Drake, *The Operas of Darius Milhaud*, 278–79. The mise-en scène was by Charles Dullin and the decors by André Masson. Ory, *Belle illusion*, 327. And see Sprout, "Music for a 'New Era,'" 39.

216. Drake, 290. Also see Sprout, "Music for a 'New Era,'" 36; and Grandgambe, 111. As the latter explains, with German operas removed from the repertoire, and an attempt to do the same with Italian works, Milhaud's was, in effect, the only new work that Rouché could allow.

217. Ibid. Also see Milhaud, *Notes sans musique*, 148; and Francis Poulenc, *Correspondance, 1910–1963*, ed. Myriam Chimènes, 481, 490. On the exodus of other musicians, including Ibert and Stravinsky, see Porcile, *Belle époque*, 398. As he points out, Milhaud left Lisbon on the *Excambion*, with Claude Levi-Strauss.

218. Wright, 395. Messiaen was taken prisoner in 1940 in Silesia. Poulenc and Bernac went on a concert tour in 1939–40 in Portugal and Italy for the office of "Propagande Musicale." Poulenc, *Correspondance 1910–1936*, ed. Myriam Chimènes, 481, 490.

219. Agulhon, *République*, 2: 71; and Wright, 395.

220. Agulhon, *République*, 73.

221. Jackson, 13. On 17 June, Maréchal Pétain announced his request for an armistice, which was declared on 25 June.

222. On the situation in the visual arts, see Michèle Cone, *Artists Under Vichy: A Case of Prejudice and Persecution* (Princeton, NJ: Princeton University Press, 1992). On music, see Myriam Chimènes, ed., *La Vie musicale sous Vichy* (Paris: Editions Complexe, 2001). Rovert O. Paxton discusses the continuities between the late Third Republic and Vichy in *Vichy France: Old Guard and New Order 1940–1944*(New York: Norton, 1972), 57.

223. As Agulhon points out (*République*, 2: 77), the Right now argued that the French lost the war because, since the 1789 Revolution, they had been "mal élevée," spoiled by a century of Republican politics.

224. Lebovics, *True France*, 175. Although Sprout, ("Music for a 'New Era,'" 79), argues that jazz was not considered so radical in 1940, noting that the Prix de Rome competition in 1933 called for it to be included in the cantata, the political conjuncture is important. In 1932 was the year a government of the Left returned to power, and its cultural politics were by now open to jazz; the government of 1940 was conservative, and frowned upon such influences. On French jazz during Vichy see Ludovic Tournès, "Le jazz: un espace de liberté pour un phénomène culturel en voie d'identification," in *La Vie Musicale sous Vichy,* ed. Myriam Chimènes, 313–332.

225. Lebovics, 175.

226. Kristeva, *Black Sun*, as cited by Winter, 172. Here my observations relate to and reinforce the revisionist view that the defeat of 1940 was not inevitable—that the nation was not completely demoralized or paralyzed. See Ernest R. May, *Strange Victory: Hitler's Conquest of France* (New York: Hill and Wang, 2000). If we look beyond conservative generals and several prominent writers, we do not necessarily see collective self-doubt, but rather a broader array of responses.

CONCLUSION

1. On the special power of cultural representation, see Louis Marin, *De la Représentation* (Paris: Gallimard, 1994).

2. On the role of symbols in political culture in France, see Maurice Agulhon. "La Place des symboles dans l'histoire d'après l'exemple de la République Française," *Bulletin de la Société d'Histoire Moderne* 1980 #3: 9–15. On networks of "cultural impregnation," see Jean-François Sirinelli and Eric Vigne, "Introduction: Des Cultures politiques," in *Histoire des Droites en France*, ed. Jean-François Sirinelli vol. 2, 1–3, 7–10.

3. On these concepts concerning the social and political role of symbols, see the works of Pierre Bourdieu, especially his "The Market of Symbolic Goods," *Poetics* 14 (1985): 13–44.

4. The close imbrication of political and stylistic conflict has been treated perhaps most insightfully and extensively by Carl E. Schorske. See his most recent study, *Thinking with History: Explorations in the Passage to Modernism* (Princeton, NJ: Princeton University Press, 1998).

5. As Schorske points out in *Thinking with History* (28), "the analysis of form can reveal meanings inaccessible on the level of ideas and discursive content."

6. See Roger Chartier, *On the Edge of the Cliff: History, Language, Practices*, trans. Lydia G. Cochrane (Baltimore: The Johns Hopkins University Press, 1997), 90.

7. Ibid.

8. On Bakhtin's concept of utterance as "the simultaneity of what is actually said and what is assumed but not spoken," see Michael Holquist and Katerina Clark, *Mikhail Bakhtin: A Biography* (Cambridge, Mass.: Harvard University Press, 1984), 207.

9. James Clifford, *The Predicament of Culture: Twentieth-Century Ethnography, Literature, and Art* (Cambridge, Mass.: Harvard University Press, 1988), 39.

10. On cultural embeddedness and texts, see Matei Calinescu, "Modernism and Ideology," in *Modernism: Challenges and Perspectives*, eds. Monique Chefdor, Ricardo Quionones, and Albert Wachtel (Urbana, Ill.: University of Illinois Press, 1986): 79–93. For the negative perspective on these works to which I refer —not isolated, but perhaps the most emphatic—see Michel Faure, *Du néoclassicisme musicale dans la France du premier XXe siècle* (Paris: Klinksieck, 1997), 254.

BIBLIOGRAPHY

SOURCES CITED

Abbate, Carolyn. "Outside Ravel's Tomb." *Journal of the American Musicological Society* 52.3 (1999): 465–530.

Adamson, Walter L. "The Language of Opposition in Early Twentieth-Century Italy: Rhetorical Continuities between Prewar Florentine Avant-Gardism and Mussolini's Fascism." *Journal of Modern History* (1992): 22–57.

Adorno, Theodor. *The Philosophy of Modern Music.* Translated by Anne G. Mitchel and Wesley V. Bloomster. London: Sheed and Ward, 1973.

Affron, Matthew. "Waldemar George: A Parisian Art Critic on Modernism and Fascism." In *Fascist Visions: Art and Ideology in France and Italy*, 171–204. Edited by Matthew Affron and Mark Antliff. Princeton, N.J.: Princeton University Press, 1997.

Affron, Matthew, and Mark Antliff. "Art and Fascist Ideology in France and Italy: An Introduction." In *Fascist Visions: Art and Ideology in France and Italy*, 3–42. Edited by Matthew Affron and Mark Antliff. Princeton, N.J.: Princeton University Press, 1997.

Agathon [Henri Massis and Gabriel de Tarde]. *L'esprit de la nouvelle Sorbonne/La crise de la culture classique/La crise du français.* Paris: Mercure de France, 1911.

Ageron, Charles-Robert. "L'Exposition Coloniale de 1931." In *Les lieux de mémoire*, 1:561–91. Edited by Pierre Nora. Paris: Gallimard, 1984.

Agulhon, Maurice. "La place des symboles dans l'histoire, d'après l'exemple de la République française." *Bulletin de la Société d'Histoire Moderne*, vol. 14, no. 3 (1980): 9–15.

———. *Marianne au pouvoir.* Paris: Flammarion, 1989.

———. *La République, 1880–1990.* 2 vols. Paris: Hachette, 1990.

Alexander, Bobby C. *Victor Turner Revisited: Ritual as Social Change.* Atlanta: Scholar's Press, 1991.

Anderson, Benedict. *Imagined Communities: Reflections on the Origin and Spread of Nationalism.* London: Verso, 1983.

Andreu, Pierre. *Révoltés de l'esprit: Les revues des années 1930.* Paris: Kimé, 1991.

Antliff, Mark. "La cité française: Georges Valois, Le Corbusier, and Fascist Theories of Urbanism." In *Fascist Visions: Art and Ideology in France and Italy*, 134–70. Edited by Matthew Affron and Mark Antliff. Princeton, N.J.: Princeton University Press, 1997.

Archives Départementales et l'Université d'Artois. *Chefs-d'oeuvre et circonstances.* Arras: Archives Départementales du Pas-de-Calais, 2000.

Aronoff, Myron J., ed. *Political Anthropology.* vol. 2, *Culture and Social Change.* New Brunswick, N.J.: Transaction, 1983.

Auric, Georges. *Quand j'étais là.* Paris: Bernard Grasset, 1979.

Austin, William. *Music in the Twentieth Century.* New York: Norton, 1966.

Bach-Sisley, J., ed. *Pour la musique française: Douze causeries.* Paris: Georges Grès, 1917.

Becker, Annette. "Musique et culture de guerre." In Archives Départementales du Pas-de-Calais, *Chefs-d'oeuvre et circonstances*, 9–14. Arras: Archives Départementales du Pas-de-Calais, 2000.

Béhague, Gerard H. "Music Performance." In *Folklore, Cultural Performances, and Popular Entertainments*, 167–78. Edited by Richard Bauman. New York: Oxford University Press, 1992.

Bellanger, Claude, Jacques Godechot, Pierre Guiral, and Fernand Terron, eds. *Histoire générale de la presse française.* 5 vols. Paris: Presses Universitaires de France, 1969.

Belmand, Pascal. "Rougemont, Denis de." In *Dictionnaire des intellectuels français*, 1006–7. Edited by Jacques Julliard and Michel Winock. Paris: Seuil, 1996.

Ben-Amos, Avner. "Les funérailles de gauche sous la IIIe République: Deuil et contestation." In *Les usages politiques des fêtes aux XIXe–XXe siècles.* Edited by Alain Corbin, Noëlle Gérôme, and Danielle Tartakowsky, 199–210. Paris: Publications de la Sorbonne, 1994.

———. "La panthéonization de Jean Jaurès." *Terrain* 15 (Oct. 1996): 49–64.

———. *Funerals, Politics, and Memory in Modern France, 1789–1996.* Oxford: Oxford University Press, 2000.

Benda, Julien. *La trahison des clercs.* Paris: Grasset, 1975 [1927].

Berkovitz, Jay. *The Shaping of Jewish Identity in Nineteenth-Century France.* Detroit: Wayne State University Press, 1989.

Bernard, Philippe. *La fin d'un monde: 1914–1929.* Paris: Seuil, 1975.

Bernard, Robert. *Les tendances de la musique française moderne.* Paris: Durand et Fils, 1930.

Berstein, Serge. *La France des années 30.* Paris: Armand Collin, 1988.

Bertrand, Paul. *Le monde de la musique.* Geneva: Palatine, 1947.

Biron, Fernand. *Le chant grégorien dans l'enseignement et les oeuvres de Vincent d'Indy.* Ottawa: Editions de l'Université d'Ottawa, 1941.

Blatt, Joel. "Relatives and Rivals: The Response of the Action Française to Italian Fascism, 1919–26." *European Studies Review* 11.3 (1981): 263–92.

Bloch, Jean-Richard. "Une insurrection contre la sensibilité." *Le monde musical* 17 (18 Sept. 1924).

———. "Prolègomènes à toute chronique musicale." *Clarté* 1925: 128–30.

Blume, Friedrich. *Classic and Romantic Music.* New York: Norton, 1970.

Bodin, Louis, and Jean Touchard. *Front populaire, 1936.* Paris: A. Colin, 1961.

Boll, André. "Pour un réveil de la musique française." *La revue musicale*, no. 193 (Aug.–Nov. 1939): 86–89.
Bonnell, Victoria, and Lynn Hunt, eds. *Beyond the Cultural Turn: New Directions in the Study of Society and Culture.* Berkeley: University of California Press, 1999.
Boschot, Adolphe. *Chez les musiciens.* Paris: Plon, 1922.
Bouffartigue, Delphine. "Mauriac, François." In *Dictionnaire des intellectuels français*, 771–72. Edited by Jacques Julliard and Michel Winock. Paris: Seuil, 1996.
Bourdieu, Pierre. *La distinction: Critique sociale du jugement.* Paris: Minuit, 1979.
———. *Ce que parler veut dire: L'économie des échanges linguistiques.* Paris: Fayard, 1982.
———. "The Market of Symbolic Goods." *Poetics* 14 (1985): 13–44.
———. "Penser la politique." *Actes de la recherche en sciences sociales* vols. 71–72 (1988) : 2–3.
Bourdieu, Pierre, and Jean-Claude Passeron. *Reproduction in Society and Culture.* Translated by Richard Nice. Beverly Hills, Calif.: Sage, 1970.
Boyd, Malcolm, ed. *Music and the French Revolution.* Cambridge: Cambridge University Press, 1992.
Brankhurst, Hauke. "Irreconcilable Modernity: Adorno's Aesthetic Experimentalism and the Transgression Theorem." In *The Actuality of Adorno: Critical Essays on Adorno and the Postmodern.* Edited by Max Pensky. Albany: State University of New York Press, 1977, 43–61.
Brothier, Jean-Jacques, ed. *La Jeune France: Yves Baudrier, André Jolivet, Daniel-Lesur, Olivier Messiaen.* Paris: Association des "Amis de la Jeune France," 1954.
Bruneau, Alfred. "Notice lue par l'auteur à l'Académie des Beaux-Arts." In Bruneau, *La vie et les oeuvres de Gabriel Fauré.* Paris: Charpentier et Fasquelle, 1925.
———. "Souvenirs inédits." *Revue internationale de musique française* 7 (Feb. 1982): 8–82.
Bruyr, José. *L'écran des musiciens.* 2nd ser. Paris: Corti, 1933.
———. *Honegger et son oeuvre.* Paris: Correa, 1947.
Buch, Esteban. *La Neuvième de Beethoven: Une histoire politique.* Paris: Gallimard, 1999.
Burrin, Philippe. *La dérive fasciste: Doriot, Déat, Bergery, 1933–1945.* Paris: Seuil, 1986.
Caballero, Carlo. "Patriotism or Nationalism? Fauré and the Great War." *Journal of the American Musicological Society* 52.3 (1999): 465–530.
Calinescu, Matei. "Modernism and Ideology." In *Modernism: Challenges and Perspectives*, 79–93. Edited by Monique Chefdor, Ricardo Quiñones, and Albert Wachtel. Urbana: University of Illinois Press, 1986.
Caron, Vicki. "The Antisemitic Revival in France in the 1930s: The Socioeconomic Dimension Reconsidered." *Journal of Modern History* 70 (1998): 24–73.
Carraud, Gaston. *La vie, l'oeuvre et la mort d'Albéric Magnard.* Paris: Rouart, Lerolle, 1921.
Carroll, David. *French Literary Fascism: Nationalism, Anti-Semitism, and the Ideology of Culture.* Princeton, N.J.: Princeton University Press, 1995.
Caumajani, Giovanni, and Detleff Gojowy. "Lourié, Arthur Vincent." In *The New Grove Dictionary of Music and Musicians.* 2nd ed. 15 (2001): 223-24. London: Grove.
Chaigne, Louis. *Paul Claudel: The Man and the Mystic.* Translated by Pierre de Fontnouvelle. Westport, Conn.: Greenwood, 1978.
Chamfray, Charles. "Enquête: Y aura-t-il une musique de guerre?" *La revue musicale*, no. 194 (Dec. 1939): 146–52.
Champigneulle, Bernard. *Les plus beaux écrits des grands musiciens.* Paris: Colombe, 1946.
Charle, Christophe. "Noblesses et élites en France au début du XXe siècle." In *Noblesses européennes au XIXe siècle*, 407–33. Paris: Collection de l'Ecole Française de Rome 107, 1988.
———. *Naissance des "intellectuels," 1880–1900.* Paris: Minuit, 1990.

Charpentier, Gustave. *Lettres inédites à ses parents*. Edited by François Andrieux. Paris: Presses Universitaires de France, 1984.

Chartier, Roger. *On the Edge of the Cliff: History, Language, and Practices*. Translated by Lydia G. Cochrane. Baltimore: Johns Hopkins University Press, 1997.

Chimènes, Myriam. "La Princesse Edmond de Polignac et la création musicale." In *La musique et le pouvoir*, 125–145. Edited by Hugues Dufourt and Joël-Marie Fauquet. Paris: Aux Amateurs de Livres, 1987.

———. "Le budget de la musique sous la IIIe République." In *La musique: Du théorique au politique*, 261–312. Edited by Hugues Dufourt and Joël-Marie Fauquet. Paris: Aux Amateurs de Livres, 1991.

———. "Poulenc and His Patrons: Social Convergences." In *Francis Poulenc: Music, Art, and Literature*, 210–51. Edited by Sidney Buckland and Myriam Chimènes. Aldershot, U.K.: Ashgate, 1999.

———. *Mécènes et musiciens : du salon au concert à Paris sous la III e République*. Paris : Fayard, 2004.

———, ed. *La vie musicale sous Vichy*. Brussels: Complexe, 2001.

Clifford, James. *The Predicament of Culture: Twentieth-Century Ethnography, Literature, and Art*. Cambridge: Harvard University Press, 1988.

Cocteau, Jean. *Le rappel à l'ordre*. Paris: Stock, 1926.

———. *Le coq et l'arlequin*. Paris: Stock, 1979.

———. *Professional Secrets: An Autobiography of Jean Cocteau*. Edited by Robert Phelps. New York: Farrar, Strauss, and Giroux, 1979.

———. *Romans, poésies, oeuvres diverses*. Edited by Bernard Benech. Paris: Pochothèque, 1996.

Coeuroy, André. *La musique française moderne*. Paris: Delagrave, 1924.

———. "Un musicien modern: Arthur Honegger." *Revue hebdomadaire* vol. 37, no. 14 (7 April 1928): 66–72.

———. "The Esthetics of Contemporary Music." Translated by Theodore Baker. *Musical Quarterly* 15 (1929): 246–67.

Cohen, Gustave. *Histoire de la mise en scène dans le théâtre du Moyen Age*. Paris: Honoré Champion, 1926.

Collaer, Paul. "L'esprit de la musique française." *La revue musicale*, no. 193 (Aug.–Nov. 1939): 79–85.

———. *A History of Modern Music*. Translated by Salley Abeles. New York: World, 1961.

———. *Darius Milhaud*. Geneva: Slatkine, 1982.

Collet, Henri. "Un livre de Rimsky et un livre de Cocteau: Les cinq Russes, les six Français et Erik Satie." *Comoedia*, 16 and 23 Jan., 1920.

Compagnon, Antoine. "L'utopie d'une république athénienne." *Le débat* (May–Aug. 1992): 42–48.

Comte, Bernard. "Pamphlet, histoire et fantaisie: A propos de Mounier, ministre de la culture de Vichy." *Le débat* (May–Aug. 1992): 49–59.

Cone, Michèle. *Artists under Vichy: A Case of Prejudice and Persecution*. Princeton, N.J.: Princeton University Press, 1992.

Conrad, Bridget. "Le langage musical d'André Jolivet." In *André Jolivet: Portraits*, 87–122. Edited by Lucie Kayas and Laetitia Chassain-Dolliou. Paris: Actes Sud, 1994.

Cook, Susan. *Opera for a New Republic: The Zeitopern of Krenek, Weill, and Hindemith*. Ann Arbor: University of Michigan Press, 1988.

Cooper, Douglas. *Picasso Theater*. New York: H. Abrams, 1987.

Cooper, Martin. *French Music from the Death of Berlioz to the Death of Fauré*. Oxford: Oxford University Press, 1951.

———. "Cortot, Alfred." In *The New Grove Dictionary of Music and Musicians*, 2nd ed. (2001) 15: 223–24. London: Grove
Coppola, Piero. *Dix-sept ans de musique à Paris, 1922–1939*. Geneva: Slatkine, 1982 [1944].
Corbin, Alain. "La fête souveraineté." In *Les usages politiques des fêtes aux XIXe–XXe siècles*, 25–38. Edited by Alain Corbin, Noelle Gérome, and Danielle Tartakowsky. Paris: Publications de la Sorbonne, 1994.
Cornick, Martyn. *Intellectuals in History: The "Nouvelle Revue Française."* Atlanta: Rodopi, 1995.
Corpet, Olivier. "La revue." In *Histoire des droites en France*. vol. 2, *Cultures*, 161–212. Edited by Jean-François Sirinelli. Paris: Gallimard, 1992.
Cortot, Alfred. "Le cas Erik Satie." *La revue musicale*, April–May 1938: 248–72.
Cossart, Michael de. *The Food of Love: Princesse Edmond de Polignac and Her Salon (1895–1943)*. London: Hamish Hamilton, 1978.
Daniel, Keith. *Francis Poulenc: His Artistic Development and Musical Style*. Ann Arbor: U.M.I. Research Press, 1982.
Darnaudet, Jean. "La musique française: Claude Debussy." *L'action française*, 1 and 15 Aug. 1915.
———. "L'orchestre wagnerien." *L'action française*, 15 January, 1917.
Daudet, Léon. *Ecrivains et artistes*. Vol. 7. Paris: Capitole, 1929.
Davenson, Henri. "D'une musique nécessaire et Arthur Lourié." *Esprit*, 1 March 1935: 824–30.
Dawes, Frank. *Debussy Piano Music*. Seattle: University of Washington Press, 1971.
Debussy, Claude. *Debussy on Music*. Edited by François Lesure and Richard L. Smith. New York: Alfred A. Knopf, 1977.
Déléage, André. "Littérature et révolution." *Esprit*, June 1933: 345–53.
Delannoy, Marcel. *Honegger*. Geneva: Slatkine, 1986.
Denis, Maurice. *Nouvelles théories sur l'art moderne: Sur l'art sacrée*. Paris: Rouart et Watelin, 1921.
Dennis, David. *Beethoven in German Politics, 1870–1989*. New Haven, Conn.: Yale University Press, 1996.
d'Indy, Vincent. "Musique française et musique allemande." *La renaissance politique, littéraire et artistique* 3 (12 June 1915): 1–8.
———. "Le public et son évolution." *Comoedia*, 1 Oct. 1923.
———. "Matière et forme dans l'art musical moderne." *Comoedia*, 28 Jan. 1924.
———. *Richard Wagner et son influence sur l'art musical français*. Paris: Delagrave, 1930.
———. *Lettres à Auguste Sérieyx*. Edited by M. L. Sérieyx. Lausanne: Cerrin, 1961.
Dioudonnat, Pierre-Marie. *"Je suis partout," 1930–1944: Les Maurrassiens devant la tentation fasciste*. Paris: Table Ronde, 1973.
Dorléac, Laurence Bertrand. "Léger, Fernand." In *Dictionnaire des intellectuels français*, p. 697. Edited by Jacques Julliard and Michel Winock. Paris: Seuil, 1996.
Drake, Jeremy. "Auric, Georges." In The New Grove Dictionary of Music and Musicians. 2: 187-88. Edited by Stanley Sadie. London: Grove, 2001.
Drake, Jeremy. *The Operas of Darius Milhaud*. New York: Garland, 1989.
———. "Auric, Georges." In *The New Grove Dictionary of Music and Musicians*. 2 : 187–88. Edited by Stanley Sadie. London: Grove, 2001.
Duchesneau, Michel. "La musique française pendant la guerre, 1914–1918: Autour de la tentative de fusion de la Société nationale de musique et de la Société musicale indépendante." *Revue de musicologie* 82.1 (1996): 123–53.
———. *L'avant-garde musicale à Paris de 1871 à 1939*. Liège: Mardaga, 1997.

Dumesnil, René. *La musique en France entre les deux guerres: 1919–1939*. Paris: Milieu du Monde, 1946.

Dunoyer, Cecilia. *Marguerite Long: A Life in French Music, 1874–1966*. Bloomington: Indiana University Press, 1993.

Dunsby, Jonathan. "The Poetry of Debussy's *En blanc et noir*." In *Analytical Strategies and Musical Interpretation: Essays in Nineteenth and Twentieth-Century Music*, 149–68. Edited by Craig Ayrey and Mark Everest. New York: Cambridge University Press, 1996.

Dupêchez, Charles. *Histoire de l'Opéra de Paris: Un siècle au Palais Garnier*. Paris: Perrin, 1984.

Duquesne, Jacques. *Les Catholiques français sous l'Occupation*. Paris: Bernard Grasset, 1996 [1966].

Durand, Jacques. *Quelques souvenirs d'un éditeur de musique*. 2nd sér. (1910–1924). Paris: A. Durand et Fils, 1925.

Eksteins, Modris. *Rites of Spring: The Great War and the Birth of the Modern Age*. Toronto: Lester and Orpen Dinnys, 1989.

Elias, Norbert. *The Germans: Power Struggles and the Development of Habitus in the Nineteenth and Twentieth Centuries*. Edited by Michael Schroter. Translated by Eric Dunning and Stephen Mannell. New York: Columbia University Press, 1996.

Entretiens 4: L'art et la réalité, l'art et l'Etat. Paris: Institut International de Coopération Intellectuelle, 1937.

Entretiens 6: Vers un nouvel humanisme. Paris: Institut International de Coopération Intellectuelle, 1937.

Fauré, Gabriel. *Opinions musicales*. Paris: Rieder, 1930.

Faure, Michel. *Du néoclassicisme musical dans la France du premier XXe siècle*. Paris: Klinksieck, 1997.

Ferro, Marc. "Cultural Life in France, 1914–1918." In *European Culture in the Great War: The Arts, Entertainment, and Propaganda, 1914–1918*, 295–307. Edited by Aviel Roshwald and Richard Stites. New York: Cambridge University Press, 1999.

Fisher, David James. *Romain Rolland and the Politics of Intellectual Engagement*. Berkeley: University of California Press, 1988.

Focillon, Henri. *La peinture au XIXe siècle*. Paris: Flammarion, 1991.

Foucault, Michel. "What Is an Author?" In *The Critical Tradition: Classic Texts and Contemporary Trends*. Edited by David H. Richter. Boston: Bedford, 1998, pps. 978–88.

Fritzsche, Peter. "Did Weimar Fail?" *Journal of Modern History* 68 (1996): 629–56.

Führer, Karl Christian. "A Medium of Modernity? Broadcasting in Weimar Germany, 1923–1932." *Journal of Modern History* 69 (1999): 722–53.

Fulcher, Jane F. "The Orphéon Societies: 'Music for the Workers' in Second-Empire France." *International Review of the Aesthetics and Sociology of Music* 10.1 (1979): 47–56.

———. *The Nation's Image: French Grand Opera as Politics and Politicized Art*. New York: Cambridge University Press, 1987.

———. "D'Indy's 'Drame Anti-Juif' and Its Meaning in Paris, 1920." *Cambridge Opera Journal*, Nov. 1990: 295–319.

———. "Charpentier's Operatic 'Roman Musical' as Read in the Wake of the Dreyfus Affair." *Nineteenth-Century Music* 16.2 (1992): 161–80.

———. "Musical Style, Meaning, and Politics in France on the Eve of the Second World War." *Journal of Musicology* 13 (1995): 425–53.

———. "The Preparation for Vichy: Anti-Semitism in French Musical Culture between the Two World Wars." *Musical Quarterly* 71 (1995): 458–75.

———. "The Concert as Political Propaganda in France and the Control of Performative Context." *Musical Quarterly* 82 (1998): 41–67.
———. "The Composer as Intellectual: Ideological Inscriptions in French Interwar Neo-classicism." *Journal of Musicology* 17 (1999): 197–230.
———. *French Cultural Politics and Music from the Dreyfus Affair to the First World War.* New York: Oxford University Press, 1999.
———. "A Political Barometer of Twentieth-Century France: Wagner as Jew or Anti-Semite." *Musical Quarterly* 84 (2000): 41–57.
———. "Speaking the Truth to Power: The Dialogic Element in Debussy's Wartime Compositions." In *Debussy and His World.* Edited by Jane F. Fulcher. Princeton, N.J.: Princeton University Press, 2001, 203–32.
Fuller, David and Bruce Gustafson. "Jolivet, André." *The New Grove Dictionary of Music and Musicians*, 2001 ed., sv., 13:174–77.
Gavoty, Bernard. *Alfred Cortot.* Paris: Buchet/Chastel, 1977.
Gênet-Delacroix, Marie-Claude. "Esthétique officielle et art national sous la Troisième République." *Le mouvement social* (1985) 13: 105–20.
Gétreau, Florence. "Le patriomoine musical de deux musées parisiens." In *La vie musicale sous Vichy*, 183–89. Edited by Myriam Chimènes. Brussels: Complexe, 2001.
Gibson-Graham, J. K., Stephen Resnick, and Richard D. Wolff, eds. *Re/Presenting Class: Essays in Post-modern Marxism.* Durham, N.C.: Duke University Press, 2001.
Gide, André. *Journal, 1889–1939.* Paris: Gallimard, 1951.
Gilliam, Bryan, ed. *Music and Performance during the Weimar Republic.* Cambridge: Cambridge University Press, 1994.
Gillmor, Alan M. *Erik Satie.* Boston: Twayne, 1988.
Golan, Romy. *Modernity and Nostalgia: Art and Politics in France between the Wars.* New Haven, Conn.: Yale University Press, 1995.
Goléa, Antoine. *Georges Auric.* Paris: Ventadour, n.d.
Grailles, Bénédicte. "Chansons de marche, lamento funèbre, et hymne de la renaissance: La production musicale imprimée entre 1918 et 1922.," In *Chefs-d'oeuvre et circonstances*, 39–46. Arras: Archives Départementales du Pas-de-Calais, 2000, pp. 39–46. In *Chefs-d'oeuvre et circonstances*. Archives Départementales du Pas-de-Calais, 2000.
Grandgambe, Sandrine. "La Réunion des Théâtres Lyriques Nationaux." In *La vie musicale sous Vichy*, 109–26. Edited by Myriam Chimènes. Brussels: Complexe, 2001.
Green, Christopher. *Cubism and Its Enemies: Modern Movements and Reaction in French Art, 1916–1928.* New Haven, Conn.: Yale University Press, 1987.
Griffiths, Paul. *Olivier Messiaen and the Music of Time.* Ithaca, N.Y.: Cornell University Press, 1985.
Gumplowicz, Philippe. *Les travaux d'Orphée: 150 ans de vie musicale amateur en France—Harmonies-chorales-fanfares.* Paris: Aubier, 1987.
Gut, Serge. *Le groupe Jeune France.* Paris: Honoré Champion, 1977.
Halbereich, Harry. *Arthur Honegger: Un musicien dans la cité des hommes.* Paris: Fayard, 1992.
Hamilton, Alastair. *The Appeal of Fascism: A Study of Intellectuals and Fascism, 1919–1945.* New York: Avon, 1973.
Hanna, Martha. *The Mobilization of Intellect: French Scholars and Writers during the Great War.* Cambridge: Harvard University Press, 1996.
Harding, James. *The Ox on the Roof: Scenes from Musical Life in Paris in the Twenties.* New York: St. Martin's, 1972.

Hart, Brian. "The Symphony in Theory and Practice in France, 1900–1914." Ph.D. diss., Indiana University, 1994.

———. "The Symphony in Debussy's World: A Context for His Views on the Genre and Early Interpretations of *La Mer*." In *Debussy and His World*, 181–202. Edited by Jane F. Fulcher. Princeton, N.J.: Princeton University Press, 2001.

Haydon, Geoffrey J. "A Study of the Exchange of Influences between the Music of Early Twentieth-Century Parisian Composers and Ragtime, Blues, and Early Jazz." DMA document, University of Texas at Austin, 1992.

Hedges, Inez. *Languages of Revolt: Dada and Surrealist Literature and Film*. Durham, N.C.: Duke University Press, 1983.

Hell, Henri. *Francis Poulenc*. Paris: Fayard, 1978.

Herf, Jeffrey. *Reactionary Modernism: Technology, Culture, and Politics in Weimar Germany and the Third Reich*. Cambridge: Cambridge University Press, 1984.

Hewitt, Andrew. *Fascist Modernism: Aesthetics, Politics, and the Avant-Garde*. Stanford, Calif.: Stanford University Press, 1993.

Hobsbawm, Eric, and Terrence Ranger, eds. *The Invention of Tradition*. Cambridge: Cambridge University Press, 1983.

Hoffman, Robert. *More than a Trial: The Struggle for Captain Dreyfus*. New York: Free Press, 1980.

Hohendahl, Peter U. *Prismatic Thought: Theodor W. Adorno*. Lincoln: University of Nebraska Press, 1995.

Holquist, Michael, and Katerina Clark. *Mikhail Bakhtin: A Biography*. Cambridge: Harvard University Press, 1984.

Honegger, Arthur. "La classe de d'Indy au Conservatoire." *La revue musicale*, (1932): 40–54.

———. *Incantation aux fossiles*. Lausanne: Ouchy, 1948.

———. *I Am a Composer*. Translated by Wilson O. Clough. New York: St. Martin's, 1966.

———. *Ecrits*. Edited by Huguette Calmel. Paris: Honoré Champion, 1992.

Hoover, Jean. "Constructions of National Identities: Opera and Nationalism in the British Isles." Ph.D. dissertation, Indiana University, 1999.

Howe, Irving. *Politics and the Novel*. New York: Avon, 1970 [1957].

Hunt, Lynn. *Politics, Culture, and Class in the French Revolution*. Berkeley: University of California Press, 1984.

Huré, Jean. *Dogmes musicaux (1904–07)*. Paris: Monde Musical, 1909.

Huynh, Pascal. *La musique sous la République de Weimar*. Paris: Fayard, 1998.

Inghelbrecht, D.-E. *Mouvement contraire: Souvenirs d'un musicien*. Paris: Domat, 1947.

Irvine, William D. "French Conservatives and the 'New Right' during the 1930s." *French Historical Studies* 8 (1974): 534–62.

Isaacs, Leonard. "Paris in 1930: The Ecole Normale de Musique." *Journal of the American Liszt Society* 38 (July–Dec. 1995): 23–26.

Jackson, Jeffrey H. *Making Jazz French: Music and Modern Life in Interwar Paris*. Durham, N.C.: Duke University Press, 2003.

Jackson, Julian. *The Popular Front in France: Defending Democracy, 1934–38*. Cambridge: Cambridge University Press, 1988.

Jacques-Dalcroze, Emile. "Une nouvelle idéale musicale." *L'esprit nouveau* 1920, 311–12.

Jankélévitch, Vladimir. *Ravel*. Translated by Margaret Crosland. Westport, Conn.: Greenwood, 1959.

Jean-Aubry, Georges. *La musique française aujourd'hui*. Paris: Librairie Académique Perrin, 1916.

Jelavich, Peter. "German Culture in the Great War." In *European Culture in the Great War: The Arts, Entertainment, and Propaganda, 1914–1918*, 32–57. Edited by Aviel Roshwald and Richard Stites. New York: Cambridge University Press, 1999.
Johnson, Douglas. *France and the Dreyfus Affair*. London: Blanford, 1966.
Jolivet, André. *Mana: 6 pièces pour piano*. Introduction by Olivier Messiaen, translated by Pierre Messiaen and Rollo Myers. Paris: Editions Costallat, 1946.
Judt, Tony. *Past Imperfect: French Intellectuals, 1944–1956*. Berkeley: University of California Press, 1992.
Julliard, Jacques. "Claudel. Paul," 268–70. In *Dictionnaire des intellectuels français*. Edited by Jacques Julliard and Michel Winock. Paris: Seuil, 1996.
Julliard, Jacques, and Michel Winock, eds. *Dictionnaire des intellectuels français*. Paris: Seuil, 1996.
Kaes, Anton, Martin Jay, and Edward Dimendberg. *The Weimar Republic Sourcebook*. Berkeley: University of California Press, 1994.
Kahan, Sylvia. *Music's Modern Muse: A Life of Winnaretta Singer, Princess de Polignac*. Rochester, NY: University of Rochester Press, 2003.
Kauppi, Niilo. *The Politics of Embodiment: Habits, Power, and Pierre Bourdieu's Theory*. New York: Peter Lang, 2000.
Kayas, Lucie. "De découverte en découverte: Le fonds André Jolivet." In *André Jolivet: Portraits*, 71–85. Edited by Lucie Kayas and Laetitia Chassain-Dalliou. Paris: Actes Sud, 1994.
Kayas, Lucie, and Laetitia Chassain-Dalliou, eds. *André Jolivet: Portraits*. Paris: Actes Sud, 1994.
Kelkel, Manfred. *Naturalisme, vérisme et réalisme dans l'opéra de 1890 à 1930*. Paris: Librairie Philosophique J. Vrin, 1984.
Kelly, Barbara. *Tradition and Style in the Works of Darius Milhaud*. Aldershot, U.K.: Ashgate, 2003.
Kendall, Alan. *The Tender Tyrant, Nadia Boulanger: A Life Devoted to Music*. London: Macdould and Jane's, 1976.
Kinser, Samuel. "Chrono-types and Catastrophes: The Cultural History of Mikhail Bakhtin." *Journal of Modern History* (1984) 56: 301–10.
Kleeblatt, Norman L., ed. *The Dreyfus Affair: Art, Truth, and Justice*. Berkeley: University of California Press, 1988.
Knights, L. C. *Public Voices: Literature and Politics with Special Reference to the Seventeenth Century*. London: Chatto and Winders, 1971.
Knowles, Dorothy. *French Drama of the Inter-war Years, 1918–39*. London: George G. Harrap, 1967.
Koechlin, Charles. "Pour Chabrier." *La revue musicale*, Jan. 1930: 8–12.
———. *La musique et le peuple*. Paris: Editions Sociales Internationales, 1936.
———. "La vraie et la fausse musique populaire." *L'art musical populaire*, May 1937, 19–20.
———. *Correspondance*. Paris: Revue Musicale, 1982.
Kramer, Lawrence. *Music as Cultural Practice, 1800–1900*. Berkeley: University of California Press, 1990.
Krance, Charles. L.-F. *Céline: The I of the Storm*. Lexington, Ky.: French Forum, 1992.
Kraus, Beate. "Henri Collet et *Comoedia*." *Revue internationale de musique française* (June 1989): 29: 29–39.
Kristeva, Julia. *Desire in Language: A Semiotic Approach to Literature and Art*. New York: Columbia University Press, 1980.
———. *Black Sun: Despair and Melancholia*. New York: Columbia University Press, 1989.

Krumeich, Gerd. *Jeanne d'Arc in der Geschichte: Historiographie, Politik, Kultur.* Sigmaringen: J. Thorbecke, 1989.
Lacouture, Jean. *Une adolescence du siècle: Jacques Rivière et "La nouvelle revue française."* Paris: Seuil, 1994.
La Laurencie, Lionel de. "Le mouvement musicographe." *Le mercure musical,* June 1907.
Laloy, Louis. *La musique retrouvée, 1902–1927.* Paris: Plon, 1928.
———. *Louis Laloy (1874–1944) on Debussy, Ravel, and Stravinsky.* Translated and annotated by Deborah Priest. Aldershot, U.K.: Ashgate, 1999.
———. "Cabarets et music-hall." *La revue musicale S.I.M.* 1913: 53–56.
Landormy, Paul. *La musique française après Debussy.* Paris: Gallimard, 1943.
Lasserre, Pierre. *L'esprit de la musique française.* Paris: Payot, 1917.
———. *Les chapelles littéraires: Claudel, Jammes, Péguy.* Paris: Garnier Frères, 1920.
———. *Philosophie du goût musical.* Paris: Bernard Grasset, 1922.
Lavignac, Albert, and Lionel de la Laurencie, eds. *Pédagogie, écoles, concerts.* Part 2 of *Encyclopédie de la musique et dictionnaire du Conservatoire.* Paris: Delagrave, 1931.
Laycock, Gary. "Olivier Messiaen's Studies and Influences during the Conservatoire Years and Their Role in the Genesis of His Style." Ph.D. diss. in progress, Indiana University.
Le Béguec, Gilles. "L'évolution de la politique gouvernementale et les problèmes institutionnels." In *Edouard Daladier: Chef du gouvernement,* 55–84. Edited by René Rémond and Janine Bourdin. Paris: Presses de la Fondation Nationale des Sciences Politiques, 1977.
Lebovics, Herman. *True France: The Wars over Cultural Identity, 1900–1945.* Ithaca, N.Y.: Cornell University Press, 1992.
Leibowitz, René. "La musique." Esprit, 1 April 1939: 140–41.
Léon, Paul. *Du Palais-Royal au Palais-Bourbon.* Paris: Albin-Michel, 1947.
Leterrier, Sophie-Anne. "Culture de guerre et musique nationale,." pp. 15–37. In *Chefs-d'oeuvre et circonstances,* 15–37. Arras: Archives Départementales du Pas-de-Calais, 2000.
Levenstein, Harvey. *Seductive Journey: American Tourists in France from Jefferson to the Jazz Age.* Chicago: University of Chicago Press, 1988.
Lindenberger, Herbert. *Opera in History: From Monteverdi to Cage.* Stanford, Calif.: Stanford University Press, 1998.
Lockspeiser, Edward. *Debussy: His Life and Mind.* London: Cassel, 1965.
Lord, Robert S. "Liturgy and Gregorian Chant in 'L'Orgue Mystique' of Charles Tournemire." *Organ Year Book* 1984: 60–97.
Loubet del Bayle, Jean-Louis. *Les non-conformistes des années 30: Une tentative de renouvellement de la pensée politique française.* Paris: Seuil, 1969.
Lourié, Arthur. *Sergei Koussevitsky and His Epoch: A Biographical Chronical.* Translated by S. W. Pring. New York: AMS, 1971.
Maillard, Jean, and Jacques Nahoum. *Les symphonies d'Arthur Honegger.* Paris: Alphonse Leduc, 1974.
Mäkelä, Tomi. "Towards a Theory of Internationalism, Europeanism, Nationalism, and 'Co-Nationalism' in Twentieth-Century Music." In *Music and Nationalism in Twentieth-Century Great Britain and Finland,* 9–16. Edited by Tomi Mäkelä. Hamburg: Von Bockel, 1997.
Mannheim, Karl. *Ideology and Utopia: An Introduction to the Sociology of Knowledge.* Translated by Louis White and Edward Shils. New York: Harcourt, Brace, and World, 1953.

Manning, Frank E. "Spectacle." In *Folklore, Cultural Performances, and Popular Entertainments*. Edited by Richard Bauman. New York: Oxford University Press, 1992, 291–99.
Marguerite, Jean. *Les fêtes du peuple: L'oeuvre, les moyens, le but*. Paris: Les Fêtes du Peuple, 1921.
Marin, Louis. *De la représentation*. Paris: Gallimard, 1994.
Maritain, Jacques. *Primauté du spirituel*. Paris: Plon, 1927.
———. *Art and Scholasticism, and the Frontiers of Poetry*. Translated by Joseph W. Evans. New York: Scribner, 1962.
———. *L'impossible antisémitisme*. Paris: Desclée de Brouwer, 1994.
Marks, Martin. "Film Music of the Silent Period, 1895–1924." Ph.D. diss., Harvard University, 1990.
Marnat, Marcel. *Maurice Ravel*. Paris: Fayard, 1986.
Marnold, Jean. *Le cas Wagner: La musique pendant la guerre*. Paris: E. Demets, 1918.
Massin, Brigitte. *Olivier Messiaen: Une poétique du merveilleux*. Aix-en-Provence: Alinéa, 1989.
Massip, Catherine, ed. *Portrait(s) d'Olivier Messiaen*. Paris: Bibliothèque Nationale de France, 1996.
Masson, Paul-Marie. *Rapport sur la musique française contemporaine*. Rome: Arman and Stein, 1913.
May, Ernest R. *Strange Victory: Hitler's Conquest of France*. New York: Hill and Wang, 2000.
Mayer, Arno J. *The Furies: Violence and Terror in the French and Russian Revolutions*. Princeton, N.J.: Princeton University Press, 2000.
Mayeur, Jean-Marie. *La vie politique sous la Troisième République*. Paris: Seuil, 1984.
Mellers, Wilfrid. *François Couperin and the French Classical Tradition*. London: Faber and Faber, 1987.
Messiaen, Olivier. *Music and Color: Conversations with Claude Samuel*. Translated by E. Thomas Glasow. Portland, Ore.: Amadeus, 1986.
Messing, Scott. *Neoclassicism in Music: From the Genesis of the Concept through the Schoenberg-Stravinsky Polemic*. Ann Arbor: UMI Research Press, 1988.
———. "Polemic as History: The Case of Neoclassicism." *Journal of Musicology* (Fall 1991): 9: 481–97.
Milhaud, Darius. "La tradition." *Atti del Terzo Congresso Internationale di Musica*. Florence, April 1938: 89–92.
———. *Notes sans musique*. Paris: Julliard, 1949.
———. *Notes without Music*. Translated by Donald Evans. New York: DaCapo, 1970.
———. *Ma vie heureuse*. Paris: Belfond, 1973.
———. *Notes sur la musique: Essais et chroniques*. Edited by Jeremy Drake. Paris: Flammarion, 1982.
Miller, Tyrus. *Late Modernism: Politics, Fiction, and the Arts between the World Wars*. Berkeley: University of California Press, 1999.
Moch, Jules. *Le Front populaire, grande espérance*. Paris: Librairie Académique Perrin, 1971.
Monsaingeon, Bruno. *Mademoiselle: Conversations with Nadia Boulanger*. Translated by Robyn Marsack. Manchester, U.K.: Chicanet, 1985.
Mounier, Emmanuel. "Refaire la Renaissance," *Esprit*, Oct. 1932, 5–51.
Musk, Andrea. "Aspects of Regionalism in French Music during the Third Republic: The Schola Cantorum, d'Indy, Séverac, and Canteloube." Ph.D. diss., Oxford University, 1999.

Mussat, Marie-Claire. "La réception de Schoenberg en France avant la Seconde guerre mondiale." *Revue de musicologie* 87.1 (2001): 145–86.
Myers, Rollo. *Modern French Music*. Oxford: Blackwell, 1971.
Nectoux, Jean-Michel. *Gabriel Fauré: Les voix du clair-obscur*. Paris: Flammarion, 1990.
Nichols, Roger. *Conversations with Madeleine Milhaud*. London: Faber and Faber, 1996.
———. *The Harlequin Years: Music in Paris, 1917–1929*. Berkeley: University of California Press, 2002.
Nora, Pierre. *Les lieux de mémoire*. 3 vols. (Paris: Gallimard, 1986).
Nouschi, André, and Maurice Agulhon. *La France de 1914 à 1940*. Paris: Fernand Nathan, 1974.
Orenstein, Arbie, ed. *A Ravel Reader: Correspondence, Articles, Interviews*. New York: Columbia University Press, 1990.
Orledge, Robert. "Indy, Vincent d'." In *The New Grove Dictionary of Music and Musicians*. 9: 220–25. Edited by Stanley Sadie. London: Grove, 1980.
———. "Tailleferre, Germaine." In *The New Grove Dictionary of Music and Musicians* 2nd.ed. 24: 930–33. Edited by Stanley Sadie. London: Grove, 2001.
———. *Charles Koechlin: His Life and Works*. London: Harwood Academic, 1989.
Ory, Pascal. "Le Front populaire et la création artistique." *Bulletin de la Société d'Histoire Moderne* 8.3 (1974): 5–21.
———. "La politique culturelle du premier gouvernement Blum." *Nouvelle revue sociale* 10–11 (1975): 75–93.
———. "La commémoration révolutionnaire en 1939." In *La France et les Français en 1938–1939*, 115–36. Edited by René Rémond and Janine Bourdin. Paris: Presses de la Fondation Nationale des Sciences Politiques, 1978.
———. *Les Expositions Universelles de Paris*. Paris: Ramsay, 1982.
———. "La politique culturelle du Front populaire français (1935–1938)." Thèse pour le doctorat d'Etat, Université de Paris X, Nanterre, 1990.
———. *La belle illusion: Culture et politique sous le signe du Front populaire, 1935–1938*. Paris: Plon, 1994.
———. "Théorie et pratique de l'art des fêtes sous le Front populaire." In *Les usages politiques des fêtes aux XIXe–XXe siècles*, 277–90. Edited by Alain Corbin, Noelle Gérome, and Danielle Tartakowsky. Paris: Publications de la Sorbonne, 1994.
Ory, Pascal, and Jean-François Sirinelli. *Les intellectuels en France de l'affaire Dreyfus à nos jours*. Paris: Armand Colin, 1992.
Oster, Daniel. "Valéry, Paul." In *Dictionnaire des intellectuels français*, 1142–43. Edited by Jacques Julliard and Michel Winock. Paris: Seuil, 1996.
Ozouf, Mona. *La fête révolutionnaire, 1789–1799*. Paris: Gallimard, 1976.
Pasler, Jann. "Paris: Conflicting Notions of Progress." In *Music and Society: The Late Romantic Era*, 389–416. Edited by Jim Samson. Englewood Cliffs, N.J.: Prentice Hall, 1991.
Patureau, Frédérique. *Le Palais Garnier dans la société parisienne, 1875–1914*. Liège: Margada, 1991.
Paxton, Robert O. *Vichy France: Old Guard and New Order*. New York: Columbia University Press, 1972.
Perloff, Nancy. *Art and the Everyday: Popular Entertainment and the Circle of Erik Satie*. Oxford, U.K.: Clarendon, 1991.
Pilmer-Taylor, Denise. "'La musique pour tout le monde': Jean Wiéner and the Dawn of French Jazz." Ph.D. diss., University of Michigan, 1998.
Pistone, Danièle. "Manifeste et musique en France." *Revue internationale de musique française* 20 (June 1986): 7–40.

———. "Beethoven et Paris: Repères historiques et évocations contemporaines." *Revue internationale de musique française* Feb. 1987 22: 7–31.
Porcile, François. *Présence de la musique à l'écran*. Paris: Cerf, 1969.
———. *La belle époque de la musique française: Le temps de Maurice Ravel, 1871–1940*. Paris: Fayard, 1999.
Poulenc, Francis. *Correspondance, 1915–1963*. Edited by Hélène de Wendel. Paris: Seuil, 1967.
———. *My Friends and Myself*. Edited by Stéphane Audel. Translated by James Harding. London: Dobson, 1978.
———. *Correspondance, 1910–1963*. Edited by Myriam Chimènes. Paris: Fayard, 1994.
Prochasson, Christophe. "Bloch, Jean-Richard." In *Dictionnaire des intellectuels français*, 155–57. Edited by Jacques Julliard and Michel Winock. Paris: Seuil, 1996.
Prochasson, Christophe, and Anne Rasmussen. *Au nom de la patrie: Les intellectuels et la Première guerre mondiale (1910–1919)*. Paris: Découverte, 1996.
Prod'homme, J.-G. *Richard Wagner et la France*. Paris: Maurice Sénart, 1921.
Prost, Antoine. "Jeanne d'Arc à la fête: Identité collective et mémoire à Orléans depuis la Révolution française." In *La France démocratique: Mélanges offerts à Maurice Agulhon*, 379–95. Edited by Christophe Charle, Jacqueline Lalouette, Michel Pigenet, and Anne-Marie Sohn. Paris: Publications de la Sorbonne, 1998.
Proust, Marcel. *Le temps retrouvé*. Paris: Gallimard, 1990.
Prunières, Henry. "Que doit-il sortir de la crise quii traverse actuellement la musique?" *Atti del Terzo Congresso Internationale di Musica*, Florence, April 1938: 78–79.
Ravel, Maurice. "A propos des Images de Claude Debussy." *Les cahiers d'aujourd'hui*, 1913: 133–38.
———. "Esquisse autobiographique." *La revue musicale* 1938, 214–17.
Rebatet, Lucien. *Une histoire de la musique*. Paris: Robert Laffont, 1969.
Reis, Frank W. *The Dance Theater of Jean Cocteau*. Ann Arbor: UMI Research Press, 1986.
Rémond, René. *Les droites en France*. Paris: Aubier Montaigne, 1982.
Rémond, René and Janine Bourdin, eds. *La France et les Français en 1938 et 1939*. Paris: Presses de la Fondation Nationale des Sciences Politiques, 1978.
Ribèyre, Charles. "Musique d'hier et de demain." *La revue musicale*, 15 March 1940.
Ritter, Naomi. *Art as Spectacle: Images of the Entertainer since Romanticism*. Columbia: University of Missouri Press, 1984.
Rivière, Jacques. Editor's introduction to *La nouvelle revue française* 70 (June 1919): 1–12..
———. "Le parti de l'intelligence." *La nouvelle revue française* 70 (Sept. 1919): 612–18.
Robert, Frédéric. "Louis Durey." *Cahiers Jean Cocteau* 9 (1981): 407–14.
Roberts, Mary Louise. *Civilization without Sexes: Reconstructing Gender in Postwar France, 1917–1927*. Chicago: University of Chicago Press, 1994.
Robinson, J. Bradford. "Jazz Reception in Weimar Germany: In Search of a Shimmy Figure." In *Music and Performance during the Weimar Republic*, 107–34. Edited by Bryan Gilliam. Cambridge: Cambridge University Press, 1994.
Roche-Pézard, Fanette. "Création artistique et idéologie politique: Futurisme et fascisme." *Cahiers d'histoire de l'art contemporaine*, May 1974: 4–11.
Roland-Manuel. *Ravel*. Paris: Editions de La Nouvelle Revue Critique, 1938.
Rosello, Mireille. *Declining the Stereotype: Ethnicity and Representation in French Culture*. Hanover, N.H.: University Press of New England, 1998.
Rosenstiel, Leonie. *Nadia Boulanger: A Life in Music*. New York: W. W. Norton, 1982.
Rosenthal, Manuel. *Jeanne d'Arc: Suite symphonique en 5 parties. Après le "Jeanne d'Arc" de Joseph Delteil*. Paris: Jean Jobert, 1936.
———. *Ravel: Souvenirs*. Paris: Hazan, 1995.

Roshwald, Aviel, and Richard Stites, eds. *European Culture in the Great War: The Arts, Entertainment, and Propaganda, 1914–1918*. New York: Cambridge University Press, 1999.
Roussel, Albert. *Lettres et écrits*. Edited by Nicole Labelle. Paris: Flammerion, 1987.
Roy, Jean. *Le Groupe des Six*. Paris: Seuil, 1994.
Sachs, Harvey. *Music in Fascist Italy*. New York: Norton, 1988.
Said, Edward. *Orientalism*. New York: Pantheon, 1978.
——. *The World, the Text, and the Critic*. Cambridge: Harvard University Press, 1983.
——. *Representations of the Intellectual*. New York: Pantheon, 1994.
Samazeuilh, Gustave. *Musiciens de mon temps: Chroniques et souvenirs*. Paris: Marcel Daubin, 1947.
Samuel, Claude, ed. *Olivier Messiaen: Conversations with Claude Samuel*. Portland, Ore.: Amadeus, 1994.
Sapiro, Gisele. "Duhamel, Georges." In *Dictionnaire des intellectuels français*, 400–401. Edited by Jacques Julliard and Michel Winock. Paris: Seuil, 1996.
——. *La guerre des écrivains: 1940–1953*. Paris: Fayard, 1999.
Saudinos, Dominique. *Manuel Rosenthal: Une vie*. Paris: Mercure de France, 1992.
Sauguet, Henri. *La musique, ma vie*. Paris: Séguier, 1990.
Schiller, Friedrich. *Briefwechsel zwischen Schiller und Korner*. Vol. 1. Stuttgart: Verlag der J. G. Cotta'schen Buchhandlung, 1892.
Schloesser, Stephen. "Mystic Realists: Sacramental Modernism in French Catholic Revival, 1918–1928." Ph.D. diss., Stanford University, 1998.
Schorske, Carl E. *Fin-de-Siècle Vienna: Politics and Culture*. New York: Alfred A. Knopf, 1980.
——. *Thinking with History: Explorations in the Passage to Modernism*. Princeton, N.J.: Princeton University Press, 1998.
Selva, Blanche. *Quelques mots sur la sonate*. Paris: Delaplane, 1914.
Senarclens, Pierre de. *Le mouvement "Esprit," 1932–1941*. Lausanne: Age d'Homme, 1974.
Serant, Paul. *Le romantisme fasciste, ou l'oeuvre politique de quelques écrivains français*. Paris: Fasquelle, 1959.
Shattuck, Roger. *The Innocent Eye: On Modern Literature and the Arts*. New York: Washington Square, 1986.
Sholl, Robert. "Tournemire, Messiaen, and the Culture of Modernity." Paper presented at the Messiaen International Conference, held at the University of Sheffield, England, 20–23 June 2002.
Silver, Kenneth. *Esprit de Corps: The Art of the Parisian Avant-Garde and the First World War, 1914–1925*. Princeton, N.J.: Princeton University Press, 1989.
Simeone, Nigel. "Offrandes Oubliées: Messiaen in the 1930s." *Musical Times*, no. 141 (2000): 33–41.
——. "Offrandes Oubliées II: Messiaen, Boulanger, and José Bruyr." *Musical Times*, no. 142 (2001): 17–22.
——. "The Science of Enchantment: Music at the 1937 Paris Exposition." *Musical Times*, (Spring 2002) 143: 9–17.
Simon, Yannick. "Les jeunesses musicales de France." In *La vie musicale sous Vichy*. Edited by Myriam Chimènes. Paris: Complexe, 2001.
Simon, Yves R. *The Road to Vichy, 1918–1938*. Translated by James A. Corbett and George J. Morrow. New York: Sheed and Ward, 1942.
Simonin, Anne. "Les nouvelles littéraires, artistiques et scientifiques." In *Dictionnaire des intellectuels français*, 843–44. Edited by Jacques Julliard and Michel Winock. Paris: Seuil, 1996.

Sirinelli, Jean-François, ed. *Histoire des droites en France*. Vol. 2, *Cultures*. Paris: Gallimard, 1992.
Sirinelli, Jean-François, and Eric Vigne. "Introduction: Des cultures politiques." In *Histoire des droites en France*, 2: 1–11. Edited by Jean-François Sirinelli.
Sordet, Dominique. *Maurice Ravel*. Paris: Tambourinaire, 1939.
———, ed. *L'initiation a la musique à l'usage des amateurs de radio*. Paris: Tambourinaire, 1935.
Soucy, Robert. "Barrès and French Fascism." *French Historical Studies* (1967) 1: 67–97.
———. *French Fascism: The Second Wave, 1933–1939*. New Haven, Conn.: Yale University Press, 1995.
———. "French Press Reactions to Hitler's First Two Years in Power." *Contemporary European History* 7.1 (1998): 21–38.
Spratt, Geoffrey. *The Music of Arthur Honegger*. Cork, Ireland: Cork University Press, 1987.
Sprout, Leslie A. "Music of the Révolution Française or the Révolution Nationale? Music and National Celebration in France, 1936–1944." *Repercussions* 5.1–2 (1996): 69–127.
———. "Music for a 'New Era': Composers and National Identity in France, 1936–1946." Ph.D. diss., University of California, Berkeley, 2000.
Stallybrass, Peter, and Allon White. *The Politics and Poetics of Transgression*. Ithaca, N.Y.: Cornell University Press, 1986.
Steegmuller, Francis. *Cocteau: A Biography*. Boston: Little, Brown, 1970.
Sternhell, Zeev. *Ni droite ni gauche: L'idéologie fasciste en France*. Paris: Seuil, 1983.
———. *Neither Right nor Left; Fascist Ideology in France*. Translated by David Marsel. Berkeley: University of California Press, 1986.
Stevenson, Robert Louis. *Across the Plains*. New York: Charles Scribner Sons, 1895.
Strauss, David. *Menace in the West: The Rise of French Anti-Americanism in Modern Times*. Westport, Conn.: Greenwood, 1978.
Stravinsky, Igor. *An Autobiography*. New York: Norton, 1962.
Stuckenschmidt, H. H. *Maurice Ravel*. Translated by Samuel R. Rosenbaum. Philadelphia: Chiton, 1968.
Suleiman, Susan. *Authoritarian Fictions: The Ideological Novel as a Literary Genre*. New York: Columbia University Press, 1983.
———. *Subversive Intent: Gender, Politics, and the Avant-Garde*. Cambridge: Harvard University Press, 1990.
Sweeney, Regina. *Singing Our Way to Victory: French Cultural Politics and Music during the Great War*. Middletown, Conn.: Wesleyan University Press, 2001.
Tailleferre, Germaine. "Mémoires à l'emporte-pièce." Edited by Frédéric Robert. *Revue internationale de musique française* 19 (Feb. 1986): 7–82.
Tannenbaum, Edward R. *The Action Française: Die-Hard Reactionaries in Twentieth-Century France*. New York: John Wiley and Sons, 1962.
Taruskin, Richard. "The Dark Side of Modern Music." *New Republic*, 5 Sept. 1988: 28–34.
———. "Back to Whom? Neoclassicism as Ideology." *Nineteenth-Century Music* 16.3 (1993): 286–302.
———. *Stravinsky and the Russian Traditions*. Berkeley: University of California Press, 1996.
Templier, Pierre-Daniel. *Erik Satie*. Paris: Rieder, 1932. Translated by David S. French. Cambridge: MIT Press, 1969.
Tiersot, Julien. *Un demi-siècle de musique française, 1870–1919*. Paris: Félix Alcan, 1924.
Toews, John E. "Intellectual History after the Linguistic Turn: The Autonomy of Meaning and the Irreducibility of Experience." *American Historical Review* 92.4 (1987): 879–907.

Tournès, Ludovic. *New Orleans-sur-Seine: Histoire du jazz en France*. Paris: Fayard, 1999.
———. "Le jazz: Un espace de liberté pour un phénomène culturel en voie d'identification." In *La vie musicale sous Vichy*, 313–32. Edited by Myriam Chimènes. Brussels: Complexe, 2001.
Tudesq, André-Jean. "Utilisation gouvernementale de la radio." In *Edouard Daladier: Chef du gouvernement*, 255–64. Edited by René Rémond and Janine Bourdin. Paris: Presses de la Fondation des Sciences Politiques, 1977.
Turner, Victor. *The Anthropology of Performance*. New York: PAJ, 1986.
Vallas, Léon. *Claude Debussy et son temps*. Paris: Felix Alcan, 1932.
———. *Vincent d'Indy*. 2 vols. Paris: Albin Michel, 1950.
Veley Vallantin, Catherine. "Le Congrès internationale de folklore de 1937." *Annales: Histoire, sciences sociales* 5.2 (1999): 481–506.
Volta, Ornella. *Erik Satie*. Paris: Seghers, 1979.
———. *L'ymagier d'Erik Satie*. Paris: Francis de Velde, 1979.
———. "Le rideau se lève sur un os." *Revue internationale de musique française* 23 (June 1987): 7–98.
Vuillermoz, Emile. *Claude Debussy*. Paris: Heugel, 1920.
———. *Musiques d'aujourd'hui*. Paris: G. Crès, 1923.
———. "Le goût moderne et la musique du passé." *Atti del Terzo Congresso Internationale di Musica*. Florence, April 1938: 21–25.
Watkins, Glen. *Soundings: Music in the Twentieth Century*. New York: Schirmer, 1988.
———. *Pyramids at the Louvre: Music, Culture, and Collage from Stravinsky to the Postmodernists*. Cambridge: Belknap Press of Harvard University, 1994.
———. *Proof through the Night: Music and the Great War*. Berkeley: University of California Press, 2002.
Weber, Eugen. *Action Française: Royalism and Reaction in Twentieth-Century France*. Stanford, Calif.: Stanford University Press, 1962.
———. *The Hollow Years: France in the 1930s*. New York: W. W. Norton, 1994.
White, Eric Walter. *Stravinsky: The Composer and His World*. Berkeley: University of California Press, 1966.
Whiting, Steven. *Satie the Bohemian: From Cabaret to Concert Hall*. New York: Oxford University Press, 1999.
Widor, Charles-Marie. *Fondations: Portraits de Massenet à Paladilhe*. Paris: Durand et Fils, 1927.
Wiecki, Ronald, V. "A Chronicle of the Pro Musica in the United States with a Biographical Sketch of Its Founder, E. Robert Schmitz." Ph.D. diss., University of Wisconsin, Madison, 1992.
Wiéner, Jean. *Allegro appassionato*. Paris: Pierre Belfond, 1978.
Willett, John. *Art and Politics in the Weimar Period: The New Sobriety, 1917–1933*. New York: Pantheon, 1978.
Williams, Christopher. "Of Canons and Context: Toward a Historiography of Twentieth-Century Music." *Repercussions* 2.1 (1993): 31–74.
Winock, Michel. *Histoire politique de la revue "Esprit," 1930–1950*. Paris: Seuil, 1975.
———. *Nationalisme, antisémitisme et fascisme en France*. Paris: Seuil, 1990.
———. *Le siècle des intellectuels*. Paris: Seuil, 1997.
Winter, Jay. *Sites of Memory, Sites of Mourning: The Great War in European Cultural History*. Cambridge: Cambridge University Press, 1995.
Wohl, Robert. *French Communism in the Making*. Stanford: Stanford University Press, 1966.
———. *The Generation of 1914*. Cambridge: Harvard University Press, 1970.

———. "The Generation of 1914 and Modernism." In *Modernism: Challenges and Perspectives*, 66–78. Edited by Monique Chefdor, Ricardo Quiñones, and Albert Wachtel. Urbana: University of Illinois Press, 1986.

———. "French Fascism, Both Right and Left: Reflections on the Sternhell Controversy." *Journal of Modern History* 63 (1991): 91–98.

———. *A Passion for Wings: Aviation and the Western Imagination, 1908–1918*. New Haven, Conn.: Yale University Press, 1994.

———. "Heart of Darkness: Modernism and Its Historians." *Journal of Modern History* 74 (2002): 573–62.

Woldu, Gail Hilson. "Gabriel Fauré as Director of the Conservatoire National de Musique et de Déclamation, 1905–1920." Ph.D. diss., Yale University, 1983.

———. "Debussy, Fauré, and d'Indy and Conceptions of the Artist: The Institutions, the Dialogues, the Conflicts." In *Debussy and His World*, 236–38. Edited by Jane F. Fulcher. Princeton, N.J.: Princeton University Press, 2001.

Wood, Marc. "Louis Durey: Homme de Tête." *Musical Times*, no. 1873 (Winter, 2000) 141: 42–46.

———. "Henri Sauguet: Springing Surprises." *Musical Times*, no.1874 (Spring 2001) 142: 23–27.

Wright, Gordon. *France in Modern Times*. New York: Rand McNally, 1974.

Zay, Jean. "Claude Debussy." *La revue musicale*, April–May 1938: 241–43.

———. *Souvenirs et solitude*. Paris: Talus d'Approche, 1987.

MANUSCRIPT AND ARCHIVAL SOURCES

Charpentier, Gustave. "Souvenirs, lettres, poésies." Bibliothèque Nationale de France. Musique. Reserve.

Debussy, Claude. "Agenda et carnet de notes, 1916–1917." Bibliothèque Nationale de France. Musique. Reserve.

Fonds Montpensier. Bibliothèque Nationale de France. Musique. Reserve.

Fonds Rouché. Bibliothèque de l'Opéra.

"La grève à l'Opéra: Dossier de presse." Bibliothèque de l'Arsenal, Paris. R0965.

Lettres autographes à Nadia Boulanger. Bibliothèque Nationale de France. Musique. N.L.A. 60.

"Lettres autographes: Fonds Nadia Boulanger." Bibliothèque Nationale de France. Musique.

Milhaud, Darius. "Albéric Magnard." Lecture given at the Ecole des Hautes Etudes Sociales, 5 Jan. 1917. Bibliothèque Nationale de France. Musique. Reserve.

———. "Paris et notre Pierre Lunaire." *Musikblatter des Anbruch*, Feb. 1922. Preserved in Bibliothèque Nationale de France. Musique. Fonds Montpensier, liasse Schoenberg.

Ravel, Maurice. "Ma vie et ma musique: Esquisse autobiographique." Bibliothèque Nationale de France. Musique. Reserve.

Ropartz, Guy. Collected Articles. Bibliothèque Nationale de France. Musique. Reserve.

Satie, Erik. "Chronique musicale." Bibliothèque Nationale de France. Musique. Manuscripts.

Satie, Erik. Dossier. 17 pieces. Bibliothèque Nationale de France. Musique. Reserve.

Satie, Erik. "Esquisses pour *Socrate*." Bibliothèque Nationale de France. Musique. Manuscripts.

Satie, Erik. "*Parade*: Esquisses autographes." Bibliothèque Nationale de France. Musique. Manuscripts.

Schmitt, Florent. Collected Articles. Bibliothèque Nationale de France. Musique. Reserve.

ARCHIVAL SERIES CONSULTED

AJ[13] Opéra. Archives of the Paris Opera. Archives Nationales.
F[21] Beaux-Arts. Paris: Archives Nationales.
F[7] Police Archives. Paris: Archives Nationales.

For Further Reference

Abel, Richard. *French Film Theory and Criticism, 1907–1939.* 2 vols. Princeton, N.J.: Princeton University Press, 1988.
Adamson, Walter L. *Hegemony and Revolution: A Study of Antonio Gramsci's Political and Cultural Theory.* Berkeley: University of California Press, 1980.
———. *Avant-Garde Florence: From Modernism to Fascism.* Cambridge: Harvard University Press, 1993.
Ades, Dawn. *Dada and Surrealism.* London: Thames and Hudson, 1974.
Adorno, Theodor. *Aesthetic Theory.* Translated by C. Lenhardt. London and New York: Routledge and Kegan Paul, 1994.
Adorno, Theodor, and Max Horkheimer. "The Culture Industry: Enlightenment as Mass Deception." In *Dialectic of Enlightenment*, 120–67. Translated by John Cummings. New York: Continuum, 1982.
Agulhon, Maurice. "Politics and Images in Post-Revolutionary France." In *Rites of Power: Symbolism, Ritual, and Politics since the Middle Ages*, 177–205. Edited by Sean Wilentz. Philadelphia: University of Pennsylvania Press, 1985.
———. *Les métamorphoses de Marianne: L'imagerie et la symbolique républicaines de 1914 à nos jours.* Paris: Flammarion, 2001.
Albertin, Pierre. *L'école en France, XIXe–XXème siècles.* Paris: Hachette, 1992.
Alexander, Jeffrey C., and Steven Seidman. *Culture and Society: Contemporary Debates.* Cambridge: Cambridge University Press, 1990.
Alexandrian, Sarane. *Surrealist Art.* Translated by Gordon Clough. London: Thames and Hudson, 1970.
Allen, Judith S. "Tonal Allusion and Illusion: Debussy's Sonata for Flute, Viola, and Harp." *Cahiers Debussy* 7 (1983): 38–48.
Amato, Joseph. *Mounier and Maritain: A French Catholic Understanding of the Modern World.* Montgomery: University of Alabama Press, 1975.
Andraschke, Peter. "Darius Milhaud's 'Opéra-Minutes.'" In *Geschichte und Dramaturgie des Operneinakters*, 337–45. Edited by Winfried Kirsch and Sieghart Döhring. Bern: Laaber-Verlag, 1991.
Andrieux, Georges. *Catalogue de vente de livres, manuscrits, documents et lettres autographes: Collection Jules Huret et collection Claude Debussy.* Aberville: F. Paillart, 1933.
Antliff, Mark. *Inventing Bergson: Cultural Politics and the Parisian Avant-Garde.* Princeton, N.J.: Princeton University Press, 1993.
———. "The Jew as Anti-artist: Georges Sorel, Anti-Semitism, and the Aesthetics of Class Consciousness." *Oxford Art Journal* 20.1 (1997): 50–67.
———. "The Fourth Dimension and Futurism: A Politicized Space." *Art Bulletin* 82.4 (2000): 720–33.
Aronowitz, Stanley. *The Politics of Identity: Class, Culture, Social Movements.* New York: Routledge, 1992.

Atkin, Nicholas, and Frank Tellatt, eds. *Religion, Society, and Politics in France since 1789.* London: Hambeldon, 1991.
Audoin, Philippe. *Les surréalistes.* Paris: Seuil, 1995.
Audoin-Rouzeau, Stéphane, and Annette Becker. *14–18, retrouver la guerre.* Paris: Gallimard, 2000.
Axsom, Richard H. *Parade: Cubism as Theater.* New York: Garland, 1979.
Azéma, Jean-Pierre. *De Munich à la Libération.* Paris: Seuil, 1979.
Azéma, Jean-Pierre, and Michel Winock. *La IIIe République.* Paris: Calmann-Lévy, 1970.
Badie, Bertrand, and Pierre Birnbaum. *Sociologie de l'Etat.* Paris: Bernard Grasset, 1978.
Bakhtin, Mikhail. *Marxisme et la philosophie du langage.* Paris: Minuit, 1977.
———. *The Dialectic Imagination.* Translated by Caryl Emerson and Michael Holquist. Edited by Michael Holquist. Austin: University of Texas Press, 1981.
Balandier, Georges. *Anthropologie politique.* Paris: Presses Universitaires de France, 1967.
Bancroft, David. "Stravinsky and the NRF (1910–20)." *Music and Letters* 53 (1972): 274–83, and 55 (1974): 261–71.
Barbusse, Henri, et al., eds. *Ceux qui ont choisi: Contre le fascisme en Allemagne, contre l'impérialisme français.* Paris: A.E.A.R., 1933.
Barrett, Linda M. "Introduction to the Life and Works of Germaine Tailleferre." Master's thesis, University of Kentucky, 1981.
Barrot, Olivier, and Pascal Ory. *Entre-deux-guerres, la création française (1919–1939).* Paris: François Bourrin, 1990.
Barthes, Roland. *Le bruissement de la langue.* Paris: Seuil, 1968.
Bartov, Omar. "Martyrs' Vengence: Memory, Trauma, and Fear of War in France, 1918–1940." *Historical Reflections* 22 (1996): 47–76.
Bataille, Georges. *Visions of Excess: Selected Writings, 1927–1939,* ed. by Allan Stoekl. Translated by Allan Stoekl, Carl Lovitt, and Donald Leslie Jr. Minneapolis: University of Minnesota Press, 1985.
———. *The College of Sociology, 1937–39,* ed. by Dennis Hollier. Translated by Betsy Wing. Minneapolis: University of Minnesota Press, 1988.
Becker, Annette. *La guerre et la foi: De la mort à la mémoire, 1914–1930.* Paris: Armand Colin, 1994.
Becker, Jean-Jacques. *Les Français dans la Grande guerre.* Paris: Robert Laffont, 1980.
———, ed. *Guerre et cultures, 1914–1918.* Paris: A. Colin, 1994.
Bell, Clara H. *Olivier Messiaen.* Boston: G. K. Hall, 1984.
Bellaigue, Camille. *Souvenirs de musique et de musiciens.* Paris: Nouvelle Librairie Nationale, 1921.
———. *Gabriel Fauré.* Paris: Plon, 1925.
Belot, Robert. *Lucien Rebatet: Un itinéraire fasciste.* Paris: Seuil, 1994.
Ben-Amos, Avner. The Uses of the Past: Patriotism between History and Memory." In *Patriotism in the Lives of Individuals and Nations,* 120–47. Edited by Daniel Bar-Tal and Ervin Staub. Chicago: Nelson-Hall, 1997.
Benoist, Luc. *Signes, symboles et mythes.* Paris: Presses Universitaires de France, 1975.
Berghaus, Gunther. *Fascism and Theater: Comparative Studies on the Aesthetics and Politics of Performance in Europe (1925–1945).* Providence, R.I.: Berghaln, 1996.
Berman, Russel A. *Modern Culture and Critical Theory: Art, Politics, and the Legacy of the Frankfurt School.* Madison: University of Wisconsin Press, 1989.
———. *Cultural Studies of Modern Germany: History, Representation, and Nationhood.* Madison: University of Wisconsin Press, 1993.
Bernac, Pierre. *Francis Poulenc et ses mélodies.* Paris: Buchet-Chastel, 1978.

Bernard, Robert. "Editorial." *La revue musicale* Aug.–Nov. 1939: 74–78.
———. *Albert Roussel.* Paris: La Colombe, 1948.
Berstein, Serge. *Edouard Herriot, ou la République en personne.* Paris: F.N.S.P., 1985.
———. *Histoire du Parti radical.* F.N.S.P., 1980.
Berstein, Serge, and Pierre Milza. *Histoire de la France au XXe siècle.* Brussels: Complexe, 1994.
Beshier, Jean-Michel. *La politique de l'impossible: L'intellectuel entre révolte et engagement.* Paris: Découverte, 1989.
Birnbaum, Pierre. *La logique de l'Etat.* Paris: Fayard, 1982.
———. *Un mythe politique: "La République juive."* Paris: Fayard, 1988.
———. *Les fous de la République: Histoire des Juifs d'Etat de Gambetta à Vichy.* Paris: Fayard, 1992.
Blanche, Jacques-Emile. *Les arts plastiques.* Paris: Editions de France, 1931.
Bloch, Jean-Richard. *Destin du siècle.* Edited by Michel Trebitsch. Paris: Presses Universitaires de France, 1996.
Bloch, Marc. *Strange Defeat: A Statement of Evidence Written in 1940.* Translated by Gerard Hopkins. New York: Norton, 1968 [1946].
Bloom, Harold. *The Anxiety of Influence.* New York: Oxford University Press, 1973.
———. *A Map of Misreading.* Oxford: Oxford University Press, 1975.
Blum, Léon. *For All Mankind.* Translated by W. Pickles. New York, 1946.
Bodin, Louis. *Les intellectuels.* Paris: Presses Universitaires de France, 1964.
Boivin, Jean. *La classe de Messiaen.* Paris: C. Bourgeois, 1995.
Bonnet, Jean–Claude, and Philippe Roger, eds. *La légende de la Révolution au XXe siècle.* Paris: Flammarion, 1988.
Boschot, Adolphe. *La vie et les oeuvres d'Alfred Bruneau.* Paris: Fasquelle, 1937.
Boswell-Kurc, Lilise. "Olivier Messiaen's Religious War-Time Works and Their Controversial Reception in France (1941–1946)." Ph.D. diss., New York University, 2001.
Bourdieu, Pierre. "Champ intellectuel et projet créateur." *Les temps modernes* 22.246 (1966): 865–906.
———. "Champ du pouvoir, champ intellectuel, et habitus de classe." *Scolies* 1 (1971): 7–26.
———. "Le Champ littéraire." *Actes de la recherche en sciences sociales* 89 (Sept. 1991): 3–46.
———. *Les règles de l'art: Genèse et structure du champ littéraire.* Paris: Seuil, 1992.
Bourdieu, Pierre, Roger Chartier, and Robert Darnton. "Dialogue à propos de l'histoire culturelle." *Actes de la recherche en sciences sociales* 59 (Sept. 1985): 86–93.
Bouvier, Nicolas, Gordon A. Craig, and Lionel Gossman, eds. *Geneva, Zurich, Basel: History, Culture, and National Identity.* Princeton, N.J.: Princeton University Press, 1994.
Brasillach, Robert. *Notre avant-guerre.* Paris: Plon, 1941.
Breton, André. *Entretiens.* Paris: Gallimard, 1969.
———. *Manifestoes of Surrealism.* Translated by Richard Seaver and Helen R. Lane. Ann Arbor: University of Michigan Press, 1969.
Britt, David, ed. *Art and Power: Europe under the Dictators, 1930–1945.* London: Thames and Hudson, 1995.
Broad, Stephen. "Messiaen: Recontextualizing His Early Career." Ph.D. diss. in progress, Oxford University.
Brody, Elaine. *Paris: The Musical Kaleidoscope, 1870–1925.* New York: George Braziller, 1987.

Brombert, Victor. *The Intellectual Hero: Studies in the French Novel, 1880–1955*. New York: J. B. Lippincott, 1960.

Brooks, Jeanice. "Nadia Boulanger and the Salon of the Princesse de Polignac." *Journal of the American Musicological Society* 46.3 (1993): 415–68.

Brown, Frederick. *An Impersonation of Angels: A Biography of Jean Cocteau*. New York: Viking, 1968.

Bruhn, Siglind. "Religious Symbolism in the Music of Olivier Messiaen." *American Journal of Semiotics* 13.1–4 (1996): 277–304.

———. *Images and Ideas in Modern French Piano Music: The Extra-Musical Subtext in Piano Works by Ravel, Debussy, and Messiaen*. New York: Pendragon, 1997.

———. *Messiaen's Language of Mystical Love*. New York: Garland, 1998.

Bruneau, Alfred. "Allocution." *La musique pendant la guerre* 8 (July–Aug. 1916): 99–101.

Buchanan, Tom. *Political Catholicism in Europe, 1918–1965*. Oxford, U.K.: Clarendon, 1996.

Buckland, Sidney, ed. *Francis Poulenc: Selected Correspondence, 1915–1953*. London: V. Gollancz, 1991.

Buckle, Richard. *Diaghilev*. New York: Atheneum, 1979.

Bullivant, Keith, ed. *Culture and Society in the Weimar Republic*. Manchester, U.K.: Manchester University Press, 1977.

Burger, Peter. *Theory of the Avant-Garde*. Translated by Michael Shaw. Minneapolis: University of Minnesota Press, 1984.

Burnett, James. *Ravel: His Life and Times*. New York: Midas/Hippocrene, 1983.

Calhoun, Craig. "Nationalism and Civil Society: Democracy, Diversity, and Self-Determination." In *Social Theory and the Politics of Identity*, 304–35. Edited by Craig Calhoun. Oxford, U.K.: Blackwell, 1994.

Canteloube, Joseph. *Vincent d'Indy*. Paris: Henri Laurens, 1951.

Carraud, Gaston. "Pour la musique française." *Le courrier musical* 20 (June 1918): 217–22.

Casadesus, Francis. "Nos festivals." *La musique pendant la guerre* 7 (April–May 1916): 99–101.

Caute, David. *Communism and the French Intellectuals, 1914–1960*. London: A. Deutsch, 1964.

Chadwick, Whitney. *Women Artists and the Surrealist Movement*. Boston: Little, Brown, 1985.

Chalupt, René. *Ravel au miroir de ses lettres*. Paris: Robert Laffont, 1956.

Charle, Christophe. *La République des universitaires, 1870–1940*. Paris: Seuil, 1994.

———. *La crise des sociétés impériales: Allemagne, France, Grande-Bretagne, 1900–1940*. Paris: Seuil, 2001.

Charpentier, Raymond. "Les grands concerts: A propos de la *Ballade* pour piano et orchestre de Mme Germaine Tailleferre." *Comoedia*, 27 May 1923.

Charpentreau, Jacques, and Louis Rocher. *L'esthétique personnaliste d'Emmanuel Mounier*. Paris: Ouvrières, 1966.

Chartier, Roger. *Cultural History: Between Practices and Representations*. Translated by Lydia G. Cochrane. Ithaca, N.Y.: Cornell University Press, 1988.

———. "Le monde comme représentation." *Annales: Economies, sociétés, civilisations* vol. 44, no. 6 (Nov.–Dec. 1989): 1505–20.

Chassain-Dolliou, Laetitia. "Les artisans d'un humanisme musical au Conservatoire de Marcel Beaufils à André Jolivet." In *Sillages musicologiques: Hommage à Yves Gérard*, 247–56. Edited by Raphaella Legrand. Paris: Conservatoire National Supérieur de Musique, 1997.

Chevrefils Desbiolles, Yves. *Les revues d'art à Paris, 1905–1940.* Paris: Entre Vues, 1993.
Chimènes, Myriam. "La musique dans les salons de la belle époque aux années cinquante." In *Musique et musiciens au Faubourg Saint-Germain,* 88–101. Edited by Jean Gallois. Paris: Délégation à l'Action Artistique de la Ville de Paris, 1990.
Clark, Priscilla Parkhurst. *Literary France: The Making of a Culture.* Berkeley: University of California Press, 1987.
Claudel, Paul. *Claudel-Gide Correspondance, 1899–1926.* Edited by R. Mallet. Paris: Gallimard, 1949.
Coeuroy, André. *Appels d'Orphée.* Paris: Editions de la Nouvelle Revue Critique, 1926.
Cogniat, G. "Le politique scolaire et culturel du gouvernement Blum vu par un parlementaire de l'époque." *Nouvelle revue socialiste,* no. 10–11 (1975): 94–99.
Colin, Mariella, ed. *Polémiques et dialogues: Les échanges culturelles entre la France et l'Italie de 1880 à 1918.* Caen: Centre de Recherches en Langues, Littératures et Civilisations du Monde Ibérique et de l'Italie, 1988.
Colin, Pierre, ed. *Intellectuels, chrétiens et esprit des années 20.* Paris: Cerf, 1997.
Collier, Peter, and Edward Timms, eds. *Visions and Blueprints: Avant-Garde Culture and Radical Politics in Early Twentieth-Century Europe.* New York: St. Martin's, 1988.
Collini, Stefan. *Public Moralists: Political Thought and Intellectuals in Britain, 1850–1930.* Oxford, U.K.: Clarendon, 1991.
Colloquium Klassizitat, Klassizismus, Klassic in der Musik, 1920–1950. Edited by Wolfgang Osthoff and Reinhard Wiesend. Wurzburger Musikhistorische Beitrage, Vol. 10. Tutzing: Hans Schneider Verlag, 1988.
Colton, Joel. *Léon Blum: Humanist in Politics.* New York: Knopf, 1966.
Compagnon, Antoine. *La Troisième République des lettres: De Flaubert à Proust.* Paris: Seuil, 1983.
Conrad, Bridget. "The Sources of Jolivet's Musical Language and His Relationships with Varèse and Messiaen." Ph.D. diss., City University of New York, 1994.
Cooper, Martin. *Opéra-Comique.* London: M. Parish, 1949.
Cork, Richard. *A Bitter Truth: Avant-Garde Art and the Great War.* New Haven, Conn.: Yale University Press, 1994.
Coutrot, Aline. *Un courant de la pensée catholique: L'hebdomadaire "Sept" (mars 1934–août 1937).* Paris: Cerf, 1961.
———. *Un journal de combat: "Sept."* Paris: Cana, 1982.
Cowling, Elizabeth, and Jennifer Mandy. *On Classic Ground: Picasso, Léger, de Chirico, and the New Classicism, 1910–30.* New York: New Museum of Contemporary Art, 1984.
Cru, J. Norton. *Témoins: Essai d'analyse et de critique des souvenirs de combattants édités en français de 1915 à 1928.* Paris: Etincelles, 1929.
Dandelot, A. *La Société des Concerts du Conservatoire (1828–1923).* Paris: Delagrave, 1923.
Darnton, Robert. "The Symbolic Element in History." *Journal of Modern History* (1986) 58: 218–34.
Daudet, Léon. "Emile Zola, ou le romantisme de l'égout." *Revue universelle,* 1920: 513–41.
Davidian, Teresa. "Debussy's Sonata Forms." Ph.D. diss., University of Chicago, 1988.
———. "Debussy, d'Indy, and the Société Nationale." *Journal of Musicological Research,* 1991: 285–301.
Dean, Basil. *Albert Roussel.* London: Barrie and Rockleff, 1961.
Debray, Regis. *Teachers, Writers, Celebrities: The Intellectuals of Modern France.* Translated by David Macey. London: New Left, 1981.
Debussy, Claude. *Monsieur Croche anti-dilettante.* Paris: Gallimard, 1926.

Decaunes, Luc, and M. L. Cavalier. *Réformes et projets de réformes de l'enseignement français de la Révolution à nos jours*. Paris: Institut Pédagogique National, 1962.
Demuth, Norman. *Albert Roussel*. London: United Music Publishers, 1947.
———. *Ravel*. London: Dent, 1947.
———. *Vincent d'Indy, 1851–1931: A Champion of Classicism*. London: Rockliff, 1951.
Depa, Daria. "Wagner and Musikpolitik in the Weimar Republic: Re-appropriations and Re-evaluations." Ph.D. diss., Indiana University, 2001.
Deuxième Congrès International d'Esthétique et Science de l'Art: Paris 1937. Vol. 2, Livre 6 : *L'art contemporain, 1: Humanisme au formalisme*. Paris: Félix Alcan, 1937.
Digeon, Claude. *La crise allemande de la pensée française*. Paris: Presses Universitaires de France, 1959.
Dillaz, Serge. *La chanson sous la IIIe République*. Paris: Talandier, 1991.
d'Indy, Jacques. *Visage inconnu de Vincent d'Indy*. Marseille: Fondation Paul Richard, n.d.
d'Indy, Vincent. *Emmanuel Chabrier et Paul Dukas*. Paris: Heugel, 1920.
———. *La Schola Cantorum en 1925*. Paris: Bloud et Gay, 1927.
Dolgin, Janet L., David S. Kemnitzer, and Daniel M. Schneider, eds. *Symbolic Anthropology: A Reader in the Study of Symbols and Meanings*. New York: Columbia University Press, 1977.
Douglas, Allen. *From Fascism to Libertarian Communism: Georges Valois against the Third Republic*. Berkeley: University of California Press, 1992.
———. *War, Memory, and the Politics of Humor: The "Canard Enchaîné" and World War I*. Berkeley: University of California Press, 2002.
Douglass, Mary. *How Institutions Think*. Syracuse, N.Y.: Syracuse University Press, 1986.
Dubief, Henri. *Le déclin de la Troisième République (1929–1938)*. Paris: Seuil, 1976.
Dufourq, Norbet. *La musique française*. Paris: A. et J. Picard, 1970.
Dufourt, Hugues, and Joël-Marie Fauquet, eds. *La musique et le pouvoir*. Paris: Aux Amateurs de Livres, 1987.
———. *La musique: Du théorique au politique*. Paris: Aux Amateurs de Livres, 1991.
Dukas, Paul. *Correspondance de Paul Dukas sur la musique*. Paris: Durand, 1971.
———. *Chroniques musicales sur deux siècles*. Paris: Stock, 1979.
Dumesnil, René. *Portraits de musiciens français*. Paris: Plon, 1938.
———. "Revue de la quinzaine." *Mercure de France*, no. 953 (1 March 1938): 408–9.
———. *La musique contemporaine en France*. 2 vols. Paris: Armand Colin, 1949.
———.*La première moitié du vingtième siècle*. Vol. 5 of *Histoire de la musique: Des origines à nos jours*. Edited by Jules Combarieu and René Dumesnil. Paris: Armand Colin, 1960.
Dupuis, René, and Alexandre Marc. *Jeune Europe*. Paris: Plon, 1933.
Edelman, Murray. *From Art to Politics: How Artistic Creations Shape Political Conceptions*. Chicago: University of Chicago Press, 1995.
Emerson, Caryl, and Gary Morson. *Mikhail Bakhtin: Creation of a Prosaics*. Stanford, Calif.: Stanford University Press, 1990.
Evans, Martha. *Masks of Tradition: Women and the Politics of Writing in Twentieth-Century France*. Ithaca, N.Y.: Cornell University Press, 1988.
Fauquet, Joël-Marie. *César Franck*. Paris: Fayard, 1999.
Faure, Christian. *Le projet culturel de Vichy: Folklore et Révolution nationale, 1940–1944*. Lyon: Presses Universitaires de Lyon, 1989.
Fauré, Gabriel. "Appel aux musiciens français." *Le courrier musical* 19 (15 March 1917): 133.
———. *Lettres intimes*. Edited by Philippe Fauré-Fremiet. Paris: Colombe, 1951.
———. *Correspondance*. Edited by Jean-Michel Nectoux. Paris: Flammarion, 1980.

Faure, Michel. *Musique et société du Second Empire aux années vingt.* Paris: Flammarion, 1985.
Fernandez, James. "The Mission of Metaphor in Expressive Culture." *Current Anthropology* 15.2 (1974): 119–45.
Ferro, Marc. *The Great War, 1914–1918.* London: Routledge, 1973.
Feschotte, Jacques. *Arthur Honegger: L'homme et son oeuvre.* Paris: Seghers, 1966.
Field, Frank. *Three French Writers and the Great War: Studies in the Rise of Communism and Fascism.* Cambridge: Cambridge University Press, 1975.
Fish, Stanley. *Is There a Text in This Class? The Authority of Interpretive Communities.* Cambridge: Harvard University Press, 1980.
Fisher, David James. "The Origins of French Popular Theater." *Journal of Contemporary History* 12 (1977): 461–97.
Flower, J. E. *Writers and Politics in Modern France, 1909–1961.* London: Hodder and Stoughton, 1977.
———. *Literature and the Left in France: Society, Politics, and the Novel since the Late Nineteenth Century.* Totowa, N.J.: Barnes and Noble, 1983.
Foucault, Michel. *L'ordre du discours.* Paris: Gallimard, 1971.
———. *Language, Counter-Memory, Practice.* Edited and translated by Donald Bouchard. Ithaca, N.Y.: Cornell University Press, 1977.
Franklin, A. David. "A Preliminary Study of the Acceptance of Jazz by French Music Critics in the 1920s and Early 1930s." *Annual Review of Jazz Studies* 4 (1988): 1–8.
Fridenson, Patrick, ed. *The French Home Front, 1914–1918.* Providence, R.I.: Berg, 1992.
Fulcher, Jane. "Style musical et enjeux politiques en France à la veille de la Seconde Guerre mondiale." *Actes de la recherche en sciences sociales* 110 (Dec. 1995): 22–35.
———. "Trajectoires opposées: La culture musicale à Paris et Berlin pendant l'entre-deux-guerres." In *Capitales culturelles, capitales symboliques (XVe–XVe siècles): Paris et les expériences européennes,* 421–34. Edited by Christophe Charle. Paris: Publications de la Sorbonne, 2002.
Fussell, Paul. *The Great War and Modern Memory.* New York: Oxford University Press, 1975.
Garafola, Lynn. *Diaghilev's Ballets Russes.* New York: Oxford University Press, 1989.
Gay, Peter. *Weimar Culture: The Outsider as Insider.* New York: Harper and Row, 1968.
Geertz, Clifford. *The Interpretation of Cultures.* New York: Basic Books, 1973.
———. "Art as a Cultural System." *Modern Language Notes* 91 (1976): 1473–99.
Gellner, Ernest. *Nations and Nationalism.* Oxford: Oxford University Press, 1983.
Gendron, Bernard. "Jamming at Le Boeuf: Jazz and the Paris Avant-Garde." *Discourse* 12.1 (1989–1990): 3–27.
———. *Between Montmartre and the Mudd Club: Popular Music and the Avant-Garde.* Chicago: University of Chicago Press, 2001.
George, Waldemar. *L'humanisme et l'idée de la patrie.* Paris: Charpentier, 1936.
Georges-Michel, Michel. *Les ballets russes de Serge Diaghilew[sic].* Paris: Galerie Billiet, 1930.
Gérard, Yves, and Anne Bongrain, eds. *Le Conservatoire de Paris: Des Menus-Plaisirs à la Cité de la Musique, 1795–1995.* Paris: Buchet et Chastel, 1996.
Gérôme, Noëlle, and Danielle Tartakowsky. *La Fête de l'Humanité: Culture communiste, culture populaire.* Paris: Messidor, 1988.
Gide, André. *Littérature engagée.* Paris: Gallimard, 1950.
Gillian, Garth. *From Sign to Symbol.* New York: Harvester, 1982.
Gillis, John, ed. *Commemorations: The Politics of National Identity.* Princeton, N.J.: Princeton University Press, 1994.

Goguel, François. *La politique des partis sous la IIIe République*. Paris: Seuil, 1946.
Gold, Arthur, and Robert Fizdale. *Misia: The Life of Misia Sert*. New York: Alfred A. Knopf, 1980.
Golson, Richard J., ed. *Fascism, Aesthetics, and Culture*. Hanover, N.H.: University Press of New England, 1992.
Goubault, Christian. *Claude Debussy*. Paris: H. Champion, 1996.
Gramsci, Antonio. *The Prison Notebooks: Selections*. Translated by Quintin Hoare and Geoffrey Nowell-Smith. New York: International, 1971.
Green, Martin, and John Swan. *The Triumph of Pierrot: The Commedia dell'Arte and the Modern Imagination*. University Park: Pennsylvania State University Press, 1993.
Greenfield, Lilah. *Nationalism: Five Roads to Modernity*. Cambridge: Harvard University Press, 1992.
Green–Le Flem, Jeanne. "Paul Le Flem." *Revue internationale de musique française* 26 (June 1988): 115–24.
Griffin, Roger. *The Nature of Fascism*. London: Routledge, 1994.
Griffiths, Paul. *A Concise History of Modern Music from Debussy to Boulez*. London: Thames and Hudson, 1978.
Guiral, Pierre. *La société française 1914–1970 à travers la littérature*. Paris: Armand Colin, 1972.
Hahn, Reynaldo. *Journal d'un musicien*. Paris: Plan et Nourrit, 1933.
———. *Thèmes variés*. Paris: J. B. Janin, 1946.
Halbwachs, Maurice. *On Collective Memory*. Edited and translated by Lewis A. Coser. Chicago: University of Chicago Press, 1992.
Haley, Christopher. *Franz Schreker, 1878–1934: A Cultural Biography*. New York: Cambridge University Press, 1993.
Hallberg, Robert von. "Introduction to the Issue on Politics and Poetic Value." *Critical Inquiry* (1987) 13: 415–20.
Hanks, William. "Discourse Genres in a Theory of Practice." *American Ethnologist*, Nov. 1987: 668–92.
Harding, James. *Saint-Saëns and His Circle*. London: Chapman and Hall, 1965.
———. *Erik Satie*. New York: Praeger, 1975.
Haskell, Francis. *De l'art et du goût, jadis et naguère*. Paris: Gallimard, 1989.
Hazareesingh, Sudhir. *Intellectuals and the French Communist Party: Disillusion and Decline*. Oxford, U.K.: Clarendon, 1991.
———. *Political Traditions in Modern France*. Oxford: Oxford University Press, 1994.
Hellman, John. *Emmanuel Mounier and the New Catholic Left, 1930–1950*. Toronto: University of Toronto Press, 1981.
Hill, Edward B. *Modern French Music*. Cambridge, Mass.: Riverside, 1924.
Hill, Peter, ed. *The Messiaen Companion*. London: Faber, 1995.
Hinton, Stephen. *The Idea of Gebrauchmusik: A Study of Musical Aesthetics in the Weimar Republic (1919–1933) with Particular Reference to the Works of Paul Hindemith*. New York: Garland, 1989.
Hirsbrunner, Theo. *Die Music in Frankreich im 20. Jahrhundert*. Bern: Laaber, 1995.
———. *Igor Stravinsky in Paris*. Bern: Laaber, 1982.
Hirsch, E. D. "Past Intentions and Present Meanings." *Essays in Criticism* 33 (1983): 79–98.
Hirschbach, Frank, ed. *Germany in the Twenties: The Artist as Social Critic*. Minneapolis: University of Minnesota Press, 1980.
Hirst, Derek, and Richard Strier, eds. *Writing and Political Engagement in Seventeenth-Century England*. New York: Cambridge University Press, 2000.

Hobsbawm, Eric. *Nations and Nationalism since 1780: Programs, Myths, Reality.* Cambridge: Cambridge University Press, 1992.
Hoérée, Arthur. "Une conférence par M. Arnold Schoenberg." *Le ménestrel,* 30 Dec. 1927: 546–47.
———. "Arnold Schoenberg à Paris." *Musique,* 15 Feb. 1928: 214–23.
———. "*Amphion,* mélodrame: Ce qu'en dit Paul Valéry." *Candide,* 25 June 1931.
Hoffmann, Stanley. *In Search of France.* Cambridge: Harvard University Press, 1963.
Hollier, Denis, ed. *A New History of French Literature.* Cambridge: Harvard University Press, 1989.
Honegger, Arthur. "Les Six ont dix ans." *Candide,* 19 Dec. 1929.
Horne, John. *State, Society, and Mobilization in Europe during the First World War.* Cambridge: Cambridge University Press, 1997.
Howlett, Jane, and Rod Menghem, eds. *The Violent Muse: Violence and the Artistic Imagination in Europe, 1910–1930.* Manchester, U.K.: Manchester University Press, 1994.
Hunt, Lynn, ed. *The New Cultural History.* Berkeley: University of California Press, 1989.
Huré, Jean. *Défense et illustration de la musique française.* Paris: A Sénart, 1915.
———. "The Immediate Future of French Music." *Musical Quarterly* 4 (1918): 74–77.
Huyghe, René, and Agathe Rouart-Valéry. *Lili et Nadia Boulanger.* Paris: Richard-Masse, 1982.
Huyssen, Andréas. *After the Great Divide: Modernism, Mass Culture, Post-modernism.* Bloomington: Indiana University Press, 1986.
Hyde, Martha. "Neoclassic and Anachronistic Impulses in Twentieth-Century Music." *Music Theory Spectrum* 18 (1996): 200–235.
Hyman, Paula. *From Dreyfus to Vichy: The Remaking of French Jewry, 1906–1939.* New York: Columbia University Press, 1979.
Iser, Wolfgang. *The Implied Reader.* Baltimore: Johns Hopkins University Press, 1974.
Ivry, Benjamin. *Francis Poulenc.* London: Phaidon, 1996.
Jackson, J. H. *Clemenceau and the Third French Republic.* New York: Macmillan, 1948.
Jameson, Frederic. *The Political Unconscious: Narrative as a Socially Symbolic Act.* Ithaca, N.Y.: Cornell University Press, 1981.
Jankélévitch, Vladimir. *La musique et l'ineffable.* Paris: Armand Colin, 1961.
Jaquet-Langlais, Marie-Louise. *Jean Langlais, 1907–1991: Ombre et lumière.* Paris: Combre, 1995.
Jay, Martin. *Force Fields: Between Intellectual History and Cultural Criticism.* New York: Routledge, 1993.
Jelavich, Peter. *Berlin Cabaret.* Cambridge: Harvard University Press, 1993.
John, Eckhard. *Musikbolschewismus: Die Politisierung der Musik in Deutschland, 1918–1938.* Stuttgart: Metzler, 1994.
Johnson, Robert S. *Messiaen.* Berkeley: University of California Press, 1975.
Jolivet, Hilda. *Avec André Jolivet.* Paris: Flammarion, 1978.
Judt, Tony. "Could the French Have Won?" *New York Review of Books,* 22 Feb. 2001: 37–40.
Junyk, Ihor. "Faces of Janus: The Revival of Classics in Modernist Paris." Ph.D. diss., University of Chicago, 2001.
Kahane, Martine, and Nicole Wilde, eds. *Wagner et la France.* Paris: Herscher, 1983.
Kaplan, Alice Y. *Reproductions of Banality: Fascism, Literature, and French Intellectual Life.* Minneapolis: University of Minnesota Press, 1986.
Kater, Michael. "The Revenge of the Fathers: The Demise of Modern Music at the End of the Weimar Republic." *German Studies Review* 15.12 (May 1992): 295–315.

———. *The Twisted Muse: Musicians and Their Music in the Third Reich.* New York: Oxford University Press, 1997.
Katz, Jacob. *From Prejudice to Destruction: Anti-Semitism, 1700–1933.* Cambridge: Harvard University Press, 1980.
Keck, George R. *Francis Poulenc: A Bio-Bibliography.* New York: Greenwood, 1990.
Kelman, Herbert C. "Nationalism, Patriotism, and National Identity: Social-Psychological Dimensions." In *Patriotism in the Lives of Individuals and Nations,* 165–89. Edited by Daniel Bar-Tal and Ervin Staub. Chicago: Nelson-Hall, 1997.
Kember, Katherine. "Is There Magic in Jolivet's Music?" *Music Review* 44.2 (1983): 121–35.
Kenney, William H. "Le Hot: The Assimilation of American Jazz in France, 1917–1940." *American Studies* 25 (1984): 5–24.
Klassen, Janine. "Theologischer Regenbogen: 'Les offrandes oubliées' von Olivier Messiaen." *Jahrbuch des Staatlichen Instituts fur Musikforschung Preussischer Kulturbesitz,* 1988: 268–76.
Kochno, Boris. *Diaghilev and the Ballets Russes.* New York: Harper and Row, 1970.
Koechlin, Charles. *Debussy.* Paris: 1927.
———. *Gabriel Fauré.* Paris: Félix Alcan, 1927.
Kornprobst, Louis J. *Guy Ropartz: Etude biographique et musicale.* Strasbourg: Musicales d'Alsace, 1949.
Kuisel, Richard F. *Seducing the French: The Dilemma of Americanization.* Berkeley: University of California Press, 1993.
Kupferman, Fred. *Pierre Laval.* Paris: Balland, 1987.
La Capra, Dominick. *Rethinking Intellectual History: Texts, Contexts, Language.* Ithaca, N.Y.: Cornell University Press, 1983.
Laclau, Ernesto. "Universalism, Particularism, and the Question of Identity." *October* 61 (1992): 83–90.
Lacombe, Nicole, and Alain Lacombe. *Les chants de bataille: La chanson patriotique de 1900 à 1918.* Paris: Belfond, 1992.
Lacouture, Jean. *François Mauriac.* Paris: Seuil, 1980.
Laloy, Louis. *Rameau.* Paris: Félix Alcan, 1919.
Landormy, Paul. *La musique française de Franck à Debussy.* Paris: Gallimard, 1943.
Langevin, Paul-Gilbert, ed. *Musiciens de France: La génération des grands symphonistes.* Paris: Richard-Masse, 1979.
Laqueur, Walter. *Fascism: A Reader's Guide.* Berkeley: University of California Press, 1976.
Large, David, and William Weber, eds. *Wagnerism in European Culture and Politics.* Ithaca, N.Y.: Cornell University Press, 1984.
Lasserre, Pierre. *Cinquante ans de pensée française.* Paris: Plon-Nourrit, 1922.
Lavignac, Albert, and Lionel de la Laurencie, eds. *Encyclopédie de la musique et dictionnaire du Conservatoire.* Paris: Delagrave, 1931.
Le Flem, Paul. "L'oeuvre symphonique de Roussel." *La revue musicale,* April 1929: 35–44.
Lefranc, Georges. *Histoire du Front populaire.* Paris: Payot, 1965.
———. "Le courant planiste de 1933 à 1936." *Le mouvement social* 54 (1966): 69–89.
———. *Le mouvement socialiste sous la Troisième République.* Vol. 2. Paris: Payot, 1977.
Léger, Danièle. *Le féminisme en France.* Paris: Sycomore, 1982.
Le Goff, Jacques. *History and Memory.* Translated by Steven Rendall and Elizabeth Claman. New York: Columbia University Press, 1992.
Leppert, Richard, and Susan McClary, eds. *The Politics of Composition, Performance, and Reception.* Cambridge: Cambridge University Press, 1987.

Lequin, Yves, ed. *La mosaïque, France: Histoire des étrangers et l'immigration*. Paris: Larousse, 1988.
Lesure, François. *Dossier de presse de "Pierrot Lunaire" d'Arnold Schoenberg*. Geneva: Minkoff, 1985.
———. *Debussy, biographie critique*. Paris: Klincksieck, 1994.
Lifar, Serge. *Serge Diaghilev: His Life, His Work, His Legend*. New York: G. P. Putnam's Sons, 1940.
Lippman, Edward. *A History of Western Musical Aesthetics*. Lincoln: University of Nebraska Press, 1992.
Lockspeiser, Edward. *The Literary Clef: An Anthology of Letters and Writings by French Composers*. London: John Calder, 1958.
Loranquin, Albert. "Claudel et Messiaen." *Le bulletin des lettres*, 15 June 1990: 209–13.
Lottman, Herbert R. *La rive gauche: Du Front populaire à la Guerre froide*. Paris: Seuil, 1981.
L'Opéra-comique pendant la guerre. Paris: Editions de la Nouvelle Revue, 1919.
Maclean, Ian, Alan Montefiore, and Peter Winch, eds. *The Political Responsibility of Intellectuals*. Cambridge: Cambridge University Press, 1990.
Maier, Charles S. *Recasting Bourgeois Europe: Stabilization in France, Germany, and Italy in the Decade after World War I*. Princeton, N.J.: Princeton University Press, 1975.
Malki-Thouvenel, Béatrice. *Cabarets, cafés et bistrots de Paris*. Paris: Horvath, 1987.
Malraux, André. *La tentation de l'Occident*. Paris: B. Grasset, 1926.
Mandel, Amy, ed. *Bakhtin in Contexts: Across the Disciplines*. Evanston, Ill.: Northwestern University Press, 1995.
Manduell, John. "Albert Roussel." In *The Symphony*. 2: 104–13. Edited by Robert Simpson. London: Harmondsworth, 1967.
Manevy, Raymond. *La presse de la IIIe République*. Paris: J. Foret, 1955.
Manning, Frank E. *The Celebration of Society: Perspectives on Contemporary Cultural Performance*. Bowling Green, Ohio: Bowling Green University Press, 1983.
Mari, Pierrette. *Olivier Messiaen: L'homme et son oeuvre*. Paris: Seghers, 1965.
Marmande, Francis. *Georges Bataille politique*. Lyon: Presses Universitaires de Lyon, 1985.
Marti, Stavronela. "Les grands concerts parisiens au seuil des années 20." *Revue internationale de musique française* (June 1989) 29: 19–38.
Martin, Benjamin F. *France and the Après-Guerre: Illusions and Disillusionment*. Baton Rouge: Louisiana State University Press, 1999.
Massis, Henri. *Défense de l'Occident*. Paris: Plon, 1927.
Matore, Daniel. "Le modernisme musical français à la veille de la Seconde guerre mondiale." *Revue internationale de musique française* (Nov. 1985) 18: 69–78.
Mauclair, Camille. *La religion de la musique et les héros de l'orchestre*. Paris: Fischbacher, 1928.
Mauriac, François. *Mozart et autres écrits sur la musique*. La Versanne: Encre Marine, 1996.
———. *Le croyant et l'humaniste inquiet: Correspondance François Mauriac, Georges Duhamel (1919–1966)*. Paris: Klincksieck, 1997.
Maurras, Charles. *La musique intérieure*. Paris: Bernard Grasset, 1925.
Maurras, Michael, and Robert O. Paxton. *Vichy France and the Jews*. New York: Basic Books, 1981.
Maxence, Jean-Pierre. *Histoire de dix ans, 1927–1937*. Paris: Gallimard, 1939.
Mayeur, Daniel. *Pour une histoire de la gauche*. Paris: Plon, 1969.
Mayeur, Françoise. *"L'aube": Etude d'un journal d'opinion*. Paris: Cana, 1982.
McLeod, Mary. "Le Corbusier: From Regional Syndicalism to Vichy." Ph.D. diss., Princeton University, 1985.

McMillan, James F. *Housewife or Harlot: The Place of Women in French Society, 1870–1940.* New York: St. Martin's, 1981.

———. *From Dreyfus to DeGaulle: Politics in France, 1898–1969.* London: Edward Arnold, 1985.

———. "Social History, 'New Cultural History,' and the Rediscovery of Politics: Some Recent Works on Modern France." *Journal of Modern History* 66 (1994): 755–72.

Mehlman, Jeffrey. *Legacies of Anti-Semitism in France.* Minneapolis: University of Minnesota Press, 1983.

Mellers, Wilfrid. *Francis Poulenc.* Oxford: Oxford University Press, 1993.

Messiaen, Olivier. "L'ascension." *Le monde musical,* 28 Feb. 1935: 48–49.

———. "La navité du Seigneur." *Le monde musical,* 30 April 1936: 123–24.

———. *Vingt leçons d'harmonie.* Paris: A. Leduc, 1939.

———. "Autour d'une partition." *Le monde musical,* 30 April 1939: 126.

———. *Messiaen on Messiaen.* Translated by Irena Feddern. Van Nuys, Calif.: Alfred, 1986.

Meylan, Pierre. *René Morax et Arthur Honegger au Théâtre du Jorat.* Lausanne: Cervin, 1966.

———. *Honegger: Son oeuvre et son message.* Paris: Age d'Homme, 1970.

Milhaud, Darius. *Milhaud-Claudel, correspondance.* Cahiers Claudel 3. Paris: Gallimard, 1966.

Milza, Pierre. *Fascisme français: Passé et présent.* Paris: Flammarion, 1987.

Mitgang, Laura. "La Princesse des Six: A Life of Germaine Tailleferre." Bachelor's thesis, Oberlin College, 1982.

Moch, Jules. *Une si longue vie.* Paris: Robert Laffont, 1976.

"Modernity and Modernism, Postmodernity and Postmodernism." Special issue, *Cultural Critique* 5 (Winter 1986–87).

Mopin, Michel. *Littérature et politique: Deux siècles de vie politique à travers les oeuvres littéraires.* Paris: Documentation Française, 1996.

Morgan, Robert P., ed. *Modern Times: From World War I to the Present.* Englewood Cliffs, N.J.: Prentice Hall, 1994.

Morris, David. *Olivier Messiaen: A Comparative Bibliography of Material on the English Language.* Ulster, U.K.: University of Ulster Press, 1991.

Mosse, George E. *International Fascism: New Thoughts and Approaches.* London: Sage, 1979.

———. *Fallen Soldiers: Reshaping the Memory of the World Wars.* Oxford: Oxford University Press, 1990.

———. "The Political Culture of Italian Fascism: A General Perspective." *Journal of Contemporary History* 25 (1990): 253–68.

———. *Confronting the Nation: Jewish and Western Nationalism.* Hanover, N.H.: University Press of New England, 1993.

Mounier, Emmanuel. *Révolution personnaliste et communautaire.* Paris: Fernand Aubier; Montaigne, 1935.

Moxey, Keith. *The Practice of Theory: Poststructuralism, Cultural Politics, and Art History.* Ithaca, N.Y.: Cornell University Press, 1994.

Murray, Michael. *French Masters of the Organ: Saint-Saëns, Franck, Widor, Vierne, Dupré, Langlais, Messiaen.* New Haven, Conn.: Yale University Press, 1998.

"La musique dans l'Exposition de 1937." Special issue, *La revue musicale,* June–July 1937.

Mussat, Marie-Claire. "Le tombeau dans la musique du XXième siècle." In *Tombeaux et monuments,* 133–44. Edited by Jacques Dugast and Michèle Touret. Rennes: Presses de l'Université de Rennes, 1992.

Nectoux, Jean-Michel. *Gabriel Fauré: A Musical Life.* Translated by Roger Nichols. Cambridge: Cambridge University Press, 1991.

———, ed. *Gabriel Fauré: His Life through Letters*. Translated by J. A. Underwood. New York: Scribner, 1984.
Nguyen, Victor. *Aux racines de L'action française: Intelligence et politique à l'aube du XXe siècle*. Paris: Fayard, 1991.
Nichols, Roger. *Debussy*. Oxford: Oxford University Press, 1973.
———. *Ravel*. London: J. M. Dent and Sons, 1977.
———. *Messiaen*. Oxford: Oxford University Press, 1986.
———. *Ravel Remembered*. London: Faber and Faber, 1989.
———, ed. *Debussy Remembered*. London: Faber, 1992.
Nicolet, Claude. *L'idée républicaine en France (1789–1924): Essai d'histoire critique*. Paris: Gallimard, 1992.
Niess, Robert. *Julien Benda*. Ann Arbor: University of Michigan Press, 1956.
Nochlin, Linda, and Tamar Garb, eds. *The Jew in the Text: Modernity and the Construction of Identity*. London: Thames and Hudson, 1995.
Noiriel, Gerard. *The French Melting Pot: Immigration, Citizenship, and National Identity*. Translated by Geoffroy de Laforcade. Minneapolis: University of Minnesota Press, 1996.
Nora, Pierre, ed. *La nation*. Vol. 2 of *Les lieux de mémoire*. Paris: Gallimard, 1986.
Norris, Christopher, ed. *Music and the Politics of Culture*. New York: St. Martin's, 1989.
Olivera, Philippe. "Le Librairie Valois (1928–1932)." Mémoire, Institut d'Etudes Politiques de Paris, 1989.
Onnen, Franck. *Maurice Ravel*. Translated by W. A. G. Doyle-Davidson. Stockholm: Continental, 1947.
Orenstein, Arbie. "Some Unpublished Music and Letters by Maurice Ravel." *Music Forum* 3 (1973): 291–334.
———. *Ravel: Man and Musician*. New York: Columbia University Press, 1975.
Orledge, Robert. *Gabriel Fauré*. London: Eulenberg, 1979.
———. *Debussy and the Theater*. Cambridge: Cambridge University Press, 1982.
———. *Satie the Composer*. New York: Cambridge University Press, 1990.
———. *Satie Remembered*. Portland, Ore.: Amadeus, 1995.
Ory, Pascal. *Les collaborateurs, 1940–45*. Paris: Seuil, 1976.
Palmer, Roy. *The Sound of History: Songs and Social Comment*. Oxford: Oxford University Press, 1988.
Paris, Alain. "La symphonie française de 1918 à nos jours." *Le courrier musical de France*, 67–68 (1979): 91–94 and 137–39.
Parker, Andrew, and Eve K. Sedgwick, eds. *Performativity and Performance*. New York: Routledge, 1995.
Parks, Richard. *The Music of Claude Debussy*. New Haven, Conn.: Yale University Press, 1989.
Pasler, Jann. "New Music as Confrontation: The Musical Sources of Jean Cocteau's Identity." *Musical Quarterly* 75 (1991): 255–78.
Pasler, Jann. ed. *Confronting Stravinsky*. Berkeley: University of California Press, 1986.
Patin, Stéphane. "La musique française et la Première guerre mondiale: Une contribution à l'étude des attitudes du corps musical dans la nation en guerre." Mémoire de maîtrise de musicologie, Université de Paris 4, 1990.
Paul, Hélène. "Présence de Ravel dans les concerts en 1930 d'après *Le ménestrel* et *Le monde musical*." *Revue internationale de musique française* (Nov. 1987) 24: 71–79.
Paxton, Robert O. "Radicals." *New York Review of Books*, 23 June 1994: 51–54.
———. "The Five Stages of Fascism." *Journal of Modern History* 70 (1998): 1–23.
Périer, Alain. *Messiaen*. Paris: Seuil, 1979.

Perloff, Marjorie. *The Futurist Moment: Avant-Garde, Avant-Guerre, and the Language of Rupture*. Chicago: University of Chicago Press, 1986.
Peter, René. *Claude Debussy*. Paris: Gallimard, 1944.
———. *Le théâtre et la vie sous la Troisième République*. Paris: Littéraires de France, 1945.
Pinçon, Frédérique. "Les oeuvres de jeunesse d'Olivier Messiaen." Mémoire de maîtrise, Université de Paris 4, 1992.
Pistone, Danièle. "Ravel et Paris: Notes sur le destin d'un oeuvre." *Revue internationale de musique française* Nov. 1987 24: 7–37.
———, ed. *Musique et musiciens à Paris dans les années trente*. Paris: Champion, 2000.
Poincaré, Raymond. *Au service de la France*. Vol. 1, *L'Union sacrée*. Paris: Plon, 1927.
Poueigh, Jean. "Doit-on jouer Wagner après la guerre?" *La renaissance politique, littéraire et artistique*, 5 Feb. 1916: 12–15.
Poulenc, Francis. *Moi et mes amis*. Edited by Stéphane Audel. Paris: Palatine, 1963.
Prochasson, Christophe. *Les intellectuels, le socialisme et la guerre (1900–1938)*. Paris: Seuil, 1992.
———. "Sur le cas Maurras: Biographie et histoire des idées politiques." *Annales: Histoire, sciences sociales* 50.3 (May–June 1995): 579–87.
Prod'homme, J.-G. "Music and Musicians in Paris during the First Two Seasons of the War." Translated by Otto Kinkeldey. *Musical Quarterly* 4 (1918): 135–60.
Prost, Antoine. *L'enseignement en France, 1800–1967*. Paris: A. Colin, 1968.
———. *Les anciens combattants et la société française, 1914–1939*. 3 vols. Paris: Fondation Nationale des Sciences Politiques, 1977.
Racine, Nicole, and Jean-Louis Bodin. *Le Parti communiste français pendant l'entre-deux-guerres*. Paris: Armand Colin, 1972.
Racine-Furland, Nicole. "Le comité de vigilance des intellectuels anti-fascistes (1934–1939)." *Le mouvement social* 101 (1977): 87–112.
Ramaut, Alban, ed. *Francis Poulenc et la voix: Texte et contexte*. Saint-Etienne: Publications de l'Université de Saint-Etienne, 2002.
"Rapports: Ligue nationale pour la défense de la musique française." *La musique pendant la guerre* 6 (10 March 1916): 86–87.
Ravel, Maurice. *Ravel par lui-même et après ses amis*. Paris: Michel de Maule, 1987.
———. *Lettres, écrits, entretiens*. Edited by Arbie Orenstein. Paris: Flammerion, 1989.
Raymond, Marcel. *From Baudelaire to Surrealism*. London: Mathuen, 1970.
Rearick, Charles. *The French in Love and War: Popular Culture in the Era of the World Wars*. New Haven, Conn.: Yale University Press, 1997.
Rebatet, Lucien. *Les décombres*. Paris: Denoël, 1942.
Réberioux, Madeleine. "Présentation" to the issue "Critique littéraire et socialisme." *Le mouvement social* (1967) 59: 3–28.
Rémond, René. *Les crises du catholicisme dans les années trente*. Paris: Cana, 1979.
Le retour à l'ordre dans les arts plastiques et l'architecture, 1919–1925. Saint-Etienne: Centre Interdisciplinaire d'Etudes et de Recherches sur l'Expression Contemporaine, 1975.
Rey, Anne. *Erik Satie*. Bourges: Tardy Quercy Auvergne, 1974.
Ricoeur, Paul. *Interpretation Theory: Discourse and the Surplus of Meaning*. Fort Worth: Texas Christian University Press, 1976.
Ridley, F. F. *Revolutionary Syndicalism in France*. Cambridge: Cambridge University Press, 1970.
Ringer, Fritz K. *Fields of Knowledge: French Academic Culture in Comparative Perspective, 1890–1920*. Cambridge: Cambridge University Press, 1992.
Rioux, Jean-Pierre, ed. *La vie culturelle sous Vichy*. Brussels: Complexe, 1990.

Rioux, Jean-Pierre, and Jean-François Sirinelli. *Pour une histoire culturelle*. Paris: Seuil, 1997.
Robert, Frédéric. *Louis Durey: L'aîné des "Six."* Paris: Editeurs Français Réunis, 1968.
———. "Pour les 85 ans de Louis Durey." *Europe*, Jan.–Feb. 1974: 4–11.
Roberts, Paul. *Images: The Piano Music of Claude Debussy*. Portland, Ore.: Amadeus, 1996.
Roche, Anne, ed. *Les écrivains et le Front populaire*. Paris: Editions du CNRS, 1986.
Roche, Anne, and Christian Tarting, eds. *Des années trente: Groupes et ruptures*. Paris: Editions du CNRS, 1985.
Rockwell, John S. "The Prussian Ministry of Culture and the Berlin State Opera, 1918–1931." Ph.D. diss., University of California, Berkeley, 1972.
Roger-Ducasse. *Lettres à Nadia Boulanger*. Edited by J. Depaulis. Paris: Spimont, 1999.
Rogers, M. Robert. "Jazz Influence on French Music." *Musical Quarterly* 21 (1935): 53–68.
Rogger, Hans, and Eugen Weber, eds. *The European Right: A Historical Profile*. Berkeley: University of California Press, 1974.
Rohoninski, L., ed. *Cinquante ans de musique française, de 1874 à 1925*. Paris: Editions Musicales de la Librairie de France, 1925.
Rolland, Romain. *Essays on Music*. New York: Allen, Towne, and Heath, 1948.
———. *Théâtre de la Révolution*. Paris: Albin Michel, 1972.
———. *Selected Letters*. Edited by Francis Doré and Marie-Laure Prévost. Oxford: Oxford University Press, 1990.
———. *Au-dessus de la mêlée*. Vol. 15 of *Oeuvres*. Paris: Albin Michel, n.d.
Rosenstiel, Leonie. *The Life and Works of Lili Boulanger*. London: Associated University Presses, 1972.
Rostand, Claude. *L'oeuvre de Pierre-Octave Ferroud*. Paris: Durand, 1957.
———. *La musique française contemporaine*. 4th ed. Paris: Presses Universitaires de France, 1971 [1952].
Rothert, Wolfgang, and Andreas Traub. "Zu einer anbekanten Ausgabe des 'Socrate' von Erik Satie." *Die Musikforschung* 38.2 (1985): 118–21.
Roy, Jean. *Darius Milhaud, l'homme et son oeuvre*. Paris: Seghers, 1968.
Russell, Charles. *Poets, Prophets, and Revolutionaries: The Literary Avant-Garde from Rimbaud through Postmodernism*. New York: Oxford University Press, 1985.
Sablonnière, Marguerite. "Le Conservatoire de musique de Paris entre les deux guerres, 1919–1939." Thèse de l'Ecole des Chartes, 1996.
Sachs, Harvey. *Toscanini*. Philadelphia: J. B. Lippincott, 1978.
Said, Edward. *Musical Elaborations*. New York: Columbia University Press, 1991.
Saint-Saëns, Camille. "L'avenir de la musique française." *La grande revue*, March 1916.
———. *Outspoken Essays on Music*. Translated by Fred Rothwell. London: Kegan Paul, Trench, Trubner, 1922.
Saint-Saëns, Camille, and Gabriel Fauré. *Correspondance*. Paris: Association des Amis de Gabriel Fauré, 1971.
Samazeuilh, Gustave. "Médée." *Le temps*, 10 May 1940.
———. *De Vichy à Bayreuth*. Vichy: Presses de l'Imprimerie Wallen, 1960.
Sanouillet, Michel. *Dada à Paris*. Paris: Jean-Jacques Pauvert, 1965.
Sanson, Rosemonde. *Le 14 juillet, fête et conscience nationale, 1789–1975*. Paris: Flammarion, 1976.
Sapir, David, and Christopher J. Crocker, eds. *The Social Use of Metaphor: Essays on the Anthropology of Rhetoric*. Philadelphia: University of Pennsylvania Press, 1977.
Sapir, Edward. *Anthropologie I: Culture et personnalité*. Translated by Christian Baudelot and Pierre Clinquart. Paris: Minuit, 1967.
Satie, Erik. *Ecrits*. Edited by Ornella Volta. Paris: Champs Libre, 1981.

Schaeffner, André. *Strawinsky*. Paris: Rieder, 1931.
Schalk, David L. *The Spectrum of Political Engagement: Mounier, Benda, Brasillach, Sartre*. Princeton, N.J.: Princeton University Press, 1979.
Schalk, Roger L. *Roger Martin du Gard: The Novelist and History*. Ithaca, N.Y.: Cornell University Press, 1967.
Schechner, Richard. *Essays in Performance Theory, 1970–1976*. New York: Drama Book Specialists, 1977.
Schlee, Thomas. *Olivier Messiaen: La cité céleste/Das himmlische Jerusalem—Über Leben und Werke des französischen Komponisten*. Cologne: Wienand, 1998.
Schloezer, Boris de. "La grande pitié de la critique musicale française." *Esprit*, 1 June 1937: 367–70.
———. "Le cas Schoenberg." *La nouvelle revue française* 52 (Jan.–June 1939): 891–900.
Schmitz, E. Robert. *The Piano Works of Claude Debussy*. New York: Dover, 1950.
Schoenberg, Arnold. "Conviction et connaissance." *Musique*, 15 Jan. 1928: 158–64.
Schor, Ralph. *L'antisémitisme en France pendant les années trente: Prélude à Vichy*. Brussels: Complexe, 1992.
Schrade, Leo. *Beethoven in France*. New Haven, Conn.: Yale University Press, 1942: rpt., New York: Da Capo, 1978.
Schwarz, Boris. *Music and Musical Life in Soviet Russia*. Bloomington: Indiana University Press, 1983.
Scriven, Michael, and Peter Wagstaff, eds. *War and Society in Twentieth-Century France*. New York: Berg, 1991.
Serant, Paul. *Les dissidents de L'action française*. Paris: Copernic, 1978.
Seroff, Victor. *Maurice Ravel*. New York: Holt, 1953.
Shapiro, Robert. *Germaine Tailleferre: A Bio-Bibliography*. Westport, Conn.: Greenwood, 1994.
Shapiro, Theda. *Painters and Politics: The European Avant-Garde and Society, 1900–1925*. New York: Elsevier, 1976.
Sharkey, Stephen, and Robert S. Dombroski. "Revolution, Myth, and Mythical Politics: The Futurist Solution." *Journal of European History* 6.23 (1976): 231–47.
Shaw, R. Paul, and Yuwa Wong. *Genetic Seeds of Warfare: Evolution, Nationalism, and Patriotism*. Boston: Unwin Hyman, 1989.
Shead, Richard. *Music in the 1920s*. London: Duckworth, 1976.
Shenton, Andrew D. "The Unspoken Word: Olivier Messiaen's 'Langage Communicable.'" Ph.D. diss., Harvard University, 1998.
Sherman, Daniel J. "Monuments, Mourning, and Masculinity in France after World War I." *Gender and History* 8 (1996): 82–107.
———. *The Construction of Memory in Interwar France*. Chicago: University of Chicago Press, 2002.
Short, Robert. "The Politics of Surrealism, 1920–1936." *Journal of Contemporary History* (1966): 1: 3–25.
Siegel, Jerrold. *Bohemian Paris: Culture, Politics, and the Boundaries of Bourgeois Life, 1830–1930*. New York: Viking, 1986.
Simeone, Nigel. *A Bibliographical Catalogue of Messiaen's Works, First Editions, First Performances, with Programmes and Documents*. Musikbibliographische Arbeiten 14. Tutzing: Schneider, 1998.
Sirinelli, Jean-François. *Génération intellectuelle: Khâgneux et normaliens dans l'entre-deux-guerres*. Paris: Fayard, 1988.
———. *Intellectuels et passions françaises: Manifestes et pétitions au XXe siècle*. Paris: Fayard, 1990.

———. *Refus et violences: Politique et littérature à l'extrême droite des années trente aux retombées de la Libération.* Paris: Gallimard, 1996.
Slonimsky, Nicolas. *Music since 1900.* New York: Scribner's, 1971.
Société des Auteurs, Compositeurs et Editeurs de Musique (SACEM). *Maurice Ravel, 1875–1975.* Paris: SACEM, 1975.
Société Internationale pour la Musique Contemporaine. *Exposition Internationale de 1937: Catalogue.* Paris: June 1937.
Solbrig, Ingeborg. "Cultural and Political Perspectives of the Weimar Republic." *Hindemith Jahrbuch* 4 (1975): 31–44.
Solomon, Maynard, ed. *Marxism and Art: Essays Classic and Contemporary.* Detroit: Wayne State University Press, 1979.
Soucy, Robert. *Fascism in France: The Case of Maurice Barrès.* Berkeley: University of California Press, 1973.
———. *French Fascism: The First Wave, 1924–1933.* New Haven, Conn.: Yale University Press, 1986.
Spycket, Jérôme. *Nadia Boulanger.* Translated by M. M. Shriver Stuyvestant. New York: Pendragon, 1995.
Stearns, Peter. *Revolutionary Syndicalism: A Cause without Rebels.* New Brunswick, N.J.: Rutgers University Press, 1971.
Steinberg, Michael, P. *The Meaning of the Salzburg Festival: Austria as Theater and Ideology.* Ithaca, N.Y.: Cornell University Press, 1990.
———. "Richard Strauss and the Question." In *Richard Strauss and His World,* 164–89. Edited by Bryan Gilliam. Princeton, N.J.: Princeton University Press, 1992.
Sternhell, Zeev. *La droite révolutionnaire.* Paris: Le Seuil, 1971.
———. *Maurice Barrès et le nationalisme français.* Paris: Armand Colin, 1972.
———. "Emmanuel Mounier et la contestation de la démocratie libérale dans la France des années trente." *Revue française de science politique* 34 (1984): 1141–80.
———. "The Anti-Materialist Revision of Marxism as an Aspect of the Rise of Fascist Ideology." *Journal of Contemporary History* 22 (1987): 379–400.
———. *Naissance de l'idéologie fasciste.* Paris: Fayard, 1989.
Strauss, David. "Notes: French Critics and American Jazz." *American Quarterly* 17.3 (1965): 582–87.
Stravinsky, Vera, and Robert Craft, eds. *Stravinsky in Pictures and Documents.* New York: Simon and Schuster, 1978.
Strelelski, Gerard. "Une année de *Comoedia.*" *Revue internationale de musique française* (June 1989) 29: 7–17.
Strowski, Fortunat. *Nationalisme ou patriotisme.* Paris: B. Grasset, 1933.
Suhami, Evelyne. *Paul Valéry et la musique.* Dakar: Langues et Littératures, 1966.
Suleiman, Ezra N. *Politics, Power, and Bureaucracy in France: The Administrative Elite.* Princeton, N.J.: Princeton University Press, 1974.
Sullivan, Jack. *New World Symphonies: How American Culture Changed European Music.* New Haven, Conn.: Yale University Press, 1999.
Tailleferre, Germaine. "Quelques mots de l'une des Six." *L'intransigeant,* 3 June 1923.
Tambling, Jeremy. *Opera, Ideology, and Film.* Manchester, U.K.: Manchester University Press, 1987.
———. *Opera and the Culture of Fascism.* Oxford, U.K.: Clarendon, 1996.
Tarasti, Eero. *Musical Signification: Essays in the Semiotics and Analysis of Music.* Berlin: Mouton de Gruyter, 1995.
Tartakowsky, Danielle. "Manifestations, fêtes et rassemblements à Paris (juin 1936–novembre 1938)." *Vingtième siècle,* July–Sept. 1990: 43–53.

Tenroc, Charles. "Le nationalisme musical." *Le courrier musical* 20 (Sept.–Oct. 1918): 273–79.
Terdiman, Richard. *Discourse/Counter-Discourse: The Theory and Practice of Symbolic Resistance in Nineteenth-Century France*. Ithaca, N.Y.: Cornell University Press, 1985.
———. *Present Past: Modernity and the Memory Crisis*. Ithaca, N.Y.: Cornell University Press, 1993.
Thibaudet, Albert. *La République des professeurs*. Paris: Grasset, 1927.
Thomson, Andrew. *The Life and Times of Charles-Marie Widor, 1844–1937*. New York: Oxford University Press, 1987.
———. *Vincent d'Indy and His World*. Oxford, U.K.: Clarendon, 1997.
Thomson, David. *Democracy in France since 1870*. 5th ed. New York: Oxford University Press, 1969.
Tiersot, Julien. *Les fêtes et les chants de la Révolution française*. Paris: Hachette, 1908.
Todorov, Tzvetan. *Mikhaïl Bakhtine: Le principe dialogique*. Paris: Seuil, 1981.
Tomlinson, Gary. "The Web of Culture: A Context for Musicology." *Nineteenth-Century Music* 7.3 (1984): 350–62.
Touchard, Jean. *La gauche en France depuis 1900*. Paris: Seuil, 1968.
———. "L'esprit des années 1930: Une tentative de renouvellement de la pensée politique français." In *Révoltés de l'esprit: Les revues des années 1930*, 195–229. Edited by Pierre Andreu. Paris: Kimé, 1991.
Tournemire, Charles. *César Franck*. Paris: Delagrave, 1931.
Valois, Georges. *Le fascisme*. Paris: Nouvelle Librairie Nationale, 1927.
Veeser, H. Aramm, ed. *The New Historicism*. New York: Routledge, 1989.
Verger, Jacques, ed. *Histoire des universités en France*. Toulouse: Privat, 1986.
Vergine, Lea. *L'autre moitié de l'avant-garde, 1910–1940*. Paris: Femmes, 1982.
Vilhelmsdóttir, Unnar. *Towards Neoclassicism: The Piano Works of Claude Debussy*. Ann Arbor: UMI Research Press, 1997.
Voldman, Danièle. "Le Corbusier (Charles-Edouard Jeannaret)." In *Dictionnaire des intellectuels français*, 689–90. Edited by Jacques Julliard and Michel Winock. Paris: Seuil, 1996. Volta, Ornella. *Satie et la danse*. Paris: Plume, 1992.
———. *Satie/Cocteau: Les malentendus d'une entente*. Paris: Le Castor Astral, 1993.
———, ed. *Erik Satie Seen through His Letters*. New York: Boyars, 1988.
Von Halberg, Robert. Introduction to special issue, "Politics and Poetic Value." *Critical Inquiry* (1987) 13: 415–20.
Von Halberg, Robert, and Lawrence Rainey, eds. Special issue, *Fascism and Culture*: Parts 1 and 2. *Modernism/Modernity* 2.3 (1995) and 3.1 (1996).
Voss, Hans Dieter. *Arthur Honegger: Le Roi David*. Munich: Emile Kalzbichler, 1983.
Wagstaff, John. *André Messager: A Bio-Bibliography*. New York: Greenwood Press, 1991.
Walker, Greg. *The Politics of Performance in Early Renaissance Drama*. Cambridge: Cambridge University Press, 1998.
Wallis, Brian, ed. *Art after Modernism: Rethinking Representation*. New York: New Museum of Contemporary Art, 1984.
Weber, Edith, ed. *Debussy et l'évolution de la musique au XXe siècle*. Paris: Editions du CNRS, 1965.
Weber, Eugen. "Nationalism, Socialism, and National-Socialism in France." *French Historical Studies* 2.3 (1962): 273–307.
———. *Varieties of Fascism: Doctrines of Revolution in the Twentieth Century*. New York: Van Nostrand, 1964.
Weber, Eugen, and Hans Rogger, eds. *The European Right: A Historical Profile*. Los Angeles: University of California Press, 1965.

Weber, William. *The Rise of Musical Classics in Eighteenth-Century England: A Study in Canon, Ritual, and Ideology*. Oxford, U.K.: Clarendon, 1992.

Weber, William, and David Large, eds. *Wagnerism in European Politics and Culture*. Ithaca, N.Y.: Cornell University Press, 1984.

Weiner, Marc. *Undertones of Insurrection: Music, Politics, and the Social Sphere in Modern German Narrative*. Lincoln: University of Nebraska Press, 1993.

———. *Richard Wagner and the Anti-Semitic Imagination*. Lincoln: University of Nebraska Press, 1995.

Weiss, John. *The Fascist Tradition*. New York: Harper and Row, 1967.

Wellesz, Egon. "Arnold Schoenberg et son oeuvre." *La revue musicale* 1 May 1923: 3–10.

Wenk, Arthur B. *Claude Debussy and the Poets*. Berkeley: University of California Press, 1976.

———. *Claude Debussy and Twentieth-Century Music*. Boston: Twayne, 1983.

Wheeler, Kenneth, and Virginia Lee Lussier. *Women, the Arts, and the 1920s*. New Brunswick, N.J.: Transaction, 1982.

Whitesitt, Linda. *The Life and Music of George Antheil, 1900–1959*. Ann Arbor, Mich.: UMI Research Press, 1983.

Whittal, Arnold. *Music since the First World War*. London: J. M. Dent, 1977.

Wild, Nicole. *Théâtres et décorateurs*. Paris: Bibliothèque Nationale, 1993.

Wilentz, Sean, ed. *Rites of Power: Symbolism, Ritual, and Politics since the Middle Ages*. Philadelphia: University of Pennsylvania Press, 1985.

Wilkins, Nigel, ed. and trans. *The Writings of Erik Satie*. London: Eulenbourg, 1980.

Winock, Michel. "Jeanne d'Arc et les Juifs." *Histoire*, Nov. 1979: 227–37.

———, ed. *Histoire de l'extrême droite en France*. Paris: Seuil, 1993.

Winzer, Dieter. *Claude Debussy und die französischen musikalische Tradition*. Wiesbaden: Breitkopf und Härtel, 1981.

Wolff, Stéphane. *L'Opéra au Palais Garnier, 1875–1962*. Paris: Entracte, 1962.

Wood, Marc. "The Influence of Stravinsky on the Music of Francis Poulenc." Ph.D. diss., Goldsmith's College, 1997.

Zeimont, Judith L., ed. *The Musical Woman*. Westport, Conn.: Greenwood, 1986.

Zeldin, Theodore. *France, 1848–1945*. Oxford, U.K.: Clarendon, 1973.

INDEX

Abbate, Carolyn, 69
Académie des Beaux-Arts, 64, 88
Académie Française, 296
Action Artistique à l'Etranger, 118
Action Française, 11, 20, 21–2, 27, 29, 32, 36–7, 40, 47, 52, 62, 89, 90, 101, 104, 112, 119, 120–22, 125–26, 130, 145, 166, 173–74, 202, 207– 242, 244, 247, 249, 277, 285, 287–88, 290, 292, 296, 310, 314
L'Action française, 37, 59, 104, 122, 150, 242, 249, 274, 315
Adam, Adolphe, 30
Adorno, Theodor, 6, 156
Aeschylus, 177
Agulhon, Maurice, 90, 153
Althusser, Louis, 6
L'ami du peuple, 242, 255
Ancien Régime, 23, 25, 41, 48, 117
Andrieu, Pierre, 247
Annunzio, Gabriele d', 83, 187, 268
Les Apaches, 65
Apollinaire, Guillaume, 71, 83–4, 156, 162, 164

Aragon, Louis, 151, 174, 180, 204, 212, 230, 304, 316
Archives littéraires des écrivains et des artistes morts pour la France, 92
Arnold, Billy, 153
Aron, Robert, 288
L'Art musical populaire, 212, 219, 221–22
L'Art pour Tous, 116
Association des Ecrivains et Artistes Révolutionnaires, 204, 224
Association des Grands Concerts, 28
L'aube, 287
Auber, Daniel François Esprit, 30, 135, 252
Auberbach, Erich, 4
Aubert, Louis, 144, 238
Auric, Georges, 83, 151–52, 154, 157, 158, 160–63, 172–75, 184, 186, 189, 190–91, 195, 212, 215, 217, 219, 221, 225, 227, 230, 232, 235, 241, 258, 270, 280, 284, 309
Austin, William, 299

Bach, Johann Sebastian, 29, 43–44, 128, 164, 169, 170, 186–87, 193, 216–17, 236, 255–56, 282, 312
Bachelet, Alfred, 105
Bach-Sisley, J., 35
Bakhtin, Mikhail, 9, 12, 153
Balakirev, Mily, 29
Ballets Futuristes Italiens, 224
Ballets Russes, 71–72, 104, 169, 195
Ballets Suédois, 151, 179, 180, 193
Banville, Théodore de, 27
Barbusse, Henri, 57, 124
Bardac, Raoul, 32
Barraine, Elsa, 284
Barrès, Maurice, 21, 33, 36, 53, 66, 72, 83, 105–6, 107, 153, 157, 248
Bartók, Bela, 33, 257, 260, 282
Bataille Syndicaliste, 127
Bathori, Jane, 146, 157
Baton, René, 34, 93
Baudelaire, Charles, 139
Baudrier, Yves, 291, 293–94, 296, 305, 308
Beaumont, Comte Etienne de, 83, 158, 160, 190, 193
Beethoven, Ludwig van, 29, 36–37, 49, 61, 93, 128, 156, 164, 175, 185, 211, 213, 218, 222–23, 236, 248, 252, 255, 282
Bellaigue, Camille, 37
Benda, Julien, 3–4, 14, 90, 108, 111–13, 124–25, 133, 176, 179, 218
Benoist, Alexandre, 313
Bérard, Léon, 138
Berg, Alban, 182, 191, 227, 277, 292, 297, 303
Bergery, Gaston, 194, 232–33, 249, 265, 272–73, 313
Berlin, Irving, 79
Berlioz, Hector, 28, 38, 129, 211, 213, 222, 253, 256, 281–82, 294, 312
Berlioz, Joanny, 283
Bernanos, Georges, 258–59
Bernard, Robert, 112–13, 168, 311
Bertin, Pierre, 157
Bertrand, Paul, 107, 278
Bizet, Georges, 26, 154, 163, 253, 274, 280, 282
Bizet, René, 254, 269
Blanche, Jacques-Emile, 279
Bloc National, 88, 90, 97, 109, 120, 183, 202

Bloch, André, 114–15
Bloch, Jean-Richard, 120, 124, 212, 224, 230, 238, 281, 316
Bloch, Marc, 314
Bloy, Léon, 120, 140, 173–74
Blum, Léon, 136, 141, 203, 237, 239–40, 242, 249, 272–73, 276, 317
Bonnat, Léon, 92
Le bonnet rouge, 192
Bonsoir, 102
Bordes, Charles, 173
Borodin, Alexander, 25, 29, 129–30
Boschot, Adolphe, 41, 104, 110–11, 117, 255–56
Boucher, Maurice, 38
Boulanger, Lili, 49, 59, 91, 118
Boulanger, Nadia, 14, 49, 116–18, 155, 169–70, 260–61, 298, 309
Bourdel, Antoine, 92
Bourdet, Edouard, 259
Bourdieu, Pierre, 7
Bourgault-Doucoudray, Louis, 130
Bourget, Paul, 66
Brahms, Johannes, 170, 285
Braque, Georges, 84, 175
Brasillach, Robert, 244, 249–50
Brecht, Bertolt, 182
Brênet, Michel, 41
Breton, André, 151, 166, 174, 179, 304
Briand, Aristide, 231
Bruneau, Alfred, 25–26, 34, 39, 88, 90, 94, 115, 217, 222–23, 257
Brussel, Robert, 118
Bruyr, José, 95
Buenzod, Emmanuel, 223
Burrin, Philippe, 273
Busoni, Ferrucio, 289

Cabellero, Carlo, 336 n. 119
Cachin, Marcel, 316
Cachin, Paul, 238
Cahiers d'aujourd'hui, 66
Caine, Hall, 55
Candide, 204, 242, 246, 248–50, 254–57, 269
Canteloube, Joseph, 107, 171
Caplet, André, 91, 96, 197
Carnet de la semaine, 84
Carraud, Gaston, 68, 84, 109–10, 115
Carroll, David, 244

Cartel des Gauches, 86–7, 91, 106, 128–31, 140, 145, 181–82, 202–3, 275
Cartier-Bresson, Henri, 316
Casadesus, Francis, 32, 58, 118, 211
Casals, Pablo, 116
Céline, Louis-Ferdinand, 299
Cendrars, Blaise, 156–57, 162
Cercle Interallié, 117
Ce soir, 226, 230
Chabrier, Emmanuel, 36, 96, 129, 154, 175, 178, 189, 217, 226, 264
Chagall, Marc, 165
Chailley, Jacques, 271
Chalupt, René, 174
Chanel, Coco, 152, 159, 160, 187
Chansons au vent, 232
"Chant du depart," 26, 270
Le Chant du Monde, 212–13, 240, 314
Charlot, Jacques, 57
Charpentier, Gustave, 26, 31–2, 39, 48, 50–52, 115, 127–28, 130–31, 217, 225, 238–39, 256–57
Charpentier, Marc-Antoine, 19
Charpentier, Victor, 28, 32
Chauminade, Cécile, 91
Chausson, Ernest, 96
Chautemps, Camille, 201, 276
Chennevière, Georges, 132–33
Cherubini, Luigi, 25, 223
Chevillard, Camille, 93, 96, 115
Chopin, Frédéric, 43, 60, 193
Chorale Populaire de Paris, 221, 230
Christian Democracy, 120, 243, 287, 295
Clair, René, 151, 161, 266
Clarté, 124–25, 296
Claudel, Paul, 125, 177, 179–80, 182, 187, 194, 230–31, 235, 238, 258–59, 268, 270–71, 272, 281, 296–97, 312–13
Clavecinistes, 54, 175
Clemenceau, Georges, 45, 90, 92, 120, 224, 251, 259, 260
Clemenceau, Paul, 137, 159
Clifford, James, 322
Cliquet-Pleyel, Henri, 171, 219, 222
Cocteau, Jean, 83–85, 93, 111–12, 126, 134, 135, 146, 150–52, 154, 156–58, 160–69, 171–72, 174–78, 182–92, 195, 216–18, 222–23, 227, 249, 251, 269–70, 278, 281, 284, 287, 293, 295

Coeuroy, André, 170, 181, 185, 248, 252, 255, 274, 278, 309, 313
Coginot, Georges, 316
Cohen, Gustave, 270
Colette, 140–41
Collaer, Paul, 302, 311
Collège de France, 166
Collet, Henri, 112, 146, 167–69, 171, 251, 259, 278
Colonial Exposition of 1931, 289, 299, 303
Colonne (and Colonne-Lamoureux) Concerts, 28–30, 56, 91, 96, 100, 155, 210, 285
Combarieu, Jules, 41
Combat, 247, 288
Comédie-Française, 23, 225, 234
Comité Franco-Américain, 49, 118
Comité de Vigilance des Intellectuels Anti-Fascistes, 203
Committee for French Restoration, 118–19
Commune, 204
Communist Party (France), 24, 89, 123, 150, 194, 200, 204, 206, 208, 213, 216, 218–19, 223, 226, 232, 240, 281, 287, 304–5, 309, 316
Comoedia, 129, 134–35, 161, 167, 169, 195
Concerts Classiques, Rouges, 28–29
Confédération Générale du Travail (CGT), 134–35, 206, 224, 234
Conférences Rive Gauche, 252
Congress of Tours, 123
Conservatoire Américain, 117–18
Conservatoire National de Musique, 10, 27, 33, 39, 42, 44, 49, 63, 66, 106, 112, 113–17, 130, 152–53, 154, 170, 173, 184–85, 189, 191–92, 207, 210, 215–16, 235, 247, 256, 281, 284, 297, 302, 308
Coolidge, Elizabeth Sprague, 141
Copeau, Jacques, 124, 157
Coppola, Pierro, 96
Le Coq, 157
Le Corbusier, 122, 188, 239, 266, 268
Cortot, Alfred, 27, 32–33, 44, 67, 278–80
Coty, François, 89, 202, 224–25
Couperin, François, 63, 68–69, 251, 312, 315
Courrier musical, 31, 44, 144, 197
Courville, Xavier de, 136
Cousin, Victor, 147

Critique, art, philosophie, 122, 197
Croix-de-Feu, 89, 202

Dada (dadaist), 15, 45, 78, 126, 134, 146–47, 151–53, 155, 158, 163, 166, 174, 176
Daladier, Edouard, 201, 203, 267
Dalamier, Albert, 23, 31
Dandieu, Arnaud, 288
Daniel, Keith, 189, 264
Daniel-Lesur, Jean Yves, 291–92, 294, 296, 305, 308
Darnaudet, Jean, 37–8, 52
Daudet, Alphonse, 27
Daudet, Léon, 37, 72, 83, 120, 204, 251, 255
Daudet, Lucien, 158
Daumier, Honoré, 75
Dauriac, Lionel, 41
Davenson, Henri, 289
David, Félicien, 135
Debussy, Claude, 12, 28, 32, 34–40, 43, 48, 50, 52–70, 92, 96, 111, 129, 135, 144, 146–47, 156, 161, 163–64, 170–71, 175, 178, 184, 188, 192, 195–96, 217, 235, 240, 253, 257, 282, 287, 296–98, 302, 304, 322
Déclaration de l'Indépendance de l'Esprit, 120, 124
Delannoy, Marcel, 107, 158, 241, 284
Déléage, André, 287
Delgrange, Félix, 157
Delteil, Joseph, 144, 271
Denis, Maurice, 101–2
Derain, André, 84
Deroulède, Paul, 27
Desnos, Robert, 180, 231, 239
Desormière, Roger, 171, 215, 219, 226, 280, 308
Devigne, Roger, 208
Dezarnaux, Robert, 141
D'Harcourt, Francis, 264
Diaghilev, Sergei, 71–73, 78, 82–83, 95, 137, 151–52, 159, 160, 175, 189
D'Indy, Vincent, 10, 25, 27–31, 33–4, 36–8, 41, 43, 48–50, 52, 54, 60, 65, 67–8, 82, 92, 93–4, 96, 97–104, 107, 110, 112–13, 117, 133–37, 140, 147, 171, 175, 177–78, 184, 195–97, 214, 221, 223, 227, 244, 246–48, 255–57, 273, 280, 282, 292–93, 298, 305, 310, 312

Donizetti, Gaetano, 25
Doriot, Jacques, 202, 243
Le Dounier Rousseau, 217
Doyen, Albert, 127, 128, 132, 295
Drake, Jeremy, 177
Dreyfus Affair, 3–4, 10–11, 20, 32–3, 46, 49, 97–8, 100, 105, 111, 136, 178, 197, 201, 205, 266, 241–42, 255
Drieu La Rochelle, Pierre, 203, 244, 247
Dubois, Théodore, 31, 115
Dubost, Jeanne, 158
Duchamp, Marcel, 154, 174, 180
Duclos, Jacques, 316
Duhamel, Georges, 17, 120, 124, 128, 173, 295
Dukas, Paul, 34, 39, 43, 96, 116, 279, 297, 299
Dumesnil, René, 105, 284
Duparc, Henri, 34
Dupré, Marcel, 116, 297–98
Durand, Jacques, 43–4, 55, 59, 60–1, 65, 87–8, 100, 298
Durey, Louis, 154, 157, 191–92, 194, 212, 219, 227, 232, 241, 318
Duruflé, Maurice, 298

L'écho de Paris, 30, 66, 242
L'éclair, 101, 161
Ecole d'Arcueil, 15, 171, 218, 222, 226–27, 258
Ecole César Franck, 216
Ecole des Hautes Etudes Sociales, 177
Ecole Normale de Musique, 116–17, 298, 308–9
Ecole Normale Supérieur, 126
Ecole de Paris, 239
Ecorcheville, Jules, 68
Editions de France, 250
Editions de la Nouvelle Revue Française, 250
Editions de la Sirène, 162
Editions Sociales Internationales, 213, 216, 221, 227, 252
L'effort, 281
Einstein, Albert, 124, 137
Eisler, Hans, 213
L'élan, 71
Elgar, Edward, 55
Elias, Norbert, 196
Eluard, Paul, 190, 259, 264, 297, 304

Emmanuel Maurice, 96
Epstein, Jean, 239
Esprit, 259, 287–91, 303
L'esprit nouveau, 167, 174
Europe, 232
Excelsior, 161, 195, 309
Expert, Henri, 96

Le Faisceau, 89, 202
Falla, Manuel de, 189
Fauré, Gabriel, 24, 32, 34, 38–40, 43, 48, 68, 87–89, 95, 115, 129, 155, 158, 184, 199, 215, 240
Fayard, Arthème, 249
Febvre, Lucien, 314
Fédération de la Jeunesse, 240
Fédération Musicale Populaire, 210–15, 218–23, 227, 230, 232, 235–36, 252
Fédération Nationale Catholique, 202
Fédération Républicaine, 119, 202
Fédération du Théâtre Ouvrier de France, 226
Ferroud, Pierre-Octave, 158, 260–61, 292
Festivals de Musique Française, 32
Fetes du Peuple, 126–32, 207, 211, 223, 237, 255, 315
Févier, Henry, 90
Le Figaro, 89, 102, 120
Flammarion Editions, 296
La fleche, 249, 273–74
Foche, Ferdinand, Maréchal, 92
Focillon, Henri, 38
Fort, Paul, 129, 194
Foucault, Michel, 7
Fourier, Charles, 127, 132
Français, Jean, 308–9
France, Anantole, 121, 124, 128, 173
Franck, César, 27–8, 38–9, 54–5, 123, 128, 156, 175, 185, 227, 256, 308
Franco, Francisco, 205, 259, 288–89
Franco-American Musical Society, 118
Franco-Prussian War, 29
Free Masons, 128
French Academy in Rome, 235
French Revolution, 23, 25, 48, 66, 128–29, 176, 179, 200, 202, 207–8, 212, 219, 223, 232, 240, 261, 315
Freud, Sigmund, 6, 14, 177
Freund, Marya, 144, 182

Gaillard, Marias-François, 59
Gallon, Jean, 297
Gallon, Noël, 91, 97
Gance, Abel, 268
Garde Républicaine, 231
Garros, Roland, 163
Gaubert, Philippe, 225
Gaulle, Charles de, 260, 317
Le Gaulois, 84
Gédalge, André. 68, 114, 132, 152, 184, 215, 256
George, Waldemar, 288
Ghéon, Henri, 97, 166
Gheusi, Pierre-Barthélemy, 23, 26, 224
Gide, André, 121, 124–25, 141, 152, 161, 166, 179, 187, 191, 204, 273, 277
Gilson, Etienne, 97
Gleizes, Albert, 73
Gluck, Christoph Willibald, 25, 30, 274, 316
Godebski, Cipa, 67, 173
Godet, Robert, 53–4
Goethe, Johann Wolfgang von, 30
Golan, Romy, 197
Gossec, François-Joseph, 25, 211, 213, 232, 235, 315
Goudimel, Claude, 186
Gounod, Charles, 56, 154, 282, 316
Gramsci, Antonio, 4
La Grande revue, 23, 30
Green Christpher, 73
Grétry, André-Ernest Modest, 213, 226
Grey, Madeleine, 253
Gringoire, 242, 246, 248, 250–52, 255, 257, 274, 315
Gris, Juan, 83
Gross, Valentine, 78
Groupe d'Etudes Philosophiques et Scientifique pour l'Examen des Idées Nouvelles, 181
Guernica, 259, 295
Guerre sociale, 192
Guilmant, Alexandre, 117
Guitry, Sacha, 238

Habá, Alois, 153
Hahn, Reynaldo, 91, 116, 225
Halévy, Jacques Fromenthal, 30, 252
Handel, George Frideric, 29, 130, 186, 213, 222

Hanna, Martha, 47, 109, 123
Haydn, Franz Joseph, 29, 50, 192
Herf, Jeffrey, 267
Hérold, Ferdinand, 30, 135
Herriot, Edouard, 114
Hervé, Gustave, 254
Hervé, Jean, 314
Hindemith, Paul, 182–83, 277
Hitler, Adolph, 200, 205, 219, 231, 270, 310, 316
Hoérée, Arthur, 214, 239
Honegger, Arthur, 15, 95, 112–13, 154, 157–58, 174, 176–78, 184–89, 192–93, 214–15, 219–20, 225, 230, 232–33, 235, 238–40, 249, 260, 265–70, 280, 285–86, 290, 305, 309, 312–14
Huë, Georges, 106, 115–16
Hugo, Jean, 173
Hugo, Victor, 27, 58, 91
Huisman, Georges, 283
L'humanité, 24, 96, 120, 124, 129–30, 132–33, 139, 183, 213, 235
Huré, Jean, 60

Ibáñez, Blasco, 106
Ibert, Jacques, 158, 219, 225, 230, 235, 238
L'illustration, 242, 315
L'indépendance, 247
Inghelbrecht, D.-E., 59, 93, 96
Institut de France, 32, 63–4, 139, 279
International Congress of Folklore (First), 208
International Congress of Writers in Defense of Culture, 203, 230
International Exposition of 1937, 212, 217, 219, 230, 233, 237–41, 254, 260, 264, 270, 278
"L'Internationale," 213, 234, 240
L'intransigeant, 53, 161, 193
Iribe, Paul, 72

Jackson, Julian, 201
Jacob, Max, 158
Jacob, Maxime, 171
Jacques-Dalcroze, E., 128, 132
Jammes, Francis, 179–80
Janequin, Clément, 70, 130, 260
Jankélévitch, Vladimir, 140

Jaubert, Maurice, 212, 230, 265, 289–90, 305
Jaurès, Jean, 89, 127, 131, 192, 270
Jazz, 13, 212
Jean-Aubry, Georges, 38–9, 40, 54, 266
Jeanne d'Arc, 59, 144
Je suis partout, 242, 246, 248, 250–51, 256–57, 276, 315
Jeune France, 16–17, 289, 291–96, 299, 302, 305, 308–10, 317
Jeunesses Patriotes, 89, 202
Jolivet, André, 16–17, 212, 215, 219, 291–92, 294, 296–97, 299, 302–7, 308–9
Le jour, 183, 242, 309
Journal des débats, 64, 104, 242
Journal officiel, 138
Jouvenel, Renaud de, 212
Judt, Tony, 305
Julien Adolphe, 64
Julliard, Jacques, 4–5

Keats, John, 269
Kelkel, Manfred, 131
Kerdyk, René, 241, 251
King Albert's Book, 55
Kochnitzsky, Léon, 236
Kodály, Zoltán, 33
Koechlin, Charles, 13, 15, 33–4, 94, 170–71, 189, 207, 212, 215–20, 225, 230, 235–36, 239, 272, 284, 314, 316
Koussevitsky, Serge, 94–5, 169, 187
Kroll Opera, 182

Lagéat, Jean, 233
Lagrange, Léo, 206–7, 210, 242
La Laurencie, Lionel de, 41
Lalo, Pierre, 84, 107, 115
Laloy, Louis, 59, 74, 97, 164, 169, 265, 287
Lamour, Philippe, 265
Lamoureux Concerts, 28, 93, 96, 115, 210, 285
Landormy, Paul, 185, 240, 248, 254, 256, 278, 297
Landowska, Wanda, 116, 189, 191
Lap, Marc, 131
La Rocque, François de la, 89, 202, 259
Lasserre, Pierre, 38, 112, 121, 164, 167, 175, 179

INDEX

Laurencin, Marie, 189, 194
Lazarus, Daniel, 215, 219–21, 224–25, 230, 235–36, 240, 249–50
League of Nations, 204, 288
Lebovics, Herman, 317
Leclau, Oierre, 250, 276
Le Flem, Paul, 161, 195, 284, 292–93, 302–3
Léger, Fernand, 84, 161, 174, 180, 238, 266
Légion d'Honneur, 14, 138–39, 144
Leibowitz, René, 290, 293
Le June, Claude, 260–61
Léon, Paul, 86, 92, 115–16
Lifar, Serge, 238, 273
Ligue des Droits de l'Homme, 273
Ligue Internationale contre l'Antisémitisme, 231
Ligue Nationale pour la Défense de la Musique Française, 31, 48, 50, 52, 65, 67, 84, 94, 138
Ligue de la Patrie Française, 10, 33
Linosier, Raymonde, 191
Liszt, Franz, 96, 138, 274, 285
Littérature, 174
Loisirs Musicaux de la Jeunesse, 231
Long, Marguerite, 116, 231
Loth, Georges, 305
Loubet, Emile, 259
Louis XIV, 19
Lourié, Arthur, 289, 297
Lully, Jean-Baptiste, 19, 24, 147, 150
Luther, Martin, 57
Lyre et Palette Concerts, 157

Mademoiselle de Nantes, 19, 25
Maeterlinck, Maurice, 232
Magnard, Albéric, 27, 109–10, 177–78, 185
Mahler, Alma, 137, 191
Mahler, Gustave, 137, 139, 191
Maison de Culture, 210, 234
Malherbe, Henry, 141
Malraux, André, 204
Manécanterie des Petits Chanteurs à la Croix de Bois, 231
Mangeot, Adolphe, 116
Manifeste pour la Paix en Europe et la Défense de l'Occident, 106
Manifeste pour un Parti de l'Intelligence, 120

Mann, Heinrich, 124
Mannheim, Karl, 8
Maré, Rolph de, 151, 159, 180, 193
Marianne, 250, 309
Mariotte, Antoine, 224,
Maritain, Jacques, 97, 120, 134, 165–66, 169, 173, 186, 259, 287, 289, 291–92, 296, 303
Marks, Martin, 151
Marnold, Jean, 66–8, 107
"La Marseillaise," 26, 28, 57–8, 234, 240, 270–71, 315
Martel, Henri, 277
Martel, Jan and Noël, 92
Martin du Garde, Roger, 105
Marx, Karl, 127
Marxist historiography, 6
Mascagni, Pietro, 226
Massenet, Jules, 141, 215, 226
Massis, Henri, 120, 157, 166, 204
Masson, André, 317
Masson, Paul-Marie, 41, 281
Matinées nationales, 27–8, 30
Matisse, Henri, 157
Maulnier, Thierry, 249, 288
Mauriac, François, 17, 258, 287, 295–96
Maurras, Charles, 21, 33, 89, 196, 207, 259, 278
Méhul, Etienne Nicolas, 130, 213, 223
Mendelssohn, Felix, 29, 118, 129
Le ménestrel, 107, 259, 278
Mercure de France, 105, 165, 168, 284, 313
Merleau-Ponty, Maurice, 265
Messager, André, 27, 34, 55, 91
Messiaen, Olivier, 16–17, 42, 114, 199, 277, 291–94, 296–310, 321
Messing, Scott, 169
Meyerbeer, Giacomo, 100, 110, 134, 257
Migot, Georges, 113, 284, 292, 308
Milhaud, Darius, 14, 152, 154, 157–62, 171, 174, 175–84, 190–92, 199, 207, 210, 215, 219, 225, 227, 230–32, 235, 237–39, 241, 249–50, 258, 270, 279–82, 284, 290, 296–97, 311, 316–17
Milhaud, Madeleine, 180, 316
Miller, Tyrus, 299
Ministère des Beaux-Arts (Ministry of Fine Arts), 27, 32–33, 42, 45, 92, 118, 205

Le monde musical, 124
Monnet, Henri, 231
Monsigny, Pierre-Alexandre, 226
Montherlant, Henry de, 268
Montespan, Madame de, 19
Montesquieu, Comte Robert de, 160
Monteux, Pierre, 28
Monteverdi, Claudio, 25, 29, 260–61
Morand, Paul, 158
Morax, René, 186
Moréas, Jean, 125
Morris, William, 208
Le mot, 72
Mounier, Emmanuel, 204, 265, 287–88, 305
Moussinac, Léon, 230
Mozart, Wolfgang Amadeus, 29–30, 110, 154, 217
Munich agreement, 276
Musée des Arts et Traditions Populaires, 207–8, 280, 314
La musique pendan la guerre, 31
Mussolini, Benito, 16, 106, 121, 170, 180, 200, 204–5, 224, 265, 267, 289, 292
Mussorgsky, Modest, 25, 161, 163, 297
Myers, Rollo, 63

Nectoux, Jean-Michel, 87
Neue Freie Presse, 253
Nietzsche, Friedrich, 163
Noailles, Anna de, 160–61
Noailles, Charles de, 191, 231
Nord-Sud, 71, 83
Les Nouveau Jeunes, 191
Le nouveau siècle, 89, 202, 256
La nouvelle revue française, 93, 124–26, 141, 144, 146, 162, 166, 174, 223, 236, 275, 278, 280–81, 290, 313
Les nouvelles littétraires, 174, 195

Offenbach, Jacques, 36, 122, 135, 141, 226, 250, 274
Oiseau Lyre, 314
Ollone, Max d', 100, 116, 225
Ondes Martenot, 108, 199, 225
Opéra-Comique, 23, 26, 31–2, 92, 106–7, 141, 210, 220, 224–26, 235–36, 284
Opéra National (Paris Opera), 19–20, 23–4, 26–7, 29–30, 71, 92–3, 95–7, 106–7, 134, 158, 182, 187, 199, 210, 224–25, 272, 316
Orchestre Symphonique de Paris, 95, 210, 308
L'ordre nouveau, 288
L'ordre public, 139
Orenstein, Arbie, 136
Orléans, Charles d', 58, 310
Orphéon Choral Societies, 129, 135, 211, 241
Ozenfant, Amadée, 71–72, 122, 174

Painlevé, Paul, 23, 136, 139, 160
Paladilhe, E., 26, 32
Pamy, Evariste-Désiré de, 141
Panassié, Hugues, 290–91
Paray, Paul, 96, 271
Parti Franciste, 202
Parti Frontiste, 233
Parti de l'Intelligence, 125
Parti Populaire Français, 202
Parti Républician National Social, 202
Parti Social Français, 202
Pasdeloup Concerts, 28, 93, 95–6, 137, 210, 285
Paulhan, Jean, 174
Péguy, Charles, 27, 90, 157, 287
La peinture, 197
Perse, Saint-John, 192
Peters Editions, 43
Petin, Philippe, Maréchal, 317
Le peuple, 131
Phonothèque Nationale, 208
Picabia, Francis, 151, 152, 161, 174, 180
Picasso, Pablo, 71, 73–7, 82–3, 146, 150–52, 157, 161, 166, 187, 234, 236, 259
Pierné, Gabriel, 96, 136, 225
Plans, 265–66, 268, 273, 286
Plato, 147
Poincaré, Raymond, 89–91, 119–20, 166, 286
Le point, 214
Poiret, Paul, 72, 83, 152, 160, 174
Polignac, Marie-Blanche de, 190, 259
Polignac, Princesse Edmond de, 83, 117, 146–47, 150, 152, 159, 160, 177, 190, 193, 260, 264, 292, 298
Le populaire de Paris, 104, 136, 141, 265

Popular Front, 15–16, 51, 124, 130, 171, 183, 198–204, 206–15, 219–27, 230–37, 239, 241–43, 245–46, 248, 251–52, 254–61, 264–65, 268–78, 281–84, 288–89, 290–91, 293, 295, 296, 302, 305, 308–10, 314, 317
Poueigh, Jean, 31, 84
Poulenc, Francis, 15–16, 54, 83, 126, 147, 150–51, 154, 156, 161, 173–74, 182, 188–94, 216, 227, 251–52, 258–65, 269, 281, 290, 296–98, 309–10
Poulet Concerts, 95
Poulet-Siohan Concerts, 210
Prévert, Jacques, 226
Prévost, Marcel, 295–96
Prix Candide, 245
Prix Cressent, 219
Prix de Rome, 59, 139, 153, 156, 210, 283, 297
Prod'homme, J.-G., 41, 93
Prokofiev, Sergey, 95, 193
Pro Musica Society, 118
Proudhon, Pierre-Joseph, 127
Proust, Marcel, 125, 160, 165
Prunières, Henry, 96, 126, 222–23, 281–82
Puccini, Giacomo, 25, 141, 226
Purcell, Henry, 29

Rabaud, Henri, 17, 106, 114–15, 225
Radiguer, Henri, 212
Radiguet, Raymond, 158, 160, 165–66
Radio elections, 255
Rameau, Jean-Philippe, 25, 54, 62, 97, 217, 308, 315
Ravel, Edouard, 138–39
Ravel, Maurice, 12–14, 28, 32–4, 48, 65–70, 94–5, 107, 111, 120, 122, 129, 136–46, 152, 156, 158, 161, 173, 185–86, 188, 191–92, 197, 214–15, 235, 240, 252–55, 257, 260, 275, 281–82, 290, 297
Réaction, 288
Rebatet, Lucien, 249–50, 153, 274
Reger, Max, 184
La renaissance, 30
Renoir, Jean, 226, 239
Réunion des Théâtres Lyriques Nationaux, 224
Reverdy, Pierre, 166, 297, 302

Revue critique des idées et des livres, 104, 122, 125
Revue des deux mondes, 64, 109, 315
La revue française, 288
Revue de France, 186
Revue hebdomadaire, 185–86
Revue des jeunes, 186
Revue musicale, 94, 96, 126, 145, 217, 223, 236, 278–81, 310–11
Revue musicale SIM, 69, 74, 275
Revue de Paris, 109, 121
La revue du siècle, 288
Revue universelle, 120, 166
Reyer, Ernest, 280
Reynaud, Paul, 260, 317
Ribèyre, Charles, 311–12
Richepin, Jean, 92
Riemann, Hugo, 50
Rieti, Vittorio, 226
Rimsky-Korsakov, Nicolas, 29, 129, 167, 297
Rivet, Paul, 208, 314
Rivier, Jean, 241
Rivière, Georges-Henri, 207–8, 284, 314
Rivière, Jacques, 93, 124–25
Robespierre, Maximilien, 129
Rocamadour, 261
Roland-Manuel, 69, 139, 145, 158, 161, 197, 280
Rolland, Romain, 46, 120, 124, 126, 187, 206, 213, 217, 219, 221–23, 230, 234, 236, 255, 268, 270
Romains, Jules, 204
Roman d'Estelle, 25
Ropartz, Guy, 49, 214
Roquebrune, Fernand-Georges, 122
Rosenthal, Manuel, 137, 144, 232, 241, 271
Rossi, Luigi, 25
Rossini, Gioacchino, 30, 154, 252, 257
Rostand, Edmond, 238
Rostand, Maurice, 270
Rouault, Georges, 165, 186
Rouché, Jacques, 19–20, 22–6, 47, 70–71, 73, 96–7, 101, 105, 158–59, 199, 224–25, 237–38, 255, 275–76
Rougemont, Denis de, 269, 305
Roussel, Albert, 13, 15, 33, 66–7, 91, 95–6, 158, 161, 197, 214–16, 219, 221–22, 225, 230, 235, 241

Rubenstein, Ida, 137, 188, 230, 268, 270–72, 313–14
Ruskin, William, 267

Sacher, Paul, 272
Said, Edward, 3–4, 14
Saint-Saens, Camille, 26–32, 39, 43, 48–9, 59–60, 64, 68–9, 86, 90–91, 97, 123, 129–30, 134, 316
Samazeuilh, Gustave, 32
Samuel, Claude, 297
Satie, Erik, 12–15, 40, 48, 54, 69–85, 112, 146–51, 153–55, 159, 160–62, 164–68, 171, 174–75, 189–90, 192, 194, 218, 222, 290
Sauguet, Henri, 15–16, 159, 171, 258–59, 309
Sauvage, Cécile, 297
Sauveplan, Henry, 212, 290
Scarlatti, Alessandro, 69
Schaeffner, André, 181, 280, 314
Schiller, Friedrich, 8
Schloezer, Boris de, 275, 280, 290, 313–14
Schmitt, Florent, 26, 33, 95, 100, 136, 158, 173, 257, 279, 315
Schmitz, E. Robert, 118, 180
Schoenberg, Arnold, 6, 33, 54, 67, 95–6, 117–18, 126, 134, 138, 141, 153, 158, 161, 163, 165, 172, 182, 191, 197–98, 220, 250, 277, 282, 290, 302–3
Schola Cantorum, 10–11, 33, 36–7, 40–41, 48–9, 52–4, 61–3, 65–6, 68, 82, 93–4, 111, 113–17, 122, 130, 140, 147, 155, 158, 173–74, 177–78, 191, 214, 216, 221–23, 246–48, 256, 261, 264, 289, 292–93, 288, 308, 312, 318
Schorske, Carl E., 138, 305
Schubert, Franz, 29, 58, 129, 275
Schumann, Robert, 96, 129
Selva, Blanche, 61
Sept, 287
Serenade Concerts, 292
Sérieyx, Auguste, 134, 150, 158
Sert, Misia, 72
Servais Concerts, 298
Séverac, Déodat, 173
Shostakovich, Dmitri, 213, 252
Silver, Kenneth, 73, 76, 83, 197
Siohan Concerts, 95
Les Six, 166–69, 171–94, 223–26

Skryabin, Alexander, 95
Socialist Party, 24, 89, 150, 207
Société des Auteurs, Compositeurs, et Editeurs de Musique (SACEM), 42
Société des Concerts du Conservatoire, 27, 95–6, 210, 293
Société Française de Musicologie, 40–41, 232
Société Internationale pour la Musique Contemporaine, 95, 241
Société Musicale Indépendante (SMI), 32–4, 58, 61, 67–8, 87, 94, 111, 136, 138, 153, 161, 215
Société Nationale de Musique Française, 32–4, 39, 60–61, 67, 91, 94–6, 129, 138, 150, 178, 195, 277, 290, 292, 298, 303
Socrates, 147
Solidarité Française, 202
Son, idées, couleurs, 71
Sophocles, 188
Sorbonne, 112, 171, 181, 287
Sordet, Dominique, 214, 249, 251, 253, 256–57
Sorel, Georges, 147, 157, 244, 247, 267, 293
Soupault, Philippe, 174
Soupault, Ralph, 249
Spanish Civil War, 16, 258, 261, 289, 316
Spender, Stephen, 9
Spirale, 292, 302, 308
Sprout, Leslie, 235, 284, 316
Stalin, Joseph, 183, 204, 310, 316
Stavisky scandal, 201
Stevenson, Robert Lewis, 8–9
Straram, Walter, 95, 298
Strauss, Richard, 184, 282, 285
Stravinsky, Igor, 14, 25, 29, 33, 50, 53–4, 58, 60, 66, 73, 76, 79, 82, 95–6, 112, 117, 126, 146, 152–55, 159, 161, 163, 165–66, 169–72, 182, 186, 188–89, 193, 195–97, 274–75, 279–8, 282, 289–90, 296–97, 314
Sulieman, Susan, 105, 194
Swift, Jonathan, 4

Tagore, Rabindranath, 191
Tailleferre, Germaine, 154, 157, 193–95, 227, 230, 232–33, 241, 270, 284, 308–9

Taittinger, Pierre, 89, 202
Taruskin, Richard, 373–74 n.434
Tchaikovsky, Peter Ilyich, 25, 29
Le Temps, 84, 138, 141, 186, 242, 284, 315
Tenroc, Charles, 31–32, 144
Thalmann, Ernest, 216
Le Théatre, 102
Thibaud, Jacques, 116
Thorez, Maurice, 316
Tiersot, Julien, 96, 252
Tombeau, 57, 69
Touche Concerts, 95
Tournemire, Charles, 114, 170, 292, 297, 305–6
Tournès, 291
Triton, 257, 260, 292
Tzara, Tristan, 151–52, 161, 174, 180

Union des Jeunes de France, 230
Union Nationale, 89, 107, 129
Union Sacrée, 25–6, 41, 44–5, 48–9, 52, 64, 78
Universal Editions, 182
Universal Exposition of 1900, 41, 240

Vaillant-Coutourier, Paul, 212–13, 230, 240
Valéry, Paul, 125, 173, 187–88, 233, 295
Vallas, Léon, 280
Valois, Georges, 89, 202, 256, 267, 293
Varèse, Edgar, 119, 214, 302–3
Vendredi, 236, 246
Vermealon, Mattÿs, 57
Vichy Regime, 17, 135, 207, 287, 311, 318, 321
La Victoire, 246, 248, 254
Vidal, Paul, 115
Vieux Colombier Concerts, 95
Vildrac, Charles, 231

Villa-Lobos, Heitor, 179
Villon, François, 57
Vines, Ricardo, 173, 189, 308
Les Virtuoses de Mazarin, 25
Voltaire, 194
Voragine, Jacques de, 98
Vuillemin, Louis, 33, 144, 196–98, 219
Vuillermoz, Emile, 33, 56, 96, 111–12, 136, 161–62, 195–96, 248, 254, 256, 278, 281–82

Wagner, Richard, 28–32, 35–6, 38–9, 49, 92–4, 96, 100–1, 104–5, 110, 127–28, 130, 134–35, 154, 156, 163, 165, 171, 184, 188, 211, 234, 248–50, 254, 257, 282, 285, 296–97, 302
Watkins, Glenn, 57
Weber, Carl Maria von, 29
Weber, Eugen, 261
Webern, Anton, 154, 182, 191
Weill, Kurt, 182
Weimar Republic, 91, 97, 114, 130, 155, 182–83, 200, 207, 209–10, 213, 218, 220–21, 223, 232, 239, 279
Weingartner, Felix, 93
Whiteman, Paul, 291
Widor, Charles-Marie, 32, 63–64, 115, 184, 292
Wiéner, Jean, 152–54, 159, 176, 181, 183, 192, 194–97, 218, 226, 230, 232, 241, 249, 268, 291, 316
Winter, Jay, 185, 188
Wohl, Robert, 154
Winock, Muchel, 4–5

Zay, Jean, 206–7, 224–25, 235, 242, 253, 259, 276, 281–83, 315
Zola, Emile, 26, 217
Zweig, Stefan, 124, 128, 137